W9-CLM-983

Marxism & Witchcraft

Marxism & Witchcraft

David Kubrin

Autonomedia

To My Children

Yarrow Lee Kubrin, Rael Caleb Kubrin Enteen,
and Mara Sonya Kubrin

ISBN: 978-1-57027-289-9

Copyright ©2020 David Kubrin

Autonomedia
POB 568 Williamsburgh Station
Brooklyn, NY 11211-0568 USA

www.autonomedia.org
info@autonomedia.org

TABLE OF CONTENTS

Interlude

Part Three — All in All, You're Just Another Brick in the Wall

Acknowledgements

A work like *Marxism & Witchcraft*, spanning many topics and quite a few decades in its writing, necessarily incorporates the ideas and work of more than one person. Any number of friends, colleagues, family, lovers, librarians, artists, my children and students appear in these pages. I only pray I can remember most of those who helped me along the way.

I might start with the book on alchemical art that Bill Gallagher and the late Sally Wellborn handed me one night in Cornish Flats, New Hampshire, in early 1969. "What do you think about *this*?" Bill asked. Bill and Sally were my "back to the land" friends and political comrades, who had also showed me an edition of Culpepper's historically important *Herbal*.

The disturbing and challenging (to me) nature of both books, as well as our many arcane conversations over tea and Sally's freshly-baked bread, were a nice launch as I sailed away to England that Fall for research into the sources and philosophical ramifications of Isaac Newton's metaphysics, with the generous support of a John Simon Guggenheim Fellowship. Thus my investigations into, among other things, the damaging effects of mining technology was partly funded, thanks, ironically, to the largess of the Guggenheim mining moneys, giving me a year to indulge my historical hunches while able to mine the hidden treasures of the British Museum, Royal Society, Greenwich Observatory, and the many nuggets located in the Bodleian Library at Oxford University, Cambridge University Library, and Trinity College, Cambridge, Library. Their librarians were unfailingly supportive, bringing frequently obscure works to my attention; so too the many US librarians at the many colleges, medical societies, and theological seminaries in Hanover, Madison, Boston, New York and the Bay Area.

In England I found a kindred soul in Bob Basarra. Our many discussions over a number of months gradually revealed themselves as a kind of *de facto* seminar we found ourselves engaged in on the worldview of the *magus*. Dame Frances Yates generously shared her insights on the Renaissance magus Bruno and his role in the scientific revolution.

It was Karen Kubrin's gift of a print of William Blake's scathing engraving of Newton that was to trigger the epiphany which is the backbone of my book. As I struggled to give form and body to this work, several people gave very much-needed encouragement at times when I was awash in self-doubt, unsure of my various heresies. Michael Pincus played a seminal role here, providing me an early platform to present an abbreviated version of this work. Riva Enteen responded to a preliminary draft with gratifying comments when they were badly needed. So too Diane di Prima and the late Christopher Hill. The late Margo Adair injected critical energy in the early stages, as well as having a transcript of an earlier lecture on the material prepared. Throughout her life she was both support and inspiration. Her partner, Bill Aal, has carried this on with very cogent editorial advice.

Special thanks are due Iain Boal, my Arch druid, who generously, painstakingly, and insightfully edited an early version of *Marxism & Witchcraft*; his rich insights and depths of knowledge of the material and of so much more benefitted me enormously. Boal's support throughout has been invaluable.

My work in Matrix is where I learned most of my magic; I am grateful to Starhawk for her inspired idea to form our group.

Shana Cohen also graciously provided valuable editorial suggestions and adroitly corrected my bearings as my project negotiated some tempestuous philosophical seas. A number of colleagues, comrades, friends and family have read the whole or sections of *Marxism & Witchcraft*, offering suggestions and critiques. Many of their comments were helpful, particularly the ones I flinched from, not willing to admit their applicability: Jake Fuchs, Marling Mast, Gina Shepard, Andrew Kubrin, Derek W., the late Moher Downing, Marian Doub, the late Prof. David Roberts, Rose May Dance, Elisa Poulos, Neil MacLean, Bill Doub, Michael Pincus, Fran Kubrin, Carolyn Merchant, Mara Kubrin, and Rael Enteen. Prof. Merchant also shared her sources and insights into some of the matters we both have been studying.

Important suggestions over our many decades since our 1961 seminar on Isaac Newton came from Prof. Robert Kargon and Prof. Wilbur Applebaum. For a number of years I benefitted from ongoing conversations on these matters with Morris Berman. At key points along the way, Margaret and Jim Jacob have been invaluable guides. So too Leonard Pitt, Tricia Case, Lee Worden, Theodore Roszak, Chris Gray, Gray Brechin (who shared a revelatory early draft of his writings on mining technologies with me). Frank Torrano, Dan Ellsberg, Doug Henwood, Will Roscoe, Roddy Erickson, Camille Mai, Antonio M., Rabbi Peretz Wolf-Prusan, Ignacio Chapela, Jorge Molina, Alison Bryant, Brook Schoenfeld, Bill Simpich, Jeffrey Alphonsus Mooney, David Solnit, Prof. Robert Proctor, Stephen Weiss, and Minoo Moallem provided valuable comments and information.

Two colleague and comrades led me by the hand to invaluable sources they knew I would never have thought to look for: Tony Ryan and the late Luis Kemnitzer.

I was thankfully able to interview key actors/experts on some of the matters discussed herein, particularly on reproductive issues: Prof. Joseph LaDou; Shanna H. Swan, PhD of the Icahn School of Medicine at Mt.

Sinai; and Ted Smith, former Director of the Silicon Valley Toxics Coalition. Roy King refreshed my memory and corrected errors in my recounting of his ordeal in jail.

For technical support, I benefitted from the electronic assists of Rael Enteen, Arturo Mendez and Steven Meeneghan and Esteban Magariños. Matthew Graham (and his mentor, Robert Heyob) are the most recent in a series of acupuncturists I have seen since 1971, always plying them with questions about traditional Chinese medical theory and practice, which helped my discussion of medical history.

To Brian Easlea, I wish to offer an apology. Early on in this project I became aware that he and I were traveling similar roads. I wanted to read his books, but was immediately struck with the compulsion to track which ideas were his, which mine, in the kind of competitive scholarship I had come to loathe, staking my claims and then his as to our respective insights and inducing stupor in any readers. To avoid such a mind-numbing exercise, I took the coward's way and put his book down after a page or two, never returning, happy that these important stories of early modern science could only benefit from two accounts.

Finally, mindful that carrying the weighty issue of human survival on its narrow shoulders, *Marxism & Witchcraft* could all too easily toss its writer into the depths of despair, I am extremely grateful to the many artists, musicians, writers, and dancers whose work has been as balm for my troubled spirits as I labored on my project.

Jim Fleming, my editor at Autonomedia, has been very generous with his time and support, as well as indulging me by incorporating many late changes as my analysis continued to evolve. For those I am deeply grateful.

It goes without saying, as the saying goes, that the final decisions of what to say and how to say it were mine alone; hence factual or interpretive errors are also mine alone.

Marxism & Witchcraft

Part One

A Marxist Theory of the Apocalypse
& An Ecological Critique of Marxism

"People do not exploit a nature that speaks to them." — Hans Peter Duerr, *Dreamtime: Concerning the Boundary Between Wilderness and Civilization* (1978)

"Nihilism is the work at the core of our culture. It is the flaw we must constantly overcome." — Lester G. Crocker, *Nature and Culture: Ethical Thought in the French Enlightenment* (1963), as quoted by Roger Shattuck, *Forbidden Knowledge: From Prometheus to Pornography* (1996).

1

Introduction:
Towards A Theory of the Apocalypse

"Indeed, the vital bond between the environment of
the Earth and the organisms upon it makes it virtually
impossible even for biologists to give a concise definition of the difference between living and nonliving
substance." — Lynn Margulis and Dorian Sagan, *Microcosmos: Four Billion Years of Microbial Evolution* (New
York, Touchstone, 1986)

i. THE APOCALYPSE AS A GROWTH INDUSTRY

In the past decades the apocalypse has become a runaway growth industry, a phenomenon reflected nearly everywhere we turn, given new impetus as we approached the year 2000 and the beginning of a new millennium. Some years ago, *Time* acknowledged the pervasive fear stalking the world that the biological entity, Earth and her inhabitants, is doomed, the planet herself identified as an "endangered species." Such imagery is no doubt overstated, with a tad of political hyperbole — there is good reason to hope that the Earth and at least some rudimentary lifeforms would survive most, if not all, of the many military, ecological, economic, and/or theological doomsdays potentially looming in our not-so-distant projected futures. Nonetheless, these doomsdays are terrifying enough— that people have (through whatever means) brought our planet to such a sorry state that so many of us should now question its vitality is simply astounding. Shocking, too, is the fact that consumer goods that prey on people's fears of impending disaster are taking off to satisfy a rapidly expanding market.

An article in the *San Francisco Chronicle* (July 29, 1992) quoted from a then-recent play, "Search and Destroy."

> Robert: Tell you what my brother says.
> Martin: What?
> Robert: Fear.
> Martin: What about it?

Robert: He thinks it's going to be very big. He thinks we're going to be
hearing a lot from fear in the '90s. It's going to be the Fear
Decade. And he says now's the time to ground-floor it.
Martin: Fear?
Robert: Fear-related industries. Blood analyzers. Viral filters. UV
screens. Totable security systems. Impact-proof leisure wear.
Very cutting edge. Very hot.

Even if some of our present world does manage to survive an outbreak of,
say, a general nuclear war (to take what just a handful of years ago was the most
obvious and virtually universally feared of these various "ecopalypses"), whatever *is* lost — of particular species; of whole habitats, of overall biotic diversity;
of scenes of wondrous grandeur; or of culture (from the carvings and astronomical alignments of Mayan temples to the songs of the whales) — the losses will
be staggering. Indeed, they already are, as we can read daily in the press.

Most people are aware of the ravages inflicted upon the spectacular lands
of Alaska by the Exxon Valdez oil spill in Prince William Sound, but the past
decades have seen literally dozens of similar disasters, including Love Canal
(1974–?), Chernobyl (1986–?), Times Beach (1985–?), Three Mile Island
(1979–?), Seveso (1976–?), Bhopal (1984–?), Windscale (1957–?), etc.,[1] each
of them in effect now a "zone of infertility" in our midst, continuing to pour
chemical or radioactive wastes out of the perforated guts of our several
social/technological infrastructures and laying waste our lands and seas. Most
of the above zones received considerable publicity when they were discovered
or occurred, though with time our attentions were diverted elsewhere. Many
others, particularly places like Chelyabinsk–40, Lake Baikal; or Semipalatinsk
Polygon in the former USSR; or Rocky Flats, St. George, Utah, Bravo–20, or
the Bikini Atoll in the US and its colonial testing grounds, all of them R & D
centers for nuclear weaponry, went largely unnoticed.

The widespread resonance of the Green critique of traditional political
parties in the face of looming ecological disasters and the growing concerns
of people everywhere over issues of the environment — by now with clear
roots in every land and various classes and races — is of capital importance,
reflecting the alarm with which the current situation and our projected futures
are widely viewed.

Since many voices from the right question whether ecological dangers are
really critical, not simply an exaggerated and skewed interpretation of a much
more complex state of terrestrial affairs, I must justify my own pessimistic reading of the evidence. Unfortunately, such justification, though forthcoming, must
be deferred, since any array of statistics, case studies, extrapolations, or painful

[1] Seveso, in Italy, was the site of a disastrous chemical explosion, which left it
massively contaminated; Windscale, a nuclear facility in England, suffered a catastrophic accident that went largely unreported in the US.

and pathetic stories at this point might all too easily be explained away by the kinds of arguments and a rhetoric whose historical development I shall be examining in great detail in Parts One and Two. By now there is an industry devoted to denial in matters of this kind. Accordingly, any assessment is best put off until we have had the opportunity to be introduced to those arguments, to see how they have functioned politically — in other words, delaying this critical discussion until we have been given some critical analytic tools. As there are many other writers, who, habitat by habitat, species by species, or pollutant by pollutant, might give a more compelling, frequently quantitatively-based, accounting, my own emphasis (which will be found in an "Interlude" between Parts Two and Three) rests on showing how certain critical Gaian "physiological" processes, so to speak, are presently facing irreparable damage from ill-conceived human activity, threats not to *all* of life, but to such a vast extent of nature's realm as to be, in anyone's ledger, an unfathomable loss.

For the present, I want to assume that the crisis is real, its true extent for now unspecified. For our purposes, it is enough that many, perhaps even most, people believe the threat to be an extremely serious one.[1] I saw this reflected in the essays I got in the 1990s from my mostly Latin-, Asian-, and African-American seventh and eighth graders in the inner-city middle school where I taught science and math for the San Francisco Unified School District, when they wrote in their journals about the world they thought their grandchildren would likely inhabit where trees no longer grew and the oceans had all dried up. I used to think my own version of the future was bleak until I encountered theirs.[2]

The torrent of ecological concern, and for many, anguish, that markedly increased as the millennial year approached, has had a number of significant tributaries feeding it. Coming of age in the 1950s and '60s, my imagined Doomsday centered on the Bomb. Like most of my contemporaries, I was possessed by fears and anxieties, by a dread that we would be the last humans to inhabit the planet.

At Caltech, which I entered as a freshman in 1957, the leader of the worldwide opposition to atomic testing, Prof. Linus Pauling, was one of our teachers in freshman chemistry, though his concerns about the effects of radiation on human health and reproduction I never heard, the Caltech faculty and administration not very hospitable to the public airing of such "controversial" ideas. His views on radioactive perils were amplified by Prof. E.B. Lewis, like Pauling a Nobel laureate

---

[1] An op-ed reflecting on the newly-released movie, "The Day After Tomorrow," wondered whether "we're suffering from apocalypse fatigue." San Francisco *Chronicle* (May 30, 2004).

[2] The students were possibly more realistic than I was. A Yale University forestry expert found that each year 15 billion trees are felled, while 10 billion are newly planted, for a loss of 5 billion trees a year. With some 3 trillion trees presently growing, that rate of loss would lead to a treeless world in about six centuries. ("News of the Day From Across the Nation," San Francisco *Chronicle*, September 3, 2015.)

and the teacher of my sophomore class in introductory genetics.[1] I later spent my junior and senior years in a Caltech/Rand Corporation seminar — the only undergraduate, the rest mostly Caltech faculty and Rand senior analysts — on issues of nuclear war and nuclear proliferation; I was already learning how to discern the language of obfuscation and deception. It seemed as if we collectively faced either a certain rapid vaporization from actual thermonuclear attacks, or a drawn-out, lower-level assault from the alpha, beta, and gamma rays that were being deployed into our lands and seas as result not only of the bomb's production and testing, but also by the resultant spread of civilian radiation technologies.

Other pollutants projected a bleak future, as well, for example the many poisonous chemicals industry and agribusiness were injecting into the environment, systematically undermining the health of organisms everywhere, so that a devastating implosion of biological variety was descending around us, the grim warning of Rachel Carson in her *Silent Spring* (1962). No longer could we assume our Springs would be filled with the songs of birds and buzz of insects. Related alarms had been sounded by Lewis Mumford, writing of the accelerating transformations of the natural and human worlds into machines, transformations begun hundreds, sometimes thousands of years ago; and by Murray Bookchin, the anarchist social theorist, writing under the *nom de plume*, Lewis Herber. In the 1970s neo-malthusians predicted the Earth's growing (human) population would rapidly exhaust all of its "resources," warily monitoring birth rates in India, China, and Latin America in particular.[2]

The Vietnam War, with its enormous escalation in utilizing the devastating power of war-making technology and the sheer tonnage of armaments unleashed against that hapless land, fueled the apocalyptic fears of many, particularly coming as it did only a few years after the terrifying showdown between the US and

---

[1] To my sister-in-law and brother, raising three young childen, I took Lewis's warnings that cows' milk should no longer be considered safe because of significant amounts of Strontium–90 contamination from nuclear tests. In his class we studied the damning statistics out of Hiroshima and Nagasaki, learned about the significantly lower life expectancy, among medical specialists, of radiologists, as well as efforts by the American Medical Association to suppress that information. At my dentist, I began refusing routine x-rays during his exam. Of course, as a kid, like others in the '40s and '50s, I had had my feet *regularly* x-rayed every time my parents took me for new shoes, the rays aimed right up my legs, no thought being given to shielding. In 1997, the US National Cancer Institute estimated that as many as 75,000 people might develop thyroid cancer as a result of drinking milk laced with radioactive iodine from atomic testing in the '50s when they were children. The report came from a study mandated by the US Congress in 1982. ("Cancer Warning From '50s Tests," San Francisco *Chronicle*, August 2, 1997.)

[2] For example, Paul Erlich, *The Population Bomb* (1968). "Resources," as we will learn later, was coined at the onset of capitalism.

the USSR over Cuba's deployment of Russian ballistic missiles. Those of us in the antiwar movement were privy (mostly through foreign press) to serious US plans under President Nixon to use its nuclear trump card as its military situation continued to deteriorate. It was axiomatic that any such move would result in a run-away, uncontrollable, totalization of the war. To be sure, neither the National Liberation Front nor North Vietnam had nuclear weapons to use in response. But the USSR did. And China would surely retaliate.[1]

Even without the use of nuclear weapons, the US military was pumping millions of gallons of the poison, Agent Orange, into the skies above Vietnam in order to kill ground vegetation (where an enemy might hide), polluting to water and land. In the process, untold numbers of US soldiers and Vietnamese were sickened, maimed, or killed, and both countries' genetic futures were given a malign bent from that chemical's gratuitous twist to the DNA of those exposed.

Nuclear power stations, the other tine of the atomic pitchfork, were nearly as worrisome as the weapons, generating mutagenic radioactive waste that would remain lethal for many hundreds of thousands of years. With the partial meltdowns at nuclear facilities in 1979 and 1986 at Three Mile Island and Chernobyl we would eventually see large chunks of the planet rendered permanently toxic, fit only for the monstrous and the mutated and, in theory, off-limits for the production of food.[2]

In my opinion, however, it was the "counterculture" of the '60s and '70s that provided a coherence and a new power to the various tributaries of Doomsday scenarios; from the 1970s on, these came together and established a mighty torrent of ecological alarm that was to be raised almost to the flood level, as a hippie ideology — with the official recognition in the US of Earth Day in 1970 and the establishment two years later of the Environmental Protection Agency (EPA) — transformed into mainstream politics. Psychedelic drugs like LSD, to the many who partook of its communion, seemed to speak of the manifold dangers to the natural world, itself revealed under the lens of acid as a many-layered mystery, the boundaries between objects vibrating with some kind of cosmic pulse in the trippers' eyes; everything was revealed as possessing a mosaic of textures and colors, nature perceived as alive in a way not explained or even allowed by the textbooks, its vitality as well as its fragility all too apparent.[3]

---

1 Because I am focusing on threats to the environment I will ignore here the protracted worldwide struggles against the Vietnam War, which played a large role in ending it and the decades-long international fight against the production, testing, and deployment of nuclear, especially first-strike, weapons, much of it successful. See Chapter 32.

2 Peasants near Chernobyl continue to eat mushrooms and other foods from contaminated areas; they have little choice in the matter. Any area behind physical barriers to protect people is quite obviously still permeable to birds, insects, bacteria, fungi, and small animals coming and going, taking outside the quarantined area anything consumed inside.

3 As shown rather nicely in James Cameron's film *Avatar*.

Some of the major corollaries to the primary countercultural themes, such as the emphasis on natural food, interest in alternative forms of healing, and the movement "back to the land" as refugees from the traumas of industrial and urban society reflected a general consensus that something very rotten was happening to the "natural" world. A dreaded endpoint loomed not so far in the future. At any rate, many voices were raised against a range of threats, joining to form a powerful chorus, one that had a decidedly apocalyptic tone to it; to seriously debate whose voice was loudest or most tuneful would, I think, be missing the point. Or, to return to the earlier metaphor, which current was most decisive?

The breadth of concern about these matters and the vast range of instances that are deeply alarming should alert us that the issues posed by our environmental crisis cut to the very core of existing social and economic institutions throughout the world; it should also suggest that what appears to be a general sickness of the biotic community on our planet might only be remedied, if at all, with a whole new set of tools, not least with a new language that's capable, for instance, of describing the many threats without implicitly providing support for the kind of thinking that produced the threats in the first place.[1] This new language should look critically at how we construct our realities by our assumptions about what *should* and *should not* be accorded ontologic status. Perhaps what we need is a way to describe phenomena more fully, not sucking "the life" out of them by rendering them objectified, flat, and dead. With the aid of such language, we will be better able to ponder anew the meaning of *place*; our modern sensibilities might take a deeper look at traditional societies and their sense of land. Perhaps such language will enable us to forge anew our sense of what it means to be alive in this world; for a theory of the end of life on this planet and how to fight against that must, I would argue, confront the question of just what life is.[2]

If our ecological crises are as bad as many credible commentators believe, in short, then a whole new way of thinking about our problems and how to respond is essential if we are to survive. Without what amounts to a new (actually, quite old in many ways) worldview, our crisis will remain critical; rather than ' escaping out from under and finding a new path, we shall simply spin in place,

---

[1] A wonderful example of such language is in David Abram, *The Spell of the Sensuous: Perception and Language in a More Than Human World* (New York: Vintage Books, 1996).

[2] This is not an easy question, as it turns out. For our sophomore biology midterm, an optional extra credit question suggested that we were facing the task of designing an experiment to determine if there were life on Mars, where a rocket was being designed to bring a robotized laboratory; our test question was, if this were so, for our experiment how would we *define life*? When our tests were returned, our professors admitted that *they* had been hired by NASA to design such experiments and had themselves to face the question, and the answer was anything but obvious, even to them.

sinking ever downward into the mire. Consequently, even initiatives that might seem to be creative and imaginative may fail if their very vocabulary and logic are the same that for hundreds or thousands of years helped mask the obvious fact that there was even a problem.

The new worldview, of course, must be informed and shaped by an understanding of how we arrived at our present fix. How could it have come to pass that in 2018, after some 5000 years of recorded history, we should face a nature no longer eager (as some of us seemed to imagine) to do our (frequently rather exorbitant) bidding, but rather, a planet taxed to her limits and obviously becoming ever-more "dysfunctional," her valued "resources" reaching the limits of their extractability, her aquifers and rivers drying up or poisoned. So much of our planet's surface now lies under concrete or blacktop and so many of her rivers are damned, so few unlogged forests remain and there is virtually no place not contaminated from plutonium, dioxin, PCB, and other deadly toxics, eating away at the core of our planet's vitality. More and more we confront points of no-return as we pass them, and ever-newer threats from biotech and nanotech, from a ramping up of both the scale and the perversity of the latest extractive modalities, as in fracking. While we watch countless species disappearing at an incomprehensible and gut-wrenching rate.[1] And witness weather patterns globally radically changing, in all probability due to human activities. How in the world did we lose sight of how much we were fouling our planet? Of the very real and pretty obvious limits of the environment's capacity to absorb our toxins? Whatever — or whoever — possessed us? Not an idle question, one we shall ponder in Part Three, Chapter 28, with some perplexing answers.

I shall show that we got into this fix partly by design, a design that can be described, traced, analyzed, and (at least in part) given parentage. To be sure, some of that design is lost in the mists of prehistory, but our discussion can cautiously and provisionally push back some of the fog, venturing educated guesses about what might have occurred based on what we can glean from artifacts and mythology. *Marxism & Witchcraft* will, of necessity, traverse such intellectual terrain, but readers should be aware that I am no archeologist, have no facility for

---

[1] Some years ago an estimate concluded that about 1000 of the world's 9000 species of birds were in danger of extinction, while about 70% (about 6300 species) were in decline; similar numbers hold for amphibians. Marine scientists on July 1, 2011 stated that ocean life is facing a devastating die-off. According to Dobrovolski ("Marx's Ecology and the Understanding of Land Cover Change," *Monthly Review* [May, 2012], pp. 31–32) 25% of mammalian, 13% of bird, and 11% of amphibian species were currently threatened with extinction. It is widely believed that the Earth is in a mass-extinction crisis. (Peter Femrite, "Big Animal Extinctions Leave Hole in Ecosystems," San Francisco *Chronicle*, October 27, 2015; Peter Femrite, "6th Mass Extinction in Progress, Study Shows," San Francisco *Chronicle*, June 20, 2015; Elizabeth Kolbert, *The Sixth Extinction: An Unnatural History* [New York: Henry Holt and Company, 2014.]

arcane languages, and with the possible exception of my discussions of archeoastronomy, most of what I say about the affairs of long ago has been said as well or even better elsewhere. For what happened millennia ago, I am a mere synthesizer, a seeker of deeper patterns. Where this work *will* break new ground in revealing the genesis of the design on the basis of my own research is for the more recent period, what many see as the beginnings of modern times, focusing particularly on the 16th and 17th centuries, when Western science, with its philosophical and social *imperium* to call the tunes for the world, took center stage. This is a topic for which I can claim some expertise. Knowing what occurred then will better enable us to imagine what might have gone on several thousand years previously, as well as to see possible common patterns. It will also, I believe, allow us deeper insight into our own times, how in the 21st century we are unknowingly being molded according to markedly similar designs, only they now can go deeper into the core of our humanity, as we shall see.

Marxism & Witchcraft is written, then, to account for how we came to this dead end and to enlarge our search for possible ways out, on the basis of new understandings of our world. To be sure, I believe that much — no, all! — of what I propose here to transform how we describe our worlds to help us pull back from the looming abyss is, in fact, *just* what we need to do; but convincing readers merely of the critical need for some new vantage point, not necessarily the one I propose, from which to view the incredible carnage would be almost as good. I especially hope to advance a discussion that, at least at the level needed, does not seem to be taking place.[1] It is long overdue. How, indeed, can we avoid our own self-destruction as a species, and the destruction of countless other species and habitats we will inevitably take with us, unless we realize the necessity of approaching our crisis with a new vocabulary and a new set of questions? It is certainly not a time to put certain topics "off limit," for what limits could conceivably hold against the possible demise of our species, of a multitude of species?[2] Of the destruction of a great deal of our planet?

[1]Though true in the 1980s and 1990s when I began writing this book, by 2020 such discussions *are* taking place.
[2] In 1998, Wade Davis wrote that from 1600 to 1900, about seventy-five species became extinct due to human activity, while from 1960 on, a conservative estimate was that about a thousand or more species *per year* disappeared. Harvard's E. O. Wilson believes that from 1975 to 2000 1,000,000 species will have disappeared, or one every thirteen minutes, a hundred four a day or 40,000 a year. (Wade Davis, *Shadows in the Sun: Travels to Landscapes of Spirit and Desire* [Washington, DC: Island Press, 1998], p. 113. Our ignorance at the rate of despeciation is compounded by the ongoing discovery of numbers of hitherto unknown species — 126 in one year by a single lab, for example. (David Perlman, "Cal Academy Team Finds New Species," San Francisco *Chronicle,* December 26, 2016.)

ii. MORE THAN THE SUM OF MY PARTS

Though at first glance the three wide-ranging parts of *Marxism & Witchcraft* may appear unrelated, there is a deep unity weaving them into a single garment. Part One, an investigation into the meaning of the "sacred" in traditional cultures; Part Two, on the assaults against and redefinitions of the "sacred" several centuries ago as a necessary foundation for the emergence of modern Capitalism and industrialism was laid; and Part Three, which focuses on these broad issues for our times and how such matters lay at the heart of our ecological crises.

Part One explores ancient meanings of the sacred by looking at its roots, widely reported for indigenous populations, in *land*, in the landscape and the life-forms it brought forth across the face of Mother Earth. An extended analysis of a largely unknown war waged against indigenous healers and healing practices that European colonialists relentlessly waged from the beginning[1] (in Europe as well against the traditional healers) provides a framework for us to better comprehend the sacred and how it functioned economically and socially in non-industrialized cultures. In indigenous societies, the shaman or healer is a guide to many sacred and profane matters, in ways that challenge the summary judgments of Marx and Engels that religion (or the sacred) are realms of illusion only. Part One critiques Marx and Engels' critique of religion as being merely an opiate of the people, suggesting that a firmly entrenched blindness at the heart of Marxist (as well as bourgeois) understanding of the ancient and virtually universal sense of the sacred is one of the important roots of our ecological crisis.

While Part One is inclusive, ranging far and wide over the continents and through the ages to marshall examples and draw its ominous conclusions, Part Two is narrower in its scope — specifically, the 17th-century scientific revolution in England, in particular the doctrines associated with Isaac Newton, the man to whom we are taught we owe the "mechanical universe," the by-now deeply engrained lesson that the universe, as well as all the bodies and creatures that are part of it, are law-driven and act like so many machines. Part Two takes a close look at Newton's alchemical research, revealing just what he was looking for and how it followed from where his *Principia* and *Opticks*, his two principal works of physics, left off. Our discussion explores the glaring contradiction between Newton the fountainhead of mechanism and the embarrassing fact that he actually repudiated mechanism, seeing it as only a superficial first step in understanding the natural world.

Marxism & Witchcraft situates the contradiction of the two Newtons within a narrative of how 17th-century mechanism served crucial social, political, economic, and especially ideological functions in early modern Europe. Science was

---

[1] At a time, it should be noted, when European medicine was not especially effective against illness, purposeful bleeding and/or giving mercury as a remedy were two of its central practices.

able, we shall see, to further two initial aims, first to further a requisite political stabilization after three centuries of vast social upheaval; and second, to provide a new way of understanding nature that could enable contemporary extractive industries, especially mining and timber, to extend the grasp and scale of their takings from nature a thousandfold, congruent with the demands of the nascent capitalist economy in 17th century England. We shall also explore how this perspective on the scientific revolution offers us a new way of conceptualizing the war against witches that tore apart early modern European society. As in Part One, struggles over the *sacred*, specifically in terms of "land-wars" regarding enclosures and the destruction of commoning, are windows through which we can observe just how *mechanism* served as the ideological antithesis of the sacred (rooted in the land and the trees, the rocks and the wind), like a hammer which was used to smash it to pieces.

The struggles over such matters over three hundred years ago, as a *particular* school of Western science came to power (institutionally and conceptually) and was able to codify the categories of peoples' perceptions and comprehensions, were critical in shaping our current ecological crisis. Specifically, the "dead" matter coded into the new mechanical reality by the Newtonian (and Cartesian) doctrine of *inertia* posited death as the ultimate reality. I shall argue that inert matter explicitly served to undercut widespread contemporary protests against the devastation of land, water, and forests that everywhere accompanied the onset of capitalism.

Finally, Part Two concludes with a second look at Marxism, exploring its origins out of a broader German critique by the "Young Hegelians" in the first decades of the 19th century against the sterility of Newtonian mechanistic and reductionistic thinking. For a number of reasons, however, the later Marx (specifically after the failures of the 1848 revolutions) ended up reconsidering and eventually re-adopting aspects of the mechanism he had once repudiated. His later mechanistic sense of science compounded an earlier problem at the heart of Marxist philosophy, in that Marx's lessons in philosophical dialectics were from Hegel, a conservative academic who had himself learned of dialectics in large measure from popular, especially rural, magic. Owing to its historical associations with popular insurgencies, Hegel felt he had to tame these, as we shall see. In thus following Hegel, Marx too ultimately uprooted his doctrines from a potentially fertile historical soil, one in which it is conceivable his ideas might have grown more profusely.

Having analyzed the 17th-century struggles over attacks on the meadows, rivers, forests, etc., including the creation of a new vocabulary used to justify them, *Marxism & Witchcraft* is now able to examine, in the "Interlude," the deferred question of whether our ecological situation today is, indeed, dire? Or, as some critics contrarily charge, are the fears over the environmental degradations largely speculative and overheated, for the most part capable of being explained in terms of age-old processes that have always been the small price we pay for humanity's domination over the natural world?[1] I show why a pessimistic reading of possible outcomes is more realistic, on the basis of the undermining of essential biotic or chemical pillars that support the Earth's biosphere. I present evidence that these threats are poised to wipe out most of our current living species.

The prospects of my successfully demonstrating to readers how our understanding of the world and our lives in it were radically reconstructed in the 17th century with an eye to justify the widespread assaults on the natural world are, I fear, slim. This is because hardly any of us are really able to grasp the non-industrial worldview that mechanical thinking banished from most of our world and our consciousness. Mechanism has succeeded in carrying out its task very effectively, so that escaping our 20th and 21st century categories is no easy matter, even if we know better, as many of us eventually find out. Consequently, Part Two's critique, for all its passion, logic, and wealth of supportive evidence will make its case at best only on the outer layers of most readers' awareness.

Yet, similar to what I describe for the 17th century, in the unfathomable impact on our thinking and ways of interacting with our world wrought by the new mechanistic science (Chapters 7 through 14), another such transformation of consciousness is underway in our world today. The fact that it is occurring *now* allows Part Three to examine up close and in daily detail how these changes are being negotiated to become embedded in our transformed consciousness. For we are living *through* it; indeed, for many of us it began when we were adults and is still permeating and altering our comprehension of everything. I refer, of course, to what is referred to as the "computer revolution" (which, given my analysis in Part Three, perhaps is better considered a computer or microelectronic *coup d'etat*).

Early on it was referred to as "hi-tech," meaning the computers and new devices, mostly digital, coming into play especially after the invention of transistors and the beginnings of the apotheosis of miniaturization. Part Three, a lengthy critique of modern (approximately post-1930s, particularly World War II and after) machinery, materials, and processes of production, argues that microelectronic communication and the digitalization of more and more aspects of our world, far from representing a way around mechanism, as is often claimed, should more accurately be described as an *extension* and *deepening* of mechanistic thinking. Now, however, mechanistic thinking can enter new domains and with a scope that poses far greater threats to the environment than ever before.

If 17th-century mechanism, as I shall argue, enabled deep mining technology, wetlands destruction, and plantation-scale agriculture to tear up landscapes of early modern history, the digital revolution will be found to vastly increase

---

[1] As one of many examples, see John Maddox, "The Doomsday Syndrome," *Saturday Review of Books* (Oct. 21, 1972), pp. 31–37. Or, more recently, Michael Shellenberger and Ted Nordhaus, "Environmentalism's Apocalyptic Daydream," *Insight: San Francisco Chronicle* (June 9, 2013).

both the scale and the dimensions of the assault on the natural realm, now indeed, mining our bodies (DNA) as well as colonizing our minds.

This is far more of an assault than anything 17th-century mechanism could ever have put into play. As before, at its heart the digital world not only is still a world consisting of *commodities*, it provides an ever-more far-reaching basis for a widespread explosion of commodification in early 21st-century capitalism.

At its core Part Three focuses on the largely unknown extreme toxicity of microelectronic production technology, the result of what I learned during the handful of years when I worked as a piping designer for several of the leading Silicon Valley hi-tech firms. From the chemicals used in their production, as we shall see in Chapter 21, devastating ecological and health problems, especially including the undermining of healthy reproduction, are as central to the ongoing computerization of our worlds as are its ubiquitous 0s and 1s.

That critique opens the door for closer scrutiny of this new tool of production, including the salient question of whether the new information technologies really "work" as promised? That is, do the military and the corporations, the two biggest sponsors of and customers for our new electronic devices, get more effective weaponry or war-making capabilities and higher productivity for their huge investments in hi-tech? The answer (in Chapter 19) will surprise many readers.

An historical and philosophical analysis of Information Theory (Chapters 22 and 23) prepares us for a critical examination of some political, economic, military, educational, aesthetic, and cultural ramifications of hi-tech, from which I propose an assessment of computer technology overall as constituting an unprecedented assault on the vitals of our natural order. Just as a mechanistic philosophy in the 17th century created an ideological justification for the plunder of natural "resources" by a nascent capitalist system (as Part Two will demonstrate), so too Information Theory (and Artificial Intelligence, Virtual Reality and the like) serve to make these newer assaults, mandated by late-20th and 21st-century capitalism on our social and cultural vitals, "reasonable."

These are no small matters, for I will argue that these vital aspects of the natural world must be defended at all costs if humanity is to have any hope of surviving. What such defenses might consist of will emerge in the course of the concluding chapters of Part Three.

The three parts of *Marxism & Witchcraft* constitute three different spears, each from a different direction, surrounding our prey — the creation of ways of thinking and feeling that came to accept ecological devastation as normal — thus cutting off its escape.

Several subsidiary questions are pushed to the fore by the wide-ranging discussions in *Marxism & Witchcraft*. One such issue is whether such profound shifts in thinking, as both Parts One, Two, and Three chronicle, really result from the machinations of the propertied classes so they can maintain control? Chapter 28 explains how such machinations, while real, end up ensnaring those who pull these levers, thus considerably complicating (as well as making more interesting) any notions of "conspiracy." Our need to reconstitute epistemology; a new look at ethics; the role of biotech in Capital's plans; and the possibility of establishing social controls over technological development all demand serious discussions, which Chapters 29, 30, and 31 venture. The two next chapters (32 and 33) address neo-pagan (animist) politics of the left and right — including the neo-pagan roots of Nazi ideology. Finally, the concluding chapter advances a theory of how left-wing dogmatism is created and perpetuated and returns once more to Marxism, to suggest that its one-sided materialism is a philosophical cul-de-sac that has prevented it both from comprehending the magnitude of threats to the environment and from being able to mount a credible attack on contemporary capitalism as a whole.

❧ ❧ ❧

Virtually all the movement organizations I worked with in the late '60s and '70s, mostly Marxist in their orientation, believed that environmental issues were simply not important to the working class. Commonly it was seen that ecological politics were hopelessly "middle class," were not strategic. My strong ecological concerns were thought to reflect my lack of serious politics. Such judgments carried ominous implications about the kind of mindset that would form them, and for the blinders that would have had to be worn to justify such an outlook. At times a kind of perverse comedy took place.[1] (Things were different in the anarchist left I later gravitated towards.)

As I try to sketch in the broad outlines for a new worldview, I shall focus on my historical interpretation of these blinders. Such blinders, of course, are not unique to the Marxist left. It is just that, in theory attuned to see the slightest injustice as it falls on the least of us, those eyes would be expected to readily see the "crimes against nature" committed in the name of civilization. That they did not is puzzling. That this blindness is similar across a broad spectrum of Marxist and bourgeois perspectives is also puzzling. I shall argue that the blinders were a social construction, put in place hundreds of years ago as a conscious enterprise. The

---

[1] In one revolutionary organization I helped form in the mid-1970s in the Bay Area we decided to have physical exercises at our Founding Congress, for we prided ourselves on the broadness of our revolutionary vision, saw the "personal as political" and valued the health of our activists. A proposal to have members do yoga at the Congress was rejected as reflecting an overly "countercultural" perspective, and instead members were led through Tai Chi exercises, the latter more in keeping with the organization's informal Maoist ideology. Yet, yoga and Tai Chi both ultimately share a common philosophical root in opposition to Western logic and scientific rationality, both part of the same undermining of the hegemony of Western assumptions that emerged in the '60s; there were merely stylistic differences between them — and the fact that socialist China had resurrected Tai Chi as a popular national pasttime.

development of a worldview blind to the desecrations being inflicted everywhere for hundreds of years was, as we say, "no accident." It was shaped, kneaded, and baked in the historical and social fires that attended the birth of early modern Europe and its construction of an ideology of the State and of colonialism.

I describe how blinders were fitted across that political spectrum. Though some of the fuller story of these matters would necessarily take us back some 5,000 years to the beginnings of centralizing States, as in ancient Egypt; to the development of metallurgy around 7,000 years ago; or to the rise of patriarchy some 3,000 years ago; or to the advent of large-scale warfare and armies; and to transformations in work, in nomadic practices, in religion, and in spirituality, most of which were in the distant past;[1] the center of our focus shall be on what has occurred in the past five or six centuries as European power and culture spread across the globe. I shall argue that it was necessary to create special blinders for the political left, particularly in the past century, and that the effectiveness of those blinders helps explain the nearly universal lack of appreciation for the depths of the environmental crisis on the Marxist left for a great many years. Those blinders help account for the painful paradox that at a time when there has been such a crying need for revolutionary uprising against power, specifically to save us from the relentless drive towards species-suicide pursued by those in command, there has been such a dearth of revolutionary theory or of ideas capable of adequately describing and making sense of the dis-order of Earthly matters.

Much of *Marxism & Witchcraft*, particularly Part Two, will show how and by whom the blinders were put in place, sowing confusion as a conceptual cloak over scenes of devastation.

* * *

As our crises deepened in the closing decades of the 20th century, a number of books have appeared which take very seriously the threats to the overall biosphere, with the result that their authors have sometimes been termed "apocalyptics." Though there is much I can agree with in each of the writer's or school's point of view, my major complaint with all of them is that they stop short, each of them dropping the story just when it starts getting good, when it develops a bite to it. If our crisis is as deep as I am sure each of them knows it to be, we must know, to whatever degree feasible, the whole story. This is hardly the time to pull analytic

---

[1] And the beginnings of cities, agriculture, irrigation, treated here only in passing to keep *Marxism & Witchcraft* within some bounds (which bounds I would hope some readers would wantonly break through). For agriculture and the deleterious effect its adoption has had on human health, culture, propensity for violence, and emotional well-being, see Spencer Wells, *Pandora's Seed: Why the Hunter-Gatherer Holds the Key to Our Survival* (New York: Random House, 2010). See also the seminal work by James Scott, *Against the Grain: A Deep History of the Earliest State* (New Hven, Conn.: Yale University Press, 2018).

punches, to dull a cutting edge. Nothing else but the full story, or as full as we can make it, will do our fight justice. To be sure, compromises will be necessary in matters of policy, of what is done — though hopefully not compromising ones. But our analysis and attempts to comprehend the source of our overwhelming problems must itself wear no blinders, must tolerate neither illusions nor timidity.

For example, Jonathan Schell in *The Fate of the Earth* (1982), a thorough examination of the nuclear threat, focused on the seeming relentless drive to nuclear war, fueled by the dynamics of an uncontrollable arms race and the proliferation of nuclear-armed states. In *The End of Nature* (1989) Bill McKibben bemoaned what he saw as the coming of a world thoroughly transformed by human hands, largely as a result of climate change (though at least for a million or so years, McKibben's touchstone of a pristine nature not transformed by humanity never really existed). Like *Marxism & Witchcraft*, *The Turning Point* (1982) by Fritjof Capra, traces the source of our out-of-balance contemporary world to the worldview born at the beginnings of modernity nearly four centuries ago, specifically singling out Descartes and Newton. But Capra doesn't tell enough of his story, treating "Newtonianism" only on the basis of a one-dimensional Newton, a pity since the three-dimensional Newton has much more to say on Capra's topic. The Cartesian–Newtonian system of the world had a history to it arising out of a particular stage in the development of early modern Europe and England and out of a particular configuration of social, cultural, and economic forces and transformations. Plans were laid in accord with certain interests. These Capra passes over too quickly. Most importantly, significant inner contradictions lie in the very bedrock of that world-view and send fissures spiderwebbing nearly everywhere (as we shall see in Chapters 12 through 14, especially), which, for those seeking to surmount Cartesian–Newtonian mechanism, provide promising footholds. These Capra largely ignores. Some more recent works in the apocalyptic vein I have examined suffer from similar limitations.

Two schools of thought among the apocalyptics deserve discussion. Deep Ecology emphasizes the importance of examining the spiritual sickness behind our society's ecological brutalizations, but, as with Capra, a political and historical void lies at the heart of their perspective, the spiritual sickness that they correctly perceive at the core of ecocide did not simply descend from the Heavens. Men wrote books justifying the need to exert control over the natural world and to squeeze from it all that could be bought and sold. Though in some measure the Deep Ecologists' insistence that humans have no more right to control, or benefit from, nature than any other species is a necessary corrective to the exclusively anthropomorphic axioms of nearly everyone else — except, of course, for the animism and pagan views common among indigenous people — we find a not-so-subtle death wish as well, a decided misanthropy in some of their positions. No good politics can ever come out of self-hatred. Self-hatred or its fraternal twin, guilt, are quicksands upon which the erection of any political or spiritual renewal is simply not possible.

Against Deep Ecology's refusal to enthrone humanity at the center stands Social Ecology, which warns of the implicit racist overtones to Deep Ecology's anti-immigrant positions and pointedly discusses their shortcomings in conjunction with a critique of the ecological views of Tom Metzger, a white supremacist. According to Social Ecology, Deep Ecology's reverence for nature is dangerous because all too easily it could be manipulated by "'Green Adolfs' for authoritarian ends."[1]

Because I have had my own interaction with such "Green Adolfs," in Part Three I shall return to this important debate between Deep Ecology and Social Ecology in my discussion in Chapter 33 of the profound ecological commitment at the heart of the early Nazi movement.

* * *

As is the case in virtually all issues of social consequence, environmental disasters are not experienced equally. A few of us are able to ride above the nearly ubiquitous storms, emerging relatively dry, while many others are overwhelmed, pretty much swept off the face of the planet in the tempest, *viz.* the poor and blacks and Latinos in New Orleans at the time of Hurricane Katrina. In general the richer, more powerful classes, races, and regions of the world have been spared exposure to some of the more extreme environmental attacks.

Poor communities and people of color are the primary eaters of the toxic stew industrial societies are continually cooking up — no exaggeration to describe it as a forced-feeding, livers engorged with industrial waste as if some kind of demonic *foie gras*, a sacrifice to the demanding Gods of Capital. In the US, examples would include immigrant farmworkers in the frequently sprayed fields in California's Central Valley; or the Navajos forced because of killing rates of unemployment to grabbing the only job available, at the bottom of a New Mexico uranium mine, their children playing on the exposed pile of radioactive tailings left *in situ* on the reservation; or the largely African American residents of Barnwell, South Carolina, where US government agencies successfully pushed for the siting of a nuclear waste dump, despite strong local opposition.

In the less industrialized areas of the world, poor countries are pressured to allow dumping on their soil of wastes, much of it toxic, that the US will not find space for on its own lands, the US essentially exporting, for a fee, the inevitable disease and death to future generations in the recipient lands. Alas, there

[1] Janet Biehl, "Ecology and the Modernization of Fascism in the German Ultra-Right," in *Ecofascism: Lessons from the German Experience* by Janet Biehl and Peter Staudenmaier (San Francisco: AK Press, 1995), p. 65. See also the stimulating discussion by Lierre Keith, "Culture of Resistance" in Aric McBay, Lierre Keith, and Derrick Jensen, *Deep Green Resistance: Strategy to Save the Planet* (New York: Seven Stories Press, 2011), especially pp. 115–26. I am grateful to Bill Aal for bringing this work to my attention .

are countries, many in Africa, so desperately poor that such trades have their takers. In the late 1980s the saga of a garbage barge from Ipswich, Long Island, was recounted as a kind of real-life serial as port after port, country after country, rejected its New-York generated, increasingly fetid, refuse, until finally a desperate host was found.

On the Mexican side of its border with the US, where a sprawl of largely US-based *maquiladora* firms have popped up in recent decades to take advantage of weak or non-existent Mexican environmental or labor protections, communities are suffering from outbreaks of clusters of babies being born without brains, or missing other essential parts of their nervous systems. Many observers believe these mutations result from high levels of toxic chemicals allowed to be discharged from the electronic, chemical, and other industries into the gutters, the drinking, washing, and playing water for the poor of the shanty towns where the industries are located.[1]

This pattern is found at the other end of production, where it is the poor who scavenge electronic devices, exposing themselves to lead and other heavy metals and to solvents.

It should come as no surprise to those who know the history of colonialism, this victimization of the poor and the non-white, though it should continue to provoke outrage and a resolve that fighting the fights of those without power, all selectively victimized, should have the highest priority in all environmental strategic thinking.

There is an hierarchy of victims among species in these wide-ranging attacks, so that soil microbes and insects, for example, are probably under more sustained and deadly assaults from the pesticides, herbicides, and fungicides than species like penguins in the Antarctic, partially (only) isolated from the toxic cornucopia modern industry has brought forth. Similarly besieged are the great schools of fish in the oceans, hunted down much as the buffalo were in the 19th century.

Yet it is also true that there are no places and no species — and no social classes or races within human societies — that do not face enormous threats to their existence due to the widespread dispersal of organophosphates, PCBs, plutonium and dioxins. The latter two are some of the deadliest poisons there are, known loose cannons in regard to reproductive processes in mammals, birds, amphibians, and insects, and now to be found in virtually all samples of human eggs, sperm, and breast milk that have been examined, no matter where they were collected. Ultimately, the frequency and severity of the resultant diseases will vary, neighborhood to neighborhood, though if everywhere noticeable amounts of dioxin or plutonium are found, everyone's safety is compromised. Especially worrisome is the fact that, as *Marxism & Witchcraft* will show, it is the capacity for reproduction itself that is under the most serious attack, whether we are the brown pelican or the human race. Rich or poor, white or black,

---

[1] San Francisco *Chronicle* (January 20, 1992).

human or *Drosophila melanogaster* (the fruit fly) may well determine what kind and how much of a nightmare your life will become, yet, in the final analysis, all will undoubtedly face night-time terrors, the distinctions somewhat mooted.

As in all wars, it is worth noting, alliances among all those under similar attacks is arguably the best strategy. That is, there is a powerful lesson in the commonality of these assaults on all of us, for while it is true that defense against ecological wars on the poor and minorities, because they are systemic and have such a long history, must take precedence, it is also true that everyone is under siege by several ongoing ecological disasters. Even if they spend their time at country estates, far from industrially compromised air, and drink pristine water, there simply is no escape from many of the toxins.

In that sense, we are all like Jews in Nazi Germany, fighting for our lives. So, even though I strongly agree with Social Ecologists' criticism of the race and class blindness of many of the Deep Ecologists, I do not believe it is on that issue that a clear ideological line in the sand is to be drawn. Not all will join the battle, but ultimately most will. Though the Social Ecologists' critique is an important one, in the end, the probability/certainty that unspeakable futures await *all* of our children if current trends persist lies a not-insignificant hope for organizing our common oppositions.

In a similar way, at least as far as the past 500 years are concerned, I will argue that there are instances where trying to determine whose grievances are most egregious in terms of race, class, gender, etc., in situations where oppression has many facets to it (and when doesn't it?) strikes me as akin to stirring up ideological whirlpools that chase round and round, in effect isolating a number of activists in a kind of stagnant backwater from the larger flows within society. Though such matters *are* important, they should not allow us to ignore the larger battles or to become cut off from each other or from the overall war in which we are engaged. Wherever possible, the aim should be to try to transform either/ors into both/ands, so long as we can do so without undercutting vital principles and issues.[1]

---

[1] I suspect that this is a more general pattern in human affairs: semmingly irreconcilable views or interests that, when looked at from a different perspective, are readily transcended, with both sides having been, though in different ways, right. Such occurred frequently in the history of science — for example, the raging controversy in 17th-century natural philosophy over *which* quantity, momentum or *vis viva*, was unchanged in any physical phenomenon involving motion. It turned out *both* were. But only after many gallons of ink were consumed in the debate. Another example would be the centuries-long battles over whether atoms (or indivisibles) truly existed. Of course they do, as we now all know, and of course they are also divisible, as the critics said, thus not really atomic at all, simply a significant level of quasi-stability in a descending hierarchy of structural coherence that ends... no one is sure.

In the transition to early modern times, then, race, class, and gender, each in its own way but largely around the same time and for related reasons, emerged as the three principal "orthogonal" axes along which oppression and exploitation were necessarily meted out as part of the process of consolidating the new, capitalist-structured social order; indeed, around the same time a fourth axis formed to represent the exploitation and oppression of *nature as a whole*, particularly of nature's wild places and of her many other species, both those which were especially useful to humans and those which just happened to get in the way.

iii. Constructing Realities

Marxism & Witchcraft is so named for a variety of reasons, some of which will be explained later in this Introduction, but for now it will suffice to point out that both Marxism and witchcraft represent kinds of philosophical and social "enthusiasms," a concept I shall discuss in great detail in Part Two; for the battle against *enthusiasm* has historically been associated with putting in place the very blinders I have referred to. To be an enthusiast has historically meant that one's ideas and life were "outside the boundaries" of what was accepted and, therefore ultimately, of what could be *real*. In the context of the 17th century, on which we will focus, as a critical turning point in world history, "enthusiasm" was the yeast thought to have encouraged the ferment of social upheaval and revolution, which in England led to the Great Rebellion against the monarchy. Due particularly to the enthusiasts, critics believed, the revolution spread radical and republican ideas and included attacks on property, sexual restraints, gender roles, class privileges, and notions of sin. Ultimately, it led to the execution of the king, the abolitions of the monarchy, the State Church, and the House of Lords, as well as a near-democratization of the Army. Limits had to be reestablished and new ones put in place if society was to be saved, many powerful people came to feel.

A society's sense of what is real (or what are the boundaries within which reality can be allowed to wander), is critical to its survival. It is the glue that holds everything else together. In our nearly ubiquitous industrialized and capitalist-dominated world, *our* sense of what is real rests nearly wholly on our science and technology.

As the historian Herbert Butterfield has observed:

> when we speak of Western civilization being carried to an oriental country like Japan in recent generations, we do not mean Graeco-Roman philosophy and humanist ideals, we do not mean the Christianising of Japan, we mean the science, the modes of thought and all that apparatus of civilization which were beginning to change the face of the West in the latter half of the seventeenth century.[1]

---

[1] Herbert Butterfield, *The Whig Interpretation of History* (London: G. Bell, 1951), p. 179. *Cf.* parallel remarks by Henry Kissinger, described in Chapter 28.

For some three to four hundred years, science has laid its claim to the central suites in the tower of knowledge constructed in the heart of the West and the lands and peoples over which it had dominion. Though others in the academy (Law, Theology, Classics, etc.) claimed those quarters as well, and on the basis of class, tradition, patrons among the aristocracy and the rich, etc., had grounds for believing the rooms were truly theirs, ultimately in the West the contest was never really in question. Through its claim to have a direct path to a knowable world, science was able to declare that it alone had a way to establish "certainty." In particular, the science making such claims increasingly was a specifically *mechanistic* science. Mechanistic science was also critical in preparing the culture for a certain kind of intellectual and social world, through the new concepts and vocabulary it introduced, much as the first roads into the wilderness prepare it for its eventual taming by civilization. Though there have been numerous times when challenges to that science-dominated outlook have become vocal, the most recent upsurge of such views began in the mid-1950s and early '60s, coinciding with the onset of the political revolt of the '60s that tore much of Western culture to tatters.

As social insurgencies nearly always do, the cultural upheavals of the 1960s brought to the fore "alternative" forms of apprehending nature, including forms of magic, non-Western forms of healing, aspects of divination (the *I Ching*), etc.[1] To some degree, such views even entered the academy for a handful of years, including some of the very best physics departments and sessions at the annual meetings of the American Association for the Advancement of Science (AAAS).[2] But more recently a coordinated and widespread counteroffensive from the scientific establishment and others reasserted the notion of an objectifiably knowable world, uniquely determined by a "scientific" or "rational" process of winnowing truth from falsehood. It is remarkable how wide a range of political persuasions are now in basic agreement with this new form of the old orthodoxy, ranging from representatives of the mainstream of the scientific community, like Carl Sagan or Gerald Holton, to left anarchists such as those associated with *Z* magazine, Noam Chomsky, or the main theoretician of Social Ecology, Murray Bookchin. What seems to fill all of them with a profound foreboding is the contemporary flourishing of ideas from various occult and pagan traditions, not only in popular, but in learned culture too. As mentioned earlier, the Social Ecologists argue that pagan views can readily lead to fascism, an end darkly hinted at by Holton and Sagan as well.

[1] See the illuminating discussion in Lierre Keith, *op. cit.*

[2] We shall see in Part Two how during the 17th century English Revolution insurgents demanded classes in astrology be taught at Oxford and Cambridge Universities. For a lucid and revealing account of both the partial acceptance, and eventual marginalization and repudiation, of such views in more modern times, see David Kaiser, *How the Hippies Saved Physics: Science, Counterculture, and the Quantum Revival* (New York: W.W. Norton, 2011).

For such a broad political consensus to emerge in the '80s and '90s suggests that a deep-seated crisis of faith is coming to the surface in our larger culture, particularly since the consensus so clearly flies in the face of considerable evidence directly contrary to the new orthodoxy, evidence from within the sciences themselves. Empirical and theoretical studies over the past few decades have dismantled many of the pillars supporting the original orthodoxy. (Especially quantum entanglement [Bell's Theorem], but also the work of Rupert Sheldrake and J. Benveniste are examples.) Yet the new orthodoxy, far from re-erecting or fixing any of those pillars, simply ignores or dismisses the studies, as if even acknowledging its critics were beneath its dignity. I want to trace where this crisis of faith comes from, because it is an important one; for even while I reject the naivete, indeed, at times, pig-headedness, behind the new orthodoxy, I respect the anguish behind its blind leaps of faith and the depth of the fears among its acolytes. Some of their fears I sometimes share.

In part a re-examination of the role of science was inevitable given its role in World War II, a conflict that on one side featured a technological and scientific fabrication of an industrial form of murder; and on the other, a technological and scientific creation of a single weapon responsible for a different kind of mass killing. Many of the scientists who had worked on the Manhattan Project took the lead in the post-war reassessment. In part, the new concern about the nature and role in the west of mechanistic science fed a new push to examine its history.

An important milestone in the re-examination of science came in the mid-1950s with Thomas Kuhn's *The Copernican Revolution*,[1] for it allowed a critical re-evaluation of the sweeping philosophic transformations in early modern Europe, focusing on the epistemological challenges facing 16th-, 17th- and 18th-century adherents of the "new science."

The revival in 1543 by Copernicus of an ancient notion of a sun-centered universe, itself rooted in an even earlier Hermetic tradition, generated many of the vexing questions faced by the European philosophical community for the next two centuries or more. A fundamental problem was that Copernicus' notion that the Earth was simply another planet, like the others orbiting around the Sun, was to many natural philosophers obviously true, yet in terms of the not-totally-unreasonable standards of intellectual inquiry at the time, Copernicus's theory could not be *proved*. Worse, reasonable arguments were put forth to disprove it, or at least to cast serious doubts that the theory had any merit. If the Earth were truly spinning on its axis, it stood to reason that a spear thrown east (in the direction of the spin) would go further than one thrown west, for example. Also, if the Earth orbited the Sun, any star viewed in January, say, should noticeably shift its position in the heavens when viewed in July, the Earth now on the other side of the solar system, because of parallax. Neither effect was observed, fundamentally challenging the new theory's credibility.

It was to be the task of the leading figures of the scientific revolution to con-

---

1 (Cambridge, Massachusetts: Harvard University Press, 1957).

struct a system of intellectual inquiry — including new standards of "proof" — to justify Copernicanism. For starters, it was clear that a new theory of motion was needed.

By the late 17th or early 18th century among natural philosophers the Copernican theory had become overwhelmingly favored, sooner in Protestant than Catholic countries after Galileo's condemnation. Kuhn argues that the sweeping victory of the Copernican vision within such a relatively short time was not primarily by the Copernicans' initially marshalling overwhelmingly convincing evidence (parallax was never seen until the middle of the 19th century) or by the clear force of their logic. Some of this victory was intellectually less heroic — the opponents of the new theory getting old and dying, while new generations grew up assuming the Copernican notion to be superior, not really needing a rigorous "proof" for something so obviously true. The new sciences that emerged after Copernicus were implicitly *charged with* erecting a "proof" that his theory was correct. And by the time of the latter part of the scientific revolution, a new criteria for truth and how assertions could be proven was, indeed, emerging. These new rules had, in effect, been the object of the 16th- and 17th-centuries' long search, a new set of standards by which to decide disagreements, after three centuries suffering religious, class, and civil wars that had ripped apart the social fabric of 15th-, 16th-, and 17th-century Europe. The warp of those deeply unsettling differences of opinion in religion, we might say, got woven together with the woof of these uncertainties about the very frame of the cosmos, whether it was geocentric or heliocentric, or, as some visionaries like Giordano Bruno proclaimed, non-centric, infinite in all directions; this created an altogether unprecedented cloak of religious and philosophical uncertainty that Europe wore at the dawn of modern times. The new "rules of reasoning." as Descartes and Newton referred to them, were simultaneously invented by philosophers and used by them and others to justify their radical new way of looking at the world. In other words, the philosophical victory of Copernicanism was in no small measure achieved on the basis of self-generated justifications, "proofs" derived from the very premises of the scientific world-view they presumed to award victory to in the battle between rival cosmologies.

This is not to minimize certain very attractive features of Copernicus's theory. It offered a stunning explanation for the puzzling phenomenon of retrograde motion, the apparent backward motion of planets on occasions in their passage across the sky. Yet Copernicus's model did not match well with actual observations of the planetary positions, was not that much more accurate. The new theory was only slightly, if at all, less cumbersome than the older, Ptolemaic theory.

The implications of Kuhn's *Copernican Revolution* seem inescapable: the choice for the new Copernican theory, which later was to form the physical basis for the 17-century scientific revolution, was founded on new rules for philosophizing drafted by Galileo, Francis Bacon, Descartes, Hobbes, Newton, Leibniz, Locke, and Hume, that had an essentially subjective side, a place where a philosopher's sense of order, symmetry, simplicity, beauty and especially God (or lack thereof), played a key though hidden role in his or her allegiance to this new intellectual order. And if *those* did become criteria, then a person's sense of religion, politics, class, or gender could easily have helped to mold the particular view of nature (s)he adopted, as we shall see in the case of Newton. Once the boogeyperson of subjectivity in the 17th-century epistemological revolution gains entrance, however, there is no telling where it may tear holes in the fabric of Western culture — which is why Kuhn's critics have gone to great pains to focus on his critical philosophic and social *gaffe*. For it is difficult not to conclude that the epistemology developed purposely to satisfy the desperately felt need for objectivity to resolve the intellectual restlessness that had engulfed Europe since the Renaissance and to put to rest the feelings of rootlessness that two centuries of religious and class warfare had brought, that epistemology only had the *appearance* of objectivity. For all its fuming against the ill-founded conceits of those who believed in earlier, pre-scientific notions, such as magic, the new science, at its foundations, still significantly rested on a core of belief, as critical as its supposed mass of evidence and use of inductive logic.

While tremendous excitement was born of Kuhn's analysis, it raised some very serious questions. It took a number of years for the alarming implications of his viewpoint to emerge, and for a while the broad vistas opened by his and related studies were filled with all manner of intriguing and colorful creations.[1] But slowly the ground underneath began to crumble. Surely one could not believe that *science* at bottom was as arbitrary as one's preferences for music or what kind of God one worshipped! — not *science*, which in the century after the Reformation that had been characterized by such worrisome skepticism, doubt, uncertainty, and social upheaval, had stepped forward to re-establish a basis for certitude. If that were true, then what other nonsense could follow on its heels?

In the end Kuhn more or less recanted, repudiating the deeper relativistic implications of his work and arguing for a privileged, knowable, reality. But it was too late. His were not the only holes made in the dike holding back the tides of subjectivity, and it would have taken considerably more than a single pair of thumbs to have stopped the serious leakage. The emerging awareness of the ecological crisis caused other troubling questions to be asked about science. So too did feminism, pointing out the troubling one-sidedness of scientific ideation. Anti-colonial voices raised similar criticism, establishing new and revealing perspec-

---

1 For reasons of brevity, I am omitting other critical studies, especially the work by E. A. Burtt, *The Metaphysical Foundations of Modern Science* (Garden City, New York: Doubleday Anchor, 1952) and Alexandre Koyré (for example, his *Newtonian Studies* (Cambridge, Mass.: 1965). Kuhn later extended his critique in his (to me, far less sucessful but hugely influential) *The Structure of Scientific Revolutions* (Chicago: Univ. of Chicago Press. 1970). Both Burtt and Koyré were, for me as a new graduate student in the history of science, enormously important in clarifying the terrain and pointing out which directions to explore.

tives.[1] Other historians and sociologists presented detailed studies of what scientists actually did. The results were revealing and troubling. Reading their journals, lab notes, and correspondence provided a deeper, sometimes contradictory understanding of what some of the key scientists actually believed, assumptions and working hypotheses which were usually not acknowledged in what was published in journal articles or treatises. In the name of post-modernism, some critics analyzed scientific statements as if they were primarily matters of rhetoric.

Owing to the crisis of the '60s, industrialization and the nation-state were called into question, the very soil where the roots of science arguably lie. At the very least, the role of the scientific community in producing a world increasingly courting annihilation through weapons of mass destruction, crystalized for many by the war in Vietnam, resulted in a number of wary eyes being cast on what they saw as the dubious premises and values of science.

All of these, I suspect, are behind the crisis of faith I mentioned a few pages ago — as soon as one has abandoned the old orthodoxy, shaky though it may be, the ground begins to dissolve. There is no telling, once started, where the disintegration will lead to or how much ultimately will be called into question. If they could dare stare into it, that is an abyss the spokespeople for the new orthodoxy (see list page 32) are profoundly shaken by. Is there anyone who does not, in some measure at least, share their vertigo? The way down *is* precipitous, with no obvious footholds or places to grab onto. Who can blame them for their attempts to latch onto the brambles of the older certitudes (physics before relativity and quantum mechanics took sizable bites out of the cause-and-effect, law-like certitudes of the older deterministic behavior of nature, before impetuous violations of common sense became commonplace), even though the soil can no longer hold their roots, rather than face the anguish of perhaps ending up having no firm ground, no basis for real knowledge, no certitude? Is there any wonder that they issue dark warnings about "the flight from science and reason?"

Yet, much as I can sympathize with their fears, and agree with a good many of their arguments, there is a fundamental difficulty in their new orthodoxy: born out of desperation, it is ready to grasp at any hopes, even when they are as puny as last year's dessicated straws. Put to a number of easy tests, they simply crumble. Admittedly, the challenge posed by Kuhn's relativism is a grave one, but to jump from one shaky foundation to another, holding to a now-untenable prequantum conception of an "objective" reality cut off from human consciousness, is no real solution. A more honest response is called for, acknowledging the many holes in the traditional views of science and either legitimately patching them or otherwise addressing those numerous critiques.

That has simply not been done. Instead, the gravest fears are carted out and a very broad brush is used to depict crude associations. The most monstrous of

---

[1] For example, Susantha Goonatilake, *Aborted Discovery: Science & Creativity in the Third World* (London: Zed Books Ltd., 1984).

fakers are paired with respected researchers, as if they represented one and the same camp. Only against one's absolute enemies is such gross exaggeration and such tendentious refusal to make distinctions normally committed. It means that Sagan, Holton, Bookchin, Chomsky, *Z* Magazine, Paul Gross, Norman Levitt[1] and scores of others who have rushed to defend the new orthodoxy have had to avert their eyes from some very responsible, well-founded research, because of their terror that acknowledging any of it would inevitably lead to the whole of it — the fortune tellers and cult-leaders and human sacrifices and cannibalism, in short order, the end of civilization as they know it. It is a very broad brush, indeed, its quite-sturdy handle made from their collective dread of the wild.

But ignored knowledge can never be a path of wisdom, nor can it be ignored forever. The new orthodoxy, at best, is but a holding pattern, a way of forestalling the inevitable. Ineluctably, in one way or another, this kind of truth will out. There is too much that is already known. We simply shall have to face the abyss and negotiate somehow its contours and precipices.

The remainder of this book, in passing, will wrestle with these challenges. I make no claim to have reached a satisfactory resolution, indeed, that has not really been my central purpose, which has been the search for a new form of thinking that might conceivably provide us a way out of the ecological nightmare that is gripping our world. Sections of this study will nonetheless attempt to clarify important issues posed by the many radical critiques of science and will propose new approaches to try resolving them.

There is a deeper purpose here, as well. Writing in the mid-19th century, Marx concluded that criticism of the capitalist society of his time should begin with a critique of its religion, its spiritual cloak. Today, however, in the first decades of the 21st century, a criticism of that still-reigning economic and political system must begin with its science, both the driver of its productive engine and its present ideological *raison d'etre.*

In the course of these pages, I must touch on a multitude of issues and topics, but one major theme will lead throughout as its *leitmotif*: this has been termed "the death of nature" by Carolyn Merchant, one of my students and colleagues, while another, Morris Berman, has suggested the need to find our way out through a "reenchantment of the world."[2] Merchant, Berman, and I entitled a session we proposed (unsuccessfully) in 1980 for a panel at the annual convention of the American Association for the Advancement of Science, "Dead on Arrival: the Fate of Nature in the Scientific Revolution." That fate (or, less hyperbolically, its unprecedented potential fate) and what we can do about it are the central pillars or themes around which the rest of my structure is built.

---

[1] The authors of *Higher Superstition: The Academic Left and Its Quarrels with Science* (Baltimore: Johns Hopkins University Press, 1994).

[2] Merchant, *The Death of Nature: Women, Ecology, and the Scientific Revolution* (San Francisco: Harper & Row, 1980). Berman, *The Reenchantment of the World* (Ithaca: Cornell Univ. Press, 1981).

All the rest is, as it should be, given the overwhelming import of all that those pillars support, mere trim, embellishment, afterthoughts.

Marxism & Witchcraft may prove to be difficult to read, I fear, harder still to digest — not because its argument is obscure or complicated. On the contrary, I believe the opposite to be the case. The argument is fundamentally a simple one. But its central thesis drains a huge and varied conceptual terrain, where there exists a great plethora of rivers, streams, brooks, creeks, springs, etc., each in its own right revelatory.

In a book of bearable length, I try to explore as many of these as feasible, though, basically, each of them repeats the same story from a slightly different perspective. In itself, this should pose little problem, but many readers may well be troubled that so many of my different stories will challenge very fundamental beliefs they have about any number of axioms, truisms, and other notions that by now pass pretty much for our culture's common wisdom. I shall be addressing these core beliefs and assumptions from a different vantage point than is usually done, in a great many cases inverting meanings that have long been taken for granted by nearly everyone. Were I to do this once, twice, a dozen times, even, I might be forgiven, perhaps applauded; but by my hundredth or two hundredth attempt to undermine the essentials about some fundamental of our culture that my reader has long held dear, my inversions may well become increasingly problematic, perhaps even tiresome.

Yet, it is precisely because the crisis of our times is so deep and so structured into the fabric of our society that I must be willing to challenge so much. Perhaps not surprisingly, if one pulls at the loose threads in the overall fabric of Western society that the devastating impact of the West on the Earth's general biotic health during the past several centuries represents, because that thread is so integral to the fabric, it proceeds to unravel. Though I have few illusions of my facility at the loom, I cannot responsibly end a book like *Marxism & Witchcraft* with my readers knee-deep in the unraveled threads of a defunct worldview, for that would invite only a deeper despair or even nihilism. So, at least provisionally, reweave I must.

One subsidiary theme of this work consists of my attempt to integrate both the political resistance movements arising in the 1960s throughout the world and the spread of spiritual and (self-) healing impulses that emerged around the same time. I shall demonstrate the very many solid points of connection and mutuality, as well as remark on the clear sense of conflict (apparent and real) between these two kinds of "movements," what have been termed the "political" and "spiritual."

The '60s political upheaval was spectacularly widespread — the US, France, Germany, Czechoslovakia, Japan, Mexico, Uruguay, China, indeed, just about everywhere,[1] but especially Vietnam, arguably the critical inspiration for most of the others. By the end of the 1960s, many if not most of the political movements and the numerous struggles spawned by the overall social ferment

---

[1] Compare this with the rapid and widespread Occupy rebellions in 2011.

had coalesced mostly around one or another variety of Marxism, with the notable exception of parts of feminism.

Though much of my analysis here will be critical of Marxism for repeated and sometimes shocking failures in the fight against a long series of historical oppressions and exploitations, a great deal of the reasoning bringing me to those conclusions was on the basis of specifically Marxist categories and theories. Indeed, the first half of the title of Part One is "A Marxist Theory of the Apocalypse…," where I shall argue that much of the modern apocalyptic disquiet stems directly from the forces generated by modern capitalist (for starters) society. That I later ("… & an Ecological Critique of Marxism") criticize Marxism for its (for our purposes, comparable to that of the capitalists') blindness to ecological issues should not mask either my obvious debt to the Marxist analysis of capitalist society or my having participated in and led any number of radical and (as we understood ourselves) revolutionary organizations that were consciously operating within a Marxist framework.

Though the shape of early 21st-century capitalism, dominated by multinational (that is to say, supranational) corporations and by quasi-public financial institutions like the World Bank and the International Monetary Fund and by international trade agreements like NAFTA, having policing mechanisms, is altogether different from the classical capitalism of 19th-century Britain that Marx studied, it is still a *capitalist system,* and so conforms to many of the same patterns and processes of its earlier incarnations. The dissolution of the USSR, the collapse of "socialism" in Eastern Europe and the marked departure from socialist ideals in the Peoples' Republic of China should not hide the fact that Marx's analysis of the relationship between those who own the means of production and those who own only their capacity to work for the others in the main holds true, even when mystified by the proliferation of supposed independent contractors and a segmenting of the hierarchies of management. The fetishization of the commodity has not changed, only revealing more bizarre sides of itself and increasingly appearing in non-tangible forms, as in financialization.

For a period of some decades after World War II, many observers prematurely concluded that some of the old contradictions between labor and capital had receded, and that a trade union-won generalized affluence was possibly attainable for advanced capitalist countries like the US. Yet the past four decades have seen a systematic counteroffensive by capital and the era of downsizing has also meant assaults on pension plans, medical benefits, social security, the eight-hour day, and, of course, unions themselves. Even slavery has made a comeback. At the same time, we see the near ubiquitous shantytowns and the large percentages of permanently unemployed or marginally employed move from the outlying "undeveloped" parts of the world into the centers of the empire and the centers of the former "Eastern bloc." The old antagonisms between capital and labor have decidedly re-emerged with a vengeance, only now with professionals and the middle class, such as teachers, becoming proletarianized.

For the "spiritual" theme, my focus is on witchcraft for a number of reasons, but the fact that witchcraft is a specifically women-oriented spiritual practice is particularly significant to my analysis. Witchcraft, additionally, has arguably had remarkable, though hidden, historical ties to ecological issues that uniquely qualify it, at least potentially, to provide critical insights and cultural roots needed to sustain us through our contemporary environmental crisis. This follows partly from witchcraft being rooted more in women's, than men's, culture, and hence its being tied to the historic social role for women in reproduction, in ensuring in every culture and every era the survival of a people. As an historian of science I also was drawn to the study of witchcraft because it represented a view of nature directly contrary to our modern mechanical scientific understanding, based as it was on magic and on primarily women adherents —as opposed to the way modern, Western science overwhelmingly has consisted, since the 17th century, of men. Not least I was drawn to study witchcraft because it is the errant sister among the other spiritual paths, the one most feared, shunned, and many times, hunted down, as during the two centuries in Europe when massive numbers of accused witches were arrested, tortured, and executed. As a Jew growing up just after the liberation of the Nazi concentration camps, perhaps, it was inevitable for me to unconsciously identify with the image of the witch at the stake.

At any rate, *Marxism & Witchcraft* will use each of these two crystalized formations of the political and the spiritual as a lens through which a refraction of the other formation is ventured.

❊ ❊ ❊

I was led to witchcraft also because during a period of political soul-searching, after a Marxist organization I had helped form underwent a painful political split in the late '70s, I was recruited in 1980 by a close friend (later my wife) into helping plan an anti-nuclear demonstration being organized as a commemoration of the first anniversary of the Three Mile Island nuclear disaster. (At the time I had been struck by how low-key the response to Three Mile Island was within my Marxist organization.) As I later learned, many of those organizing the commemoration were Bay Area witches.

The march was conceived as a ritual, as an ongoing theatrical performance, evoking in its fluid passage of floats; theater troops; dancers; people chanting; paper-mache statues; contingents honoring the traditional elements of air, fire, water, and Earth; statues representing the sun; and a mock nuclear reactor repetitively going out of control,[1] the vast and ordinarily numbing totality of the horrors of the nuclear age, making it palpable, viscerally more than intellectually.

---

[1] I played a scientist on the reactor-float, vainly trying to establish control in a skit we performed over and over on a flat-bed truck.

With three notable exceptions, there were to be no speeches.[1] It was the most effective political event I had ever been part of in my decades of activism.

Much to my shock, a year later I was practicing witchcraft. I had received a phone call from Starhawk, who had been one of the main organizers of the procession. She proposed that she and I and a handful of others form a political affinity group to participate in the upcoming blockade of the Diablo Canyon nuclear-power facility near San Luis Obispo, then under construction. Our group, she elaborated, would do magic as part of our political activism.

Through several conversations we had over the months since the TMI demonstration, and a lecture of mine she had attended, Starhawk knew I had been drawn to the study of magic as a scholar trying to investigate Newton's alchemy. She also knew that I had come to see a fundamentally important political and ideological role that magic had historically played in the 17th-century English revolution. On the basis of research I had done a decade earlier, it had become the focus of my writing.[2] Now she was asking me to join a group that would use magic as part of *our* organizing, making magic a component of a 20th-century *US* movement. How could I not find Starhawk's proposal compelling? It resonated with so many of my beliefs and interests. I eagerly joined.

Our group, Matrix, began at the time of the 1981 Diablo Canyon blockade, but as we learned from that and participated in other campaigns, our engagement broadened from its initial focus on nuclear power and weapons. Indeed, the nuclear issue was but one aspect of a colossus that we had to confront. A brief discussion of our work can be found in Part Three, Chapter 32.

---

[1] We had planned no speeches, but one element in our procession was a GI veteran who participated in the US atomic-bomb tests as a soldier stationed a couple hundred yards from Ground Zero, as were tens of thousands of other troops who were involuntarily given high radiation doses as part of this despicable government experiment. During the march he repeatedly told their dismal stories of cancers and early deaths and a government denying all responsibilty. We also invited delegations of Hiroshima/Nagasaki survivors and representatives from the American Indian Movement as guests, and both chose to speak at the march's end.

[2] My early work on magic and the left during the English Civil War, based on research conducted in England on a Guggenheim Fellowship, was put out in mimeographed form and mailed to people I thought might be interested, under the title "How Sir Isaac Newton Helped Restore Law'n'Order to the West." Part One, a general introduction, was printed in *Liberation* magazine in their May, 1972 issue, Part Three, a poem, in "Alternative Sources of Energy." Later I published a summary in a volume dedicated to my PhD advisor, Henry Guerlac, *The Analytic Spirit: Essays in the History of Science in Honor of...*, ed. Harry Woolf (Ithaca, New York: Cornell Univ. Press, 1981), under the title "Newton's Inside Out! Magic, Class Struggle, and the Rise of Mechanism in the West."

In graduate school I had been presented with lectures regarding the "paradox" of witchcraft in Western history — the torture and execution of those countless (mostly) women did *not* occur in the medieval "Dark Ages," as most people, educated or not, assumed, but *precisely* at the time Europe supposedly was undergoing an unprecedented transition to early *modern* times. The transition included:

* the emergence of the first nation-states, a new form of political entity;

* large-scale mining (and other extractive industries) fueled both by increased warfare, and by the rapid expansion of trade, premised on the belief that it would have a free hand in taking anything wanted from nature, and from ancient times closely associated with warfare;

* the rapid and irreversible dispossession of peasants across Europe from their customary land base through a process of "enclosures," essentially an expropriation or privatization of common lands; similar dispossession occurred in the new colonies;

* European powers extending their grip on the Americas, Asia, and elsewhere, establishing the infrastructure and rationalization for colonialism;

* the industrialization of slave-taking and selling;

* the emergence of a world-wide capitalist economy, based on a new logic of exchange;

* most significantly, science coming into its power as a new way of comprehending the natural world and investigating its properties, along with a rise in what is considered "reason."

Remarkably, some of the major defenders of persecuting witches were the scientists themselves or their propagandists. To most historians of witchcraft, this overlap, persecution of the witches against a background of the rise of science, has constituted a major mystery, many of them retreating into explanations of the mass execution of witches as some kind of historical aberration, "mass hysteria," or, in more recent years, as a kind of sociological phenomenon, the consequence of particular historical stressors.[1] The more I investigated magic, the more inadequate such "explanations" seemed. I offer an alternative hypothesis in Chapter 10, arguing that the repression of witches in Europe was a necessary corollary to the simultaneous subjugation of indigenous spiritual beliefs and practices in the Americas and elsewhere, as well as to the taming of nature herself that the new extractive industries were required.

———————

[1] For claims of mass hysteria, see, *e.g.*, Cullen Murphy, *God's Jury: The Inquisition and the Making of the Modern World* (Boston: Mariner Books, 2012), p. 197. Though I do not accept his overarching thesis that the onset of syphillis in Europe was the causative agent of the "witch craze," Stanislav Andreski's critique of sociological explanations is instructive. Andreski, "The Syphilitic Shock," in David Hicks (ed.), *Ritual and Belief: Readings in the Anthropology of Religion* (New York: McGraw Hill, 2002), pp. 370–93.

The phenomena of witchcraft and the war against it, I shall argue, played a key role in the history of European civilization that has barely been hinted at, despite the many decades of detailed scholarly studies of those bloody centuries.

iv. An Epistemological Stew

Having been trained at elite academic institutions, first in physics and then in historical scholarship, I base a great deal of my analysis (especially in Part Two) on the standard tools of the historian's craft, marshalling my array of primary sources and commentaries by contemporaries or authorities in an effort to sweep readers to the unavoidable conclusion that it must have happened quite as I claim.

But I also demonstrate in Part Two that to a substantial degree, such a mode of argumentation rests far less on its purported logic and weight of evidence and far more on naked class (and race and gender) interests than is generally realized. Though it has its decided merits, the method of the scholars also has huge, somewhat consciously chosen, blind spots, frequently used as a tool for casting aside of crucial forms of intelligence, knowledge, and wisdom. That is, there are serious limitations to the scholarly approach precisely because it is a method *designed* to justify some arenas as being "off limits." For these and other reasons, it is both right and necessary to supplement its insights with ones arrived at by altogether different paths, by direct experience, by poetry, etc. My goal has not been an illusory "objectivity," but to present an honest and faithful explanation of the matters at hand.

So, may my readers be aware of my assumptions and "mere" hunches, the better to arm themselves, I would hope, against any biases, any improper shadings or ignoring of contrary evidence that my political and social proclivities, despite my best efforts, might easily spawn, I try to clarify which of my claims are speculative, which rest on more-or-less solid foundations.

There is no doubt a danger in my method, for some readers, less critical of the norm of objectivity than I, may well be put off by my flagrant violations of the cardinal rule of distancing myself from my depictions of the scenes of historical crimes; since the overall theme of this book is the creation of the ideological foundations that have enabled dire threats to humanity and to innumerable other species, as well as the disappearance of a similarly incalculable number of irreplaceable habitats, to become manifest everywhere, I am especially loathe to speak or write dispassionately. If senseless death is frequently an occasion for anger, sometimes to outrage or raw fury, how much more so to the senseless death of the countless creatures and the disappearance of so much beauty and vitality from our world? I simply cannot find it in myself to write of such matters as if, at some deeper level, it did not matter; for the very *act* of writing of such affairs *as if* they did not matter, I will argue, is one of the roots of the problem and helps account for a collective numbing of our sensibilities to which, as a culture, we have become complicit.

v. An Apology of Sorts

When I began *Marxism & Witchcraft* I realized I had to go broader, at the expense at times, of deeper. To get to the heart of our ecological catastrophe, I had to learn anthropology, ethnography, to explore the labyrinth of what is called "earth mysteries," to find out about ethnobotany, to study magic, mythology, and language, medicine and other forms of healing, to immerse myself in music. For a book on the ecological crisis, all of these and more are critical, for, at least in the West, that crisis did not develop its deeply rooted presence across the face of the planet without embedding its malign DNA into every institution, common practice, and received wisdom. For these I have tried to read widely, but I make no claims to scholarship.

It was also critical that my book be some 600-odd pages, not 6,000 — or even 60,000. Certainly the breadth of concerns, if each were discussed judiciously and in-depth, would necessitate a corresponding lengthening of the text. But that would also so restrict its readership, to experts and the rare foolhardy enthusiast equal to a gargantuan time-consuming read. Our crisis is too dire to so lock up this discussion. It concerns all of us, indeed, crosses boundaries even between species.

Hence a number of compromises, stories told but not demonstrated, counter-examples left out, a historical narrative that at times skips decades, even centuries, as the story unfolds. These compromises, however, do not compromise my argument.

A more thorough book, also a considerably longer one, would have tried to document all of it, taking not only many more hundreds of pages, but decades longer to write. I decided it was far better to finish the book while I was still alive.

Structurally the book is arranged in a spiral, for a number of themes and topics that are central or emblematic to a telling of the convoluted roots of our manifold environmental problems are visited repeatedly: themes such as, not surprisingly, health and healing, magic, Marxism, science, and the creation of an ideology able to mask the many desecrations inflicted on nature so that they appear to be something else; but also, less obviously, topics like music and dance, time and myth, colonization and military weaponry, and, most critically, the seedbeds of agriculture, education, and language. In a sense, these constitute the woof upon which my tellings will be woven.

Each successive time we visit one of these topics it will be from a new, broader, perspective, at times affording a higher, more complete vision of the overall conceptual terrain. If the multiplicity of themes is perplexing, at times the discussion seemingly unfocused, it is because in order to grasp how our crisis has managed to get to this point, it is important for us to examine at least a small handful of the many fronts on which something so fundamental as a meltdown of our planetary biotic realm is being played out.

If not all of my stories are "provable," a wealth of evidence exists for most of them. For all of them, however, if not a proof, I have a convincing narrative of what I think transpired. Taken as a whole, I believe that they offer us the most coherent framework for looking at and comprehending all that we, as a society, are experiencing as we rush headlong into what might well be our demise. I believe thus we may be able to navigate the turbulent times ahead of us. For the ecologically disastrous futures we are confronting, those stories potentially may provide us with a pathway to species-survival.

Accordingly, readers may choose to hold in suspension their need to accept or reject my various pronouncements, re-interpretations, and inversions, simply allowing them to accumulate, to percolate in their consciousnesses, watching to see if the brew becomes strong enough to convince them. Eventually it should at least become clear how much the many stories and the numerous inversions are but different aspects of one and the same story. At that point, the reader may well decide if that story makes sense and judge the degree to which my interpretations are or are not able to make things seem rightside up at last.

2

Colonialism & The Hypodermic Needle

> Western medicine was a key weapon in the campaign
> to weaken indigenous culture and promote allegiance
> to European institutions and modes of thought. —
> Malcolm Nicolson, "Medicine and Racial Politics:
> Changing Images of the New Zealand Maori in the
> Nineteenth Century," (ed.) David Arnold, *Imperial
> Medicine and Indigenous Society* (1986).

i. HEALING & IMPERIALISM

Having talked about everything under the sun and promised the moon, I must now bring matters down to earth. This I shall do by demonstrating how my two titular, polar opposites, Marxism and witchcraft, can and must be made congruent. A detailed history and analysis of healing in relation to imperialism will illustrate how interpenetrating the two categories are, as well as offering us a promising path to take into our extended, more general discussion of the roots of our present environmental crisis, a path affording us the opportunity of examining up close the soil of false ideology from which those roots have historically drawn their toxic sustenance.

Because of this false ideology, a monumental confusion has so muddied the waters of consciousness that, until recently, nearly all of us, but particularly those on the political left, were prevented from grasping the magnitude of the environmental collapse that we have been headed towards for a very long time.

The outward expansion of European power for the past 500 years and, in this and the previous century, its seeming retreat and recrudescence, form the foreground of this story. That our discussion of the ecological crisis should begin with a history of colonialism should come as no surprise, for arguably the origins of the crisis arose out of the confrontation of civilization with the "wild." Though there were examples of the wild in the European past, by the 16th century they were few enough to be marginalized, seen, as in the remote hills of Scotland, as isolated instances. But in the Americas, Africa, parts of Asia, and Oceana, there were tribal people, "wild" people, people outside the boundaries, and yet who, from the very beginning, were integral to the political economies of the mother colonizing powers. *They* could not simply be made incidental or be ignored, so it was ideologically necessary to reconstruct, on a new and firm basis, a notion of *otherness* that could swallow up the whole of the colonized people, a process that occurred in conjunction with new understandings crystalizing just then about the nature of matter, of how things are and how they become something else, thanks to the stirrings of what came to be known as the "scientific revolution."[1]

European conquest, eventually of most of the rest of the planet, was a long and complex process, but from early on sickness and how it was to be treated played a vital role in the victory European societies eventually won. Not all of what occurred was as malevolent or as conscious as the reported provision by Lord Jeffrey Amherst to the Native American tribes he was trying to subdue of blankets taken from smallpox victims.[2] Nature itself was seemingly an ally of the European powers and, in many respects, disease vectors were as important as the cannons the conquerors arrived with.

On the two continents of the Americas that for millennia had been mostly isolated from the rest of the world and presumably populated much later than the African or Eurasian landmasses, the aboriginal Americans were "naive" and innocent in terms of many of the pathogens and disease entities that had historically afflicted African and Eurasian populations.[3] With the latter's established trade routes and a tradition of large numbers of domestic animals living in close proximity to a human population with whom they shared some pathogens, Eurasian urban centers especially had long lived with epidemic diseases as perennial scourges that were simply one of their facts of life. Disastrous as such diseases as measles, German measles, smallpox, or typhus could be, their preva-

---

[1] In the first instance, the *other* stood for the wild of the colonies and for their dark-skinned people, but it could and would stand too for the female, for the nonurban, those who spoke another mother tongue, or for insects, trees — or, at other times, for the homeless, the sexual others, those of other classes or those who merely act weird, the "crazies." With the coming of the early modern world, acceptable norms of just about all those categories get increasingly narrowed.

[2] Seemingly good evidence of Amherst's biological warfare existed in his time, but according to William H. McNeill, *Plagues and People* (New York: Doubleday, 1976), p. 222 it has disappeared and the reports cannot be confirmed. However, in a letter to a subordinate officer, Amherst wrote: "Could it not be contrived to Send the Small Pox among the Disaffected Tribes of Indians?" and insisted they must use "every Strategem in our power to Reduce them." The letter is quoted in Roxanne Dunbar-Ortiz, *An Indigenous Peoples' History of the United States* (Boston: Beacon Press, 2014), p. 68.

[3] My discussion is heavily indebted to Alfred W. Crosby, *Ecological Imperialism: The Biological Expansion of Europe, 900–1900* (Cambridge, England: Cambridge Univ. Press, 1986) and McNeill, *op. cit.*, as well as by Virgil J. Vogel, *American Indian Medicine* (New York: Ballantine Books, 1973).

lence over the centuries and millennia at least meant that many adults had been exposed to them in childhood. Quite a few died. But some survived. The constant presence of these diseases thus ensured that eventually some sort of partial immunity existed among the population.

No such medical background had existed in the Americas, and Native Americans North and South were totally unprepared for contact with the Europeans and the diseases they carried. For some places, more than the cannon (though always in conjunction with it), illness served in a critical capacity of "softening up" the population for their eventual domination by the Europeans.

Medical statistics for the Americas prior to Columbus are non-existent,[1] but skeletal remains of pre-Columbian Indians, at least those not in the tropics (where the environment is supportive of all life, including that of vermin and pathogens), have revealed a remarkable story of good health.[2] Considerable evidence suggests the absence not only of infectious diseases in general, but of such major degenerative diseases as cancer and heart problems. Some categories of illness simply cannot be found:

> Whole important scourges were [in pre-Columbian times] wholly unknown.... Cancer was rare.... There was no [leprosy].... There were, apparently, no [skin tumors].[3]

Diseases of the skin, and perhaps mental disorders,[4] were much scarcer than they would be among whites after they settled the land. Explorers initially found few if any cases of palsy, toothlessness, body deformity, gout, kidney stones, asthma, eczema, lameness, blindness, scurvy, dropsy, diabetes, paralysis or arteriosclerosis; even diseases arising from nutritional deficiencies appeared rare. Native Americans *were* afflicted primarily by pleurisy, arthritis, tuberculosis, rheumatism, leishmaniasis, cleft palette, dysentery, worms, and other stomach disorders.[5]

Indeed, based on this and other evidence, the historian William McNeill has concluded that in the Americas, legends of a Golden Age, at least in terms of health, might have had some basis, quoting elders who, after several decades of contact with the Spanish had such a devastating epidemiological effect on native populations, claimed that in their youth disease simply had not "existed in

---

[1] See my discussion in Chapter 4, pp. 99f.

[2] My examples are from Vogel, *op. cit*, p. 149, and David Arnold (ed.), *Imperial Medicine and Indigenous Society* (Manchester, England: Manchester Univ. Press, 1988, p. 41.

[3] Vogel, *op. cit.*, p. 149.

[4] The practice of trepanning went on in pre-Columbian South America, possibly to treat mental disorders.

[5] Vogel, *op. cit.*, pp. 1–11, 150–51. My thanks to Tricia Case, who helped me understand the role of leishmaniasis.

any form."[1] (A little later, we shall examine such claims in more detail.) A similar story was told by John Savage, a surgeon, in 1806 in regard to the Maori of New Zealand, whom he had investigated.[2]

Given not only the Native American's lack of previous contact with numerous European diseases, but the ability of many wild Eurasian plants and animals quickly to wreak havoc in virgin but uprooted ecologies, which were as unprepared for wild pigs or plantain, say, as their human populations were for smallpox or typhus, in many cases, including in the Americas, native economies and ecologies simply crumbled.[3] The effects were, as is well known, catastrophic, though it is still difficult for us to grasp the magnitude of it all. Almost instantly, smallpox wiped out about one-third of Native American populations, followed quickly by other diseases like typhus and, later, influenza (the latter possibly a new disease for the Europeans, as well, who were also devastated by the flu). Within fifty years of contact, native populations commonly had fallen to ten per cent of their pre-Columbian size.[4] In some places populations levelled out at one-twentieth or one-twenty-fifth of what they had been, of course not only because of disease, that being only one of several forms death might take as colonialism took root in its "new" world.[5]

Modern examples can be even more telling, though by now disease itself plays a more minor role. One South American tribe in 1903 had contact with a single missionary who was especially cautious, well-aware of the devastating effects that contact with whites usually had brought to isolated natives. Despite his precautions, the tribe declined from approximately seven thousand in 1903 to only 500 by 1918. A decade later, only 27 of the tribe still survived; by 1950 they had been reduced to two or three individuals. The tribe quite simply had disappeared in the space of five decades.[6]

Because of the location and isolation of the Americas, the effect of European expansion on Native Americans is most dramatic and probably the best known, but similar experiences befell indigenous populations in southern Africa (the Hottentots, among others), the Aborigines in Australia, other Pacific Islanders, and inhabitants of Siberia.[7]

---

[1] McNeill, *op. cit.,* p. 177; Wade Davis, *Light at the Edge of the World* (Vancouver, Canada: Douglas & Mcintyre, 2001/07), p. 124 on the "essentially disease-free" nature of native society upon contact.

[2] Arnold, *op. cit.,* p. 69.

[3] Prior to contact, other ecological collapses had occurred, most notably from the overhunting of the wooly mammoth and other Pleistocene animals, although this has been challeged by Charles C. Mann, *1491: New Reveations of the Americas Before Columbus* (New York: Vintage Books, 2006), p. 176; Crosby, *op. cit.,* p. 56.

[4] McNeill, *op. cit.,* p. 180. Dunbar-Ortiz questions the emphasis on disease, pp. 39ff.

[5] *Ibid.,* p. 190; Ralph Davis, *The Rise of the Atlantic Economies* (Ithaca, New York: Cornell Univ. Press, 1973), p. 11.

[6] This example is from McNeill, *op. cit,* pp. 180–81.

[7] *Ibid.,* pp. 192, 281.

With the non-American, other non-European countries undergoing colonization, such as China, India, or Turkey, or because they were part of the same land
mass as Europe and thus had both greater epidemiological experience and disease
patterns in common with Europe, sickness was related in a more subtle way to
colonialism's ultimate victory. Though not under assault by a corps of new disease
entities, these cultures underwent another kind of medical attack, both ideological
and institutional, white authorities attempting to destroy native healing traditions.[1]
This was, indeed, the pattern everywhere. Even when, as in Mexico, newly-arrived Europeans found a population that enjoyed extraordinary sanitation facilities, handling waste and fresh water with great technical skill, as well as benefitting
from a medical care exceeding anything found in Europe — with research institutions collecting and studying plants and animals for possible medical uses, a
medical academy, ongoing experimental medical research, and licensing procedures — nearly immediately the Conquistadores set out to destroy all of it.[2]

In the Americas, the historic collapse of native healing arts in the face of
colonialism would seem as natural a process as the progress of the diseases
against which local populations had no protection. One might, that is, expect
that the shattering experience of devastating epidemics would have called everything in question for many of the conquered peoples.[3] But far more was involved. For the scorched-earth campaigns, the harsh treatment of natives who
were enslaved, the destruction of local economies of subsistence agriculture or
fishing, and the resultant starvation or severe malnutrition of natives fundamentally undermined both social and political institutions and peoples' health.[4] European contact generally resulted in a great weakening of local economies,
established systems governing exchange, often where land was held in common,
and of traditional hunting, herding or growing practices that had formerly
brought food to people's stomachs. In the Indian Ocean, for example, Portuguese ships "were able to disrupt Arab trade routes at will and forced trading
concessions from the rulers of coastal and island states."[5]

---

1 Arnold, *op. cit.*, pp. vi, 3, 8, 16–17, 51, 78–79, and 127.

2 I learned about Mexican pre-conquest medicine from the anthropologist, the
late Luis Kemnitzer. At the same time Spanish authorities were dismantling indigenous organs of healing, an expedition led by Francisco Hernandez was sent
to study the natural history of New Spain, including questioning the medicine
men about the herbs they used. (David Goodman, "Philip II' s Patronage of Science and Engineering," *British Journal for the History of Science* 16 [1983], pp.
62–65.) A similar suppression of native medicine occurred in the Ellice Islands
when in 1892 they became a British Protectorate. Richard Rudgley, *The Lost
Civilizations of the Stone Age* (New York: Simon & Schuster, 2000), p. 124.

3 McNeill, *op. cit.*, p. 181.

4 *Ibid*, pp. 181f.

5 Arnold, *op. cit.*, p. 46; Davis, *op. cit.*, p. 11.

In New Spain, huge amounts of what had been rich agricultural land on which the Otomi Indians raised a variety of vegetables were transformed into grazing land for sheep and cattle. The number of animals exploded, going from about 41,000 sheep in the 1540s (tended by African-slave shepherds) to some 2,000,000 by the mid-1560s. By then the Otomi were rapidly dying out. A few rich Spanish men owned the animals, some with as many as 150,000 head by 1579.[1] Such shifts in land and animal usage meant introducing and forcibly maintaining the private ownership of land, in cultures that previously had known only land held in common.[2]

In the Valle de Mezquital (source of the above figures) the arrival of the flocks and herds rapidly changed the overall terrain, in many places transforming what had been a lush vegetable cover into bare soil. Forests in the Valle were cut down, both to increase land for pasture and to supply nearby mines with wood for support beams and for fuel. Semi-arid species of plants began to take over and the hillsides became heavily eroded. Springs on which the farmers had depended began to disappear. By the end of the 16th century only an eroded and gullied mesquite desert was left.[3]

In society after society, European contact generated hungry, landless people who ended up in small towns or cities, which swelled with the destitute, scraping by if they were lucky. New laws would criminalize them, as their growing numbers led to penalizing the poor, as in Europe, with its recently dispossessed peasantry. One mining town in Bolivia, Potosí, where the workers were mostly enslaved Indians, by the middle of the 16th century had become one of the largest cities in the world.[4]

Swollen with new inhabitants and (in the Americas) with new kinds of domesticated animals, such as horses and pigs, that carried diseases capable of infecting humans, villagers and town-dwellers would soon find their pathways and roads awash with a variety of fecal matter — pig, horse, dog, chicken, and human — which soil and water could no longer process (in lower densities, arguably not that problematic), leading to outbreaks of disease.[5] Because of extensive mining development — by the last half of the 16th century both the

---

[1] In Spain, herds had rarely been over 800 to a thousand head.
[2] See E. P. Thompson, *Customs in Common* (New York: New Press, 1993) for an illuminating discussion of the parallel processes of teaching private ownership to the English and to the people being colonized.
[3] Alexander Cockburn, "A Short, Meat-Oriented History of the World: From Eden to Mattole," *New Left Review* 215 (Jan.–Feb., 1996), pp. 16ff.
[4] Davis, *op. cit.*, p. 52.
[5] I believe I witnessed something like this process in Nepali villages I visited in 1970, finding the pathways just as I describe them here. Any scratches or insect bites on bare or sandaled feet easily became infected under such conditions. See Crosby, *op. cit.*, pp. 19, 76, 173–76; Davis, *op. cit.*, p. 46.

Peruvian and Mexican economies were dominated by mining and the industries and services it required — toxic chemicals, such as mercury (Mexico, c. 1550, Peru, 1573) and lead further fouled their waters and degraded local health.[1] In the meantime, outraged by the "excessive" liberty Indians were accustomed to, Spanish administrators insisted on imposing forced labor on natives. The fouled and poisoned water supplies, along with the hunger and overcrowded urban centers filled with makeshift shelters, and, of course, the outright massacres combined to kill many of those who survived the initial wave of epidemics.

> Spain built a new society in America... but Spain's principal gift to America was the destruction of its people....[2]

The numbers involved in this destruction are mind-boggling, but since we are pursuing the mentality that has today led humanity to the edges of self-annihilation, it is instructive to look at the scales involved. In 1912, after several hundred years of colonialism, an agent wrote to Sir Edward Gray, the British Foreign Secretary:

> The numbers of Indians killed either by starvation — often purposely brought about by the destruction of crops over whole districts or inflicted as a form of death penalty on individuals who have failed to bring in their quota of rubber — or by deliberate murder by bullet, fire, beheading, or flogging to death, and accompanied by a variety of atrocious tortures, during the course of these twelve years, in order to extort these 4,000 tons of rubber, cannot have been less than 30,000, and possibly came to many more.[3]

The agent was writing in 1912, well before the job of "risk assessment engineer" had been invented, someone whose job it now is to calculate how many maimed, diseased, mangled, or dead bodies a given industrial practice is "worth." The agent's accounting works out, at any rate, using his conservative estimate, to approximately 7.5 dead Indians per ton of rubber, or 2,500 per year.

Overall figures for the loss of native life in the Americas are exceedingly difficult to obtain, in large part because of huge uncertainties about the population prior to contact with Europeans. For just the region of Amazonia in South America, Hecht and Cockburn estimate that the 200,000 Indians at the time they wrote are what remains of the some six to twelve million Indians who inhabited the Amazon basin in 1492. Taking note that estimates for pre-contact

[1] Davis, *op. cit.*, pp. 42ff, 47, 50–53.

[2] *Ibid.*, p. 55.

[3] Michael Taussig, *Shamanism, Colonialism, and the Wild Man: A Study in Terror and Healing* (Chicago: Univ. of Chicago Press, 1987), p. 20.

population appears to be steadily increasing among scholars, they suggest the possibility of a final figure closer to fifteen million. This would indicate a ratio of survivors for the low population estimate (six million) of one out of thirty, for the high (fifteen million) one out of forty-five.[1]

After an extended discussion of the enormous difficulties in arriving at any population estimate, Charles C. Mann in *1491: New Revelations of the Americas Before Columbus*, comes to something of a modern consensus figure of forty million indigenous in the Americas prior to contact.[2]

In the face of all this demographic collapse, it should come as no surprise that European victory came so relatively easily. There were times the cannons did not even have to be used. To be sure, resistance was immediate and persistent, including a rebellion by indigenous people that killed all of the crew Columbus left behind in "Hispaniola" while he returned to Spain (taking *indios* as slaves back with him) to prepare for a second voyage of conquest and plunder. For decades and centuries, Native Americans fought back, frequently with arms, against Ponce de Leon, the Pilgrims, the French, English, Spanish, and Portuguese, against Canada and, of course, what became the United States throughout the 16th, 17th, 18th, 19th, and 20th centuries — and still, in the 21st, it goes on. Along with rebellion, there was also acquiescence, sometimes after a long period of resistance that was finally suppressed. Citing increased instances of suicide or infanticide among the colonized, McNeill speaks of a "wholesale demoralization and simple surrender of will"[3] among Native Americans. "Faith in established institutions and beliefs," he continues, "cannot easily withstand such disasters; skills and knowledge disappear."[4]

To both Europeans and some natives, it was hard not to see the former's relative immunity to the diseases devastating the latter as anything but a clear message of divine favor/anger. With no doubt undue (and arguably racist) exaggeration, McNeill claims a "stunned acquiescence" to Spanish superiority and a docility in following the orders of whites in South America.[5] Missionaries proudly reported mass conversions.

Elsewhere, as late as 1831 in the Middle East, an area used to Eurasian diseases, a particularly devastating cholera epidemic evoked a popular terror that "helped to discredit traditional authority within the Moslem world and opened the way for reception of European medicine."[6] Something much deeper than a simple fleeing from an obviously sinking ship was taking place as native healing arts weakened and lost ground to colonial medicine, for at the same time, par-

1 Susanna Hecht & Alexander Cockburn, *The Fate of the Forest: Developers, Destroyers and Defenders of the Amazon* (New York: 1990), pp. 3, 282n3.
2 Mann, *op. cit.*, pp. 147–48. Dunbar-Ortiz estimates a western hemisphere population of between fifteen and one hundred million (*op. cit.*, p. 17).
3 McNeill, *op. cit.*, p. 182.
4 *Ibid.*, p. 181.
5 McNeill, *Ibid.*, pp. 183–84.
6 *Ibid.*, p. 234.

ticularly in the Americas, many whites came to appreciate the potent, effective, and skillful healing arts of the natives, as we shall see.[1]

At the same time, however, no matter where we look it is clear that the suppression of native healers and the effort to bring sickness under the sway of Western medicine from early on was a primary objective of the colonial powers, and played a critical role, in fact, in the worldwide victory of colonialism.[2] From the earliest times, missionaries were as essential as the soldiers on board the ships of the colonial forces and if in their one hand they held Holy Writ, in the other eventually a hypodermic needle would appear. In Africa, in the late 19th century, missionaries sought to use medicine in such a manner, sometimes being recruited specifically on the basis of their prior medical training.[2]

Healing arts among the American native peoples were the responsibility of their medicine people, including their shamans. These healers, some with specialties in different healing modalities, were viewed by the colonials as doubly dangerous.[3] First, at a time of a demonization of the indigenous people that served the ideological function of debasing the colonial *subject,* so that they were reduced to *objects,* upon whom cruel and despicable tortures and murders, starvation and being worked to death could be (and were) done, the Indian healers reflected the diabolical infestation that invested trees, springs, special rocks, etc. with divinity — an infestation that the Conquistadores and later waves of colonialists sought to wipe out. Second, native shamans and healers not infrequently emerged as the leaders of local resistance to the colonial powers, as in Peru, with the Taki Onqoy millennial movement against the colonialists.[4]

An Ecclesiastical Council in Lima in 1567 issued a decree that priests should "extirpate the innumerable superstitions, ceremonies, and diabolical rites" of the indigenous people. Authorities worried about native drunkenness and were appalled at their "inordinate fondness" for music and dancing.[5] Shrines and talis-

---

[1] Arnold, *op. cit.;* Vogel, *op. cit.;* David Kubrin, Marcia Altman, John Kwasnik, and Tina Logan, "The People's Healers: Healthcare and Class Struggle in the United States in the 19th Century,"dittoed, 1974.

[2] Arnold, *op. cit,.* On Columbus' second voyage, five "religiosos" sailed, both for the colonists and to "bring the indigenous people into the bosum of the Church." Collen Murphy, *op. cit.,* p. 218.

[3] Arnold, *op. cit.,* pp. 51, 78–79.

[4] Silvia Federici, *Caliban and the Witch: Women, the Body, and Primitive Accumulation* (Brooklyn, N.Y: Autonomedia, 2004) pp. 225–26.

[5] *Ibid.,* p, 200. European observers sometimes commented on the parallels between the suppression of native rites and crackdowns on carnival and other festivals in Europe. In general authorities tended to fear celebrations as "springboards for rebellion against white [or upper-class] rule…" and were apt to equate the indigenous of the new world with the lower classes of the old. (Barbara Ehrenreich, *Dancing in the Streets: A History of Collective Joy* [New York: Metropolitan Books, 2006], pp.160–61, 168–73, 177–78.)

mans were to be destroyed and their "witch-doctors," who "guard the *huacas* [i.e., springs, or mountains] and converse with the devil" were to be arrested.[1] In 1533 and 1543, when the Cupul in the Yucatan Peninsula rose in insurrection against the Conquistadores, it was at Saci, an ancient religious center, where it began; more than three centuries later, Jose Maria Barrera led Mayan revolutionaries to a holy well in the rainforest, I would think so as to seek spiritual protection and inspiration for their planned insurrection.

Given the clear priority in crushing any signs of resistance to colonial rule, authorities focused especially on native spiritual leaders, who were the healers.[2] Western leaders were convinced that victory over the natives turned on the question of whose healing traditions, their own or that of the Europeans, native people followed. Captain John Burke, a late 19th century US Army officer in the Indian wars, for example, wrote that the Indian healers were "an influence antagonistic to the rapid absorption of the new ideas and the adoption of new customs." Indeed, only "after we have thoroughly rooted the medicine men [*sic*: there were women healers] from their entrenchments and made them an object of ridicule," could whites "hope to bend and train the mind of our Indian wards in the direction of civilization." His sentiments and attacks on the medicine men by then had a long history.

> The hostility of the Christian missionaries to the medicine men
> is revealed in many of their accounts. Thus all the principal forces
> of European erosion of Indian society have been brought to bear
> in the assault against the medicine men. To the extent that his
> influence was weakened, white influence was able to penetrate.[3]

Elsewhere among colonized people, the same pattern is found. Missionaries had as their primary goal destroying the authority of Inuit shamans.[4] In Africa, Christian missionaries pitted the miracles of their God against those of the African deities.[5] In Nigeria, the British outlawed the traditional native healers. Nicole Maxwell's *The Jungle Search for Nature's Cures* portrays how the Catholic and Protestant missionaries were trying in the 1950s to win natives over from their shamanic medicine, partly because that change — their swallowing penicillin instead of animistic magic — was the most tangible measure of their degree of civilization, of just how reasonable they were willing to be, how acculturated and

---

1 Federici, *op. cit.*, p. 200.

2 Hans Duerr, *Dreamtime* (Oxford, England: Basil Blackwell, 1987), p. 214, n. 107.

3 Vogel, *op. cit.*, pp. 31–32.

4 Davis, *Shadows in the Sun*, p. 24.

5 Michael T. Taussig, *The Devil and Commodity Fetishism in South America* (Chapel Hill: Univ. of North Carolina Press, 1980), p. 41.

6 Maxwell, *op. cit.*, (New York: Star, 1961). Presumably even priests, modern "project managers of the souls," need to have "hard" data from which to argue their effectiveness to their Boards of Trustees when pleading for more money for the future, and so must record their successes. See also Arnold, *op. cit.*, p. 16, 79.

assimilated.[6] At the time of Maxwell's researches, native healers were losing a lot of power and influence. Tribal cultures, not surprisingly, were crumbling.[1]

These assaults on indigenous healing are no minor skirmishes on the periphery of colonialism as a system, for undermining a native healing tradition, whether in Africa or in South America, is a direct scientific, social, economic, political, and (above all) ideological blow against the vitals of that culture — in essence, destroying the ability of a people to reproduce and sustain themselves, to remain autonomous as a society, able to resist invasions by outsiders hell-bent on subverting their values and institutions in an all-out effort to subjugate them.

For example, John D. Rockefeller's money and influence helped to found the Peking Union Medical College — not only to teach Western medicine, but also to train people to Western values, and more generally to help form a new technocratic Chinese elite, wedded to Western logic and serving as the core of a new *comprador* class to ease colonial penetration of China.[2]

The Peking Union Medical College, we can be sure, taught a particular form of medicine, based, especially by the early part of the last century, on a powerful arsenal of chemical medicines (purporting to offer medical miracles) and a heavy reliance upon the invasive techniques of surgery. (More on Western medicine below.) With drugs, too, the mentality behind Lord Amherst's use of biological warfare against Native Americans in the 18th century has become more cunning by far. After World War I, the giant German chemical cartel, I.G. Farben, notorious later for its central role in the Nazi Reich, thought it had developed a cure for sleeping sickness, responsible for so much death and misery in parts of Africa. Through medical intermediaries, the German government proposed to the British that they should give back part of the African colonies taken from Germany under the dev-

---

1 No doubt shamanic healing traditions today, in the early 21st century, are experiencing a kind of modern "renaissance " in places like the Bay Area; but even so, globally, they are unquestionably a thousand times more endangered now than when Maxwell wrote half a century ago, if only because so many non-industrial habitats are rapidly disappearing from the face of the planet, particularly, as is well-known, in the equatorial rain forests. The "renaissance" is problematic, too, for too often it comes in the guise of neo-colonial exploitations of shamanic culture, with "New Age" hucksters trying to launch lucrative careers peddling native wisdom, or healing practices, torn from their sacred matrix and tied to a fee-for-service commodity structure. Rick Vecchio and Paul Elias, "Root From Peru at Center of Dispute," San Francisco *Chronicle*, January 7, 2007. For the use of ayahuasca ceremonies for US corporate CEOs, see Chris Colin, "In the Mountains of Peru, an Ayahuasca Retreat Tailor-Made for the Start-Up Set," *California Sunday* (n.d., San Francisco *Chronicle*, 2016.)

2 San Francisco *Chronicle*, Dec. 9, 1996, and Jan. 2, 1997; "Is Well Enough?" University of California at San Francisco *Magazine*, April, 1997.

3 Arnold, *op. cit.*, p. 16. See also E. Richard Brown, *Rockefeller Medicine Men and Capitalism in America* (Berkeley: University of California Press, 1979.)

astating Treaty of Versailles, in return for which Germany would allow them to share in their cure for sleeping sickness. Access to that claimed cure, the Germans pointed out, would greatly expand British power throughout the whole of Africa.[1]

ii. Healthcare, Culture, & Dependency

The above examples demonstrate the central importance of the fight Western powers waged against the healing traditions in the countries undergoing colonization. The struggle was, however, not as one-sided as my discussion so far would suggest. For one thing, disease can, at other times, act as an impetus to strengthen native healing traditions when indigenous medicine proves more effective, as occurred, for example, in a 1918 influenza outbreak in Southern Rhodesia (modern Zimbabwe), where the death rate was higher in regions where European medicine was primarily used than in remote areas. Here indigenous people had the merits of their own medical traditions confirmed.[2]

Natives, as we shall see in the next chapter, used their medicine as weapons in their war to survive; and it is clear that they were as conscious as the colonizers, if not more so, of the larger issues involved.

Despite the centrality of these issues, not even a hint of this critical aspect of colonialism can be found in Lenin's *Imperialism, the Highest State of Capitalism,* the starting point for the Marxist analysis of how imperialism functions as a global system. One could easily argue that such a topic would have been far from Lenin's object, as indeed it was, for he did not consider the cultural aspects of colonial relations in *Imperialism.*

However, later Marxist analyses of imperialism until quite recently have also mostly ignored what was obviously a central aspect of how imperialism operated. Only now is this gap being admirably filled, with the recognition that "medicine was itself a primary vehicle for imperial ideas and their application, [and offers] richly suggestive insights into the general character of European expansion," as John M. MacKenzie, the editor of the *Studies in Imperialism* series, has written.[3] In the series volume, *Imperial Medicine and Indigenous Societies,* David Arnold and others track the use of medical interventions as a form of propaganda for Western culture and the capitalist societies sponsoring it by Rockefeller Foundation leaders hoping to open Asia up to American commercial and industrial investments.[4] In relation to Southern Africa, one writer emphasizes that "Western medicine was a key weapon in the campaign to weaken indigenous culture and promote allegiance to European institutions and modes of

---

[1] Richard Sasuly, *I. G. Farben* (New York: Boni & Goer, 1947), p. 30.

[2] Arnold, *op. cit.,* pp. 177–78.

[3] In Arnold, *op. cit.,* p. vi.

[4] *Ibid.,* p. 16.

[5] Malcolm Nicolson, "Medicine and Racial Politics: Changing Images of the New Zealand Maori in the Nineteenth Century," in Arnold, *op. cit.,* p. 79.

thought."[5] In particular, the same author pointed out the mandate Western doctors were given "to wean the natives from witchcraft."

Ignoring, for the moment, Arnold's volume, which appeared quite late in the game, this is no small topic for the Marxist canon to have ignored. For the question of who heals — whether it is the professional medical doctors (or their native apprentices) whose talents, outside the missions, are available for a fee, or the indigenous healers on the basis of native medical arts that are rooted in their traditions, often thousands of years old — is essential for the question of whether their culture (and their society, for the one is essential to the other) survives or not.

In the course of the 1970s as I thought, wrote, and lectured on such matters, I began to realize that the lack of interest in environmental issues I encountered among nearly all my political comrades and the lack of analysis of health-care issues in relation to colonialism in the Marxist literature grew from the same tree. Both these instances of political and ideological blindness followed, I concluded, from the fact that in traditional societies issues of health and survival, of life and death, are inherently *sacred* matters, while the *sacred* has become pretty much anathema for Marxists.

Survival of a people and their culture (language, music, poetry, ceremonies, and especially healing traditions) are at the center of their spiritual cosmos. In large measure it is from those strands that a peoples' story is woven so that a break in any one of them ultimately may lead to an unravelling. Throughout the world, for the most part, these matters spring from the ground of popular magic, the seedbed out of which indigenous healing traditions in particular arose in non-industrial societies. And magic assumes that the world as such is to be understood as alive. Magical systems are all based on such animism, which we shall see made them rather problematic to authorities at times of unrest.

Since Marx and Engels' time, however, the concept of sacred has become an embarrassment in the culture of the left. Indeed, doing battle against all matters of the spirit has been one of the highest priorities of the various Marxist movements, parties, and governments.

To understand how this came about, we need to take a close look at the critique of religion by Marx and Engels.

3

A Critique of Marx and Engels' Critique of Religion

> The ancient Poets animated all sensible objects with Gods or Geniuses, calling them by the names and adorning them with the properties of woods, rivers, mountains, lakes, cities, nations, and whatever their enlarged & numerous senses could perceive. And particularly they studied the genius of each city & country placing it under its mental deity; Till a system was formed, which some took advantage of & enslav'd the vulgar by attempting to realize or abstract the ment.al deities from their objects: thus began Priesthood.... — William Blake, *The Marriage of Heaven & Hell* (1790?)

> Even though the followers of the old religion were cruelly persecuted, the authority of native ritualists did not necessarily diminish. Called *brujos*, witches, or sorcerers by the Spanish, such ritualists perforce led a secretive existence. Preconquest religion did not die out; it went underground in the form of "magic"and dissimulated itself in a variety of ways. — Michael T. Taussig, *The Devil and Commodity Fetishism in South America* (1980)

i. Mediterranean, Patriarchal Religions: the Real Opiates?

The severe limits of Marx and Engels' well-known critique of religion have generally escaped attention. In their critique it is only in passing that they touch upon what arguably has historically been the spiritual home for the overwhelming majority of the Earth's inhabitants, what Marx refers to as "popular religions" — in other words, "religion" before it became "organized," the spiritual beliefs, actions, and ceremonies of indigenous people nearly everywhere, widely found, as well, among hunters, peasants, miners, seamen, people in general who work in and with natural forces and who thus have an ongoing relationship with nature in its various manifestations. These beliefs were contemptuously dismissed by the two philosophers as simply "man's childish attitude[s] towards nature," "these various false conceptions of nature, of man's own being, of spirits, magic forces, etc." Indeed, so far beneath contempt were the spiritual beliefs of prehistoric people that Engels concluded that it was pointless to try to account "for all this primitive nonsense" on the basis, as normally Marxists would insist, of "economic necessity" being the engine driving human understanding. Engels blamed these "erroneous, primitive conceptions" for the "low economic development of prehistoric people."[1]

If, unlike Marx and Engels, we include such beliefs and practices in our analysis of religion we shall find a radically different picture of the forms, uses, and, most importantly, the social function of religion than the one they arrived at in their critique. In actuality, their's was but a critique of Christianity, Judaism, and Islam, all patriarchal, Mediterranean-based, Abrahamic religions.[2]

The specific context for Marx's oft-quoted dictum that religion "is the *opiate* of the people" was a particular time and place, early 19th-century Germany. In one of his earliest essays (1844) Marx noted that for Germany, "criticism of religion is the premise of all [other, i.e., social and cultural] criticism." The "*world of man*, the state, society" "produce religion" as a moral sanction, a "source of consolation and justification" of existing social relations. [3] "The struggle against religion," Marx went on, "is therefore indirectly a fight against *the world* of which religion is the spiritual aroma. Thus the criticism of religion turns into the criticism of the earth."[4] In other words, one must begin one's fight against the State and society with a critique of its theological justification, religion.[5]

But what may have been true of Germany in the first half of the 19th century does not necessarily turn out to be true for the rest of the world, or to be true for all the religions that have informed the souls of its varied peoples, or true for all times. Far too broad a brush has been used, as we shall see. As I shall argue below, the social role of religion in many of the cultures encountered by Europe as it began its outward expansion frequently was strikingly at odds with Marx and Engels' simple dictum. Especially is this so for people whose spiritual traditions or religions are closer to shamanism, totemism, or other forms of animist religion. Continuities of symbols, themes, and rituals lead many students to see those forms of spirituality as nearest to the religions of early humanity, dating back at least to near the end of the last Ice Age, some 20,000 years ago; sometimes these are termed "nature religions."[6] Though important exceptions

[1]Marx, Engels, *On Religion* (Moscow: Progress Publishers, 1975), pp. 84, 229, 248.

[2] On the patriarchal nature of the Abrahamic religions, see Elaine Pagels, *The Gnostic Gospels* (New York: Vintage Books, 1981), p. 57.

[3] Karl Marx, "Introduction" to *Contribution to the Critique of Hegel's Philosophy of Law*, in *On Religion*, p. 38.

[4] *Ibid.*, pp. 38–39.

[5] *Ibid.*, p. 39; emphasis in the original.

[6] See, for example, Hans Peter Duerr, *Dreamtime: Concerning the Boundary Between*

exist, these nature religions are frequently found in cultures least integrated into rigid hierarchies of class, race, and gender or of urbanized social roles. (I, too, am obviously utilizing a broad brush, but I am making such claims not for these cultures in *general*, simply that a significant number of such existed.[1])

Throughout the world, including down into modern times, varieties of what, for convenience, I will refer to as animism, based partly on such traditions as shamanism, totemism, witchcraft, etc. are widespread. Not infrequently, the animism might be hidden, partly buried beneath outer, more orthodox, garments that may be Christian, Jewish, Islamic, Buddhist, or Hindu in form, religions or spiritual practices which historically have frequently been imposed on conquered populations.

It is important to determine whether the shamanic, magical, or animist religions or spiritual beliefs were or are simply or primarily "opiates" of their people. Marx believed that the earliest societies were atheistical and that the notion of gods or similar religious sentiments only arose in connection with the development of a "property-owning elite" and a separation between a public and a private sphere, so that, even in such early forms, religion serves as the "chief ideological disguise" for property and the State. Though Marx and Engels' remarks on religion as opiates of the people were made in the context of the Germany in which they lived, in absence of later retractions or qualification, it has been seen as a general truth, applicable now and in the distant past, not simply true of 19th-century Germany.[2]

Wilderness and Civilization (Oxford, England: Basil Blackwell, 1985); Wade Davis, *Shadows in the Sun;* David Abram, *op. cit.;* Jeremy Narby, *The Cosmic Serpent: DNA and the Origins of Knowledge* (New York: Putnam, 1998) (I am grateful to Chris Carlsson for bringing me to this important book); Arthur Evans, *Witchcraft and the Gay Counterculture: A Radical View of Western Civilization and Some of the People It Has Tried to Destroy* (Boston: Fag Rag Books, 1978); Arthur Evans, "The Mythic Proportions of Halloween," *Coming Up!* (October, 1984); and Gary Snyder, *Earth House Hold: Technical Notes & Queries to Fellow Dharma Revolutionaries* (New York: New Directions, n.d.).

[1] Leaving the question of "significance" to be resolved by those who think history is decided by numbers. Engels's writings on women and Native Americans (*The Origin of the Family, Private Property, and the State, in Light of the Researches of Lewis H. Morgan* (New York: International Publishers, 1970) did not much change this.

[2] There is good evidence that Marx in his later years was radically reformulating his ideas on the customs, social stru cture, and political significance of the tribal peoples who largely embody such animist spirituality, profoundly changing his views, for example, on the active political resistance offered by present-day Native Americans, Australian aborigines, and Russian peasants against their oppression, as a result of a close reading of Lewis Henry Morgan's *Ancient Society.* Yet, his sensitive reading of Morgan and of other ethnologists did not substantially change Marx's negative views towards religion of any kind. He continued to believe that the earliest human societies were atheistic, that gods and such only arose in connection with property-owning, and that religion essentially serves as an ideological disguise.

Let us utilize the methodology of Marxism itself, that is, by undertaking a "class analysis" of the role played by the shamans and witches in indigenous cultures to see if we agree with Marx and Engels. Of course, we have the benefit, for better or worse, of over a century of ethnological research since their observations were made. What social roles did religious "leaders" play and what kind of people fulfilled them in non-Abrahamic religions, in those other societies? What exactly did the shaman or witch or the priests and priestesses of these religions do, and how did their activities affect, if they did, the larger functioning of the societies of which they were a part? If we wish to remain faithful to Marxist methodology, which for the time being, at least, I do, we should specifically look to see what their role was, if any, in *production*? As we shall presently see, their role there was often central. Far from parasitical or instrumental in peddling illusions about reality, the shaman plays a vital role in putting food on the table and providing a roof overhead. Let us take an extended detour to look at such roles.

ii. THE POLITICAL ECONOMY OF MAGIC IN HUNTING/GATHERING & EARLY AGRICULTURAL SOCIETIES: CALENDARS, HEALING, & REPRODUCTION

Shamans or witches[1] in nonindustrial societies engage in a variety of activities arising out of their respective spiritualities. The tasks performed vary widely, including what Western culture would tend to separate off as the "spiritual," the "medical," the "political," and the "economic" functions, but it is doubtful that a Hopi shaman would see any essential differences in his helping to increase the yield from the corn planting (to us, economic); healing illnesses of her people (medical); or observing, honoring, and mimicking through sympathetic magic the Fall descent of the sun towards more southern latitudes as the length of the day heads towards its minimum (magic, science).[2]

Among other things, the shaman and witch are keepers of the time, observing the turns of the years and months and constructing, interpreting, or honoring the elaborate and often exceedingly accurate calendars that have emerged in virtually every human culture. My high school and college texts quickly passed over the creation of calendars in Middle East cultures without acknowl-

---

[1] I will mostly use these two forms of often tribal-based spiritual practice as a shorthand, realizing that they are sometimes inappropriate or even, for some of their practitioners, unacceptable terms. Otherwise I would be forced to spell out in each instance the full range of spiritual traditions I am referring to.

[2] Cf. Hill: "Wakuenai curing rituals are simultaneously musical, cosmological, social, psychological, medical, and economic events, a multidimensionality that embarrasses the categories of Western scientific and artistic cultures." ("A Musical Aesthetic of Ritual Curing in the Northwest Amazon," in *Portals of Power: Shamanism in South America*, E. Jean Matteson Langdon and Gerhard Baer (eds.), (Albuquerque: Univ. of New Mexico Press, 1992, as quoted in Narby, *op. cit.*, p. 215 n.2).

edging the magnitude of their task or the fact that people nearly everywhere have constructed quite accurate calendars out of a rather complex array of celestial phenomena, varying according to the day, hour, and latitude of any observation. The texts also do not mention the crucial economic role a calendar necessarily plays in the life of any people having to feed itself in tune with the rhythms of the planetary cycles — as all people historically have had to do until very recent times. Only as I began decades later to observe the heavens more closely myself did I come to appreciate the intricacies of deciphering the array of interpenetrating cycles found in the heavens and the level of observational acuity and theoretical comprehension the ancients must have exercised in order to bring into focus the manifold appearances of the night skies.

That their achievements should have been so exceptional could not have been foreordained, but surely their need to navigate the mysterious waters of time was universal among our earliest ancestors (something other animal, bird, and plant species, it is increasingly obvious, do as well). People feeding themselves by hunting, gathering, fishing, or even by a rudimentary agriculture would have had to govern virtually every one of these "economic" activities according to a certain rhythm, corresponding to cyclical changes of light, heat, precipitation, and perhaps winds, no matter where they were. Whether it was a tribe awaiting the return of caribou to their traditional hunting lands or a small community anticipating the best moment to put the rye seeds into the ground, there were cycles that had to be carefully followed and listened to. If the timing of a community or tribe is off, seeds may not sprout or may grow stunted, may be eaten more readily by pests, or may rot; and the caribou may have long been gone by the time the hunters go looking for them. Fishers, hunters, gatherers, growers: all have to be acutely sensitive to the cycles that shape their work, most of these being themselves reflections of the parental rhythms established by sun, Earth, and moon in their cosmic dance.[1]

The accuracy of these early calendars is striking, as well as how early and how widely they emerged in human society. Bones with notches, for example, marking off the days, longer notches every twenty-nine or so days, were widely used over ten thousand years ago to keep track of full moons.[2] Complex calendrical instruments dating from 34,000 years ago have been found in Siberia.[3] Astonishingly, these early observations, record-keeping, and theoretical considerations revealed an exceedingly minute cycle of changes in the Earth/Sun system. According to the findings of Professors Giorgio de Santillana and Hertha von Dechend, one quite subtle cycle in the heavens called the "precession of the equinoxes" served a framework for mythology worldwide. Ancient peoples were

---

[1] Such cycles are themselves subject to transformation, as Ice Ages, tsunamis, or plate tectonics redistribute the mass of our planet. Also, the Earth's mass is increased from the continental rain of debris, as with meteorites.

[2] Kenneth Brecher and Michael Fertig, (eds.), *Astronomy of the Ancients* (Cambridge, Mass.: MIT Press, 1981), p. 40.

[3] Rudgley, *op. cit.*, p. 100.

both aware of and obsessed with this minor motion of the Earth's axis of rotation, a slight wobble that takes about 26,000 years to complete one turn. Yet, it was widely known many thousands of years ago among our planet's early inhabitants, in many scattered parts of the world, as de Santillana and von Dechend show.[1]

Similar tales about a world axle that slipped from an earlier, symmetrical position, thereby throwing time out of joint (creating seasons) form an underlying theme in mythological tales the world over, stretching back to Paleolithic times, according to de Santillana and von Dechend. Until recently, historians of science have believed that it was only with the advent of classical Greek science (modern Europe's intellectual spawning grounds, according to traditional historians), around the 4th century B.C.E., that this fundamental but minute motion was first discovered. As a result of their researches, however, de Santillana and von Dechend found that this was not the case, but behind this revelation lay an important secret: the core of ancient mythologies the world over was *astronomical!* As von Dechend explained her breakthrough, it was after many months of trying to comprehend Polynesian mythology that:

> the annihilating recognition of our complete ignorance came down upon me like a sledge hammer: there was no single sentence [in some 10,000 pages she was then attempting to decipher] that could be understood. But then, if anyone was entitled to be taken seriously, it had to be the Polynesians guiding their ships securely over the largest ocean of our globe, navigators to whom our much praised discoverers from Magellan to Captain Cook confided the steering of their ships more than once.

She knew that Polynesian mythology, the basis for their fabled skills as navigators, had to be looked at as more than a collection of "tall tales." It was when she followed up one clue that she realized that

> astronomy could not be escaped. First it was still "simple" geometry — the orbit of the sun,... the seasons — and the adventures of gods and heroes did not make much more sense even then. Maybe one should *count* for a change? What could it mean when "returning" at intervals, "falling into space," coming off the "right" route? There remained, indeed, not many possible solutions: it had to be planets.... If so, planets had to be constitutive members of every mythical personnel; the Polynesians did not invent their strain by themselves.[2]

---

1 Richard Rudgley *The Lost Civilizations of the Stone Age* (New York: Simon & Schuster, 2000), p. 100.

2 The references to irregularities in a hero's progress would have been allusions to a planet's retrograde motion, where the relative motions of the planet and of the Earth

Though we are only now beginning to understand what Neolithic astronomy might have been looking for or found, there are a remarkable number of ancient structures that suggest that it was a very subtle and powerful science in its own right. It was that science, we may presume, that guided those, whoever they were, who built Stonehenge. But, in addition to Stonehenge, in Great Britain alone nearly a thousand stone circles or similar sites have survived; many others have been destroyed as stones were diverted to other uses or structures torn down for offending orthodox Christians.[1] In the Great Plains, some five to six million stone rings, from five to ten feet in diameter, are still intact. Around the world many more sacred sites, often quite different in appearance but probably many having similar purposes, have been identified.[2]

from time to time combine to give the illusion of a negative speed for the planet, so that from the Earth the other planet appears as if it has temporarily reversed direction across the skies. Giorgio de Santillana and Hertha von Dechend, *Hamlet's Mill: An Essay on Myth and the Frame of Time* (Boston: Gambit, Inc., 1969), pp. ix–x.

[1] In recent years a number of works have been published in the new field of archeoastronomy — the study of ancient astronomical knowledge and techniques based on an analysis of ancient sacred sites and mythology. Three books that offered early introductions were John Michell's *The View Over Atlantis* (London: Sage Press, 1969); Gerald Hawkins, *Stonehenge Decoded* (Garden City, NY: Doubleday, 1965); and A. Thom, *Megalithic Sites in Britain* (Oxford: Clarendon Press, 1967). A general overview is provided by E.C. Krupp, *Echoes of the Lost Skies: The Astronomy of Ancient Lost Civilizations* (New York: Harper and Row, 1983) and Brecher and Fertig (eds.), *Astronomy of the Ancients*. Keith Critchlow in *Time Stands Still: New Light on Megalithic Science* (London: Gordon Fraser, 1979) provides a wonderful theoretical overview. Preliminary reports of the investigations into some of Britain's stone circles can be found in Don Robins, *Circles of Silence* (London: Souvenir Press, 1985), Paul Devereux, *Places of Power: Secret Energies at Ancient Sites. A Guide to Observed or Measured Phenomena* (London: Bradford, 1999), and Paul Devereux, John Steele and David Kubrin, *Earthmind: Communicating with the Living World of Gaia* (Rochester, Vt.: Destiny Books, 1992). See also Peter Lancaster Brown, *Megaliths, Myths and Men: An Introduction to Astra-Archaeology* (New York: Harper & Row, 1976); Martin Brennan, *The Stars and the Stones: Ancient Art and Astronomy in Ireland* (London: Thames and Hudson, 1983). An early pioneer in the field was J. Norman Lockyer, *The Dawn of Astronomy: A Study of the Temple Worship and Mythology of the Ancient Egyptians* (Cambridge, Mass.: MIT Press, 1964; first ed., 1894).

[2] Brecher and Feirtag, *Astronomy of the Ancients*, p. 5; "'Magical' Solar Etchings Left By Ancient Indians in Desert," San Francisco *Chronicle* (January 10, 1983), reporting on petroglyphs designed to "mark the sun's movements." "What we have found almost uniformly is that the function of petroglyphs was to serve as a yearly calendar," the research astronomers concluded. The focus was on determining precisely the moment of solstice with devices like "a dagger of sunlight that runs precisely on the edge of a single carved [petroglyph] circle at both Winter and Summer Solstice, as a shadow bisects a spiral at dawn on the Summer Solstice."

The stone circles in the British Isles, to a naive observer, often look rather bent-out-of-shape, as if our Neolithic forebears did not have the intellectual or technical wherewithal to notice that the "circles" they so painstakingly built were so obviously asymmetrical, indeed, lopsided. With characteristic cultural arrogance, most of us assumed that people four to five thousand years ago did not know any better. Recently, however, exhaustive surveys by the engineer Alexander Thom of numerous British sites have shown that the constructions actually reflected a very conscious and technically ingenious use of one of six possible circle-like geometries. Two of the six are the circle itself and the ellipse. Four other geometries found in the constructions incorporated, in every site Thom surveyed, either a flattened or an egg-shaped circle-like figure, made by two or three different "radii " sweeping around the same number of "centers" to create one contiguous figure.[1] (See *Figure 1,* below.)

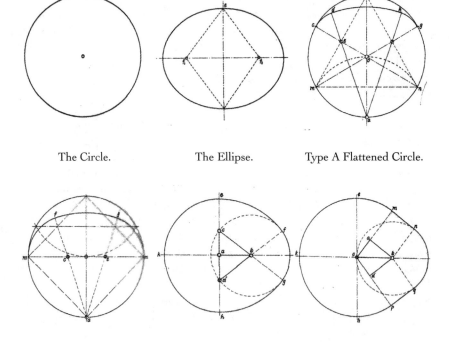

The Circle.   The Ellipse.   Type A Flattened Circle.

Type B Flattened Circle.   Type I Egg-Shaped Ring.   Type II Egg-Shaped Ring.

Figure 1
THOM'S STONE CIRCLE GEOMETRIES

---

[1] Critchlow, *op. cit.,* pp. 32–33; Michell, *View,* p. 33. A. Thom, *Megalithic Lunar Observations* (Oxford, England: Clarendon Press, 1978).

Remarkably, on the basis of their novel designs, these figures (except, of course, the circle itself) were able to incorporate circle-like functions without having to depend on the unique circle-enabler of pi (π), a troublesome irrational number. In fact, these circle-like forms (that to our eyes simply appear "crude") allowed rational numbers to be used instead to connect their "diameters" to their "circumferences" — unlike the cumbersome, and to the Greeks intellectually loathsome, irrational number our geometry uses, whose exact value can never be known.[1]

It would take us too far afield to go into the details of the many ancient sites in Britain and around the globe hinting how very much seems to have been known by whatever sages designed and built the sites. Isaac Newton, however, credited the persistent legends attributing a vast astronomical sophistication to ancient astronomer-seers, and he read widely to track down whatever information he could about their theories, believing that his own comprehension of the workings of the cosmos was but a pale reflection of what they had known. As many early authors did, Newton cited legends that the ancient wisdom had been encoded by those sages in particular structures built in antiquity, especially temples. Newton particularly focused on the Temple of Solomon and the Great Pyramid, both of which he analyzed mathematically.[2] A few decades later, his biographer, William Stukely, on the same quest, looked rather to Stonehenge and Avebury in Britain for clues as to the encoded ancient wisdom.

The tradition that Newton and Stukely drew upon taught that ancient temples were designed so as to incorporate certain key *ratios* in their structures, being built on the basis of dimensions that reflected critical features or scales of the cosmos. Temples were built to the order of the cosmos around us.[3] As Newton himself wrote:

---

[1] Since Classical Greek philosophy was invested in the rational order of things, and had a powerful belief in numbers as the basis of reality (as. for example, in Plato), the discovery of the irrationality of the diagonal of a unit square was seen as an outrage, even scandalous. See John Burnet, *Early Greek Philosophy* (New York: Meridian Books, 1960; first ed., 1892), pp. 101, 105; *Astronomy of the Ancients*, p. 182.

[2] Newton pursued this in his studies of the Temple of Solomon and in his investigations of the Great Pyramid. See Richard S. Westfall, *Never at Rest: A Biography of Isaac Newton* (Cambridge, England: Cambridge Univ. Press, 1983), pp. 346–48, 354, and Newton, *A Dissertation upon the Sacred Cubit of the Jews and the Cubits of Several Nations; in which, from the Dimensions of the Greatest Egyptian Pyramid... the... Cubit... is Determined* in John Greaves, Miscellaneous Works of... (London: 1737), vol. 2; Newton, *Chronology of Ancient Kingdoms Amended* (London: 1728).

[3] See John Michell, *View Over Atlantis* and his many subsequent books, especially *City of Revelation, Or the Proportions and Symbolic Numbers of the Cosmic Temple* (New York: Ballantine Books, 1972).

[The ancients] would have [this one God] dwelt in all bodies whatsoever as in his own temple, and thence they *shaped ancient temples in the manner of the heavens* [even as the] entire universe was rightly designed a Temple of God.[1]

William Stukely, one of the first to study Stonehenge and Avebury seriously, elaborated on this theme:

The ancients indeed did make huge temples of immense pillars in colonnades, like a small forest; or vast concaves of cupolas to represent the heavens; ... but to our British Druids was re-serv'd the honour of a more extensive idea, and of executing it. They have made plains and hills, valleys, springs and rivers contribute to form a temple of three miles in length. They have stamp'd a whole country [at Avebury] with the impress of this sacred character and that of the most permanent nature.[2]

The same general idea of the *temple* is found, far afield and considerably later, in Black Elk's words describing the construction of the Sun Dance Lodge:

I should explain to you here that in setting up the sun dance lodge, we are really making the Universe in a likeness; for, you see, each of the posts around the lodge represents some par-ticular object of creation, so that the whole circle is the entire creation, and the one tree at the centre, upon which the twenty-eight poles rest, is Wakan Tanka, who is the centre of everything.... And I should tell you why it is that we use twenty-eight poles. I have already explained why the numbers four and seven are sacred; then if you add four sevens you get twenty-eight. Also the moon lives twenty-eight days [between full moons], and this is our month....[3]

---

[1] Emphasis added. Quoted in J.E. McGuire, "Forces, Active Principles, and Newton's Invisible Realm," *Ambix* 15 (1968), p. 200; cf. Westfall, *op. cit.*, p. 354 and Betty Jo Teeter Dobbs, *The Janus Face of Genius: The Role of Alchemy in Newton's Thought* (Cambridge: Cambridge Univ. Press, 1991), p. 151.

[2] Quoted in Michell, *View*, p. 6.

[3] This central pole represents the world axis, around which the heavens revolve, and the main protagonist in the saga of the precessing equinoxes. Keith Critchlow, *op. cit.*, p. 60.

Certain numbers of astronomical significance found their way around the world and into a number of sacred structures and texts. For example, 864,000, the diameter of the Sun in miles (to within 0.05%) was made the basis for the temporal unit, the second, 86,400 of which fill a 24-hour day. Factors of that number pop up in a variety of sacred traditions. The Aion of Heraclitus is 10,800 years (or ⅛ x 86,400) in duration, and the Babylonian Great Year is 432,000 years (or ½ of 864,000). The *Rigveda* has 43,200 syllables. The Indian fire altar consists of 10,800 bricks; Angkor Wat has 108 stone figures along each of the five roads leading to its gates. There are 1080 *minims* in the Jewish hour, 108 beads in Hindu and Buddhist rosaries. One hundred and eight, according to the present Dalai Lama, is a favorite number for Tibetans. A season of the Hindu Kali Yuga has 108,000 years. In the *Griminismal*, 432,000 *einherier*, warriors who fell in combat on Earth and who now reside in Valhalla, emerge from the 540 (¹/₁₆₀₀ x 864,000) gates to do battle.[1] In the *Vedas*, Mahu's reward for saving humanity and the "seed of all living creatures," includes giving him powers allowing him to reign for one *manvontara*, equivalent to 64,800,000 (108 x 600,000) years.[2] The Greek astronomer Hipparchus (*fl. c.* 146–127 B.C.E.) and Galileo both incorporated a special role for 108 in their astronomies.

In miles, 1080 is the mean diameter of the moon. A series of geometrical and cabalistic exercises derives the same number, 1080, from the relationship between 5040, the product of 1 x 2 x 3 x 4 x 5 x 6 x 7, and 7920, the product of 8 x 9 x 10 x 11. Note that each of these special numbers — 7920, 5040, 540, 1080, 43,200, 108, and 108,000 — according to the cabalistic technique of *gematria*,[3] adds up to the magical number, 9.

Tracking the extremely minute changes in the length of the day that ushers in Winter or Summer Solstice was obviously one of the central goals of those archaic astronomers; additionally, it appears that local planting conditions, tidal patterns, or rainfall cycles would dictate some of the particular foci for individual megalithic sites. Though Stonehenge was a particularly elaborate temple, even the simpler sites erected nearly everywhere in the world appear remarkably able to detect the subtle differences in day-length at the solstices, a difference only amounting to a matter of seconds for a period lasting more than a week. Modern scholars may not agree whether a given site was meant for observational or ritual purposes, but their confusion simply reflects a modern mania for separation of things into distinct categories.

---

[1] de Santillana and von Dechend, *op. cit.*, p. 162; John Michell, *At the Center of the World: Polar Symbolism Discovered in Celtic, Norse and Other Ritualized Landscapes* (London: Thames and Hudson, 1994), pp. 167–69; Peter Thompkins, *Secrets of the Great Pyramid*, with an appendix by Livio Stecchini (New York: Harper & Row, 1971), p. 210.

[2] Graham Hancock, *Underworld: The Mysterious Origins of Civilization* (New York: Three Rivers Press, 2002), p. 138.

[3] Where, for example, the number 126 = 1+2+6=9 and 73=7+3=10=1+0=1.)

Rituals would not have been carried out separated from astronomical observations, nor observations made divorced from ritual magic; the observation, I believe, would have been *part of* the magic.

At any rate, rituals served as a kind of timepiece for a culture, ushering in changes in nature and signaling corresponding variations in human activity, especially critical for planting cycles in agricultural societies. Among the Tukano hunting/gathering tribe in the Columbian northwestern Amazon,

> it is the energy of the sun, imagined by the Tukano in terms of seminal light and heat, that causes plants to grow and fruit to ripen, that makes mankind and animals reproduce, and that is thought to be creative not only in a germinal, biological sense, but also in the sense of spiritual illumination and the attainment of esoteric wisdom.[1]

The energy that enters our world is seen by the Tukano as flowing in a loop or circuit, for only so much creative energy exists, passing among rocks, rivers, animals, people, and the other creatures of the world. Whatever energy is taken by an individual or a group, say in a hunt, must be "reincorporated into the circuit" in some other form to maintain a healthy flow.[2] Knowing how and when to do this is the responsibility of the shaman.

> The shaman... interferes quite directly with hunting, fishing, gathering and most other harvesting activities. For example, a shaman will personally control the quantity and concentration of fish-poison to be used on a certain stretch of a river; he will determine the number of animals to be killed when a herd of peccary is reported, and he will decide on a suitable harvesting strategy for the gathering of wild fruits. He will determine which fish have to be thrown back into the water after a haul has been made, and occasionally he even might completely prohibit the killing of certain animals in a restricted area of the forest. He will also control such technological activities as the construction of a communal house, the manufacture of a canoe, or the opening of a trail. All these activities obviously affect the natural environment since trees have to be felled and many plants have to be destroyed or used in the process, and the shaman's *role as a protector of game and plant-life*

---

[1] G. Reichel-Dolmatoff, "Cosmology as Ecological Analysis: A View from the Rain Forest," *Man, New Theories*, vol. xi, no. 3 (September, 1976), p. 309. I am grateful to Prof. Carolyn Merchant for bringing this article to my attention.
[2] *Ibid.*, p. 310.

explains why animals and plants figure so prominently as his
spirit-helpers.[1]

Early hunting/gathering people learned to communicate directly with the
animals they hunted. Rituals were designed to that end, and songs and prayers
were created to speak directly to the soul of the hunters' prey. Spirits of the animals, they believed, answered those prayers and taught the shamans rules and
taboos that the hunters and their people should observe in order that the animals
would allow themselves to be caught, and so feed the people.

> Before there was agriculture and ceremonialism directed to-
> wards the growth of domestic plants, hunting was the pri-
> mary means of survival — hunting and the gathering of roots
> (tubers), plants, nuts, and berries. In the northernmost re-
> gions of this [North American] continent the native people
> did not have agriculture until the late nineteenth century, and
> today some still depend only on hunting and gathering (and,
> of course, nowadays, commercial food). These cultures in-
> clude the Eskimo of the Baffin Bay area, the Crees in the
> Northeast and the Athapaskan tribal people in the North-
> west. The Navajo... were primarily a hunting and gathering
> people [until the 16th century], with shamanism at the center
> of their religious system.... By examining the relationships
> that were established in the aboriginal hunting culture be-
> tween animals, plants, and human beings, it can be seen how
> these principles of balance and ecology helped create sacred
> beliefs and procedures of human beings. And observing the
> role and function of the shaman in diagnosing diseases, it is
> easy to see how closely related his/her work is to those of the
> early hunters.[2]

Creation and origin stories of Native Americans gave methods by which animals
were to be killed or roots collected in order to maintain balance in the cosmos.
Arrows and firearms were never to be pointed indiscriminately, so went one rule
that the deer gods laid down to the Deer People. Nor were game animals to be
talked about in disparaging terms when the men hunted. If hunters encountered
four of the animals, one had to be spared. Prayers and rituals were specified for
the last kill of the season. Rules for the use and disposal of the parts of killed

---

[1] Emphasis mine. *Ibid.*, p. 309.

[2] Peggy V. Beck, Anna Lee Walters, and Nia Rancisco, *The Sacred: Ways of Knowledge, Sources of Life* (Tsaile, Arizona: Navajo Community Press, 1992), pp. 104–05.
I am grateful to Luis Kemnitzer for drawing my attention to this important work.

animals were also specified. Another story taught the lesson that hunters were always to keep their knees bent.[1]

If hunters held to the rules and maintained proper attitudes, then

> *you will always have enough meat to eat. It does not matter how many people there are, you will always get enough if you hunt right, if you prepare the animals correctly, if you bring them home properly, and if you dispose of the bones in the prescribed manner.*[2]

These stories conveyed not just rules for the hunt, but a theology of the animated world and the vital place of deer within its pantheon, along with the mountains, rainbows, sunlight, lightning, and insects.[3] In general, the songs and proper names of the game animals help hunting people know "the order and structure of things."[4]

iii. THE SHAMAN & PRODUCTIVE LABOR

We began our inquiry several pages back with a specific question: what role did the shaman (or witch) play in *production*? As we have just seen, their role, in what some call the "economic sphere," was often a considerable one. It is clear that the tasks they performed in relation to production were far from marginal or parasitic. Their activities connected hunting/gathering or agricultural people to the material world and its patterns and aided in their transformation of that world in order to survive.

The same, with an even greater emphasis, could be said about the role played by shamans and witches in *re*production. She attends the bringing of new life into the world as midwife — one of two (the other, of course, being death) sacred gates that all shamanic (actually, all religious) wisdom invests with great sanctity.

---

1 *Ibid.*, pp. 105–06, 111.

2 *Ibid.*, p. 106. In the past century, encroachments by Western culture and adoption of some of its technology have led to many changes in some of these rules, as "many fragile ecological relationships and balance between [Native Americans] and the natural world have been put in danger. 'For example, the Eskimo people of the Baffin Islands have recently begun to notice with some anxiety that trust between animals and humans has broken down. They say that the noise of the motorboats, snowmobiles, and rifles has scared the older seals away and only the young animals can be 'coaxed within shooting range.'" The Baffin Islanders have come up with compromises in an effort to rebalance their relationship with nature, stipulating certain periods of the year for the selling of crafts since it takes the hunters out of the hunted seals' habitats, giving them a respite for a while from the hunt and so allowing their young to mature (p. 111).

3 *Ibid.*, pp. 104–06, 110.

4 *Ibid.*, p. 110.

Ancestors of the living, the dead, are accessible to shamans and witches. In many traditional cultures, part of shamanic knowledge includes secrets of controlling pregnancy — by interfering with conception, aborting of fetuses, and/or ensuring fertility. This knowledge, as Nicole Maxwell found out (see below) is among the most closely guarded mysteries of a healing tradition, jealously kept from outsiders — and in tribes where patriarchal power has undermined women's autonomy, likely to be a source of conflict between the men and women.[1]

Their role in reproduction forms the central core of a more general responsibility witches and shamans have for healing. Through their use of local herbs, massage, purging, sweating, and other techniques (spiritual as well as physical), they maintain the well-being of a tribe's members, enabling the people and the culture to renew themselves.

Native American and African American healers have also used healing practices as integral parts of their overall resistance to colonialism, just as colonial governors felt free to deploy medical policy as a weapon in the fight for Western hegemony, as we saw in the last chapter. For example, in the 19th century, Southern US medical journals carried reports about the use of abortive and contraceptive methods by slaves apparently unwilling to allow their lovemaking to serve as "productive labor" for slavemasters anticipating broods of marketable slave children. Numerous slave families, it was noted, simply failed to produce *any* children. One physician reported a plantation where several slave women "of the proper age to breed" had, over a twenty-five year period, brought only two children to term. The plantation's owner kept replacing some of the apparently infertile men and women with other couples, but still no children were "produced." After many years of trying to determine how conception was being prevented, the owner was shown a weed used by his slaves to prevent pregnancy. Other contemporary reports mention herbal and manipulative means used to interfere with reproduction.[2]

Plantation owners were in a serious bind in regard to their black healers. Originally trained in the healing arts in Africa, in many instances they were able to make contact with Native American healers, from whom they learned the particular powers of North American herbs and how they were prepared. Having traditionally been the religious and political leaders of their people in Africa, these men and women were potentially quite dangerous — as Southern whites

---

[1] This is discussed in Frank Waters, *The Man Who Killed the Deer* (New York: Pocket Books, 1971), as well as by Nicole Maxwell, *The Jungle Search*, pp.186ff, 190, 249ff.

[2] For indigenous knowledge of birth control and abortants, see Federici, *Caliban and the Witch*, p. 131 n. 78; Jerry Mander, *Four Arguments for the Elimination of Television* (New York: Morrow Quill Paperbacks, 1978), p. 72; Taussig, *Shamanism, Colonialism, and the Wild Man*, p. 22; Eugene P. Genovese, *Roll, Jordan, Roll: The World the Slaves Made* (New York: Vintage, 1976), pp. 496–97.

learned soon enough. In the mid-1830s a suppressed slave insurrection that was to have stretched across the heart of the South was organized by healers associated with a widespread Thomsonian popular healing movement. This movement had experienced a huge upsurge of support following a devastating cholera epidemic in 1830, when a higher mortality rate in patients treated by regular physicians, compared to the fate of those treated by Thomsonians, was widely noted. Among those implicated and lynched for this failed uprising were several slave healers.[1] I suspect that some of the notorious laws passed by Southern states making it illegal to teach slaves to read were specifically aimed at African American healers, men and women who had a great influence in slave quarters and enjoyed the freedom to go from dwelling to dwelling, plantation to plantation, delivering babies and treating the sick. Such mobility made them easy carriers of information or plots.[2]

Despite this clear and present danger of allowing slaves to practice their traditional healing arts, few slave owners wanted to see their investments in chattel be affected by sickness or preventable deaths. While white doctors sometimes were used to treat slaves on plantations, so too were slave "herb" doctors, and not only to treat other blacks, but occasionally also to treat whites. In fact, the reputation of the black healers in plantation country was quite high. Some planters, themselves physicians, preferred the black herb doctors. As John Hamilton wrote, "It is seldom that I call in a physician. We Doctor upon the old woman slave and have first-rate luck." The historian Eugene Genovese documents one slave owner who hired out a healer he owned to treat whites and blacks — a practice that may well have been not uncommon.[3]

Finally, there is a long tradition of healers in non-industrial societies acting as leaders of resistance to encroachments by colonial powers or central authorities, a tradition that has a rich history and reaches into the present. We shall examine this in the next chapter, encounter it later in the English Civil War and Revolution, and in Part Two shall suggest ways Newton's science was thereby affected. Today, opposition to tropical rainforest destruction in Brazil, Hawa'ii, and elsewhere is led by shamans.

In sum, in the shamanic toolkit the healing arts are a kind of hub from which most everything radiates out.

---

[1] A history of this popular movement was sketched by Barbara Ehrenreich and Deirdre English, *Witches, Midwives and Nurses* (New York: Feminist Press, 2nd ed., 2010); and in more detail in David Kubrin, Marcia Altman, John Kwasnik, and Tina Logan, "The People's Healers." Information regarding the 1830s aborted slave insurrection emerged in our research for a planned print edition, which, alas, never made it off of our collective desk.

[2] This was first suggested to me by John Kwasnik.

[3] Eugene Genovese, *op. cit.*, pp. 62, 224–260.

iv. SURVIVAL AS A SACRED QUESTION

In general terms, in tribal or other nonindustrial settings, forms of shamanic magic frequently play a vital role in ensuring continued existence and vitality, culturally as well as physically, of a people. Shamans navigating the river of time and the hunting and gathering protocols and skills in the healing arts they bring back from those trips to the spirit world introduce forms of organization, of structure, that are central to their people's survival. (Undoubtedly there are magical dimensions to their activities and rules, though readers more comfortable [for now] in an orthodox rationality might choose to focus more on the practical aspects, on the shaman as *time-reckoner* or as *healer*.)

Clearly, if we broaden the category of religion to include shamanism and witchcraft — "religions," we should note, specifically of colonized people and of women — their social role is not at all simply that of providing an "opiate" to a people in order to dull their critical faculties. In fact, once we widen our analysis of religion beyond a provincial focus on the "Mediterranean cradle" and on forms of worship, as in Judaism, Christianity, and Islam, that explicitly mandate the subjugation of women by men, quite the reverse appears to be the case.

Undoubtedly, some of these non-Abrahamic religions or forms of spirituality are oppressive, perhaps of women, or of unbelievers, or the poor. I would argue that any such oppressive roles arise out of a particular historical matrix in which they operate, rather than as an essential aspect of religion or spirituality *per se*. In other words, while religion may well act as an opiate, it by no means does so as a general rule.[1]

v. A DIALECTICS OF MAGIC & SCIENCE

We shall find that a critique of the Marxist critique of religion of necessity will unfold to become a critique of the Marxist conception of science and technology — in Marxism (as in much of post-Enlightenment culture) functioning in a kind of dialectical tension with regard to religion. The "productive" aspects of shamanic knowledge discussed above would not have occurred to the militant atheists Marx and Engels, partly because of their overwhelming faith in Western science and technology, not least as the motor force pushing the development of ever-newer modes of production.

Indeed, in the years after their *Communist Manifesto* (1848) and particularly in the wake of the crushing of the revolutionary insurrections that spread across

---

[1] We get a glimpse of the older traditions being transformed "into a booming business" in Dan Levin, "Shamans' Spirits Crowd Air of Mongolian Capital: Ulan Bator Journal," *New York Times* (July 21, 2009). Once banned under communist rulers, shamanism is being revived, but now traditional shamans must compete with self-created practitioners with self-created ceremonies, for whom it is simply a business.

Europe in 1848, Marx and especially Engels insisted that their socialist politics were grounded in empirical reality, were, in fact, a science. Not for them the utopian and moralistic conceptions of socialism, rather a scientific analysis demonstrating the inevitability of Capitalism's destroying itself because of its inherent contradictions.[1]

We can explore this dialectic between the shamanic and the scientific by considering, once again, the healing arts, a domain that is both shamanic and scientific. It is in the transition to industrialism that eventually the balance shifts from the former to the latter. Pre- or non-industrial cultures generally rely on healing practices rooted in the soil of magic, while in the modern, industrial world, healing has become increasingly industrialized. At first this occurred within powerful chemical firms like I.G. Farben or Dow, where in one of their corporate divisions new drugs were devised to control diseases by waging war against bacteria in general,[2] while another division of the same firm deployed resources to devise new technologies of killing (explosives, poison gases or rocket fuels for the military, fungicides and herbicides for agribusiness) in a kind of reverse alchemy. With chemical drugs as the main weapon in their arsenal since the 20th century, Western medicine has waged a scientific and technological war against sickness and disease.

It is worth noting that it is precisely those societies based on scientific medicine where the origin of the threat to the Earth as a community of living creatures is found. And it is because of the historical agenda of those societies these past few centuries that today we face the traditional big questions, those of life and death, in an historically absolutely unique way, posed now as a question of the life or death (again, somewhat hyperbolically speaking) of the Earth herself.

Matters of life and death of individuals and of a people as a whole are the focus of rituals, songs and creation myths and are found at the heart of every culture. Such questions of life and death, the passage into or out of existence, are inherently *sacred* questions — all the more so when it is the planet herself whose vital signs we are monitoring — questions that serve as a kind of window from which each of these dialectically opposed realities can glimpse the other. In those domains, the shaman and his or her journeys to the ancestors' world demonstrate how porous are the boundaries between the two. All non-industrialized cultures have understood this, and feel a proximity to their ancestors. It is our own that has lost that elementary truth. And, alas, the Marxist tradition, with its embarrassment about and hostility to the *sacred*, is ill-equipped to reclaim it.

---

[1] A discussion of how this claim to being "scientific" affected late-19th-century social theory, can be found in H. Stuart Hughes, *Consciousness and Society: The Reconstructing of European Social Thought 1890–1930* (New York: Vintage, 1958).

[2] Arguably far more important for the overall health of the Earth than humans, and comprising some quarter of a million species. See Margulis and Sagan, *op. cit.*; Erin Allday, "Tracking Body's 100 Trillion Bacteria," San Francisco *Chronicle* (July 5, 2013).

We need to take a closer look at that sense of the sacred, to glimpse, if possible, what our Paleolithic forebears may have perceived when they gave voice to their archaic visions, describing the cosmos as they comprehended it. For that we need to understand the world of magic.

4

Magic As a Portal to the Spirit World

For the people of the Andes, matter is fluid. Bones are not death but life crystallized, and thus potent sources of energy, like a stone charged by lightning or a plant brought into being by the sun., Water is vapor, a miasma of disease and mystery, but in its purest state it is ice, the shape of snowfields on the flanks of mountains, the glaciers that are the highest and most sacred destination of the pilgrims. When an Inca mason placed his hands on rock, he did not feel cold granite; he sensed life, the power and resonance of the Earth within the stone. Transforming it into a perfect ashlar or a block of polygonal masonry was service to the Inca, and thus a gesture to the gods, and for such a task, time had no meaning. — Wade Davis, *Light at the Edge of the World* (2007)

Without *Contraries* is no progression. Attraction and Repulsion, Reason and Energy, Love and Hate, are necessary to Human existtence. — William Blake, *The Marriage of Heaven & Hell* (1790?)

i. INTRODUCTION

Magic is a special map of the whole of the cosmos. Like any map, used correctly it can help its user travel to the domains it depicts. Magic can both "explain" the world (within limits) and help the magus effect changes in it. (More later on how these changes are brought about.) Initially, my own very tentative descent into the subterranean world of magic (certainly a rash step for the Caltech student of the late '50s, where I carried the banner of Martin Gardner and Bertrand Russell) occurred simply because I wanted to "understand."

In the early '60s I had become one of a small army of scholars eagerly devouring the newly published *Correspondence* and crucial early drafts of key works by Isaac Newton so as to pin down that intellectually elusive founder of celestial mechanics, whose *Principia* (1687) and *Opticks* (1704) had been the culmination of the scientific revolution of the 17th century. As were several others, I was trying to comprehend his mysterious concepts of how new motion emerges in the cosmos. For Newton had, audaciously, added a new *entity* in his analysis of nature — force. It was force — particularly the force of gravitational attraction, but not only that — which caused change, which started things to move differently, which, in effect, activated the dead world of the supposedly inert bodies that were thought to constitute the cosmos. To try (unsuccessfully) to justify his notion of force, Newton was obliged to consider all the ways new motion is brought into being.

By the 1960s it was becoming clearer and clearer that Newton's supposedly mechanical universe had a hidden, magical side, something first noted by John Maynard Keynes in 1947.[1] Why? What, if any, was the role of magic in his scientific thought? The widespread availability of important Newtonian texts, recently published, opened these questions anew. Getting my bachelors degree in physics from Caltech, I entered graduate school in 1961 in a field just beginning to find an academic niche, the history of science. Under the tutelage of Prof. Henry Guerlac, my first graduate school seminar met weekly in the Fall and Winter of 1961 and soon had me and a handful of other PhD candidates picking at the contradictions at the heart of Newton's theory of matter, as we, too, shall pick in Part Two. Soon enough I was hooked on the profound historical problems posed.

My initial foray into the mysterious waters of magic, then, was as an historian, in 1969 newly blessed with a Guggenheim Fellowship to pursue Newton's cosmogonical speculations, a topic I had more or less invented, since prior to my work it was universally believed that Newton had condemned such theorizing. His cosmogony, I eventually realized, had a magical core. Yet it would be dishonest to leave the story there, for the same year I was sitting in the British Museum puzzling over Newton's magic, I also took LSD for the first time and saw the world in a different light. This was the '60s, and if my days were frequently spent organizing anti-war activities on my campus, my nights were spent under headphones listening to the latest music while perusing the *I Ching*. I began to understand the importance of eating a non-agribusiness diet, learned about alternative forms of healing like acupuncture, homeopathy, yoga or herbology; and, on their basis, was able to effectively banish my asthma without medication for the first time in my thirty years.

So it should not be a surprise that I eventually found my interest in magic was more than that of a scholar. I was filled with a very troubled but growing conviction that the world magic described was quite "real" and that it was able to explain the mysterious cosmos in which we live as well as anything I had previously learned. Newton had obviously thought so, and so, following his steps,

---

[1] Lord Keynes, "Newton, the Man," in *Newton Tercentenary Celebrations*, (ed.) the Royal Society (Cambridge, England: 1947).

did I. I saw common patterns. Sources, sometimes from traditions separated by millennia or several continents were in fundamental agreement, though of course their terminologies and frameworks might diverge widely.

One final clarification before I begin a detailed description of what I learned about magic: a major difficulty in understanding it lies in the manifold realities it encompasses. On the one hand, once glimpsed, magic becomes manifest everywhere, so prosaic as to make numinous the simplest of interactions between the creatures of our world: a bee landing on a flower, two lovers meeting, the discovery of language by a child, the preparation of a meal, the making of a tool or a piece of pottery — all of these reflect, as poets have long recognized, the essence of magic. On the other hand, it is equally clear that at times magic also encompasses the fabulous and supposedly "supernatural": the flying of a witch, the travels to and from the realms of the dead by yogis and shamans, shapeshifting from human to some other form, the creation of gold out of "lesser" metals, and the ability of some shamans to manifest themselves, as if in two separate bodies, in more than one place at a time. These too are part of what is generally understood as magic. And I believe all of them to have "really" occurred any number of times (even if there might have to be some discussion of what "really occurred" means), though I do not doubt that on many other occasions, probably a larger number, hoaxes have been perpetrated by fakers trying to convince others of their "miraculous" powers. But reading in the literature of magic, some years learning, observing, and practicing it, have convinced me that other demonstrations of magical powers were not bogus. Some of these things, as I shall recount in Part Three, I have witnessed or been a part of.

Credible accounts, some involving Newton, exist of alchemical transmutations,[1] for example, as I learned when I read both what Newton himself wrote and accounts by his contemporaries. I shall also[2] describe several remarkable healings I observed or participated in. Put into trance for the first time by my teacher, I was shaken to realize that I was "experiencing" my body as that of a spider, feeling the web I was on vibrate when prey was caught, though at the same time I was dimly conscious of my other, human, body, to which I was still obviously connected. Oral traditions of countless cultures fairly burst with their innumerable stories of miraculous feats done by *saddhus*, shamans, wise women, healers, medicine men and women, *brujos*, witches, and alchemists that can be ignored only by turning a blind eye to the accumulated mass of evidence, even when it is credible — just as the Jesuit priests refused to look through the telescope Galileo insisted could convince them of the new worlds he had discovered circling around the planet Jupiter, which he believed lent credence to the Copernican theory of the solar system. Like those Jesuits, modern scholarship treats the stories of magical deeds, despite any evidence that *might* exist, as axiomatically impossible, to be understood simply as one more demonstration of peoples'

[1] See Part Two.
[2] Part Three, Chapter 32.

consummate ignorance and built-in propensity for superstition. And woe to any serious scholar or scientist who credits such outlandish tales.

So magic is the mundane *and* the miraculous, the small and the grand, and while its loftier realms are usually only accessible to the experienced traveler, mighty initiates in the arcane traditions, there are aspects of magic that are experienced by virtually all of us every day. For we all live in a world in which magical relations tie everything and all of us into a marvellous web of mutually acting presences, vibrations in an ocean of energy, whose harmonic cross currents resonate and clash in a kind of symphonic splendor. Truly powerful shamans or witches are different from the rest of us in that they can navigate these currents with more precision and control of where they are headed because they are knowledgeable of the maps that describe them; therein lies their "miraculous" powers, their ability to affect the world of matter. But these are powers that all of us, in some measure, possess.

To the best of my ability, insofar as I have traveled some of these roads and pathways and know of others through my scholarship or direct observation, and given both that this is only a sketch and that such matters should be experienced, not read about, I shall be describing this terrain — a living terrain, for as I shall repeatedly emphasize, magic most of all arises out of a complex of relationships that ties all of us into the web of life.[1]

II. MIND OR MATTER?

To begin our analysis, let us go to the core: central to magic is the belief that mind and matter interpenetrate one another, so that what occurs in the one realm is reflected — or, better, resonates — in the other. Unlike the main traditions of Western philosophy, where a sharp cleavage is maintained between matter and spirit, magic maintains their essential unity. The core of magical techniques consists of various practices that enable a *magus* to influence the material world through the use of images, symbols, words, sounds, smells, and so on, techniques that rely upon that interpenetration and on the magical axiom that similar things often have mutual affinities. In the modern syntax and mode of discourse, it is difficult to avoid assumptions of "causality," but in order to escape the trap of seeing only a distorted apparition of magic, born of the very false consciousness I wish to critique, we should try to understand that the *magus* does not so much try to control what happens as he or she will "dance" among the currents making

---

[1] It goes without saying that my descriptions and analyses of magic reflect my experiences, reading, work with others, and participation in rituals; I have tried to be general in my descriptions, but others will surely have other emphases or disallow altogether some of my categories. There is no one true current; perhaps once there was, but by now, after millennia of having to exist in the shadows and subject to various suppressions, the waters of the occult flow in a multitude of ways, sometimes even at cross purposes.

up the world and attempt to nudge the play of events in this direction or that. Just as no real dancer believes his or her partner to be purely passive, a mere object to be acted *on,* and no good hunter or fisher treats his or her prey as just a thing, so too magicians see the cosmos they seek to transform as a living creature, and therefore prone to have a will of her own. More than someone who tries to *control* reality, in a sense a *magus* attempts to *seduce* it. As Duerr explains,

> the "magic rituals" are less an *intrusion* into the events, as envisaged by· those who would consider them a "protoscientific technique of manipulation," but instead they are rather a participation in the cosmic crisis, which is both a threat to and a condition for life.[1]

When in the late 1960s and early '70s I first began to take magic seriously, for me to talk about the ability of mind or consciousness to be used to work one's will on the world of material things, or that one could dance with reality, was not easy. As the various civil rights and anti-war movements I had been involved with pointed to the need for a general revolutionary approach to the many entrenched problems of racism and war we confronted, along with countless others I eventually gravitated towards the great theoretician of revolutionary change, Karl Marx. Though frequently intertwined with anarchist and populist strains and themes, my radical analysis of things took on the major Marxist categories of class, exploitation, alienation, and the like, and I understood the struggle of the Vietnamese, Cambodians, Brazilians, and others against US-imposed regimes in neocolonial terms.

Accordingly, my conviction that the core of magic bore validity posed a clear contradiction. Within the Marxist tradition, notions that *consciousness* could actually change *material reality* would be summarily dismissed as inherently "idealist," a clear violation of accepted categories and methods. As a materialist theory, Marxism made the material world, so I learned, the prime mover of everything else. Later, I shall discuss this question in more detail,[2] but for now let me simply say that such judgments, whether by others or from my own inner voices (actually it was more like my inner whine), not only rest on a manifestly false ideology, it is that ideology which is integral to Gaia's ecological crisis.

In order to show the limitations of defining things as belonging *either* to the material *or* to the mental realm, as if these were adequate or exclusive categories, I shall analyze music and dance, for there the severe deficiencies of this approach become readily apparent. Music, too, is a good example of the sheer *ordinariness* of much of magic, of how commonly we experience it, daily and even moment-to-moment in our lives. Finally, as with all magic I know of, music is structured around an axis of time.

---

[1] Duerr, *op. cit.,* pp. 43–44; also Taussig, *Devil,* p. 157.
[2] Part Three.

When I dance, the music "moves" me, it literally enters my bones and I can feel my body gyrating as normally it could not, exercising joints of which my non-dancing self is thoroughly oblivious; I am quickly in a state of trance. My energy — especially some years ago, when I first wrote this — seems limitless, and I could dance for hours, dancing beyond the capacity of my breath to sustain movement — and yet, I still move, never winded. When I look around, many of those on the dance floor are similarly transfixed, and I realize the subtle ways in which we are all connected, feeling each others' presence. Frequently I dance with eyes closed on crowded dance floors, yet rarely do I bump into anyone. My experience of dancing is transcendent, and brings me joy that hardly anything else can.

At those moments, I am undoubtedly experiencing a deep, yet quite common, form of magic. I am outside of myself, connected to currents beyond the limitations of my body or (sometimes) ego, or, indeed, anything narrowly confined to my being. It is an experience common to many, arguably most of us. Music, after all, is the universal language. Though not everyone dances, most are moved by some music; and not all so moved are *homo sapiens*. Yet, if we try to decide what is it that is causing all these things to happen to us, we run into a mess of troubles, mostly stemming from a fundamental confusion regarding the mental/physical boundaries at the heart of Marxist (and bourgeois) thought. Is the heart of music, presumably the entity that is moving in and through me when I dance, *material* — or is it *mental*, a "mere" idea? In the case of music, we reach an immediate impasse, for music is clearly both. There is no well-defined line that separates the one from the other.

To be sure, most of us are aware that music does consist of certain notes, and these can be described in terms of certain frequencies in the vibrations that constitute the sound, vibrations in the air (usually) produced by the various instruments and forming a pattern of excitation in the molecules pressing upon our eardrums. Numbers can be assigned to these notes, establishing their identity or frequency as a *thing*. These notes also exist in a certain temporal progression and ratio, repeating themselves in still another kind of pattern (that can be given other numbers). And of course they are loud or soft and the gradations in between. It is certainly possible to focus, as was done during the scientific revolution, exclusively on those molecular vibrations and mathematical patterns, relationships of amplitude, frequency, and rhythm, and understand the *material* basis of the music's influence on me.[1]

Yet it is obvious that much more is going on. When I lose much of my ego (obviously, not the part prone to boasting) listening to the music that I find moving, that literally begins to move *through* me, I *experience* the music inside me as a pattern of vividly-shaped relationships and designs that form, transform, and dissolve. The shapes interact, they are sculpted and move in relation to one another. The music swirls around me, is *palpable*. I feel as if I am bending the con-

---

[1] Part Three.

tours of space and time to my purposes, based on what I am hearing, but it goes beyond sound. It is those shapes and patterns, I believe, that get me moving, for it is those that it feels like I am dancing *with,* that become my dance *partners.* My appendages and the articulations between them bend this way and that in response to the changing topology in my mind's eye.

No amount of mathematical notation or description can capture the patterns or shapes conjured up by the music that I can "see" and feel; no mathematical discourse can describe the terrible abandon and grace these shapes induce in me and the others on the dance floor as we cut loose. To believe in the power of those numbers of the frequencies and harmonics, of amplitude and rhythm, to sum up those experiences is the worst form of reductionism, that assumption that all complex phenomena can ultimately be traced back to simpler, more basic components, of which, in Euclidean terms, they are the mere summation. For if music is pulsation in the molecules of air, it is also pure form, an organizing idea that creates symmetries and patterns in the warp of time. Music simply cannot be explained in *either* material *or* idealistic terms, for it is both and neither.

And music, too, in many ways symbolizes the essence of magic, initially coming forth out of a seed and creating form and substance out of "mere" idea, which, as we shall see, is the essence of all magic. For music the seed may be any number of things, a harmonic progression, a particular interplay of rhythm, a mood, a vision, a texture, etc., but it begins with idea and then becomes manifest in a single or multiple performances, in people's listening and responding, or in a recording, or symbols imposed upon a staff. All art is similar; which is why a deep affinity exists between artists and magic.

Not much magic occurs *without* the use of sound (if not always sound that is organized around particular harmonics). The transformation in the sound patterns that envelop me will, through dance, induce me into trance, a state where I am in touch with something outside my own boundaries, something I feel I am sharing with the other dancers on the floor. I move somewhat without volition, for my body seems to acquire a mind of its own, a mind beyond mine. One of the profound mysteries of dance is this: that it is *through* my body that I am most readily able to move *outside* it.

III. Mysteries of Life & Death & the Ritual of Sexuality

Life itself, of course, is a dance, and in magic the mystery of the life process is the central metaphor for everything else on Earth, for the whole of the cosmos. All craft is seen by magic as a reflection of that metaphor, all human (and animal) activity mirrors the overall life cycle. When an Indian woman throws a pot or weaves a garment or a troubadour creates a new song, when Nepali peasant women sow their bright green rice seedlings into the fecund soil of the monsoon-soaked paddy or a smith forges a new plow blade in his hammer's fire: in all of these the cycle of life and death is manifest.

Though not all of nature's creatures necessarily reproduce through sex, for the part of the world we are closest to, the animal kingdom, it is sexuality, that mysterious root of the tree of life, that underlies the life cycle.

Sexuality can result in pro-creation, through the coming together of opposites in the formation of a new life; but it is also re-creation, a joy simply of union, the most intimate and powerful form of ecstasy, and much of it, as in non-coital sexuality or sex between man and man, or woman and woman, is quite apart from reproduction. In magic, sexuality is seen as everywhere in our daily world — an overlap that has been shamelessly exploited by modern advertising in order to create artificial desires among would-be consumers — providing in magic (and advertising) a metaphor and sacred image that can be glimpsed any place we look. To the Tukano, for example, "the hunt itself is more than a mere food quest in that it is imagined as a courtship in which the prey has to be seduced to submit to the hunter."[1] Because of the resonances of sexuality in all spheres of life, magic often incorporates sexuality for ritualistic expression and as a way, quite literally, of making the magical work fertile. And yet, sometimes, to the contrary, magical relationships require sexual abstinence for a task to be accomplished. Among the Tukano, besides having to gain permission from the Master of Animals before a hunter is able to kill a game animal, preceding the hunt he must not eat certain foods; must undergo cleansing by fasting, bathing, and taking emetics; and must forgo any sexual activity for a number of days. In some tribes, the male hunter cannot even talk to or see a woman for a period of days preceding a hunt.

Food and sexuality to the Tukano are closely related, perhaps even, when considered symbolically, equivalent. Eating certain foods is regulated according to the stages in a person's life.

> Especially strict prohibitions keep people from eating normally while engaged in the acquisition of esoteric knowledge and, similarly, all rituals of the individual life cycle involve temporary dietary restrictions... during pregnancy, childbirth and menstruation; during mourning periods or while gathering medicinal herbs; during the couvade [when husbands take "sick" when their wives go into labor] or while engaged upon the preparation of poisons, narcotics or love potions, people carefully control their food intake and, as a general rule, refrain from eating the meat of game animals.

Eating and sexuality are both among the most significant ways in which the life energies are moved from place to place within the Tukano cosmos.

Sexuality frequently lies hidden at the core of much of traditional spirituality, especially in, but not limited to, ancient and non-industrial cultures. There

---

[1] G. Reichel-Dolmatoff, "Cosmology as Ecological Analysis: A View From the Rainforest," *Man*, vol. 21(3), (September, 1976), p. 307ff.

are numerous examples. Tibetan Buddhist *tankas* often portray male and female divinities in conjugal embraces, as images of the union of all oppositions within the cosmos. Certain yogic and Buddhist traditions are built upon the freeing of the *kundilini* (serpent) energies around the spine through ritualistic sexual practices. Witches will sometimes energize their spells by having a "Great Rite" involving two or more people making love.

Much to *my* shock, having grown up in a conventional Jewish household, I found out that sexuality formed a central core even in the ancient Hebrew religion. During the last century of the existence of

Figure 2
TIBETAN BUDDHIST *TANKA*

the Second Temple of Jerusalem, Hebrew sages tried to suppress the practice of ending certain festivals in frenzies of sexual activity.[1] Later on, in medieval times, with the development of cabala, a central role in the divine mysteries was played by the female Matronit, whose sexual union with the King of the cabalistic tetrad was described in detail in the *Zohar*, the central text for the cabala. One early 4th-century manuscript by a Spanish cabalist, in discussing the holy letters used in the name of God, described how

> the Holy one, blessed be He,... pours out the good oil to the Matronit.... The letter *het* [ח] is open to receive the male, that is, the letter *zayin* [ז], which is called the Covenant.... The letter *het* hints at the Matronit: as the woman is closed on three sides and is open on the fourth side to receive her husband, so the letter *het*, which is the Matronit, is open to receive the *vav* [ו], the King, the Lord of Hosts. For the legs of the *het* are the legs of the Matronit, which are open, and the beam on top is the body of the Matronit. And the *zayin* is the Covenant in relation to the *het*, and is complete, and the letter *het* is as in the human body with its two legs spread out.... Moreover, woman is also like the letter *he* [ה] but in the letter *he* the son does not cleave to her, while in the *het* he does cleave and suck from her.[2]

---

[1] Raphael Patai, *The Hebrew Goddess* (New York, Avon Books, 1978), pp. 84–85.
[2] *Ibid.*, pp. 164–65.

Agricultural communities across the world commonly had ritualistic couplings in their newly-plowed fields, frequently after dancing around the maypole–phallos, a celebration of life that enacted in the revelers' bodies the very drama they ritualistically invoked for the seeds to perform in the ground below.[1] It is a classic form of sympathetic magic, where the logic of metaphor and the multiple levels of reality, rather than some notion of causality and mechanistic interaction, informs beliefs, actions, and presumably outcomes.

Creating a child is a sacred act, probably the most sacred of acts, and so too must be the copulation at its root. But magic's celebration of sexuality is not limited to the kinds of couplings that might end in procreation. In cultures that freely express sexuality as part of their sacred life, there is the presence of *both* a playful androgyny, the wearing of costumes so that man becomes woman, or woman, man; or indeed, either of them becoming some animal or other, in the many guises taken on, or a joyful sexual activity, man to man or woman to woman and the various combinations that might in the course of things arise, and a celebration of the sexual union between polar opposites.[2] In fact, witchcraft and deviant sexuality became virtually synonymous in the eyes of witchhunters in early modern Europe, according to Arthur Evans; and gay men were tied together and placed at the foot of the stake on which a witch was to be burned to serve as her tinder — as "faggots" for her burning pyre.[3]

iv. TIME & SEASONS, RITUAL & POWER

Sexuality has its rhythms, whether they are the rhythms of sexual maturation and decline in the life of an individual or the rhythms of gestation in fetuses as form and function take on embodiment, or, of course, the rhythms of the sexual acts themselves, of whatever is being done, the two (or more) energies conjoining, merging, and building before a resolution into a final merging, the earthy dance behind all other dances. But behind *that* dance of sexuality is the heavenly dance, the play of Earth, sun, and moon, the dance of time. All of life follows the cycles of time: the seasons of the year, month, day and night. And magic reflects this, uses it, celebrating that deepest of mysteries, time. Whereas modern science insists on the isomorphism of one unit of time with another, so that any genuine scientific phenomenon (as in cold fusion) should be able to be replicated pretty much any time (as well as anywhere and by nearly anyone), magic insists on everything having its proper time (and place, etc.). For there are subtle en-

[1] Janet and Colin Bord, *Earth Rites: Fertility Practices in Pre-Industrial Britain* (London: Grenada, 1982), p. 137.

[2] This is nicely treated in Arthur Evans, *Witchcraft and the Gay Counterculture.* See also his *God of Ecstasy: Sex Roles and the Madness of Dionysos* (New York: St. Martin's Press, 1988).

[3] Evans, *Witchcraft and the Gay Counterculture,* p. 12–13; Ehrenreich and English, *op cit.*

ergies whose flow is molded by the movements of the planets through various signs of the zodiac belt, perhaps in harmony with the four quarters of the year as the sun's energies appear to wax and wane, or perhaps in time with the moon, that regulator of tides, of women's fertility, of feelings. In accord with these cycles and transitions, rituals are enacted, and these, as observations of those cycles —literally taking them into ourselves — become tools of power, means of navigating the currents of transformation.

According to magic, we should seek the great patterns of the cosmos less in the laws supposed to govern the transformation of this thing into that one, and more in the rhythmic patterns that lie behind all change, for where those common patterns are grasped, understanding one thing is apt to open up a comprehension of all things, of the All. As the *Emerald Tablet*, a central text that has survived out of the legendary ancient past of alchemy, explains:

> That which is above is like that which is below: and that which
> is below is like that which is above to accomplish the miracles
> of one thing.

This, then, is the basis for the profound ties that bind the microcosmic minutiae of our everyday lives to the macrocosmic grand patterns that rule over certain moments or whole eras. And if change is all, then change itself is the mystery, just as it is the given. An understanding of those overall patterns of change is therefore key to swimming with their currents rather than being buffeted about by them.

v. CHANGE & DIALECTICAL LOGIC

Underlying all relationships, all transformations in the world, according to magic, is a dialectical logic that is quite different in form and content from the logic we have been taught in our schools, which is based, as it sees itself, on a certain form of scientific reasoning. A number of Marxists, ex-Marxists, and apparently even Marx himself, have noticed the distinctly dialectical form of discourse found in magical teachings. That a kind of dialectical logic, in fact, predates Hegel, Marx's source for this invaluable tool of philosophical, historical, economic, and political inquiry, is enormously significant for the political history of Marxism itself. The young Marx praised Jakob Boehme, the 17th-century German alchemist and agitator whom we shall meet in greater detail in Part Two, in 1842 calling him a "'great philosopher.'"[1] A few years earlier, Engels, too, had written approvingly of Boehme.[2] Yet, Marx's (and especially Engels') growing emphasis on their own *scientific* socialism, which they contrasted with

---

[1] Franklin Rosemont, "Marx and the Iroquois," (Brooklyn, New York: Red Balloon Collective, 1989), p. 4.

[2] *Ibid.*, p. 47.

utopian versions, effectively banished such appreciative feelings towards occult thought to the margins, where they rapidly disappeared from view. Later I shall argue that these tensions played an important part in putting in place the special blinders worn by much of the revolutionary movement during the past century that have made environmental issues seem so irrelevant to the overall struggle.

For now let me only emphasize the crucial importance dialectical logic has historically played for centuries in both the revolutionary and the magical traditions. In creative hands this logic can tie together widely divergent parts of social or shamanic reality, illuminating the hidden threads and then weaving a single garment out of what at first appears to be but tattered shreds of yarn; but in other hands, alas, it can become a tool of deadly rigidity, ossifying rather than recreating the patterns of the world around us, while anaesthetizing its adherents, as in Stalinism.

Within the magical (as well as the revolutionary) tradition, dialectics has a fourfold presence: as a logic; as a theory of how change occurs; as a theory of being (called by philosophers, *ontology*); and as a theory of how we know things (*epistemology*). Yet it is important to see also the unity behind dialectics, for it is the same unity that holistically integrates every facet of the world as a whole into that larger whole. Everywhere around us, unfortunately, this unity is nearly invisible, and division is all we can see.

Change and inconstancy, according to dialectics, is immanent in the world for an important reason: everywhere, in every entity and every situation, there is a profound inconsistency, for every thing contains within its own opposite, in fact, is shaped and nurtured by it. Death gives meaning to and shapes the contours of life, and similarly dry with wet, sweet with bitter, and even rich with poor. No single one of those polarities could conceivably exist without its opposite. We tacitly recognize this when we acknowledge the fine lines between love and hate, bitter and sweet, at times even between power and impotence. This is all very different from our modern scientific logic that governs modern discourse, based as it is on an earlier, Aristotelian logic, according to which something must be *either* "A" *or* "not-A," with no possibility of hedging, no middle grounds, no smooth emergence of the *this* from the *that*. In contrast, dialectical logic (as in the well known *yin/yang* symbol) holds that if an entity is "A"— bad, hot, wet, destructive, or any other quality we can think of — it is at the same time, at least in part, "not-A" — good, cold, dry, constructive, etc. Into all things, all relationships, there is built an internal conflict. According to the anthropologist Levy-Bruhl,

> The collective representations and interconnections which constitute such a (primitive) mentality are governed by the law of participation and in so far they take but little account of the [Aristotelian] law of contradiction.[1]

---

[1] As quoted in Owen Barfield, *Saving the Appearances: A Study in Idolatry* (New York: Harcourt, Brace & World, 1957), p. 31.

The "primitive" mind ignores the core of our Western logic, where the essence of an entity must always remain the same until some *external* agent makes it change. Thus the magical mentality has a far different sense of things than one based on scientific logic, with its "law of identity."

The alchemist Thomas Vaughan, writing about the Creation during the period of social upheaval in England in the mid-17th century, put it more directly, explaining that the material matrix of the Creation was

> a miraculous *substance*... of which you may affirme *contraries* without *Inconvenience*. It is very *weake*, and yet most *strong*, it is excessively *soft* and yet there is nothing so *hard*. It is *one* and *all*: *spirit* and *body*; *fixt* and *volatile*, *Male* and *Female*: *visible* and *invisible*. It is *fire* and *burns* not: it is *water* and *wets* not, it is *earth* that runs, and *Aire* that stands still.[1]

From the law of opposites (or the "unity of opposites," as it came to be called within Marxism) there follows the great ubiquity of change, of transformation everywhere, for the tension between opposites is a dynamic one. Isaac Newton, writing a little after Vaughan, and celebrating the dynamism of nature, in his youth put it thus:

> For nature is a perpetual circulatory worker, generating fluids out of solids, and solids out of fluids, fixed things out of volatile, and volatile out of fixed, subtile out of gross, & gross out of subtile, Some things to ascend, & make the upper terrestrial juices, Rivers, and the Atmosphere; & by consequence others to descend for a Requitall to the former.[2]

So hot passes over into cold, life into death. No one has expressed this dynamic better, perhaps, than William Blake, the late-18th-century radical poet and engraver (he savored the fact that his images were created only where he had *not* carved on his block):

> The road of excess leads to the palace of wisdom.

> Prisons are built with stones of Law, Brothels with bricks of Religion.

---

1 [Vaugha]N. [Thoma]S., *Aula Lucis, or the House of Light* (London: 1652), p. 14; *cf.* Newton's alchemical manuscript, Babson Ms 420, quoted in Dobbs, *Janus Face*, p. 162.

2 *The Correspondence of Isaac Newton* (ed.) H.W. Turnbull, F.R.S. (Cambridge, England: Cambridge Univ. Press, 1959), vol. 1, p. 366. Newton to Oldenburg December 7, 1675.

You never know what is enough unless you know what is more than enough.

If the fool would persist in his folly he would become wise.[1]

A late-20th-century example of the unity of opposites can be seen in the US effort in the 1960s and '70s to subjugate the Vietnamese, trying to demonstrate to the world its capacity to compel the submission of uppity Third World nations that dared to try throwing off colonial and neocolonial domination. In fact, the US achieved precisely the opposite in its dramatic Mayday, 1975, defeat: on worldwide TV the vivid demonstration of how vulnerable the mightiest military and economic power the world had ever known was in the face of a determined and disciplined peasant-based insurgency by one of the poorest and (initially, in the south of Vietnam) most poorly armed populations in the world.

Not only is change everywhere, but according to dialectics it emerges for reasons that are *internal* to a thing or situation, not owing to some *external* agent — as the US, to its peril, never understood in Vietnam. Things change primarily because of themselves, rather than serving as passive objects against which outside forces act, as in the post-Newtonian European consciousness that is the subject of Part Two of this book. For both magic and for the left, as I shall discuss later, this was especially crucial. On the basis of dialectical logic, then, the universality of change was explained, and behind it was seen the interconnectedness, the unity of all things. Using it, Marx was able to explain capitalism by his detailed analysis of the "commodity," its central actor, metaphor, and fetish.

vi. MAGIC & HEALING: YOGA, ACUPUNCTURE, HERBALISM, ETC; OR, WERE WE ALL DYING LIKE FLIES BEFORE PASTEUR? STATISTICS & COLONIALISM

Every magical tradition I have studied is firmly rooted in an art of healing, whether it be acupuncture, which originally arose in connection with Taoist magic; the herbal therapies used in witchcraft; or the physical and spiritual healing practices historically associated with alchemy. This critically-important connection between magical traditions and healing is a reflection of magic's focus on the life cycle, on beginnings and continuations. In nonindustrial societies, such concerns constitute the very foundations of culture.[2] The centrality of healing to all magical traditions obligates us to take a rather lengthy look, once again, at the history of a handful of those healing traditions in the hopes that they will help us better grasp how magic functions in those cultures where it plays a significant

---

[1] William Blake, "Proverbs of Hell," in *Marriage of Heaven & Hell* (London and Paris: Oxford Univ. Press & The Trianon Press), pp. 7–9.
[2] The World Health Organization claims that approximately 80% of the population in developing countries relies primarily on traditional, rather than Western, medicine for their primary health care. (Wade Davis, *Shadows in the Sun*, p. 117.)

role in shaping matters. We shall find, not unexpectedly, that a book on our eco-logical crisis needs to pay close attention to healing on any number of occasions.[1]

When ancient magical healing arts are discussed, it is common to hear that such archaic traditions may be very interesting, and because of the many centuries of "trial and error," perhaps even useful for a small number of ills, but certainly no one could want to return to preindustrial healing practices, to what amounted to mere *hocus-pocus*. If there is any place where the advance of modern civilization over the distant past is irrefutable, it is medicine, the healing arts. Prior to modern medicine, we are taught, people were dying in the gutters and lived in squalor, covered everywhere by flies. The very real horrors of the Black Death in Europe are thereby extended both backwards and forward in time from the 14th century, and outward from Europe, universalized so as to include virtually all premodern times and the whole of the world. These are, as we shall see, very questionable extrapolations.

Our suspicions should be aroused at any rate regarding any supposed "history" that is so openly and widely used, as this particular medical legend is, to justify the crimes of colonialism. It is a particularly damaging "history, " because many who might think that the transformation of natives into job-holding consumers was an insufficient justification for the barbarities committed by Westerners in the name of civilization readily turn to this masqueraded medical apologetics as support for colonialism. It seems to make it all turn out "for the best." As Hubert Lyautey put it, "Le seule excuse de la colonisation c'est la médicien," ameliorating the "harsh aspects" of colonial rule. For historic figures such as Florence Nightingale and David Livingstone, "medicine was taken as a prime examplar of the constructive and beneficial effects of European rule, and thus… as one of the most indisputable claims to legitimacy."[2]

I suggest we examine this medical legend in some detail. In it we can see how scientific mystification is propagated through a false version of history that serves nakedly ideological ends. Certainly epidemics and plagues have erupted down through the ages, but as I discussed above, they were not by any means universal phenomena. Reflexively, when attempting to weigh the pros and cons of rival medical practices, we reach for statistics in order to settle any questions of "better" or "worse."

Unfortunately, statistics as a form of mathematical analysis historically arose quite late in the game, in fact only *after* European colonialism had begun to reshape the world. Statistical arguments were first used by John Graunt, a London tradesman in the 1660s who analyzed the Bills of Mortality issued by London authorities since 1527, to deduce medical patterns and form "various political and social conclusions from them."[3]

---

[1] We shall return to the broader, trans-healing meanings of magic on pp. 108ff.

[2] Arnold, *op. cit.*, p. 3.

[3] Robert Kargon, "John Graunt, Francis Bacon, and the Royal Society: The Reception of Statistics," *Journal of the History of Medicine and Allied Sciences*, vol. 18 (1963), p. 341.

I do not know how long it took before Graunt's new methodology began to be widely used to look at the health of natives in the various lands undergoing colonialization, but undoubtedly, when it was, it too was with the larger goal of deriving "political and social conclusions" from them. I suspect it occurred fairly soon after Graunt showed the way. What kind of medical situation would a newly arrived statistician have found upon beginning his investigations? If he travelled to one of the previously isolated areas of the world, such as New Zealand, he would obtain quite different data than if he went to some part of Asia, such as India, which was more-or-less part of the same landmass as the colonizing country. Whether the land was tropical or temperate, mountainous or plained, wet or dry would have also shaped the data. But everywhere the data would have reflected the devastation greeting him, for once the data starts being collected, colonialism has already had a devastating impact.

Previous native economies based on hunting and gathering, simple trade, subsistence agriculture, or combinations of these, and with forms of ownership (most likely, the lack thereof), particularly of land, many with an ethos that ensured a sharing of whatever food was produced, were simply uprooted. Within a handful of years of European contact, many patterns of production and distribution had been destroyed, replaced by slavery, forced work for the colonized, or the widespread growth of crops for export to Europe. Soon after contact, European plants and animals began to take over the terrain, in some areas replacing critical native stocks, sometimes wiping out animals, plants, or fish traditionally forming a crucial part of the local diet, as in the Canary Islands, New Zealand, and the West Indies.[2]

As discussed earlier, starvation, landlessness, the crowding of urban centers that were soon choking on accumulated garbage, shit (human and animal), and dead bodies far beyond anything the environment could handle, exacerbated the patterns of disease. People crowded into makeshift shelters, drank polluted water, and, particularly in mining towns like Potosí, were exposed to poisons such as lead and mercury and breathed smoke and the stench of decay. No doubt European-bred pathogens marched doubletime through the weakened bodies and spirits such conditions bred in the colonized lands. And the catastrophic rates of disease and dying, in turn, served to accelerate the process by which the local economy collapsed, sometimes aided by overt violence directed against its wares, as in India, where handicrafts were smashed so they could not compete against the inferior European imports.

The collapse generally paralleled the erection of a European-centered economy that increasingly called the important shots. Not all aspects of the new economy, of course, had to be directly in European hands, and opportunities for locals existed. Some natives, no doubt, would have admired the new power, and

---

[2] Crosby, *Ecological Imperialism*, pp. 93–97, 245, 265–66.

for a variety of reasons and perceived advantages sought to make their peace with it. Some initial converts were brought as slaves to the towns, put into Christian churches, and taught, at least by the 17th century, about Western science. In the 18th or early 19th century, European medicine was aggressively promoted, mobilized, in fact, largely to fight the very epidemics and diseases brought over by the Europeans. The extent of healing to be done was enormous: whole peoples and complex ecosystems were in the process of being wiped out.

Paradoxically, even as the indigenous economies were being undermined, simultaneously, in a process whose results were not apparent for some time (and so perhaps were rarely considered by the indigenous population) the lands undergoing colonization were having their plants systemically exported to the colonial powers as curiosities for their scientists to study and display. For a critical number of them, seeds were exploited as an important new basis for agriculture in the mother country —corn, potatoes, and tobacco, for starters, but the list is quite a lengthy one and includes many of the major crops currently under cultivation by the farms and plantations of Europe, the US, and Japan. In effect, the scientists were transforming the seeds from the colonized lands into *capital* that was invested in the farms of Europe, only the earnings on the capital flowed solely into the European banks.

> The data... provide a means of empirically assessing one of the principal issues in the current controversy over plant germplasm. The six regions that contain nearly all of the world's less developed nations (Chino-Japanese, Indo-Chinese, Hindustanean, West Central Asiatic, African, Latin American) together have contributed the plant genetic material that has provided the base for fully 95.7 percent of the global food crop production. By contrast, those regions with dependency indices greater than 90 percent (North American, Australian, Mediterranean, Euro-Siberian) contain all of the world's advanced industrial nations (with the exception of Japan), yet have contributed species accounting for only 4.3 percent of world food crop production.[1]

In particular, Latin America and West Central Asia provide over 75% of North American, 85% of Euro-Siberian, and 85% of Mediterranean food crop production in terms of the original provider of seeds. Similar patterns hold for the regions where current industrial crops (rubber, jute, tobacco, flax, etc.) were first found.

---

[1] Jack Ralph Kloppenburg, Jr., *First the Seed: The Political Economy of Plant Biotechnology, 1492–2000* (Cambridge, England: Cambridge Univ. Press, 1988), pp. 178 [Table 7.9], 179 [Table 7.10], and 181. My thanks to Iain Boal for bringing this work to my attention.

Several pages ago I raised the question of judging relative merits of healing traditions by the use of statistics, but we can now see that it was only *after* the prior onset of these many degradations of how people lived and struggled to survive that the first statistician would have arrived — after the beatings, enslavements, attacks on the economies, nutrition, morale, etc. His investigations of the sad state of affairs inevitably would have established a totally inaccurate baseline that later assessments of the health of the native population would use for comparisons. Relative to the grim situation that presented itself as the statistician first landed, later patterns of sickness and death, even though mostly dire themselves, might indeed look like a dramatic improvement — especially if questions of the health (or survival) of native cultures are passed over, as they nearly always are. The argument can then be made, as both bourgeois and Marxist historians have done, that colonialism ultimately was historically "progressive," a painful but necessary snag on the road to Progress.

Let me illustrate what I mean about precolonial health with an example close to home: Native American health prior to Columbus. As discussed above, Native Americans on the eve of contact with Europeans had a remarkable tendency to be free of most of the diseases that have plagued humanity, and heart disease, cancer, plague, cholera, typhus, measles, and, of course, smallpox were either unknown, or very rare. Diseases of the skin and most mental disorders were uncommon. Existing evidence suggests that Native Americans suffered primarily from rheumatism and arthritis, digestive problems (especially among the young and old), worms, eye problems, respiratory illnesses, and mastoid infections.[1]

The first settlers and explorers were in agreement as to the good health Native Americans enjoyed, noting their astounding longevity, many living into their nineties. Aside from infant mortality, both their general health and the power of their healing traditions elicited favorable comments from many contemporaries. One Dutchman wrote in 1624 that there was not "an ailment they have not a remedy for." Whites widely reported being treated successfully by Native American healers for everything from snake bites to rheumatism, throat infections, worms, ulcerated legs, yellow fever, blood poisoning, toothache, burns, herpes, scurvy, and gunshot wounds.[2] To European settlers, the new land itself seemed blessed with healing energy and visits to the North American colonies were recommended to the English as curative. A Jesuit missionary reported from the Huron mission that no European associated with it had died of natural causes in sixteen years, "while in Europe those years are few when some one does not die in our Colleges, if their inmates are at all numerous."[3]

Writing of Indian medicine, the evangelist John Wesley wrote in his popular *Primitive Physic* (1743) that

---

[1] See Chapter 2.
[2] Vogel, *op. cit.*, pp. 42, 139f.
[3] Crosby, *op. cit.*, pp. 282–83; Vogel, *op. cit.*

[t]heir diseases, indeed, are exceedingly few; nor do they often occur, by reasons of their continual exercise.... But if any are sick, or bit by a serpent, or torn by a wild beast, the fathers immediately tell their children what remedy to apply. And it is rare that the patient suffers long; these medicines being quick, as well as generally infallible.[1]

A number of settlers in the US in the 19th century published popular healing manuals — especially useful when one is at far remove from urban centers where (rarely affordable) doctors might be found — claiming to base them on Indian methods, such as the *Indian Doctor's Practice of Medicine or... Family Physician* (1848). Indian remedies were so extremely well-regarded and sold so well that later in the century, a number of charlatans flooded the market with fake "Indian" patent medicines in order to capitalize on its reputation for effectiveness.

Indeed, although a nearly universal assumption exists that Third World societies unequivocally benefitted from the imposition of the Western medical theory, practice, and personnel accompanying European ships, perhaps much more was lost than gained. It is especially ironic that nearly always it is vaccination we think of as one of the major superior life-saving medical interventions that colonialism brought to natives. In fact, the introduction of vaccination to European society, like the seeds for corn, came out of similar practices that had been carried on in the lands being colonized, in this case, Asia. Vaccinations were first reported in Europe in two pamphlets published in English in the early part of the 18th century by two Greek doctors in Constantinople familiar with Western medicine from their days at the University of Padua. In Constantinople, the doctors wrote, "the practice of inoculation had long been familiar among Greek peasant women of the Morea and Thessaly." According to William McNeill,

> smallpox inoculation seems to have been known and practiced *at a folk level* [my emphasis] throughout Arabia, North Africa, Persia, and India. Reports of a more elaborate Chinese method, involving the insertion of a suitable infected swab of cotton inside the patient's nostril, reached London in 1700.[2]

McNeill suggests the practice had been introduced in China in the 11th century, but variolation (a related practice) with smallpox culture is described in the classic text of acupuncture, *The Inner Classic of the Yellow Emperor* (*Huang di Nei-Jing*), compiled about 100 B.C.E., but by legend dating from much earlier. From China it is probable that some form of vaccination spread to the Moslem world around the 14th century. McNeill concludes that "it therefore seems probable that deliberate inoculation of children with smallpox had been a folk practice in much of Asia for

---

1 *Ibid.*, p. 69.
2 McNeill, *Plagues and Peoples*, pp. 223–24.

centuries, long before it came to the attention of European doctors...."[1] Because of its different history and social structures, England became familiar with vaccination before the Continent; and it was adopted earlier in the American colonies than in England itself, largely owing to a suggestion an African made to Cotton Mather when an epidemic was raging in New England. By the first few decades of the 19th century, in rural as well as urban England, vaccination was being widely practiced. On the Continent it was Napoleon's armies that spread the practice.[2]

With that thumbnail history, let us examine more closely McNeill's analysis of this story, especially his instinctive use of the term, "folk practice," for it is symptomatic of the kind of thinking that has created the medical legend of the unquestionable superiority of colonial over native medicine and thus has served as a justification for colonialism. McNeill (among others) assumes, first, that these "folk practices" in the countryside arose wholly in a hit-or-miss fashion and existed apart from any real medical tradition or body of theory, which is certainly not the case for Chinese medicine and the *Inner Classic*, which plays a role roughly akin to the Hippocratic corpus in the medical arts of the West. It is also usually taken for granted that the treatments of folk medicine were mostly based on what is curtly dismissed as "superstition," and that those treatments that were effective were either "lucky guesses" or the result of simple, blind, trial and error. Thus, after the preceding account, McNeill has the audacity to negate the significance of Asian vaccination by explaining that it "had been a matter of folk practices analogous to the innumerable other customary rules of hygiene that human beings had everywhere worked out and justified to themselves by a variety of naive and ingenious myths."[3] To illustrate a point about such "naive and ingenious myths," McNeill cites a Near Eastern folk tradition in which a person being inoculated was understood "as 'buying' the disease," and to make the transaction effective, had to give ritual gifts to the person vaccinating him or her.[2] This practice, it would appear, strikes McNeill as more "naive and ingenious" than our own Western tradition of providing inoculation, like all our medicine, in exchange for a fee, healing, like everything else, making perfect sense (to those like McNeill) only once it had been packaged as a commodity.

Far from being an exception, McNeill is more like the norm. Given a near universal contempt (though this is finally starting to change in some quarters) held by Western medical authorities and the historians who for the most part share their biases about earlier medical practices, we should be wary of "naively" overlooking what terminology such as "folk practice" often tacitly implies about the low levels of skill and lack of conceptual framework such practices reflected. I would argue, to the contrary, that behind those "folk practices" we can frequently find an historical tradition consisting of one of several different kinds of healers, for the most part trained by some kind of apprenticeship, be they

---

[1] *Ibid.*

[2] *Ibid.*, pp. 221ff.

[3] *Ibid.*, p. 225.

midwives, "cunning men," witches, shamans, medicine men, etc.; these approaches are likely to share certain attitudes regarding nature's healing powers, though their specific beliefs and practices might well vary.

That such folk practices generally are not conducted in cities, or in offices; are practiced by "non-professionals" who usually engage in other kinds of productive work in addition to their healing; usually cannot be found summarized in books written by one of its practitioners; and are frequently provided for barter or even for free if the sick person cannot pay, instead of being exchanged for a fee: all these should not blind us to the profound medical wisdom many of these traditions have accumulated. To compound the irony, not only is Western medicine generally regarded as superior because of a medical technique, vaccination, that it learned of only through reports of peasant practices common throughout much of Asia, but it turns out that it was only after the widespread adoption of this practice by European doctors that Western medicine "began for the first time to contribute to population growth in a statistically significant fashion."[1] McNeill dismisses the significance of the likelihood that Chinese medicine performed a similar feat in China by its use of inoculation long before 1700, again because it had arisen there only in the context of a "variety of naive and ingenious myths."

So what *was* the net effect of the victory of Western medicine in the colonies? As we have seen, this is a particularly sensitive question since its answer has so often served to celebrate the triumph of colonialism.

To do justice to this question and give due consideration to the often subtle points that need pondering would require another book altogether, more likely a series of books; that would take us far from the direction of our main inquiry. And yet I cannot forego a few words about what some of those discussions might involve.

To be sure, based largely on invasive therapeutics of synthetic chemical drugs and surgery, Western medicine *is* a profoundly powerful weapon to have in one's arsenal in the fight against disease. But note how much has already been conceded in way this last sentence has been framed. The belief that disease is an enemy to be defeated already no longer grasps its role in the larger economy of life and death that a community or individual must always contend with, and has clearly lost sight of the fundamental truth that life can only emerge *out of* death, and that without some of us dying, others could not be born — a mistake no traditional culture would ever make. Certainly the explicitly military metaphor I used was no accident, either, given this manner of thinking.

What is expecially striking about Western medicine is that a great many of the very things Western therapeutics are so effective against are the very kinds of traumatic injuries and wasting diseases that Western society is particularly adept at inflicting on its denizens in the first place: major traumas, such as modern industrial machinery and automobiles excel in creating, or debilitating ill-

---

[1] *Ibid.*

nesses like heart disease and cancers largely unknown among the aboriginal inhabitants of the Americas. Indeed, this is as it *should* be; the healing priorities for any society should reflect the real problems its people and animals face. However, efficacy against what are essentially local problems can in no way establish the basis of any claims Western medicine might make as to its universality.

Modern medicine, on the basis of its use of drugs, can lay some claim that its interventions have had a notable impact on survival rates for pneumonia and typhus. Treatment of malaria and syphilis was effective for a time, but (partly due to resistence acquired by mosquitos to pesticides) it did not last. Polio, measles, and whooping-cough treatments have also seen successes due to vaccines. Mortality from TB, tetanus, diphtheria, and scarlet fever has declined, but, according to Ivan Illich, not because of drugs.

Even for treatment of traumatic conditions, questions can be raised as to whether, as a general rule, Western therapeutics are the most effective, as the following examples will demonstrate. In 1958, floated by a small grant from a pharmaceutical company, Nicole Maxwell travelled deep into the Amazon rainforest in search of medically useful plants, conferring with local healers when possible.[1] She observed the following herb-based treatments used by the tribal people:

• One plant, applied carefully as a resin to any tooth that is rotten gradually loosens it until it falls out in tiny pieces over a period of about a month, without any inflammation, bleeding, swelling, or discomfort. If the tooth was already in severe pain, the first touch of the resin to the nerve completely stopped it. (Her tribal informant, told of the Western alternative, extraction of the tooth by force, thought it was "barbaric.")

• Noticing exceptionally well-shaped and preserved teeth among the elders of the Witelo tribe, Maxwell learned that they (though not the younger, more acculturated tribal members) every once in a while chewed the leaves of the Yanamuco tree; such treatment turned the teeth entirely black for about a week, with a much longer period of speckling, which is one reason the youth tend to avoid the treatment. But teeth so treated did not decay between treatments..

• The Witelos also have a plant whose leaves are given to children who show a tendency to pudginess. Lifetime thinness results, and consequently overweight people do not exist among them. (Nor, let us hope, anyone with anorexia or bulimia.)

• Maxwell saw a plant whose pale green leaves —applied in one instance within minutes of critical burns on the head and chest from a gasoline explosion, and in a second case first administered a full month after a pot of boiling stew had horribly burned a woman's legs — brought instant relief from pain. In both cases, despite the seriousness of the burns involved, no scars were visible, even in bright sunlight, following treatment. The woman with burned legs had been

---

[1] Nicole Maxwell, *Nature's Search*, pp. 4, 41–43, 54–55, 91, 161–62.

bed-ridden for a month prior to her treatment, but the day after taking this remedy, she was up and able to walk.

• Maxwell was shown a tree with smooth pale bark whose sap stops postpartum hemorrhaging or bleeding from bad cuts.

• Maxwell heard about (this was one remedy she did not actually see used) a plant whose tea breaks up gall or kidney stones into small pieces that are easily passed; and she was told by a trusted informant about using the fats and viscera of jaguars, crocodiles, monkeys and vultures to cure snakebites, bronchitis, and pneumonia.

Needless to say, these remedies have no equivalent within the Western pharmacopoeia. But the most remarkable of Maxwell's finds, and the reason for planning her expedition in the first place, were a pair of plants used to control contraception. (This was in the '50s, before the birth-control pill.) She had heard rumors of such miraculous plants. Native healers, she found, were quite reluctant to share information about these herbs, since they controlled the very opening of the sacred gate between life and death. A leaf from one of the plants was given in a single dose to Witelo girls at puberty, resulting in their being infertile for a period of six to eight years. Repeated doses could extend the infertility. Another tribe had a root that rendered a woman similarly infertile, though a reversal root was available to enable her — or a woman who had not taken the infertility root — to conceive easily.[1]

Maxwell's findings were quite dramatic, but Western herbalism (that is, based on European traditional usage) has its own powerful plants. Comfrey is widely used to speed up the healing of bruises, sprains, breaks, and abrasions; bruised tissues and bones treated with comfrey will mend more rapidly, with less swelling and pain in the process. (I try to carry comfrey leaves with me to demonstrations.)

Western medicine simply has no drug or treatment able to bind wounds and speed recovery, and for extensive abrasion or wounds will often prescribe antibiotics "in case" infection results. Surely, however, the best way to prevent infections in such instances is to provide for the rapid healing of the wounds, giving fewer opportunities for any infection to take up residence. Of such remedies, Western-trained doctors are ignorant. If, in fact, infection does occur, there are plant-based remedies, such as golden seal or garlic, to treat many of them.

This is not to argue that in all cases, non-industrial medicines are superior, though perhaps, except possibly in emergencies, they should be the remedies first tried, since they are less invasive, if the sick person's vitality is still intact. I am arguing, however, that the case for or against the different approaches to healing, Western or traditional, is much more complex an issue than is generally realized.

---

[1] *Ibid.*, pp. 186f, 249.

DAVID KUBRIN

vii. Eye of Newt, Anyone?

Let us return to the more general aspect of magic, to *what* the *magus* or shaman actually *does*. Can I give a more detailed "job description," as our current social fetish calls for? What such magical practitioners do, of course, varies considerably depending on the particular cultural tradition (Jewish cabalist, Cheyenne shaman, Balinese *lejaks*, etc.) and the modality (divination, healing, hexing, alchemical transmutation, etc.) that he or she is engaged in, so my remarks will necessarily be somewhat general.

All magic is based on the multi-dimensional nature of reality. Whereas in the post-Newtonian world, rooted in notions of scientific causality, a modern person wanting to effect a particular situation or object (let us say, a war in Nicaragua) likely will focus on all the forces or things having an obvious relation to that situation (so, in our example, the soldiers and *materiel* on both sides, transportation, weather and terrain, public opinion, economic considerations, etc.). A *magus* or witch, on the other hand, is likely to pay attention more to representations of that war on "other planes," those reflections, so to speak, of different, other dimensional, levels of reality. These other planes can have different names and functions in separate traditions, but they include "places" reached through dreams, deep-trance work, or by meditation, fasting, drumming, chanting, some herbs, dancing, and quite often, a combination of many or all of these. The *magus* knows that what occurs on those other planes can very much have a bearing on realities elsewhere — on what we can call the material, day-to-day world, such as, in my earlier example, the progress of the US war in Nicaragua during the Reagan years.

I am drawn to this example in part since for the coven I worked in, it was an arena in which we focused much of our efforts in our visits to those other planes; but I was later intrigued to learn that Augusto Sandino, the anti-colonial leader who in the 1930s fought to overthrow the domination of the US in Nicaragua and after whom the Sandinistas (devils incarnate for President Reagan) are named, frequently used magic in his military operations against US marines sent in the '30s to suppress Nicaraguan rebels. Sandino is known to have communicated with his men telepathically. He also used divination as a way of analyzing the movement of enemy troops (US marines and the Nicaraguans under their command).[1]

In *The Spell of the Sensuous* David Abram argues persuasively that for the shaman these other planes are where humans can more directly communicate with the creatures with whom we co-habit the Earth, and indeed, in some profound manner, find a way to enter into the consciousnesses of those flora or fauna. In Native American spiritual traditions such animals become the spirit guide for clans

---

[1] Gregorio Selzer, *Sandino* (New York: Monthly Review Press, 1981), pp. 117–21. Donald C. Hodges, *Intellectual Foundations of the Nicaraguan Revolution* (Austin: Univ. of Texas Press, 1986). I am very grateful to Tony Ryan for bringing these important works to my attention.

(Deer, Badger, Bear, etc.) and individuals after vision quests. Feathers and claws are tools to this end. The ability to enter into these other awarenesses in traditional cultures is frequently extended to the trees, the rocks, the healing (and other) plants, especially notable ones like extraordinary trees or springs whose waters possess special powers.[1] With numerous shrines and burials, ancestors, one's parents and grandparents, sisters and brothers and cousins, are sown back into a consecrated landscape that a people inhabits, Such beliefs persist well into sedentary agricultural societies. Abram:

> humans, in an indigenous and oral context, experience their own consciousness as simply one form of awareness among many others. The traditional magician cultivates an ability to shift out of his or her common state of consciousness precisely in order to make contact with the other organic forms of sensitivity and awareness with which human existence is entwined. Only by temporarily shedding the accepted perceptual logic of his culture can the sorcerer hope to enter into relation with other species on their own terms; only by altering the common organization of his senses will he be able to enter into a rapport with the multiple nonhuman sensibilities that animate the local landscape.... His magic is precisely this heightened receptivity to the meaningful solicitations — songs, cries, gestures — of the larger, more-than-human field.

On the basis of his analysis *and* his own entrance into the consciousness about which he is writing, Abram provides his own summary of magic as "the experience of existing in a world made up of multiple intelligences," and that living in such a world rests on the

> intuition that every form one perceives from the swallow swooping overhead to the fly on the blade of grass, and indeed the blade of grass itself — is an *experiencing* form, an entity with its own predilections and sensations, albeit sensations that are very different from our own.[2]

The shaman or witch will know that the other planes not only are connected with our day-to-day world (in actuality, the two domains interpenetrate one another), but that these other worlds are often easier for a person or small group to affect than the day-to-day world. The *magus* can also create a version of the "material world" which is smaller, more manageable, easier to manipulate, or, to use my earlier image, to seduce. Since on one level these other realities are projections

---

1 Taussig, *Devils*, p. 185.
1 David Abram, *op. cit.*, pp. 9–10.

of our inner selves, they are in principle as easy (or as difficult) to control *as* our selves — as our vision, as our will. What makes this other than a totally solipsistic view of the world — or, to Marxists, idealist — is that "our selves" are in no way independent of the material world we inhabit. For our selves both create and are created by the material world. What the *magus* or witch understands is how mutual this interaction, this dance, is, and how active a role our inner visions can play in shaping the unfolding of all of our multi-dimensional realities. And, in principle, there is no reason this cannot include things as concrete as wars, or the functioning of a whole political economy. Because of this interpenetration, though, an object from the day-to-day world can be a bridge to other planes if it has the special energies, resonances, or attributes that directly relate it to the object or situation the *magus* wishes to invoke or influence — thus, the proverbial pieces of clothing or the hairs, photographs, or doll representations of someone being healed or hexed. Or for our coven one winter solstice night, a few rocks and plants plucked by Roy from the north, east, south, and west perimeters of a major military base, whose functioning furthered the likelihood of nuclear Armageddon, for which reason we *i-magined* — that is, used magic — to conceive of an alternative future. Into or through our imagined vision, we used our magic to energize it, to propel our hopes/prayers into its manifestation.

At its core, magic is created out of imagination, imagery, as indicated by its root, *mag* (from the Greek, μαγοσ, and Persian, 𐎶𐎥𐎢𐏁, a wise man or member of the priesthood)[1] and the *image* at its foundation is both created and honed inwardly by a variety of means, including poetry, song, dance, ritual, representations in symbols or metaphors, etc.; it is in like manner projected outward, so that it may become manifest, since symbols are portals from one reality into another, which is why traditionally artists of all kinds are so often drawn to magic and understand it in their souls. It is the staff of their creative lives. Indeed, art itself *is* magic, the bringing forth out of an idea, image, or feeling a purposeful manifestation, be it through dance, words, paint, wood, or welded pieces of metal.

One of the most powerful sources for the awareness of the *magus* is the map to the bridges themselves, what has been called the Doctrine of Signatures, which teaches that emblematic hints of their probable connection to other realities can be discerned in the objects themselves.[2] For example, the root of the lotus flower, a very effective herbal remedy for breathing problems, such as asthma, in cross-section looks like the air sacs of lungs. (See *Figure 3*, p. 107.) Initiates into some spiritual traditions might have alternative understandings, but I think that it was that correspondence that guided the first healer who thought to try lotus root for someone having trouble with his or her breathing.

Indeed, the centrality of breathing exercises in many of the spiritual traditions of the East probably accounts for the frequency with which one encounters

---

[1] I am grateful to Athandsios Paroadopoulos and to Jake Fuchs for the Greek and to Minoo Moallem for the Persian entomologies.

[2] For example, see Maxwell, *op. cit.*, p. 163.

Figure 3
PIECES OF LOTUS ROOT

the lotus in the iconography of those practices. The body and its perceptions, and the soul of the *magus*, are instrumentalities in a dialectical creation, using representations to bridge different worlds — hence the emphasis not only on breathing exercises, but on fasting, chanting, adopting special body postures, using power plants like peyote, psilocybin, ayahuasca, and similar means of focusing/defocusing/refocusing the body and its attentions.

I learned how "spirits" can gain entrance to our world once when my eight-year-old son, Yarrow, was home with a high fever. He spent the day with a babysitter, while I was at work (designing equipment for an aquifer-depleting, coal mine in Wyoming). At home the previous night I had done my first deep trance with my magic teacher, during which the classic "scary" witch — Hecate, the hag who watches at the gate of death, and with whom my teacher worked in her own magic — had "come" in response to her invocation. At the time Hecate scared me, for despite my conscious understanding, I still associated death only with bad things. The hag, as she sometimes appears, had *not* become manifest to me in my trance, and I did not want to think too much about her appearance in my partner's. But I had no choice: when I got home from work I found out that my son had seen her. Though Yarrow knew that I practiced witchcraft and had come with me to a number of solstice, equinox, or moon rituals, I had not told him of my work the night before. But when greeting me he said that he had seen the "mean witch" that day. When I asked what he meant, he explained that the sitter had cut open a kiwi fruit for his lunch and, no doubt helped by the dissociation caused by his high fever, he saw the face of the hag in patterns made in the tiny black seeds embedded in the fruit's green flesh. I suppose from Hecate's point of view, her coming into my teacher's trance the night before had opened our house to her, and she had taken it as an opportunity to use what most of us might simply see as random black seeds as a means of in-forming her presence in the fruit, making their pattern her own. Did some local spirit thus appear to Moses in patterns of the bush in flames (I make no claim to being able to account for the origins of the fire itself)? Or is this how the Virgin Mary, the Roman Catholic version of the archaic goddess of fertility found across the world, frequently manifests to believers in the patterns appearing in trees, plaster walls, or tortillas?

On another occasion Yarrow was again my teacher. He was then about eleven and we were hiking one Sunday on Mount Tamalpais, sacred to local Native Americans, taking a trail that we had been on a number of times before. As we entered the woods from the parking lot, my son began to chant, "We all come from the goddess, and to her we shall return / Like a drop of rain, flowing to the ocean," a simple and haunting chant common in our pagan circles. I joined in and we chanted as we walked, which, given what occurred, I believe put both of us in receptive spiritual states. We had been walking about twenty minutes when Yarrow pointed to a distinctive madrone tree growing out across the trail. "Look at that tree, Dad," he pointed. I stared. The tree had taken on an exceedingly clear pattern where its bark had unevenly worn away, of a bird goddess. I saw her immediately, though Yarrow, it turned out, had merely sensed something very remarkable about the tree, *some* presence. It was a large and majestic madrone. leaning out over half of the trail. As Yarrow and I sat there and experienced the tree and its fantastic power and image, other hikers passed. Feeling I was in the presence of some sacred mystery, I said nothing to these others about the image, curious whether they would see it. All who passed felt *something* about that tree, noticed it in some way. One group who stopped consisted of a father and two small boys, one riding on his back in a carrier. The children, like Yarrow, were especially drawn to the tree, though it was clear that neither they nor their father nor, for that matter, anyone else we saw that day explicitly saw the image of the bird goddess or any other representation. (See *Figure 4*, p. 113.)

Yet, as the reader can see from the photograph, the figure was clear and distinct and not the least bit ambiguous. From pudendum to navel to breasts to birdlike head, she is very present; actually, a *second* figure is apparent to some others who look at the tree or photograph. Numerous times since I have closely examined the bird-goddess figure, and so far as I can tell, nearly all of it is the work of the tree, or what is immanent in the tree, rather than the result of human art. Someone with a knife does seem to have completed a line or more of the left outer thigh, and the rear part of the goddess's hair was probably added on. The rest I believe to be the tree's doing. Everyone I brought in the next few years to the tree was able to see the image, but I had already told them what we were looking for.

Now the Doctrine of Signatures would suggest that the madrone is the embodiment of some power, probably the mountain's sacred spirit had become manifest in that tree. The tree possesses a numinous quality. It subsequently became a power spot where I went to commune with the spirits, seeking visions there with the aid of peyote for a challenging episode in a novel I was trying to write, and it was there, too, that my second wife and I did a ceremony to ask that our efforts to make a baby would be blessed with fertility. From the day that baby was born, Yarrow has had an intense bond with his baby (half) brother, possibly because of the tree he had discovered.

Figure 4
"BIRD GODDESS"
MADRONE TREE,
MOUNT
TAMALPAIS,
CALIFORNIA
(author's photo)

viii. WHOSE REALITY IS IT? IS MAGIC INHERENTLY LEFTIST, RIGHTIST, OR NEITHER? OR IS IT ROOTED IN THE CONCRETE HISTORICAL DIALECTIC?

Are there any inherent politics of spirituality or of magic? Or of religion, taking it as a more formalized, rule-bound, hierarchical, historically-later version of spirituality? Am I arguing that it consistently takes on a leftist coloration? What about rightwing magic — that of W.B. Yeats, for example, or the terror-based magic of groups such as the Ku Klux Klan, or the Nazis? Some readers, no doubt, will find the very concept of magic abhorrent, conjuring up perhaps images of a "black" Satanic worship; or of the magic of the Roman Catholic mass; or of Brahmanism, with its pious santification of privilege on the basis of karmic justifications of "lower" castes; or of cults like Scientology, EST, or the Moonies. These are, indeed, some of the many shapes magic can take. However, these are particular forms of magic, all thoroughly imbued with patriarchal values, if not, indeed, actually centered around blood sacrifices, as Nazism, the

KKK, and Catholicism are.[1] In other words, does magic *have* a politics, or is it, as many believe, like much of culture, inherently neither left nor right?

Historically magic has had both left- and right-wing forms. But it is the latter we tend to know about (the Nazis, the Bohemian Grove, *Opus Dei*, Skull and Bones). Because history is written by the winners (including by those who can write), a critical part of our history has been kept from us, a story of the historic defeat of a broad-based revolutionary movement that was strongly influenced by magical ideology (caballa, alchemy, astrology) some three and a half centuries ago. The insurgencies were everywhere in the period we will be examining, but in England things came to a bloody head. A crucial showdown eventually defeated the magical insurgents, as we shall see.[2]

Had it been otherwise, had that revolutionary ideology been victorious, it would have radically altered the face of early modern Europe in the 17th and 18th centuries and, I think it is safe to speculate, sent the trajectory of history off in an altogether different, arguably more balanced, set of tangents. The insurgency and the campaign to crush it unquestionably played a key role in the development of modern consciousness, I will argue below.

Since few, on the left or not, know this history, and because it provides a stark contrast with the modern mentality that was victorious and that provided a cover for ecological despoilation, Part Two will offer an extended look at the forces involved and especially at the ideological function magic played in the 17th-century English Civil War and revolution. This rebellion, a key chapter in the emergence of nation-states at the time, was the first generalized uprising in early modern times against centralizing (monarchical) authority — accordingly, the model for the rebellions and revolutions to come in France, Germany, the US, Russia, as well as elsewhere in successive centuries.

With the possible exception of the Nazis,[3] the forms of patriarchal magic mentioned above are manifestations of a spirituality that is based on what Starhawk calls "estrangement," forms in which the central theme is one of separateness.[4]

---

[1] Thus the central theme of Christianity in general, the crucifixion — and historically the many millions who died with the blessings of Roman priests in the Conquest, the Crusades, the Inquisition, witch hunts, and the burning of heretics, a central motif, as well, that perhaps Rome is finally putting behind it.
[2] Chapters 5 through 11 and 14, where we will discuss in detail how that defeat was carefully planned and executed, and why it was so critical.
[3] The focus of Part Three, Chapter 33.
[4] Since I learned much of my magic from working with Starhawk, practicing it regularly in our coven for a number of years, and rely, as in what follows, on a great deal of her perspective in my own interpretation and practice of magic, I think it important to clarify where our views diverge. Though I largely agree with her that the hideous interpretation of witchcraft that is common in our culture — as Satanic and as practiced mostly by demonic fiends — was *largely* a projection of orthodox Christians centuries ago, in a vicious campaign to un-

dermine widespread support for pagan spirituality among the peasantry, by grossly distorting the beliefs, behaviors, and aims of the witches, I do not think that is the whole story. For even in non-Christian cultures, there is still a dark shadow associated with the idea of sorcery, witchcraft, and shamanism. Were the transformation of the old pagan gods (such as Pan) into Satan *only* a matter of the Christian churches' blaspheming of pagan deities and doctrines, we would not expect to encounter similar (though often greatly attenuated) senses of foreboding toward African sorcery, the *brujas* of the US Southwest, etc. Abram suggests that the necessary removal of the shaman from his or her hunan nexus, the degree to which, as the precondition for shamanic power, the shaman's primary allegience is not to the human world, but to the more-than-human worlds (as "the primary strategist and negotiator in any dealings with the Others") is why their presence within human society is so problematic. "For the magician's intelligence is not encompassed *within* the society; its place is at the edge of the comuunity, mediating *between* the human conmunity and the larger conmunity of beings upon which the village depends for its nourishment and sustenance." (Abram, *op. cit.*, pp. 6–7). Because they are thus removed from the human world, they are feared within it.

More importantly, I have never felt comfortable with Starhawk's definition of magic, which she, following Dion Fortune, says is "the art of changing consciousness at will." Were this only a passing phrase of hers, I might not pay it so much attention, but Starhawk works this definition into everything of hers I have read and makes reference to it at many rituals. When I first heard her formulation, what bothered me was that it rendered magic into such a flat, even boring, entity, robbing it of both mystery and power. While I certainly agree that magic is ordinary, since it pervades the whole of our lives, I am troubled by the absence in her definition of its less mundane, more mysterious, aspects. The point, as I see it, is not merely to change consciousness, but that such changes in turn help transform the outer, or material, world. I agree with Abram who sees in this a dismissal of *why* one would want to alter one's consciousness, which, he emphasizes, is precisely to take on the extradimensionality of being able to perceive not just as a human, but as a jackal, a hummingbird, a cricket, a river, or a rock overhang. Starhawk's (and Dion Fortune's) definition strikes me as narrowly psychological, too inwardly-focused. This rather surprises me, since in our coven magic was much more a matter of our projecting our political will outward, onto the workings (more often, the non-workings) of the Diablo Canyon nuclear-power facility, the wars in Central America, etc., a focus emphasized in public rituals and in her ongoing political engagement. Other issues where Starhawk's and my views diverge are, I believe, not related to this basic philosophical disagreement about magic, and involve questions about the cultural, magical, ecological, and spiritual implications of hi-tech. For this latter issue, see Part Three.

Estrangement begins with the separation between we who live on this world and a transcendent Being who is *out* of this world, or far beyond the reach of everyone except possibly a selected priesthood. Estrangement seeps inevitably into everything else, until it mandates, or at least accounts for, the separation between all people, the universal sense of solitude painfully carried in the depths of each of our modern souls. Naturally enough, alas, there follows the separation and divorces most of us feel from the parts of our own atomized and scattered selves — a sickness of the soul, as I shall argue in Part Two, that directly emerged out of the ideological teachings of late-17th-century science. Starhawk explains that

> [E]strangement is the culmination of a long historical process. Its roots lie in the Bronze-Age shift from matrifocal, earth-centered cultures whose religions centered on the Goddess and Gods embodied in nature, to patriarchal urban cultures of conquest, whose Gods inspired and supported war. Yahweh of the Old Testament is a prime example, promising His Chosen People dominion over plant and animal life, and over other peoples whom they were encouraged to invade and conquer. Christianity deepened the split, establishing a duality between spirit and matter that identified flesh, nature, woman, and sexuality, with the Devil and the forces of evil. God was envisioned as male — uncontaminated by the processes of birth, nurturing, growth, menstruation, and decay of the flesh. He was removed from this world to a transcendent realm of spirit somewhere else. Goodness and true value were removed from nature and the world as well.[1]

The forms and ideology of estrangement are those of hierarchy, and ultimately it may be immaterial whether it is the hierarchy of an established male priesthood based on the theory of apostolic succession or the hierarchy of a *Fortune* 500 multinational corporation.

Along with the consciousness of estrangement, of alienation and powerlessness, however, another form of consciousness exists, to a limited degree surviving into the modern era. In Starhawk's terminology, it is the consciousness of "immanence," which she defines as "the awareness of the world and everything in it as alive, dynamic, interdependent, interacting, and infused with moving energies; a living being, a weaving dance."[2] In what follows, when I speak about issues of estrangement or immanence, following Starhawk I shall mean them as embodying respectively, "power-over" or "power-from-within" relationships among creatures and things.

---

[1] Starhawk, *Dreaming the Dark: Magic, Sex & Politics* (Boston: Beacon Press, 1982), p. 9.
[2] *Ibid.*, p. 9.

This consciousness of immanence historically has been the basis for numerous forms of left-wing magic, a magic which we rarely learn about. Yet a striking number of instances of such magic can be found:

• The just-mentioned insurgency in mid-17th-century England, which will be described and analyzed in depth later, and so to which here I will only make a cursory nod.

• As mentioned above, Augusto Sandino, the historic founder of the military and political resistance to the humiliating treatment by US Marines in the 1920s and '30s, dictating dos and don'ts to the Nicaraguans in order to benefit local oligarchs and US investors, was a serious student of the occult, using his mastery of magic for military purposes. For example, Sandino successfully anticipated the movement of enemy troops through divination and communicated with his soldiers telepathically. More importantly for us, Sandino drew his inspiration for revolution from the occult teachings of theosophy, Freemasonry, and especially a movement called the "Magnetic–Spiritual School," established in 1911 and on the basis of a distinct spiritual war declared on all religion, was eventually to spread widely across Central America. It brought a program of establishing agricultural and industrial cooperatives managed by the workers where "each produced what he can and consumes what he needs."[1] Organized in *cathedra*, or schools, by its peak just before World War II, there were about 250 *cathedras* spread across the continent. Sandino was closely associated with its founder, Joaquin Trincado (1836–1935), an Argentine of Basque origin. In 1931, Sandino was appointed the Magnetic–Spiritual School's regional trustee for Nicaragua. On the basis of this appointment, he established an agricultural cooperative in Wiwili in 1933 to implement his vision of anarcho-communism. To Sandino, Spiritism (as the Magnetic–Spiritual School styled its spiritual program) provided a spiritual justification for his anarchism.[2]

• When the Romans conquered the Celts in the first century B.C.E., it was the druids or priests who urged resistence to the invaders, organizing rebellions and prophesying victory in their protracted struggle.[3]

• The example of the druids is emblematic of a more general pattern whereby traditional spirituality is responsible for fighting off colonial powers, as the numerous examples that follow illustrate. This is widely seen in Native American history and is the reason for the US government's frame-up of Leonard Peltier. Earlier shamanic resistance was embodied in Rolling Thunder, Geronimo, Crazy Horse, and Leonard Crow Dog, among many others.[4]

---

[1] Hodges, *op. cit.*, p. 41.

[2] *Ibid.*, pp. 40–48.

[3] Evans, *Witchcraft and the Gay Counterculture*, p. 22.

[4] For Peltier, see Peter Matthiessen, *In the Spirit of Crazy Horse* (New York: Penguin Books, 1992).

• In Peru, the rubber companies exploiting the forests singled out shamans in the workers' camps and sent them away as prisoners, perhaps mindful of their role two centuries earlier in encouraging slaves to run away.[5]

• In the 1560s, as a result of the huge costs of Spain's colonial warfare, authorities racheted up the level of required labor, and hence the torture of any natives that resisted. The natives organized the Taki Onqoy movement, a millennarian attempt to form a pan-Andean collaboration of the different local gods and goddesses to defeat colonialism. The movement spread widely across Peru and into what is now Bolivia, causing the Spanish to panic and declare all-out war against the shrines of the local gods (*huacas*).

> Idols were destroyed, temples burned, and those who celebrated native rites and practiced sacrifices were punished by death; festivals such as banquets, songs and dances, as well as artistic and intellectual activities (painting, sculpture, observation of stars, hieroglyphic writing) — suspected of being inspired by the devil — were forbidden and those who took part in them mercilessly hunted down.[1]

• The same pattern is perhaps seen in an aborted plan for a slave insurrection in 1741 in New York that principally involved the Papa, Igbo, the Malagasay, and the Akan, African slaves who worked along the waterfront and which involved a central role by an "obeah man," an Akan shaman.[2]

• In 1791 insurrection was not aborted and the successful Haitian slave rebellion that defeated army after army sent after it is somewhat well-known, but few are aware that this only successful slave uprising began at a Vodoun ceremony on August 14, 1791, near Marne Runge, when a priestess was possessed by a spirit and spoke in the voices of Ogoun, calling for war. By morning of the next day, plantations had been torched and the uprising was on the march. For over a decade the rebellion flourished, defeating French, Spanish, and English forces sent against them and their "outrageous" demand for an end to slavery, and it was able to establish a black republic that, to this day is still treated as a pariah by the international community, continually occupied and forced to have a sham election due to the need to demonstrate the folly of their "cheeky" resistence.[3]

• Three decades earlier, in Jamaica in 1760, an uprising against slavery was led by obeah men of the Akan religion who practiced spirit possession and contact with ancestors; it lasted over a year. When "Tacky's Revolt" was finally suppressed, hundreds of natives and sixty whites had been killed and a host of

---

[1] Baudez and Picasso, *Lost Cities of the Maya* (1987), quoted in Federici, *op. cit.*, pp. 225–26).

[2] Peter Linebaugh and Marcus Rediker, *The Many-Headed Hydra: Sailors, Slaves, Commoners, and the Hidden History of the Revolutionary Atlantic* (Boston: Beacon Press, 2000), pp. 179–86.

[3] Davis, *Shadows in the Sun*, pp. 4, 51f.

newly-enacted restrictions were in place, including the death penalty for practitioners of *obeah*. Revolts in 1761 and each of the following years broke out
across the surrounding islands into the late 1770s.[1]

• After a particularly harrowing uprising of hundreds of slaves demanding
their freedom broke out in Barbados in 1816, burning nearly a quarter of the
sugar-cane crop, one observer claimed that the organizational skills evident in
the planning and execution of "Busso's Rebellion" resulted from "a new kind of
leadership; this was the leadership of the religious preacher, literate in the English language and in the African religious practices."[2]

• In the 1790s a synthesis of Baptist Christianity and Akan and Yoruba,
called myalism, inspired by an American preacher, Moses Baker, and taught to
African slaves, invoked river spirits in their rites. Myalism was believed at the
time to constitute a "hotbed of slave rebellion."[3]

• Weston La Barre, Juan Victor Nunez Del Prado B, and Adolf F. Bande-
lier have all observed that beneath the outward Christian forms, the Aymara
around Lake Titicaca, the Quecha, and other Indians, despite over 400 years of
attempts to eliminate them, persist in their pagan beliefs and practices, with Ban-
delier concluding, "The Indian of Bolivia is a Catholic, at least nominally.... But
in case of a general uprising, I doubt very much (and in this I am confirmed
by... reliable parish priests) whether the Indians would not return openly to a
paganism which at heart they still profess and in secret actually practice."[4]

• In the late 19th century in Columbia a sorcerer, Jose Cenero Mina, was
a guerilla commander in the War of A Thousand Days (1899–1902), able, it was
believed, to shapeshift into an animal or plant if pursued.[5]

• Parallels existed in Asia, as well, as in the Sinyasin Revolt, a guerrilla
war led by ascetic priests.[6] In India, also, a Bengali Terrorist movement took its
inspiration originally from Hinduism, especially the goddess, Kali. They established temples in places far from cities, where the air was pure. (Though at first
not driven by Western ideology, in the 1930s the Bengali Terrorists had for the
most part become communists.)[7]

• By far the deepest affinity between rebellion against hierarchy and authority and a magical worldview is found among the Taoists in ancient China.
The adherents of one dominant school of Taoism lived in the mountains and
forests, removed from the unnatural feudal order, where they meditated on the
order of nature. The other school came out of the ancient magic and shamanic

---

1 Linebaugh and Rediker, *op. cit.*, p. 222.

2 *Ibid.*, p. 302.

3 *Ibid.*, p. 302.

4 *Ibid.*, p. 306.

5 Taussig, *Devil*, pp. 160–61.

6 *Ibid.*, p. 65.

5 Peter Linebaugh, *The London Hanged: Crime and Civil Society in the Eighteenth Century* (Cambridge, England: Cambridge Univ. Press, 1992), p. 243.

tradition, practiced alchemy, and enjoyed deep roots among the common people. Taoism has been repeatedly associated in China with movements of liberation, of political revolution. Taoists placed the element of water, the most protean of substances, at the center of their philosophy of nature, a comprehension consonant with their belief in "leadership from within," as well as congruent with their pronounced feminist political leanings, as they extolled water both for its overwhelming strength and for its utterly yielding nature. The rigidity of feudal society was the opposite of yielding. Opposing such a society sent the Taoists to the mountains and to an ideology that looked to the collectivism of villages before a formal priesthood, a warrior caste, and lords emerged. For over a thousand years all the revolts against the established order in China were associated with the Taoists.[1]

• In the 10th century C.E., a movement centered in Basra formed, the Ikawan al-Safa', or the Brothers of Sincerity, a semi-secret society with close ties to Sufism and with egalitarian and socialist or communist political leanings and an outlook on the world that Joseph Needham calls "nature mysticism." Eventually, the Brothers of Sincerity, along with a broader, Qarmatian movement established deep roots in Baghdad, too, from where they waged perpetual war throughout the 10th century against the caliphate.[2]

• Afro-Christianity at times seemed to encourage insurrection, as in 1776 in Saint Bartholomew Parish in South Carolina. Led by black preachers, including two female prophets, the plot did not succeed but managed to terrify whites.[3] The same tendency can be seen in the dominant role played by black churches in the early phases of the civil rights movement in the US South; bombings of black churches were frequently carried out by the Ku Klux Klan and its sympathizers as retaliation and Klan-inspired arson of churches continues to this day.

Societies (or movements) whose outlooks on the world were rooted in immanence generally have different comprehension of material reality than do the estrangement-rooted. In opposition to traditions that divorce matter from spirit, matter from good, matter from energy, and matter from God (or the gods and goddesses), the consciousness of immanence puts value and life into matter itself. Far from being a dull, lifeless, lump into which, always from the outside, *spirit* is injected so as to give life, purpose, will, or an inherent worthiness, to the immanentists *matter,* by virtue simply of its existence, already has *intrinsic* value. The world around us, the trees, brooks, foothills, all of it, including the myriad crea-

---

[1] A very fine analysis of the Taoists can be found in Joseph Needham, *Science and Civilization in China* (Cambridge, England: Cambridge Univ. Press, 1956), vol. 2, Chap. 10 (pp. 33–164). Needham also discusses the general phenomena of left-wing magic that we are exploring here very insightfully.
[2] *Ibid.,* pp. 95–96.
[3] Linebaugh and Rediker, *op. cit.,* p. 226.

tures with whom we share the skies and seas and the newly discovered bacteria that live 24 miles beneath the surface of the earth[1] — all participate in this divinity. Translated into social terms, immanence means that any one, regardless of station, income, gender, race, age, education, species, has worth and intrinsic power.

It is not difficult to understand why such notions, particularly at times of political and social upheaval, when many of the political, economic, and cultural traditions are suddenly called into question, can have an essential democratic ethos to them. The significance of this should be noted: that a theory of matter — what material substance is and how its properties are determined — has historically tended to embody an inherent political ideology. What is meant by an "inherent ideology" will be clarified in Part Two.

I shall argue that as the immanent form of magic became identified with radical assaults on the emerging hierarchy and property relations of modernity (although this tension and those battles somewhat predate the coming of modernity), the propertied classes increasingly realized an overriding imperative to repress magic altogether — or at least to control knowledge of its history so that only its patriarchal forms could be known, and so that certain questions could never again be raised. Such fears and precautions had arisen among the ruling classes in earlier epochs, but always there were contradictory tendencies and in the absence of "objective" science, the weapons with which to carry out their ideological assault against the redoubts of magic had been relatively impotent.[2]

---

[1] *Discover*, special issue, "Invisible Planet" (n.d.), p. 80.

[2] As we shall see in Part Two, the wave of persecutions against witches that occurred in Europe and England in the 15th, 16th, and 17th centuries was only the most bloody and most visible part of that assault. Far from the witchcraft persecutions, overlapping historically with the rise of science, posing an historical conundrum, then, the two phenomena should be understood as complementary aspects of the process by which the cornerstones of modern consciousness were cemented in place.

Part Two

Tunneling Into the Future:
Isaac Newton & The Ideological
Roots of Modern Times

"Historians of European culture are in substantial agreement that in the late 16th and early 17th centuries, something like a mutation in human nature took place."—Lionel Trilling, quoted in Barbara Ehrenreich, *Dancing in the Streets: A History of Collective Joy* (2006)

"If the body were truly a set of closed or predetermined mechanisms, it could never come into genuine contact with anything outside of itself, could never perceive anything really new, could never be genuinely startled or surprised. All of its experiences, and all its responses, would already have been anticipated from the beginning, already programmed, as it were, into the machine. But could we ever, then, call them experiences? For is not experience, or more precisely, perception, the constant thwarting of such closure?" — David Abram, *The Spell of the Sensuous: Perception and Language in a More-Than-Human World* (1997)

"The rise of... detached inquiry into phenomena is, like the rise of a western art and literature, called the Renaissance. But nothing was reborn: not even the most arrogant of the Greeks had quite attained to this notion of inquiring into nature as if man stood god-like outside it. Galileo, Leeuwenhoek, Newton, were, in their methods, expressing the peculiarly Judeo-Christian idea that men were God's principal tenants, the rest of creation the fittings and stock let with the property. The method led, of course, to what are sometimes called the triumphs of science. Great discoveries were made, and it is not [my intention] to discuss whether the practical application of these discoveries has justified the faith of rational men in science. One of the last trades to which science, the method of inquiry into nature, but not of living as a part of nature, was applied, was that of the farmer. It would be almost impossible to exaggerate the disasters which ensued." Edward Hyams, *Soil & Civilization* (1952)

5

Remarking the Boundaries of Nature

The soil is the great connector of lives, the source and destination of all.... It is alive itself. It is a grave, too, of course. Or
a healthy soil is. It is full of dead animals and plants, bodies
that have passed through other bodies. For except for some
humans — with their sealed coffins and vaults, their pathological fear of the earth — the only way into the soil is through
other bodies. But no matter how finely the dead are broken
down, or how many times they are eaten, they yet give into
other life. If a healthy soil is full of death, it is also full of life:
worms, fungi, micro-organisms of all kinds, for which, as for
us humans, the dead bodies of the once living are a feast....
Given only the health of the soil, nothing that dies is dead for
very long.....

Because the soil is alive, various, intricate, and because its
processes yield more readily to imitation than to analysis, more
readily to care than to coercion, agriculture can never be an
exact science. — Wendell Berry, *The Unsettling of America: Culture & Agriculture* (1977)

i. CONTOURS OF MODERNITY

The natural world came under an unprecedented assault from the twin on-
sets of the conquest of the Americas (soon extended to Africa, Asia, etc.)
and the erection of a capitalist world system at around the same time.
Fortunes were made, empires built, in every instance on the basis of the pieces
of the natural order that were taken and sold, precious metals or minerals, trees
and pelts, sugar and rum, and millions of humans as slaves to work those mines

and plantations, all were cut down or dug up, transformed into commodities, the ultimate ontological priority in the new order. A vast new scale was afoot: whole forests were cut down, huge plantations were given over to monoculture, and mines — which, with few exceptions, such as Rio Tinto in Spain, in antiquity and medieval times had not dug much below the Earth's surface — now dug much deeper into the flanks of the planet, shafts hundreds and then thousands of feet deep, devastating the streams and any nearby trees.

At the same time, a new understanding of what that natural order *was* was being erected, in what is sometimes called the "scientific revolution," to explain it all. Proponents of the 17th-century scientific revolution insisted that the proper comprehension of nature required adapting thinking to a new set of assumptions about the world: about space, time, the nature of matter, motion, causation, and so on. Assumptions about the natural order, as we shall see, that ended up serving as a kind of ideological blinder, especially in agrarian areas, where a desecrated spring or woods, stream, wetlands, or heath might well be met with a measure of shock and anger, and ways to deflect that anger would have been eagerly sought by the desecrators. The new way of understanding nature emerged even as a rapid *denaturalization* of the Earth from the 16th century on rapidly became the dominant pattern popping up here, there, and then nearly everywhere with terrifying rapidity ever since.[1]

No less than a wholesale assault on nature — in the towns and the countryside, in the European centers of trade and the plantations at the far reaches of the nascent empires — erupts nearly all over. In Europe and the newly-claimed Americas, for example, mining for both precious and armaments-related metals intensified, as if building to a never-realized climax as early embodiments of both capital accumulation and (not-unrelated) an arms race began; extensive deforestation was carried on also in both the "old" and the "new" worlds; a system of agricultural "improvements" began transforming European and English farming practices, even as a new plantation system to grow things like sugar, tobacco, and coffee began its eventual rapacious remake of land usage, divvying up the "resources" in the new colonial domains.[2]

These developments were bound up with a massive removal of the peasantry in many areas, as their land was appropriated for more profitable activities and a veritable forced march of the new, landless ex-peasantry from the countryside into the towns and cities (again in both European countries and the proto-colonies) began, an astounding population transfer that generated cities

[1] Within a century of the 1607 founding of Jamestown, the ancient Eastern woodlands of North America were facing destruction, in the largest and most rapid deforestation in human history — until now. Scott Wallace, *The Unconquered: In Search of the Amazon's Last Uncontacted Tribes* (New York: Crown Publishers, 2011), p. 10

[2] The word "resource" was coined in 1611, according to the *Shorter Oxford English Dictionary.*

out of towns with the human detritus from the enclosures of common land in the countryside, essentially privatizing vast stretches of what traditionally had been part of the means of subsistence for those ex-peasants.[1]

The enclosed land facilitated the spread of agricultural monoculture, and the further cutting down of woods, draining of wetlands, and the progressive departure from the fields of whole *kinds* of animals and the absolute decrease in habitat for *all* animals. In these and many other ways the emergence of new social and economic forms in early modern England and Europe and the colonies mandated a transformed attitude towards, and behavior in relation to, the airs, waters, and places of the planet.[2]

Under the dual pressures of increased trade and intensification of warfare in early modern Europe, mines went deeper in their feverish search for gold and silver to pay for the former, and lead, brass, and iron to make possible the latter — and in England, coal, since what little wood was still left there went to building ships for her expanding fleets. The mines' deeper shafts, and the expansion to more marginal deposits, necessitated greater investments in machinery to drain those shafts of seeped-in-water or to vent bad (poisonous or explosive) air from them. Such investments — in 1700 in England, £2000 was not an uncommon amount spent to reach just one seam; and it cost nearly £20,000 simply to install drainage tubes against flooding in one mine — required far greater profits; that push inevitably meant less-safe working conditions and many more crushed, broken, poisoned, or diseased miners' bodies — in places like Scotland, including the bodies of substantial numbers of young children and women.[3] Streams and rivers became poisoned near the mines. Woods were cut down to build the shafts. Fish and animals disappeared.

The scientific revolution came to dominate European and English intellectual life during this period, reaching a peak of sorts in the 17th century in the investigations and writings of Johannes Kepler, Galileo, William Harvey, René Descartes, and especially with the theories and experimental researches of Isaac

---

[1] Good overviews of these transformations can be found in Federici, *op. cit.* and A. L. Morton, *A Peoples' History of England* (London: Lawrence & Wishart Ltd., 1968). See also the incisive analysis of Kirkpatrick Sale, *The Conquest of Paradise: Christopher Columbus and the Columbian Legacy* (New York: Plume, 1990). (Unfortunately I only am reading Sale's rich book as this work is close to publication.) Sale contends that in some parts of Europe similar processes were in place as early as the 11th century. Sale also would doubt that the desecration of woods and streams would get noticed in a Europe that was uniquely alienated from nature (pp. 76–82, 87, 91), though later Sale exempts from that judgement rural areas —a huge exemption (p, 249).

[2] A classic of the Hippocratic medical corpus, and the basis for his environmental medicine, was *Airs, Waters, and Places*.

[3] J.U. Nef, *The Rise of the British Coal Industry* (London, 1932), 2 vols, especially vol. II, Part 4, chap. 3 and 4; and Taussig, *Devil.*

Newton, whose accomplishments both summed up and extended to unimaginable realms the challenge of explaining the workings of nature.

Optics, explicating the nature of colors, lenses, and rainbows, and inventing a new kind of telescope; the motion of bodies, explaining the mysterious workings of Earth, moon, sun, and planets under the guidance of Newton's new theory of gravitation; and mathematics, now equipped with the penetrating tool of the calculus, creating in the *derivative* a virtual double dynamically reflecting any and all "smooth" transformations in nature and thereby rendering them up for careful analysis: all revealed their inner workings under Newton's (and, in the case of the calculus, Leibniz') masterful inquiries.

In turn, to explain those Isaac Newton needed to define the nature of matter, space, time, and how we are to understand change itself. He told, too, how he investigated nature, and who, after all, would know better? His views, which were to create a whole conceptual universe, rapidly became the views of educated and of literate people, first in England but soon enough just about everywhere in the world. Newton's teachings can be seen as the main gatepost through which, historically ever since, regions or individuals entered into modern times.

Though in what follows I tend to focus on one particular way of looking at Newton's work, indeed, a whole system of ways, and at the social significance of the scientific revolution, which embeds the story, I do not want to be understood as meaning that this way was the *real* cause of everything else or that things happened in *just* the manner I describe, which of necessity is frequently in isolation. Reality, thankfully, is more complex than that. Historical transformations as fundamental as the scientific revolution should not be seen as emerging from single causes.

Rather, I shall be focusing on certain social and ideological aspects of the scientific revolution not only because they reveal a framework of that cultural watershed that has not yet been seen, and they throw into new relief many hitherto indistinct facets of the philosophical upheaval, but primarily because my new rendering will illuminate critical and largely unknown aspects of our present environmental crisis. Newton's conceptual redefinitions of matter, space, time, and the rest of it, I shall argue, played a decisive role in a fundamental ideological war regarding nature that was being waged in the 17th century, determining the shape of modern society and still continuing to define its contours. Though my interpretation is, of course, *one of several* ways of looking at the vast transformation in worldview that was developed during the scientific revolution, in an age like ours, facing an unprecedented ecological meltdown, arguably it is *the* most important way.

ii. LEARNING NOT TO MIND YOUR MOTHER

Under pressure from the development of capitalism as a major force in the economies of England, the Netherlands, and elsewhere in early modern Europe, the boundaries of nature, both in practice and in theory, had to be renegotiated. Given the centrality of trade to the merchant and entrepreneurial classes, early on these new practices and theories made their ways from Europe to the colonies.[1] Thus, by the second half of the 16th century, both Peru and Mexico had economies that were dominated by mining, and toxic chemicals such as lead and mercury, used in refining the ores, were fouling their waters. Discovered in 1546, the Mexican silver deposits attracted a sizable mining camp in a few years, having fifty different mine owners, and stamp mills, refineries, slave and Indian workers, as well as roads to bring in the necessary supplies. Within about two decades, water-powered crushing machinery was operating in both Peru and Mexico.[2]

Potosí, a city in the Bolivian highlands that formed after the discovery of silver there in 1545, had a population of 120,000 by 1570, larger than any city in Spain or in the Americas.

European scientific concepts also were exported to the Americas, as we shall see, for the expressed purpose of teaching natives about the "passivity" of brute matter, a concept utterly alien in their animist worldview, in the hope that they might be won over to the European view that private ownership of land, whose resources could then be exploited, was nature's (as well as God's and the King's) way.

The consequences of the 17th-century conceptual transformation of nature were quite dramatic. At the beginning of the century it was believed just about everywhere that the Earth was a living creature, literally a kind of Mother to all life on the planet. By about 1700, quite the opposite was *the* central tenet in the emerging scientific culture, participation in which was the touchstone of educated people. This included many who had no formal schooling but had heard or seen in Sunday sermons or in pamphlets this new physical theology espousing how the Protestant (or Catholic) God required *lifeless* matter for the substrate of the cosmos.[3]

A core principle of the scientific revolution, vouched for by Galileo, formally enunciated by Descartes, and made the foundation of Newton's momentous *Principia Mathematica Naturalis Philosophiæ* (1687), was the concept of inertia, which taught that matter left by itself does not change its state of motion. All change in a body's motion must come from *outside* of the body, and since *any* change was thought to be rooted *in motion*, change itself always had an *external* origin, according to Newtonian inertia. In essence, material bodies are passive by nature, suffering, but never initiating, transformation.[4] In other words, they are mere objects. They are *dead*.

---

[1] For the reverse processes, from the colonies to Europe, in relation to the economy, see Linebaugh, *London Hanged*, pp. 66, 159.

[2] Davis, *op. cit.*, pp. 50–55.

[3] I have discussed this at more length in Chapter Two of Devereux, Steele, and Kubrin, *Earthmind*.

[4] Accordingly, both in Aristotelianism and in the scientific revolution, matter was understood as "female."

This was not an altogether new belief. Both the Church and Aristotle taught that matter is passive, needing *animus* or spirit to undergo changes, to become active, but that passivity did not extend to the various features of the world, to her rivers, forests, and hills, her cliffs and springs. This is what now changed. Inertia sounded the death-knell for anything made of "mere" matter, including such wordly features as rivers, etc.

Not that the concept of inertia was without significant scientific import, for with it natural philosophers were able to resolve some of the thorny paradoxes about motion that so perplexed adherents of Copernicanism.

In a world already understood as essentially dead, nature is left defenseless, for scars in the countryside that result from mining, deforestation, wetlands draining, etc., ultimately are insignificant. To be sure, local consequences, including serious human costs, can result, but any transcendent value associated with a particular meadow, forest, mountain, or stream, in a world of dead matter, would go unrecognized. Once it is seen as essentially dead, land becomes incapable of mounting sacred claims.

It is instructive to examine shifting meanings of the words "dirt" and "dirty" during this period. "Dirt" originally came from the Middle English, "drit," which meant excrement, hence, something unclean. Of course, peasants have long known the association between manure and soil, how the one eventually becomes the other; but it was not until the end of the 17th century that "dirt" comes to take on the meaning of "earth" or "soil." Thus the Earth, obviously the end product, among other things, of shit, became essentially identified with it.

The adjectival form, "dirty," was first used around 1530, according to the *Shorter Oxford English Dictionary*, denoting that which was soiled or foul. By the end of the century, however, "dirty" has added certain sexual connotations, in particular, an association with "smutty." Within a mere decade, other moral judgments were added, dirty now identified as well with the despicable or repulsive.

By the end of the 17th century, when dirt becomes synonymous with Earth, that sense of smut and repulsion are part of the package, at least implicitly. "Soil," too, changes. Associated in Middle English with the Earth, by 1608 "soil" has come to mean filth and has become a synonym for shit, as in "nightsoil," coined a year earlier. As a verb, "to soil" had been used earlier to mean giving a laxative to horses or cattle, or to refer to adding manure to the land. Thus, by the first decade of the new century a shift in language had transformed the meaning of the Earth's substrate, dirt, now associated with excrement, the unclean, and sexual smut. These newer connotations served to symbolically dig the ground out from under pagan sensibilities.

iii. Clearing the Conceptual Landscape
for Industrialization: The Mechanization of the World

The increasing industrialization[1] of the natural world in the past 400 to 500 years, driven by the ideological strawboss of capitalism, was and has been devastating in its extremism, and its single-minded need to dominate and control by now has created a terrifying scale of destruction of habitats and species.

At the root of today's environmental crisis we can find a critical ideological transformation occurring in the 16th and 17th centuries. Antecedents, some of them undoubtedly important, no doubt existed, but in a fundamental way the forces undermining our planetary future grew from seeds planted a mere several hundred years ago.

The central drama, on which the latter part of Part Two of *Marxism & Witchcraft* will focus, is that Isaac Newton — whose ideas more than anything else established a widespread belief in a world of inert, dead, bodies, where planets and moons, apples and beams of light follow, blindly, the necessary laws of material bodies — did not himself really believe such mechanical depictions of nature were the real story. More than once he revealed his central notion of a world everywhere pregnant with life. The matter, which in his *Principia* appears to move in predetermined pathways, according to the one or several forces acting on it, was, at a deeper level, the subject of a lifetime of alchemical research by Newton, whose central premise was the lifefulness of the whole of nature, including its "mere" matter. In brief, almost transient passages, we can see this alchemical vision scattered throughout Newton's published work, including in his two masterpieces of analysis, his *Principia* (1687) and his *Opticks* (1704), as well as in extended discussions in his (till recently, almost entirely unpublished) alchemical works.

That Newton, ostensibly its creator, disavowed his supposed creation of what has been called the "machine universe," surely calls out for careful, extended examination, one to which I shall later attempt to do justice. Just how did *that* model of the natural world emerge victorious after a mere century where opposing visions of the world did battle? In a word, it was the machine universe more than anything else that paved the way for the assaults against nature so common in the modern world. This mechanization was a victory for a point of view that could

---

[1] By "industrialization" I do not necessarily mean factories, though in the woolen industry, they existed early on, nor urban enterprises. Much of the impetus for industrialization arose in mining, frequently in rural areas. Sidney W. Mintz comments that the plantations were organized industrially in the way labor, time, and discipline were structured (*Sweetness & Power: The Place of Sugar in Modern History* [New York: Penguin Books, 1985], pp. 50–52); Linebaugh, *London Hanged*, makes the same point about ships of the late 17th century, which could have as many as 700 to 900 sailors on board (p. 60).

finally claim the power for which it had been contending for centuries, enshrining the principle that the whole of reality is reducible to a gigantic mechanism. In what follows, I shall be showing how these fundamental transformations in human thinking about the world have brought us to our present peril.

iv. THE PROPRIETIES OF PROPERTY: FROM OURS TO MINING

Though the assaults against nature are found across the map of the world in the early modern period, it will greatly simplify (without distorting) matters if we focus on one emblematic industry, mining, in one country, England. Both in mining in general and in English mining in particular, the patterns are simply incised deeper into the social terrain and so stand out in bolder relief. In England the assaults were exacerbated by the decision of Henry VIII, following his break from Rome (both to fill his depleted coffers and to break the power of the Roman Church in England) to sell off the extensive land holdings of the Church. Huge tracts of land thus became commodities, now objects of speculation, and entered private hands.[1] (One of those benefitting from the new availability of land was Sir Nicolaus Bacon, father of Francis, who had become Lord Chancellor under Elizabeth, as his son did later under James I.) Unlike medieval times, when land was controlled but not owned in the modern sense, since feudal lands were part of a complex of political and military obligations, now land would be *free* to be sold to any bidder; he who owned it was now free, in turn, to do with it as he chose, no matter how such usage might affect the creatures living on it. He could destroy a meadow, poison a woodland, transform numerous habitats; if the land were his (rarely hers, especially by the 17th century), he could do as he willed.[2]

The subjugation of nature came to play a central role in the English understanding of that holy-of-holies within capitalism, their sense of *property*. When John Locke tried to explain the meaning of property, he claimed that dominion, and hence ownership, was established by actions to make the land *productive*, i.e., ratcheting up its exploitation through logging, mining, and enclosures so as to use the land for new purposes. He thus made it clear that mere subsistence and commoning, where fish and fowl or pig and goat are caught or raised on a shared

---

[1] About 25–30% of real property in England before the Reformation was owned by the Church. Henry VIII sold about 65% of that, or from 16 to 19% of the total (Federici, *op. cit.*, p. 121 n. 22).

[2] I am simplifying a process that was gradual, especially in England, and had to contend with claims on property from rights of commons going back to medieval times and which, in many instances, took a century or more of litigation and Parliamentary law before the absolute rights to property were fully realized. See Thompson, *Customs in Common*. See also Peter Linebaugh, *The Magna Carta Manifesto: Liberties and Commons for All* (Berkeley: University of California Press, 2008).

commons, didn't cut it anymore. He claimed that there was no way that the indigenous encountered in the Americas and elsewhere, living off the bounty of their ancestral land, actually *owned* it (as Indian custom would surely agree) since they were clearly improvident in not "working" their lands harder — so, making way for the rightful, colonial, owners.[1]

The world, according to Locke in his *Second Treatise on Government,* was given to people "in common" and its fruits and beasts are "produced by the spontaneous hand of nature." But this commons, belonging to no one, is subject to the taking. It was by mixing of his labor with that commons that one is able to "make[s] it his property."[2] "[S]ubduing or cultivating the earth, and having dominion, we see are joined together."[3] Unlike European traditions, wherein property ownership meant an "exclusive and absolute right of dominion," Locke's concept of property rights was more flexible, including coincident use-rights, rights that lasted as long as one was alive, as well as absolute rights. By the 18th century, those nuances had fallen away, leaving "'virtually unlimited and saleable rights to things'."[4] As that right became codified, commons and use-rights of the plebian orders were progressively taken away.

The land of the indigenous in the Americas was akin to the world where all is in common, and the Indians were poor "for want of improving" their land. Since it was labor and improvements that constituted the basis for property rights, the dispossession of Indian land by colonialists was easy to justify.[5] The forests and other commons even in England and Europe were but "[N]urseries of idleness and Insolence," as John Bellers claimed, that make "the Poor that are upon them too much like the Indians."[6]

---

[1] A senator in the late 19th century complained of the indigenous Americans that "there is no selfishness, which is at the bottom of civilization," (Dunbar-Ortiz, *op. cit.,* p. 158). The word "civilization" was first used, interestingly, in 1601, defined as the antithesis of "barbarism." John Lukacs, *The Hitler of History* (New York: HarperCollins, 1997), p. 267.

[2] *Customs in Common,* p. 160.

[3] *Ibid.,* p. 170.

[4] *Ibid.,* p. 161.

[5] Indeed, the indigenous *did* "improve" their lands, for example, making the Amazon one extended orchard and landscaping the plains to encourage foraging by elk, bear, and deer. See Mann, *1491,* and M. Kat Anderson, *Tending the Wild: Native American Knowledge and the Management of California's Natural Resources* (Berkeley, Univ. of California Press, 2005) and Anderson, "Tending the Wilderness," *Restoration and Management Notes* 14 (2): 154–66. See also Rebecca Solnit, *Savage Dreams: A Journey into the Landscape Wars of the American West* (New York, Vintage Books, 1994), pp. 304ff. Perhaps native improvements did not rise to the level of devastation necessary for whites like Locke to recognize their "cultivation."

[6] Quoted in Thompson, *Customs in Common,* p. 165.

Figures 5–11 MINING TECHNOLOGIES From Agricola's *De Re Metallica* (1556)

METHODS OF DRAINING MINES *(Note the felled trees.)*

A–TIMBER PLACED IN FRONT OF THE SHAFT. B–TIMBER PLACED AT THE
BACK OF THE SHAFT. C–POINTED STAKES. D–CROSS-TIMBERS. E–POSTS OR
THICK PLANKS. F–IRON SOCKETS. G–BARREL. H–ENDS OF BARREL.
I–PIECES OF WOOD. K–HANDLE. L–DRAWING ROPE. M–ITS HOOK.
N–BUCKET. O–BALE OF THE BUCKET.

DRAINING
TECHNOLOGY

A–WHEEL WHICH IS
TURNED BY TREAD-
ING. B–AXLE.
C–DOUBLE CHAIN.
D–LINK OF DOUBLE
CHAIN. E–DIPPERS.
F–SIMPLE CLAMPS.
G–CLAMP WITH
TRIPLE CURVES.

PUMP TECHNOLOGY
(Note logs and miner boring out one of them to make a pipe.)
A–SUMP. B–PIPES. C–FLOORING. D–TRUNK. E–PERFORATIONS OF TRUNK.
F–VALVE. G–SPOUT. H–PISTON-ROD. I–HAND-BAR OF PISTON. K–SHOE.
L–DISC WITH ROUND OPENINGS. M–DISC WITH OVAL OPENINGS.
N–COVER. O–THIS MAN IS BORING LOGS AND MAKING THEM INTO PIPES.
P–BORER WITH AUGER. Q–WIDER BORER.

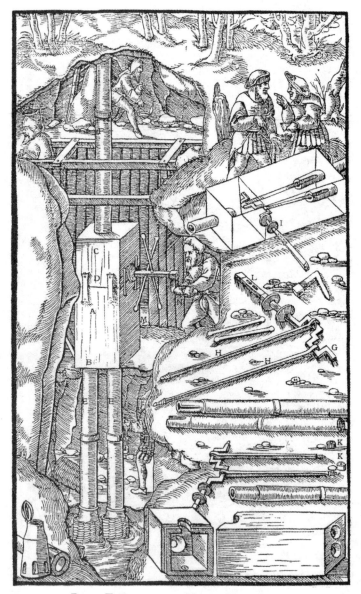

PUMP TECHNOLOGY, USING MANPOWER

A–BOX. B–LOWER PART OF BOX. C–UPPER PART OF SAME.
D–CLAMPS. E–PIPES BELOW THE BOX. F–COLUMN PIPE FIXED ABOVE
THE BOX. G–IRON AXLE. H–PISTON-RODS. I–WASHERS TO PROTECT
THE BEARINGS. K–LEATHERS. L–EYES IN THE AXLE. M–RODS WHOSE
ENDS ARE WEIIGHTED WITH LUMPS OF COAL. N–CRANK.

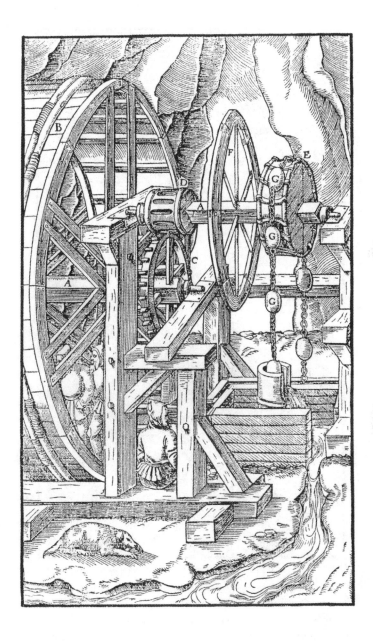

PUMP TECHNOLOGY, OPERATED BY MEN IN GEARED TREADMILL

A–AXLES. B–WHEEL WHICH IS TURNED BY TREADING. C–TOOTHED
WHEEL. D–DRUM MADE OF RUNDLES. E–DRUM TO WHICH ARE FIXED
IRON CLAMPS. F–SECOND WHEEL. G–BALLS.

BELLOWS TO VENTILATE MINE,
OPERATED BY HORSEPOWER AND HUMAN FOOTPOWER

A–MACHINE FIRST DESCRIBED. B–THIS WORKMAN, TREADING WITH HIS
FEET, IS COMPRESSING THE BELLOWS. C–BELLOWS WITHOUT NOZZLES.
D–HOLE BY WHICH HEAVY VAPOURS OR BLASTS ARE BLOWN OUT.
E–CONDUITS. F–TUNNEL. G–SECOND MACHINE DESCRIBED. H–WOODEN
WHEEL. I–ITS STEPS. K–BARS. L–HOLE IN SAME WHEEL. M–POLE.
N–THIRD MACHINE DESCRIBED. O–UPRIGHT AXLE. P–ITS TOOTHED
DRUM. Q–HORIZONTAL AXLE. R–ITS DRUM WHICH IS MADE OF RUNDLES.

VENTILATION, USING WINDPOWER AND MANPOWER

A–BOX-SHAPED CASING PLACED ON THE GROUND. B–ITS BLOWHOLE.
C–ITS AXLE WITH FANS. D–CRANK OF THE AXLE. E–RODS OF SAME.
F–CASINGS SET ON TIMBERS.
G–SAILS WHICH THE AXLE HAS OUTSIDE THE CASING.

The right to use ownership as a license to do as one wished was especially important in the case of mining, for building or working a mine or refining the ores dug have historically been devastating to the lands adjacent to the works. From ancient times to the present, writers have been awed by the reign of death and desolation that mining enthrones in its environs. The mines themselves have been described by more than one observer as "Hells on Earth," and the havoc they wreaked on their airs, waters, and places portrayed in the most horror-filled terms.[1] For example, an Englishman who had seen the ancient Rio Tinto mines in Spain a little over a century ago wrote:

> No tree or green thing breaks the view;
> On every side death reigns supreme,
> for six long miles no life is seen
> But barren ground and charred stumps
> …
> Her poisoned breath, polluted air;
> Which, withering every blossom fair
> Has left instead of nature's plenty
> A howling desert bare and empty.[2]

v. THE DREAD TERRAIN

If *around* the mines scenes of barren desolation took "root," the *insides* of the mines were even grimmer. Mines are, as Lewis Mumford has observed,

> the first completely inorganic environment to be created and lived in by man…. unbroken by trees, beasts, clouds, or sunlight. Day has been abolished and the rhythm of nature broken: continuous day-and-night production first came into existence here. The miner must work by artificial light even

---

[1] Thus, Justinian said that being condemned to work in the mines was nearly as bad as a death sentence. Miners at times encountered materials that would eat wounds down to the bone, others that ate away at their hands and feet. In one mine, 400 workers died in a single day. George Rosen, *The History of Miners' Diseases: A Medical and Social Interpretation* (New York: Schuman's, 1943), pp. 31, 60, 63.) It is estimated by Taussig (*Devil*, p. 200) that some eight million Andeans died in mines during the colonial period. Rosen says that in mining areas, children and adolescents, many of whom worked in the mines, some as young as 5 or 6, had death-rates four to five times greater than those of agricultural districts (Rosen, *op. cit.*, pp. 430–31).

[2] John Allen, "A Modern Inferno," quoted in Gray Brechin, *Imperial San Francisco: Urban Power, Earthly Ruin* (Berkeley, Calif., Univ. of California Press, 2007), p. 27. I am very grateful to Brechin for generously sharing early drafts of his seminal work with me.

though the sun be shining outside; still further down in the
seam, he must work by artificial ventilation, too.[1]

Into such living hells, few voluntarily went. Except for prospectors, "no one entered a mine in civilized states until relatively modern times except as a prisoner
of war, a criminal, or slave."[2]

Mining was seen as a particularly heinous form of punishment, combining
"the terrors of the dungeon with the physical exacerbation of the galley." Rich
veins, such as at Rio Tinto, justified extensive machinery even in antiquity to
get as much of the ore as possible. Huge water wheels, powered by slaves, were
used there to pump water out of the shafts. Tens of thousands of slaves worked
in these mines, where life expectancy was but a few weeks. The mines were the
object of fierce rivalry between Rome and Carthage.[3] While miners, historically,
have produced riches in staggering amounts, nearly always, though literally
wearing out their bodies by their labors, they themselves earned (if they were
not slaves or prisoners, who got nothing at all) but a pittance. Already in antiquity the critical lesson had been learned that large-scale mines required both
military discipline for their workforce and an actual proximity of the army to
put down the frequent actual rebellions, strikes, and riots by the miners, all the
more common because the tools of mining were readily adaptable as weapons
of war. Fearful of such revolts, the Roman Senate in the 2nd century B.C.E.
banned altogether any mining on the Italian peninsula.[4]

vi. TUNNELS INTO THE FUTURE: THE SUBTERRANEAN ROOTS OF MODERNITY

After a period in early feudal times when mining of the Earth had greatly diminished, discovery of silver in the 10th century in the Harz Mountains in the
Duchy of Saxony created a sudden wave of miners. Eventually, they branched out
into parts of central Europe, including Bohemia — which will later emerge as a
major arena where the patterns at the heart of this essay most starkly stood out —
and Hungary and areas of the Alps. Increased trade in the 15th and 16th centuries
required more gold and silver to pay its way, exacerbating the lust for precious metals
that drove the conquistadors to inflict unspeakable cruelties on Native Americans.
Even Cortés admitted the European lust was "a disease of the heart," but he went
on, falsely, to claim that if they got access to gold it would be "a certain cure." Into
the 16th century, Saxony remained the leader in development of mining techniques.

[1] Lewis Mumford, *Technics and Civilization* (San Diego: Harcourt, Brace, Jovanovich, 1963), p. 70.

[2] Brechin, *op. cit.*, p. 20.

[3] Brechin comments on how mines traditionally have formed the basis of empire
(*Ibid.*)

[4] Brechin, *op. cit.*, p. 21; Rosen, *History of Mining Diseases*, p. 181. The military
had to be used against rebellious miners in 1785, for example. (*Ibid.*).

As mentioned earlier, in 16th and 17th century England the mines were primarily for iron and coal: iron because England, having no copper to alloy to make bronze for arms, successfully tried a new form of cast iron to manufacture cannons and cannonballs. To smelt the iron, as well as to fuel emerging cottage industries and for cooking and heat, England was forced to use coal, its forests now nearly depleted, in large part because of the many ships built for expanding English fleets.[1] As England became a worldwide naval power, on the prowl for slaves, empire and plunder, English ships were sent to North America and Ireland in the last half of the 17th century to bring back cargoes of trees from the clearcut forests to make more masts and spars. In Ireland, also, to deny refuge for hiding rebels.[2] Quantities of coal dug out of the ground increased asymptotically in early modern England. From 33,000 tons a year shipped out of Newcastle in the 1560s to 57,000 tons a year in the 1570s, nearly twice as much; by the 1590s, two decades later, about 145,000 tons a year are being shipped, and at 240,000 tons a year in the first decade of the 17th century, there had been a 725% increase relative to the 1560s. In the 1680s, 620,000 tons a year left Newcastle, almost 19 times as much as in the 1560s.[3] (See Table 1 and Graph 1.)

The drive to obtain more coal led to the opening of increasing numbers of new mines, existing ones sunk many more shafts, and the shafts themselves went deeper, by 1700 as far as 300 to 400 feet. Increased depths exacerbated age-old problems of mining, for drainage, ventilation, explosions, cave-ins, and poisonous fumes, so that the machinery of mining got ratcheted up several more notches. The tunneling, refining, ventilating, assaying, transporting ores, etc., as they acquired new complexities and scale, necessitated ever more complicated and massive framing, the more aggressive use of pumps, wheels, axles, and (often toxic) chemicals for refining in an effort to extract ever more, forever more, from the Earth.[4]

---

[1] As the oak forests of northeastern America during the 18th century were cut down, shipbuilders had to turn to southern pine. Marcus Rediker, *Slave Ships: A Human History* (New York: Penguin Books, 2007), p. 53.

[2] Leonard Pitt, *A Small Moment of Great Illumination: Searching for Valentine Greatrakes, the Master Healer* (Emeryville, Calif.: Shoemaker & Hoard, 2006), p. 128, describes the whole province of Munster being intentionally deforested, partly to destroy potential hiding spots for rebels. Deforestation occurred in North America and, also to destroy refuge, in Scotland. I am grateful to Neil MacLane for telling me about the case of Scotland. In the 1690s, Irish deforestation was carried out for raising cattle. (Linebaugh, *op. cit.*, p, 319). In Barbados, it took 40 years to clear the forests (Linebaugh and Rediker, *op. cit.*, p. 125).

[3] Nef, *op. cit.*

[4] Rosen, *History of Miners' Diseases*, p. 90, reports that around 1670, gunpowder was being used to set off underground explosions in mining operations in what can be seen as a literal war against the Earth.

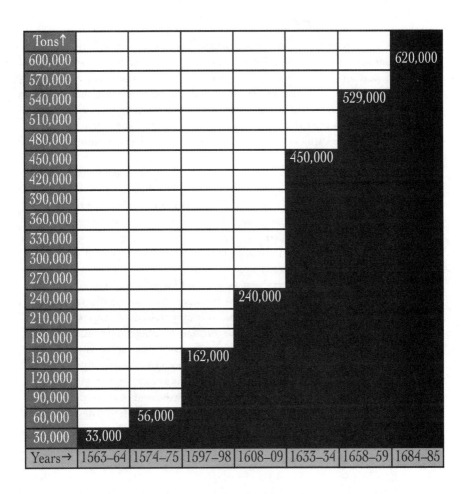

Tons↑						
600,000						620,000
570,000						
540,000					529,000	
510,000						
480,000						
450,000				450,000		
420,000						
390,000						
360,000						
330,000						
300,000						
270,000						
240,000			240,000			
210,000						
180,000						
150,000		162,000				
120,000						
90,000						
60,000	56,000					
30,000	33,000					
Years→	1563–64	1574–75	1597–98	1608–09	1633–34	1658–59	1684–85

Table 1
TONS OF COAL SHIPPED FROM NEWCASTLE
1560–1700[1]

---

[1] John Ulric Nef, *The Rise of the British Coal Industry* (London, England: George Routledge and Sons, 1932).

vii. DIALECTICS OF CLASS

As in Germany and eastern Europe earlier, these more extensive technologies required extensive investments. Partners, eventually absentee investors, entered the picture. Rather quickly in the history of mining, only a few could afford the necessary machinery and most miners were reduced to scratching out a bare — frequently short-lived — subsistence, working for a mere handful of owners, a process made considerably more common by a widespread speculation in mining shares that, since the 15th century, had also been part of the economy of the mining industry.

By the 16th century, after the defeat of a guild system which had offered some protection for miners, they had been reduced to the status of wage-slaves, the modern proletariat.[1] Not coincidentally, it was then, too, that we find the origins of the first (of many) of the great families, in this case the Fuggers, whose vast riches and power play such decisive roles at every turn in European history. The Fuggers leased the ancient mines at Rio Tinto and were instrumental in the new spice trade with India; served as bankers for popes; and extended substantial loans to emperors, for which they were granted large feudal lands and made counts, thus entering the aristocracy. The Fuggers' was but the first of the great fortunes built on mining. Later would come the Rothschilds, Morgans, Mellons, Hearsts, Guggenheims, and (if oil is included) Rockefellers and Gettys.

From the beginning, too, a close relationship tied mining to arms-making.[2] A persuasive logic drove this history: devouring wood for shoring up shafts, tunnels, and galleys, for railroad ties (historically, trains are associated with mining), and for smelting and fuel, mines necessarily have to expand, since they rapidly exhaust the wood and other resources around the minehead itself. Inevitably, this meant infringement on other peoples' lands, and this was possible only with arms.

The association of mining with war was noted by Plato, Seneca, and others in antiquity. In the 16th century,

> Royalty, nobles, and the papacy all borrowed heavily from the Fugger bank to fight wars with which to acquire more land and mines. Mines were needed both to increase the power of the borrowers and to repay their creditors with interest. Since royalty could, at any time, renounce its debts by citing the church's ban on usury, the Fuggers charged high rates of interest to cover their risk while taking as collateral the European, then American, mines and crown lands. Those mines in turn financed the warfare necessary to reimburse the bankers.

---

[1] *Ibid.*, p. 46.
[2] Grey Brechin develops this link masterfully in *op. cit.*, pp. 17ff.

Of course, the Fugger mines, smelters, and foundries were brought into play to make the necessary weaponry. Brechin remarks,

> To this new kind of businessman — the international financier
> — national boundaries meant little, except insofar as nations
> provided the armies to protect and defend their properties and
> to collect taxes needed to repay loans…. Through their access
> to the state treasuries, the Fuggers and their fellow bankers
> became Europe's de facto tax collectors and grew even richer
> on public revenues.[1]

viii. TEARING DOWN THE MOUNTAINS

It is instructive to look at the long-range trajectory of the mining industry, peeking ahead to the California Gold Rush some centuries later, where a vast hydraulic network was constructed to facilitate mining. Each year gigantic wooden flumes were erected as part of what was termed "river mining." With "hydraulic mining," still another level of attack against nature was reached, as cast-iron pipes played high pressure streams of water against rocks, shattering them and dissolving mountains. For this process, a "vast network of dams, flumes, and ditches reached higher into the Sierra to give the mines their necessary head" of pressure.[2]

Streams were moved bodily from one watershed to another, carrying their water across the bridges and trestles and through tunnels built for that purpose, radically transforming the Sierra's waterways and creating havoc for all of those downstream, particularly as hastily-constructed dams fell apart in spring runoffs. Such practices allowed ever more mammoth profits, but the cost to the rivers and valleys of California was both unprecedented and permanent, as river after river had its bed filled in by the silt, mud, and gravel the miners dredged up. By 1869 even the purest of streams were changing into "thick yellow mud."[3] Flooding got worse and worse, until finally a vast system of dikes and levees had to be built in the Central Valley, and the city of Sacramento was raised up, block by block, out of the mud onto landfill. Within a few decades after 1849, the bed of the Yuba River had been raised as much as 60 feet. By 1880, the State Engineer of California reported that 40,000 acres of farmland had been destroyed, with another 270,000 severely damaged.[4]

Later, the development of the Comstock silver mine not only took the scale of machinery and overall operation to whole new levels, it involved penetrating a vol-

---

[1] Brechin, *op. cit.*, pp. 23–24.

[2] *Ibid.*, p. 34.

[3] *Ibid.*, p. 50.

[4] *Ibid.*, pp. 48, 50.

canic formation that was still quite hot. Comstock mines were known as the deepest and hottest on Earth. Rivers of boiling sulphuric water and toxic gases filled some of their shafts. Dealing with the immense size of the ore bodies in the Comstock also required a new framing system built of heavy timber, which made the mines, as a reporter said, "the graveyard of the Sierra forests."[1] The mines ate up the pinyon pines of the desert and then the mountain forests, as the Sierra Nevada slopes, from the Eastern side, now were denuded. Even some of mining's advocates were appalled at the scale of the destruction. One mining attorney wrote, "The Sierras were devastated for a length of nearly 100 miles to provide the 600,000,000 feet of lumber that went into the Comstock mine, and the 2,000,000 cords of firewood consumed by mines and mills up to 1880," and he lamented the "majesty and beauty" being "fed into the maws of those voracious sawmills."[2]

In 1878, in reaction to the construction of a debris tunnel to the Yuba River, an Anti-Debris Society was formed by downstream farmers and townspeople. They sued the Hydraulic Miners' Association, winning a landmark decision against any more dumping into the Yuba.[3] Unfortunately, their loss simply led the mining interests to apply their newest methods elsewhere, by the 20th century exporting their know-how to new mines in South Africa, the USSR, and Chile.[4]

Popular awareness of the corrosiveness of mining technology did not, however, have to wait for the scale of the devastation to reach that of the California and Nevada gold, silver, and mercury mines of the 1850s, '60s, and '70s. Such awareness seems to date back pretty much to the earliest days of mining.

ix. TESTIMONY FROM THE GODS & GODDESSES

Carolyn Merchant has dug up a number of places in the 15th and 16th centuries where popular opposition to destructive mining is recorded in literary works and legal documents. An allegory from Lichtstadt in Saxony near the end of the 15th century, for example, reflects strong opposition to mining's destructive bent. In the allegory, Mother Earth files matricide charges against a miner and calls as expert witnesses a number of pagan deities: Bacchus, who complains about the miner's uprooting his vines and desecrating his most sacred groves; Ceres, who similarly laments the devastation to her fields; Pluto, who complains that the hammering and pounding of the miner's hammers and axes resound through the shafts and caverns underground; and water spirits, who note the drying up of fountains and the diverting of underground water. Laws were passed in Florence throughout the 15th century to ban destructive mining practices.[5]

---

[1] Quoted in *Ibid.*, p. 46.

[2] *Ibid.*, pp. 46–47.

[3] *Ibid.*, p. 51.

[4] *Ibid.*, pp. 52ff, 64.

[5] Merchant, *op. cit.*, pp. 32–33, 36.

Opposition to mining was so extensive, in fact, that Georg Agricola, the writer of the classic encyclopedic work on mining technology, *De Re Metallica* (1556), felt obliged to begin his large treatise, a virtual manifesto on mining practice and theory, by acknowledging there were widespread fears about mining. According to Agricola, people were complaining that

> mining is a perilous occupation... because the miners are sometimes killed by the pestilential air which they breathe; sometimes their lungs rot away; sometimes the men perish by being crushed in masses of rock; sometimes, falling...into the shafts, they break their arms, legs, or necks....

More than miners were affected by mining practices:

> [T]he strongest argument of the detractors [of mining] is that the fields are devastated by mining operations.... [T]hey argue that the woods and groves are cut down, for there is need of an endless amount of wood for timbers, machines, and the smelting of metals. And when the wood and groves are felled, then are exterminated the beasts and birds, very many of which furnish a pleasant and agreeable food for man.[1]

Washing ores, moreover, further "poisons the brooks and streams," destroying their fish. The disappearance of animals, birds, and fish is devastating to the food supply for those who live near the mines.[2]

We should assume that Agricola was summarizing many such complaints made in scattered mining regions, some dating from classical times. Interestingly enough, Agricola's answers to the charges that animals, fish, and fowl are exterminated where the woods are torn down by miners are the very ones we hear today whenever protests mount against the destruction of streams, hillsides, or wetlands: after blaming the miners for their carelessness ("operator error," in the modern lexicon), Agricola goes on to say that any loss of woods or streams and the small animals, fish, and birds they harbor is more than compensated for by the new fields where crops may be planted or by the vast number of smaller animals that may be *purchased* by the riches created by the mines ("job-creation" in today's terminology). Another link between Agricola's apologetics and today's: thanks to Herbert Hoover, in turn mining engineer and president of the US, there is a modern translation by the future president and Lou Henry Hoover in

---

1 Agricola, *De Re Metallica,* trans. Herbert Clark Hoover and Lou Henry Hoover (New York: Dover, 1950), pp. 6, 8.

2 Seneca and Ovid, among others, decried the cruelties and loss of life and limb associated with mining.

a handsome edition, complete with the wonderful woodcuts of the original, several of which I reproduce here.

By Agricola's time, the division of the workday into three shifts of seven hours each, extending work around the clock (the other three hours were for shift changes) had been put into effect in the mines. Outlines of other aspects of modernity — e.g. railroads are first found deployed in mines — emerge in connection with mining practices.[1]

x. Clearing the Land of People and Peopling the Ranks of the Destitute: The Creation of the Modern Proletariat

To peasants under assault by the extended process of enclosure, further disappearance of a woods, wetlands, stream, or meadow, where animals once might have been grazed or game hunted, or a woods where fuel or boughs for construction might have been gathered, according to age-old customs, was simply one more shovelful thrown on the coffin whereby their traditional way of rural life was being buried. Buried as a result of the seemingly inexorable forces of capitalist development, driven by an ideology of Progress, an ideology constructed in significant measure with concepts taken from the new theories of the scientific revolution.

In general, the transition from the Middle Ages was brutalizing for much of the population of Europe. From the 14th century on, numerous rebellions, uprisings, revolts, and insurrections erupted against the conditions and strictures of the emerging new order nearly everywhere. Much of this took the form of peasant uprisings, which were by the end of the century "endemic, massified, and frequently armed."[2] Fighting over land was not uncommon, particularly over land traditionally held *in* common, where a duck or a pig could be kept, but also the woods, lakes, and hills, places where rebels could escape to because survival there was easier. "[W]e can go to the woods," serfs claimed in the middle of the 12th century, "and take what we want, take fish from the fish pond, and game from the forests; we'll have our will in the woods, the waters, and the meadows." On the other hand, there was a constant appropriation of land from the peasantry, many of whom were now forced to survive by hiring themselves out as laborers. When the nobility in England tried to fix a maximum wage in 1381, a peasant uprising, involving a march of thousands from Kent to London, erupted.

Workers, too, rebelled against the conditions they faced. In 1377, cloth workers in Flanders fought with arms against their employers. Similar rebellions broke out in Bruges in 1348, in Ghent in 1335 and 1378; so too in Germany and Italy, where in Florence in 1379 the workers seized power.[3]

In France, a "'whirlwind of revolution'" broke out from 1379 to 1382 in Montpellier, Bezier, Carcassim, Orleans, Amiens, Rouen, Paris, and Tonrnai.

---

[1] Potosí, by the end of the 16th century, was on a double shift (Taussig, *Devil*, p. 202.)
[2] Federici, *op. cit.*, p. 25.
[3] *Ibid.*, pp. 43–46.

Some of these rebellions became full-scale wars, as in Spain in the 15th century, for example, involving thousands of combattants and lasting nearly a quarter of a century.[1]

In the 16th and 17th centuries especially a form of agrarian "improvements" in England resulted in the enclosure of common lands and the destruction of traditional forms of land tenure and usage. Anti-enclosure riots began in the late 1400s and continued for over two centuries, sometimes escalating into mass uprisings, such as Kett's Rebellion in 1549.[2]

As land was privatized, food became more expensive and the work load increased. What an artisan in 1500 could make by working for fifteen weeks, fifty years later took forty weeks. Whereas in the late Middle Ages the average person ate 100 kilograms of meat per year, by the middle of the 16th century, meat virtually disappeared from workers' tables.[3]

In France, more than a thousand uprisings took place from 1590 to the 1690s. In Spain, Italy, and England, it was likewise.

Creating a reliable workforce for the emerging capitalist economy was not easy, nor quickly done.[4] Control had to be put *into* the bodies of workers, with numerous attempts to regulate how people moved, ate, etc. "To pose the body as mechanical matter… was to make intelligible the possibility of subordinating it to a work process that increasingly relied on uniform and predictable forms of behavior."[5] Indeed, *"the machine was becoming the model of social behavior,"*[6] *and control when working required control when not;* hence the beginning of table "manners" and rules for how to laugh, walk, sneeze, etc.[7] Vesalius, the great 16th century anatomist, portrayed the human body as a factory.[8]

Throughout the long period of threatened enclosures, etc., those able to remain on the land, painfully scratching out a subsistence on the margins, witnessed neighbors, friends, and kin as they all struggled to maintain connections to the countryside until finally, eventually for nearly all of them, they were forced to leave, many of them abandoning the way of life of their family from time im-

---

1 *Ibid.*, pp. 43–49.

2 On enclosures, see Morton, *op. cit.*, pp. 166–70.

3 Federici, *op. cit.*, p. 77.

4 Taussig, *Devil*, p. 19; Federici, *op. cit.*, pp. 135–36.

5 *Ibid.*, p. 144. Cf. G. Gordon Liddy, the architect of COINTELPRO, in his autobiography, *Will* (New York: St.Martin's Press, 1980), on his transformative realization as a child when his father showed him a locomotive: "What extraordinary power they had! Machines could go on forever. They never tired, never hurt, just kept putting out all that power, day after day, week after week, year after year, world without end, amen. A flash of inspiration struck me. *I would make myself into a machine.*"

6 Federici, *op. cit.*, pp. 135–136.

7 *Ibid.*, p. 153, 145.

8 *Ibid.*, p. 157 n. 14.

memorial, and most of them destined to join growing urban mobs. Over decades and centuries some of them were reluctantly drawn into waged labor, but the availability of such employment usually lagged far behind the numbers dispossessed, since capitalism was much more efficient, at least in the short run, in land-clearing than in its job-creating capabilities. Thus was created the pool in which was spawned the modern proletariat.[1]

xi. Limiting the Take or Raising the Stakes?

From ancient times mining has been fraught with dangers, and from ancient times also miners have observed certain rituals and held specific beliefs about the spirits ruling individual mines. A complex relationship governs the taking of treasures from the inside of Mother Earth. Fasting, setting out offerings at altars, prayers, and formal rituals as new mines or new shafts were opened or on particular sacred days are commonly found in many different periods of history and several continents in relation to mining.[2] Limits were observed in how much was taken out of the mine, and miners offered gifts to the spirit of the mine in the hopes that he would provide prosperity and spare the lives and limbs of the miners. Less than a bribe, gifts were given so that a balance could be maintained between the taking and the giving, a profound sense of reciprocity underlying social as well as spiritual relationships that is assumed in many traditional cultures.[3]

As mentioned earlier, as late as 1600 the lifefulness of the Earth — and for many, of the material substrate that constituted the tangible world — was taken for granted nearly everywhere. Nurturing the fish, birds, animals, humans, plants, and insects as a Mother to them all, the Earth was perceived in a multitude of resemblances to other living creatures, her hills like the contours of a woman's body, rivers and streams akin to blood vessels, and grasslands like hair. The natural features of such a world were sacred aspects of the body of this Mother; to violate them, say, by indiscriminate digging or by taking in excess, was a desecration of the sacred order of Creation. Age-old sanctions against such behavior had helped keep most mines close to the surface.

When mining occurs on a small scale, such acts of piety in relation to the spirits or deities ruling the mineshafts and galleries, indeed, the mountain itself, are possible. As the new mines emerged, however, as one of a new breed of industrial and capitalist enterprises beginning forever to alter the economy and social order of Europe, England, and the rest of the world, and availability of transport, costs of extraction, access to water and labor-power, and distance to markets became virtually the only considerations governing what is dug up, this

[1] Thompson, *Customs in Common*; Linebaugh, *London Hanged*.

[2] For Europe, Berman, *Reenchantment*, p. 88; Merchant, *op. cit.*, p. 4; Duerr, *op. cit.*, p. 344 n. 41. For Latin America, see. Taussig, *Devil*, p. 146.

[3] Taussig, *Devil*; Taussig, *Shamanism*.

had to change. Any desire to observe limits in what and how much, or any manifestation of respect for a sacred part of Mother Earth is unacceptably anachronistic, a barrier to Progress pure and simple, to be rapidly destroyed so that the business of production might continue to grow unabated. A capitalist economy has its own deities, shaping the flows of labor, material, and finished goods with their invisible hands, and these are jealous gods, unwilling to coexist with a Mother Earth.[1] It is here that, as we shall see, the ideology of the new science would prove to be particularly serviceable. By 1600 limits against indiscriminate mining had long been breached. It took another century, however, for the beliefs supporting such limits to be successfully dug up, to yield to overwhelming historical forces. By 1700, if not before, the comprehension of nature had been dramatically transformed. Nature was no longer seen as alive, but as a thing, a dead object. We shall be studying this transformation in detail throughout Part Two.

xii. A SPIRITUAL UNRAVELLING

The lifefulness of nature had long been a primary principle of all magical belief. Paradoxically, the 16th century Reformation both made magic a pejorative for Protestants to hurl at the Roman Church and apparently was responsible for a marked increase in the belief in, and the use of, magic by rural people.[2]

Perhaps it was the growing pains of the societies of western Europe and England in the decades after the colonial project was launched that led to the shattering in early modern times of the only kind of unity, an ecclesiastical one, that Europe had known for a thousand or more years. Though frequently it was an illusory unity, especially in the 14th century, when the Church itself split into two or more antagonistic camps, at its best the Roman Church offered a cohesiveness of vision and of law that could be found nowhere else.

Luther's crisis of faith, his despair at not finding God in the context of a Roman Church awash in avarice, lust, and luxury, led to his questioning the Church's role as *the* source of salvation, its claims to being the necessary intermediary with God. According to the Church, all salvation came through its priestly function, its possession of the means of bringing forth the power that flowed through the sacraments. Only thus could sin be absolved and salvation attained. By means of *that* Church — although Luther was one of its priests, monks, and theologians — he could imagine no convincing salvation. In 1517 he took the first step away from its path. As his proposed reforms were resisted and then fought, he was driven to see the enormity of what he had to do. As Luther came to understand, salvation had to come through *faith*, not through the Church, *any* church. Christ was not to be found in the Institution that professed to speak for Him, but in Scriptures, a record of Christ's life and words and redemptive mission.

---

[1] Taussig, *Devil*, pp. 199–201.
[2] Keith Thomas, *Religion & the Decline of Magic* (New York: Charles Scribner's Sons, 1971).

Luther's notion of a priesthood of all believers, interpreting for themselves the meaning of the Bible, was to undergo serious revision as other reform leaders such as John Calvin, Ulrich Zwingli, John Knox, and others, joined the battle and added their particular slant or national perspective to Luther's original theses, but the Reformation they formed powerfully shaped the history of the world for the centuries to come. Within a decade wars of religion began between the two camps. The fight whether a State or principality was to be Catholic or Protestant and, in the latter case, over whose form of the reformed church should prevail — Luther's, Calvin's, or another's — tore various countries and regions into warring political, military, and cultural fragments. In some places, like England, neither side obtained a decisive victory for a century and a half, during which time intrigues, plots, assassinations, civil wars, secret negotiations between the Crown and Catholic powers on the Continent, and ongoing doctrinal strife all corroded the life of the nation.

Despite Luther's own conservative social leanings, his *de facto* democratization of religion, taking responsibility for salvation away from the Church and putting it in the hands of individual believers, was to play a central role in encouraging rebellious acts and beliefs by peasants, artisans, and the dispossessed in early modern times. Luther was horrified when combatants in the Peasant Wars invoked his notion of religious freedom to justify their battle for political and social freedom, unequivocally advocating the repression of their subversive notions, pointing out that "nothing can be more poisonous, hurtful, or devilish than a rebel."

It was too late. Already, Thomas Müntzer was beginning his rebellion against Luther's vision of reform in Zwickau, a booming silver mining town that was a center of the Waldensian "heresy," charging that "faith" was meaningless to miners or weavers incapable of feeding their families. Müntzer denounced the rich and attacked the princes, who "bleed the people with usury and count as their own the fish in the stream, the bird of the air, and the grass of the field, and Dr. Liar [i.e., Luther] says 'Amen'."

Müntzer emerged as head of the peasant insurrection in Thuringa in 1525, which, on the eve of their military defeat, numbered about 8000 combatants. Nearly ten years later, Anabaptists under his leadership were able to take over the town of Münster, where they instituted revolutionary policies that hinted at a return to the communism of primitive Christianity, including the abolition of money and private property, mandating that inhabitants eat collectively, and forcibly imposing polygamy.

For the rulers, Münster had to be retaken and crushed. Following a siege of 481 days and after several earlier failures, troops of Bishop von Woldeck finally were able to mount a successful assault and overcome Münster's defenses. Most of its men and about half of its women were slaughtered, in all about three or four thousand.[1]

---

[1] Otto Friedrich, *The End of the World: A History* (New York: Coword, McCann & Geoghegan, 1982), pp. 153–58, 163–76.

In another manner, too, Luther was a social radical despite himself, for if each person, guided by Scriptures, was to find the basis for faith, then it was necessary to expand literacy, even to women; public schooling did increase in many of the strongholds of Lutheranism, while different vernacular versions of the Old and New Testaments fueled the rapid spread of printed works in the 16th and 17th centuries.

The Reformation nurtured what became a flowering of works dealing with New Testament prophecy, in a sense transforming earlier preoccupations with death and despair — born of the devastations of the Black Death and the disruption of peoples' social and economic lives as their agrarian world began to unravel — into an obsession with the Last Judgment and millennium. By the 17th century, many of the leading Protestant thinkers were convinced that the world was approaching its preordained end, to be followed by a Kingdom of God ruling the worthy. Interpretations of the Book of Revelation and the Book of Daniel attempted to determine exactly when certain stages had or would come to pass.

xiii. SEEDBEDS OF MAGIC

The Roman Church was certainly not comfortable with magical beliefs, since they undercut the role of God as Creator of all things, but it nonetheless relied on magical notions as the basis of many of its doctrinal tenets and rituals, most notably the Mass and rituals of purification. After the Reformation, Protestant churches were even less sympathetic to magic, singling out the Roman Church's magical doctrines as one of its most egregious errors.[1] Popular beliefs, at least in the countryside, on the other hand, were not affected by this dispute. European and English rural areas were riddled with magical beliefs and practitioners who treated the sick and led rituals when seeds were first put in the ground, or crops harvested, or at numerous special times like solstices or sacred days.[2]

Sometimes these healers were midwives. They might have been called "cunning men," "wise women," wizards, or witches. While Christianity had claimed England and Europe centuries before, frequently it had to merely co-exist with older, pagan traditions (even as is frequently the case with *indios* in Latin America) perhaps indigenous since Paleolithic times, that involved invoking nature spirits and holding rituals in accord with the rhythms of the year and months.

---

[1] Rupert Sheldrake, *The Rebirth of Nature: The Greening of Science and God* (London: Century, 1990), pp. 19–20; also Thomas, *Religion and the Decline*.

[2] In *Night Battles: Witchcraft & Agrarian Cults in the 16th & 17th Centuries* trans. John & Anne Tedeschi (New York: Penguin, 1983) Carlo Ginzburg claims that the rural areas of Italy, and the rest of Europe was "overrun by healers, sorcerers, and witches who cured every sort of malady through the use of ointments and poultices seasoned with magic and superstitious prayers.... " (p. 78).

Special rocks, particular springs or wells, streams or caves might be where the nature spirits were most easily encountered in a given locale. Coming later, the Catholic Church frequently appropriated these holy sites — rocks or springs, for example — from the older religion, building its own churches there.[1]

Whether one's livelihood came from planting grain in the fields, or through fishing in the storm-tossed North Sea, the rhythmic turnings of nature molded nearly everyone's lives to its contours and it were wise to give pause at the critical nodal points. The cycles of the moon ruled more than the fertility of women, and solstices and equinoxes marked crucial balance points in the world that needed to be observed. Planting and harvest were attended by specific rituals, large and small, as were the setting out of a flotilla of fishers or the opening of a mine.

In the past several decades, historians have realized the extent to which magical beliefs and practices saw a sharp increase in the periods of social turmoil such as exploded across Europe and England from the 15th to the 17th centuries. This was particularly true during the English Civil War and revolution that broke out in 1642.

Magical beliefs, as we shall see below, had important roles to play in the course of that revolution and its aftermath. I want to focus especially on two forms of magical belief and practice: alchemy and witchcraft. Both alchemy and witchcraft shared certain core beliefs and attitudes with a broad array of magical practices, including astrology, numerous kinds of healing, cabala, the study of Arabic philosophy, soothsaying, and prophecy. These traditions frequently had more in common, in terms of central tenets, than they had peculiarities that separated them from one another. Alchemy is especially important for us because it is there that ideas about the powers of matter were explored and discussed and because Isaac Newton, the man largely responsible for our modern conceptual universe, was a careful and dedicated craftsman in pursuit of alchemical secrets. It was into her chambers that Newton descended in his quest to understand the makings of the natural world. It was there, too, that Newton continually renewed his (secret) belief in the inherent lifefulness of nature. Finally, alchemy is important because of its central concern with healing, which became the basis for a profound political role alchemical arts played in the intellectual and social ferment in the first half of the 17th century.

To the best of our knowledge, Newton did not meet secretly with witch covens the way we now know he did with small circles of alchemists (to some of whom he contributed money), but witchcraft is worth our careful attentions by virtue of the highly unusual social issues involved in the 15th, 16th, and 17th

---

[1] In Peru, natives were known to have buried mummies or other sacred objects underneath the crosses erected by Catholic priests, in effect, reconsecrating the ground in the spirit of their own deities (Taussig, *Devil*, p. 173). The priests sometimes coopted the magic of the natives in an effort to convert them. Steve Chawkins, "Parishioners See the Light at Mission During Solstice," San Francisco *Chronicle* (December 22, 2011).

centuries' war against the witches. All forms of magic came under strong attack in the last half of the 17th century, for the core beliefs of magic were seen as an impediment for the new social and economic order then emerging. But while most magical crafts, for example, alchemy and astrology, were simply ridiculed and eventually excluded from "serious" discussion in the following decades, only the witches were hunted down, subjected to excruciating tortures, and often — though less so in England than on the Continent — executed: burned at the stake on the Continent, in England, hanged.

xiv. THE ROSICRUCIAN SEDITION

While the roots of alchemy were planted in prehistory, it was in the early 17th century that it flowered as a politically powerful organized brotherhood,[1] which simultaneously pursued science, healing and spirituality. The anonymous appearance of a series of tracts, beginning with the *Fama Fraternitatis* in 1614, announced the mysterious arrival in Germany of this Brotherhood as a foil to the (in part) Jesuit-inspired Counter-Reformation. Waging an intellectual and magical campaign against the Jesuits, the highly influential Rosicrucian order, publicly "appeared" in the wake of the *Fama* and several other publications that followed in each successive year. All were addressed to the learned of Europe and proclaimed that the goal of the Brotherhood was to fulfill the general reformation of the world, based upon the alchemical magic and cabala of the East.

Members of the Brotherhood were called upon to teach and to treat the ill. The description of their work emphasized its spiritual nature. Its members would serve anonymously, nothing they wore setting them apart from others. They would not allow others to know who they were. And they would accept no payment for their healing of the sick.

The impact of these tracts was enormous. Their message had apparently fallen on a fertile and well-prepared European soil, figuratively turned over by the previous few centuries of warfare and upheaval. The Rosicrucian literature invited the learned to contact them— though how to do so was never spelled out, and remained a mystery and source of great frustration to many[2] — resulting in "a river of printed works," many by men who claimed to have unsuccessfully tried to contact this shadowy new Brotherhood.

---

[1] Scholars question whether the Rosicrucians were, in fact, an organized group, as opposed to a handful of writers of the several tracts. But, of course, clandestine groups always try to make obscure their activities, so a lack of clarity in this regard is to be expected and cannot be taken at face value.

[2] Baillet, the 17th-century biographer of Descartes, reports the rumors that only by magical means, "by thought joined to the will, that is to say in a manner imperceptible to the senses," could one contact the Rosicrucians. Descartes apparently tried and, according to Baillet, failed.

Quite a number of these authors were receptive to the Rosicrucian program of wiping out hunger, poverty, disease, and ignorance, and expressed anxiety at their failures to reach the new Brotherhood. There were others, however, who denounced it as fomenting "political insubordination or sedition," and of being "subversive."[1] As the controversy developed and spread, Rosicrucianism created considerable havoc, first in Germany, then in France, and finally, in a somewhat adulterated form and under radically different social, political and religious conditions, in Civil War England.

Above all the Rosicrucians were a spiritual movement, concerned with peoples' salvation. Unlike traditional Christianity, which disdained the temporal, as opposed to the heavenly, world, Rosicrucian spirituality rested on a theory of, as well as practical work with, the world of *matter*. Alchemical beliefs and practices were a cornerstone of the Rosicrucian literature, which announced that magic and cabala were central to their reformation.

Besides ending poverty and hunger, the Rosicrucian transformation of the world and general reformation had as a primary aim the banishing of disease. Their alchemy was the perfect vehicle to that end. While its belief that it is possible to transmute ordinary matter into gold is well known, this fundamental role of healing in alchemical beliefs and practices is not. The legendary Philosophers' Stone, said to be capable of transmuting base metals into gold or silver, could also, by virtue of the same power, transform a sick into a healthy person.[2] Tales of miraculous healings, even immortality, fill the historical ledgers of alchemy, not all of them, arguably, necessarily legend only.

Indeed, if there was a spiritual river that constituted the inner current of the alchemical tradition, healing was the canyon in the human world that this river carved out down through the ages. The transmutation of base matter into gold has an isomorphism with the healing of a diseased person, involving a cleansing followed by a reconstitution, based on a seed or an inner potential (for "goldness" or for health) already present. To true adepts, it was this latter, medical. and even more, the spiritual mastery it rested on, that was truly their goal, the material gold they created more like a signpost that mastery over the spiritual and material world had really been achieved.[3]

---

1 My discussion here and in the next chapter leans heavily on Frances A. Yates, *The Rosicrucian Enlightenment* (Boulder, Colo.: Shambala, 1972); on "subversion," see pp. 97–98.

2 The miraculous powers alleged in some such healings, I have read in several sources, are operant under the constraint that the sick person's vital organs are still intact and that he or she retains some vitality.

3 My interpretation here differs from that of Lawrence M. Principe whose pioneering work on Newton's and Boyle's alchemical research I have greatly benefitted from. See, for example, his *The Aspiring Adept: Robert Boyle and His Alchemical Quest* (including Boyle's "Lost" Dialogue on the Transmutations of Metals) (Princeton: Princeton Univ. Press, 2000).

In the tumultuous years of the 17th century in Europe and England, and especially in the English Civil War and revolution at the middle of the century, alchemy was brought in to even greater prominence; the social upheavals caused certain issues to become major concerns for the swollen ranks of the expropriated peasantry and the large numbers of demobilized and restless soldiers from both sides. Issues were brought into sharper definition by the wide-ranging social discussions and debates that epitomized this upheaval, particularly with the effective end of censorship that resulted from the breakup of Church authority. Under the new liberties, an explosion of pamphlets and treatises on all manner of topics and from a wide range of perspectives erupted.

I shall speak, for convenience, of a Rosicrucian or alchemical tradition even though, especially as the 17th century reached its midpoint, more and more those traditions branched out into other, related doctrines, many of which, like astrology, numerology, cabala, or natural magic, already existed. Certainly by the English Civil War, a flowering of occult ideas of all kinds burst forth. Demands for Oriental studies at Oxford and Cambridge Universities were part of a more general intellectual ferment centering around the doctrines of Paracelsus, the German healer and alchemist, and Jakob Boehme, another radical alchemist from Bohemia, among many other mystical points of view. The point to remember is that the doctrines and mystical practices were not necessarily distinct from one another; that a student or dabbler in astrology most likely can at some point be found investigating alchemy, an enthusiastic advocate for Boehme later found as a follower of the Seekers. Though divergent beliefs and practices characterized these different traditions, for our purposes I believe their commonalities were more basic, that though exceptions certainly existed to the general pattern I shall depict, it is, to a remarkable degree, a useful and valid guide.[1]

On that basis, let us take a closer look at what was probably one of the major wellsprings of Rosicrucianism.

---

[1] On this point, see Christopher Hill, *The World Turned Upside Down: Radical Ideas During the English Revolution* (New York: Viking Press, 1972), p. 153, where he descibes militants "pass[ing] rapidly from sect to sect, trying all things...." Winthrop S. Hudson describes the tendency of many who "embarked upon a spiritual pilgrimage, moving from group to group in search of the assurance and security to be found in the true church." "Mystical Religion in the Puritan Commonwealth," *Journal of Religion,* XVIII (1948), p. 54.

6

The Spiritual Imperialism of John Dee

> [S]he [Queen Elizabeth]... sent [Dee] word... to doe what he would in Alchymie and Philosophy, and none should controule or molest him.... — Elias Ashmole, *Theatrum Chemicum Britannicum. Containing Severall Poeticall Pieces of our Famous English Philosophers, who have written the Hermetique Mysteries in their owne Ancient Language* (1652)

> "...'the worst of all witch persecutions, the climax of the European craze' were the persecutions which broke out in central Europe in the sixteen-twenties 'with the destruction of Protestantism in Bohemia and the Palatinate' and the Catholic reconquest of Germany." — Frances Yates, *The Rosicrucian Enlightenment* (1972) quoting H.R. Trevor-Roper, *Religion, the Reformation, and Social Change* (1967)

i. QUEEN ELIZABETH & "HYR PHILOSOPHER"

However the strange history of Rosicrucianism in the 17th century is untangled and subjected to ongoing reinterpretation, the figure of John Dee, English *magus* and close advisor to Queen Elizabeth, will no doubt be seen as central. As a *magus*, Dee's powers were legendary. In this, as in his strong influence on the interests and actions of a near-mythical monarch, Elizabeth, there is an uncanny parallel to the figure of Merlin in Arthur's Camelot.

Dee was arguably the foremost mathematician of the late 16th century and was a key figure in the circle of thinkers that formed around Sir Phillip Sidney. Dee was quite involved with another influential group that the "Wizard Earl," (as Henry Percy was called), gathered with, known for its far-reaching speculations about poetry, religion, philosophical questions, mathematics, and natural philosophy.[1] Dee constructed detailed Tables of Navigation, meant to aid English ships, and wrote treatises on navigation as well. These were not, however, mere extensions of his mathematical interests, put to practical use for England's expanding fleet, but integral to an elaborate and specifically *imperialist ideology* that Dee articulated, developed, and, over a number of years, organized on behalf of.

In Dee's vision England was to serve as the instrument to bring about the fulfillment of a general worldwide reformation, where the long-awaited (and to a great many of his contemporaries, now drawing near) millennium would finally be realized, ushering in a reign of universal peace. Dee had apparently played an important role in promoting voyages of exploration to North America by his friend, Sir Francis Drake, and he used information from these and inflated precedents gleaned from ancient maps and legends to posit a legal and moral right, even an obligation, for England to claim these newly "discovered" lands across the Atlantic.[2]

While a strong advocate for the kinds of liberties asserted by the several Protestant churches in their fight against Rome, Dee's pretensions on behalf of England, with Elizabeth cast as Empress, were thus premised on the notion that the European powers had fair claim on lands so obviously already inhabited. Native people simply did not count; where they lived was clearly there to take. The critical liberties, especially as relates to property, were apparently for Europeans only.

Accordingly, the core of Dee's vision, proclaimed as an idea of liberation, was from a decidedly colonialist angle. In audience after audience that she granted him, Dee pressed his visions on Elizabeth, dedicated works on the imperial theme to her, and in his frontispiece portrayed her as surrounded by celestial forces ready to help her historic, indeed, sacred, task should she choose to follow Dee's advice. Elizabeth was said to hold Dee in high regard, valued his ideas, calling him, a contemporary claimed, "hyr philosopher," and sent word to him that he should "doe what he would in *Alchymie* and *Philosophy*, and none shall controule or molest him...."[3]

1 Peter J. French, *John Dee: The World of an Elizabethan Magus* (London: Routledge & Kegan Paul, 1984), pp. 171–72. Benjamin Woolley, *The Queen's Conjuror: The Science and Magic of Dr. John Dee, Adviser to Queen Elizabeth I* (New York: Henry Holt and Company, 2001), pp. 63, 186.

2 French, *op. cit.*, pp. 179–80, 183 n1, 197–98.

3 French, *op. cit.*, pp. 6–7. Elias Ashmole, "Annotations and Discourse, upon some part of the preceding Worke," in *Theatrum Britannicum. Containing Severall Poeticall Pieces of our Famous English Philosophers, who have written the Hermetique Mysteries in their owne Ancient Language* (New York: Johnson Reprint Corp., 1967 reprint of 1652 London ed.) (ed.) Allen G. Debus, p. 483. The idea of Elizabeth as a new Constantine, bringing peace, strength, and stability, is discussed in Bernard Capp, "The Fifth Monarchists and Popular Millenarianism," in *Radical Religion in the English Revolution* (ed.) J. F. McGregor & B. Reay (Oxford: Oxford Univ. Press, 1986), p. 181. Elizabeth was intrigued by the possibility that the Philosopher's Stone might help preserve her youth. Anne Whitelock, *The Queen's Bed: An Intimate History of Elizabeth's Court* (New York: Picador, 2013), p. 9.

Dee's magical work was often conducted with Edward Kelley, a man with whom his life became tragically and scandalously intertwined. A confidence man and forger, Kelley also had remarkable powers as a medium, and served as Dee's access to realms, creatures, and visions Dee himself could not experience directly. Kelley reportedly had obtained an old alchemical manuscript and some mysterious powders that had been taken from the tomb, at Glastonbury Abbey, of a rich bishop who had died some years earlier. It was these powders and the manuscript that initially gained Kelley a meeting with Dee, where Kelley was able to demonstrate some of his powers as a medium, as well as allowing Dee to try the powder's potency at a goldsmith's.[1] Thus began years of tumultuous and adventuresome collaboration between the two men, taking them halfway across Europe on a secret mission for Elizabeth, and casting both of them at various times into disrepute or jail because of their widely known necromancy and their swapping of wives.

In 1583 Dee and Kelley journeyed to Prague to confer with the Holy Roman Emperor, Rudolf II, who had moved the imperial capital to Prague, where he established alchemical laboratories to actively pursue the ancient art. For six years the two men stayed in Europe, working on philosophical, religious, and magical matters, keeping an ear to the ground so as to avoid imprisonment (not always successfully) and conferring with a number of courts, kings, and philosophers. Rudolf II was one of their closest contacts and they tried "to interest the Emperor in his [Dee's] imperialist mysticism," according to Frances Yates. Finally in 1589 a summons from Elizabeth brought Dee back to England, to report, Yates surmises, on the mission she had dispatched him to undertake six years previously.[2]

Dee, it is worth noting, at its request provided the Privy Council "the crux of a fledgling, yet well-oiled espionage network" critical for an England in ongoing conflict with Catholic Spain, and the Protestant Queen confronted with an underground network of disloyal papists. As a master mathematician, Dee was expert in devising codes or cyphers, crucial both for his magic and communicating with agents and informants of the nascent Empire, a kind of early version, if you will, of Allen Dulles. (Keep this in mind when in Chapter 28 we return to Dee and a speculation as to his relation to contemporary crises.)[3]

Remarkably, it was in the places in Germany near where the England-bound Dee passed that the Rosicrucian movement, again according to Yates, first arose some twenty-five years later. The early Rosicrucian manifestos alluded

---

[1] Several sources for Kelley's powder and manuscript are discussed in Woolley, *Queen's Conjuror*, p. 169.

[2] Yates, *op. cit.* Her argument has been critiqued by Didier Kahn, "The Rosicrucian Hoax in France (1623–24)" in *Secrets of Nature: Astrology and Alchemy in Early Modern Europe* (ed.) William R. Newman and Anthony Grafton (Cambridge, Mass.: MIT Press, 2001), pp. 235–344.

[3] Susan Ronald, *The Pirate Queen: Queen Elizabeth I, Her Pirate Adventurers, and the Dawn of Empire* (New York: Harper Perennial, 2007), p. 182.

to a "more secret philosophy" which symbolically was identified as John Dee's, Yates claims.

Dee died in 1608, a man broke and broken, hounded by public suspicions about his magical activities and his conjuring of demons. Indeed, when in 1589 he had returned to England from Prague, he found that his immense library (said to have been the best in England, with some 4000 volumes) had been destroyed by a mob. And when Elizabeth died in 1601, her promised protection for Dee did not extend from the beyond. She was followed onto the throne by the first of the Stuarts, the magic-fearing James I.

ii. THE DEMONIZING OF MAGIC

James I's hostility to magic may have stemmed from a ferocious storm at sea that occurred when he sailed with his new wife in 1591; there were rumors of a witchcraft-inspired origin to the storm, in which James and his wife almost lost their lives.[1] Before ascending the throne of England, James, at that point James VI of Scotland, had written his *Daemonology* (1597), a work strongly antagonistic to magic of any kind. The first year he reigned as James I, he made witchcraft *per se* a capital offense; previously, it had only been felonious *acts committed* by witches that had been so punished. Despite his marked hostility towards the occult arts, however, Yates believes that James I played a critical role in an occult drama whose outcome was to have grave consequences for the whole of European history that followed.

Behind the mystery of the Rosicrucian manifestoes that appeared from 1614 on lay not only the alchemical and political ideas of John Dee, but, Yates argues, the development of political and spiritual adventures in the second decade of the 17th century in the Palatinate and Prague. Those developments, in turn, built on a possible secret alliance of Protestant leaders established in the mid-1580s to defend Protestantism against the Catholic League, representatives of King Henry of Navarre, the King of Denmark, and the Queen of England (Elizabeth) meeting and agreeing to a common defense.

It was the death of the Emperor Rudolf II in 1612 that set off a remarkable train of events, according to Yates, involving an attempt to institute an alchemical reign of peace and well-being across Europe, in which James I played a critical role. Indeed, a major watershed in the war between the Protestant forces and those of the Catholic Counter-Reformation, fighting for the future of Europe and of the lands undergoing colonization, was crossed in the course of a crucial 1620 battle over the control of an alchemically-infused realm.

---

1 The story of the storm is widely repeated, but Julio Caro Baroja, *The World of the Witches*, trans. O.N.V. Glendinning (Chicago: Univ. of Chicago Press, 1965), pp, 126f claims that the couple were unable to sail because of the storm.

Two years earlier, in 1610, Henri IV of France had been assassinated, and a new leader was needed for the loose alliance that was the center of Protestant resistance to the Catholic Hapsburg domination and its attempt to push back the Protestant footholds in Europe, particularly in the Netherlands and England, parts of Germany, and some of France. For a number of historic and other reasons, the logical choice for a new leader of the Protestant resistance was Frederick V, the young Elector Palatine.

Rudolf II's death two years later meant a new Emperor had to be selected, as well. The most likely candidate for this was the Archduke Ferdinand of Styria, a Catholic and a Hapsburg, a Jesuit-educated zealot known for his intolerance of "heresy." When Ferdinand was crowned as King of Bohemia in 1617, he immediately set out to destroy the cosmopolitan and tolerant city of Prague, fashioned by Rudolf II as a place where cabalists, alchemists, Jews, Catholics, Protestants, astronomers, prophets, and mystics of various stripes had lived amidst peace and intellectual ferment.

Instead, Fedinand tried to impose his brand of intolerance on the unique Renaissance culture of Prague. He suppressed the Bohemian church which, under the leadership of John Hus, had led one of Europe's first attempts for a church reformed along national and anticlerical lines and a continual source of radical theology. To some observers, the real beginning of the Thirty Years War that soon brutalized so much of central Europe and whose fallout was felt over much of the globe are to be found in that move against the Bohemian church. Before long, Bohemia was in open rebellion against the Archduke Ferdinand, justifying their revolt with a theory that the crown of Bohemia was elective, so that they could offer it to their alternative, Frederick V, Elector Palatine. In August, 1619 this is what they did. If Frederick V accepted, he would then have two votes in the upcoming imperial election, a valuable asset in the campaign against Hapsburg reaction.

Frederick V's position was dangerous, but it looked as if he had exceptionally strong cards to play. Through family he enjoyed close ties to the Netherlands, the cornerstone of Protestantism at the time. In France, he had strong connections with the Protestant Huguenots. By tradition, as Elector Palatine, he was also the obvious leader of the Union of German Protestant Princes. Not least, one year after Rudolf II's death, Frederick V had married the Princess Elizabeth, daughter of James I, in an elaborate ceremony on St. Valentine's Day, 1613, attended by representatives from the most important courts of Europe and staged as a major event in Europe at the time.

Clearly the wedding was a moment of great significance for England. The marriage and the carefully orchestrated ceremonies attending it, were seen as signalling James I's support for Frederick V in his role as defender of Protestant interests.

Towards the end of September, 1619, Frederick V accepted the Bohemian offer. By now the situation was more complicated, for around the time of the Bohemian rebellion, Ferdinand of Styria had been elected Emperor. Accordingly, Frederick V's acceptance of the Bohemian Crown was now a clear act of rebellion against his feudal lord.

On the 27th of September, 1619, Frederick V, the Princess Elizabeth, and their son, Prince Henry, began their journey to Prague from Heidelberg. A story of epic proportions unfolded as many in England enthusiastically cheered them on from afar, seeing the Princess as the reincarnation of Elizabeth I and following news of this latest "holy family" carrying the hopes of Protestantism with them. The Bohemian adventure, Yates concludes,

> was not merely a political anti-Hapsburg effort. It was the expression of a religious movement which had been gathering force for many years, fostered by secret influences moving in Europe, a movement towards solving religious problems along mystical lines suggested by Hermetic [alchemical] and Cabalist influences.

She further suggests that the outbreak in Germany of the Rosicrucian movement was "the delayed result of Dee's mission" — perhaps under Elizabeth's direction — "in Bohemia over twenty years earlier."[1]

A closer look at the Rosicrucian manifestoes is illuminating. In elaborate allegories they spoke of a new reformation and of the millennium it would usher in. The first treatise, *The Fama Fraternitatis*, told of the rediscovery of an ancient philosophy, based on alchemy and closely tied to healing, that is also intertwined with numerology, geometry, and the creation of mechanical marvels.[2] Above all, it is "an illumination of a religious and spiritual nature." The second manifesto of the Rosicrucians alluded to the "more secret philosophy" — the cabala and alchemy of Dee, Yates maintains.

It was one year after the seeming fateful alliance between the Palatine and England in opposition to Hapsburg reaction was sealed in 1613 that the first Rosicrucian manifesto appeared. For a while, each year saw a new treatise from the Rosicrucian camp, eliciting a huge outpouring of printed works in response to the Brotherhood's challenge, with more than 200 such works published between 1614 and 1623.[3] Many of the authors wrote of their interests in cooperating with the announced enterprise of the Brotherhood, though the writers' appeals to make contact apparently met only silence, Yates believes. Yet, an underground movement seen by many as subversive might simply have kept any responses se-

---

[1] Yates, *op. cit.*, pp. 34, 40.

[2] *Ibid.*, pp. 44–45.

[3] *Ibid.*, p. 49; F.T. Moran, "Alchemy, Prophecy, and the Rosicrucians: Raphael, Egonus and the Mystical Currents of the Early 17th Century," in (ed.) P.M. Rattansi and Antonio Clericuzio, *Alchemy and Chemistry in the 16th and 17th Centuries* (Dordrecht: Kluwer Academic Publishers, 1994), p. 114.

cretive.[1] Nonetheless, a profound debate about a general reformation, rooted in the alchemical studies that Rosicrucianism argued for, was set in motion.

iii. ENGLISH EQUIVOCATION

Support from the English Crown for Frederick V's challenge to the Hapsburgs was critical. As a result of his daughter's very public marriage to Frederick V, many assumed that James I strongly supported the Elector Palatine's cause. James I, however, was absolutely determined not to antagonize the Hapsburgs, which meant balancing the Princess Elizabeth's marriage with a mirror-image match of James' son to a Hapsburg. James I's equivocation proved fatal to the cause. Frederick V's other allies, sensing confusion, hesitated and hedged.

The war between Spain, the center of Hapsburg power, and the Netherlands had ended in 1613 with a shaky truce that was due to end shortly; many expected the war to resume. Frederick V's revolt, in effect, was the spark needed. The Catholic forces were led by the Duke of Bavaria, those of Frederick V by Christian of Anhalt, a key strategist both in the anti-Hapsburg movement and closely connected with occult figures, including the Bohemian followers of the late John Dee.

In November, 1620, at the Battle of White Mountain outside of Prague, Frederick V's forces were routed, ending the reign of the "Winter King and Queen of Bohemia," as he and the Princess Elizabeth were subsequently called, and ushering in both another generation of Hapsburg domination and the onset of the Thirty Years War that was to devastate Europe. The crushing of Frederick V's forces and what he stood for was total. Frederick V, the Princess Elizabeth, and their two children narrowly escaped from Prague, leaving everything behind. Spain invaded the Palatinate. In Bohemia there were mass executions to stamp out any resistance. The Bohemian church was crushed. A violent counter-reformation took place in Austria and in Silesia. And the course of European history was unalterably transformed.

Frances Yates paints a picture of what was lost with the defeat of Frederick V and the Princess Elizabeth:

> The alchemical and esoteric interests encouraged by Rudolph II had represented a more liberal Renaissance atmosphere than that which the [Hapsburg] Reaction wished to impose…. [With the coming of] the Princess Elizabeth, bringing with her influence from the late Renaissance flowering in Jacobean London, [there was]… a hope of powerful support against the forces of reaction. Heidelberg castle [the center of Frederick V's power], with its magic-scientific models, Heidelberg Uni-

---

[1]Yates, *op. cit.*, pp. 44–45.

versity, center of Protestant learning, became the symbols of a resistance movement during the years between the wars....[1]

IV. The Failure of the "Rosicrucian Dawn"

The failure of what Yates refers to as a "misunderstood Rosicrucian Dawn" brought about the destruction of the famous libraries of the Palatinate as a "whole world vanished... its monuments defaced or destroyed, its books and written records vanished, its population turned into refugees — those who could escape — or destined to die by violence, plague, or famine in the terrible years to come."[2] The world destroyed was closely associated with an alchemical vision and its mission of free healing for the sick. Thus, Ferdinand's attempt to suppress the Bohemian church and the subsequent revolt of Bohemia had set off a major showdown, wherein Frederick V carried a banner for a different kind of State than what came to be established, as early modern Europe was fashioned out of the remnants of feudal Europe, ending in 1648 with the Treaty of Westphalia, which was to codify what constituted nation-states.. Yates takes pains to point out what a turning point Frederick V's loss was for the whole of European history. While clearly one battle alone cannot decide the fate of an intellectual/spiritual movement having such deep roots in the soil of human consciousness, still it is apparent that the Battle of White Mountain represented a key event at the birth of modernity, a critical turning away from alchemy — an alchemy, I again wish to emphasize, standing for an alternative vision of the role and character of natural philosophy, and carrying profound social and religious resonances, all the more powerful for having in some fashion allied with a sovereign power.

And with the defeat of that movement at the hands of the Duke of Bavaria at the Battle of White Mountain, without warning the earlier steady stream of Rosicrucian publications suddenly dried up, though not without parting polemics, such as the 1621 *Warning Against the Rosicrucian Vermin,* published in Heidelberg.[3]

Writers before Yates, not knowing of the connection between Rosicrucianism and the campaign of Frederick V, have been puzzled by this sudden silence. To Yates, on the other hand, the reason for the precipitous drop of Rosicrucian ferment and widespread debates was obvious: the movement for Rosicrucian reform had just been dealt a near-fatal blow.

What remnants were left were rapidly pulling back and regrouping, preparing to defend themselves against physical and legal threats from the Hapsburg invaders who now controlled Prague and the Palatine. Mocking attacks on Rosicrucian ideology pilloried the retreating Frederick V and the Princess Elizabeth

---

[1] *Ibid.*, pp. 27–28.

[2] *Ibid.*

[3] Richard Watson, *Cogito, Ergo, Sum: The Life of René Descartes* (Boston: David R. Godine, 2002), p. 103.

as they fled to their exile in The Hague. The atmosphere of ridicule, weakness, fear, and disillusion/dissolution was not conducive to open advocacy.

v. A REGROUPING IN PARIS

A number of members of the legendary Brotherhood apparently must have fled Germany, for in 1623 placards suddenly appeared in Paris to announce the arrival there of the Brotherhood. By then the *Fama* had already made a stir in Catholic France. As in Germany nearly a decade earlier, when the first treatises appeared, these placards whipped up a storm of rumors, although, forearmed by what had occurred in Germany, the French critics seem to have been prepared. One work attacked these newcomers as devil worshippers, and recounted the specific diabolical pacts they supposedly made. The Rosicrucians are heathen, a Jesuit claimed, going on to judge them to be "really wicked sorcerers, dangerous to religion and the state."[1]

Another writer, who was encouraged by the Church to write against the Rosicrucians, was the young René Descartes. His friend and patron, Marin Mersenne, a Minorite monk, also feverishly attacked them. The campaign to discredit Rosicrucianism, Yates suggests, may well have been the catalyst for what H.R. Trevor-Roper describes as "the worst of all witch persecutions, the climax of the [two centuries long] European craze" following "the destruction of Protestantism in Bohemia and the Palatinate...."[2]

This campaign also played a crucial role in the coming English Civil War and revolution at the middle of the century, as we shall see in the next chapter.

(We are not done with Dee. A much later Chapter 28 will speculate about a possible deep structural connection between Dee's work and the troubles of our time.)

---

[1] Merchant, *op. cit.*, p. 198; Yates, *op. cit.*, pp. 97–98.

[2] Yates, *op. cit.*, p. 105, quoting H.R. Trevor-Roper, *Religion, The Reformation and Social Change.*

7

Spiritual Insurgency in the English Civil War

What was not foreseen in this simple-minded economics of religion was that it is not possible to devalue the body and value the soul. The body, cast loose from the soul, is on its own. Devalued and cast out of the temple, the body does not skulk off like a sick dog to die in the bushes. It sets up a counterpart economy of its own, based also on the laws of competition, in which it devalues and exploits the spirit. These two economies maintain themselves at each other's expense, living upon each other's loss, collaborating without cease in mutual futility and absurdity....

The damages of our present agriculture all come from the determination to use the life of the soil as if it were an extractable resource like coal, to use living things as if they were machines, to impose scientific (that is, laboratory) exactitude upon living complexities that are ultimately mysterious.

If the soil is regarded as a machine, then its life, its involvement in living systems and cycles, must perforce be ignored. It must be treated as a dead, inert chemical mass. If its life is ignored, then so must be the natural sources of its fertility — and not only ignored, but scorned... [A]nimal manures are "wastes"; "efficiency" cannot use them. — Wendell Berry, *The Unsettling of America: Culture and Agriculture* (1977)

In 1649 to St. Georges Hill
A ragged band they called the Diggers came to show
       the people's will.
They defied the landlords, thy defied the law,
They were the dispossessed reclaiming what was theirs.

We come in peace they said, to dig and sow,
We come to work the land in common & to make the
       wastelands grow.

This earth divided we will make whole,
So it will be a common treasury for all.

The sin of property we do disdain.
No one has any right to buy & sell the earth for private gain.
By theft & murder they took the land,
Now everywhere the walls spring up at their command.

They made the laws to chain us well.
The clergy dazzle us with Heaven or they damn us into Hell.
We will not worship the Gods they serve,
The God of greed who feeds the rich while poor folks starve.

We work we eat together, we need no swords.
We will not bow to the masters or pay rent to the Lords.
We are free people though we are poor,
You Diggers all rise up for freedom, rise up now.

From the men of property the orders came.
They sent the hired men & troopers to wipe out
          the Digger claim.
Tear down their cottages, destroy their corn.
They were dispersed, but their vision lingers on.
          — Leon Rosselson, "The World Turned Upside Down"

i. The Great Unravelling

The next staging ground for the Rosicrucian spiritual insurgency was provided by the Civil War in England two decades later. Not, obviously, that Rosicrucianism was the *cause* of the war, only that the ideals of the Brotherhood became a central part of the ideological debate the rebellion elicited; in that debate the intellectual framework for modern times was first hammered into place.

I shall argue that the attacks on Rosicrucian ideology and ideas by Descartes, Mersenne, and Gassendi in France and by Thomas Hobbes, Walter Charleton, and Robert Boyle, among many others in England, together with the parallel contemporary war against witchcraft (Chapter 10) served to define the broad outlines of the consciousness of the emerging modernity.

These attacks effectively crafted the concepts and principles regarding the shape of the natural world and the way it can undergo changes that was used to mold an orthodox "reality." This new orthodoxy constituted an ideological forceps that was instrumental in the birthing of the systems of nation-states and of capitalism[1] that were beginning to play such formidable roles in early modern European (and world) history.

Isaac Newton's system of the world, meaning his ideas on motion, light, forces, matter, mathematics, and methods of finding the truth about the world will be shown[2] to be a carefully crafted (though often unconscious) negotiation of the allowable spaces reality could then occupy in the newly crafted framework, in which a largely hidden dialectic can be seen playing back and forth between inner and outer layers of the doctrines Newton believed.

James I's refusal to go along with the tremendous support for the campaign of the Elector Palatine in Bohemia, and his conduct of a foreign policy with a conciliating attitude towards the Hapsburgs, at such odds with powerful voices in England, could be seen as the first major rupture in the newly established Stuart monarchy. Ultimately the crisis of the early Stuarts would prove to be the undoing of his son, Charles I. By the time matters of State broke down completely and Civil War broke out in 1642, any number of fundamental differences between the Crown and the Parliament had bubbled to an already fairly fetid surface, and a variety of reasons for the apparent rottenness were in contention: religious differences; disagreements over foreign policy; trade; the finances of the State; the prerogatives of the Crown, especially in legal and taxation matters; constitutional differences over who could exercise what powers; and so on, all at a time of poor harvests (1637 and 1660–61, especially)[3] amidst an unprecedented outpouring of pamphlets arguing a rich blend of causes, particularly once censorship ended. After Charles I had accused five leaders of the House of Commons of treason and, accompanied by a few hundred soldiers, first demanded their surrender and then unsuccessfully attempted to seize them, Parliament began to raise its own army. Charles I prepared to meet it. There is no need here to follow the course of the Great Rebellion, as it came to be called. We shall concern ourselves only with broad patterns, how, at critical moments, the dust appeared to be settling, and how certain key questions came to be posed.

The Civil War and revolution of 1642–1649, however, was the first of its kind in Europe and carved out the mold in which subsequent revolutionary upheavals in European history (in 1789, 1848, 1871, and 1917) were pretty much, for better or worse, cast. Its features, accordingly, carry considerable historical inertia, so to speak.

The Civil War between the Parliamentary and Royalist forces lasted seven years. Within the Parliamentary side, there existed several divisions, primarily, on the one hand, between the more democratic and more radical (politically

---

[1] There is, of course, a vast sea of books on the origins of capitalism. One I found particularly illuminating is Ellen Meiskins Wood, *The Origin of Capitalism* (New York: Monthly Review Press, 1999).

[2] Chapters 12 through 14.

[3] Sidney Mintz, *op. cit.*, pp. 76, 241 n. 8.

and religiously) army, and, on the other, the Parliament, more representative of moneyed and landed interests; other, often volatile, differences arose, especially towards the end of the Civil War, between the more hierarchical Presbyterians and the followers of the several more anarchistic Independent sects; between the propertied and those utterly without; and there were important regional differences.

It was a Parliament from which the Army forcibly ejected some members that eventually put an end to the on-again/off-again bargaining with the already militarily-defeated Charles I. Throughout a series of military and political setbacks, the King had steadfastly refused to accede to Parliamentary demands and had pursued secret negotiations with third parties with whom he thought he could cut a better deal. Instead the "Rump Parliament," what was left after nearly 100 members were removed by the Army, voted to bring Charles I to trial for treason. When the House of Lords refused to go along with such "extremism," the Commons simply declared itself the sole seat of legislative power and proceeded to try Charles before a high court, where he was sentenced to death. In January, 1649, Charles I was beheaded.

Power now lay in a Council of State, led by Oliver Cromwell (who had commanded the Parliamentary armies[1]) under a Commonwealth and then from 1653 a Protectorate until 1660. During this time the monarchy, the House of Lords, and the Church of England were all abolished.

The dialectic within the Civil War between the more moderate Parliament, with its legal prerogatives, and the more militant army, which felt it had a more legitimate claim to power and had the might to back its claim, resulted from the far more inclusive social base of the Cromwellian army and was reflected in the move to radical democracy within its ranks. At its most radical, assemblies of the rank-and-file soldiers debated important policy decisions and selected their officers by vote.

The divisions between Parliament and the New Model Army of Cromwell were also religious, with Parliament more sympathetic to a hierarchical, Presbyterian form of church, while the Army was dominated at times by Independents who tolerated an astoundingly wide range both of church forms and doctrinal positions.

ii. RADICAL VISIONS

It was within the ranks of the Independents, or of the assemblies in which they constituted a major voice, that some of the more interesting debates occurred in the course of the English revolution. Though socially and numerically in no position ultimately to enforce their demands, by virtue of the extreme actions being taken, and their own situation as a sometimes dominant voice within

---

[1] Originally, Cromwell had risen to prominence as the "Defender of the Fens," or wetlands; in effect, for defending the "wild places" against capitalist development.

the Army, the Independents often got to set the agenda, to pose the questions of the day that other social groupings then needed to address.[1]

The broadest implications of the ferment would have been readily apparent at the time, all the more so in light of the uprising in Naples in 1647, several years after the onset of the English rebellion. The uprising had begun as a simple

---

[1] We can see a parallel to this example of political radicals playing an historic role vastly disproportional to their numbers in the US in the 1960s, when a relatively small (and, by conventional accounts, Marxist and bourgeois alike, economically and hence socially marginal) sector of the population, the Southern black sharecroppers, in conjunction with young (frequently college student) activists, managed to make *its* agenda in large measure that of the country (and soon the world) as a whole; a little later a similar process occurred with the student-led opposition to the Vietnam (by its end, the Indochinese) War.

In both cases, relatively small groups were able to define the issues that needed to be resolved because *their* concerns managed to spread to other, less marginal, social strata. In the case of the student anti-war and anti-racist left, this critical point dramatically occurred with the San Francisco State College student strike, for unlike the earlier outbreaks of student insurgency at Columbia University, Cornell University, the University of Wisconsin, or Berkeley — more or less residential institutions of the elite or near-elite — San Francisco State was attended by a largely urban working class, and included students who at night went back home to one or another of the city's black, Japanese, Chinese, or Latino ghettoes and *barrios*, which is why the suppression of the rebellion there was a much higher priority for ruling circles; indeed, it won a Senate seat for S.I. Hayakawa, the "heroic" president of S.F. State at the time.

I would argue that in England in the 1640s the Civil War and revolution pushed to the fore certain questions that mainly the far left were willing to bring out into the open. In that lay their not-inconsiderable power and influence, which was much greater than a mere counting of adherents would lead one to expect. Similarly, I would think, the Student Non-Violent Coordinating Committee (SNCC), a few hundred students of working-class background, through its design of the Mississippi Freedom Summer in 1964, was able decisively to shape the historical moment in 1963 and '64 by posing, through their actions, the questions that history needed to have asked, as did the Students for a Democratic Society (SDS) several years later. In playing roles such as these, groups that appear, on a quantitative or even a structural basis, to be of little or no significance, may emerge as major actors, though ultimately their lack of real power prevents them, in 1653 as in 1969, from being decisive in how matters are resolved and in reinventing the whole of society on a new basis. (See, on SNCC's role, Charles M. Payne, *I've Got the Light of Freedom: The Organizing Tradition and the Mississippi Freedom Struggle* [Berkeley: Univ. of California Press, 1995].) Thanks to Susanna Martinez for sharing her insights about the San Francisco State College strike.

protest against a new tax imposed by their Spanish viceroy on Naples' prized fruit. It was led by a Neapolitan, Masaniello, a fisherman, and involved a broad array of "market women, carters, porters, sailors, fishermen, weavers, silk winders, and all the other poor" in Naples.[1] Within days, over 150,000 were in the streets, opening prisons, burning tax records, and distributing free books to students. Restrictions on what garments the nobility would be allowed to wear were issued and their furnishings dragged from palaces and burned in the streets, while their palaces were set to be destroyed. Looting was strictly prohibited, so "that all the World may know, we have not enterpris'd this businesse to enrich ourselves but to vindicate the common liberty." Prices of bread fell. As the luxuries of the aristocracy burned, one revolutionary proclaimed. "These Goods are got out of our Heart's Blood; and as they burn, so ought the Souls and Bodies of those Blood-suckers who own them, to fry in the Fire of Hell."

The rebellion was short-lived (ten days), but as the "first time the proletariat of any European city seized power and governed alone," it both shocked and inspired contemporaries, including many in England, which recently had begun sending a few thousand sailors a year to Naples as English sea trade expanded. The sailors brought back news of the rebellion.

In 1649, a play was published, *The Rebellion of Naples or the Tragedy of Massenello... Written by a Gentleman who was an eye-witness... upon the Bloody... Streets of Naples*, and an Italian history of the uprising was translated into English one year later. In *The Rebellion of Naples*, a major theme is that of solidarity and the cry (from a mutiny of 1626) is raised, "One and all, One and all, One and all." An advisor to Massenello, one character in the play, promises to "level the high walls of government with the earth they stood on: The Axe is already laid to the root."

The issue of slavery was a central theme in both the play and the 1650 history; some of the rebels had in fact been slaves. The history commented on the armed women and girl street-fighters. Massenello had a black daughter, and in the play she sings a song praising blackness.

Authorities in the American colonies (Maryland, New York, Massachusetts, and Virginia), as well as those in London, condemned the Neopolitan rebels. In November, 1647, four months after the revolt, in the middle of the central debates (at Putney) on what should now be done by the English revolution, a London speaker proclaimed, "The same business we are upon is perfected in Naples, for if any person stand up for monarchy there, he is immediately hanged at his door."[2]

---

1 My discussion of the rebellion of Naples and all of the quotations are from the remarkable analysis in Linebaugh and Rediker, *op. cit.*, pp. 112–16.

2 It was at the tine of the Putney debates that the political meaning of the word "revolution" first emerged, according to Benjamin Woolley, *Heal Thyself: Nicholas Culpepper and the Seventeenth Century Struggle to Bring Medicine to the People* (New York: Harper Collins, 2004), p. 260.

In these wide-ranging debates of the English Civil War, fundamental is-sues were aired in an attempt to decide how England should now be gov-erned. The hierarchy of the Church of England, the bone of contention for many decades, was dissolved, and though that ended the forced tithing to pay for clergy, it hardly settled the multitude of contentious issues. Precisely who — what classes? what gender? — was to have a voice in England was widely discussed; so too the role of women as possible preachers, the question of whether they, too, should be educated. The limits to religious toleration, the rules governing sexual behavior, the nature of sin, the wider implications of ownership of property — all these and more were debated openly, or implic-itly negotiated in actions taken.

These abstractions will acquire color, texture, and specificity in a cursory survey of the wide range of groups constituting the Independents.[1] As was com-mon at the time, the Fifth Monarchy Men focused on the imminence of the mil-lennium, and the literal reign of Christ that was about to begin. But they then went further, armed themselves, and carried out a series of uprisings with the goal of removing the ungodly impediments (officials) to the reign of Christ and installing true Saints, to rule civil society until the final conflagration. Mean-while the Fifth Monarchists drew up the laws that should apply during the Kingdom of the Saints.

The Behemists, another Independent sect, were followers of a German shoe-maker, Jakob Boehme, an alchemist, occult thinker, healer, and radical democ-rat.[2] Anabaptists, whom we met as the radical wing of the Reformation early on, and who in the 16th century had seized control of the city of Münster, ruling it as a Christian theocratic republic, were very active in the English uprising. Goods and some spouses were shared by their believers. The Friends, forerun-ners of today's Quakers, then as now focused on the process of resolving ques-tions, concerned lest they reproduce within their own ranks the very qualities they were determined to extirpate from the established Church.[3]

---

[1] P. M. Rattansi, *The Literary Attack on Science in the 17th and 18th Centuries,* 1961, doctoral dissertation, London School of Economics, pp. 77–78, 107–08. For an eye-popping glimpse of the beliefs and practices of the Independents, see Hill, *op. cit.*; also, Margaret Bailey, *Milton and Jakob Boehme: A Study of German Mysti-cism in Seventeenth Century England* (New York: 1914), p. 232.

[2] On Boehme, see Yates, *op. cit.,* p. 99.

[3] A very nice discussion is found in Hudson, *op. cit.,* pp. 51–56. On the Fifth Monarchy Men, see Louise F. Brown, *The Political Activities of the Baptists and Fifth Monarchy Men in England During the Interregnum* (Oxford: 1912), and my Cornell University doctoral dissertation, *Providence and the Mechanical Philosophy: The Creation and Dissolution of the World in Newtonian Thought. A Study of the Relations of Science and Religion in Seventeenth Century England* (1968), Chapter Four. Also, P. G. Rogers, *The Fifth Monarchy Men* (London: Oxford Univ. Press, 1966).

Levellers were acutely conscious of issues of class and the rule of property. The Diggers, sometimes known as the True Levellers, under the leadership of Gerrard Winstanley, on April 1, 1649, gathered on St. George's Hill on the outskirts of London to dig the waste land for cultivation, since, as Winstanley put it, "the earth should be made a common treasury of livelihood to whole mankind, without respect of persons."[1] Authorities feared that the two or three dozen laborers at St. George's would soon grow to four or five thousand and that "they have some design in hand."[2] The Diggers, too, were acutely tuned to class differentiation and privilege.

(That Winstanley chose April 1, All Fools Day, for his action is surely significant, for that was the day when distinctions of class and station were traditionally flouted at will, a day when the "lower orders" could violate with impunity the rules of deference that were used to enforce the gross inequalities between the classes, a custom dating back to prehistoric times. Presumably All Fools Day was a kind of historical shadow cast from earlier eras when distinctions of station did not exist and the gross inequalities which defined social classes were rare, a ritualized act of collective remembering and reenactment that, I would think, was the small concession extracted from the masters when they first were able to enforce their new prerogatives and supremacy. Indeed, might this be a shadow of a not-so-mythical Golden Age? Whether my conjecture be correct or not, it seems obvious that Winstanley would have chosen April 1 for this attempt at taking back commons as a way of proclaiming that the social reversals allowed on that *one* day were to be extended for *all* days in a new, classless society.)[3]

Other Independents also focused on class distinctions and stations. The Family of Love, whose roots go back to a 16th-century movement that had been composed, at least in the 1570s, primarily of the "mean people" like cowherds, clothiers, etc., believed that heaven and hell were only in this life, that the Bible was only an allegory and the Sabbath just another day. They were drawn to schemes of sharing property and other agrarian communist notions. John Dee had some connections with them.[4]

Many of the sects believed that the Civil War was really in order to complete the Reformation and to establish a New Jerusalem, where true piety could flourish. There was considerable agreement that private property (a *sine qua non*

---

[1] Hill, *op. cit.*, pp. 88–90.

[2] Quoted in Hill, *op cit.*, pp. 88–90, from the Clark Papers.

[3] G. E. Aylmer, "The Religion of Gerrard Winstanley," in (ed.) J. F. McGregor and B. Reay, *op. cit.*, p. 102, suggests there were other sites besides the one established by Winstanley himself on St. George's Hill near London, probably as many as seven; Hill (p. 99) suggests nearly a dozen.

[4] For the Family of Love, see Merchant, *op. cit.*; Hill, *op. cit.*; Yates, *op. cit.*; Federici, *op. cit.*; and Evans, *Witchcraft and the Gay Counterculture*, pp. 60–61. Also, Woolley, *Queen's Conjuror*, pp. 63, 186.

for capitalism) blocked any path to holiness. Indeed, Winstanley claimed it was the cause of the Fall and the source of all sin.[1]

Besides the Familists, many of the Independent sects believed in a kind of agrarian communism, where property, and for some, spouses, were shared. Other stretching, or in some cases, abandonment, of sexual boundaries took place, and the Ranters were accused of naked and drunken orgies, sometimes in churches, which they said were their rituals.[2] Some Ranters said that an act is sinful only if the person doing it perceived it as such. With that in mind, we can interpret Clarkson's and Coppe's practices of sexual freedom, as well as the latter's claim to have been taken into the bosom of "the King of Glory" by means of sexual passion.[3] Winstanley complained about Ranters that they had too much emphasis on "meat, drink, pleasure and women."[4]

At the end of this period of wild experimentation and debates over sexual roles in England, demands for instilling a much narrower range of acceptable behavior mounted, and it is this reaction that we have come to know as the Puritan revolution. But Puritan strictures against display in language, dress, dance, theater, and so on, were in part reactions against the earlier public displays that had flagrantly violated conventional Christian mores.

iii. The Nature of the Dispossessed

As the questions about how to make terms with the defeated Charles I were debated, and when, after his execution, a newly constituted society faced further, even more fundamental questions as to how the English should now rule themselves, discussions ranged far and wide. Especially important for our inquiry were the views of nature articulated by the Independents. Understanding their thoughts about nature will allow us to comprehend the significance of the reaction *against* their view that exploded in the mid-1650s.

Against the extreme positions advocated in the course of the revolution, new views of nature, defined precisely in terms to fundamentally differ from the

---

[1] Hill, *op. cit.*, pp. 131, 255.

[2] Cynics might see only self-serving rhetoric in such claims, but sexual union as a form of ecstatic worship, as discussed in Chapter 4, has a long history in popular religion and magic, in witchcraft, for example, and possibly in alchemy. There is also a tendency in periods of insurgency to question sexual and gender boundaries, as is nicely illustrated in André Malraux's novel of the early (1927) days of the Chinese Communist Party, *La Condition Humain* or *Man's Fate* (1933), where on the eve of a planned insurrection, May tells her lover of her desire to start an affair with another comrade. On the charges against the Ranters, see Linebaugh and Rediker, *op. cit.*, p. 86; Merchant, *op. cit.*, p. 124; Evans, *Witchcraft and the Gay Counterculture*, p. 22; McGregor and Reay, *op. cit.*, p. 130.

[3] Hill, *op. cit.*, pp. 161, 254.

[4] G. E. Aylmer, "The Religion of Gerrard Winstanley," in McGregor and Reay, *op. cit.*, pp. 106, 130..

views of the Independents, were advocated by powerful voices in English society, as we shall see. These new, anti-Independent notions, in turn, came to shape the concept of reality that constituted the scientific revolution and have continued to dominate modern consciousness ever since.

For a great many, if not most, of the Independents, nature was alive. Their God was *in* nature, not *above* and *separate* from it; as in pantheism, nature was everywhere infused with spirit, with deity, everywhere numinous; everything in some measure was sacred. The Muggletonians, followers of Lodowicke Muggleton, and the Ranters were accused of proclaiming that the only God was nature. Muggleton expressed indifference towards any afterlife, content to "but lie still in earth for ever...." Many others tended to equate God and nature, including some of the Seekers and the Family of Love. Winstanley stated that the only preachers needed were the objects of creation.[1]

Many were the currents, large and small, contributing to the mighty river that magical/animist thinking had become by the time of the Civil War. Ideas from Arabic and Hindu treatises, English folk magic, Rosicrucianism, astrology, the alchemical theories of Paracelsus (the 16th-century German healer), cabala, the Hermetic doctrines espoused by Renaissance Neoplatonists like Ficino, Pico della Mirandola, and Giordano Bruno, and German mystical theology all had their adherents, their own tributaries.[2]

Following the arguments of Frances Yates, I shall tend to refer to the overall contours and temper of these as "Rosicrucian," without meaning that all who believed in occult ideas during the Civil War period and after were members (if indeed, the Rosicrucians *had* actual members) or narrowly adhered to their tenets, as opposed to, say, cabalistic views. I use the catchall phrase "Rosicrucian" primarily for two reasons: first, I agree with Yates that it was their advocacy of a broadened view of reformation that started the particular 17th-century ferment over alchemical doctrine; and second, because very frequently the critics of the Independents accused them, as we shall see, of all being under the sway of Rosicrucian notions. Rosicrucian theories are an important focus here, too, because far more than in Hindu theology or astrology or mystical theology do we find in alchemy a developed picture of nature and how she works. What I label "Rosicrucian" therefore, should be understood to have become, by the time of the Civil War, a broad movement, encompassing diverse currents.

However we choose to label them, though, there is little question that, as Piyo Rattansi has pointed out, "the natural magic tradition attained unprecedented in-

---

[1] *Ibid.*, pp. 139, 143, 165. Thomas Edwards, in his *Gangrena* (London: 1646), charged that the heresy that each creature "that hath life and breath being an efflux from God" was a dangerous contemporary belief. ("Introduction" in McGregor and Reay, *op. cit.*, p. 13).

[2] Hudson, *op. cit.*, pp. 54–55. John Dury, *A Seasonable Discourse* (London, 1649) called for the study of Oriental tongues and Jewish mysteries.

fluence and attention in England during the Puritan Revolution...."[1] In the midst of far-ranging debates on who should be able to vote or about agrarian issues, the Independents made demands for courses on alchemy at Oxford and Cambridge. More books on astrology, alchemy, and Paracelsian medicine were translated in England in the decade from 1650 to 1660 than in the whole of the previous century,[2] bringing out into the open beliefs common in the countryside. Many continental works of magic and alchemy were now translated into English, as were the Rosicrucian manifestos, nearly three decades after their original appearance. Familists were involved with alchemy and astrology; one of them translated the works of the legendary founder of alchemy, Hermes Trismegistus.[3]

A Seeker leader, William Erbery, was drawn to the ideas of Jakob Boehme, as was Muggleton, and, according to critics, so too were the Quakers. An attack on the Ranters claimed astrology was very popular in their ranks. Lawrence Clarkson, the Ranter, was a practicing astrologer; another such was the Fifth Monarchist leader, John Spittlehouse. There were widespread astrological interests among other Ranters, Seekers, Familists, Quakers, and Anabaptists. Winstanley had alchemical sympathies.[4]

In order to comprehend why such Rosicrucian ideas spread so broadly in the midst of England's Civil War and to understand their wider significance, it will be helpful to make a cursory taxonomy of the dispossessed in 17th-century England. In his masterful *The World Turned Upside Down*, the English historian Christopher Hill draws our attention to the people who, while outside the fight between Parliament and the Crown, having little stake in either side's winning, were *not* outside the broader debates over issues the Civil War brought forward.

The extended process of expropriation of the peasantry, well underway by the mid-17th century in England, had created a large mass of what Hill calls the "masterless people," meaning those on the margins, frequently transients or squatters in forests and removed from the rule of either clergy or landlord. The masterless might include immigrants, pedlars, hired laborers, vagabonds, petty criminals, and growing numbers of journeymen in numerous crafts as the onrush of capitalism rendered them superfluous. Travelling performers, jugglers, musicians, acrobats, and players, were also often found among those at the mar-

---

[1] The first formal lodge of the Freemasons in England, according to Thomas De Quincey, was in 1646, though he believed it possible that private meetings had occurred earlier. De Quincey, "Historico-Critical Inquiry into the Origins of Rosicrucianism & Freemasonry," *London Magazine* (1824), p. 259; P. M. Rattansi, "Paracelsus and the Puritan Revolution," *Ambix* XI (1963)1: pp. 24–32.

[2] Allen Debus, *The English Paracelsians* (London: Oldbourne, 1965), pp. 125–26, 178; Bailey, *op. cit.*, p. 60f; Allen Debus, *Chemical Dreams of the Renaissance* (Cambridge: 1968), p. 26. Thomas, *op. cit.*, p. 227.

[3] Hill, *op. cit.*, p. 149, 232–34.

[4] *Ibid.*, pp. 114, 232–33, 240.

gins. At one point, Cromwell's army had to confront armed masses whose issues differed markedly from those heard in Parliament.[1]

Given the roiling social situation, even those whose social standing removed them from formal debates over policies and church doctrines could participate in other ways, especially given the explosion of pamphlet literature that the end of censorship facilitated.

iv. Marginal Issues

To return to the question raised above: why *did* the "masterless people" or men and women in the Independent sects turn to Rosicrucian ideals and ideology during the Civil War and after? What at first glance seems puzzling, at a closer look reveals a clear pattern of several overlapping interests, points of view, and doctrines that were shared between Rosicrucianism and the radical Independents.

First, both the political movements intent on a thorough reformation in religious matters and those involved in Rosicrucianism or other occult traditions shared a marked hostility to the Church of England, once it was clear that reforming it was out of the question. The forced tithing to support clergy, many of whom never even appeared in their churches, was intolerable. The Church's rigid hierarchies, generous and exclusive State subsidies, lack of toleration, and exclusive male voice, among other things, made the Church an obvious target for both political radicals and occultists.

Second, the various streams of occult thought rested on categories and processes that readily lent themselves to radical agitation. Magic, alchemy, astrology, cabala — all assume a logic of polarities, where all that is exists in a state of tension between contrary forces, perhaps between a number of contraries, and the playing out of those oppositions is what shapes and forms things, events, and history, as was discussed in Part One.[2]

Both the Aristotelian logic (that came to dominate formal thought in the late medieval period) and the scientific logic (that emerged victorious in the course of the scientific revolution) rejected the notion, advanced by the mystics and sectarians, that reality is fluid and inherently dynamic. The Aristotelians, and in the later scientific revolution the scientists, asserted that a thing had to be defined by its classification as only *one* of any pair of oppositions — for example, as wet *or* dry — that it be *either* "A" *or* "not-A," hot or cold, sweet or bitter, not, as the magical doctrines claimed, that it can be both hot *and* cold, wet *and* dry, can be bittersweet or a case of love/hate.

Emphasizing the transitory state of all reality, this logic establishes *transformation* or *change,* rather than *things,* as what is ontologically primary. Such a logic intuitively appeals to those in the thick of social struggles to transform their

---

[1] Hill, *op. cit.,* p. 20.
[2] See pp. 95–98.

world, as well as to adepts seeking to transmute matter from one form to another. This logic sees all change as arising *internally*, due to tensions between the several polarities, not, as with Aristotle (somewhat) and the later science, *externally*.

We would expect, given their emphasis on one's inner voice and individual conscience rather than outside authority as the definers of a person's actions, that the Independent sects would easily understand how such a logic of opposites, what we can accurately identify as a "dialectical" logic, could serve them as an ideological tool, justifying any of their insurrectionary activities.[1]

Third, the logic of polarities readily offered succor and encouragement to "enthusiasm" — that behavior during the Civil War and revolution that so outraged the men of sobriety and property when they saw boundaries rudely breached by men and women in the grip of their passions. The word itself, used for the first time in 1603, comes from the Greek and literally means "full of gods." It was enthusiasm that explained the beheading of Charles I, the seizure of land from their "lawful" owners, the abolition of the House of Lords, or the reported fucking in the churches done by some Ranters as part of their rituals. Religiously, enthusiasm, to which we shall frequently return in the remainder of our discussion, was the free spirit let loose without any external authority and could include speaking in tongues or prophesying.

Taken at another level, we might say that the Rosicrucian concept of the inherent *activity* of all matter fed the ongoing *activism* of the enthusiasts.[2] The world's inherent lifefulness, seen in its incessant transformations and based on the immanence of divinity, could encourage the self-confidence needed by militants to allow them to do battle against such unspeakable odds and to take on the most powerful of institutions, the most exalted of beliefs. Emphasizing the individual man or woman's ability to act upon the world, enthusiasts found in magic a pathway to their inner sources, thus emboldening would-be "gnostic saviors" that both the Hermetic myths and the Civil War quite literally brought out of the woods.[3]

Readers should note: I am suggesting that popular movements in the past gravitated towards a dialectical logic because it emboldened them to act, long before a Marx arrived on the scene to codify in a formalized language this method of understanding the world that he had learned from the German philosopher, G.W. Hegel. In fact Hegel, as is clear from his *History of Philosophy*, developed his own dialectical approach in part by studying Giordano Bruno,

---

[1] Other scholars, Marxists or ex-Marxists, have noted this dialectical quality in forms of occult thought, most notably Joseph Needham and Christopher Hill.
[2] Thomas Harmon Jobe, "The Devil in Restoration Science: The Glanvill–Webster Debate," *Isis* 72 (1981): "The theology of the sects tended to support immanentalism, or the presence of God in things, and illuminationism, or the immediate inspiration of the individual by God," p. 345.
[3] I owe this phrase to Alison Coudert, in remarks given at the 1987 conference on "Latitudinarianism, Science, and Society," in Los Angeles at the William Andrews Clark Library of UCLA, where we both delivered papers.

Jakob Boehme, and the popular movements in 17th-century England that I have just discussed.[1]

Fourth, I suspect both the marginalized masterless people and the practitioners of ceremonial or other forms of magic would have stood shoulder to shoulder in opposition to the continual assault on nature, on the wilderness. The woods that were cleared, the streams damned, or the meadows torn up were not only where the marginalized population frequently subsisted, squatting in the woods or hunting in the wetlands. They were also where one found the holy wells, sacred trees, or large, singularly shaped rock outcroppings where the village people from time immemorial had lit their bonfires, danced, and feasted at solstices, equinoxes, full or new moons, or at particular stages of the planting cycle to help their harvests, insure the fertility of their animals and of the village women, and help usher in changes in the seasons or of the moon. As Janet and Colin Bord write about such celebrations in England:

> Observation of the natural cycles, together with experience, taught the first farmers how they could promote the fertility of their land and crops and healthy cattle were not achieved solely by keeping the land fertile, important as that was; there were other invisible forces at work. Innumerable rituals were followed as man [*sic*] attempted to reinforce these subtle forces and to influence them to work in their favour: rituals to encourage the return of the life-giving sun, rituals to energize the sprouting seed, rituals to cause the rain to fall....[2]

Fifth, and last, after centuries of religious and political warfare, the 17th century in England and Europe was awash in millennarian views, widespread expectations of renewal, of fulfillment of ancient prophecies, of a time of universal peace and unlimited possibilities tied into apocalyptic upheavals and massive destruction. Such expectations describe alike the ends sought by radical Independents and the ideals of Rosicrucian visionaries.

* * *

I must immediately issue some important qualifications to all the generalizations I have just advanced. Important exceptions certainly existed to these five overlapping commonalities. Not every Rosicrucian came from the Independents; undoubtedly, there were aristocratic occultists — alchemists, for example.[3] Even

---

[1] As we shall discuss at the end of Part Two.

[2] Bord and Bord, *op. cit.,* p. 115.

[3] It is thought Charles II was interested in alchemy. Betty Jo Teeter Dobbs, *The Foundations of Newton's Alchemy or "The Hunting of the Greene Lyon"* (Cambridge, England: Cambridge Univ. Press, 1983), p 78, as was Philip II of Spain (French, *op. cit.,* p. 69) as well as Sir Robert Moray and of course, as we shall see, Robert Boyle.

so, in the minds of their critics at the time, there was a profound linkage that bound left-wing activism and the forms of magic I have been describing. Their accusations, in turn, rested on a substantial number of overlappings.[1]

v. MECHANIZATION TO THE RESCUE

Reaction against the Rosicrucian view arose, as described above, very soon after the first manifestos were published in 1614. With the crushing defeat of Christian of Anhalt's Protestant troops in the Battle of White Mountain in 1620, the attacks increased both in number and fury. It was not until after the Rosicrucians were rumored to have resurfaced in 1623, however, that a systematic attempt was really mounted to undermine and destroy each of the Rosicrucian premises and conclusions. The world-view that was thus constructed is the outlook, for the most part, still dominant today.

The remainder of Part Two will consist of an extended look at the new conceptual cosmos and how it was created in the latter part of the scientific revolution, as well as an analysis of how it served to re-mold the natural world from a place that traditionally had been viewed by the peasantry in awe and reverence into the "repository" of "resources"[2] more suitable for a capitalist reckoning. Theories of material reality that would come to dominate discourse within the community of natural philosophers by the second half of the 17th century would take as their premise the utter passivity of dead matter, the need for understanding all change as coming to any object or being from the outside — usually from the impact of another object or being, in a philosophical construct called the "mechanical philosophy." That Isaac Newton, who is credited with this conception, did not himself believe in such views, in the final analysis did not matter, for reasons we shall explore later.

Some scholars have argued that Newton's very real departures from this strict mechanical worldview (the subject of Chapters 12 through 14) was not so unusual, that others — most notably Robert Hooke — similarly used non-mechanical explanations not rooted in impact causality.[3] That others besides Newton

---

[1] On alchemy and political reform, see Dobbs, *Foundations*, p. 59. While chapter and verse might be cited for some of these general commonalities I have suggested (notably, the fifth one, having to do with millennarianism), some of it, of necessity, is more speculative (the fourth, concerning the destroyed meadows as places of ritual), and the rest are a little of both (the first, opposition to the Church of England, second, their common dialectical logic, and third, enthusiasm) Inasmuch as my purpose here is to make plausible what otherwise seems merely odd, a certain degree of conjecture and *just supposing* is, I would hope, acceptable.

[2] As mentioned earlier, the word "resources" was first used in 1611.

[3] See John Henry, "Robert Hooke, the Incongrous Mechanist," in *Robert Hooke: New Studies* (ed.) by Michael Hunter and Simon Schaffer (Woodbridge, England: The Boyloll Press, 1989), pp.149–80.

should find that strict adherence to the axioms of the mechanical philosophy was impossible should not, however, detract from my argument here, for all of the *public* pronouncements of the mechanists repeatedly emphasized the utter passivity of the underlying matter that was acted on by impact from other bodies. This is the view that came to define orthodoxy.

Though rural people certainly did not relinquish their comprehension of a living nature overnight, and for many of them, ever, it was a belief now under serious attack, quite literally undermined by the new understanding of nature resulting from the scientific revolution and, so it appeared, from the laws of nature discovered by Newton. Holding nature in awe, as revealing a sacred presence and therefore to be treated respectfully and with restraint, was henceforth considered more and more by people with education as mere superstition.[1]

While the rest of Part Two will demonstrate just how this view prevailed, Part Three will extend the analysis begun here to demonstrate how Information Age ideology simply pushes the 17th-century view of the dead world further along in the direction it was already headed, but now with far graver ecological, political, and cultural ramifications. For now, let us turn to a more detailed discussion of how the attack on living nature was carried out.

---

[1] Interesting that the Greek word, εκρταριρ (ecstasy) is sometimes translated into Latin as *superstitio*. Barbara Ehrenreich, *Dancing in the Streets*, p. 48.

8

Subverting the Imagination

In our fear to deal with the material world we make matter inert, and then we conjure up spirits to enliven it. Reality falls apart, split into the alternate domains, equally unreal, of the grossly material and the purely spiritual: the dark and the light, the passive and the active, matter and energy, prostitute and princess, masses and elite, heaven and hell. Repression polarizes the world into opposites that are both nonexistent, obverse sides of a single fantasy that once had been the world. — Bert Alpert, *Inversions* (1973)

The cornerstone of the scientific method is the postulate that nature is objective. In other words, the *systematic* denial "true" knowledge can be reached by interpreting phenomena in terms of final causes — that is to say, of "purpose".… This pure postulate is impossible to demonstrate, for it is obviously impossible to imagine an experiment proving the *non-existence* anywhere in nature of a purpose, or a pursued end. But the postulate of objectivity is consubstantial with science, and has guided the whole of its prodigious development for three centuries. It is impossible to escape it, even provisionally or in a limited area, without departing from the domain of science itself. — Nobel laureate Jacques Monod, a molecular biologist, *Chance and Necessity: An Essay on the Natural Philosophy of Modern Biology* (1971), as quoted in Jeremy Narby, *The Cosmic Serpent: DNA and the Origins of Knowledge* (1998).

The storage of fragmented reality in mechanically delimited compartments, manifesting itself in productive relations as bureaucracy, is also visible socially in formal manners, psychologically as compulsion, and scientifically and philosophically as mechanistic method and theory. In all these the common characteristic is a strict isolation of things and people and of parts of things…so that they seem to exist in and of themselves in disparate, particulate fragments. The details become detached as do the persons, interacting but never interpenetrating, arriving and departing, but never transforming, a dead world of fixed forms that replace each other as cause-and-effect in quick succession — like so many cinema frames which give the appearance of motion but are after all only the operation of a wound-up machine." — Bert Alpert, *op. cit.*

I. Taking Aim at the Occult

Marin Mersenne was particularly horrified by the appearance in 1623 of the Rosicrucian placards in Paris. The pretensions of the alchemists were extremely dangerous, Mersenne believed, and had to be exposed even as the sect itself was destroyed. To that end Mersenne devoted his life, gathering around him like-minded thinkers, many of them the cream of the second half of the 17th-century scientific community. To an astonishing degree Mersenne succeeded in his enterprise, what amounted to a multifaceted intellectual counter-revolution. Together with philosophical allies, he undertook a series of campaigns to redefine the totality of European culture, from music to language to natural philosophy. The shape of European formal thinking, as a result, was forever transformed.

What Mersenne, who later became a monk of the Minorite order, most feared about Rosicrucianism was its bid to become a "sort of counter-church," providing a path to "salvation without faith." Initially Mersenne set out to refute the English writer, Robert Fludd, who was allied with the Rosicrucians, directing his *Questiones in Genesim* (1623) against Fludd's 1616 defense of Rosicrucianism. He believed Fludd to be a heretic, an evil magician, and a defiler of Christianity. Attributing power to matter itself, as alchemy did, not only undercut the power of God, it threatened to become "the sole religion of mankind." Alarmingly, some alchemists openly compared the work of alchemy with the miracles performed by Christ.[1] Mersenne argued that since the Earth has no sense organs, it makes no sense to think of it as alive.[2]

---

[1] Berman, *Reenchantment*, pp. 107–10; Henry Khunruth, a 16th-century alchemist, identified the Philosophers Stone as Jesus Christ (Dobbs, Foundation, pp. 54–57), Boehme as Holy Spirit (Hillel Schwartz, *The French Prophets: The History of a Millennarian Group in Eighteenth Century England* (Berkeley: Univ. of California Press, 1980), p. 244.

[2] Merchant, *op.cit.,* p. 197.

Joining Mersenne in his campaign was another Minorite, Pierre Gassendi, who also first arrived in Paris in 1623, the year the Rosicrucian leaflets appeared there. In 1631, Gassendi was able to publish *his* critique of Fludd, deepening as well as broadening the attack. Gassendi sought to demolish the very basis of magical thinking, forever severing the network of pathways connecting the macrocosm, the vast cosmos and all that it contained, with the microcosm, or individual human.

It was those special connections that allowed the Rosicrucians to discern meaning in the trivial and mundane. For everything was *not* random, patterns and meanings could be gleaned from events, so insisted those who believed in magic. Those patterns are what allows the alchemist to monitor progress in the unfolding of the Great Work, wherein the mysteries of matter are finally mastered and brought under control.[1]

Gassendi took aim at Fludd's dialectical logic by arguing that the supposed polarities of light and dark are really not "opposites," but only gradations along a single scale.[2] Gassendi's lifework was to be a systematic revival of ancient atomistic theories as an ontological weapon for the attack on the worldview of the Rosicrucians, by constructing a mechanistic alternative.[3] Using a somewhat Christianized version of ancient Greek Epicurean atomism, Gassendi claimed that all phenomena in the world could be understood as the result of interactions among atoms, out of which all objects were constructed — and not just any interactions, but specifically *mechanical* ones. These consisted only of impacts of one atom against another or of some kind of pattern inherent in the atoms' motions relative to one another — for example, all of them moving along parallel lines. The atoms themselves were *without* qualities, save for their sizes, shapes, and motions. Using these kinds of explanations, Gassendi developed models of how fluidity, electrical attraction, heat, firmness, etc. were caused.

The ontological foundation of the macrocosm/microcosm nexus was the holistic realization that the whole is reflected in each of its parts It was this comprehension that Gasendi sought to destroy forever. A thorough analysis of nature

---

[1] As well, such patterns are the reason that "[wo]man is the measure of the universe," and they explain how new lovers search for signs in their first times together. Similarly, belief in such patterns encourages a coach to sense trouble when a couple of "bad breaks" mar a season's opening. In the hands of those who through gifts of training can traverse such webs from node to node, and at specific times in the lives of many of the rest of us, such signposts may make miracles possible. But it is fraught as well with the temptations of self-deception, perhaps more so for those not trained in the nuances of the map linking one realm to another — but ultimately in everyone. Meaning there are no guarantees — but then, that holds true for all ways of knowing.

[2] Merchant, *op. cit.*, pp. 199–200.

[3] Robert Kargon, *Atomism in England from Hariot to Newton* (Oxford: Clarendon Press, 1966).

showed that if one got down to basics there were only meaningless, random, ties between any two entities. The particle in one's blood cared not a whit that at some earlier point it had been part of some plant supposed to be beneficial to your particular ailment, or to the phase of the moon — nor could it. Once God had created the material world, according to Gassendi, blind mechanism took over and that is all there is.

A third French philosopher who played a major role in the concerted refutation of Rosicrucianism was René Descartes, himself, just returned to Paris in 1623, the year of the appearance of the Rosicrucian leaflets there, from travels abroad. During his travels, indeed, he had been in the Battle of White Mountain, fighting as a mercenary against the armies of Frederick V. Despite this, on his appearance in Paris in 1623, rumors spread that he himself was a Rosicrucian. Wanting to demonstrate that the suspicions were false, according to Descartes' 17th-century biographer, Descartes "made himself visible," that is, in contrast to the proposed code of the Rosicrucians, he was publicly outspoken and allowed himself to be readily identified. Even so, as Shea and Richard Watson have argued, contemporaries might have had good reasons to wonder about Descartes' possible ties to the shadowy Brotherhood.[1]

II. DESCARTES' SACRED TASK: THE PACIFICATION OF NATURE

Descartes' choice of *how* he would be "outspoken" was dramatic. When one evening he attended a gathering of French thinkers, including Mersenne, at the home of the papal nuncio, for a presentation by a man named Chandoux of his new alchemical philosophy, Descartes found his direction. Offering a refutation of Chandoux's alchemical theory following the presentation brought Descartes to the attention of Cardinal Bérulle, who was a leading voice in the Counter-reformation's Catholic League, and who advised Descartes that pursuing his line of attack should be understood as his sacred task.

Important differences separated Descartes' system from Gassendi's — the former denying that either atoms or a void could exist, while the latter made them fundamental elements of his theory. They both differed from Mersenne's system, too. But together with those of the English natural philosophers Thomas Hobbes, Walter Charleton, and Robert Boyle, who had all participated in Mersenne's weekly meetings during their exile during the Civil War, these thinkers established a new foundation for Western thought, what they called the "mechanical philosophy."[2]

---

1 William Shea, *The Magic of Numbers and Motion: Scientific Career of René Descartes* (Canton, Massachusetts: Science History Publications, 1993), Chap. 5. Descartes studied in 1620 with Johann Faulbaber, who contemporaries believed to be in a Rosicrucian order.

2 See below, pp. 190f. Watson, *op. cit.*, especially pp. 103–08.

The mechanical philosophy took as its axioms that all causation, indeed, all change in the natural world, was the result of "matter and motion." By hypothesizing certain-sized or -shaped particles or atoms and endowing them with appropriate theoretical motions, the mechanical philosophers sought to explain all of the world — its hardness, softness, sweetness, bitterness, coldness, stickiness, magnetic properties — all fell within the theoretical ken of the mechanical philosophers. Transformation of a body, it was clear to them, had to begin from *outside* the body, the result of an impact by another body. Thus the smallest particles or atoms themselves (hypothetical only, for they could not be observed) undergo no change, except that through impact they are moved hither and thither in their submicroscopic world. At their most basic level, then, there is no change; there is no alteration to the fundamental particles themselves, for they only undergo a form of "changeless change," as the historian of science Alexandre Koyré has expressed it.[1]

According to Locke, all land requires an outside mover, man, to subdue it by bringing it to a higher state of productivity, just as all brute matter, to the mechanical philosopher (of which Locke was one) is simply inert, lifeless, able to act (to change) only under the influence of outside forces: for land, this meant becoming someone's property, for the particles of matter, moving at a different speed and/or direction after being hit by another particle.

The central axiom of the mechanical philosophy was its insistence that matter *per se* was inert. Enunciated gradually, and with increasing clarity by Galileo, Kepler, and Descartes, inertia emerged, finally, in Newton's *Principia* as his first Law of Motion and, fundamentally, as the basis for his other Laws: "Every body continues in its state of rest, or of uniform motion in a right [i.e., straight] line, unless it is compelled to change that state by forces impressed upon it."[2]

Stated more plainly, Newton's law of inertia says that a body at rest will *stay at rest unless an outside force acts on it,* just as a body moving at a constant speed and in a straight line will *keep that constant motion unless an outside force acts to change it.* It

---

[1] See his *Newtonian Studies*, pp. 9–10, but also his *From the Closed World to the Infinite Universe* (New York: Harper & Bros., 1957). See Chapter Fourteen for my critique of Koyré, whose influence on Newtonian studies, including mine, was immense.

[2] Isaac Newton, *Mathematical Principles of Natural Philosophy and His System of the World* (ed.) Florian Cajori (Berkeley, California: Univ. of California Press, 1934), p. 13: "Law I." Henceforth, *Principia*. For our purposes, it is the mature mechanical philosophy that is of most interest. An encyclopedic treatment of how mechanism came to be can be found in E.J. Dijksterhuis, *The Mechanization of the World Picture* (Oxford, England: Oxford Univ. Press, 1961). Rupert Sheldrake, *Science Set Free: Ten Paths To New Discovery* (New York: Deepak Chopra Books, 2012) gives a more detailed history, along with a nuanced, insightful critique of mechanism.

is changes in motion, not motion itself, that henceforth require explanations ("forces") — thus giving an ontological priority to sameness, to stability.

"The word "inert" appeared in the English tongue in 1647. In ancient Rome it had referred, among other things, to idle people: sluggish, unskilled, and unemployable.[1]

iii. DEAD ON ARRIVAL: THE FATE OF NATURE IN THE SCIENTIFIC REVOLUTION[2]

These notions of the mechanical philosophy and of inertia redefined the matter of the cosmos as essentially passive. Nothing changed *of itself.* Change always came from elsewhere. Gassendi, according to Carolyn Merchant, believed that there "was no place for spontaneity in nature itself, nor could it be sanctioned in the human soul…. Spontaneity was an impulse of nature, of passion."[3]

Gassendi was not the only one to make the essential jump to human behavior. A banishing of spontaneity was the crux of the matter; indeed, it would come to serve as the template for the modern mentality. As nature goes, it was implied, so too people, their actions the result of external impositions on otherwise essentially passive beings in interactions with one another and with the world at large. In point of fact, the teaching *began* with the critical necessity to curtail the actual things, under the sway of enthusiasm, *people* were doing in the 1640s and '50s, in a word, to pacify them.

All that behavior would become, so these mechanists hoped, mechanical and machine-like, bereft of spontaneity, in a word, safe, as the lessons of the mechanical philosophy took hold and spread out from Europe and became part of popular culture.

Against the pantheistic[4] world of the enthusiasts, where every tree, rock, or stream reflected the wonders of the Creation, manifesting the sacredness of the world, the many new voices of philosophical moderation arising near the mid-17th century claimed that at the deepest level, reality consisted only of the "matter and motion" of the submicroscopic underlying atoms or particles they hypothesized made up each thing in the world.[5] To the mechanical philosophy it was the quantitative aspects of its matter and motion (size, shape, speed, direction of movement, etc.) that served to define any given reality and accounted for all subsequent change it underwent. The worlds that we perceive — an ob-

---

[1] Julian Jaynes, "The Problem of Animate Motion in the Seventeenth Century," *Journal of the History of Ideas* XXXI (April–June, 1970): pp. 219–34.

[2] See Part One, p. 41, for an explanation of the origins of this heading.

[3] Merchant, *op. cit.,* p. 202.

[4] A word coined only in the beginning of the 18th century.

[5] Though many a popularizer of science, say a Carl Sagan, could still sing nature's praises in a rhapsodic poetic affirmation, such paeans to the world's splendor always serve as mere introducttions to the *deeper* explanations of the blind mechanism underlying it all.

ject's colors, sounds, textures, smells, and tastes — were merely the consequences ("secondary qualities") of those quantitative ("primary qualities") factors. "Explanations" of a range of natural phenomena, based on such primary
causes, were ventured by the adherents of the mechanical philosophy with bold
strokes. In fact, it is no exaggeration that for many natural philosophers the
mere fact that a theory *was* framed in terms of the categories of "matter and motion" was enough for them to believe the theory to be correct.

Since in essence these hypothesized submicroscopic particles of the mechanical philosophy are themselves incapable of self-activity, according to the
new views, matter is really dead. This implicit lesson was to have an incalculable
impact on the subsequent history of our planet, for it made the *actual* delivery
of death to a woods, a brook, a grassland, or an estuary inconsequential, masking
the desecrations taking place nearly everywhere in the onrush to Progress that
by the late 18th century had been raised to a secular theology.

The Mersenne circle actually conducted three major crusades that set out
to remake not just the boundaries of science, but those of music and language
as well.[1] All three (overlapping, to be sure) campaigns were conducted, it is
clear, in direct response to a contagion of enthusiasm that was threatening
France and seemed close to achieving substantial control of England. A number
of the major English voices in this sudden crusade against enthusiasm had gone
into exile during the Civil War and had become part of the circle that gathered
weekly in the monastic cell of Mersenne. In this cell, which Berman has called
"the virtual nerve center of European science,"[2] ideas were discussed, manuscripts exchanged, and Mersenne's correspondence with natural philosophers
everywhere was freely shared.

English *emigrés* who regularly came included Thomas Hobbes, Boyle,
Charles Cavendish, William Petty, and William and Margaret Newcastle. Sir
Kenhelm Digby corresponded with Mersenne on a regular basis. All of them
were leading figures in the discussions about natural philosophy in England during the first half of the 17th century. It was these men and women, along with
John Wilkins, Thomas Sprat, and Walter Charleton who hammered home the
critical need to rein in the passions through a reinterpretation of natural philosophy that subdued nature —the goal, as well, of the parallel campaigns in music
and language — in order to combat enthusiasm.

The timing of their attacks is significant. By 1653, when their campaign in
England shifted into high gear, a critical political shift had taken place in the Civil

---

[1] The attempts in England and France to establish effective control over their
emerging nation-states established parallel pressures on policing of language, as
in the attempts by Cardinal Richelieu in France to standardize French usage.
Ivan Illich, *Medical Nemesis: The Expropriation of Health* (New York: Pantheon
Books, 1976) p. 164.

[2] Morris Berman, *Coming to Our Senses: Body and Spirit in the Hidden History of the
West* (New York: Bantam Books, 1990), pp. 111, 239; Merchant, *op. cit.*, p. 206.

✗ Cromwellien Thermidor 1653

War and revolution. Cromwell had gradually consolidated his power over the army of the nation over the previous several years. In 1647 he was able to begin bringing the Levellers, who had challenged his policies, to heel, as well suppressing the Diggers and Ranters. A Scottish invasion of England on behalf of Charles I was readily defeated by Cromwell's army the next year. In 1652 Cromwell succeeded in crushing the Irish uprising that had been under way for over a decade. The following year he moved to bring Parliament into line, ejecting the "Rump Parliament" and establishing a "Barebones Parliament" more attuned to the interests of the army than its predecessor. Cromwell then set up a new form of government called the Protectorate, which ruled England until the Restoration of the monarchy in 1660 (one year after Cromwell's death). Under the Protectorate, Cromwell was Lord Protector; within two years England was essentially ruled by the army under his control.

Cromwell's consolidation of power was paralleled by the decline (from a 1649 high point) in the power of the Independents, most particularly the Levellers, who lost their influence in the army and many of its leaders. It was at this low point that the former *emigrés* stepped up their critique of the enthusiasts.

iv. SOUNDING THE RETREAT

The overall character of the Mersenne program is seen clearly in his efforts to reform music. From time immemorial music has been a major conveyance for transporting people's souls to other realms. This is why we find music at the center of every religion in all cultures.[1] With the revival of magic in learned circles during the Renaissance, this soul-carrying aspect of music was clearly articulated — by Ficino, for one, who wrote about the use of sound to reach states of trance. Music was able to take the meditative self on fantastic journeys, ushering someone outside of his- or herself, frequently inducing states of ecstasy.[2]

By the mid-1640s it was clear that states of ecstasy and states of insurrection were at times indistinguishable. The necessity of preventing anyone not only from boarding that vehicle of the soul's journeys, but even from knowing that such a ride had ever existed for ordinary people, was obvious to authorities.

This is what Mersenne consciously set out to do. This particular campaign was more Mersenne's than his circle's doing. In a series of pioneering treatises, he rewrote the rules of harmony.[3] His theoretical work was a critical part of a more general 17th-century reform of musical structure and harmony, including the "tempering" of the scale by Bach and others. While the new definition of harmonic intervals that was adopted gave musicians new freedoms to create, play together, and extend the range of musical expression, it did so at the ex-

---

[1] Sometimes this is in the form of drumming or chanting, and may lack melodic content. Even the Taliban, who banish music, use chanting in the call to prayer.
[2] French, *op. cit.,* p. 134.
[3] Berman, *Coming,* pp. 237f.

pense of abandoning certain "natural" harmonies that earlier more "natural" scales had contained. After the 17th century, "pure tones" were no longer used; key tones were all fudged a little (in terms of their frequencies) in order to make certain harmonies easier. Now harmony was put solely on a quantitative basis, instead of on the, arguably, more "felt" "inner harmonies" heard by the ear and stressed by Pythagorean, Platonic, cabalistic, and other harmonic theories since antiquity.

Mersenne focused on the analytic aspects of harmony, showing how it *worked*. To make music supportive, rather than subversive, of social tranquility, he sought to abandon its affective power, its ability to *move* people emotionally and spiritually, not to mention kinesthetically. Harmony was now a matter of acoustics, to be explained in terms of the physics of vibrating bodies.

To effect such a subversion of music, to transform the harmonic basis on which it rested, harmony was *reduced* by Mersenne *to* merely vibrations. The walls of Jericho fell, and David was able to cure Saul with his harp, in Mersenne's reinterpretation of sacred myths, only because of the vibrations that the music in each instance consisted of. Aside from those vibrations, Mersenne insisted, music is *nothing*.[1]

v. RESTRAINING THE PASSIONS

Mersenne acknowledged that his aim in mechanizing music was in order to subvert its ability to serve as the primary means for achieving ecstasy. The role of the musician, he claimed, was "to *restrain* the passions."[2] With this in mind, Mersenne thus analyzed the mechanics of vibrating strings, for the first time establishing rules based on the length, mass, diameter, tension, etc., of a string. He and his followers worked out precise rules for the bowing of string instruments, for executing ornaments.

In opposition to how music had generally functioned in the past, this prescription for a musical sedative — conceptually (and anachronistically) a kind of Baroque version of muzak — amounted to no less than an inversion of what music historically had meant to a culture and its people. For Mersenne, true piety required subdued states; musical harmony thus became a means to that end, and through that, to social stability. Mersenne's campaign won significant victories, indeed, perhaps even the overall war itself. According to Jacques Attali, the tonal music that developed in Europe in the century following Mersenne's treatise on harmony served to emphasize a particularly bourgeois sense of harmony, a harmony *in* order, "*by shaping what* [people] *hear*."[3]

[1] *Ibid.*, pp. 240–41.

[2] *Ibid.*, p. 243; my emphasis.

[3] Quoted in Berman, *Coming*, p. 246; cf. John Zerzan, "'Tonality and the Totality," in *Future Primitive and Other Essays* (Brooklyn and Columbia, Mo.: Autonomedia & *Anarchy: A Journal of Desire Armed*, 1994).

Language, too, was a critical arena in which the Rosicrucian madness had to be combatted. Any language allowed some things to be true while forbidding others. With a suitable language, might not alchemy simply be unthinkable? More generally, control of discourse offered control of just about everything else. Creating such a new language, once more, was a task assumed by Marin Mersenne, though as a Frenchman his influence on the way English was used was indirect. Others, men like John Wilkins and Thomas Sprat, influenced by Mersenne, conducted the syntactic and ideological battles to tether the mother tongue in England to the necessary new constraints.

Interest in language reform arose out of a more general reformation of all learning sought by many thinkers in the 17th century, trying to establish a new basis for thinking. The more general reform would ride on methodological breakthroughs for the study of the world, beginning with the study of nature.

To begin with, this approach narrowly focused on questions of *fact*, while questions having to do with *value* or *ultimate meaning* were shunted off to the sidelines, something of an embarrassment. The new science, as we shall see, was boldly promised to authorities, just as Mersenne had done for music, as a guarantor of sobriety. It, too, would encourage social harmony among the different classes and orders. For that sobriety to take hold, in theory the scientists themselves had to relinquish personal concerns about the topics they studied, and the results they found had to be "objective." In this ideology, scientific disagreements were framed to have little emotional force. The Earl of Newcastle, an influential supporter of the new science, had written Charles II after he was safely seated on the restored throne, that "controversye is a Civill War with the pen which pulls out the sorde soon afterwards."[1] To the contrary, to ensure that the sword always stayed in its sheath, controversy would now be carefully limited to certain questions, effectively muted with a new set of conventions and scientific protocols in place. Establishing "facts" as a kind of "conceptual atom," the new learning attempted to divorce these "facts" from context, from emotionality.

Not surprisingly, in the first instance, this cutting away from context was to be done to alchemy. Mersenne did not actually propose *abolishing* alchemy (at the root of which lay subversive Rosicrucianism). Instead he proposed establishing *state-sponsored* academies where the claims of alchemy could "objectively" be put to the test.[2] In this way, alchemical frauds and clear nonsense could be purged, while nuggets of useful information, freed from their alchemical dross and considered apart from one another, could be mined and refined.

Two important methodological principles were to guide such academies, according to Mersenne: first, a reform of alchemical language — emphasizing the necessity of using only terminology firmly grounded in empirical reality; second, banishing any questions of a religious, ethical, and philosophical nature from all alchemical discussions.

1 Report to Charles II, http://www.walter9.info/Cavendish/html/antwerp.html
2 Berman, *Reenchantment,* pp. 110–11.

But the body of Rosicrucianism, where spiritual and ethical questions, as well as a general theory of material reality, form its core, would inevitably be eviscerated by any such strictures. It was no less deadly to alchemy in general, because classically alchemy was first and foremost a spiritual pilgrimage, a vehicle for an adept to achieve his or her own salvation.

vi. A SANCTIONED REALITY

In different writers we find slight variations in the boundaries between the realms they stressed had to be kept separate — facts versus values; truth versus beauty, according to John Wilkins; facts versus religion, ethics, and philosophy for Mersenne, as, earlier, for Galileo — but using this approach of forever dividing things from one another, brought to a single-minded ontologic weapon in Descartes' *Discours sur la methode* (1637), the new science was able to reach and secure three key inter-related redoubts in its war to establish a new State-sanctioned reality:

First, the conceit of objectivity, the bizarre notion that a thing or question is best looked at from outside itself, as a concrete, static, *object*; theoretically rendering scientific controversy irrelevant, except as to questions of facticity, of what *is*. Since all experience, by definition, *is* subjective (since it is experienced by someone), this mandate to render it objectively actually forces the greatest distortion in attempts to render reality faithfully. Arguably, this is the *least* "objective" of methodologies. And what initially was the aim for scientific matters was soon enough extended to all manner of topics.

Second, as Berman observes, this is really the beginning of scientific positivism, whereby all ultimate questions are banished as unnecessary or, for some, an actual encumbrance in the pursuit of truth.[1]

Third, the isolation of the different realms or different parts of a given thing from one another drove a stake through the heart of most significant matters. Holistic analyses are in principle eschewed. Thus, serious epidemiological investigations can be carried out which ignore environmental aspects; or research into a particular critter's digestion can proceed blissfully ignorant of how it shelters itself, or its reproductive modalities. Though in theory a reintegration of all the parts into a whole, only now a well-understood whole, is supposed to happen somewhere down the line, in practice it rarely does. Dissociation provides a metaphysical isolation out of which a widespread alienation is fostered. For if separation into parts is the first step and can be done without limit, then ultimately everything may be rendered into ever-more minute, separate, self-sufficient entities.[2]

---

[1] *Ibid.,* p. 109.

[2] Thus, almost as if on purpose, modern institutions (particularly those of State or finance) on the basis of such un-holistic analyses, create crises without solu-

Mersenne's language reform focused on how words would be defined. Sadly, alchemy was generally construed from a vocabulary that was obscure and poetic (if for no other reason than to maintain the secrecy necessary to keep potentially dangerous powers over the material world out of unscrupulous or unworthy hands). The alchemical text was a highly metaphoric code, at times revealing in its accompanying illustrations things purposely made muddy in the text itself.

But the problem, as the language reformers saw it, was much broader than alchemy.[1] The Ranters and other 17th-century sectarians denied key tenets of the social and religious conventions that bound society together, and their delusions were similarly rooted in their use of a language of fancy. The Blasphemy Act of 1650 took aim at those who claimed to be God or equal with God or who denied the inherent shamefulness of swearing, adultery, drunkenness, theft, and so on, or who said that sin occurred only when a person's acts were so "perceived" by that person.[2]

The many men and women who emerged as prophets during the revolutionary decades also used language that sometimes was obscure, inflated, wildly metaphorical. Indeed, in times of social upheaval, what else but the gifted tongue of a fiery orator, able to erect a metaphoric scaffolding that allows his or her listeners (and in the English Civil War and revolution, there were eloquent men *and* women lay preachers in great number) to scale unimaginable heights, so as to set in motion acts of incredible vision and derring-do? Such excesses in words had to be pruned if England (for Mersenne, France) were to be able to regain social stability, whether the threat came from alchemical, prophetic, or agitational unrestrained rhetoric.

---

tions — as in allowing the widespread development of nuclear power facilities, even basing whole national economies on it, without any inkling of how nuclear wastes (some of them extremely toxic for many *hundreds of thousands* of years) could ever be disposed of in a safe manner; or, how a nuclear state such as the US became in the 1950s and beyond was built around a command and control military system whose most critical links relied on the ubiquitous AT&T (mostly) telephone lines, despite known vulnerability to those lines from the EMF effects of nuclear blasts and the quite different risks arising from the internal financial concerns of the telecommunications industry, making such lines obviously unreliable. Paul Bracken, *The Command and Control of Nuclear Forces* (New Haven: Yale Univ. Press, 1983), pp. 215ff.

All of these and a multitude of others are instances of "rationality" run amok, freed, on the basis of piecemeal and uncoordinated analyses, from any responsibility for actually making anything truly work, and so tolerating, if not sometimes actually encouraging, the "parts" working against each other, in defiance of any "whole."

[1] Pioneering work on the language reform movement and its effects on English usage was done by Richard Foster Jones; see his Jones, *et. al., The Seventeenth Century: Studies in the History of English Thought and Literature from Bacon to Pope* (Stanford, Calif.: Stanford Univ. Press, 1969), upon which my discussion is largely based.

[2] Hill, *op. cit.,* p. 167. Such as advocated by Muggleton, among others.

In the reformed language that Mersenne proposed, words would have to satisfy certain criteria. Words that were too exotic would simply be banished altogether. Nonexistent things, such as fauns, should no longer have terms to designate them, according to John Wilkins, since words should refer only to what is real.

vii. THE WAR AGAINST THE ENTHUSIASTS

As the Civil War, revolution, and Protectorate succesively failed to come to terms with the underlying problems in England that had led to revolt, a concerted effort was mounted to discredit the rebellion, feeding and being fed by a disillusionment among the increasing numbers of Englishmen and women growing tired of the uncertainty, the upheavals, the excesses, the turmoil and sheer unsettledness of the whole thing. Cromwell's non-monarchical autocratic rule alarmed many, and the stew of social debate began to simmer anew. One year into the Commonwealth, the ideas of the Mersenne circle on how to fight enthusiasm began to be articulated widely in England. Several seminal critiques of the enthusiasts were published, arguing the case that the late social turmoil was a result of enthusiasm.

Guided by the writings of, among others, William Petty, John Wilkins, Thomas Hobbes, Walter Charleton, and Robert Boyle (all members of the Mersenne circle) large numbers of English thinkers early in the Commonwealth turned strikingly against the Rosicrucian magic at the core of enthusiasm. We see, instead, the mechanical philosophy put forth as the underpinning of a new reality, including its axiom that all natural occurrences were to be explained only by "matter and motion," to replace the magical, animist nonsense that had so clearly encouraged enthusiasm.

Attacks on the political radicals that were mounted from the mid-1640s and into the '50s and '60s made it clear that magic had been centrally responsible for their many excesses. John Wilkins wrote of the enthusiasts that of late they had been

> much cryed up and followed... [but they do] in the opinion of many sober and judicious men, deliver only a kind of cabelistical or *Chymical, Rosecrucian* Theologie, darkening wisdom with words, heaping together a farrago of obscure affected expressions and Wild allegories.[1]

The campaign against the "turmoil of religious fanaticism and revolution" was the focus, according to Wilkins' biographer, of much of Wilkins' work. He disliked the separatism of the sects, "their lower-class membership, but above all their mys-

---

[1] Wilkins, *Ecclesiastes: or, A Discourse of the Art of Preaching* (London: 1646), p. 71, quoted in Barbara Shapiro, *John Wilkins, 1614–1672: An Intellectual Biography* (Berkeley, Calif.: Univ. of California Press, 1969), p. 273; see also pp. 32, 66, 71.

ticism and excessive zeal."[1] Another critic attacked the educational reformer, John
Webster, by attributing to him a "Familistical–Levelling–Magical temper."[2] Seth
Ward attacked the "canting Discourses" of the Rosicrucians. After the Restoration,
Bishop Samuel Parker claimed that, in contrast to the mechanical philosophy,
Rosicrucianism had led people to "the wildest and most Enthusiastical Fanati-
cisme, for there is so much Affinity between Rosi-Crucianisme and Enthusiasme,
that whoever entertains the one, he may upon the same reason embrace the other."
Both were considered the same as sedition.[3] Anthony à Wood charged that the
people claiming to have revelations, visions, and inspirations were "aiming at an
utter subversion in [the universities], church, and schools."[4] Such attacks were
repeated and amplified in pamphlets and treatises by Robert Boyle, Joseph
Glanvill, Ralph Cudworth, Christopher Wren, Isaac Barrow (Newton's tutor at
Cambridge), Simon Patrick, Walter Charleton, and many other Englishmen.

One of the more remarkable of the propagandists against enthusiasm was Henry
More, a Cambridge Platonist who, similar to other critics, had himself come under the
sway of magical notions during the 1640s and even later.[5] More's tract, *Enthusiasmus Triumphatus* (1656) provided a full taxonomy of enthusiasm, exposing its several roots in the
use of overly florid language, indulgence in unbridled imagination, and states of ecstasy
and lust. The philosophical root of enthusiasm, More emphasized, can be traced to
alchemy, and he singled out the ideas of Paracelsus, whose followers thought they found
God "in every object of their senses." More particularly condemned the beliefs that "Nature is the Body of God," that the deity may be found in all that can be perceived.[6]

Moreover, he argued that the major prophecies had already been fulfilled
at the Reformation, thus discrediting the prophets, denouncing the pointless
armed uprising instigated by the Fifth Monarchists when they judged it the eve
of Armageddon.[7]

---

[1] *Ibid.*

[2] Rattansi, "Paracelsus and the Puritan Revolution," *op. cit.*, p. 29; *Thomas, Religion and the Decline*, p. 374; Hill, *op. cit.*, p. 233.

[3] Samuel Parker, *A Free and Impartial Censure of the Platonick Philosophy...* (Oxford,
England: 1666), quoted by J. R. Jacob, *Robert Boyle and the English Revolution: A Study
in Social and Intellectual Change* (New York: Burt Franklin & Co., 1977), p. 163.

[4] Anthony à Wood, *The Life and Times of Anthony à Wood* in *The Broadview Anthology
of Seventeenth-Century Verse and Prose* (ed.) Alan Rudrum, Joseph Black, & Holly
Faith Nelson (Peterborough, Ontario: Broadview Press, 2000), p. 1021.

[5] See M[ore], H[enry], *Psychathanesia, or the Second Part of the Song of the Soul, Treating of the Immortality of the Soule...* (Cambridge, England, 1647).

[6] More wrote the work after a heated exchange with the alchemist Thomas
Vaughan in 1650–51. *Enthusiasmus Triumphatus; or, a Brief Discourse of the Nature,
Causes, Kinds, and Cure of Enthusiasm* (London: 1662; reprint, Los Angeles: William
Andrews Clark Memorial Library, 1966); 1st ed., 1656), pp. 31f, 34, 45, 30.
Thomas Harmon Jobe, *op. cit.*, p. 349).

[7] More, *Enthusiasmus*, p. 22.

Figure 5
MECHANICAL MAN, COMPOSED OF AGRICULTURAL IMPLEMENTS
(16th Century German engraving)

Eventually a monarchy was restored (with some of its powers now shared with Parliament), along with the re-empowered House of Lords and restored Church of England, and repressive legislation (the Clarendon Code) so as to uproot any threats to the new configuration of power and privilege. Coffee houses, which had first appeared in England in the 1650s and were notorious for spreading dissent, were kept under close surveillance and were proscribed in the 1670s.[1] So too were sporting events, fairs, carnivals, markets — just about anywhere people were apt to gather and different classes mix.[2]

[1] We return to this in Chapter 11.

[2] This radical constriction of public space in the 1660s in reaction to the turmoil of the 1640s and '50s has a parallel in the reaction in the US and elsewhere to the un-

It would be exceedingly difficult to *overestimate* the overall impact of the new laws, codes, surveillances, and new standards of natural philosophy. With the Restoration, a tidal shift in ideas and practices relating to religion, philosophy, science, poetry, rhetoric, and music had calmed the seas of culture as something called "Latitudinarianism" became established in the Royal Society, Church of England, and other major institutions of cultural hegemony. The Latitudinarians, advocating a middle way between the two extremes of the Catholics and the Independents, were closely allied with the new science.

All of these strategems appear to have worked, for there was a massive transformation of people's behavior as well as attitudes in the following decades. Writing about the differences in England between the 17th and 18th centuries in his study of political stability, the historian J.H. Plumb (among others) has commented on 18th-century England's "adamantine strength and profound *inertia*" (NB) and argued that it was in the decades right after the Restoration that the basis had been established for this highly rare and (by the rulers and propertied) much desired state of political stability[1] — though beneath its apparently placid surface, there were significant stirrings.[2]

Henry More's influence on the cultural tidal shift was particularly immense. He was especially important early on in arguing that the mechanical philosophy could not in itself, without the presence of spiritual agencies, satisfactorily explain nature. Previously More had played a central role in popularizing the ideas of Descartes in England, advocating a religious settlement after the Restoration allied with the new science. Then More began to have doubts. He started to see how, according to the Cartesians, the God of the mechanical philosophy had precious little to do once Creation had occurred. Eventually turning against Descartes, More became an impassioned advocate for a mechanical philosophy that was explicitly combined with spiritual agencies, so as to preserve God's present Providence in the natural world, His necessarily ongoing role in affairs of the cosmos.

One of the thinkers very much taken with More's approach to the burning issues of the day was the young Isaac Newton, newly arrived in Cambridge in 1661, seeking out More who, like Newton, was from Grantham in Lincolnshire. The young student took notes on their discussions, as he later did in the margins of a number of More's treatises. These issues and concerns were to continue guiding Newton as he set about reconstructing our comprehension of the natural world, as we shall see in Chapter 12.

rest of the 1930s by similar restrictions in the late '40s, as seen in the development of centerless suburbs; urban renewal; massive freeway construction that ripped apart communities (frequently of color); and the spread of malls as ersatz public space, owned privately. In response to the insurgencies of the 1960s, neo-liberalism was born with its inherent antipathy to the public sphere and its "structural adjustment programs," and its push to privatize schools, prisons, clinics, and public lands.

[1] J. H. Plumb, *The Growth of Political Stability in England* (London: 1967), p. 13; my emphasis, Max Beloff, *Public Order and Popular Disturbances, 1661–1715* (Oxford, England: 1938), pp. 20–24.

[2] Linebaugh, *London Hanged.*

9

State-Sponsored Natural Philosophy: Obedience School for the Intelligentsia?

There is probably no general and universal answer... to the question of whether carnival functioned as a school for revolution or as a means of social control. We do not know how the people themselves construed their festive mockeries of kings and priests, for example — as good-natured mischief or as a kind of threat. But it is safe to say that carnival increasingly gains a political edge, in the modern sense, after the Middle Ages, from the sixteenth century on. It is then that large numbers of people begin to use the masks and noises of their traditional festivities as a cover for armed rebellion, and to see, perhaps for the first time, the possibility of inverting hierarchy on a permanent basis and not just for a few festive hours.
— Barbara Ehrenreich, *Dancing in the Streets: A History of Collective Joy* (2006)

For such a candid, and unpassionate company [as met at Oxford during the English Civil War]... and for such a gloomy season, what could have been a fitter Subject to pitch upon, then *Natural Philosophy?*... It was *Nature* alone, which could pleasantly entertain them, in that estate. The contemplation of that, draws our minds off from past, or present misfortunes, and makes them conquerers over things, in the greatest publick unhappiness: while the consideration of *Men*, and *humane affairs*, may affect us, with a thousand various disquiets; that never separates us into mortal Factions; that gives us room to differ, without animosity; and *permits us to raise contrary imaginations upon it, without any danger of a* Civil War.
— Thomas Sprat, *The History of the Royal Society of London, For the Improving of Natural Knowledge* (1667), italics in original, except for last two lines

I. TEACHING "THE BEST PRAESERVATIVE AGAINST DISOBEDIENCE"

Charles II began his reign with the founding of a new institution, the Royal Society of London for the Improving of Natural Knowledge. Finally receiving its official charter in 1662, the Royal Society was the first of its kind. Eventually societies very much like it would spring up in Paris, Berlin, St. Petersburg, Philadelphia — indeed, in just about any important city and State throughout the world. Having a local scientific society became, in fact, a critical way in which urban centers and States announced their own coming of age in the 18th-century Enlightenment.

Numerous studies in the 1960s suggested one or another origin for the Royal Society: did it come from the efforts of those savants who met at (Royalist) Oxford during the Civil War, as Sprat and others claimed? Or, as another camp argued, did it spring forth from the experimental philosophers who had been meeting during those same years in (Parliamentarian) London and were in contact with City tradesmen and craftspeople?[1]

Such debates strike me as akin to arguing over which one of the tributaries to a mighty river is the most important in determining its course. Just like a river, the currents of human history are generally far too turbulent to justify such linear analysis. That such questions have the considerable power they do in our culture is a measure of how much mechanical thinking has taken over our modalities of understanding, since scientific "method" and ideology have come to dominate, one by one, the higher grounds in the culture of modern times.

I would think that the establishment of the Royal Society was a confluence of a number of major intellectual and institutional tributaries, including earlier proposals for research that had been advocated and/or tried since the Renaissance in Italy, France, and England. Instead of focusing on questions of origins for the Society, here we will marvel at the degree to which it was able to serve as a platform for the Latitudinarian philosophy, including the idea of using natural philosophy as a weapon in the fight for political and religious "moderation."

Religious warfare in 17th-century England had become polarized between those favoring ritual and hierarchical priestly powers and dogmas, if not that of the Catholic Church, something close to it, and those whose total condemnation of Roman avarice, pomp, and hypocrisy led them into rigid advocacy of what they thought was its opposite. Agreement on just what that opposite was became points of contention among the Puritan sects, which tended towards schism, especially during the years just prior to the Civil War and revolution, as Puritan opponents of the Stuart monarchy and Church were

---

1 By the 1960s, when I was in graduate school, a veritable industry had developed attempting to find the origin of the Society. Insofar as eventually I decided the numerous studies did not clarify much, I did not continue following the debate.

sometimes able to combine the zeal of religious fanaticism with the self-right-eousness of political radicals. In the 1660s, the Latitudinarians would condemn both extremes, Catholic and radical Puritan alike. They sought, through the use of "reason," a middle way built on a certain broad agreement on matters of faith and worship and toleration of other views — but only up to a point. Catholics and radical Puritan sectarians were beyond the pale — and were neither included in the Latitudinarian "toleration" nor allowed a voice in the newly restored Church of England.

The newly established Royal Society came under serious attack shortly after its establishment. Members of the old guard in England feared that the Society would help destroy the basis for order and authority in England with its new method of questioning everything. Former leaders of the Independents, on the other hand, charged the Society with lacking a truly new vision of how science could *free* people, such as had been the premise of the Rosicrucian-inspired visions of science in the early part of the century. The Royal Society had consciously set out to bury *that* vision. Now, in defense of its beliefs, activities, and investigations, the Society decided to construct an official history of its six short years; Wilkins' protege, Thomas Sprat, would write it. The work would show the value of their experiments and deliberations, as well as providing samples of its inquiries, reprints of individual researches, and tables of data discovered. The Society appointed a committee, in which Wilkins played a major role, that met in secret to advise Sprat on what to put in the defense he was drafting[1]

Sprat's *History of the Royal Society* (1667) is a most remarkable document, skillfully weaving together the interests of the State and those of the community of natural philosophers coming together in England into a strikingly attractive (and by today, a very well-worn) ideological garment. Sprat argued that support for the work of the Royal Society in itself would help ensure an era of social, religious, and political peace, because the study of science would prove to be "the best praeservative against disobedience."[2]

Like the other critics of enthusiasm, Sprat had his woeful tales of the terrible things done by those caught up in the "infinite pretences to *Inspiration* and *immediate Communion with God* that have abounded in this Age," as a result of enthusiasm. In contrast, men drawn to the study of natural philosophy during the same years of the Great Rebellion had, according to Sprat, been nurtured on a *"sober* and *generous knowledge* [and so] were invincibly arm'd against all the in-

---

[1] For the close supervision of what Sprat should write, see P. M. Rattansi, *The Literary Attack on Science*, pp. 66, 77, and Thomas Birch, *A History of the Royal Society for Improving of Natural Knowledge...* (London: 1756–57) facsimile (Darmstadt: 1968), vol. I, p. 507 for December 21, 1664 and vol. II, p. 47 for May 16, 1665).
[2] Thomas Sprat, *The History of the Royal Society of London, For the Improving of Natural Knowledge* (London: 1667) reprint (ed.) Jackson I. Cope and Harold Whitmore Jones (St. Louis: Washington Univ. Studies, 1958), p. 428.

chantments of Enthusiasm."[1] Sprat enumerates the many ways sober natural philosophy acts to cool down the political passions, and actually claims that the study of nature

> draws our minds off from past, or present misfortunes, ... that never separates us into mortal Factions; gives us room to differ, without animosity; and permits us to raise contrary imaginations upon it without any danger of a *Civil War*.[2]

What a remarkable promise to make to Charles II, to whom Sprat's *History* was dedicated, only seven years after the end of the rebellion that had cost Charles' father, Charles I, his head! Even more strikingly, we will see that the promises made by this fawning publicist for the budding scientific community, vying for royal patronage, were historically more than mere puffery.[3]

Natural philosophy breeds caution, Sprat (and Wilkins) argued, in contrast to the enthusiast's "rashness of setting upon causes" of things. The method used by the Royal Society, based on a "singular sobriety of debating" and "slowness of consenting" forestalled the appearance of factions, according to Sprat, simply by preventing the ingredients that allow them to form. A kind of consensus was in effect at meetings of the Society, Sprat implies, since conclusions can be reached only if everyone present agrees, making "their deliberations... so tedious"

---

[1] *Ibid.*, pp. 375–76, 53.

[2] *Ibid.*, p. 56; cf. Wilkins' modern biographer, who claims that the new science served as a "haven from religious dogmatism and conflicts." (Shapiro, *op. cit.*, p. 250). Joseph Glanvill similarly wrote that none of the natural philosophers of the mid-17th century were "zealous Votar[ies] of a Sect." (*Essays on Several Important Subjects* [London: 1676], quoted in Barbara Shapiro, "Latitudinarianism and Science in Seventeenth Century England," *Past and Present* no. 40 (1968), p. 35.

[3] For example, in 1958 Fred Iklé of the RAND Corporation submitted a report to the Pentagon where he proposed establishing an official board of inquiry into a hypothetical accidental nuclear explosion as "an important device for temporizing." If such an accident were to occur in a remote area, the government, Iklé suggested, could simply lie, or if news leaked out could claim "it had been an experiment." During the months such a board of inquiry took to prepare its report, called by Iklé a "delaying period," news media could be deluged with information about rehabilitation and relief, so that "[w]ithin a relatively short time... interest in rehabilitation [will] tend[s] to crowd out reports about destruction and casualties." Fred Iklé with J. E. Hill, U.S. Project RAND Research Memorandum, May 8, 1959 (RM–2364), quoted in Eric Schlosser, *Command and Control: Nuclear Weapons, the Damascus Accident, and the Illusion of Safety* (New York: Penguin Books, 2014), p. 195. On nuclear issues the AEC, NRC and Pentagon have, from the beginning, routinely lied.

Sprat, *op. cit.*, pp. 91, 104, 426.

that usually by the time they *might* act on some issue the opportunity for doing so has long since passed. Serious questions demand thorough study, for this "Gentle, and easy *Method*"[1] takes patience; such effort ensures that the prejudice of one experimenter will be balanced by those of others. There was a marked effort to avoid answering larger questions (reaching conclusions), and discussions, Sprat insisted, were designed only for matters of *fact* to be decided. Articulated thus, *any* criticism would be the death knell for a theory, for "Every rubb is... to be smooth'd: every scrupple to be plained: everything to be forseen...."[2] The moderation of language Sprat (and Wilkins) advocated lends a hand to this, too.[3]

Here, the methodological rules of the new science, its vigorous examination (up to a point) of all theories, its mania for splitting all topics into an ordered hierarchy of semi-autonomous subdomains, which can be, and in practice are, solved with little reference to the totality from which they were torn, the emphasis on facticity — all of these were brought forth at the Restoration in order to serve clear ideological and political ends of delaying effective political action, in large part through the creation of conceptual and procedural quagmires.

II. REALITY IN BONDAGE: THE WAR AGAINST AMBIGUITY

Two of the main proponents of language reform in England were Wilkins and his disciple, Thomas Sprat. Wilkins, who was to be made a Bishop in 1670, had been trying to reconstruct language from the 1640s on, alarmed at both the rampant social upheavals and the inflammatory words that sparked the tinder of discontent into a conflagration.[4] Wilkins tended to come to terms with whomever was in power and in the 1640s became brother-in-law to Cromwell, as after the Restoration he was favored by the monarch.

Using the Royal Society as a base from which to propagate their views, both Wilkins and Sprat were able to engineer real transformation in English usage. Sprat advocated a particularly severe restriction on language: *each thing* was to be assigned *only one word* to represent it, while *each word* was to refer to *one thing only*. Additionally, Wilkins wanted to reduce words to symbols on a page.[5]

---

[1] Sprat, *op. cit.*, pp. 91, 104, 426.

[2] *Ibid.*, p. 104.

[3] The notion that technical matters insulate individuals from social and political controversy can be seen in the shift of some social science researchers — two thirds of whom had been questioned by FBI agents in 1951 as part of J. Edgar Hoover's "Responsibilities Program," and more than 1000 of whom were fired — to investigations of statistical or quantitative questionsd. Betty Medsger, *The Burglary: The Discovery of J. Edgar Hoover's Secret FBI* (New York: Alfred A. Knopf, 2014), pp. 358–59.

[4] Shapiro, *John Wilkins.*

[5] Jackson I. Cope, *Joseph Glanvill, Anglican Apologist* (St. Louis: Washington Univ. Studies, 1956), p. 150.

As language reform became more closely associated with the Royal Society, a committee was appointed in 1654 to improve the language of the English, setting John Wilkins the task of instructing the committee how to proceed.[1] Their aim, quite surprisingly, was the impossible one of abolishing all ambiguity in language. The domain of truth had to be protected from both shades of meaning and from empty phraseology.

Both Wilkins and Sprat took careful aim at the conceit of eloquence, Wilkins priding himself on the plainness of his own discourse "that shewed he had no design upon his hearers." "When the notion it self is good, the best way to set it off is in the most obvious plain expression."[2] Wilkins warned against "puerile worded Rhetoric." He thought eloquence was the sign of "low thought and designs," a clear indication that the polishing of phrases, rather than the substance itself, was the writer's priority. Just as God need not be approached with inane and Latinized incantations, as the Papists did, so truth had no need of fancy garb and fine words to be conveyed. Sprat considered proposing "that *eloquence* ought to be banish'd out of *civil Societies,* as a thing fatal to Peace and good manners," but decided such a rule would only allow a clear field for the "uncontested use of eloquence" by the enthusiasts, and changed his mind.[3] Thomas Hobbes, too, in his *Leviathan* (1651), warned against *"all metaphysicall Speeches, tending to the stirring up of Passion."*[4]

Metaphors or other figures of speech, the use of words to refer to more than one reality at a time, seemed to many like loaded weapons in the hands of the agitators, capable of blasting huge holes in the social fabric of revolutionary England. Such fancy wordcraft had to be drastically curtailed. Several years after the Restoration, Bishop Samuel Parker pushed the attack on enthusiastic language to a logical (albeit totalitarian) conclusion, proposing a Bill in the House of Lords making it illegal for preachers to use "fulsome and lushious Metaphors."[5] He also attacked caballa.[6]

Language could be useful for identifying who was a "real man," too, judging from Bishop Parker's criticism that enthusiastic ranting represented only "Schemes of *Effeminate Follies.*" Joseph Glanvill, wanting to be admitted to the Royal Society, rewrote his earlier *Vanity of Dogmatizing* (1661) — his "Corrective of Enthusiasm" — so as to tone down his prose, each of its two succeeding editions showing more pruning; as he started rewriting, he confessed to preferring the more "manly sense" in his recent prose, as opposed to the "Caprices of

---

1 Jones, *op. cit.,* p. 103 n. 49.

2 *Ibid.,* p. 78. But how easily Willkins violated his own dictum, see our Chapter 8, p. 18, where he heaps *eloquent* scorn on the enthusiasts.

3 Sprat, *op. cit.,* p. 111.

4 Hobbes, *Leviathan Or the Matter, Forme and Power of a Commonwealth Ecclesiasticall and Civil,* (1651), as quoted in Jones, *op. cit.,* p. 81; emphasis in the original.

5 Jones, *The Seventeenth Century,* p. 118, 108 n.

6 Parker, *op. cit.* pp. 104ff.

froathy imagination" that had characterized his former style. After his second edition, with its inclusion of a new, lengthy, "Address to the Royal Society," the Society elected Glanvill to membership, where he joined Sprat as one of its most effective propagandists.[1]

III. Victory of the New Word Order

Under the Royal Society's leadership, a new canon of how to use the English language, with stylistic and linguistic rules of conduct, and a "new standard of expression"[2] first gained a foothold in scientific deliberations and then, as the new science gathered prestige, spread to larger circles. The literary historian R. F. Jones, claims that "science exerted by far the most powerful force upon [the English] prose of the last part of the 17th century. Plainness, lack of ambiguity (by fiat, ambiguity becomes impossible if they could manage to restrict each word to a single referent and vice versa), abandonment of imagery, and a new structure for language were the essential guidelines in this campaign. What had become a new word order was adopted by Glanvill as subject → verb → object[3] (Jones, p. 97), and this "natural" form eventually became the norm. Cadence, rhetorical questions, lengthy deliberations, and exclamations were to be shunned in the new canon.[4]

Jones maintains that a price had to be paid in adopting these new standards for language, for the scientific spirit dominating discourse ended up "destroying the sheer joy in language," a joy that was (and is) the very soul of poetry — perhaps helping explain why Shakespeare, Donne, and Milton from the first half of the 17th century still command the heights of English literature, for such joy is fundamental to oral and written language both. No matter, as a major source of enthusiasm, the impetus to sculpt discourse with one's words — mindful of their sounds, revelling in their shadings, delighting in the free play of creativity in putting the words, and hence the world, in a certain order — by the 1650s has been reviled as too dangerous. It was a time for reining in the spirit itself, an essential step if one's ultimate target was to undermine any sense of the Earth's sacred value. For if mine owners were to be able to dig deeper and further, gouging wounds into the flanks of the planet at their wills, such views could no longer be tolerated.[5]

---

[1] Jones, *op. cit.*, pp. 89–91 and notes 29 and 31, p. 117, note 14; Cope, *Glanvill*, p. 5.

[2] Jones, *op. cit.*, p. 76.

[3] *Ibid.*, p. 97.

[4] A canon, readers will have already noticed, I frequently flout, suspecting it ultimately to be a tool for "dumbing down" much of written expression.

[5] This proscription, too, is still operative, as when RAND Corp. circa 2005, in an effort to keep itts analyses free of emotion, tried to banish all adjectives and charged language. Alex Abella, *Soldiers of Reason: The RAND Corporation and the Rise of American Empire* (Orlando, Florida: Harcourt, Inc. 2008), p. 307.

The Royal Society, in effect, also became the codifier and enforcer of a new concept of nature's reality that emerged after the Restoration, and, through the impact in the following decades and centuries that the new science had on how people across the planet experienced the world, the codifier of reality as a whole.

As did its sister institutions, the Académie Royale des Sciences (founded 1666), the Berlin Academy (1700), the American Philosophical Society in the American colonies (1767),[1] and many others, institutions commonly used by the nation-states to adjudicate when scientific matters have a bearing on public issues.[2]

The new reality, the campaign to rein in language (in France, as well, under Mersenne's guidance), the criteria that were established to decide questions of fact — all of this went hand-in-hand with a war against the imagination itself. *Imagination*, too, perhaps especially, is an enemy of social tranquility, as several writers made clear, for it feeds the spirit of enthusiasm by encouraging alternative visions to thrive, by keeping alive its root, *mag*,[3] and hence, magic itself.

Perhaps no one understood better the deeper meaning of this attack on the imagination and the spirit than Johann Amos Comenius, the Moravian occultist and visionary whose schemes for world reform, a reign of universal peace based on education for everyone, and the improving of peoples' livelihoods through the use of science and technology, were enormously influential in England, particularly during the 1640s upheaval when his notions had important support in Parliament. Comenius' manifesto for a "Universal College" circulated in manuscript in England as early as 1641, having a critical impact on thinking about the need for new approaches to education, and is thought to be one of several streams of thought leading eventually to establishment of the Royal Society.[4]

Around the time Sprat's *History* appeared, Comenius wrote that though he welcomed the founding of the Society, he worried that in its pursuit of natural science without any but utilitarian ends and divorced from the earlier, utopian visions (such as is seen in Rosicrucian alchemy and the occult schemes of Boehme, Dee, Paracelsus, and Comenius himself), the Royal Society's work would utterly lack any spiritual basis.[5]

From an early-21st-century vantage point, it is not too difficult to see how that utter lack of spiritual basis has served in modern times as an ideological en-

---

[1] Following a proposal by Benjamin Franklin in 1743, an earlier society had been formed, but it was unsatisfactory and did not last.

[2] As, for example, in the condemnation of Mesmer in 18th-century France and of Wilhelm Reich in the United States in the 1950s, or in assessing and prescribing for the energy needs of the US in the 1970s and beyond with a plan to make much of the Southwest a "national sacrificial zone," by giving free rein to mineral extraction.

[3] For a discussion of the root, "*mag*," see Chapter 4, p. 106.

[4] Cope and Jones, edition of Sprat's *History*, Appendix A, p. 65; Shapiro, *Wilkins*, pp. 26f; Yates, *op. cit.*, pp. 156ff; Hill, *op. cit.*, p. 232.

[5] Yates, *op. cit.*, pp. 191, 233.

abler, in the absence of transcendent values, opening the door to the wholesale economic "development" of wild places and thereby facilitating humanity's pell-mell rush, even conceivably to the demise of our (and countless other) species. Perhaps this, indeed, was even what Comenius dimly and painfully anticipated. A direct result of the retreat in the 17th century from that earlier sense of science as a source for liberation of people, as a leveller of fortunes, was the victory of a shadow self and the birth, I am arguing, of a form of knowledge that secretly and perversely, somewhere deep inside, craves annihilation and destruction.

IV. The Son of Science

Yet, the story of the retreat of science from its earlier spiritual (Rosicrucian) connections and its consequence for our culture is known at most by a handful of scholars and even that only rather recently; in society as a whole, not only are people generally unaware of this crucial battle and its outcome, but the story that virtually everyone *does* learn, instead, regarding the divorce of science from any and all values, is Galileo's; his trial and tribulations. We are taught how his views led (around the same time as the crushing of the Rosicrucians) to a nasty confrontation with the Catholic Church, in which Galileo, the Son of Science, was forced to recant his deeply-held belief that the Earth moved around the sun, as Copernicus had proposed in 1543, rather than the sun around the Earth, as the older, Ptolemaic theory had it.[1] Galileo's works in support of the new Copernican heliocentric view and the physics and epistemology he helped create to expose the weaknesses of Aristotelian physics and to justify the apparent new structure of the cosmos had encountered strong opposition in some quarters of the Church. In effect, the story of his martyred fight against the closed minds of some Church leaders and, ultimately, by his supporters, against the Church itself, has become a monument on the pathway to the modern world, symbolically pointing out the ultimate victory of "truth" over "superstition," with its poignant demonstration as to why science must be kept separate from the rigid tenets of religion, indeed, separate from any sense of values, as modern scientific positivism has steadfastly, and successfully, demanded.

But the "necessary" separation of science from any values, ethics, purpose, etc., central to most strands of Western culture since the Enlightenment, is widely accepted as essential to the modern world only on the basis of this true, but utterly one-sided, example of Galileo. In reaction to the ill-conceived attempt by the Roman Church to grasp Science (Galileo) in its talons and to subject his theories to the Church's hierarchy and dogmas, people take for granted that science has won its right to what is essentially an autonomous zone. Galileo's story has thus become a central pillar of the common mythology of

---

[1] For example — they are legion — see Paul R. Gross and Norman Levitt, *op. cit.*, p. 148.

our culture.[1] Yet, this necessary "insulation" from political and religious inter-ference, precisely because it is built on a societal amnesia concerning the par-allel, but opposite, contemporaneous campaign by the Rosicrucians and their allies, who advocated for a science that would serve to liberate people from sickness, ignorance, and poverty — especially since that amnesia is obviously the result of explicit ideological and political controls over what gets told in the dominant culture — is demonstrably a lie. It is really more like a *false* autonomy, one that serves to mask the very real political boundaries within which science has had to operate in modern societies.

The scientific community at the Restoration in England, forsaking political and religious issues in their debates (thus, implicitly, taking a side in such dis-cussions), had to promise as well to eschew *scientific* debate (over causes, frame-works, overall theories). In this way it continued its anti-enthusiastic politics and religion, the middle way of the moderate Latitudinarians. Even as the moun-tains, waterways, and marshes were increasingly fouled by development (min-ing, plantation agriculture, wetlands draining, etc.), "moderate" science acted in accord with the need to help preserve social stability by actively suppressing passions and enthusiasm through its lessons about the objective, dead, nature out of which those mountains and rivers and were all made.

v. A Cry for Perspective!

But wait! Surely I cannot be critiquing Mersenne's creation of a new aesthetic in music, wherein he reduced it to *nothing but vibrations*, by reducing his theory of harmony to *nothing but a framework for insuring social cohesion*, any more than I can claim that Newton's system of the world, with its implicit lesson that nature is only laws of reaction and forces and the consequential movement of dead particles, was *nothing but a device to encourage social stability and access to the coal* — though how it did just that will be the subject of the rest of this essay —for that would be to mir-ror Mersenne's (and to a lesser degree, Newton's) one-dimensional treatment of their subjects with my own, in effect negating my own analysis.

No, Mersenne's help in tempering the scales and reformulating the roles and rules of harmony, no matter what his intent was, were more than only social control. Mersenne (and others) did give new powers to music, and listening to Beethoven's string quartets or Mozart's "Jupiter Symphony," we have been its obvious beneficiaries. To appreciate those works does not mean, however, that we cannot be aware, as well, of all that have been abandoned, for they, too, are considerable: the pure tones, harmonies that are felt, rather than calculated, the

---

1 This is not to deny the role of contemporary examples (e.g., Lysenko, Cre-ationism) in keeping the myth alive, but I believe their import does not negate my argument here. At any rate, Galileo may have got the last laugh. His remains are kept in the Church of Santa Croce (Florence) "as if they were the relics of a saint." Cullen Murphy, *op. cit.*, p. 127.

gateway to ecstasy that anyone can enter with ease, harmonies without an explicit hierarchal tonality. And what was put in place was equally weighty: the complete subordination of rhythm to melody in European classical music from the 18th century on.[1]

Like Mersenne, Newton had larger social aims, and a conceptual lens through which he could judge notions about the cosmos he continually encountered, pondering the many mysteries he was driven to solve. No less than Mersenne, Newton was a survivor of the social upheavals of his youth, and like Mersenne, searched for patterns and processes in nature that could encourage certain solutions and not others to the problems of social instability— though I doubt very much that such was generally Newton's conscious intent.

Yet, Newton, too, required peace. Whether we should attribute it primarily to Newton's own tortured psyche[2] or whether that, too, was primarily a product of the revolutionary decades is not certain, but we shall see how Newton was driven to rage by criticisms of his science. As a result, increasingly he tried to write about his notions so as to deflect criticisms, and pushed into the shadows any ideas that revealed too much of the alchemical schema by which, increasingly, he understood the material world.

Yet, like Mersenne, Newton's physics was more than simply a wrapping around his social aims.[3] His scientific theories had a depth and breath that is unprecedented in the history of humanity, and dazzles our imaginations. We should be able to appreciate the wondrous aspects of Newton's creation, while still recognizing what he surrendered, for just as was the case for Mersenne, it was monumental. For since his theories became the basis of the post-Enlightenment world's common sense, Newton's obfuscations as to his true thoughts, I will argue, to a significant degree can be seen as what has landed us in the present horrific trap — caught up in an economy, an extensive machine-driven social structure, and an ideology that all too frequently appears to be driving our species over some kind of ontological edge.

vi. AFTER ABOVE BUT BEFORE BELOW

It is enlightening to step backwards from these ideological battles, situating them within a more general framework and over a longer timespan. Prior to the specific 17th-century reform movements in music, language, and natural philosophy just discussed, a far broader movement across Europe had been engaged in campaigns to fundamentally reconstruct the body of popular culture. Clergy and laity alike, Catholics and eventually Protestants, from about 1500, had mounted coordinated fights involving a wide swath of practices and beliefs with the aim of suppressing or at least thoroughly distorting popular culture, aiming

---

[1] As will be discussed in Chapter 18.
[2] To be discussed in Chapter 12.
[3] As we shall see in some detail later.

in particular at public gatherings, festivals whose participants were wont to cavort in "over-indulge[s] licence," taking part in markedly savage and pagan behaviors and singing songs whose intonations were troubling. Erasmus, for example, disapproved of the Carnaval he witnessed in Siena in 1509, complaining of its "traces of ancient paganism."[1] Parallel efforts to suppress the "inordinate fondness for music and dancing" were undertaken by the missionaries to America.[2] As Barbara Ehrenreich notes, in connection with the Americas, celebration was seen as a "springboard for rebellion against white rule;" in Europe, it would have been against class rule.[3]

This broader reform movement sought to uproot fundamental cultural values and instill new, more modern, ones, suitable to the new world Europe was fashioning. Where traditional European culture had honored generosity and spontaneity, and tolerated a substantial degree of disorder, for example, the reformers now emphasized the importance of self-control, frugality, hard work, and order, and erected firm lines of demarcation between sacred and profane matters, against the older view of the sacred nature of the land and its cycles.[4]

Activities now discouraged included many with roots in popular magic, including divining, mask-making and -wearing, card-playing; puppetry and theater; and dancing, as well as witchcraft and other forms of explicit magic. Use of folk healers was discouraged. Even Christian plays were thought to be dangerous, for they too engaged the imagination.[5] Coffee-houses, which first appeared in London in 1652, during the rebellion, were now suspect, seen as meeting places for enthusiasm, which is to say, for rebellion.[6]

After numerous civil wars, peasant uprisings, and urban unrest during early modern times, certain aspects of popular culture — especially given the spread of literacy — became even more worrisome to the rulers. Popular rituals were notorious for having egalitarian structures; festivals frequently ended in riots or rebellion. Gatherings of people easily got carried away. An assembly of peasants in Berarac in 1594 ended with cries of "liberté!" Huge demonstrations occurred during England's Civil War. Fifteen thousand people signed the Root and Branch Petition in England in 1640 and twice that number another petition demanding justice against the king's minister, Strafford.[7] Ways to discourage (or short of that, to control) crowds seemed essential to officials.

---

1 Peter Burke, *Popular Culture in Early Modern Europe* (New York: Harper & Row, 1978), p. 209; I am indebted to Prof. James Jacob for bringing this critical work to my attention.

2 Federici, *op. cit.*, p. 200.

3 Ehrenreich, *Dancing in the Streets: A History of Collective Joy* (New York: Metropolitan Books, 2006), pp. 160–61, 164.

4 Burke, *op. cit.*, p. 213.

5 *Ibid.*, p. 212.

6 Cope, *Glanvill*, pp. 36, 43; Mintz, *Sweetness and Power*, p. 111.

7 *Ibid.*, p. 263.

This remarkable broader reform movement seems to fall roughly into two different phases, a first, more general one, dating from about 1500 to 1650, during which *suppression* of followers of the occult was the aim, and a second phase, from the mid-17th century to about the end of the 18th, in which reformers instead tried to *ridicule* occultists.

> Earlier reformers of popular culture… had believed in the efficacy of the magic they denounced as diabolical, indeed, there would be a case for including the great witch hunts… in this [first] movement of reform. However, a number of reformers of the second phase no longer took witchcraft [or other forms of magic] seriously at all.[1]

While the first phase, in other words, focused on how magic was inherently evil, the second emphasized that it was simply a preposterous idea, nonsense that only fools could believe. The campaign against enthusiasm that erupts in the mid-1650s should thus be viewed against this more extended reform movement of which it was the particular crystalization, taking the stage only after a long period of challenging peasant beliefs had come to this particular focus, with the outbreak of the English Civil War so vividly raising the ultimate question of who had power.

vii. The Controlled Experiment as an Ideological Construct

The new science created, as might be expected of any new all-encompassing worldview, a new theory of what could be known and how to know it, most explicitly codified in what came to be known in treatises, textbooks, and lectures, as the "scientific method," adapted and simplified, as auxillary fields like the studies of the economy, society, psychology, ethics, etc., were sooner or later moved to don the cloak of "science" in an effort to make their nascent disciplines more credible. With each telling, *the* scientific method more and more represented its procedures for pursuing knowledge as a *timeless* standard for the seeking of truth, against which *all* inquiry, in whatever era, was measured, with the sages of antiquity like Thales, Anaximander, or Lao Tse frequently ranked by how much of the method they had presciently grasped.

But the method was used not only to evaluate the sages, but additionally to allow the wholesale jettisoning of "superstition," much of it during the Enlightenment. Superstition was simply the traditional knowledge and practices, rituals and sayings, healing potions and a whole range of beliefs going back, in some cases, millennia.

These traditional forms of knowledge, in the "New" World, included the creation myths and healing traditions of indigenous people who were the object

---

1 Burke, *op. cit.*, p. 241.

of colonial agendas.[1] In Europe, the traditional forms were the beliefs and practices of village healers, midwives, wisewomen, and witches.

In the scientific method, observation and experiment are of course key, but
the pinnacle of *proof* was the notion of a *controlled* experiment, where all variables
but one were kept constant in order to pin down with certainty the central question
of *agency*. If all parts of a system save X remained the same, X alone allowed to vary,
and the system under study changed, X was thereby fingered as a central actor.

Of course, the traditional knowledge of the shamans — knowledge that in
many cultures[2] was critical in shaping the hunting, gathering, growing, building,
and healing that is done in order to survive — did not use controlled experiments. Nor could it have. In those traditions, healers do not believe that sickness
is for the most part an identical entity for each person who might manifest its
symptoms, for one person might also have a compromised kidney, another a history of bowel problems, a third a life full of bitterness, hence treatment is not
necessarily the same for all.

The shaman's knowledge *is*, nonetheless, the product of relentless observation, but it is a different form of observation. It is observation of creatures and
phenomena embedded *in*, not abstracted *from*, their worlds. A shaman would
not catch a butterfly and pin its dead body onto cardboard in order to teach
about it; his or her students would instead spend endless hours, perhaps weeks,
in minute observation of many individual flora and fauna as each operates in
league with the rest of its world, the rivers and winds, the cycles, the movement
of stars and herds.

Nor, coming from different landscapes, from mountains or deserts, islands
or river valleys; having different languages and different mythic traditions; and
blessed with a varied availability of power plants,[3] should we imagine that a
shaman or witch from the Ibo, the Hopi, or the Tukano would understand or
treat, what to a Western physician was the same illness, in identical ways.

Controlled experiments are anathema in shamanic healing additionally since
the notion that an ill person should receive only *one* out of a handful of potentially
helpful treatment modalities in order to establish causal relationships would be
considered some kind of violation, as would the use of "placebos," in essence an
attempt to trick the sick person. That is not how healing is to be done.

This is not the place[4] to argue the relative merits of the two distinctly different medicines associated with scientific vs. traditional healing, except I cannot
forbear pointing out that a quite large number of medicines that form the modern
Western pharmacoepia, in fact, were developed by Western scientists from
plants or other substances first used by traditional healers, often for thousands

---

1 See Chapter 2.

2 As shown in Chapters 2, 3, and 4.

3 That is, plants taken by the shaman on his or her journey during healings or
other magical feats, such as peyote or ayahuasca.

4 See Chapter 4.

of years, including, among many others, aspirin, digitalis, quinine, birth control pills, and the opiates, among many others. Though grudgingly admitting to any number of successes in the shamans' use of these remedies, Western scientists (indeed, Western culture in general) embodies its contempt for these traditions with its insistence that any such instances were "of course" discovered by "trial and error," a rhetorical tool of ideology allowing inquiry to dismiss outright any possibility of theoretical frameworks that one might imagine as having pointed the way as to which leaf or root should be taken or applied to a wide variety of injuries and ailments.

Though it is obvious that in many instances conceptual frameworks *are* used in those healing traditions, to a Western eye most of it looks, as it is, like a scaffolding made only of the mud and straw of mythology and incantations. In many instances, when asked how they know which plant to use in a treatment, shamans will reply that the plant told them. In a culture where talking with trees and rocks is part of one's spiritual life, such an answer cannot be lightly discounted, though to a Westerner, raised to see only a world of dead matter, such explanations will immediately be seen as what they clearly *are*, mere "superstitions."

In other words, though the Western scientists — who from the 16th century on, were increasingly on board the voyages of discovery and conquest into the New World — frequently observed the advanced mastery of native healing traditions, they took special pains to discredit and destroy the shamans.[1] From this one is perhaps safe in concluding that *their* observational objectivity was seriously undermined by their ideological prior committment to mechanism as the only way the world could *be,* and could be *understood.* Observation, yes, to be sure — but apparently only certain kinds of observations were what really counted. (What did not fit could be dismissed as "anecdotal.") This is an aspect of the scientific method that is mostly never discussed.

---

[1] As discussed in Chapter 2.

10

A New Model of the Witchcraft Wars

For what else is woman but a foe to friendship, an unescapable punishment, a necessary evil, a natural temptation, a desirable calamity, a domestic danger, a delectable detriment, an evil of nature... — Heinrich Kramer and James Sprenger, *The Malleus Maleficarum* (1489)

[F]rom the fifteenth through the seventeenth centuries, with its power consolidated, European Christianity mounted a rigorous attack against paganism to try to eliminate its hold on popular feeling, while the spread of the market and the development of modern class society altered social morality. Jules Michelet went so far as to argue that the European devil of the early modern period was a figure emerging from popular paganism who was seen as an ally of the poor in their struggle against landlord and Church....

In their efforts to stamp out idolatry, the Spanish credited Indian gods with power and invincibility. A further difficulty preventing the extirpation of indigenous religion was that it permeated every day life, birth, death, agriculture, healing, and so on. Moreover, their icons were largely ineradicable since they were the mountains, rocks, lakes, and streams that composed the sacred geography of nature. — Michael T. Taussig, *The Devil and Commodity Fetishism in South America* (1980)

In a science dominated by men, women have been deemed especially prone to empathy, hence anthropomorphic error and contamination. Long considered inferior to men precisely on the ground that they feel too much, women were thought to overidentify with the animals they studied. This is one reason why male scientists for so long did not encourage female field biologists. They were too emotional; they allowed emotions to sway judgments and observations. Women, it was felt, were more likely than men to attribute emotional attitudes to animals by projecting their own feelings onto them, thereby polluting data. Thus did gender bias and species bias converge in a supposedly objective environment. — Jeffrey Moussaieff Masson and Susan McCarthy, *When Elephants Weep: The Emotional Lives of Animals* (1995)

i. The War Against the Witches In Context

The war against witches in early modern Europe and England was an historical turning point, one at which, as I have stressed, even the best historians, in trying to retrace our collective pathway, have mostly lost their footing. Situated just at the entrance to modern times, the campaign of extermination and torture of witches, killing some hundreds of thousands of mostly women, was contemporaneous, as mentioned before, with the emergence of the first nation-states; with the development of capitalism; and with the relentless drive on the part of continental Europe and England to take control over the other continents and islands of the seas; so too the emergence of ocean-spanning slave trade; and with the beginnings of the inexorable drive to reduce all of nature into "natural resources." And, finally, it was when a new way of thinking, what has been characterized as the "scientific revolution," was being hammered out.

Yet, while reasonable efforts have been made to explain the rise of nation-states; capitalism; the international slave-trade; the scientific revolution; etc., witchcraft, as well as its unprecedented persecution, has gone begging for plausible accountings. As discussed earlier, most people simply assume the campaign and the resultant masses of burned bodies date back to the Dark Ages — a thousand years too early — and, given the presumed pathology of that dismal time, leave it at that.

Legions of historians who do know the correct chronology have gone digging amongst some of the relevant, mostly court, documents, scattered among thousands of civil and ecclesiastical jurisdictions, but for the most part their conclusions — a self-righteous *tsk-tsk* of disapproval — are based on the assumption, rarely justified, that there really *were* no witches, that the massive pile of corpses was actually some kind of ghastly mistake.[1]

When early in the 20th century one anthropologist, Margaret Murray, suggested that witches did exist, regularly meeting for rituals, just as they said they did, and that they held notions similar to ancient beliefs in a nature goddess, she was roundly criticized (her method, her critics said, was quite flawed) and her

---

1 Cullen Murphy (*op. cit.*, p. 197) describes historians of the war against witches as "looking to explain the origins of mass hysteria."

theory summarily dismissed in vitriolic attacks.[1] "Witch hunt," in the modem idiom, especially on the left, has come to mean a highly visible campaign against chimeras, enemies who exist only in the mind. With rare exceptions. scholars seem determined to believe there were no witches.[2]

There are several things that strike me as quite odd about this. *First,* and most obviously, it is difficult for me to attribute so many dead bodies, spread over such an extended geographical and temporal range, to something so inconsequential as a mistake or so general as mass hysteria. *Second,* there is more than a hint of racism in this denial of witches *really* existing in early modern Europe, for many of the same historians who make such claims readily accept the reality of witches or *brujas* in Africa or Latin America. On what basis do they suppose Europe should have been different? *Third,* why are we taught that witches did not exist when no one bothers to deny the existence of their brother and sister occultists at the time — the alchemists, astrologers, natural magicians, cabalists, etc? What is the difference? Apart from the piles of dead witches, mostly women, littering the historical landscape of early modern times? To be sure, astrologers, alchemists, and their like wrote and published treatises on their respective arts, which we do not have from witches before the present century or so.[3] Witchcraft, in general, has remained an oral tradition, not generating much of an accounting by its practitioners, partly, no doubt, as a result of its historic suppression.

Astrologers, cabalists, alchemists, and practitioners of other occult arts also tend to operate solo or as small units, perhaps reading each other's manuscripts and books and possibly maintaining informal contact with one another. But except for the Rosicrucians, who may not have actually existed as more than a shared ideology, and later the Freemasons, there were no organizations of alchemists, astrologers, etc., that we know of. So, *fourth,* witches, by contrast with

---

[1] Thus, H. R. Trevor-Roper claims that Murray's "fancies" were "justly…. dismissed by a real scholar as 'vapid balderdash'," citing C. L. Ewen, (Trevor-Roper, *The European Witch-Craze of the Sixteenth and Seventeenth Centuries and Other Essays* (New York: Harper & Row, 1967), p. 116 n. 1. Even so later historians such as Carlo Ginzburg, *Witchcraft & Agrarian Cults in the Sixteenth and Seventeenth Centuries,* transl. John & Anne Tedeschi (New York: Penguin Books, 1985; Italian orig., 1966), p. xix, though accepting that Murray made serious errors, argue that her fundamental thesis is prevailing.

[2] Carlo Ginzburg suggests such an aversion to thinking that witches could have actually existed stems from the fear, common among historians, of yielding to sensationalism or credulity regarding magical powers, as well as uncertainty about how to handle the "absurdity" of things like flying to their sabbaths or other beliefs common among witches. Ginzburg, *Ecstasies: Deciphering the Witches' Sabbath.,* trans. Raymond Rosenthal (New York: Penguin Books, 1992), p. 11).

[3] Be assured, despite the figure of the witch as hag, a number of the witches, especially in England where literacy was high, would have been able to read and write, so that was not the isssue.

the other occultists, were said to meet regularly in small groups, called covens, where they conducted their magic in accord with the lunar and solar calendars. Besides the fact that must of the witches *were* women, witchcraft, *fifth,* was portrayed as a practice in which women bore most of the responsibilities, notwithstanding lurid tales of secret coupling with the presumably male devil.

Even more notable is that contemporaneous with the war against witchcraft in Europe was the even bloodier war against indigenous people in the lands being explored and then colonized by the Europeans. There, too, the shamans or healers were especially singled out for punishment and execution, as we saw in Chapters 2 and 4. In the proto-colonies, shamans may have been singled out, but the whole population was at risk. While a number of the colonized who died as a result of European contact were. like the witches, wiped out by violence,[1] many more fell because of strange new diseases from Europe to which natives had no immunity at all. Also different was that the indigenous victims had to contend with the havoc inflicted on their local ecology by newly-arrived foreign plants (for example, plantain) and animals (feral pigs) tearing up the countryside and wiping out staples of the indigenous diet. Additionally, the sheer scope of the disruption of essential features of their social, economic, and spiritual systems that had traditionally kept people fed and taken care of delivered a devastating blow to indigenous people — though a parallel of sorts existed for the European peasants uprooted by land enclosures.

The two sets of victims had some profound similarities as well. For example, both the natives of the colonized lands and the witches of Europe or England saw their world in magical, animist terms. Like that of the natives, the spiritual fabric of women-focused witchcraft was polytheistic, and had been woven out of the skeins of an animate vision of nature, a world alive in every nook and cranny and flowing with a vitality out of which traditional healing systems were, in culture after culture, constructed. In Part One, readers may recall, we saw how native healing traditions (which in at least some instances we know to have been remarkably effective), were forcibly suppressed by the colonial powers, and the medicine of their Western colonizers, including the philosophical basis on which it rested, imposed. This was the case even though for the poor the colonizers' medicine was frequently unavailable, for unlike indigenous healing it was quite costly and often much less effective.

Let me suggest on the basis of all this a different interpretation of the "witch craze" (as it is sometimes called) of early modern Europe, one which starts with three of the anomalies I have just discussed. First, the fact of all those dead bodies, demanding an explanation of substance; second, the common denial that there actually *were* any witches; and third, the remarkable coincidence in time of the *external* extermination of peoples undergoing colonization with this similar *internal* campaign of mass destruction, both of them perfuming the air with the stench of burning flesh.

---

[1] As described in Part One.

I shall offer in the form of a working hypothesis an alternative approach to the witchcraft wars, hoping that these speculations might help clarify many matters otherwise enigmatic, starting with the central fact — vast numbers of dead.[1] It is sensible to assume a massive, geographically extended and long-lasting campaign of extermination arose, for some important reason or other,[2] we must wonder what such a purpose might have been. Let me suggest it was precisely because witches were obvious impediments blocking the way to modernity, and particularly (in hindsight) to the modern capitalist State, that their systematic extermination over a period of two centuries became such a high priority for certain elites. Once capitalism was playing a significant economic role — and in some areas of Europe we can find this as early as the 14th century — it demands that resources be freely accessible. For the "free," as in "free enterprise," really means "free" to take from the rivers, the rain forests, and the ground, and "free," in turn, to return a degraded environment, liberally awash with poison and wastes, with generous portions of fouled air, water, and soil, the slag heap that capitalist (initially) industrial development commonly leaves in its wake.

This process was already well underway and generally understood by many in early modern Europe. The freedom for which men and women struggled in the end applied less to them than to the near-absolute freedom of *property* — land as privately-owned property, especially, a concept unknown in feudal Europe, just as it is not found in most indigenous cultures; land able to be bought and sold, subject only to standard contractual rules developed then so as to keep ownership clear and enforceable.[3]

Those who followed the old ways, who stood for customary rights over land so that everyone could, though in different measures and manners, share in its bounty and uses, those who saw nature as alive and the Earth as sacred were un-

---

[1] Because of the many jurisdictions, ecclesiastical and civil, involved in the persecution of witches, not to mention the centuries over which it was spread, reliable estimates as to the numbers actually killed are quite difficult to arrive at. In the 1980s, some feminist scholars estimated several million witches were killed in Europe, perhaps unconsciously reaching for a number in the range of those killed in the Nazi Holocaust, but more recent scholarship, while acknowledging the difficulty in establishing a reliable figure, suggests a number closer to two hundred thousand. Christina Larner, *Witchcraft and Religion: The Politics of Popular Belief,* (ed.) Alan Macfarlane (Oxford, England: Basil Blackwell Ltd., 1985).

[2] Eric Hobsbawm, *The Age of Extremes: A History of the World, 1914–1991* (New York: Vintage Boks, 1994), in a different context, makes this point.

[3] Linebaugh, *op. cit.,* and Thompson (*Customs in Common*) elucidate with many fine examples the way in which these new rights were contested and negotiated over many decades, which here I must telescope, focusing on final rules.

[3] For a modern perspective on what this feels like, see Ann Pancake's very fine, movingly written, *Strange As This Weather Has Been* (n.p.: Shoemaker Hoard Publishers, 2007), about mountaintop-removal mining in West Virginia.

willing to go along with the ideological degradation of that natural world to the "resources" demanded by the capitalist economy. Witches, whose worship focused on the natural world of moon and heath, were such. But so too, I believe, were a lot of the population in the countryside; if we can assume the toxic effects of the now-voracious mines would have grown much worse since Agricola's time, as well as people's outrage at the devastation, the desecration. In the colonized lands of the Americas, Africa, and parts of Asia, virtually everyone would have been horrified.[3]

At any rate, especially with the onset of the Civil War in England, rebellion itself became synonymous with witchcraft. As Woolley explains

> At the outbreak of the Civil War, one of the charges levelled against radicals was the biblical nostrum that "Rebellion is as the sin of witchcraft." The royalist newspaper *Mercurius Aulicus* claimed that witchcraft was a "usual attendant on former rebellions," and others noted that, since the outbreak of hostilities, the number of witches had proliferated "more… ever this Island bred since the Creation." The *Parliamentary Journal* observed that "it is the ordinary mirth of the malignants of this city to discourse with the association of witches."[1]

Given such associations, it is no wonder that there were more reported instances of witchcraft throughout the early modern period.

The colonized *did* come under the gun or over the pyre and were subject to a host of other threats to their safety or life, just as the witches, but in Europe it was witches (and other heretics) alone who were hunted down. Though occasionally a *magus* like Bruno was burned or, like Dee, had to take flight, these were infrequent. Why were there no *autos da fé* against astrologers? Or cabalists? Was there some way witches, more than cabalists or astrologers, both of whom were also seen as dangerous by authorities, stood out as more of a threat, one requiring mass extermination? These, it would appear, are important questions to pursue. To help in this regard, let us take a look at changing social roles of women in early modern times.

ii. GENDERED BATTLEFIELDS IN EARLY MODERN TIMES

Two key differences were identified earlier. First, witchcraft was mostly of and about women; second, witches are supposed to have been organized, meeting in small circles for ceremonies on a regular basis. Larger assemblies were thought to be held once a year or more. As such, witches had the potential to serve as alternative centers of power, out of the control that central authorities were feverishly trying to consolidate in those tumultuous times. Part of that tumult amounted to a generalized campaign against women specifically.

---

[1] Woolley, *Heal Thyself*, p. 215.

Women in those times were subject to special surveillance, and new forms of control; new laws that applied specifically to them, a number of which carried death sentences, and other restrictions on their rights and freedoms, were being increasingly imposed in early modern Europe.

For one thing, from the 15th century on, authorities and the guilds placed severe limits on what kinds of work women could engage in. In medieval times, women butchers, smiths, candlestick makers, hatters, brewers of ale, carders of wool, furriers, harness makers, and retailers could be found in towns. In Frankfurt, there were some 200 different occupations for women between 1300 and 1500. Out of eighty-five guilds in England, seventy-two had women members. In the 14th century one could find women schoolteachers, doctors and surgeons.[1] Peasant and farm women — in addition to bearing and raising the children and performing various tasks women traditionally had in relation to the animals — engaged in whatever duties and crafts were necessary to run their households and farms, which included making cheese, soap, cloth, and beer, as well as gardening, cooking, and healing. Unmarried women might be employed as servants or as laborers in mowing, reaping, etc. Urban women worked in various crafts or trades, and some were members of craft guilds, as mentioned earlier. Noblewomen supervised their estates and frequently would keep the accounts.

This all begins to change in the late-15th century, when craft workers, probably reacting to women being paid lower wages, tried to exclude women from membership. In the 16th and 17th centuries, new laws established restrictions on women. In France they could no longer be a party to a contract, nor represent themselves in court. In Germany, middle-class widows had their affairs taken over by tutors. Also in Germany, women were unable to live with other women. In England, women's presence in public places began to be stigmatized.[2]

In all classes, married women ended up being more economically dependant on their husbands. Among the propertied classes, women were expected to display in the domestic sphere the trappings of their leisure and of their husbands' successes.[3] Whereas in Elizabethan times, such women often managed the family estates if widowed or when their husbands were away, after the 1660 Restoration in England a "lady of quality" was identified *by* her leisure, her life increasingly defined by religious and charitable activities. Involvement in productive work was discouraged for such women; to them were reserved the qualities denoting "refinement."

Wives of yeoman farmers and husbanders, also involved early in the 17th century in productive activity on their lands, were increasingly replaced by day laborers and servants, and simply withdrew into leisure activities as the gentry prospered. Underpinning the new restrictions on women from these classes entering the recognized economic sphere was a new ideology that emphasized women's essential helplessness.

---

1 Federici, *op. cit.*, p. 171.

2 *Ibid.*, pp. 100–02.

3 See Thompson, *Customs in Common*, pp. 74–75, on ostentation and display.

For women in families without property, of course, the new conventions were even more constricting. Under capitalist agriculture, many male farm laborers, now without access to land on which to grow food, substantially depended on wages for themselves and their families. If the woman in a family worked out of the house, her wages were much less than her husband's. Women deserted by husbands or widowed now frequently became destitute. In lean times, even women "lucky" enough to remain married often went hungry, along with their children, while if their husbands worked they would be fed at work as part of their wages. Infant mortality was very high in the frequently lean times in 17th-century England.

In the trades, too, the growing mass of capitalist production in the 17th century drove craftsmen and journeymen from small shops into wage-labor, and a wife who, in earlier times when the household was the dominant unit of production, had helped or ran the business herself if widowed, was now relegated to the shadows of the official economy. In some of the women's trades, such as cloak- or hat-making, women still were able to become apprenticed, but in crafts like baking, butchery, brewing, or fishmongering, rules and statutes were adopted in an effort to limit the numbers able to work, and women lost their former economic status. By the end of the 17th century, the brewing trades, for example, once monopolized by women, saw control pass over to men.

In a variety of occupations and classes, therefore, by about the end of the 17th century, women had been pushed out of the sphere of production. Simultaneously, more and more women were relegated to the sphere of reproduction.

Reproduction and sexuality in general became central battlefields in what amounted to a war against women. Partly, the authorities were mindful of the devastating effect — higher wages, for one — of the mass die-off brought about by the bubonic plague in the 14th century. But with the decreasing availability of land, combined with new restrictions on guild membership, some peasants and artisans limited conception (with the use of certain herbs, for example). In the 16th and 17th century this became highly contested terrain. By the middle of the 16th century, all the governments of Europe "began to impose the severest penalties against contraception, abortion, and infanticide."[1] In France new laws mandated that all pregnancies had to be registered. In effect, reproduction was literally turned into a form of forced labor.

In the medieval period, prostitution was often tolerated,[2] and some brothels were state-run. Now it became criminalized. In France, rape of prostitutes was decriminalized, even as the number of prostitutes increased.[3] Childbirth by unmarried women was outlawed, and infanticide and adultery became capital crimes.[4]

Midwifery was where the battles against women was particularly intense — an especially apt thread to follow in a book on ecology, on the fight to safeguard the

[1] Federici, *op. cit.,* p. 88.
[2] Federici, *op. cit.,* p. 49.
[3] *Ibid.,* p. 94.
[4] *Ibid.,* pp. 186 and 214 n. 27.

processes of bringing forth. By the end of the 17th century, birthgiving, traditionally a realm wholly under the control (after conception) of women, as it had been at the beginning of the century, had passed out of their hands. Midwives, providers of abortions as well as live births, came under suspicion.[5] During the Thirty Years War (1618–48), nearly all the midwives of Cologne were executed (as witches).

Early in the 1600s a family of male physicians challenged the monopoly of women in delivering children. Dr. Peter Chamberlen and his son, also a physician and also a Peter, attempted in 1616 to form a corporation of midwives. Midwives resisted joining, doubting the doctors' motives and fearing it was only a ruse to get control of their craft. They also opposed the Chamberlens' advocacy of forceps-delivery of babies, charging that such births were based on "extraordinary violence." The forceps had been invented by the Chamberlens and, as an instrument authorized for use only by surgeons, was a convenient "technological" means of driving women out of midwifery.[1] In a petition midwives submitted, they also complained that "Dr. Chamberlane... hath no experience in [midwifery] but by reading." Numerous attacks by physicians against midwifery practices were published, including treatises by both Drs. Peter Chamberlen (1616), by Peter Chamberlen III (1647), by Hugh Chamberlen, the Elder, by Paul Chamberlen (1665), and by William Harvey (1651), who denounced midwives' attempts to aid women in lessening their pains, and disparaged using massage as a means to open the birth canal.[2]

Jane Sharp and Elizabeth Cellier, both English midwives, responded by publishing handbooks of midwifery so as to improve education for its practitioners. So too did Nicolas Culpeper, the radical herbalist who was involved in several challenges to the monopolies of power and knowledge physicians assumed. A school for midwives was established in France for the same purposes.

It is not clear how successful the Chamberlens, Harveys, and others opposed to midwifery actually were. Merchant claims that by 1700 "childbirth was passing into the hands of male doctors and 'man-midwives'," while Woolley believes the campaign, at least until mid-century, was "successfully resisted."[3]

Women and the idea of the feminine also served certain critical ideological functions, at a time when the exploitation of nature's "resources" was emerging

---

[1] *Ibid.*, p. 89; Duerr, *op. cit.*, p. 194 n. 48.

[2] No doubt not the first, and clearly not the last time a change in technological deployment was used for political and social reasons; other examples include the early use of computerized machinery in the manufacturing of aircraft, as will be discussed in Part Three, and the introduction of mechanized cotton-picking in the US South in the middle of the 20th century.

[3] Massage to open the birth canal is still used by midwives. It is noteworthy that the male physicians believed forceps, metal instruments, cold, unyielding and unfeeling, to be preferable to soft, warm, yielding, and sentient human hands for delivery, reflecting, one might suspect, besides their sexual anxieties, preference for machines.

as the central priority in the new political economy. Nature and the feminine had long been virtually synonymous. Operating as a metaphor or as metaphysics, we can understand how this could have especially powerful consequences: in order to tame nature, as required by the new capitalist social order, women had to be brought under clear control. Witches were women not under control, or at least under any control that really mattered; their subjugation (and a very public sub-jugation at that) could be an absolute priority for the emerging social order of early modern times. Worse, their being organized into a network of covens sug-gested to authorities the threat of an alternative system of control, so that their subjugation (and a very public subjugation at that) could be an absolute priority for the emerging social order of early modern times!

Finally, it was undoubtedly the case that the places chosen for development, for quarries, sheep-grazing enclosures, or wetlands slated for draining to create arable areas, were frequently the very sites where the presence of holy springs, sa-cred trees, or a circle of rocks stood, places of power and veneration for the peasants for as long as anyone could remember and where witches might hold rites at equinoxes, solstices, full or new moons. Such rites, and especially those who led them, must have been intolerable, formidable barriers in the way of modernity.

There is one further historical pattern that I shall suggest in this hypothet-ical social and ideological accounting for the warfare against witches in early modern Europe. As Taussig has pointed out, in the Bolivian Andes in more re-cent times, as the taproots of colonialism force their way into the soil of the social system, and many peasants are driven to work the mines (or the plantations), experiencing and witnessing the utter misery and chaos that is commonly now their lot as waged laborers (or slaves), not uncommonly they react by concluding that the devil has obviously taken over. Only thus can the peasants explain the sudden generalized suffering everywhere they look.

Accordingly, in Bolivia rituals begin to be enacted specifically to seek pro-tection from the malign entity in control, for if he is not given his due, he is likely simply to take it, perhaps in ways especially horrific. To the miners, especially, the reality of Hell is palpable: lives getting crushed in instants from cave-ins, explosions, or falling; miners drowning, suffocating, getting poisoned by mer-cury, lead, or arsenic, and frequently suffering from a myriad of mining-related diseases, many of which are fatal. Such dangers often lurk beneath the ground, but they do not remain there, for some of the poisons follow the miners home, on their clothes or shoes or hair, to affect spouses, lovers, parents, children, an-imals. Even some of the Spanish colonialists referred to the largest mining city, Potosí (in Bolivia), as a "mouth to hell."[2]

And so altars are built for those demons and on them offerings are made — not necessarily because these Bolivian natives Taussig describes truly worship

---

[1] An illuminating discussion of the multitude of Doctors Chamberlane is in Mer-chant, *Death of Nature*, pp. 153–55. Woolley, *op. cit.*, p. 308.

[2] Taussig, *Devil*, p. 202. Rosen, *History of Mining Diseases*.

the devil, but because they believe that giving him offerings will make it less likely it will be their own crushed body lying under the pile of rocks next time.

It should not be too much of a stretch of our imaginations, given Taussig's analysis, to consider the real possibility that similar experiences and feelings erupted in England and Europe during the explosive rise there from the 15th century on of an industrial mining technology and large agricultural and pastoral operations. As English and European peasants lost *their* land and were forced to rely on waged labor to survive, as they were driven into the hellholes of German silver or English coal mines, wouldn't they, too, have seen the disintegration of their communities and families and concluded that the devil had begun calling the shots? Under these circumstances, might they similarly have thought it best to make altars for offerings to such evil spirits in an effort to appease their demonic hungers? To a clergy overzealous on the topic of heresy, as was the case in the 16th and 17th centuries in Europe, these offerings or sacrifices could readily be interpreted as evidence of widespread and growing worship of the devil, thus creating the impetus for carrying out a thorough purge against those who had been worshipping the older gods and goddesses in the countryside.

In sum, the war against witches ran concurrently with a war against women in the economic, social and reproductive worlds of early modern times. Since historically fights against desecration of the woods, rivers, and estuaries tend to be led by women,[1] demonization of witches and the reign of "Burning Times," as those two centuries are called by contemporary witches, cleared the landscape of opposition in what should be understood as a war of terror against women.

To be sure, some of the above analysis is conjectural, and some rests on my belief — not accepted by many scholars — that the witches who obviously did exist in early modern Europe and England, as the discredited Margaret Murray claimed, and as was later validated in many respects by the more recent researches of Carlo Ginzburg (*The Worm and the Cheese*) and Julio Caro Baroja (*The World of the Witches*), pursued forms of spirituality that can roughly be described as "pagan." Some of the broad outlines of their rituals and beliefs can be traced back to Paleolithic times and the worship of the Great Goddess and her consort over extensive areas of North Africa and Europe, especially troublesome given the predominance of women (especially prone to heresy, noted Bishop Irenaeus), slaves, and the lower orders of society.[2]

Against these potential warning signs, that my model and its claims might be too rooted in my own values and beliefs, however, there stands the fact that my analysis at least provides a coherent explanation of the long-lasting and widespread bloody campaign against witches, which is currently incoherent. It also

---

[1] As in Love Canal, the campaign to save the San Francisco Bay, Greenham Commons, Judi Bari, Vandana Shiva, etc.

[2] Hill, *op. cit.*, p. 250; Ehrenreich, *op. cit.*, p. 35; Evans, *God of Ecstasy*, pp. 40, 42, 52, 110, 140; Duerr, *op. cit.*, pp. 13, 25; Evans, *Witchcraft and the Gay Counterculture*, p. 22; Pagels, *op. cit.*, p. 70; Baroja, *op. cit.*, p. 123; Sale, *op. cit.*, p. 249.

has, to me, the distinct advantage that it draws the witches from the margins, where they were singularly out of place, in to the central stage of the coming of modernity. Far from being a ghastly mistake, the witch persecutions are revealed as central gears in the machinery that pulled the new social order of the 16th and 17th centuries — the slave trade, nation-states, colonialism, capitalism, and ecological devastation everywhere — into place. And as well, it reveals the centrality of the punishment, repression, and exploitation of women as an integral part of the same process by which racial and class categories were made central to the structures of oppression and exploitation in that new order.

11

Signs of Life in Brute Matter?

Even though the followers of the old religion were cruelly per-
secuted, the authority of native ritualists did not necessarily
diminish. Called *brujos*, witches, or sorcerers by the Spanish,
such ritualists perforce led a secretive existence. Preconquest
religion did not die out; it went underground in the form of
"magic" and dissimulated itself in a variety of ways....
     The Christian Fathers in the Andes had the supremely dif-
ficult task of supplanting pagan views of nature with Church-
derived doctrines. They had to effect a revolution in the moral
basis of cognition itself. Many of the *huacas* [sacred places such
as holy springs] populating and coordinating nature could not
be removed. The Church, as the Fathers said, had therefore
to root them from the Indians' hearts. If the signs could not be
eradicated, then their signification had to be. A new semiotic
had to be written, as large and as all-encompassing as the universe itself. The Indians had to be properly taught the sources
of springs and rivers, how the lightning is forged in the sky,
how the waters freeze, and other natural phenomena, which
their teacher will have to know well. Two issues stood out: the
implications of the regularity of nature and ontogeny. —
Michael T. Taussig, *The Devil and Commodity Fetishism in South
America* (1980)

i. The Common Touch of a Gnostic Savior

Despite the public campaigns against enthusiasm and warnings about
the dangers of popular culture in general and of alchemy, prophecy, or
astrology, natural magic, and witchcraft, in particular, those dangers
continued into the Restoration. Passions ran too deep and issues were too intertwined for easy resolution. The newly restored monarchy was to be an ideo-

logical bedrock, anchoring a sober repudiation of the "excesses" of the revolutionary years, but that role was hard to discern against a background of a court
well-known for its licentious carryings-on. Whereas Puritans had managed to
get Parliament to ban maypoles in 1644, constables mandated to destroy them.
With the Restoration they reappeared, though by 1717, one in London had been
reappropriated as a stand to hold Sir Isaac Newton's new telescope.[1]

Beneath the surface of the new social order, dissent against the Restoration
simmered from the onset, and authorities were on the alert for plots and signs
of rebellion.[2] Six years into the new monarchy, when disaster hit England, open
conflict seemed once more imminent. Being the 666th year of the second millennium, the year 1666, in that most apocalyptic of centuries, had already received prophetic attentions. The important astrologer William Lilly, among
others, had issued special prognostications for the fateful year, including one of
a huge fire. When England was hit in 1664 (London in 1665) by bubonic plague
and then, in 1666, the great fire of London, such visions and many others seemed
vindicated. Additionally, natural disasters are widely interpreted across the
world as nature's plebiscites on the rulers of a land.[3]

That same year a powerful healer/seer emerged out of obscurity, soon acquiring a substantial following in England. Such figures have appeared from
time to time in Europe, Coudertian "gnostic saviors." Valentine Greatrakes, also
known as the "Irish Stroker," in 1662 was able to self-heal his own persistent
arm pains and then experienced an inner calling for him to attempt healing the
sickness then known as the "King's Evil," a swelling of the glands in the neck

---

[1] Bord and Bord, *op.cit.*, p. 183.
[2] For mobs hostile to the Restoration settlement and authorities fearing a return
of Civil War, see Max Beloff, *op. cit.*, p. 35. A standing army to put down disorders
was introduced at the Restoration; its size was increased in 1662 (*Ibid.*, pp. 144f);
R. Bosher, *Making of the Restoration Settlement: The Influence of the Laudians,
1649–1662* (Westminster, 1951), p. 145. Joseph Glanvill warned of a return to
the "chaos of the fourties." (Cope, *Joseph Glanvill*, p. 38.) The year 1662 was worrisome because a prevailing high price for food and a scarcity of money combined
with new taxes to cause an upswell of discontent. Rumors of risings in successive
years egged on the repressive acts of the Clarendon Code, according to the noted
historian David Ogg, "passed when the air was heavy with rumours of rebellions
and insurrections; it needed only a few genuine plots to justify such fears in the
minds of the legislature." (Quoted in Beloff, *op. cit.*, pp. 35–36.). The Clarendon
Code, enacted over a period of four years, was a series of Parliamentary shackles
to repress all forms of religious dissent or possible *foci* for political resistence.
[3] Traditionally, this was a recurring theme in Chinese history, but we see it as
well in Nicaragua under Somoza, when a great earthquake that levelled Managua
played a role in his downfall. On Lilly, see Bernard Capp, "The Fifth Monarchists," in McGregor and Reay, *op. cit.*, pp. 176–77.

and inflammation of the joints and mucous membranes. According to tradition, this disease could be alleviated only with the personal touch by a monarch, an ability they possessed by virtue of their divine anointment. Greatrakes, a gentleman but not an aristocrat, found that he *could* successfully treat sufferers of the King's Evil, the implications of which were most unsettling. After all, it had not been that long since republicans had denied the legitimacy of monarchical power. Here was proof that such power might be in anyone. Like the Rosicrucians, Greatrakes refused to take money for the treatments he gave.

As the Irish Stroker began to heal people suffering from a wide range of diseases, his cures became legendary. Edward, Viscount Conway, called Greatrakes to his English estate to treat his wife, Lady Anne Conway, for her long-standing migraines. Lady Anne was a central figure in the Latitudinarian movement, with close ties both to important transitional figures within Hermeticism, such as the Van Helmonts,[1] and to Henry More and Robert Boyle and other figures significant in Restoration natural philosophy. Against Lady Anne's headaches, Greatrakes had no success, but in the nearby city of Worcester he was able to cure huge crowds of the sick and lame. His reputation spread even more broadly, to wider social circles. Greatrakes' treatments were witnessed by many — Robert Boyle personally saw and wrote about some sixty or more successful healings in London by the Stroker.

In the previous year, 1665, avoiding crowds because of his fear of the plague then spreading in England, Charles II had abandoned performing the office of the Royal Touch to those with the King's Evil. For similar reasons, most physicians had stopped treating the sick. Accordingly, the Irish Stroker's healings especially stood out. Hearing of Greatrakes, Charles II summoned him to court in London to demonstrate his powers. The Stroker came and his obvious successes at court won him a massive following in England, including nobles, clergy, and "people of all ages, sexes, and conditions." The Solicitor General of England worried at the huge number of Greatrakes' followers, accusing him, according to Greatrakes, of creating "the greatest faction and distraction between clergy and layman that any one has these 1000 years," an astounding accusation coming only a handful of years after the Civil War and revolution. Another critic of the Stroker, David Lloyd, charged that Greatrakes' cures might well be part of a republican plot against the monarchy, for if ordinary citizens could heal, Lloyd deduced, they might as well "give laws to the world." He suspected either republican or Catholic involvement in the matter, and was certain it would bring about an increase in atheism and sedition. Another writer anonymously claimed to see a connection between Greatrakes' work and the imminent millennium.

---

[1] J. B. Van Helmont was an influential physician and alchemist, whose works were publshed by his son F. M. (for Mercury) Van Helmont.

ii. POWERS IN NATURE?

Greatrakes' cures did become grist for the mill of one important republican theorist, Henry Stubbe, a man associated during the Civil War not only with republican, but also regicidal, politics. Stubbe was also one of the most pointed of the critics of Thomas Sprat, after Sprat had published his ideological *History of the Royal Society* in 1667. According to Stubbe, the miraculous aspects of the Stroker's cures demonstrated that there were powers *in* nature, and he dared to draw parallels between Greatrakes' abilities and the healings attributed to Jesus. Stubbe's wild assertions undermined the orthodox Christian separation between God and His supernatural powers, on the one hand, and nature, on the other, and were especially worrisome, given Stubbes' republican and pagan views,[1] dangerous enough to mobilize Robert Boyle, who was incensed by Stubbe's radical ideas.[2]

Boyle was the wealthy son of Richard Boyle, the first Earl of Cork and one of the most powerful men in early-17th-century England. The first Earl's enormous wealth came from his interests in Ireland, where he had purchased considerable land from Sir Walter Raleigh. Robert, Richard's youngest son, is worth examining in several regards. He played a key role in establishing belief in the mechanical philosophy, though for all his life he was a practicing alchemist. He was a central figure in the founding of the Royal Society. Not least Boyle had crucial roles to play in several critical economic, religious and social institutions that loomed large in Restoration England, as the foundations for the English Empire were, as J.R. Jacob shows, laid in earnest. Jacobs argues that Boyle's economic and social goals helped shape the nature of his theory of corpuscularianism.

Boyle was the governor of the Company for the Propagation of the Gospel in New England, which was chartered in 1662, the same year as the Royal Society; was an active member of the Council for Foreign Plantations; and was a Governor of the New England Company, responsible for overseeing trade with the colonies there. In all of these positions of power, we can see the characteristic themes of Latitudinarian ideology, in which science is mandated to serve consciously the interests of empire, trade, and religious (Protestant) reform.

In New England, for instance, Boyle clearly stated his aim was to pry the Native Americans loose from their tribal ways, not only including what some missionaries saw as their "idle and lecherous habits," but also their superstitions

---

1 J.R. Jacob believes those views more or less survived the Restoration, though under conditions of heavy censorship, Stubbe expressed them only in veiled statements. Jacob, *Henry Stubbe, Radical Protestantism and the Early Enlightenment* (Cambridge, England: Cambridge Univ. Press, 1983).

2 Boyle might have been concerned had he known that, early in his attempts at healing, Greatrakes obtained a book of spells, which he later burned; he also tried using charms and magic, but later abandoned those as well (Pitt, *A Small Moment*, p. 148).

and "ridiculous Notions" about the workings of nature. Their degenerate view of land, that it was not proper to buy, sell, or own it, was, possibly, the most worrisome of these. To help in the fight against the Catholic powers, it was necessary to expand England's empire, which required the conversion of Native Americans to Protestantism. The "idle" natives would then be put to work. The discipline of hard work would convey a host of vital lessons, from bringing to those who had mastered its dos and don'ts access to an array of commodities, to forcing the heathen natives to abandon those former idle and lecherous practices.[1]

Along with others in the Royal Society, Boyle also advocated work schemes meant to undermine the heretical behavior of English sectarians, engaging them in activities that could consume so much of their time and energy that they would have had none left for heretical studies or enthusiastic carryings-on.

Like many other Fellows of the early Royal Society, Robert Boyle had been involved in a project to survey the natural "wealth" of New England that might be extracted by native labor. Charles II was an early supporter of the plan. Along with Samuel Hartlib, John Dury, Benjamin Worsley and others in the late 1650s, Boyle had earlier been part of a plan to build an academy for research along the lines originally proposed by Francis Bacon and J.A. Comenius on land confiscated by Cromwell in Ireland, as the English campaign against that sorry land dramatically extended its reach.

Boyle and the early Royal Society emphasized the need to base all knowledge in natural philosophy on a foundation of experimental investigations. How nature actually worked was to be key. Among other things, Boyle hoped, an experimental philosophy would allow the English to gain "social control of native people within the empire," peacefully winning them over from their mistaken tribal *mores* that were formidable barriers to their successful colonization.[2]

---

[1] J.R. Jacob, *Robert Boyle and the English Revolution,* pp. 139, 150–52, 155. See also Jacob, *Henry Stubbe.* This campaign to coerce natives into waged labor would have been quite an uphill battle, as it is whenever a workforce is first introduced to waged-work, what Taussig refers to as the "indifference or outright hostility of peasants and tribespeople the world over" necessitating a massive effort, frequently based on force, to bring them over. (Taussig, *Devil,* pp. 19f; also, Thompson, *Customs in Common*). Cf. Davis, *op. cit.,* p. 49 on how loss of their lands was used to cure them of the "excessive liberty" natives enjoyed. Linebaugh (*The London Hanged,* p. 410) comments, for a later period, on the alliance of science and a culture of command, and rationality to impose discipline on the workers in the London shipyards. The prominent English jurist, Sir Mathew Hale, upon visiting a plantation in Barbados, admired the orderliness of its slave workers, hoping the workhouse would instill in the London poor a similar work habit. (Linebaugh, *London Hanged,* p. 68.) Boyle believed that getting men to work decreased the threat of subversion from below. (Jacob, *Stubbe,* p. 85.)

[2] Jacob, *Robert Boyle,* p. 151.

iii. THE "HIGH ROAD" OF HERMETICISM?

The center of Boyle's grand design, the merging of scientific inquiry with the other central strands of his vision — completing the Protestant Reformation; building an English empire; and extending and expanding commerce — rested on Boyle's "corpuscularian philosophy," his gloss on the mechanical philosophy. Indebted as he was to certain prominent alchemists, such as Paracelsus and J.B. van Helmont, Boyle nonetheless sought a "high road" of Hermetic alchemy, built of bricks made from the mud and straw of the mechanical philosophy's matter and motion.[1] Like the key continental mechanists, Mersenne, Gassendi, and Descartes, Boyle took particular exception to the notion of a world soul, or *anima mundi*, separate from God and governing the motions of the parts of Creation. Boyle's corpuscularianism was in opposition to the implications of an *anima mundi* that attributed perception, volition, and even an ethos to "brute matter."

The centrality of this anathema in Boyle's program made the healings by Greatrakes (many of them witnessed by Boyle) — particularly as interpreted by Stubbe as demonstrating powers in nature — all the more troubling. To make matters considerably worse, Greatrakes' own political associations were problematic. Robert Phaire, Greatrakes' former regimental commander, someone he was still in touch with, was one of those involved in the execution of Charles I and was a Ranter. Though the Stroker himself was not a member, he was sympathetic to the Muggletonians and to Lodowicke Muggleton.[2]

Even more ominously, at the Restoration a new self-identified circle, having connections to the aristocracy and calling for a reformation of learning based on alchemy and pagan teachings, began to worry authorities. When its members discussed God, according to an informant, s/he was "such a one, as is not really distinct from the animated and intelligent universe."[3] Their main spokesman, John Heydon, attributed motion to the agency of the *anima mundi* and claimed to worship the sun, moon, and other heavenly bodies. Seditious movements of sectarians in Ireland and England were reported by Robert Boyle's brother, the Earl of Orrery, in 1663, 1665, and the millennially-associated 1666, that Bishop Samuel Parker linked to the Heydon circle.[4]

Boyle argued against Stubbe, Heydon, and others that at the beginning God had set everything in motion, mechanism controlling all that came after. Trying to base his arguments on experimental investigations, he provided speculative

---

[1] Boyle brought Peter Sthael, a Rosicrucian, to Oxford in 1659 to lecture to a small group, including John Locke. (Henderson, L & T. Wilkins, pp. 98–99.)

[2] Pitt, *A Smnall Moment*, pp. 41, 146–48.

[3] Jacob, *Stubb*, pp. 144–46; Michael Hunter, "Alchemy, Magic and Moralism in the Thought of Robert Boyle," *British Journal for the History of Science*, 23 (1990), 4: pp. 389–410.

[4] Jacob, *Robert Boyle*, p. 163.

explanations of how common phenomena like hardness, fluidity, magnetic attraction, and so on, *could* be explained on the basis of "matter and motion." For example, to explain the supposed "horror" of a totally empty space or vacuum that nature was said to show, which historically had been used to explain certain suction forces, Boyle had recourse to a corpuscular counter-explanation based on the weight and assumed "springiness" of hypothesized air corpuscles.[1]

As a result, Boyle's "Hermeticism" was transmuted in two major respects: tied to social conservatism, benefitting now the people of property, instead of poor and rich alike, as the earlier Rosicrucian vision had it; and integrated into a theory of the world stripped of its lifefulness, its world soul. A "Hermeticism" thus divorced from a living nature, confined, instead, to the framework of the mechanical philosophy and at odds with its earlier vision of everyone sharing in the fruits of the land, their labor, and the knowledge provided by an experimental science, is really no Hermeticism at all.[2]

Probably because he was able to divorce Hermeticism from both its animism and social utopianism, Boyle has the historical reputation as the man who disproved alchemy, and accordingly has been awarded a conceptual paternity by many historians, who point to him as the "Father" of modern chemistry. That Boyle played an important historical role in the defeat of alchemy is no doubt partly correct, given the constraints with which he bound it, but that role must be reinterpreted in light of the clear evidence that Boyle was also a practicing alchemist and very much believed in the reputed goals of the alchemical quest of transmutation that he is wrongly thought to have exposed as nonsense.

When he died in 1691, parts of his recipe for philosophical mercury, a key agent in the alchemical arcana that was vital to the "Great Work" of transmutation, were exchanged between Isaac Newton and John Locke. As I shall recount in Chapter 14, when Newton received both what Locke had and a sample of a certain "red earth" that was to be used, he began a series of quite remarkable alchemical researches.

Boyle was an alchemist, but not a Hermeticist, as that term had been used to describe certain thinkers in the decades before the Restoration. His scientific work was part of a larger, Latitudinarian ideology, wherein science facilitated the ends of empire, the pursuit of commerce, and the cause of Protestantism, more particularly of the broad, but Anglican, church advocated by the Latitudinarians. That ideology was built on the tenets of matter and motion, which was able simultaneously to undermine the beliefs of two distinct enemies faced then by England: *internally,* the political and religious sectarians of the Civil War and the years after; and *externally,* the heathen in North America (and elsewhere around the world) who had to be converted to Christianity in order to win over

---

[1] "Horror" of a vacuum, needless to say, explicitly ascribes consciousness as well as volition to nature.

[2] And yet, in a letter, Boyle wrote that he wished to leave a "kind of Hermetic legacy to the studious disciples of that art…." (Hunter, *op. cit.,* p. 403.)

their souls, thereby to mold a compliant workforce, using the necessity for work as a means of forcing them to forsake their "lecherous habits."

For both these ends, it was vital that "brute" matter be shorn of its vitality, of any hint of powers inherent in nature. That question was very much being mulled over by the key thinkers in Restoration England, when a young Isaac Newton entered Trinity College, Cambridge, in 1661, as we shall see in the next chapter.

iv. THE RELUCTANT ALCHEMISTS' REMARKABLE THRICE-REVEALED TRANSMUTATION

A central chapter in the tale of the 17th-century transformation of thought must be the story of Johannes Friedrich Helvetius, who was very much a critic, as neither Boyle or Newton were, of what he understood to be alchemy's pretensions and outlandish aims. Yet Helvetius ended up unmistakably in the alchemists' camp. There is, to my mind, no story about alchemy more outlandish or instructive than his.

Physician to the Prince of Orange, Helvetius had recently published his *Pyrotechnic Art,* in which he had argued that a true alchemical transmutation of one kind of metal into another was not possible, when he was visited by one of those "mysterious strangers" who, in the annals of alchemy, frequently show up bearing critical gifts at just the right time. The physician judged the stranger who appeared at his door to be in his mid-forties and to have been born, given his speech, in North Holland. Wearing "a plebeian habit," the man was beardless, had black somewhat curly hair, and a long face with pock marks.

He begged Helvetius' pardon for his boldness, but confessed to being a "great lover" of alchemy and to having read some of the physician's treatises critical of the art. He asked Helvetius whether he doubted that a medicine might exist "which could cure all diseases, unless the principal parts (as lungs, liver, &c) were perished, or the predestined time of death were come." The physician asked the stranger if *he* were a physician, too, but the man said, no, that he was a brass founder. Over the years, however, he explained how he had come to appreciate how one might extract certain medicinal principles from metals.

At this point the man asked Helvetius if he thought he would recognize the legendary Philosophers' Stone if he saw it. Helvetius said no. The stranger then took from an intricately carved ivory box three lumps about the size of small walnuts. While the physician examined them, he listened to a "recital of its wonderful curative properties," as well as its astounding powers to transmute metals. Helvetius begged the man to allow him a tiny piece of it, but was told it would not be lawful. Nonetheless, while handling the matter, the physician secretly scraped a miniscule amount under his fingernail. Meanwhile, the man was telling Helvetius "many rare secrets of its admirable effects in human and metallic bodies, and other magical properties."

He then asked if there were a private place where the two could continue their discussion. Removed to a back room, the stranger displayed to the physician five pieces of gold, made in the alchemical way he claimed, that "so far ex-celled" gold that Helvetius had previously seen "that there was no comparison for flexibility and color...," and he recounted the story of his apprenticeship to a true alchemical adept.

As soon as the man departed, Helvetius rushed to his laboratory to cast his purloined bits of the "Stone" onto a quantity of melted lead. Nothing happened.

When a few weeks later the brass founder did return, Helvetius again begged him for a tiny piece of his Stone. This time the man, having apparently got per-mission from his adept, handed Helvetius a piece "as big as a rape or turnip [s]eed." Helvetius expressed disappointment at its miniscule size, whereupon the brass worker took it back and returned a piece only half as big as before, telling him that he still had more than he needed. At this point, Helvetius confessed to his earlier theft and recounted the failure in his attempt to transmute lead with his tiny piece of the alleged Stone. Hearing this, the stranger laughed and said he was a better thief than at using the stone, and explained that Helvetius had failed to wrap the piece in wax in order to protect it prior to throwing it into the melted lead. The stranger had to leave, but he promised to return the next day to demonstrate how the Stone was to be used.

The stranger did not show up the next morning, but a note promised he would come later that day. He did not. In fact, he never did return. In the meantime, spurred on by his wife, also a student of alchemy, Helvetius again tried out the man's claimed Stone, but this time he coated it in yellow wax before casting it into about half an ounce of melted old lead pipe. Within about fifteen minutes, accord-ing to the physician, all of the lead had been transmuted into the "finest gold."

Helvetius and his wife rushed the still hot ingot to a nearby goldsmith, who not only confirmed that it was gold, but raved that "it was the finest gold he had ever seen," and tried to buy it from them.[1]

Lest a reader be misled by the antiquity of this story into doubting the tes-timony of the people involved, I should point out that, as one of the world's lead-ing commercial powers at the end of the 17th century, when mercantile capital was at its peak, the Netherlands certainly possessed men (and probably women) quite qualified to judge just what was or was not gold. Keep this in mind as this very strange story becomes weirder, much weirder.

Word of the supposed transmutation spread to many in Amsterdam, one of whom was the General Assay Master of Holland, a man named Porelius, re-sponsible for examining the coinage of Holland. He asked Helvetius if he could have the new "gold" tested. The two men took the ingot to a celebrated Dutch

---

[1] John Frederick Helvetius, *Golden Calf, Which the World Worships and Adores: In Which Is Discussed The Most Rare Miracle of Nature in the Transmutation of Metals. Viz.: How at the Hague a Mass of Lead Was in a Moment of Time Changed into Gold by the Infusion of a Small Particle of Our Stone*, reprint (Edmonds, WA: The Alchem-ical Press, 1987). F. Sherwood Taylor, *The Alchemists* (New York: Collier Books, 1962), pp. 142–150.

goldsmith, Buectel. When Buectel dissolved the newly-made substance, together with some silver, a most astounding thing appeared to happen: after a series of experiments had been carried out, the three men found that the quantity of gold had actually *increased* since Helvetius and his wife's initial transmutation, seemingly transmuting some of the silver into gold. Initially, the incredulous men suspected the increase in weight resulted from an insufficient separation of the gold from the silver, but when they melted the gold once more to see if such was the case, *another* small increase in the weight of gold occurred!

The conclusion the three men reached after considerable discussion was that the Philosophers' Stone utilized by Helvetius had not, in its initial use by the physician and his wife, exhausted its power and was therefore able to continue its transmutations in the two subsequent tests.

News of this astounding series of pyrotechnic experiments spread and others investigated to satisfy themselves as to what really happened. None other than Baruch Spinoza, the Jewish Dutch philosopher, himself a sceptic regarding alchemy's extravagant claims, interviewed all of the principal parties, except for the never-again-seen stranger, including the assayers and goldsmiths. Neither Spinoza, whose account can be found in his *Posthumous Works*,[1] nor any other contemporary investigator, could ever find reasons to disbelieve the account given by the physician.

Were the Helvetius story unique, perhaps it might be dismissed as a mere chimera. But it is not. In his papers, Robert Boyle recounts having witnessed two actual alchemical transmutations. Given Boyle's chemical expertise and experience, he would not have been easily fooled.[2] In scattered museums there are numbers of coins and medals, labelled as having been made from gold that had been transmuted at a witnessed Great Work, many accompanied by signed statements by credible witnesses as to what was done, by whom, when. Of *course* fraud had to be involved — though evidence for such chicanery isn't even necessary, for by now it's simply axiomatic.[3]

Thus when the phenomena of radioactivity were uncovered in the late 19th and early 20th centuries, early experiments by the chemist Frederick Soddy (1876–1956) and the physicist Ernst Rutherford (1871–1937) revealed that radioactive thorium was changing into an inert gas, an altogether different element. In a state of "exaltation" Soddy exclaimed to his collaborator, "Rutherford, this is transmutation!" To which Rutherford, shocked, replied, "For Mike's sake, Soddy, don't call it *transmutation*. They'll have our heads off as alchemists." Even

[1] *Ibid.*, pp. 144–49; Jacques Sadoul, *Alchemists and Gold* (trans. Olga Sieveking (New York: G. P. Putnam's Sons, 1972), pp. 140–45.

[2] Hunter, *op. cit.*; Principe, *op. cit.*, pp. 98–106, 217, 296ff. Robert Hooke recorded in his *Diary* of Boyle's telling him of a chemist, Wansell, who "made projection," *i.e.* a transmutation. *Diary of Robert Hooke, M.A., M.D., F.R.S., 1672–1682*, ed. Harry W. Robinson and Walter Adams (London: Taylor & Francis, 1935), p. 147.

[3] V. Karpenko, "Coins and Medals Made of Alchemical Metal," *Ambix* 35 (1988), pp. 65–76.

so, the new atomic physics suggested to many at the time, including ultimately Rutherford himself, illuminating affinities with the alchemical tradition, Rutherford himself later publishing a book of lectures about radioactivity called *The New Alchemy* (1937). Indeed, as shown so well in Mark Morrison's *Modern Alchemy: Occultism and the Emergence of Atomic Theory*, a rich collaboration emerged between a recrudescent alchemy in the late 19th and early 20th centuries and the new sciences of atomic physics.[1]

v. *Who* Disproved Alchemy?
The Case of the Missing Debunker & His Philosophical Castration

Characteristically, Helvetius' remarkable story has not had an impact on the history of the scientific revolution or the specific history of chemistry. It is only in recent years that it has begun to be discussed by "serious" scholars. Previously the story was simply dismissed, since it was known that alchemy had been "disproved." When and by whom this refutation occurred, if one actually looks, is not at all clear, however. Certainly not by Robert Boyle. Nor, as we shall see, by Newton. Nor by anyone else, so far as I can determine.

Thus, the historical myth of modern science is founded on a denial of what did occur, and the glorification of something (the refutation) that did not. It is more accurate to say, then, as Morris Berman has, that "alchemy was never disproved, it was suppressed."[2]

Most likely this suppression was the work of men like David Hume, the Scottish philosopher, who in 1738 wrote that any miracle, such as are commonly claimed in the holy writings of many religions,

> is a violation of the laws of nature; and as a firm and unalterable experience has established those laws, the proof against a miracle, from the very nature of the fact, is as entire as any argument from experience can possibly be imagined.

Hume went on — and since this is probably what is meant by the "refutation" of alchemy — its historical import compels me to quote at some length the tortured logic by which Hume justified his outlandish argument. His "proof" is as circular as the epicycles of the old, Ptolemaic system, over which the new science so confidently trumpeted the superiority of its own models. Hume argued that even if "proof" of a miracle *did* exist,

> it would be opposed by another proof, derived from the very nature of the fact, which it would endeavour to establish. It is

---

[1] Morrison, *Modern Alchemy...* (Oxford, England: Oxford Univ. Press, 2007). p. 4.
[2] Conversation at Orr Hot Springs, Ukiah, California, sometime in 1979 or 1980.

> experience only, which gives authority to human testimony, and
> it is the same experience, which assures us of the laws of nature.

Lest we believe this to be circular reasoning, in which a proposition cannot be true because it can not be true, Hume pulls out an epistemological calculator to make his point clearer:

> When, therefore, these two kinds of experiences are contrary;
> we have nothing to do but subtract the [number of instances
> of the] one from the other, and embrace an opinion, either on
> one side or the other, with that assurances which arises from
> the remainder.[1]

Such an argument is simply absurd! Hume is saying that since miracles, if such exist, are by definition *extraordinary* occurences, they can simply be swept under an ontological rug by using the (by definition) "mass" of the greater number of *ordinary* occurrences. In other words, the very meaning of miracles predicates their non-existence. This is Wilkins' banishing of words for non-existent things like unicorns now seemingly embodied in philosophy and logic. Quoting Bacon, Hume extended this argument specifically to the "outlandish" claims of magic and alchemy.

Quite plainly, Hume's argument is philosophical sleight-of-hand.[2] It would be remarkable that he got away with it, especially in an age known for its philosophical rigor, but for this — Hume's readers were already looking for reasons to believe alchemy (and the rest of the occult) impossible. It was a conclusion they had been driven to on other than logical grounds, and as a result of a long-lasting campaign, orchestrated with a studied precision and even, some of the time, considerable forethought.

But this is obviously to get ahead of our story, for Hume came later, from a different age in many ways, even though he was separated from Helvetius and Boyle and Newton by only a handful of decades. Hume's target was only indirectly alchemy, his real goal being to discredit Christianity and other revealed religions. Initially, his "Essay on Miracles" was written in the 1730s, a few years after Newton's death, but after showing it to a few of his friends, Hume decided to delete it from a larger treatise he was then preparing. His self-censorship must have been dreadfully painful, judging from the imagery used in a letter to Henry Home (December, 1737): "I am at present castrating my work, that is, cutting

---

1 David Hume, *Essays Moral, Political, and Literary* (ed.) T.H. Green and T.H. Grose (London: 1882; reprint Darmstadt, 1964), vol. I, p. 93; vol. II, p. 105.

2 As a freshman at Caltech in 1957, I first encountered Hume's arguments in my Humanities reader, part of a compilation of Enlightenment philosophy put together by the Humanities faculty for all Caltech freshmen to read. In the 1990s, the reader was still being used.

off its nobler parts." He explained his actions ("cowardice" is what he called it) by pointing out that he would not be able to mount an attack on enthusiasm while revealing himself as "an enthusiast in philosophy,"[1] as he felt his argument against miracles did, probably because of its overt skepticism, which would be taken as support for atheism.

It was only after another ten-year delay that Hume felt secure enough to publish his "Essay on Miracles," as part of his 1748 *Enquiry Concerning Human Understanding.* By that time revealed religion, at least for many of the educated, was on the defensive; and alchemy had, indeed, been rendered wholly marginal, the pursuit of cranks and obscure thinkers one hardly ever encounters, except in the alchemical literature or as occasionally cited signposts for sideroads not taken at critical junctures on the highway of Progress, onto which the 18th and 19th centuries had so resolutely turned.[2] Nor until very recently could readers learn that the leading mainstream thinkers, such as Boyle, Locke, and Newton, were secretly disciples of the alchemical arts. A particular history to be taught, so notably at odds with what actually occurred, but vital to the myth of Western rationalism that the West needed for its enterprise to succeed.

vi. CRITICS OF THE MECHANICAL PHILOSOPHY

I would be remiss to describe the emerging consensus in late-17th-century philosophical circles in favor of a mechanical world-view without touching on a few notable nay-sayers. Even for them, the power of the Cartesian metaphysics of *res extensa* versus *res cogitans* was so powerful that though the three philosophers we shall now discuss — Baruch Spinoza, Lady Anne Conway, and Gottfried Wilhelm Leibniz — were fundamentally anti-Cartesian, the systems they proposed instead began with a close examination of the Cartesian metaphysics. With his ontologic dualism, Descartes had established a precisely bordered field on which all philosophical jousting would henceforth be conducted; even the anti-Cartesians

---

[1] Peter Gay, *The Enlightenment: An Interpretation. The Rise of Modern Paganism* (New York: Vintage Books, 1966), pp. 404–05.

[2] Thus Maurice Crossland, "The Chemical Revolution of the 18th Century and the Eclipse of Alchemy in the 'Age of Enlightenment'," in Martels, "Alchemy Revisited," p. 71, quoted in Betty Jo Teeter Dobbs, "Newton as Final Cause & First Mover," in *Rethinking the Scientific Revolution*, ed. Margaret Osler (Cambridge, England: Cambridge Univ. Press, 2000), p. 32, argues that alchemy in the 18th-century was not so much attacked as ignored; Baroja (*op. cit.*, p. 212) claims that "[T] he battle between those who believed in magic and those who attacked it wholeheartedly was nearly at an end by the middle of the eighteenth century ... at least as far as the ruling classes were concerned"; and Ginzburg argues that during the 17th century the belief that the activities of witches were only the "delirious fantasies of old women" gradually came to predominate. (Ginzburg, *Night Battles*, p. 21.)

posed their questions and began their answers in Cartesian terms, for example, using his criteria of "clear and distinct" as the measure of an idea's validity.

Spinoza (1632–1677) lived in Amsterdam, where he received training as a rabbi. His increasing philosophical radicalism caused a profound ostracism from the Jewish community there, which denounced him as a heretic. Though he wrote an analysis of Descartes' physics and metaphysics and reflected on matters of optics, for the most part Spinoza's concerns were more focused on ethics, political theory, and psychology. Even in these, Spinoza's approach was in step with the scientific and mathematical logic of the age, his treatises (like the *Ethics*) organized more like Euclid than Plato, into propositions, corollaries, and lemmas.

As in Descartes and most of his critics, it was the nature of "substance" that was central to Spinoza's system. Unlike the others, however, Spinoza held that only one substance existed, that in effect God and nature were one and the same. In contrast to Descartes, who made an absolute distinction between thought and matter, Spinoza held both to be aspects of God. God contained all things, in effect, *was* all things. Individual souls, even individual material objects, were simply aspects of God. God — hence the universe — was self-contained and neither free will nor chance existed. Time, too, is illusory, for the future is wholly fixed, just as the past is.

Spinoza's radical monism, what some decades later would be termed "pantheism," was a critical presence in the late 17th century, for his was a consistently articulated and thoroughly heretical position, in opposition to which most thinkers of the time, Newton among them, felt the need to distinguish their own position. Boyle and More, too, were moved to clarify what set their own notions apart from those of Spinoza's.

Lady Anne Conway (1631–1679) will stand not only as our token female philosopher in a parade of mostly men in this critical period, but also demonstrates how and why her theories were marginalized and rejected as a result of her gender and her gender's philosophical proclivities, their collective take on matters not taken seriously by the community of natural philosophers.[1] As discussed earlier, Conway was a central figure in Restoration Latitudinarian circles, holding discussions at her estate at Ragley with a wide range of influential philosophers, including the Cambridge Platonists Henry More, Ralph Cudworth, and Benjamin Whichcote, as well as Joseph Glanvill, and the alchemist Francis Mercury Van Helmont. The latter came to England in 1670 bearing letters to More from Princess Elizabeth of Bohemia (daughter of the Winter Queen) for a planned short stay, but he was persuaded by More to stop at Ragley, where he ended up remaining for eight years. Under Van Helmont's influence, Conway studied texts of the Quakers, the Behemists, Seekers, and Familists, eventually becoming a Quaker herself.

---

[1] Contemporary portraits show women looking away in horror from the animals being asphyxiated by the newly-developed vacuum pump while the male philosophers look on in wonderment.

At her death in 1679, Conway left behind her manuscript for *The Principles of the Most Ancient Philosophy*, a full-fledged attack on the presumptions of the mechanical philosophy and a defense of philosophical vitalism. Conway saw her philosophy as fundamentally in opposition to Descartes' system. While Descartes had taught many "excellent and ingenious things concerning the Mechanical part of Natural Operations," Conway insisted that nature's operations were "far more than merely Mechanical."[1] Nor was nature to be seen as analogous to a clock, a common 17th-century trope for the maturing community of natural philosophers.

The Cartesian notion that body and spirit are essentially different substances was roundly rejected by Conway. Rather than extension being an attribute only of matter, both body and spirit exist spatially, though to different degrees. Spirit, for example, is capable of both expanding or contracting itself. Like body, spirit can be divided, for both of them infinitely so, endlessly spinning off more infinitesimals. Rather than an ontologic divide between body and spirit, then, Conway believed that bodies could become spirits, and spirits, bodies.[2]

In her *Principles of the Most Ancient Philosophy*, Conway drew from the aquifer of the *prisca sapiente*, the legendary wisdom of the ancients, a source later on for Newton's philosophical thirst as well (as we shall see, in the following chapters). It was a heady draught. The insights of the *Kaballah denuda* of Knorr von Rosenroth were frequently cited, as well what she had learned in her studies (mostly with Van Helmont) of caballa and the doctrines of the key radical Independent sects, the Behemists, the Ranters, Familists, Seekers, and Quakers. In the late 1660s she had corresponded with Henry More about Boehme and the Familists. More, her tutor in some of these studies, disapproved of the "enthusiasm" of the sects and their abandonment of reason, Conway herself, for the most part, did not.[3]

In her magical ontology, beings and essences were in continual exchange, this a kind of bleeding over between matter and spirit, between one creature and another, so that her pages are filled with examples of life springing anew out of nothing, out of dirt, transformation and transmutation in a world that is fundamentally alive, death itself a mere pause between reanimations, the universe everywhere vital and nakedly thumbing its nose at the "inert" bodies of Descartes and the rest of the mechanical philosophers.[4] "[A]ll things have life,

---

[1] Anne Conway, *The Principles of the Most Ancient Philosophy. Concerning God, Christ, and the Creatures, viz. of spirit and as well matter in general, whereby may be resolved all those probems or difficulties which neither by the school nor common modern philosophy nor by the Cartesian, Hobbesian or Spinosian could be discussed...* (London: 1692); modern edition, Peter Laptson (The Hague: Martinus Nijhof Publishers, 1982), p. 222. As we shall see, Newton agreed with this.

[2] *Ibid.*, p. 191.

[3] Conway, *Principles*, p. 175, where she criticizes the Ranters.

[4] *Ibid.*, pp. 182–84, 219.

and do really live in some degree of measure."[1] Body was but condensed spirit, spirit a more volatile and subtle form of body. Against Descartes' insistence that vivisected animals' screams were akin to the screeching made by unoiled gears, and that animals, lacking souls, were only machines, Conway insisted that animal life had spirit, had knowledge, sense, and love.[2]

If spirit had no extension, no location, she argued, they would not feel pain, which obviously they do, for if a body is hurt, it is felt by the spirit.[3] She took a further swipe at the holes in the mechanical philosophy by focusing on the different behaviors of light in relation to solid, impenetrable yet *transparent* objects, such as some crystals, in contrast to very porous yet *opaque* materials, like wood.[4]

To Conway, both spirit and matter are divisible to infinity, into basic units she called "monades," self-contained entities that were what existed from the first Creation.

Since God is incapable of creating death, its appearance is "not the Annihilation of these Things; but a change from one kind and degree of Life to another... for "God made not death... he made no dead Things."[5]

Given Henry More's railings against alchemical beliefs in his *Enthusiasmus Triumphatus* (1654), it might seem strange to learn that at Ragley he and Francis Mercury Van Helmont, Conway's other tutor, engaged in alchemical experiments in the lab Van Helmont made at the estate,[6] a reminder that some of our philosophers may say one thing and do another, or that beliefs and ideologies can change over time.

It was with Francis Mercury, the son of the alchemist J.B. Van Helmont, that Conway did much of her study and it was he who saw to the publication of the *Principles* in 1690, after her death in 1679. The absence of an author on its title page, owing to Conway's being a woman, meant that for over two centuries the work was wrongly attributed to the younger Van Helmont.

It was he, too, who in 1696 went to Hanover where for several months he met with the German philosopher, G.W. von Leibniz each morning to discuss philosophy, with Van Helmont in the role of tutor. Much of their study, according to both men, centered around the teachings of Conway, whom Leibniz cred-

---

[1] *Ibid.*, p. 219.

[2] *Ibid.*, p. 214. Though I would be reluctant to think that such was Descartes' conscious motive, his notions would provide a welcome justification for ranchers when, within a century, herds of as many as 150,000 head of cattle (in New Spain, a thousand in European Spain) existed for the inevitable suffering of the animals that would have emerged. (Figures from this work, p. 56.)

[3] *Ibid.*, p. 228.

[4] *Ibid.*, p. 228.

[5] *Ibid.*, pp. 210, 196.

[6] Merchant, *op. cit.*, p. 255. Dobbs (*Foundations*, pp. 115ff) argues that More was not opposed to alchemy as such, but only when it sought to explain too much, encouraging system-making.

ited with showing him that "all things are full of life and consciousness, contrary to the view of the Atomists,"[1] i.e., the mechanical philosophers.

Carolyn Merchant convincingly argues that it was from Conway, transmitted through Van Helmont during his 1696 visit, that Leibniz got the concept of the *monad*, using the idea and term for the first time after their long discussions.

Leibniz' philosophy, too, was profoundly shaped by the Cartesian categories. In the mid-1660s, the German philosopher fell in with mechanical explanations. However, following his exposure to the ideas of Christopher Wren and Christian Huygens on motion and collisions, the problem of the cohesion of material bodies began to perplex Leibniz. He found the various mechanical philosophers' explanations as to why the particles or atoms of any body stayed together as a unit unsatisfying. In a 1670 letter to Henry Oldenburg, Secretary of the Royal Society, Leibniz wrote that cohesion is a quality that is central to hardness, softness, tenacity, flexibility, fragility, and friability. A satisfactory explanation for cohesion, accordingly, is all the more important. Gassendi's explanation, hooks and barbs in the numerous particles, so that they can "latch on" to each other, Leibniz thought unconvincing: what accounts for the cohesion of those hooks and barbs? Bringing in, as Gassendi did, the deity to explain this feature would unnecessarily make cohesion a perpetual miracle. Nor did Hobbes or Descartes provide adequate explanations of cohesion. The use of incorporeal agents to solve the problem was not a satisfactory answer either (I suspect Henry More is Leibniz' target here, whose work he knew.)[2]

To Leibniz the phenomena of cohesion implies that *vacua* — small empty spaces — must exist between bodies,[3] since a body can go from hard to soft (for example, the melting of ice) and in the re-arrangement of its particles spaces would open up. In this 1670 letter, Leibniz proposed his own theory of cohesion, premised on an aether-like substance (akin to the *pneuma* of the ancient Stoics), along with light or by itself, circling the Earth in a direction contrary to the Earth's rotation, an aether that was itself the universal vital principle in nature. Such an aether, Leibniz believed, could explain gravity, as well as magnetism. Chemical behavior, too, now can fall into place: solutions, precipitations, fermentations, sympathies and antipathies, as well as how a chemical reacts to some chemicals but not to others.

Leibniz decided that *extension* could not be an attribute of any one substance, since extension involves *plurality*; hence extension must be a property of an aggregate. He rejected the possibility of atoms, in part because nature never acts in

---

[1] *Ibid.*, p. 257.

[2] Leibniz to Oldenburg, 18 September 1670, in Henry Oldenburg, *The Correspondence of Henry Oldenburg* (ed. and transl.) A. Rupert Hall & Marie Boas Hall, vol. VII (Madison: Univ. of Wisconsin Press, 1970), pp. 166–70.

[3] A hotly debated issue among the mechanical philosophers, Descartes denying the existence of a vacuum, Gassendi for, and Hobbes early on accepting small vacua but eventually rejecting the notion altogether.

jumps.[1] All bodies are aggregates, so much so that an infinite number of substances exist within any one thing. Rather than explaining physical phenomena, like that of bodies' impacts — the key interaction to study under the mandates of the mechanical philosophy — on the basis of inert, extended, substance, as the Cartesians and other mechanical philosophers did, Leibniz began to organize his explanations on the basis of a mind-like substance. It was this that underlay all motion, an active, vital being that was able to overcome the natural passivity of matter. Without the aether, "all things will return to incoherent, dead dust."[2]

In other words, to explain the motion of matter, Leibniz returned to the forbidden (by the mechanists) notion of a world soul to account for a universe filled with spirit, a "panorganic vitalism," as Mercer calls it, where "principles of life [are] diffused throught all nature."[3] Without allowing such a spirit, the origins of motion would be impossible to satisfactorily explain.[4]

In psychology, as well, Leibniz fell out with the mechanical philosophers, who believed that the motion of their hypothetical particles or atoms would lead to impacts against the various sense organs — taste, vision, smell, touch, and hearing resulting from such interactions. On the contrary, Leibniz argued, if such organs were vastly increased in size so that a person could physically enter them, s/he would find only parts in motion, but still no perception *per se*, nor any explanation for perception.[5]

Leibniz radically departed from the impact physics of the mechanical philosophy to account for the behavior of material bodies. Bodies behave as they do not because of impact, but on the basis of *internal* principles, principles embodied in their spirit. Since Leibniz believed that extension necessarily involved plurality, any thing, that is, any substance, must consist of an infinity of substances that cohere, what, following Conway, Leibniz began to call "monads," each substance endowed with "its own mind-like principles of activity."[6] The spirit present through all of nature knows what will happen because of a "pre-established harmony" established at Creation and this knowledge is manifest in every monad, which moves bodies in accord with their cosmic plan.

There is much more to Leibniz's physics, how the material world acts according to that plan in place from the beginning; or Leibniz's vigorous disputes over whether it was the product of *mass* and the square of the velocity (mv^2), what Leibniz called the "living force," that remained constant throughout all

---

[1] Leibniz, *Selections* (ed.) Philip P. Wiener (New York: Charles Scribner's Sons, 1951) from the *Journal des Savans* (1692), p. 71.

[2] Christine Mercer, *Leibniz's Metaphysics: Its Origin and Development* (Cambridge, England: Cambridge Univ. Press, 2001), p. 279.

[3] Leibniz, *op. cit.*, "Considerations on the Principles of Life, and on Plastic Natures...," *Histoire des Ouvrages des savans* (1705), p. 190.

[4] Mercer, *op. cit.*, p. 277.

[5] Leibniz, *op. cit.*, *The Monadology* (1717), p. 536.

[6] Leibniz, *ibid.*

physical interactions (Leibniz's belief) or, rather, the product of mass and the velocity (mv) that stayed the same.[1]

But a discussion of those matters or of the ferocious debate over who, Newton or Leibniz, really invented the calculus (both, as we now realize) would take us too far afield from our concerns in *Marxism & Witchcraft*. What is important for us is that Leibniz's animist alternative to the mechanical philosophy gained few adherents in the decades and centuries that followed and it was destined, for reasons delineated in the previous chapters, to remain in the station while the trainload of theories assembled by the community of mechanical philosophers roared away into an ecologically devastating future.

It was the system of Isaac Newton, especially, that eventually took control of that locomotive, driving that train and successfully explaining celestial dynamics and the rest of it and establishing a basis for the sciences of heat, electricity and magnetism, chemistry, geology, and a growing array of others to board at successive stations.

We can now turn to our focused discussion of Isaac Newton. I intend to demonstrate how only a particular, one-sided representation of Newton's inner visions and beliefs was allowed to define for the public just what his system *was*, part of a crafting of a narrowed view of the scientific enterprise that was premised on the concerns of men like Henry More and Robert Boyle, of Mersenne and John Wilkins, philosophers obsessed with the threat posed by enthusiasm and in agreement with the promise made by Sprat that science could be a force to cool down the passions; it was that sense of science that pointed the way to the Enlightenment and beyond. That it was a one-sided version of Newtonianism bore considerably on just what baggage that train had on board, what it brought to (and what it took away from) those successive stations as the Newtonian local eventually brought us all to the early 21st century, antibiotics lacing our meats and pesticides swimming in our drinking waters. And with us, it appears, in the opening stages of a long period of ever-deepening and devastating environmental collapses, while our movie screens depict apocalyptic fantasies of endtimes.

---

[1] As noted above (p. 34, n.1) it was finally concluded that both were conserved, but the latter involving not just magnitude, as mv^2 does, but a directionality as well.

12

Newton & The Lifefulness of Nature

No machine starts from small beginnings, grows, forms new structures within itself and then reproduces itself. Yet plants and animals do this all the time. They can also regenerate after damage. To see them as machines propelled only by ordinary physics and chemistry is an act of faith; to insist that they are machines despite all appearances is dogmatic. — Rupert Sheldrake, *Science Set Free: 10 Paths To New Discovery* (2012)

For nature is a perpetuall circulatory worker, generating fluids out of solids, and solids out of fluids, fixed things out of volatile, & volatile out of fixed, subtile out of gross, & gross out of subtile, Some things to ascend & make the upper terrestriall juices, Rivers and the Atmosphere; & by consequence others to descend for a Requitall to the former. And as the Earth, so perhaps may the Sun imbibe this Spirit copiously to conserve his Shineing, & keep the Planets from recedeing further from him. And they that will, may also suppose, that this Spirit affords or carryes with it thither the solary fewell & materiall Principle of Light; And that the vast aethereall Spaces between us, & the stars are for a sufficient repository for this food of the Sunn & Planets. — Isaac Newton, Letter to Henry Oldenburg, (7 December 1675) in *The Correspondence of Isaac Newton* (1959).

i. WILL AS AN ACTIVATING PRINCIPLE

Because of the pivotal role Newton played in ushering in the modern view of all things, an extended examination of his system and how he came to it is central to our inquiry. Though it took decades for his ideas to spread from country to country, region to region, class to class, and male to female,[1] there was a profound transformation of society whenever a pre-Newtonian culture, anywhere, underwent its almost inevitable Newtonianization. The passage between the two is through nothing less than the gateway to modernity. The shape and texture of just about everything changes once a society or individual has negotiated that rite of passage.

We are fortunate to have one of the earliest of Newton's notebooks, written as a young student at Cambridge University in the early 1660's, enabling us to see the unfolding of his inchoate ideas.[2] It is clear that young Newton, like many of the thinkers at the time, looked to the matter and motion tenets of the mechanical philosophy for explanations as to the nature of reality. At the same time it is obvious that Newton's reading of, and discussions with, Henry More have had a profound impact on his thinking.

More's ideas about the immateriality of the soul, the immanence of God, the nature of space, and the insufficiency of inertia to explain all natural phenomena were to have deep resonances in Newton's theories.[3] In particular, Newton was aware of phenomena that begged to be interpreted on the basis of other principles besides the simple ones of the mechanical philosophy.

A creative tension between two polar approaches, that of the mechanical philosophy and that of some forever-under-construction alternative, in fact, was to help map out the path Newton blazed as he negotiated the philosophical terrain of the late 17th century. In his early optical work, to help explain how mind can cause an arm or leg to move, for example, Newton had recourse to a "secret principle of unsociablenes,"[4] reminiscent of the forces of antipathy in the older magical tradition, not generally a category to be found in the lexicon of the mechanical philosophy.

---

1 The latter "translation" was undertaken by Francesco Algarotti, *Sir Isaac Newton's Philosophy Explain'd for the Use of the Ladies*, trans. Elizabeth Carter (London: 1739) from the 1737 Italian edition.

2 Isaac Newton, "Qu[a]estiones quaedam Philosophiae," Cambridge Add Ms 3996; published (ed.) J.E. McGuire and Martin Tamny as *Certain Philosophical Questions: Newton's Trinity Notebook* (Cambridge, England: Cambridge Univ. Press, 1983).

3 This is explored nicely in Burtt, *op. cit.*; Westfall, *Never at Rest*; and Koyré, *Newtonian Studies*.

4 Newton to Oldenburg, 7 December 1675, *Correspondence*, vol. I, p. 368.

Certain key themes of Newton's character are also evident at an early age — his great skill at making mechanical things (tiny treadmills for mice, for example); his dreaminess and ability to immerse himself in his thoughts, becoming oblivious to everything else, frequently for long periods of time; and his enormous temper and inability to bear criticism. At a young age Newton also revealed his paranoia, his brooding suspicions against potential rivals, his fears that they would attack him or get credit for his work. Criticism of his ideas would typically send Newton scurrying for cover, enraged at detractors and determined to hide any of his questionable tracks so as to elude their chase.[1] The paranoia only intensified Newton's awareness at what had to have been obvious to anyone in Cambridge right after the Restoration, that Hermetic notions were widely viewed as leading to enthusiasm and social chaos. We should keep these tendencies in mind when we read Newton's explanations of what he was trying to do and what he thought, for it is foolish to take them at face value.

Yet, perhaps inevitably, Hermeticism beckoned to Newton. More's strictures against too much reliance on the bare mechanical philosophy had focused on the need to provide a mediation between Descartes' two antithetical realities — *extended things* (matter) and *unextended things* (mind or spirit). Spirit that could move *into* matter, in effect, energizing it, what More called "essential Spissitude,"[2] was his suggestion for this intermediary. Something like this notion may have been the portal through which Newton entered in his initial forays into the alchemical mysteries. If not via More, it was an obvious world to explore for someone of Newton's prodigious curiosity and piercing intellect searching to understand the manifold aspects of matter.

For while "brute matter," defined by its inertia and law-like apparent predictability, was the focus for the construction of Newton's new science of the laws of motion, it was the aspect of matter that Newton found of lesser interest. Early on, Newton's attention was drawn to more "disorderly phenomena," phenomena arising, in *every* instance, out of the life-processes. Living — or recently living — matter putrefies, it effervesces, it is digested, it ferments, it grows, it can perceive, it has will, it can (under certain conditions) gestate, it will eventually die. Precisely in these mysteries of the numerous life processes, Newton, surmised, lay the secrets of transformation, of change itself. Accordingly, he set himself the critical challenge of comprehending living matter.

---

[1] Frank E. Manuel, *A Portrait of Isaac Newton* (Cambridge, Mass.: Harvard Univ. Press, 1968). Also see a penetrating series of articles by Richard Westfall: "Short-Writing and the State of Newton Conscience, 1662 (1)," *Notes and Records of the Royal Society* 18 (1963), pp. 10–16; "Newton's Reply to Hooke and the Theory of Colors," *Isis*, 54 (1963), pp. 82–97; and "Newton Defends His First Publication: The Newton–Lucas Correspondence," *Isis* 56 (1966), pp. 299–314.

[2] Henry More developed these ideas especially during the 1660s. See his *Antidote against Atheism: Letters to Des Cartes, &c; Immortality of the Soul; Conjectura Cabbalistica*, in More, *A Collection of Several Philosophical Writings...* (London: 1712).

While all the magical traditions have in common an animistic framework for the world, it is alchemy, especially, that focuses on the phenomenal transformations of matter and how they conform to the patterns of living creatures. The creation of the Philosophers' Stone is perceived as an obstetrical process, the alchemist a kind of philosophical midwife. Many of the material changes in matter have sexual roots, in a kind of chemical coition. Others are akin to breathing, to dying, to excreting, etc. To understand the life of matter, it is to alchemy one should turn. This Newton understood.

Newton's introduction into philosophical discussion of the bizarre notion (to a mechanical philosopher) of an attractive *force* of gravity between any separated bodies as an explanation of the workings of the solar system, and his suggestion of other forces of attraction and repulsion, were understood by many of his contemporaries — themselves newly converted to the axioms of matter and motion — as reversions to older, magical ways of thinking. And deny as he might such charges, it was in fact to alchemy especially that Newton turned in his quest to understand the nature of these mysterious "forces."

The faculty of the will was the way in which living creatures exerted force. A person who *wills* it can move his or her arm, an eye, a toe. Newton looked at will as a particularly clear window into these mysteries, referring to it often in his many drafts on the subject. In one of his early attempts to account for the properties of matter, his *de Gravitatione et Aequipondio Fluidorum* (estimated by Westfall and the Halls to have been written in the late 1660s, by Dobbs in the mid–1680s), Newton hypothesized that God could have created matter by an act of His will. Were the Deity to restrict certain regions of space from being penetrable, in effect, such spaces would constitute the "particles" of which the material world, to a mechanical philosopher, is made.

> So God may appear (to our innermost consciousness) to have
> created the world solely by the act of will, just as we move our
> bodies, by an act of will alone.

Newton would have it both ways — the particles of the mechanists, but made by an animating (i.e., spiritual) force. The role of the will would be one of Newton's recurrent themes.[1]

In two early alchemical papers, Newton mapped out broad principles to follow in his research. The first, named by historians "The Vegetation of Metals," dates, according to Westfall, to at least as late as Spring, 1669, and based its reasoning on four fundamental propositions:

> All things are corruptible
> All things are generable

---

[1] Isaac Newton in A.R. and Marie Boas Hall, *Unpublished Scientific Papers of Isaac Newton* (Cambridge, England: Cambridge Univ. Press, 1962), p. 141.

> Nature only works in moyst substances
> And wth a gentle heat.

Both papers were inquiries into a "vital agent diffused through everything in the earth" that if put with a mixture of ordinary matter acts to "putrefy and confound them into chaos; then it proceeds to generation."[1]

This vital spirit is the secret principle underlying the "vegetative actions of nature." It is "vegetative principles" that lead to growth. Without such principles, "nothing could ever yet be made," for it is how nature creates all substances. The metals of the Earth, indeed, the whole of the mineral kingdom, conform to the vegetative principle.

And yet, Newton makes clear, there are significant differences between the growth of minerals and growth of other living things. Only minerals, for example, can "grow without air." Also, while in plants and animals the seeds out of which a new creature can grow (what elsewhere he referred to as nature's "only agents, her fire, her soul, her life") are but a tiny portion of the whole creature, with minerals, in contrast, any part can act as a seed for further growth (as in crystallization).

Putrefaction was another process of life that had particular power, according to Newton. He was especially impressed by the fact that it is through putrefaction that a dry body can "relent to water." Should this occur in the open and under the sun, soon only vapors will remain; in effect, a dissolution of matter, as Newton saw it, had occurred. In the reverse process, mineral seeds can also bind with water; after a number of iterations, Newton believed, it could account for solid bodies emerging from spirit and for the formation of crystals — in other words, for the *creation* of matter.[2]

In effect, at the core of Newton's quest, as for other alchemists, were the chemical secrets of how God had created the world in the beginning (as modern cosmologists, if they could only keep God out of it, might possibly agree.)[3] Through deeply spiritual practices, including fasting, inducing trance states, meditation, chanting, and so on (generally not part of the accepted methodology of today's cosmologists), alchemists literally sought out the mind of God.

In his early alchemical essay, Newton characteristically was drawn to the juncture *between* worlds, for that is where he believed the most critical interactions can be assumed to occur. Newton frequently looked for the secret of how things are put together and taken apart in the "middle state" between gross matter and aethereal spirits. "All nature's operations are twixt things of differing dispositions. The most powerful agent acts not on itself," he wrote in "The Veg-

---

[1] Burndy Ms 16 in Westfall, *Never at Rest*, pp. 305–07. I am grateful to the Burndy Library for allowing me to see a copy of the manuscript.

[2] Newton, "Of natures obvious laws & processes in vegetation," in Dobbs, *Janus Face*, pp. 260, 262, 263.

[3] Debus, *Chemical Dream*, p. 14.

etation of Metals." He thought that various chemical salts, with their many crystalline formations, were "mean[s] twixt the mineral and other kingdoms." It was there that he believed he would learn how the world was put together.[1]

In alchemy the key mediating agent is called "philosophical mercury." Newton and his alchemical circles focused on how to create this remarkable substance, which can dissolve gold and other metals. This agent causes the gold to grow and create formations that had all the appearances of life. Among Newton's papers was found a glowing report of the workings of this special mercury, long attributed to Newton, though perhaps something he transcribed from Thomas Vaughan, but compatible with Newton's own beliefs:

> I have in the fire manifold glasses with gold and this mercury. They grow in these glasses in the form of a tree, and by a continued circulation the trees are dissolved again with the work into new mercury. I have such a vessel in the fire with gold thus dissolved, where the gold was visibly not dissolved by a corrosive into atoms, but extrinsically and intrinsically into a mercury as living and mobile as any mercury found in the world. For it makes gold begin to swell, to be swollen, and to putrefy, and to spring forth into sprouts and branches, changing colors daily, the appearances of which fascinate me every day. I reckon this a great secret in Alchemy....[2]

Newton was fascinated with the vegetative principle, because it acted, not *upon* (as in the mechanical philosophy), but *in* the gross materials it in-formed with its essence, just as seeds act in their food, the soil, altering it "to their one temper and nature" in order to sprout and grow.

At other times and in other contexts, Newton likened the Earth to "a great animall or rather inanimate vegetable" that daily takes in "aethereal breath" for its "dayly refreshment and vitall ferments," later breathing out any wastes. These inhaled aethereal spirits eventually become fixed in the Earth in minerals and salts, where they serve in effect as the seeds of solidification, of body-ness. In 1675 Newton used the continued raining down of this aethereal spirit on the planet (balanced by an opposite rising up of various forms of air, beginning the process back into an aethereal state where the substance "relents & is attenuated into its first principle") to account for the gravity of an Earth whose "vast body" "may be everywhere to the very center in perpetuall working...." In this paper, which Newton sent to be read to the Royal Society, he elaborated on this "perpetuall working" to suggest that "the whole frame of Nature may be nothing but

---

[1] Burndy MS 16, fol. 5ᵛ, in Dobbs, *Janus Face*, p. 267.

[2] Quoted in Westfall, *Never at Rest*, p. 371; the case for Vaughan is made by William R. Newman, "Newton's *Clavis* as Starkey's *Key*," *Isis* 78 (1987): 564–74; see also Dobbs, *Janus*, p. 15 and Principe, *op. cit.*, p. 174.

various Contextures of some aethereall spirits or vapors condens'd, as it were, by praecipitation...."[1]

It was light, especially, that became Newton's focus, for light, in particular, had to be at the center of the key mysteries. The spirit in aether, he speculated, "perhaps is ye body of light," since they both had "prodigious active principle[s], both are perpetual workers." If supplied with enough heat, Newton observed, "all things may be made to emit light," suggesting an inner, more intimate, connection between light and heat. Moreover,

> [N]o substance so indifferently, subtly, and swiftly pervades
> all things as light, and no spirit searches bodies so subtly, pierc-
> ingly, and quickly as the vegetative spirit.[2]

This inner significance of light served Newton later in life, when in the first two decades of the 18th century he published several editions of his long-anticipated *Opticks* and used the famous "Queries" at its end as a forum for ongoing and wide-ranging speculations on the nature of the cosmos. Here he continued to ponder the ties between light and bodies, in Query 30,[3] posing the question whether bodies obtained their active principles from particles of light entering them and wondering, since nature "seems delighted with Transmutations," "why may not Nature change bodies into Light and Light into Bodies?"[4] In drafts (most from the 1690s) for the *Opticks* and its Queries, Newton circled around the heretical notion that the laws of motion of *living* bodies seem to apply to *all* bodies, "may be of universal extent...." The instance of will (or thought) moving, say, an arm, demonstrates, he argued, that other laws of motion, besides those delineated in his *Principia,* must exist. That he repeatedly chose *not* to publish such material would suggest a measure of caution before using these drafts as evidence, while the numerous iterations, of these and related notions, not all of them crossed out, would suggest his virtual obsession with the idea, as he wrote, that "we cannot say that all Nature is not alive."[5]

ii. A WORLD OF DECAY?

In the early "Queries," published a few years into the 18th century, Newton's thoughts on the activating agent were drawn again to the concept of "active principles," a necessary entity, he insisted, since from *inertia* alone motion could not long exist in the world.

---

[1] Newton to Oldenburg, 7 December, 1675, in Newton, *Correspondence* Vol. 2, pp. 367–86.

[2] Burndy Ms 16, fol. 3; Westfall, *Never at Rest,* p. 306.

[3] Originally, in the 1705 *Optice,* Query 22.

[4] Queries 31 and 30 in *Opticks, or A Treatise of the Reflections, Refractions, Inflections & Colours of Light* (New York: Dover Publications, 1952), pp. 378, 374–75.

[5] Cambridge Univ. Add MS 3970, fol. 619, 618ᵛ, 620ʳ.

Motion [in the world] is more apt to be lost than got, and is always upon the Decay. Seeing therefore the variety of motion which we find in the World is always decreasing, there is a necessity of conserving and recruiting it by active Principles....[1]

It was after his 1693 nervous breakdown (of this, more later) that evidence of the decay of motion and of sources of instability began to accumulate for Newton. In a fundamental way, Newton's real aim in science had been and continued to be finding energizing principles to infuse and renew activity in the cosmos; over the decades he adjusted and sometimes altered his ideas, vocabulary, and theoretical working of the principle(s) that served to reinfuse life into things so as to enable the cosmos and the Earth to continue. In an alchemical memorandum, Newton was attentive to processes that kept the life *within* matter:

That the white spirit must be rectified seven times from its (?calx) without separating any flegm from it, & that in rectifying, it will endour any heat without losing its life.[2]

In his long paper on light sent to the Royal Society in 1675, where he theorized about a living, breathing earth, he included a lyrical paean to the protean quality of the natural world that would serve as a *leitmotif* for his wide-ranging thoughts in the decades that followed:

For nature is a perpetuall circulatory worker, generating fluids out of solids, and solids out of fluids, fixed things out of volatile & volatile out of fixed, subtile out of gross, & gross out of Subtile....[3]

He continued in this vein, suggesting that the Sun, as well as the Earth, might drink in this spirit for fuel and to replenish the source of its gravitational pull on planets, and he speculated that the same spirit might well serve as the "material Principle of light" that the sun drinks from the space between us and the distant stars.[4]

---

[1] Query 31 in *Opticks*, p. 398.
[2] Newton, "Memorandum," March, 1695/6 in *Correspondence*, vol. IV, p. 196. [3] Newton to Oldenburg, 7 December, 1675, *Correspondence*, vol. I, p. 360.
[4] Burndy MS 16, fol. 4. I have dealt with the question of stellar fuel in Newton's philosophy in my "Newton and the Cyclical Cosmos: Providence and the Mechanical Philosophy," *Journal of the History of Ideas*, vol. XXVIII, no. 3 (July–Sept. 1967): 325–46.

iii. The "More Subtle, Secret, and Noble Way of Working"

Given Newton's role as the father of the mechanical universe, in essence, the Moses of the modern age who has brought down from on high the Lord's Laws of Motion and the rest of it, we should fully understand the depths of his critique of the mechanical philosophy and appreciate how important that critique was to his overall work. Though Newton's scathing indictment of mechanism is most explicit in the early "Vegetation of Metals," the ideas expressed there resonate and are sometimes echoed in formulations he was to put forth throughout his life.

While Newton realized the power of mechanical analysis to explicate the interactions *between* gross bodies, the subject of his famed *Principia,* he regarded such an approach as woefully lacking in its ability to penetrate to the center of things, to the vegetative principle that *truly* revealed nature's inner workings. The mechanical philosophy, in short, does not operate *in* matter, as the vegetative principle does, but *upon* it. Newton realized that to our five senses, the changes in nature might

> appear to be nothing but mechanism or several dissevering & associating the p^{ts} of ye matter acted upon & that becaus severall changes to sense may be wrought wthout any act of vegetation....[1]

This is appearance only, however, and not at all a basis for real understanding. Unlike "vulgar chemistry," which is about such crude "mechanicall coalitions or seperations of particles," in order to obtain true knowledge "we must have recourse to some further cause," "a more subtle, secret, and noble way of working in all vegetation.... "[2] Thus, the mechanics behind the *Principia* is but a crude approximation of what nature really does, unlike the more sophisticated approach through alchemical studies.

Alchemy was the place to look for these spirits pervading nature. Newton's assistant and amanuensis, Humphrey Newton (no relation), recounted that Newton's "fires were almost perpetual," and that he was so oblivious during his spring and fall alchemical researches to the need for food and sleep[3] that it "made me think he aim'd at something beyond ye Reach of humane Art & Industry."

Richard Westfall, Newton's biographer, has judged that Newton's alchemical researches, his prodigious reading and laboratory investigations, so preoc-

---

[1] Burndy, MS 16, fol. 5^v; *Janus Face,* p. 268.

[2] Ibid., *Janus Face,* p. 269.

[3] Alternatively, Newton might have been consciously *fasting* and or *meditating* as he was conducting his alchemical researches. Westfall, *Never at Rest,* p. 371.

cupied him in the 1680s and early '90s that it would not be inappropriate to view the *Principia* (1687) as "an intrusion" into his primary alchemical concerns.

Alchemy was dangerous work. While authorities from time to time were drawn to the allure of its gold-making claims, alchemy's spiritual challenge to orthodox Christianity and its seditious political nature made both Church and State wary, if not outright hostile. Internally, there were dangers that were even greater. Rushing through laboratory processes that are inherently slow, even tedious, can cause the whole procedure to fail. Worst, the alchemists' quest to know the mind of God may easily overwhelm the would-be adept, plunging him/her into a personal Hell, as Berman puts it, quoting the traditional alchemical slogan, "Not a few have perished in our work."[1] Especially problematic was the troublesome role of the alchemist, as he was conducting his alchemical researches, who in finding the Philosopher's Stone and projecting its miraculous power into other matter, is creating part of the world even as the Creator did at the beginning, acting as a midwife to bring forth what before was only latent. Unless carefully tempered, the spiritual teaching of alchemy that God is found *within* can easily lead to spiritual arrogance and megalomania (as today is sometimes found in gurus or some weapon scientists). Newton was well aware of the connection between God's will and power and his own. In the "Vegetation of Metals," he wrote:

> Of God Whatever I can conceive wthout a contradiction either
> is or may bee made by something, that is: I can conceive all
> my owne powers, (knowledge activating matter, &c) wthout
> assigning them any limits. Therefore such powers either are
> or may bee made to bee....[2]

Indeed, the various yoga-like activities — fasting, meditating, chanting, etc. — engaged in by alchemists are to prepare them to meet such spiritual challenges without succumbing, without becoming intoxicated and overtaken by a cosmic hubris.

---

1 Berman, *Reenchantment of the World*, p. 86.
2 "Of natures obvious laws & processes in vegetation," Dibner MSS 1031B in Dobbs, *Janus*, Appendix A, p. 266.

13

Newton's Alchemical Cosmogony

So... as on the First World, Sótuknang called on the
Ant People to open their underground world for the
chosen people. When they were safely underground,
Sótuknang commanded the twins, Pöqánghoya and
Palöngawhoya to leave their posts at the north and
south ends of the world's axis, where they were stationed to keep the earth properly rotating.

The twins had hardly abandoned their stations
when the world, with no one to control it, teetered off
balance, spun around crazily, then rolled over twice.
Mountains plunged into the seas with a great splash,
seas and lakes sloshed over the land; and as the world
spun through cold and lifeless space it froze into solid
ice. — Frank Waters, *Book of the Hopi* (1963)

We have all been split away from each other, the
earth, ourselves. — Susan Griffin, *A Chorus of Stones:
The Private Life of War* (1992)

i. NEWTON'S COMETARY REBUTTAL TO HOOKE'S "GREAT STIR & PRETENDING"

According to Westfall, Newton's monumental *Principia* might be seen as an
interruption of his ongoing alchemical researches. Rather, I think it especially illuminating to see how Newton, because of the *Principia*, had the opportunity to extend his alchemical investigations *into* the cosmos, constructing over
the years a rather elaborate alchemical cosmogony that sought to explain details of
the "perpetuall circulatory worker" that kept the solar system, and perhaps even the
universe as a whole, going. The cosmogony relied on the recently discovered peri-
odicity of comets. As Newton explained to Halley in 1686, nearly two months after
the manuscript of his unprecedented opus had been presented to the Royal Society,

The third [Book still] wants ye Theory of Comets. In Autumn
last I spent two months in calculations to no purpose for want

of a good method, wch made me afterwards return to ye first
Book & enlarge it wth divers Propositions some relating to
Comets others to other things found out last Winter.

Alas, he announced this even as he threatened to withhold the crucial third book,
since Hooke's claim (see below) to have been responsible for some of his notions
made Newton realize that

Philosophy is such an impertinently litigious Lady that a man
had as good be engaged in Law suits as have to do with her.[1]

Indeed, his cometary theory was to play a cental role in the legendary battle
Newton had with his lifelong nemesis and rival, Robert Hooke.

In 1672, Hooke, having recently published his own ideas about light, had
the thankless, if not, indeed, sacrificial, role of criticizing the epochal paper on
light that a young and still largely unknown Isaac Newton had sent to the Royal
Society, the paper in which he first explicated the mysteries of prisms, and related the different colors of light, the hues of the rainbow, to the phenomenon
of refraction. Newton's response to Hooke's critique and the questions he posed
were characteristic; slowly his explosive rage gathered its head as he wrote draft
and draft of a reply, each angrier and more scathing, as Westfall has skillfully
shown. The challenge by Hooke was to make Newton gunshy in the future, apt
to hold onto his work and even to threaten to abandon philosophy altogether.[2]

Early in the making of Newton's *Principia*, the decade-old rivalry with Hooke
exploded anew. The story has been told many, many times, as its telling too is part
of the ongoing replenishment of the legend about the onset of modern times, but
a crucial part of the story has always been left out. Once put back in place, this
piece reveals the true shape and character of the famous Newton–Hooke enmity,
which, in turn, has critical ramifications for our understanding of Newtonianism.[3]

---

[1] Newton to Halley, 20 June 1686, *Correspondence*, vol. II, p. 437.

[2] See footnote 1, p. 251 above, and Westfall, *Never at Rest*, pp. 446ff.

[3] I have shown elsewhere how this new framework allows us to see, as a piece,
Halley's scientific career and research interests, to discern an overall form to
much of Hooke's work, as well as revealing an unknown aspect of Newton's
concept of the cosmos. David Kubrin, "'Such an Impertinently Litigious Lady':
Hooke's 'Great Pretending' vs. Newton's *Principia* and Newton's and Halley's
Theory of Comets," in (ed.) Norman J. W. Thrower, *Standing on the Shoulder of
Giants: A Longer View of Newton and Halley. Essays Commemorating the Tercentenary
of Newton's Principia and the 1985–1986 Return of Comet Halley* (Berkeley: Univ. of
California Press, 1990), pp. 55–90. See also my article "Edmond Halley," *Ency-
clopedia of the Scientific Revolution from Copernicus to Newton* (ed.) Wilbur Applebaum
(New York: Garland Publishing, 2000).

It was Halley's presentation to the Royal Society of Newton's manuscript for the first draft of the *Principia* that provoked Hooke's claim that Newton had taken some of its chief notions from him. Historians have ignored Hooke's own continued explanations of his meaning over the following months and years, instead grabbing onto what *they* think was the *one* issue Hooke meant by his boast — that Newton had stolen Hooke's idea that the force of attraction due to gravity decreased as the square of the distance between any two bodies (the $1/r^2$ term in the equation for the gravitational force, a key part of what we think of as Newton's law of gravitational attraction.) Correspondence between Hooke and Newton had occurred several years prior to the writing of the *Principia* on the question of what path a falling body would take as it fell to the Earth, and Hooke had corrected a mistake Newton had made, where the differences between Hooke's and Newton's solutions rested on how one thought the attractive force acted *inside* the Earth.

ii. The True Shape of the Newton–Hooke Enmity

But, as Hooke continued to argue over an extended period, the $1/r^2$ question was simply a key to a number of other fundamental philosophical issues, chief of which was the shape of the Earth's surface. Following similar considerations as those Newton later developed in his *Principia,* Hooke had deduced from the $1/r^2$ rule that the Earth's shape was a compressed spheroid, larger in the equatorial, than in its axial, circumference. This is the missing piece in the Hooke-Newton rivalry, the real "theft" Hooke most resented, for to Hooke the shape of the Earth was the linchpin of an elaborate general system of natural philosophy he had discovered, what Hooke himself called his "excellent System of Nature" that tied earthquakes, fossils from no-longer-existing creatures, the changes to species over time, the varying axial orientation of the Earth, volcanoes, and the formation of the planet's continents, as well as the vicissitudes in the planet's vitality, into one grand overarching system.

Indeed, as Hooke marshalled his arguments and elaborated his schema in the years that followed, a wide range of phenomena hitherto lacking explanations seemed to follow as a consequence of understanding "the Cause and Reason of the present Figure, Shape, and Constitution of the Surface of this Body of the Earth, whether Sea or Land...."[1]

It has always been assumed that when Halley confronted the boastful Hooke about his false claims against Newton's treatise and his pretense of having done certain critical investigations himself, and in response told Hooke, in effect,

---

1 Robert Hooke, *The Posthumous Works of Robert Hooke... Containing His Cutlerian Lectures, and Other Discourses Read at the Meetings of the Illustrious Royal Society....,* (ed.) Richard Waller (London, 1705), repr. (New York: Johnson Reprint Corp., 1969), (ed.) Richard S. Westfall, p. 334; cf. p. 371.

to put up or shut up, that Hooke simply shut up. That is patently not the case. In fact, as we shall see, Hooke eagerly and quickly responded to Halley's mocking challenge that "unless he produce another differing demonstration [of the $1/r2$ relationship] and let the world judge of it," no one would believe him.[1]

In June, 1686, one month after his initial claim, Hooke began a series of lectures to the Royal Society that occupied him for the next twelve years, initially on successive weeks lecturing the Society on the latest installment of his extended, serial, theoretical schema, laying out the details of his "excellent System of Nature." The set of lectures (after 1688, delivered by a broken and increasingly blind Hooke), which he presented on and off until 1699, are known as his *Lectures on Earthquakes,* and have been judged by their modern editor, Richard Westfall, to be Hooke's most prominent work. Certainly they stand out against a background of Hooke's deserved reputation for not sticking to a subject, of generally jumping from one topic to another before adequately exploring the possibilities of the first.[2] In contrast, his *Lectures on Earthquakes* is an extended philosophical inquiry into his subject — in this case, the shape of the Earth. No one, however, has realized that Hooke's driven fury in delivering them was because of his frantic race with the presses that were themselves struggling (once even coming to a halt for a matter of months) in their epochal mission to bring Newton's Laws (in the *Principia*) to the world.

In April, 1687, the manuscript of Newton's Third (and last) Book of the *Principia* ("System of the World") was presented to the Royal Society, providing them with Newton's demonstration of how a spinning Earth would experience a tendency at its equator to bulge outward, partially counterbalancing the effects of gravity, so as to mold the Earth into a compressed spheroidal shape. In reporting on this to the natural philosopher John Wallis, even Halley acknowledged Hooke's earlier demonstration of the spheroidal shape.[3] The *Principia*, published by Halley, was finally presented to the Society in early July, 1687.

It is clear that Hooke had certainly broadcast his intentions in relation to Halley's demand that he "show his stuff." At the beginning of his first lecture, in June, 1686, Hooke promised to demonstrate a new way of doing natural philosophy, adding "but I understand the same thing will now be shortly done by Mr. Newton in a Treatise of his now in the Press."[4] That a race was on would have been clear to anyone present.

Hooke's speculations and the treatise on his "excellent System of Nature" actually had begun with investigations sometime prior to 1668; in that year he gave,

---

1 Halley to Newton, 29 June 1686, Newton, *Correspondence,* vol. II, p. 442.
2 In part this was because Hooke worked *for* the Royal Society and was frequently told what investigations to undertake, usually by Boyle.
3 See Halley to Wallis, April 9, 1687 in *Correspondence and Papers of Edmond Halley,* (ed.) Eugene Fairfield MacPike (London: Taylor and Francis, Ltd., 1937), p. 80.
4 Hooke, *op. cit.,* pp. 329–30. The date of this discourse is uncertain; it might have been given on 8 December.

as a kind of small memorandum summarizing his ideas about the natural form of the Earth, a lecture to the Royal Society. In it Hooke mapped out a methodological approach, discussing the kinds of evidence available to guide natural philosophers in such matters. If gravity alone acted upon the first Earth, as Hooke supposed it must have, the different substances forming the planet would have settled out in the form of concentric spheres, "not unlike... the Shells... of an Onion," according to their differing densities. Huge earthquakes must have then changed it, forming the valleys and mountains seen in the present world, and with their stupendous energy, also shifting so much matter around on the inside of the planet that its very center of gravity could easily have been changed. Changing the center of gravity, however, would likely change the axis of rotation for the planet. He argued in this early discourse that comparisons of ancient with modern night skies indicated that such axial transformations had already occurred.[1]

Because a spinning Earth undergoes, as Christian Huygens had argued, a centrifugal force, any significant change in the direction of the spin axis would create absolute havoc, the planet becoming axially compressed and equatorially bloated, its surface decreasing radially in some new latitudes while radially expanding in others. As a new equator pushed outward and the new poles collapsed in, the planet's continents might well crumble and/or be covered with seas, and former ocean floors might be left high and dry.[2] This could explain the otherwise bizarre fact that sea shells and fish fossils — and Hooke was an early expert on fossils and aware of many extinctions — to the puzzlement of naturalists and travellers alike, had been found on mountaintops (e.g. the Alps). It might even account for the cause of Noah's deluge, Hooke suggested.[3]

Hooke's system thus utilized the Earth's shape as a platform upon which he erected a multitude of ancillary theories of the planet, encompassing theories of earthquakes, volcanoes, continent formation and dissolution, changes in time to the species living on the planet, variations of the Earth's magnetic forces, and how the Earth's orientation in space changes in time — a sweeping set of Earth-based hypotheses that can plausibly justify Hooke's boast of it as constituting his "excellent System of Nature."

Hooke devised schema to determine whether changes to the axes had, indeed, occurred, comparison of ancient and modern astronomical data and a plan to use a very long telescope to take measurements in future years.[4]

---

[1] Hooke's early work can be found in *Posthumous Works*, pp. 279–328. See especially pp. 313–14 and 321–27. Hooke claimed, (in *Dect. de Potent Restito*, p. 86) to have lectured on earthquakes at Gresham College as early as 1664 and 1665.

[2] Thomas Birch, *History of the Royal Society* in 4 volumes (London, 1756/57), vol. IV, pp. 521–22.

[3] *Posthumous Works*, p. 328. I discuss Hooke's theories in more detail in my "'Such an Impertinently Litigious Lady'," as well as in Chapter Six of *Providence and the Mechanical Philosophy* (doctoral diss., 1968).

[4] *Journal Book* of the Royal Society, February 9, 1687/88.

No wonder Hooke argued so passionately for his claim against Newton, since if it were accepted by his peers, or by posterity, he would be widely seen as the architect of an overall framework of the cosmos arguably as grand and profound — though quite different in scope — as the system of Newton.

Historians may have been misled into thinking Hooke's claim against Newton was limited to the l/r2 rule, but Newton certainly realized the full extent of Hooke's challenge. Beginning several months after Hooke's first discourse, in December, 1686 and extending for the next several decades, Newton created his own, rival, cosmogonic theory to counter Hooke's. Fighting Newton's battle, as his proxy, was Edmond Halley, the man responsible for the *Principia's* publication, and the first to realize what a dozen or so other disciples of Newton, men such as Roger Cotes, William Whiston, David Gregory, Richard Bentley, John Keill, and a host of other young men, soon found out: that their major role would be to fight for the integrity and truth of Newton's theories, and on occasion to reveal key axioms and speculations that Newton was hesitant or afraid to put out in his own name.[1]

iii. COMETARY *DEI EX MACHINA*

In an anonymous article in 1687, the year the *Principia* was published, Halley offered an alternative theory to Hooke's.[2] Halley actually accepted much of the general outline of Hooke's schema, such as that the Earth was a compressed spheroid and that any change in its axis of rotation would create vast terrestrial upheavals; the laws of motion, even though just then newly codified in Newton's treatise, were clear in their predictions. Halley accepted, too, the onion-like nested spheres model of Hooke's, making it his own by extending its structural specificity and using it as the basis for a complex model of geomagnetism, particularly for those aspects that changed over time. Halley disagreed with Hooke, however, about the heavens, arguing that they did not show that axial displacements had already occurred. Comparing recent astronomical observations with ones made 200 years earlier in Nuremburg and those made nearly 1900 years ago in Alexandria, Halley judged the differences to be so small as either simply to be the result of observational

---

[1] For the heavy hand of Newton holding the pen of his disciples, see William Whiston, *Memoirs of the Life and Writings of Mr. William Whiston. Containing Memoirs of Several of His Friends Also,* 2 vol. (London: 2nd ed., 1753), pp. 131, 155; for Newton's seeking "plausible deniability," see Newton to Roger Cotes, March 28, 1713 in (ed.) Joseph Edleston, Newton, *Correspondence of Sir Isaac Newton & Professor Cotes...* (London: 1850), p. 157, where he wrote, "If you write any further Preface [to the second edition of the *Principia,* which Cotes edited], I must not see it, for I find that I shall be examined about it." Cotes' most urgent task in his Preface was an attempt to justify Newton's highly suspect notion of the attractive forces, seemingly *in* matter.

[2] *Journal Book* of the Royal Society, February 1, 1687/88 in Halley, *Correspondence and Papers,* pp, 210–11.

error, and claimed that the kinds of catastrophic upheaval proposed by Hooke (or by the story of Noah) could never have happened in this manner.

To explain the kinds of catastrophes capable of wiping out whole species and of transforming seas into land and lands into seas, Halley instead proposed a possible impact upon the Earth of "some transient Body, such as a Comet."[1]

Thus was created what became an ongoing elaboration of a Newtonian cometary cosmogony, begun, really, with Newton's own hint in the first edition of the *Principia* that comets were special kinds of bodies, having peculiar qualities. Indeed, comets played two major roles in Newton's cosmology. On the one hand, he used their free passage through the heavens with no apparent resistance as a club to beat on Descartes' theory of vortices, which, based on material substance, would have impeded their passages; on the other hand, it was clear that comets had important functions, different from those of stars, planets, or moons, to fulfill, "indicating a divine hand," he said to David Gregory.[2] It was around the time of his writing the *Principia* that Newton first accepted that comets, like planets, orbited the sun, a position he had argued against in 1680/81 to John Flamsteed, the Astronomer Royal.[3] Newton's treatment of comets and their orbits was, as mentioned above, to be the crowning touch of the *Principia*, as well as its grand finale. When Newton was thrown into an explosive rage by Hooke's claim in relation to the *Principia* and he threatened to withhold the critical last book containing his theory of comets, Halley, who had bankrolled as well as edited the monumental work's first edition and stood to lose on his substantial investment, had to exercise the utmost care to make sure it did not happen.

What was so startling about comets — the Earth had witnessed a few spectacular ones in Newton's student years — were their tails, able to grow in a matter of weeks from a barely visible smudge in the sky to something reaching hundreds of millions of miles in length and stretching over a third of the way across the heavens. Whatever made up these tails, if it was material in nature, must be very rare and subtle, Newton deduced. Moreover, the tails were always pointing *away* from the sun, which indicated that some principle was actually counteracting the universal gravitational force — and from the beginning of his recorded speculations about nature, Newton had given special consideration to

---

[1] Teachings about the shifting position of the North and South Poles can be traced back to Pythagoras, whose influence on Newton was enormous; Pythagoras is said to have learned it from the Egyptians, who in turn learned it from Indian sages. See Elizabeth Gould Davis, *The First Sex* (Baltimore: Penguin Books 1972), p. 22. Similar myths are found in Native American traditions, for example, the epigraph for this Chapter from *The Book of the Hopi*.

[2] Memorandum by David Gregory; 5–7 May, 1694, in Newton, *Correspondence*, vol. III, p. 336. For an account of Newton's changing views on the nature of their orbits, see *Ibid.*, vol. IV, note 2 to Letter 528, pp. 165–66.

[3] Newton to Crompton for Flamsteed 28 February 1680–81, *Correspondence* vol. I, pp. 340f.

forces of repulsion. In the first edition of the *Principia*, Newton noted that these tails appeared to slowly dissipate into space and that he believed their substance would then gradually be attracted to the various planets, mixing with their atmospheres, oceans, and fluids.[1]

Indeed, this is but his earlier vision of the Earth drinking in aethereal spirit from above, as in his alchemical image of the living and breathing planet that he had sent to the Royal Society in 1675, only now it is generalized from Earth to *all* of the planets, and Newton in the intervening years had come to suspect that "it is chiefly from comets that spirit comes, which is indeed the smallest but most subtle and useful part of our air, and so much required to sustain the life of all things with us."[2] Newton proposes in the *Principia*, in other words, that comets are carriers of the principle of life, and suggests that they are necessary for the circulation of spirit throughout the solar system.

iv. MOTION "ALWAYS UPON THE DECAY"

Initially, Newton saw certain limits to this cosmic circulatory system. Since their tails always point away from the sun, his schema is unable to "feed" the sun and stars as it does the planets, and so, unlike in his 1675 letter to the Royal Society, they go unnourished.

Another difference between his *Principia* and the earlier alchemical speculations is that whereas nature had formerly been a "perpetual circulatory worker," now there are certain one-way processes, which threaten ultimately to create chaos in the workings of the cosmos. For example, in 1675 there was enough air rising up out of the Earth to balance the aethereal spirit being absorbed; by 1687, Newton believed, to the contrary, that "the bulk of the solid earth is continually increased...."[3] In 1694 he would elaborate on this in a conversation with Halley, pointing out that the Earth must be growing in bulk and that this would cause the moon to speed up in its orbit, perhaps even eventually to spiral down onto the Earth.[4] Twelve years later, in the "Queries" to the 1706 *Opticks*, Newton discussed a variety of unidirectional processes in nature. He had determined certain perturbations in the orbits of planets that introduced irregularities into the frame of nature and if allowed to continue would require a reformation of the world. Moreover, numerous mechanical interactions resulted

---

[1] Newton, *Principia* (1687, first ed.) p. 506. Newton's changing notions of the role of such cometary emissions and how eventually he came to see them as "feeding" a kind of cosmic nourishment to stars, too, are described in my "Newton and the Cyclical Cosmos," pp. 325–46.

[2] Sir Isaac Newton, *Mathematical Principles of Natural Philosophy*, p. 530.

[3] *Principia*, 1st ed., p. 506; Cajori (ed.), pp. 529–30.

[4] *Journal Book* of the Royal Society, October 31, 1694.

in an overall loss of the amount of motion, so that, as Newton ruefully put it, motion "is always upon the Decay."[1]

We shall return to the larger meaning of these forms of dissolution emphasized by Newton from the mid-1690s on, but for now it is important to stress that, when eventually Newton solved the various problems of the system's irregularities, it was comets that, once again, were called upon to put things right.

Indeed, in the hands of the Newtonians, there was no end of things that a properly situated comet, of the right mass and velocity, might accomplish, say in an impact with, or close passage by, the Earth. In 1692 Halley returned to speculations regarding cometary impacts on the Earth by proposing a probable internal structure of the Earth, where two (or more) nesting spheres each contains a pair of magnetic poles; such an Earth (an adaptation of Hooke's onion model), if hit a glancing blow from a passing comet, so that the outer, but not the inner, pair of magnetic poles was set spinning, could account, he believed, for many of the complexities observed about the changing strengths and directionality of terrestrial magnetism. Two years later, he followed up in a discourse proposing that such an impact might "produce a new axis & poles of diurnal Rotation, a new length of the Day, & year..." essentially giving Hooke's hypothesis of the changes to the Earth's axis a new spin, due to the proposed impact of comets. Such a collision might well account for the depression of Hudson's Bay and could have been the cause of Noah's Deluge. One week later, Halley suggested that such cometary hits might well have occurred "once or oftener," destroying former Earths.[2] There is good reason to believe this latter notion came from Newton.[3]

William Whiston, another early disciple of the master, extended Halley's hypothesis in 1696, proposing such periodic cometary visitations as the occasion for the original Creation of the Earth (out of the remains of a former comet) and then for both the Fall from innocence and the subsequent Deluge; one day, Whiston had no doubt, it would be a comet that brought on Armageddon.

Newton had provided another disciple, the astronomer David Gregory, with deeper explanations of cometary machinations, which he recorded in memoranda and then elaborated on in his *Elements of Physical and Geometrical Astronomy* (1702), where he showed how a comet might crash into a planet and change its

---

[1] Newton, *Opticks*, pp. 398–99.

[2] Halley, "An Account of the Cause in the Change in the Variation of the Magnetical Needle," *Philosophical Transactions of the Royal Society*, no. 175 (1692); *Journal Book* of the Royal Society, December 12, 1694 in Halley, *Correspondence and Papers*, p. 234; Halley, "Of the Cause of the Deluge," *Philosophical Transactions and Collections..., Abridged...* (ed.) John Lowthorp (London: various dates), vol. 6 (2), p. 38ff. (Henceforth *PTA*).

[3] Kubrin, "'Such an Impertinently Litigious Lady,'" pp. 71f.

orbit and period.[1] Should a *moon* be hit by a comet, it could be knocked out of its orbit around its planet, becoming, under the right conditions, a planet in its own right. A decade earlier, in the memoranda of their conversations, Gregory had recorded Newton's ruminations on the possibilities that the moons of Jupiter and Saturn "can take the places of the Earth, Venus, Mars, if they are destroyed, and be held in reserve for a new Creation."[2]

What finally enabled Newton to use comets to *fully* resupply the vital stuff of the cosmos was the realization, while working on his theory of comets for the long-awaited second edition of the *Principia* (1713), that the comet of 1680/81, in each of its successive passages, was likely to be pulled closer and closer to the sun, eventually (perhaps after five more orbits) crashing down into it. He believed this could well be the fate of many comets. When Newton had originally supposed in the *Principia* that the vital energy was circulated by comets, they were capable of delivering the goods only to *planets* and *moons*, since the sun (and presumably other stars) pushed comets' tails, where he figured such spirits resided, away from it. Now, with solar infusions too, it was clear the energizing spirits could feed stars, as well. And so, for the second edition of the *Principia*, Newton added the following explanation for novas:[3]

> So fixed stars, that have been gradually wasted by the light
> and vapors emitted from them for a long time, may be re-
> cruited [*i.e.*, nourished] by comets that fall upon them.

Towards the end of his life, Newton gave the fullest explanation of his cometary cosmogony to John Conduitt, in a contemplative mood one night telling Conduitt some of his deeper cosmological views:

---

[1] In Gregory's memoranda, "Of Comets" is the first heading, underscoring the importance Newton assigned to these cosmic "messengers" in his overall framework of nature. See Gregory, *The Elements of Physical & Geometrical Astronomy*, 2 vols., transl. from the Latin (London: 2nd. ed., 1726), vol. 2, pp. 716, 852–54 on cometary tails possibly being baneful or as bringers of vital fluids to the sun and planets. The Newtonian J.T. Desagulier in *A Course of Mechanical and Experimental Philosophy* (n.p., n.d), pp. 354–55, answers the objection that comets are so miniscule that they could not provide much by way of fuel to a star by noting that even if they were "in solidity the Ten hundred thousandth Part." it may amount to "as much as the Sun in many Years may lose in Light...."

[2] Memoranda by David Gregory, 5–7 May 1694, in Newton, *Correspondence*, vol. III, p. 336.

[3] In 1572 and again in 1604, such "new" stars, what are today called "novas"or "supernovas," were seen in the supposedly immutable heavens, greatly confusing natural philosophers. Newton, *Principia*, 1712 ed., p. 481, in Cajori, ed., pp. 540–41.

that it was his conjecture (he would affirm nothing) that there was a sort of revolution in the heavenly bodies that the vapours & light emitted by the sun which had their sediment in water and other matter had gathered themselves by degrees in to a body & attracted some more matter from the planets & at last made a secondary planett [i.e., a moon]... & then by gathering to them... more matter became a primary planet, & then by increasing still became a comet....[1]

A comet whose tail, he believed, consisted of a "living universal innate spirit, wch in form of an aereal vapour perpetually descends from heaven to earth to fill its porous belly...."[2] Such comets would eventually fall into the sun, refueling it. Newton made clear to Conduitt that the Earth itself had "visible marks of ruin upon it," which a mere deluge could not have made.[3]

So though it is certainly true that Newton's system of the cosmos resembles the "billiard ball" universe attributed to him, *that* image ignores that the "cue balls" of Newton's cosmos, comets, were really magical, alchemically-charged agents, serving as a kind of cosmic regenerative force, able "to nourish & vivify all nature."[4] More accurately, we might say that the "father" of the mechanical universe, Newton, in actuality abandoned and repudiated (albeit not entirely disinheriting) his alleged offspring.

After the publication of the first edition of his *Principia,* Newton continued to press his line of inquiry about the kinds of rare and subtle matter found in

---

[1] Memorandum by John Conduitt, Kings College (Cambridge) Manuscript Keynes 130, no. 11, reprinted with some changes in Edmund Turner, *Collections for the History of the Town and Sake of Grantham containing Authentic Memoirs of Sir Isaac Newton* (London: 1806), pp. 172–73.

[2] Newton, "[Notes] Out of La Lumiere sortant des Tenebres," quoted in Dobbs, *Janus,* p. 280; probably written between 1687 and 1692.

[3] Compare Halley's comments, above, p. 265. Cometary impacts on the Earth are finally seen as playing major roles in terrestrial history. Mike Reynolds, "Earth Under Fire," *Astronomy* (August, 2006), pp. 40–45. As carriers of organic molecules to the Earth to start life, see "New Theory On Origin of Life on Earth," San Francisco *Chronicle* (September 28, 1978); "Comet Lovejoy Found To Be All Hopped Up on Alcohol," San Francisco *Chronicle* (October 27, 2015); David Perlman, "Mysteries of Mass Extinction Cleared Up," San Francisco *Chronicle* (October 2, 2015).

[4] Newton, "[Notes] Out of La Lumiere," p. 284. In drafts for the Queries for the *Opticks* drafted in 1706 and later, it is clear that Newton sees the materials brought to the Earth as embodying the alchemical vegetative principles. See Cambridge University Library, CUL Add. 3970, fol. 244r, for example, a draft possibly for Query 26, where Newton is discussing the sources of new motion inside the Earth.

comets' tails. He was particularly intrigued by the possibility of *structure* being a way to explain varying gross properties of different kinds of substance, their selective reactivities, different densities, and the like. The extremes of density suggested a powerful nesting of levels of matter inside other levels, and so on, each nesting being accounted for by a subtle shift in a geometric hierarchy of forms, which ultimately rested on hard bodies. These bodies themselves were the result of an intricate patterning of *force centers* having diminishingly small dimensions — sources of powerful forces of resistance that, at extremely short distances, were so huge as to prevent bodies from being penetrated. Such point centers produced around them the effect of hardness — akin, perhaps, to the act of God's will that Newton had posited in his early manuscript *De Gravitatione* as the manner in which the material world was originally created. Variations on the same architecture would, Newton hoped, account for the differing reactivities of the variety of substances, some prone to react violently to nearly everything, while others were overwhelmingly stable. In the end, Newton believed these nearly point-sized centers of resistance forces were so small that all the truly hard matter in the universe could fit inside a single nutshell![1] Newton's "machine universe," then, was built of gears, pulleys, and levers that were themselves very nearly immaterial.

v. A WORLD FROM ETERNITY?

Newton's and Halley's speculations regarding a series of ruins that had thoroughly transformed past Earths had more in common with the myths of the succession of Ages than it did with Genesis. Such cyclic theories could be found in Stoic or Hindu mythology, with which Halley would surely have been familiar, or even Native American cosmology.[2] Halley, in fact, came under serious attack because of widespread rumors about his unorthodox religious views, particularly the alarming heresy that the world was eternal, a doctrine especially dangerous in England in 1691 and '92 for political reasons, as I have argued elsewhere.[3] As Halley wrote to Abraham Hill in 1691, he had been denied an appointment he had been seeking as Savilian Professor of Astronomy at Oxford because of reports of such beliefs. He needed to "clear myself" on charges of "asserting the

[1] Arnold Thackray, "Matter in a Nut-Shell: Newton's *Opticks* and Eighteenth Century Chemistry," *Ambix* 15 (1968), 29–53; Karin Figula, "Newton As Alchemist," *History of Science* 15 (1977), pp. 102–37.

[2] Hindu legends would have become known during the upsurge of study of Eastern philosophies that swept across England during the radical 1640s and '50s; Native American ideas came under attack, as we saw in Chapter Eleven, by leading elements of the Royal Society in the 1660s.

[3] Kubrin, "Such an Impertinently Litigious Lady;" Kubrin, *Providence and the Mechanical Philosophy*, doctoral dissertation, Chap. 9; also Chapter 2, "The Eternity of the World."

eternity of the world."[1] Indeed, rumors of Halley's "infidel" opinions periodically arose during his life.[2]

To the task of clearing himself Halley turned his considerable talents, initiating in 1692 a series of astronomical and geochronological investigations, all designed to demonstrate unidirectional patterns in nature, the clear implications of every one of them being that the world "must have had a beginning," as he explained, even as he kept out of print (for three decades, as it turned out) his earlier talk to the Royal Society about former Earth's being destroyed by cometary impacts.[3]

His effort to clear his name was singularly rewarding. In those pursuits, Halley was to uncover a number of new phenomena, ones which are integral to his reputation as a prolific and talented astronomer, such as his finding the secular acceleration of the moon; his discovery of stellar proper motion; his announcement of the variation in the length of the year; his establishing a theoretical protocol to date the age of the oceans by periodic measurement of their (presumably always linearly) increasing salinity and extrapolating back to a presumed non-saline origin — all these and more flowed from the need to clear his name in terms of impiety.[4]

It appears, as well, that Halley's strategem of putting a new slant on his axial cosmology worked. At least, when in 1703 a new Savilian Professorship (this one of Geometry) was open, Halley sought its appointment; with the help of the Earl of Nottingham, this time Halley was successful. Years later he was Astronomer Royal of England and given responsibility for the strategically important Greenwich Observatory.

Even so, in 1713, when the second edition of Newton's *Principia* was finally published (the first, over 25 years old, long unavailable and now with many wishing to attempt its fabled ascent) its editor, Richard Bentley, boldly and unilaterally changed Halley's famous "Ode" to Newton placed at the beginning of his *Principia*, modifying several lines that seemed to imply that the frame of nature had stood forever. Halley was extremely upset, and managed to get Newton to promise that in any further editions, the "Ode" would be restored to its original form. But when the third, 1726, edition appeared, a year before Sir Isaac's death, the offending lines of the "Ode," far from being reinstated, had been al-

---

[1] Halley to Abraham Hill, 22 June 1691 in Halley, *Corresponddence and Papers*, p. 88. He allowed to Hill that he was "sensible that he might have adventured" too far.

[2] Bodleian MS Rawl. J 4°, 2, fol. 103^r–103^v; Thomas Hearne, *Remarks and Collections* iii (May 25, 1710–Dec. 14, 1712 (ed.) Ce. E. Doblem (Oxford, England: 1889), pp. 472–73.

[3] *Journal Book* of the Royal Society, in *Correspondence and Papers*, pp. 229, 232.

[4] Kubrin, "'Such an Impertinently Litigious Lady,'"; Halley's "An Attempt to Find the Age of the World by the Saltness of the Sea" (1715) *PTA* vol. V, pp. 216–19.

tered yet again, by Henry Pemberton, its new editor, in a further effort to dissociate Newton's grand synthesis from anything implying the eternity of the world.[1]

Till his death, Hooke, too, kept up his end of the ongoing public debate with Halley/Newton, often returning to the central questions of cosmogony and proposing tests to uncover the variations he claimed lay at the heart of his "excellent System of Nature," and reminding his audience from time to time of the ongoing rivalry with references to "an *Hypothesis* I have formerly acquainted this Society with, *somewhat* [my emphasis] of Mr Newton hath printed."[2]

Like Halley, Hooke proposed long-term measurement projects — in his case, of the meridians and latitudes of specific terrestrial locations — to find out if the patterns he predicted, centering around variations of the Earth's axis of rotation, actually existed in nature. Hooke continued, too, to mock some notions of the Newtonians, making snide comments to the Royal Society about Whiston's avowal (an elaboration of Newton's own notions) that gravity itself existed due to an act of God's special Providence.[3]

vi. Newton's Passive Earth

Newton's and Hooke's agreement that *something* periodically upset the axis of the Earth perhaps reflected common Pythagorean roots for both men, but, at the same time, a profound chasm lay between them.[4] For Hooke, it was the Earth itself that precipitated these mighty shifts in axial location, through an earthquake or volcanic transfer of massive amounts of matter from one location to another, thereby changing the planet's center of gravity. Newton (and Halley), however, in this regard truer to the ideology of the mechanical philosophy, insisted that only outside bodies (in their view, transient objects, like comets) had caused the axial changes, by striking the Earth; their Earth was transformed, superficially at least, only by impact, by outside agencies.

Their fight went on till Hooke's death in 1703 and even beyond. One year

---

1 Though Bentley was reputed to be the foremost classicist of the age, the Latin of his version was reportedly not as good as Halley's. Bentley was a confident emender of the texts of others, defending his version of Milton in which hundreds of lines were struck out as "spurious." The three versions of the "Ode" are in Halley, *Correspondence and Papers*, p. 5. See Memoranda by John Conduitt, Kings College, MS Keynes 30, no. 7 (published in *Ibid.*, p. 206).

2 Hooke, *Posthumous Works*, p. 377.

3 Kubrin, *Providence and the Mechanical Philosophy* dissertation.

4 Kubrin, "'Such an Impertinently Litigious Lady.'" It is clear that Pythagoras is the source of Newton's thoughts on comets. An interesting window into this is found in Isaac Newton, "Out of Cudworth," William Andrews Clarke Memorial Library, manuscript, fol. 1^r.

after the death of his clear nemesis, Newton finally allowed the publication of his much-anticipated *Opticks*, able to do so now without having to hear still again from Hooke on any of its matters.

The 1690s had taken a steep toll on Newton, however, as we shall see in the next chapter. Psychologically, politically, and philosophically, he appears to have negotiated a precipitous divide sometime in the first half of the decade, probably in relation to his 1693 nervous breakdown, for in the course of his recovery, certain quandaries seem to have been, for better or worse, worked through. Since many crucial questions end up having significantly different approaches and answers for Newton after that breakdown, it is worth our while to look in some detail at just what occurred; perhaps thereby we can glean something about this crisis in Newton's psyche and see how his resolution of the burning issues at the heart of his ongoing philosophical investigations might bear on our own vexing times.

14

Newton's Alchemical Breakdown

> [T] he purpose of the [military] drill is to instill *automatic response to orders*. It was Frederick the Great who [in 1686] first understood this.... inspired to invent the Prussian drill by the newly emerging scientific view of the universe as a great machine. The peasants in his army were to be like cogs in the mechanism of official will. — Susan Griffin, *A Chorus of Stones. The Private Life of War* (1992) [emphasis hers]

> I have already stated my opinion that one major result of modern science has been to make people doubt what they would otherwise accept as true from their own observation and experience. Science, medicine, psychology and economics all deeply depend on people being mystified by their own experience and blind to the strict limits of scientific method. — Jerry Mander, *Four Arguments for the Elimination of Television* (1978)

> This mechanical and atomistic view of reality, the basis of which was outlined in the works of Descartes and Galileo, found its most perfect expression in the physics and metaphysics of Isaac Newton, who may with all justice be regarded as the father of modern science and as the man who gave to capitalist apprehension the legitimizing and final smack of approval that only science can now endow. — Michael T. Taussig, *The Devil and Commodity Fetishism in South America* (1980)

i. THE *NIGREDO* OF NEWTON'S SOUL

The reality of Newton's nervous breakdown is well-documented. All of a sudden, incoherent and paranoid letters were sent to his close friends, John Locke and Samuel Pepys, confessing to earlier beliefs that they both had "designs" upon him and that Locke in particular had attempted to entangle Newton in emotional liasons with women. Newton condemned what he saw as a campaign of theirs to get him a position in the apparatus of the State, apologized for wishing death upon Locke, and declared his desire to end the friendships he had long had with both of them. Reports of Newton's bizarre behavior also spread through international philosophical correspondence.[1]

Newton's own explanation of his emotional turmoil blamed severe sleep deprivation, the careful tending of his alchemical fires that required his keeping constantly by his furnaces, to the effect that "I had not slept a night for a fortnight together & for 5 nights together not a wink." Reports of a fire that destroyed some of Newton's crucial manuscripts have been cited by others as a possible cause of his odd behavior and it has been suggested that Newton was the victim of mercury poisoning from continuous exposure during his intense, continuous alchemical research. But a fire, though real enough, appears to date from another time and the symptoms of mercury poisoning are inconsistent.[2]

A close examination of the period immediately preceding his breakdown suggests a radically alternative explanation for the crisis. Here too it is alchemy that looms largest in the picture. With the publication of his *Principia*, Newton had returned, as Westfall documents, to his earlier alchemical obsessions. One good reason for turning from the mechanics and celestial dynamics of the *Principia* to alchemy was that in those mysteries he could conceivably find answers to the many questions his *Principia* had posed without answering, most explicitly those raised by his bizarre notion of a universal gravitational attraction between all bodies in the universe.[3] To contemporaries, there was more than a hint of magic in this idea that the axiomatized "inert" bodies of the mechanical philosophy were capable of exerting forces, or pulls, across the empty reaches of millions of miles of space — and according to a precise quantitative measure of both of the masses involved and the distances between them at that![4] There was

---

[1] Along with the official institutionalized journals of scientific research — begun in the last half of the 17th century in Italy, in London (with the debut of the *Philosophical Transactions of the Royal Society*), in Paris, and in the plethora of other places where philosophical bodies were spawned — letters focusing on natural philosophy from one savant to another, often bearing enclosures, perhaps copies of letters from a third philosophical party, or copies of secretly-passed manuscripts, or newly published works unable to be published in the recipient's country, at this time of effervescent intellectual ferment, acquired a new legitimacy for the creation and transmission of learning and culture.

[2] Westfall, *Never at Rest*, pp. 534ff; Frank Manuel, *op. cit.*, Chapter Ten.

[3] Notions of influence acting across space without intervening agents are still profoundly disturbing, even anathema, to scientists, despite the fact that Bell's theorem implies that at the quantum level such "non-local" effects do exist. For an illuminating recent history, see Kaiser, *op. cit.*

[4] Leibniz thus in a review of a work by John Freind, a young chemist known as a Newtonian, criticized his use of the concept of forces for chemical phenomena as a philosophical return to "a certain fantastic scholastic [i.e., Aristotelian] phi-

more than a hint, too, of the *anima mundi,* or world soul, here. In a planned second edition of the *Principia,* which was supposed to be published in the early to mid-1690s, it was understood that Newton would address his critics' concerns and explain what he really meant.[1]

Let us savor the many layers of Newton's ambiguities and appreciate the historical significance of his tortured relationship with the "mechanical universe" that history has portrayed as his legacy. Ultimately, modern consciousness itself was being shaped in the complex cross currents, as Newton struggled with these challenges in the critical period after the 1687 appearance of his *Principia.* For Newton the central question was how did matter become "active," that is, how did it act in utter defiance of the canonical inertness of all matter in the universe? Any answer to this question was, Newton well knew, most apt to be found in alchemy.

As it happened, Robert Boyle died in 1691 and in his Will had named Locke and Drs. Cox and Dickison to examine his extensive papers. Earlier, Boyle had given different parts of a treasured alchemical recipe to Locke, Newton, and perhaps others. Not long after Boyle's death (in January 1691/92), Newton wrote Locke mentioning a red earth and a mercury, implying that he and Locke should share what each had been separately given by Boyle.[2] Obviously, both men were under oath to Boyle to be secretive about the process. By early July, 1692, it is clear that Locke had sent Newton a supply of the red earth and a description of part of the procedure.[3] Newton's return letter expressed great reservations about the overall value of Boyle's parcelled-out secrets. Despite his skepticism, however, Newton wished to try out the first part (the "entrance") of the recipe.

His next letter again expressed doubts about Boyle's process, but Newton had found himself a dodge about the issue of secrecy: since Boyle had given only part of the recipe (in characteristically alchemical fashion leaving out crucial parts), Newton felt free to violate his oath of secrecy "so yt I may reccon my self at my own discretion to say or do what I will about this matter...."[4]

ii. IN PURSUIT OF FATIO

Fatio de Duillier had become the central figure in Newton's life around this time. Contacting Newton shortly after the appearance of his *Principia,* Fatio

---

losophy, or even the *enthusiastic* philosophy of Fludd." (My emphasis. Quoted in Westfall, *Never at Rest,* p. 730.) Leibniz and Newton at the time were engaged in a parallel dispute over who had created the calculus. Leibniz published his gibe in the *Acta eruditorium,* arguably the most important European scientific journal of the time, anonymously. But the Newtonians recognized its authorship.

[1] As mentioned earlier, the second edition was not published until 1713.

[2] Newton to Locke, 26 January 1691/92 in *Correspondence,* vol. III, p. 193.

[3] Newton to Locke, 7 July 1692, *Ibid.,* p. 215.

[4] Newton to Locke, 2 August 1692, *Ibid.,* pp. 217–18.

quickly established an exceedingly close relationship with the reclusive scientist. The two men shared a number of vital interests, including prophecy and alchemy. Soon it became known that it would be Fatio who was the planned editor of the eagerly awaited new edition of the *Principia*. Fatio had even worked out an explanation of gravitational attraction that was supposedly consistent with the mechanical philosophy, and for a while Newton was said to favor it. Most significantly, a strong emotional attraction developed between the two men.[1]

For a man free of strong ties to nearly anyone besides his mother, Newton's love for Fatio stands out in stark relief. Whether the two men ever were sexually intimate is unknown, but it is clear from their letters that it was on both their minds. Given the central role Fatio played in Newton's life, and the curtain that suddenly fell on that play precisely at the time of Newton's breakdown, I suggest taking a close look at their truncated courtship to see if it might shed some needed light on our matters.

A particularly intense exchange of letters between the two men began in the Fall of 1692 — as Newton's alchemical experiments, following Boyle's newly coherent recipe, were reaching a peak — concerning the decline of Fatio's health and Newton's alarm at hearing that the illness could well prove fatal.[2]

Newton's reply urged Fatio to go to a physician, for which he would pay. Learning from a subsequent letter that Fatio' s illness remained serious, Newton advised him to escape London's notoriously bad air by coming to stay with him in Cambridge. Fatio's reply was to the point; his health had now improved somewhat and a recent inheritance might even allow him to remain in England, mainly at Cambridge. But if Newton wished his presence, however, "and have for that some other reasons than what barely relateth to my health and the savings of charges, I am ready to do so; But I could wish in that case You would be plain in your next letter."[3]

Plain, however, Newton was utterly incapable of being, particulary in matters of this sort, and his next letter to Fatio is almost businesslike, searching for ways of getting money to his young friend (for medicine they had shared and for books he had borrowed and now wished to buy from Fatio), but in closing, supposedly in reference to Fatio's discussion towards the end of his letter about prophecy, a mutual interest of the two men, Newton added, "but I feel you indulg too much in fancy in some things."[4] Fatio replied, acknowledging his receipt

---

[1] Manuel, *op. cit.*, Chap. 9 on Newton and Fatio. Newton's oft-reported repudiation of Fatio's explanation for gravity, it should be noted, was written later, as is obvious in the manuscript but not published version from the different color ink and its placement off to the sides; when we do not know. Royal Society MS Gregory, fol. 71^v.

[2] The relevant letters are found in Newton, *Correspondence*, vol. III, pp. 229–30, 231–33, 241, 242–43, 243, 245, 260–61, 262, 263, 265–66, 267–70, 391–92.

[3] *Ibid.*, Fatio du Duillier to Newton, 30 January 1692/93, p. 243.

[4] Newton to Fatio, 14 February 1692/93, *Ibid.*, p 245.

of the £14 Newton had sent for the medicine, alchemical books, and a box of brass rulers, and then coyly remarked, "S^r if Your design hath been to put an obligation upon me You have done it effectively."[1] In the next sentence Fatio confessed that he found the prospect of living at Cambridge attractive, "chiefly if it was practicable and proper that I should hire the chambers which You had next to Yours."[2]

Alas, those adjacent chambers were already occupied, but Newton repeated his invitation to the younger man. Fatio's reply, a month later, affirmed his affections. "I would wish Sir to live all my life, or the greatest part of it, with you, if it was possible, and shall always be glad of any such methods to bring that to pass" that were not burdensome for Newton. Fatio told Newton that Locke had invited him to his estate at Oates, but that Fatio believed Locke "would have me to go there only that You may be the sooner inclinable to come"[3] — in other words, that Locke was using him as bait for the reclusive Newton.

In early May, Newton heard what seemed like good news from his ailing friend. He was feeling considerably better, and was looking forward the next day to trying a remedy that had been given him by a new acquaintance, a man Fatio was now working with on alchemical matters who had assured him it would cure him in just a few days.

Most interestingly, this remedy was made from a quite remarkable new mercury Fatio had seen; he had also been told how to prepare this mercury. He described its actions in detail, how out of a metallic putrefaction and fermentation arises a "heap of golden trees," due to a vegetative action. Fatio repeats the recipe in his letter, which he instructs Newton to destroy after reading, and he passes on an invitation for Newton to see it himself, presumably in London.[4]

When surrounded by sand, placed inside a sealed container and heated, an amalgam of this mercury and gold filings "do presently swell, and puff up, and grow black and in a matter of seven days go through the colors of the Philosophers" tell-tale Peacock-like signs described in the alchemical literature to indicate to any would-be adept that s/he is on the right pathway. A "heap of trees… grows… out of the matter, and a slow transformation of colors takes place, the trunk of the trees a copper or violet color, while the branches are gold and silver in color." Having seen it, Fatio excitedly reported, "[T]here is plainly a life and a ferment in that composition."[5] From what Newton later wrote, it is clear he too (quite possibly in Fatio's laboratory) had seen the same transformations.

[1] Fatio to Newton, 9 March 1692/93, *Ibid.*, p. 262.

[2] Fatio to Newton, 9 March 1692/93 in Correspondence, vol. III, p. 262.

[3] Fatio to Newton, 11 April 1693, *Correspondence*, vol. III, pp. 391–92.

[4] Newton did not follow Fatio's instructions. An earlier letter from Newton to Fatio has three places, probably names of other alchemists, where words have been carefully cut out. Newton, *Correspondence*, vol. III, p. 45 (10 October, 1689).

[5] Fatio to Newton, 4 May 1693, Ibid., vol. III, pp. 265–66. Compare this description to that in the quotation in Chapter 12, p. 254.

Fatio's health continued to improve and two weeks later he was writing for Newton's advice on business matters. His new alchemist friend had offered to teach him how to make the same remedy that had so helped him. In greater detail he again described the preparation of this special mercury. By the end it becomes a most remarkable, very dense, vapor that is nearly invisible; but after several days, if kept cool, it will settle into a liquid capable of dissolving any metal or gem. Fatio believed this mercury was able "to go on to ye Noblest operations" in alchemy; that is, it would form the basis for the making of the Philosophers' Stone.

It was Fatio's uncertainty about his financial standing that dominated his last letter. The larger inheritance he had expected looked doubtful. Fatio sought Newton's advice: should he take advantage of his new friend's offer and learn how to make this powerful medicine? His friend had given the remedy free to more than 10,000 people, according to Fatio, sometimes to 500 in one day. Fatio thought he could "cure for nothing thousands of people and so make it [the remedy] known in a little while." Then (readily abandoning the Rosicrucian principle of philosophic medicine for free) once this initial trial period was over, "it would be easie to raise a fortune by it." His scheme, however, might require being supported for several years. He welcomed Newton's advice, obviously open to an offer of financial backing or perhaps even being led to some form of preferment from the older scientist.[1]

Shortly after receiving this letter, Newton took leave of Cambridge to go to London. Westfall believes it was in order to visit Fatio, and suggests jealousy towards Fatio's new friend as one possible reason.[2] Assuming there are no lost letters during this time between them, Newton certainly would have noted the dramatic change of feelings reflected in Fatio's latest letter. Additionally, he certainly would have been drawn to see the making of this new mercury that so obviously had "a life."

iii. "A Life and a Ferment"

It was probably shortly later that Newton wrote his most important alchemical treatise, *Praxis*. In it be refers to Fatio's letter of May, 1693, so it must date after that period of intense personal and alchemical exchange between the two men. In *Praxis* we find a quite astounding claim:

> Thus you may multiply each stone 4 times & no more for they will then become oyles shining in y^e dark & fit for magicall uses. You may ferment them w^{th} $\odot$ [gold] by keeping them in fusion for a day, & then project upon metals. This is y^e multiplication in quality. You may multiply it in quantity by the

1 Fatio to Newton, 18 May 1693, *Correspondance*, vol. III, pp. 267–70.
2 Westfall, *Never at Rest*, p. 533.

mercuries of wch you made it at first, amalgaming ye stone
wth ye ☿ [mercury] of 3 or more eagles & adding their weight
of ye water, & if you design it for mettalls you may melt every
time 3 parts of ☉ wth one of ye stone. Every multiplication
will encreas it's [sic] vertue ten times &, if you use y^e ☿ of y^e
2d or 3d rotation wthout ye spirit, perhaps a thousand times.
Thus you may multiply to infinity.[1]

This is, needless to say, an extraordinary document! It appears to be a summary statement on the hows and whats of alchemical laboratory practice, if I
read it correctly. If the language is obscure to us, to a practitioner of the art it
would be clear enough. Unlike some of *Praxis*, which reads more like a summary
of alchemical *theory*, this part of the work reads as a how-to manual, giving times,
quantities to use, and degrees of refinement ("of ye 2d or 3d rotation.") Given
his overall concerns, we should realize that this is a draft for a treatise that for
Newton was every bit as important, if not more so, as his justly celebrated *Principia* and *Opticks*. This is true even if, as is likely, Newton never intended the
Praxis for publication.

Westfall, whose writings on Newton's alchemy have done so much to clarify
what Newton was looking for, quotes this astounding document at length, before
immediately urging readers to dismiss its contents, alluding to the nervous
breakdown Newton went through about the time he wrote *Praxis* and caution-
ing, "We should probably read its extravagant claims in the light of that stress."[2]
In other words, having all along argued strenuously and brilliantly that we
should take Newton's alchemy seriously, Westfall, when the really good stuff finally arrives, can only avert his eyes, like a child watching tender or loving embraces in a movie, too embarrassed to actually look except by blocking out whole
parts of the scene.

Extravagant, indeed! Able to "multiply to infinity" or to obtain an oil that
shines in the dark and has "magical uses," the adept with such a Stone has the
means of discovering the secrets behind Creation and can work its transformative powers to coax the world to go from one form to another — "multiplication
of ye stone in quality" — besides being able to use these powers to cure the sick
and diseased! These are no small matters.

Let me now use the preceding account of Newton's involvement with
Fatio and the sensational claims made in *Praxis* to propose a new theory of
Newton's puzzling nervous breakdown in 1693. I shall need to venture onto
historiographical terrain considerably more unsettled, where the magma of
free-flowing conjecture has not yet congealed into well-defined, hard ground,
more speculative than is normally my wont and aggressively pursuing intrusive
conjectures about purely "personal matters" for the reasons stated previously:

---

[1] *Never at Rest*, p. 530; Dobbs, *Janus Face*, p. 304.
[2] *Never at Rest*, p. 530.

that the Newton before and the Newton after the 1693 crisis have different orientations on a number of central concerns. In Newton's most fundamental notions regarding the cosmos; in his manner of living; and in his relationship to power: all had been profoundly transformed. As I insisted earlier, given the degree to which Newtonianism established the parameters of modern consciousness worldwide, our finding out as well as we can how it was formed from the ideological and cosmological and psychological pushes and pulls is a matter of overriding importance, justifying what, given its sexual nature, in other places might seem like mere tendentious and salacious conjectures, suitable for *National Enquirer,* but not *here.*

I offer my account of Newton's breakdown as a *plausible* version of what happened, merely one *possible* explanation consistent with the key evidence: but for me it has the not-inconsiderable advantage of explaining considerably more than alternative accounts advanced by other scholars and biographers. In what follows I shall indicate where my argument is purely speculative.

To begin with, like Westfall I assume that when Newton departed Cambridge in June, 1693, it was to go to London to do alchemical experiments with Fatio and his new friend. I also agree with Westfall's view that there was a strong element of jealousy towards Fatio's London benefactor. However, given what I have written about John Dee and Helvetius above, it should be no surprise that my interpretation of *Praxis* is radically at odds with Westfall's. Instead of dismissing it as a delusional document, reflecting Newton's obvious nervous collapse, I want to use it as the basis for a critical inquiry into why, *after* he had reached its stunning conclusions, Newton underwent a nervous breakdown.

The passage in the *Praxis* about making the Philosophers' Stone and employing it for "magicall uses" reads to me like a detailed description by someone who has seen it done, unlike some of Newton's other alchemical writings (including other parts of *Praxis*) that read as if they are more of a compilation out of his reading. For example, the following description is very broad and general:

> How salt turns to a hard stony pellucid stoney substance insoluble in water whence sand christall & all pellucid stony concrescences are produced & glorious gemms also if the matter be pure & pervaded by pure & variously coloured metalline fumes before it be hard.[1]

Or, in the earlier sections of *Praxis* we can read

> This is the metallique fixt salt by the help of wch Mercury (after he had his wings brought ye most high up to his throne & thereby become ye Caduceus) established an everylasting

---

[1] "Vegetation of Metals," in Dobbs, *Janus Face,* p. 262. Dobbs prints Newton's deletions; I do not.

Kingdome [Snyders ib. c. 6 p. 16] This is the sharp sp[h]ere of Mars & sith [scythe] of Saturn.[1]

In contrast to such broad generalizing, we find other parts of *Praxis* that are much more specific, suggesting experiments that Newton has done or at least seen done:

This pouder mixes also w[th] melted metalls Regulus's & in a little quantity purifies y[m] (as was hinted) but in a greater, burns & calcines them....[2]

Or, consider this:

Imbibe this pouder first wth an eight part of its weight of the animated spirit then wth a seventh then wth a sixt then wth a fift, & ever after wth a fourth, interposing a weeks digestion between every imbibation till y[e] matter be moderately dry & then distilling off y[e] flegm.[3]

One knows when this part of the work is nearing completion, for the substance "grows white & fluxible as wax & will ascend...."

Newton is known to have fudged his data on occasion, as many of the early, iconic, scientists are thought to have similarly done; and his claims against Leibniz or Hooke in matters of priority may not always be in strict accord with the record as historians have reconstructed it: but I am aware of no instance where Newton is known to have lied about the phenomena he observed in his decades of tireless, painstaking, and quite often brilliant experimentation. If the parts of *Praxis* that read as specific recipes he (or someone he observed) had used to get the startling results he described are, in fact, fabrications, it would be out of character for Newton.

✿ ✿ ✿ ✿ ✿

Let me suggest, then, as a speculation that Newton's visit to Fatio and his alchemist friend in London for alchemical experiments was rewarded with a stunning success, and that on the basis of this richly productive working, Newton wrote the more astounding accounts in *Praxis*. As to Newton's other purpose for this visit to Fatio, to check out Fatio's new friend and to assess their relationship and find out how it affected his own with Fatio, I believe the results

---

[1] Dobbs, *Ibid.*, p. 300.

[2] *Ibid.*, p. 302.

[3] *Ibid.*, p. 304.

(as Westfall suggests) were nothing short of a disaster, one which, alas, pulled Newton's psyche inside out, pushing him over an emotional edge.[1]

In fact, after his presumed London visit there is a near complete and permanent break in the intense relationship between Newton and Fatio. Since their relationship is the only strong emotional bond we know that Newton ever formed outside the maternal one, this complete break, coming as it does on the heels of the heated correspondence between them in the months leading up to his visit, is quite remarkable, and begs for an explanation — all the more so because of the enormity of what followed. It was a month or so after his visit to London that Newton suffered his nervous breakdown.

Newton's relationship with Fatio had a multiplicity of layers. The reclusive natural philosopher opened up to the young Swiss *emigré* as he had to no one else, at once teacher, benefactor, father figure, beloved in an intense emotional attachment, and collaborator on the path to the Great Work, as the making of the Stone is known in alchemy. Newton's visit, during a period of extended and driven alchemical experimentation both in Cambridge with only his assistant and in London with Fatio and his alchemical friend, came just after his outpouring of anticipated grieving and — virtually unknown elsewhere for Newton — the articulation of deep feelings suffusing his letters at a time both men thought Fatio was dying. Newton went to London to see Fatio *and* his London friend. I imagine him finding a worrisome relationship between Fatio and this new collaborator on their common path. This man has not only healed Fatio — and reportedly thousands of others — of his grievous illness for free, but he was a true adept, capable of creating the legendary Philosophers' Stone that was, as Newton put it in the above passage, "fit for magicall uses."

iv. "A Scent of Dead Mens Bones"

Let me repeat: as I read and reread the key passages of *Praxis*, they appear to be digested laboratory notes. Immediately following his extravagant description of being able to create a Stone having virtually infinite powers ("vertue"), Newton went on with specific directions to enable someone to find and follow the procedure as he did.

> But if you would whiten Latona then distill not ye red spirit
> but cohabite ye white spirit upon ye black matter wth interposed digestions till it bring over all ye red spirit with it w^{ch}
> you shall know by its the black matter a light dry pouder.[2]

After a little more work, described above, one finally gets what Newton calls the "white Diana."

[1] See my "Newton's Inside Out!"
[2] Dobbs, *Janus Face*, p. 304.

> Imbibe one part of this sublimate [the white Diana] wth three
> of ye spirit digest for 24 hours & distill, imbibe ye remainder
> wth thrice its weight of new spirit, digest 24 hours & distill,
> Imbibe & digest a third & 4th time & all will ascend. Circulate
> it for eight or nine weeks & you have the Alkahest....[1]

that is, the agent which can reduce ordinary substances back to their original *chaos*, in order for the Great Work to start from the very beginning even as God had created the world. Newton continues, providing more details for specific modifications of the basic preparation. For example, one may rectify and dilute with rain water "ye oyle of good & well purified Hungarian Vitriol" in order to get an even higher form of the Alkahest, and he indicated another variation to obtain "Snyders his most general ♀ of both a solary & lunary nature." He wrote how a certain mysterious "earth," that is in fact the chaos from which the path to the Stone begins, is made, this substance that is unlike "any thing y^t is grown, that is neither to stones nor minerals," and — though as an afterthought Newton crossed this last out — he added "& y^t it hath a scent of dead mens bones....[2]

If one possessed a familiarity with the purposefully poetic language and a key to decode some of the more obscure terminology, much of this reads, as the overall title of the work would have it, as *praxis*, that is, as laboratory procedures undertaken to prepare the Stone. If this is correct, then we should see *Praxis* as Newton's report based on having been present when the Philosophers' Stone was made.

Made, I believe, by Fatio's new benefactor, healer, and, I strongly suspect, new paramour, perhaps even a man closer to Fatio's own age, and maybe, as a healer, even cast in the mold of Boehme, Paracelsus, or others of the "gnostic saviors," a man having a presence and possibly a charisma that Newton, the solitary and reclusive Cambridge savant, utterly lacked.

"Not a few have perished in our work,"[3] an alchemical slogan, reminds us of the fatalities along the path, and I suspect the reference is more to the psychic dangers than to the poisonous vapors or occasional explosions suffered by would-be adepts. Despite the fact that for Newton, seeing the legendary Stone made was finding the Holy Grail itself, ultimately he was unable to avoid the spiritual abyss that this philosophical pathway skirted. Given the evidence of his frequent rages, jealousies, emotional distancing, and bouts of paranoia, it is fair to conclude that Newton's ego was a damaged one. There is no telling how much strength of character or integrity *is* demanded if one acquires such vast, ultimately superhuman, powers, able to transform the elements of the material world *at will* and to heal the sick with the "universal medicine" of the Stone, pos-

---

[1] *Ibid.*

[2] *Ibid.*, pp. 304–05.

[3] Berman, *Reenchantment*, p. 86.

sessing the powers of the Creator Him — or Her — self! Newton, in my view, succumbed, more vulnerable by far to the dangers surrounding him as a result of the emotionally wrenching blow he suffered as Fatio's attentions gravitated elsewhere, essentially abandoning him for another, conceivably at the conclusion of their chemical working.[1]

Rather than using the extraordinary claims of *Praxis*, then, like Westfall, as *evidence* of Newton's breakdown, I am driven to take an opposite approach. Let me suggest that what Newton experienced with Fatio and his London friend, as described in *Praxis*, was in large part *responsible for* his breakdown, coming as it did inextricably bound up with his break-up with Fatio. Instead of concluding that Newton could not have seen what he clearly describes in the *Praxis*, and that his temporary insanity accounts for his descriptions, let us assume Newton *had* seen what he described — and that *that* vision, *that* power, that gnostic myth fulfilled, proved too much for him. Together with the period of extreme sleep deprivation described by Newton and an effective end to his relationship with Fatio, Newton suffered a severe mental breakdown that lasted at least three or four months, and by some contemporaries was said to have gone on for a year and a half. That Newton's and Fatio's budding romance, whether ever finally consumated or not, essentially ends at this time is clear from the *Correspondence*.[2]

For a number of years after Newton's visit to Fatio in 1693, Fatio virtually disappeared from Newton's life. There was complete silence for some time; except for some overlapping concerns about prophecy, Fatio and Newton appear to encounter each other only casually, as part of larger gatherings. A decade later some minor business arrangements put them briefly in contact, but in effect Newton and Fatio ended their ties sometime during the summer when Newton "lost it." For lose it he certainly did. The letters at the time to John Locke and Samuel Pepys make clear Newton's going over the edge. His charge that Locke had tried "to embroil me with woemen" is certainly significant, given Fatio's earlier letter to Newton where he had joked that he thought Locke was mainly using him as bait to lure Newton to his estate at Oates. If Locke had tried to fan the embers of their affection, a disasterous break from his young crush could understandably embitter Newton towards Locke. His letters to both Locke and Pepys are filled with resentment towards what he believed was a campaign to involve him in the system of patronage and position, proclaiming "I never designed to get anything by your [Pepys'] interest, nor by King James's favour"and declared angrily that he was "now sensible

---

[1] See Manuel, *Portrait of Newton*.

[2] On the basis of a list of Newton's alchemical purchases in the first decade of the 18th century, Dobbs believes that Newton and Fatio may have resumed their alchemical study together, but the evidence for that is slim. (Dobbs, *Janus Face*, pp. 183–84.)

that I must withdraw from your acquaintance and see neither you nor the rest of my friends any more....[1]

v. The Reconstruction of Newton;
Making Peace with the Mechanical Philosophy

The Newton who finally emerges some months later, having regained his composure, was a man in the process of re-orienting his life and rethinking some of the fundamentals of his worldview. We see this in a number of disparate areas.

First, not only does his break with Fatio date from his collapse, but we know of no other emotional attachment Newton formed after that; in effect an emotional wall of some solidity had been erected, creating a great divide.

Second, there was a marked shift in Newton's alchemical attentions. Though alchemy remained an active passion for him, in effect his own laboratory work was nearly over. He was now more apt to read and comment on alchemical books or manuscripts, which he continued to collect in great numbers, or visit alchemists, some of whom he probably supported financially.[2]

Third, a Newton who had articulated his fears of city air and city manners, after 1693 leaves Cambridge for good, moving to London where he seeks and gains honors, place, and power, is appointed Master of the Mint in England and later elected President of the Royal Society. In 1705, Newton was knighted, becoming Sir Isaac and behaving autocratically, carried around London in a sedan chair, for example, and ostracizing from the Royal Society any who disagreed with him. At the Society he instituted new rules that moved it in authoritarian directions, including establishing a seating plan for the President and other officers (just as at the Royal Court); banishing whispering, talking, and loud laughter at its meetings; and greatly expanding honorary memberships for foreign dignitaries.[3] From his letters written as he was in the throes of his breakdown, we saw that seeking preferment and a comfortable position were extremely troubling to Newton, something he greatly feared; by the mid-1690s, he had no apparent qualms about such new roles and appeared to relish his authority and new positions of power. As Master of the Mint, counterfeiters became his special prey and over them, since theirs was a capital crime in Restoration England, he had the power of life and death.

Fourth, Newton abandoned his plans for a second edition of the *Principia*, the one Fatio had been about to edit. (It would be another two decades before a new edition of the by-then very rare *Principia* was finally published.) Newton seriously rethought many of the fundamentals of his theoretical framework in the 1690s, substantially recasting some of his assumptions and constructs, particularly about

---

1 Newton to Pepys, 13 September 1693, *Correspondence*, vol. III, p. 279.
2 Westfall, *Never at Rest*, p. 53 n. 215.
3 Manuel, *Portrait of Newton*, Chapter Thirteen.

matter. That it took twenty years before some of these additions to the second edition, for which numerous drafts from the 1690s survive, made it into print suggests that the issues they raised for Newton tore at his philosophical soul like nothing else. The question of gravitational attraction was still his most vexing problem. How could he justify it? When Fatio formulated a mechanical theory for the cause of gravity, for a while Newton had looked favorably on it, planning to include it in his aborted second edition. After his nervous collapse, however, while once more wrestling with the problem of gravitational attraction, he was able to see the logical absurdities of impact causative agents: for the impact of lesser particles to be a cause of (say, a spherical) body's gravitation towards another body would produce a force proportional to the *surface area* (r^2 if r is the *radius*) of the first body, rather than to its *mass*, distributed throughout the three dimensions of that body and thus accordingly proportional to the volume (r^3).[1] And of course it was *mass*, not area, in his gravitational equation.

Newton began to abandon mechanical explanations altogether, favoring spiritual agencies to carry the strange attractive power. In so doing, however, Newton simultaneously adopted one of the key tenets of the mechanical philosophy, the idea that all bodies had certain "essential" or *primary* qualities (such as extension, inertia, and impenetrability) that they can never, even in theory, lose. Accordingly, though nature to Newton still "delighted" in transformations, as he had once written, now only those that were of the body's *secondary* qualities (that is, an object's colors, smells, textures, tastes, and shapes, those aspects we can actually perceive) were transformable. These secondary qualities are now (as with the other mechanical philosophers) seemingly to be explained *on the basis of* "matter and motion," the reigning slogan of the new philosophy. The experiential world now had a second-class status, ontologically inferior to the mathematical abstractions of hypothetical invisible particles. This was an epochal watershed for Newton to have crossed, eventually taking, as he did, the whole of the modern world along with him.[2]

In 6th and 5th century B.C.E. Greece, the philosopher Parmenides had come forth to banish a troubling philosophical chaos he thought was the result of his predecessors' emphasis on sense experiences; Parmenides proposed as a solution that the cosmos as a whole should be understood to be a gigantic, unchanging sphere of Being, so that motion and even transformation are illusions. The ancient atomists had partly adopted this view, only they proposed possibly an infinite number of such spheres, the unchanging atoms. Newton's espousal of key aspects of the mechanical philosophy was in many ways similar, accepting certain categories of bodies as being *essential* and unchanging (extension, impenetrability, inertia, and hardness), except as to degree. In effect, Newton has stabilized nature. Only relative changes could now occur, changes that redis-

[1] On Fatio's mechanical hypothesis, see p. 278, n. 1, above.
[2] J.E. McGuire, "The Origin of Newton's Doctrine of Essential Qualities," *Centaurus* 12 (1968), 233–60.

tributed the *matter* and reapportioned its overall *motion*, themselves the change-less and ontologically privileged essences of reality. Not coincidentally, around this time Newton also downplayed earlier statements of his that bodies could transform into one another.

Perhaps in reaction to this, *fifth*, as mentioned earlier, Newton after his break-down began to note mechanisms of decay in nature that, over a long time, would immobilize the cosmos, or at least the solar system. A loss in the amount of overall motion and a growing disequilibrium in the motions of planets and moons in the solar system would some day need fixing, or everything would fall apart. In 1692 Newton had written to Richard Bentley, then preparing his "Boyle Sermons," that cosmogonic speculations were unwise, but now, having seen such manifestations of nature's falling short of the "perpetuall circulatory worker" a younger Newton had sung the praises of, he continued to pursue cosmogonic speculations about possible cosmic counterforces, using Whiston, as well as Halley, to float some of his cometary "mechanisms," theories he got, it is clear, from Pythagoras.[1] While allowing Whiston, Halley, and Gregory to suggest various cometary *deus ex machina*, Newton himself in the 1706 *Opticks* publicly-denounced cosmogonic the-orizing, reinforcing in the public's (though not his disciples') mind the idea of na-ture's unchanging timelessness as a central tenet of Newtonian thought.

Sixth, in the later 1690s when a Hermetic enthusiast of some notoriety, John Toland, tried to justify his radical and heretical ideas by referring to Newton's theory of matter, since gravitational attraction was clear evidence of powers *in* nature such as he himself was proposing, Newton took great pains to draw clear lines of demarcation between his own notions and their republican or levelling misuse by men like Toland. An Irish freethinker educated at Edinburgh Uni-versity under David Gregory, one of Newton's very early disciples, Toland was active in many different political and social circles, associating with atheists, skeptics, and other freethinkers. He conjured up all-too-vivid memories of the republican enthusiasts of the recent English Civil War.

Toland's philosophical skepticism was based on his notion of self-active matter, which he said Newton's work clearly implied. To be sure, these were positions Newton himself disagreed with; and yet, in some measure, he and Toland, both Hermeticists, and both, in their own ways tending towards pantheism (a term in-vented by Toland), overlapped enough to make Newton increasingly edgy. To dis-tinguish his own views from Toland's, and from the philosophical monism of Baruch Spinoza and the materialism of Thomas Hobbes, Newton orchestrated public an-nouncements, using his position as Trustee for the series of sermons established by Boyle's Will. As he had with Bentley, Newton pushed Samuel Clarke, another young disciple, to give the 1704 sermons, where he delineated these necessary po-litical and philosophical distinctions; later, Newton would facilitate the publication of Clarke's sermon. Shortly afterwards the publication of Newton's Latin *Optice*

---

[1] Pythagoras is found front and center in the all-important confidences Newton shared with David Gregory on several occasions.

provided its author with still another opportunity, in its "Queries," to spell out the crucial differences between his views and those of Toland, Spinoza, and Hobbes.[1]

Yet even so, in Newton's famous debate, using Clarke as his proxy, with Leibniz over their radically different visions of the physical (and spiritual) cosmos), Newton in 1716 faulted the German philosopher for ashering to "the Hypothesis of the materialists, viz., that all the phenomena in nature are caused by mere matter [added in between lines, "and motion"] & man himself a mere machine."[2]

vi. Interim Conclusion 1: Newton's Shadow

In sum, the Newton who survived his psychic breakdown in 1693 had significantly altered his course. He had turned his back on some of his most cherished earlier ideas, such as the superiority of explanations based on the vegetative principle over those that only dealt with surface phenomena and interactions, that did not penetrate *inside* the matter of things. Having armored himself against the blows that had laid him low in that crisis year of 1693, he emerged *out of* the shadows, to a significant degree, *as* his shadow. He had made his peace with some earlier doctrinal anathemas, even, to a considerable extent, key aspects of the mechanical philosophy whose profound limitations he had earlier spelled out. *Not* that he *really* abandoned his alchemical vision. Not entirely. And yet, these visions were so filtered so as to render them, ultimately, nearly irrelevant. Somehow, Newton did manage to have it both ways, letting go of certain youthful perspectives without entirely relinquishing them, but in the end the distinction made no difference.

Newton's growing circle of disciples surely knew the brilliance and breadth of the Master's visions, for nearly all of them at one time or another served as point men, with Newton on the sidelines dictating texts to one disciple or another, his champion in this particular fight (literally so in the cases of Gregory, Cotes, Clarke, and Keill, for whom we have extant memoranda or letters of what they were told to say or not say), and it would have been in trying to justify the more troublesome aspects of his theories that Newton would most have had to make these young men privy to those inner convictions and schema, which his paranoid temper would never allow him to put in his own treatises.

Alas, however much of that magical core and that nearly immaterial essence of matter did get passed along to the inner circle of the disciples, those doctrines

---

1 Samuel Clarke, *A Dissertation of the Being and Attributes of God: More Particularly in Answer to Mr. Hobb's, Spinoza, and their Followers* (London: 1705), p. 46; M.C. Jacob, "The Church and the Formulation of the Newtonian World View," *Journal of European Studies* (1971): 128–48; Margaret Candee Jacob, "John Toland and the Newtonian Ideology," *Journal of the Warburg and Courtault Institute*, vol. XXXII (1969): 307–31.

2 Alexander Koyré and I.B. Cohen, "Newton and the Leibniz-Clarke Correspondence," *Archives Internationale d'Histoire des Sciences* XV (1962) 58–59, p. 113.

did not long survive Newton's death. Newton's own sense of what he could and should not publish was endorsed by Dr. Thomas Pellet, from the Royal Society, who after Newton's death examined his unpublished manuscripts and wrote on many of them, "Not fit to be printed."[1]

Thus, within a generation at most, the Newton that the world learns became fixed as Newton the mechanist, bringer of Law to the unruly cosmos, showing us how predictable the hard, inert bodies that make up the matter of the universe are. The Newton who reduced it all to an elaborate machine, like a gigantic clock.

The Newton no one was allowed to remember, for a complex set of social, religious, economic, and political reasons, was the Newton who believed his *Principia* dealt with the superficial, less significant and less interesting, aspect of the natural world, the Newton not so taken with the doctrine of inertia that he projected it (as nearly all adherents of the mechanical philosophy did) as *the* ontological state of the cosmos, with the world in itself (as with Boyle) essentially dead. The hidden Newton is the natural philosopher who focused *his* attentions on finding what agent could act *in* matter (not *on* it, as in the mechanical philosophy) so as to give it the range of activity Newton found fecund matter everywhere experiencing, particularly living matter — but to Newton perhaps all of it was alive. Though Newton would never *print* such a notion about a living world, it appeared in the drafts for the *Opticks*, for example.[2]

The world was thus allowed to see only the hard outer shell of Newton's theories — but this, after all, was the part of his doctrines that Newton himself chose to expose to the public. This was especially true of his theory of matter, where the living matter of his alchemical researches was now buried beneath the construct of "hard bodies." Wrested from the Hermetic context in which they had their birth and from which they took their deeper meanings, his conceptions were sure to be misconstrued.

Given the globalization of Newtonian culture and the manner in which, upon its conceptual and supposed methodological footing, were eventually erected systems of philosophy, theology, psychology, political theory, ethics, aesthetics,[3] not to mention the equally significant manner in which government and trade and bureaucracy in general built a social machinery, which, to the 18th and 19th century men (and women) who put it together, was clearly understood

---

1 Westfall, *Never at Rest*, p. 872.

2 See above, p. 255. Newton, Cambridge Univ. Library Add. MS 3970.

3 Thus, as Cullen Murphy comments, "The rationalists of the Enlightenment conceived of a government as a machine; something that had 'levers' and 'wheels' and 'springs' and that if properly built would run with minimal intervention." Murphy, *God's Jury*, p. 235. Narby comments on how, as from the 1930s, "anthropology obsessively sought order in its study of others, to elevate itself to the rank of science. In the process it transformed reality into next to incomprehensible discourses," quoting a mind-numbing example of verbal gibberish from Claude Levi-Strauss as an example (*op. cit.*, p. 12). I also remember

as a pale reflection on Earth of what Newton had revealed as the order of the heavens; and given the generations of civil servants, administrators, estate agents, overseers, ministers, headmasters, lawyers and judges, and the rest of those who had to serve as agents for His Majesty's plan for the world, beginning in the 18th century if not before, men, we may be sure, who were lectured to at Cambridge, Oxford, or Eton and Harrow or who sat through sermons where the same lesson, as to the larger meanings of the order in the heavens thus revealed and codified by Newton, was said in different ways; given all that, though it was not quite an about-face that Newton executed, the utterly one-sided perspective we have been culturally marinated in as a representation of his ideas over the centuries, in effect lends it that overall significance and meaning. His ideas having been distorted beyond all measure, this watershed passage in Western history invites, again, an even closer look.

The main difference between the nature Newton thought about and the one he bequeathed through his published writings to posterity was that the former was alive and the latter one is not. Whatever else the scientific revolution accomplished and however the mechanical philosophy may have served to establish a framework for systematic "scientific" thinking in the 18th and 19th centuries, one major achievement of the mechanical philosophy, and the scientific revolution whose emblem it became, was its systemic assault on the idea of a living Earth.

Indeed, once the pillars of the mechanical philosophy are in place there is no way for notions of living matter or a Mother Earth, in academic and learned culture at least, to take root; the soil for such conceptions was henceforth utterly barren, paved over with the idea of Progress and its inherent passion for control. Though such conceptions as Mother Earth are maintained in popular culture and have had a strong, even living, presence wherever people worked with natural forces (for example, miners, farmers, fishers, tree-fellers), in official, academic culture the world consisted of dead particles that had aggregated together

---

fellow graduate students at Cornell suffering in their government majors from having to plow through Talcott Parsons and Edward Shils (ed.), *Toward a General Theory of Action: Theoretical Foundations for the Social Sciences* (New York: Harper & Row, 1962), in which we are taught (paragraph picked at random): "Thus consideration of the place of complementarity of expectations in the processes of human interaction has implications for certain categories which are central in the analysis of the origins and functions of cultural patterns. There is a *double contingency* inherent in interaction. On the one hand, ego's gratifications are contingent on his selection among available alternatives. But in turn, alter's reaction will be contingent on ego's selection and will result from a complementary selection on alter's part. Because of this *double contingency*, communication, which is the precondition of cultural patterns, could not exist without both generalization from the particularity of the specific situations (which are never identical for ego and alter) and stability of meaning...." (We have suffered enough.)

in various forms. Any hint of the notion of a world soul, of a matter that was by nature animated, in a thinker's conceptual vocabulary and his or her work would quickly be dismissed in respectable forums.[1] Belief in the axiom of a machine universe, made up of its dead, insensate bodies, was simply the price of admission to the domains where one would be allowed to participate in that official culture, at least in England, and, in differing ways, eventually nearly everywhere in the "developed" or industrialized parts of the world.[2]

The mechanical philosophy thus cut the ground out from the valuation, in sacred terms, of the natural order, of the Earth. Each time a forest is felled, a hillock levelled, a wetlands filled in, local peasants — and frequently more than just them — understand that it is an assault on lifefulness of the terrain[3] and the well-being of the local spirits, who are venerated through such natural forms as springs, rock outcroppings, caves, or special trees.[4] Indeed, it is an assault on those peasants

---

[1] See the discussion of Lady Anne Conway, Chapter 11.

[2] In addition to overt sexism in admission policies, this ideological bias towards the necrotic in the scientific community in the West has arguably played a major role in the near-exclusion of women in the major institutions of science, until a few decades ago.

If we remember that mining has from the beginning characterized colonialism's enterprises in the lands under subjugation, it is clear that "developed" and "industrialized" are not necessarily synonymous. Historical studies of the past decades have shown a far greater integration economically and socially between colonizers and colonized than was understood earlier.

[3] I do not want to imply that alteration to the Earth is always to be avoided. Ditches and canals, for example, make water transfer feasible. Certainly alterations of some kind was done to create megalithic circles like Stonehenge, not to mention the kinds of transformations necessary to make a harbor safer or to create arable land. Hunter-gatherers, such as Native Americans, engaged in a substantial amount of transformation of their terrain, according to Rebecca Solnit and Kat Anderson (Solnit, *Savage Dreams*, pp. 304f). Assemblies to decide the kinds of alterations to the landscape that do not undermine the living communities of a particular terrain and so can be tolerated or even encouraged, as opposed to those that are done in the name of a small segment of all those affected and that benefits primarily them, to the expense of the rest of the creatures, would be a formidable, but not insurmountable, task, one that no doubt occurs in many traditional cultures.

[4] Recently Japanese research by Dr. Qing Li (Nyron Medical School) and Yoshifumi Miyazahi (Ciba University) demonstrated how after brief periods in a cedar forest levels of cortisol associated with stress decreased. The trees gave off aromatic compounds (phytoncides) that when inhaled bolstered immune systems, lowering blood pressue as well as providing relief of symptoms of heart disease, depression, cancer, and anxiety. *Time,* vol. 188, no. 4 (July 25, 2016). Forests were being leveled for mines, to deprive rebels of refuge, and to build galleons from the 16th century on.

and their animals. There is really no answer to those who level charges of this kind, for on their own terms, they are obviously right. The *only* hope of elites is to render such charges senseless, in effect undercutting them by creating a new vocabulary and framework of logic in which those accusations no longer can even be conceptualized, for the expressions and even the syntax for such charges no longer exist. Since it is, indeed, living nature that the peasantry and others venerate, it would have been obvious how difficult mourning the destruction of a creek would be, if in the popular understanding, nature everywhere has already been ideologically killed off, in effect, assassinated.[1]

That a man of such towering intellect and profound insight into the workings of the cosmos as Newton should, ultimately as a result of overwhelming social pressures, finally be reduced to a spokesman for a worldview he did not really even believe in, is, of course, a profound tragedy, one that is social and cultural as well as personal.[2] For *we* have been robbed not only of our opportunity to know the true ideas of the man who, more than anyone else, established the boundaries of modern civilization. But upon the basis of the *false* consciousness thus set in place have been erected the collective edifices of modern society — the armies and laws, the nation-states, the transportation and communication networks, the multinational corporations, in short, the administrative apparatus of the various institutions and megastructures of the social and cultural order that, for the most

---

[1] It is difficult for me to forego saying, "of course, this is what was meant to happen." But such a statement would imply a someone(s) who so meant it to happen, and I doubt it works that simply. And yet, I also cannot shake off a sense that the emerging political economy, with its heavy base in extractive industries like mining and deforestation or its industrialization of traditional enterprises such as agriculture and shipping, where *control* of nature is a major preoccupation, *needed* the mechanical philosophy. They got what they needed, in large measure, of course, because they do control the production and dissemination of ideas (through control of the universities, schools, pulpits, foundations, patent offices, courts of law, legislatures, and, under censorship, the presses, among a great many other institutions of culture), as Marx said, but that is only part of it. There is more, I feel, whether it is some kind of "natural selection" that operates on conceptual frameworks, or the agency of a sort of Hegelian-like spirit guiding History, or by means of some other meta-historical process, I do not know; but it seems to me that at the level of ideology, the formation and spread of ideas acts "as if" there were, indeed, a "guiding hand." (Readers might keep this in mind when reading Part Three.)

[2] My profound hope that Newton's betrayal of his deepest beliefs will still shock some readers is tempered by my fear that in an age when major "personalities" from sports heroes to poets to classical musicians publicly appear to endorse, for a fee, on international TV this product or that, few will feel the tragedy of Newton's fundamental misrepresentations.

part, we still inhabit, and that are increasingly widely understood to be fundamentally dysfunctional.

While I believe Newton's doctrines *did* act to justify the new order, I realize that a multitude of considerations, mediations, and hesitations necessarily intervened along the way from the prerogatives of the mining industry in the early 17th century to the *Principia*. Yet Newton's cosmos, as it was publicly known, was a gigantic step towards precisely what the owners of the mines needed most from both their workers and those who lived among the effluents and the decimated woods the mines always brought: belief that nature was essentially a collection of purposeless, dead, inanimate bodies —in short, of "resources."

vii. Interim Conclusion 2: Was Newton Essentially a Pawn of Capital?

Some readers may have noticed parallels between my argument for the social roots of Newtonian mechanics and those of the Russian historian, B. Hessen. The reaction to Hessen's Marxist theory of the scientific revolution, presented in 1931 to the International Congress of the History of Science and Technology in London, dominated the historiography of science when I entered graduate school in the history of science at Cornell University in 1961. The dominant figures in the field, my guiding lights during my apprenticeship as an historian, were still arguing against Hessen's sweeping theory of class forces at play in the shaping of early modern science given in his *The Social and Economic Roots of Newton's Principia* (in *Science at the Cross Roads*).

Hessen's thesis in a nutshell was that the scientific revolution could clearly be understood as a response by 17th-century natural philosophers to the needs of capitalism and the early modern State. In England especially mining technology demanded an understanding of air pressure and the vacuum (to deal with the intensive problems of pumping water out of shafts), both of which loomed large in the attentions of the natural philosophers. Similarly the widespread warfare that marked the birth of early modern Europe, by requiring a deeper understanding of ballistics, gave birth to mechanics. Other practical problems drove much of the research done at the time.

There is much to admire in Hessen's masterly analysis, and yet, alas, a great deal to mourn. For Hessen's Marxism was formulaic, decked out in the pseudo-scientific terminology of "scientific socialism," in a word, the mechanical Marxism that had been problematic in the working-class movement since at least the late 19th century (as described in the following chapter) and had by the 1930s become structurally part of the Soviet state under Stalin.

Lenin, as well, was capable of a mechanical heavy hand, but there were times he also showed great creativity and historical acumen in his analysis and practice. This is gone under Stalin.

It is difficult for me today to comprehend how much of my critical reaction when *circa* 1962 I first read Hessen was an aversion to his mechanical analysis and how much I was simply suspicious because of the anti-communism I had been draped in as a high-school student in the early 1950s — an anti-communism I was in a sustained dialogue and uneven retreat from throughout the 1960s as I became an organizer in the New Left involved in the civil rights and antiwar struggles in the United States.

One of Hessen's greatest critics was the brilliant historian of science, Alexandre Koyré, a man whose writings were enormously influential in the development of my understanding of Newton. Koyré was a dogmatic anti-Marxist, sniffing his nose at even a hint of economic interests in relation to scientific work. Koyre's fundamental guiding principle, seen through his seminal studies on Galileo, Newton, and other early scientists, was that at its heart science was an activity *of* the mind and so required an explanation based *on* mind, on spirit. To Koyré there were philosophical principles, traceable in the case of Newton to his theological ideas, involved in the monumental intellectual constructs of early modern science. That, not the need for accurate ballistics nor the requirement for more metals, more mines, that trade and war required, was the driving force of the scientific revolution. Newton's deepest ideas of space, of force, according to Koyré, emerged out of his religious conceptions, his ideas of God. This is the Newton I initially was introduced to in my eager reading of the seminal analyses of Newton by Koyré, Hessen's arch-nemesis.

What Koyré (and many others) seems to have overlooked was a concluding section of Hessen's essay, where he explicitly discusses the ideological and philosophical component of the scientific revolution, making some of the same associations that Koyré was to later claim.

Delving more deeply into Newton's theoretical development at the same time as I began to read Marx seriously,[1] two things stood out — that last, largely overlooked section in Hessen where he discusses the philosophical and theological grounds of the scientific revolution in terms not so different from Koyré's; and the astounding selective vision Koyré had chosen, basing his interpretation of Newton on religious ideas without even acknowledging that when Newton was born, England had entered into a convulsive Civil War and revolution, ending just before he entered Cambridge in 1661, in which *religion* and *class* were key elements in what was being fought over. In other words, if one grants Koyré his anti-Marxist formulation that essentially religious ideation was the font from which early science drank deeply, should we

---

[1] The impetus for my study was a request from a black student activist at Dartmouth in the Fall of 1968 that he take a reading class from me on revolutionary theory. I admitted I knew not much more than he, and we proceeded to read Fanon, Che, Lenin, Marx, Malcolm X, and others, discussing the many ramifications for the political struggles of the late '60s that both of us were part of, and he wrote papers on the readings.

not ask whether those ideas, in turn, might have been affected by the fermentation seen in the convulsive religious and social upheavals of Newton's youth?

My historiography, presented here, is an effort "to turn [Koyré] on his head," as was said of Marx's own reaction to the idealism of Hegel, *his* youthful mentor — to plant Koyré's reluctant feet in the soil of the *real* England in which Newton lived, where one's religious sensibilities and beliefs had quite *material* meaning.

In conclusion, I admire Hessen's work; am in awe of the effect it had in driving several decades of subsequent historiography; am obviously (even if at times unconsciously) influenced by especially its last section; but ultimately I find Hessen's analyses part of an increasingly sterile mechanical Marxism that was widespread in the 1930s, and hope that my own efforts here may correct some of his oversights.

viii. INTERIM CONCLUSION 3: AS "RAYS FROM A CENTER"

Certainly Adam Smith recognized the importance of Isaac Newton's doctrines that were "'everwhere the most precise and particular that can be imagined, and ascertain[s] the time, the places, the quantity, the duration of each individual phenomenon,'" and Smith noted the resemblances between Newtonian "principles of union" (gravitational attraction) in the world of matter and parallel processes in the human world "which take[s] place in all other qualities which are propagated in rays from a center."[1]

Smith, the theoretician of the political economy of capitalism, well knew another system with influences radiating out from its center — the capitalist firm, with its hierarchic ordering of power and privileges and its taken-for-granted acquiescence by the end of each ray to the will expressed at that center.

For the system of capitalism to function, ultimately, all individuals must be broken of their dignity. No more than a private in the army can be allowed to question a general's decisions, can the individual cog in the machine (factory or other enterprise) interfere with the turning of the wheels of production. To accomplish the end of creating such weakened individuals, many things had to happen, not least the successful establishment of the modern fear of starvation — "modern," insofar as in the capitalist, detribalized, world, where most people have been torn loose from their former base on the land, more often than not one starves as an individual or as a single family, while others around are eating their fill and more. In other words, people can and do die of hunger not, as before, because there *is* no food, but because what food there is is *distributed* in a way that allows some to starve while others glut.

To that indignity is added another, equally troublesome aspect of modern times: that since the products made under wage labor, just as in all other

---

1 Smith, quoted in Taussig, *Devil*, p. 34.

forms of production, necessarily include some of the worker's very life essence (as all prior societies freely acknowledged), and because such an essence enters into anything made from an individual's labor, under *wage labor* this essence is *taken from* the worker in return for the wage, so that inevitably workers end up confronting *part of themselves possessed*, by virtue of his control of capital, by *the owner* of the firm.

Ultimately, this form of alienation, in which individuals are systematically turned against their own spiritual being, is abetted by the new consciousness early modern science fosters by teaching that all big problems are to be broken down, piece by piece, into their "component" parts; in these more manageable forms, these atomized sub-problems are to be solved, as Descartes advocated, in isolation from one another. This tearing down of the whole (i.e., the multitude of systems through which the world *actually* operates) in favor of isolated components, whose essence obviously is assumed to be self-contained, in order to "comprehend" the world, ends up splitting living from dead, men from women, white from black, health from sickness, humans from animals, and so on, until, inevitably, it splits any individual into the innumerable shards of him- or herself. Soon it is extremely difficult for these pieces any longer to see the whole, indeed, even to remember that there is, or ever had been, a whole.

Aspects of this alienation had long been present, of course, deeply rooted in the Judeo-Christian ethic,[1] but the "17th century watershed," as it has been called, extended them, deepened their hold, and finally fixed these particular forms of alienation in the human psyche, not only cementing them permanently into the framework of psychology, but justifying them on the basis of Newtonian physics — on the basis, that is, of the new "reality." Soul from body, body from mind, mind from morality, morality from day-to-day activities to earn a living — once the ideal of dissociation takes hold, it figuratively tears every thing, being, and relationship to pieces. Thus the disappearance of forests would be analyzed in isolation from the mass depression that took hold.[2] Fragmentation, then, inevitably emerges as more than a social mandate, for it becomes the basis of the fractured mold in which, perforce, more and more our lives are being recast, especially in these most maddening of times.

Should we be surprised, then, to learn that it was in the decades following the scientific revolution that asylums for the "insane" were established

[1] According to Lynn White, Jr.'s seminal work, a major source of our environmental problems. See Lynn White, Jr., "The Historical Roots of Our Ecology Crisis," in *Ecology and Religion in History* (New York: Harper & Row, 1967).

[2] Barbara Ehrenreich writes: "Beginning in England in the seventeenth century, the European world was stricken by what looks, in today's terms, like an epidemic of depression." *Dancing,* p. 129.)

in Europe and England, for quite literally, the emergent culture, seen from outside itself, was crazy (though, of course, it had its many experts, some of them scientists and academics, to say it all made good sense), and this general insanity was facilitated by new agreements and procedures that could isolate or banish outright those who disagreed with official reality, people capable even of "hallucinating" other possible worlds.[1]

Those who were able successfully to make their peace with the new reality, who learned not to ask certain questions and not to acknowledge particular kinds of (their own) experiences, especially learned how *not to feel* in the fragmented reality. If the mechanical philosophy taught that ultimately the cosmos consisted of hard, inanimate bodies, devoid of all but quantitative properties such as extension, inertia, and shape, and forever and unalterably divorced from mind and spirit, then it was not long before some men (and it was mostly, though never wholly, men) took as their goal the reduction of themselves to similar "hard" objects, casting off all that would not fit and reconstituting themselves in the mold of the dominant cultural ontology, particulate matter. Those men and of late women tended to be the ones who gravitate to positions of power, where human feelings would only get in the way; in such a manner, as they harden, such people lose touch with their emotions, are out of touch with their bodies, their spirits.

Of course, the "higher" one advanced in the social structure, the more mandatory was it to learn the lessons of divorcing oneself from his (or her) feelings: only thus, we might imagine, has it been possible again and again for the orders to be given, and forever followed, that continue to destroy rivers, forests, and creatures — that, in the older view of things, were actually essential parts of ourselves — with the sickening "reality" of a stream forever damned or fouled with irradiated water, of a mountaintop shorn off and bereft of trees and of the flora and fauna that played and danced in their shadows, or of a brightly colored songbird that disappears forever from the face of nature as the rainforest (or the empty city lot) where it lives falls to the bulldozers of Progress.

---

[1] See Michel Foucault, *Madness and Civilization* (New York: 1965); George Rosen, "Irrationality and Madness in Seventeenth and Eighteenth Century Europe."

15

Marx & The Phenomenon
of "Mechanical Marxism"

All these deformations and a row of other less important ones
were inflicted on Marxism by its epigones in the second
phase [roughly from the crushing of the 1848 revolutions to
the end of the 19th century] of its development, and they can
be summarized in one all-inclusive formulation: a unified
general theory of social revolution was changed into criticisms of the bourgeois system of education, of bourgeois religion, art, science and culture. These criticisms no longer
necessarily develop by their very nature into revolutionary
practice; they can equally well develop into all kinds of attempts at *reform*, which fundamentally remain within the limits of bourgeois society and the bourgeois State, and in
actually practice usually did so… [a] distortion of the revolutionary doctrine of Marxism itself — into a purely theoretical critique that no longer leads to practical revolutionary
action… — Karl Korsch, *Marxism and Philosophy* (1932)

i. The Dissent of the *Naturphilosophen*

I shall forego any detailed attempt to bridge the three-hundred-year gap
between Newton's late 17th century and our own beginning of the 21st,
since it would too much extend the scope and length of this work. For
the most part, the overall schema of dominant scientific thinking (and of the
ecological blindness), despite the many changes to conceptions of the world,
did not in its essentials vary from the mechanism that had been articulated
at the core of the scientific revolution. The new science of thermodynamics
simply extended mechanistic interactions into new domains, confirming their
powerful reach. And for all James Clerk Maxwell was able to synthesize
the findings of Coulomb, Faraday, Oersted and Ampère with his equations
elucidating the intricacies of the electromagnetic *field*, seemingly a non-mech-
anistic construct, to explain its hidden workings, Maxwell fell back on hypothetical miniscule pulleys and wheels.

There were some scientists like Joseph Priestley who continued to use traditional understandings about a vitality in nature, but mostly such views remained on the margins. When vital powers were more generally attributed to matter by the scientific community, as in Priestley's mid-18th-century Scotland, it was part of a system of theorizing that served as scaffolding for a schema of social reintegration, the project of powerful and moneyed social circles in Scotland, seeking to stanch recent rebellions and repair the serious fraying of the social fabric. Such moments were few and tended to be limited in their impact.[1]

Though the need to limit the sweep of our inquiry makes it inadvisable to follow such intriguing 18th and 19th century counter-examples, one in particular deserves a closer look, for it directly bears on some of the major issues in our story. In the late 18th century, "romantic" reaction against mechanistic thinking that had many of the same criticisms of the mechanical philosophy as advanced in *Marxism & Witchcraft* acquired considerable influence in England and Germany, especially. In Germany a more-or-less distinct philosophical school, *Naturphilosophie*, formed, strongly critical of the mechanistic explanations of natural phenomena and of what it saw as an overly, indeed, virtually totalizing, quantitative analysis taking over the sciences. *Naturphilosophie* sought to find the reality behind phenomena, something more basic than mere perception, though intimately embedded in experience and sensations. In some of the *Naturphilosophen*, this was some kind of ineffable soul of nature an ultimate reality or "Absolute."[2]

Let us situate the *Naturphilosophen* in context: by the time of their emergence, the steam engine was beginning to demonstrate, at least in England, its awesome power, implanting the notion that eventually it or something like it would be used nearly universally for productive processes of all kinds. Not everyone sang hymns to Progress, however; to those with a certain kind of vision, the outlook was bleak, indeed: as if witnessing the land increasingly parcelled out and tamed and machines spring up next to, and eventually supplanting, humans and animals, some saw it as the soul being drained away from the world around them. Literature bore witness to their lamentations as they anticipated the doleful spread of this blight. William Blake, Samuel Coleridge, and William Wordsworth suffered these loses; so, too, Emerson

---

[1] Steven Shapin, "Social Uses of Science," in G. S. Rousseau and Roy Porter (ed.), *The Ferment of Knowledge* (Cambridge, England: Cambridge Univ. Press, 1980), pp. 128ff.

[2] I benefitted from participation in a seminar of L. Pearce Williams in 1962, where the *Naturphilosophen* were given some close study, and also from conversations with Robert Kargon at the time. See also, for a negative assessment of the *Naturphilosophen*, John Theodore Merz, *A History of European Thought in the Nineteenth Century*, in 4 volumes, (New York: Dover Publications, 1965), vol. 1, pp. 178 n.1, 207.

in the US and in Germany Goethe and the *Naturphilosophen,* Friedrich von Schelling and Johann Gottlieb Fichte. Ultimately *Naturphilosophie* was defeated, especially in its Anglo-American schools of science, its history in the natural sciences eclipsed or baldly distorted so that it appeared as little more than a quaint but futile attempt to sidetrack understanding; but particularly in Germany its real influences on the sciences were notable.

ii. GOETHE'S ANTI-NEWTONIAN THEORY OF COLORS

A deeper understanding of the *Naturphilosophen's* critique might be helped by a brief examination of Goethe's researches in natural philosophy. He investigated and did experiments on plant growth, geology, comparative anatomy, and light, the latter including numerous inquiries into the nature of color. This research led Goethe to a forceful critique of the baneful influences of Newtonian science. Trying out a prism one day, Goethe insisted that he saw something altogether different from what he thought Newton had described, and this is what energized his subsequent research. His *Theory of Colours* (1810) recorded his numerous experiments on vision and colors. Its starting point was the process of vision, how the eye and retina interact with light. It was also about psychology, how light is experienced. Many of his experiments had to do with contrasts, between bright and dark, or between complementary colors, for example, or with the after-images resulting from certain progressions of viewing, especially those that had to do with opposites. Like other *Naurphilosophen,* Goethe's interpretations of these phenomena centered on hypothesized polar forces, whose interactions generated powerful rhythms that were woven through all natural phenomena. Thus,

> The retina, after being acted upon by light or darkness, is found to be in two different states, which are entirely opposed to each other....
>
> In the act which we call seeing, the retina is at one and the same time in different and even opposite states.[1]

Demonstrating how vision conforms to the patterns of all living processes, he wrote:

> every vital principle is forced to exhibit [a silent resistance] when any definite or immutable state is presented to it. Thus inspiration already presupposed expiration, thus

---

[1] Johann Wolfgang von Goethe, *Goethe's Color Theory* (ed). Rupprect Matthei, transl. Herb Aach (New York: Van Nostrand Reinhold Co., 1971), p. 215. Readers might benefit from reviewing the earlier discussions of dialectical logic in Chapters 4 and 6.

every systole its diastole. It is the universal formula of life which manifests itself in this as in all other cases. When darkness is presented to the eye it demands brightness, and *vice versa*: it shows its vital energy, its fitness to receive the impression of the object, precisely by spontaneously tending to an opposite state.[1]

Not realizing how close his views were to Newton's own secret alchemical notions, Goethe emphasized that the world everywhere showed its lifefulness, its vital energies, and that nature everywhere "is in harmony with herself."[2] "To the attentive observer [Nature] is nowhere dead nor silent...."[3] At a fundamental level, nature in fact was nothing *but* undulations to Goethe, as we perceive in the reverberations of bells, or when a glass filled with water is rubbed around its rim, producing a tone, or when ripples spread out from where a stone has been thrown in a pond. Such undulations were behind the phenomena of halos (auras) that can form around living creatures.[4]

Goethe saw his theory of color in practical terms, something immediately useful to artists, dyers, or other craftspeople and manufacturers who worked with colors. Such people had been among the first to see the marked inadequacies of Newton's "entirely false notion on the physical origin of colors...."[5] Goethe saw Newton's optical theories as deeply flawed, based as they were on abstract notions, so unlike his own, more physiologically-based, theories. Too, Newton's system was overly complicated and hid more than elucidated the true nature of colors.

Like the other *Naturphilosophen*, the German philosopher G.W.F. Hegel evoked the agency of an "Absolute Spirit," a force moving through History as well as through nature, and encompassing the divine and human minds. The Absolute Spirit, so Hegel seemed to say, became embodied in the State and was made manifest through History. In the aftermath of 1789 and again 1830, when uprisings across Europe had given voice to demands for freedom, liberty, justice, and the like, Germany too was stirred by these ideals. As a society not dominated by either capitalism or industry as England or even France were, the Germanic stirrings expressed themselves primarily in abstractions and found focus in the writings of a group that came to be known as the "Young Hegelians," writers, most of whom were academics. It was as part of the Young Hegelians that Marx and Engels were first drawn to criticism; and it was in making a break in the mid-1840s from the detached academic nature of the other Young Hegelians that they moved decisively towards communism.

---

[1] *Ibid.*, p. 217.

[2] *Ibid.*, p. 220.

[3] *Ibid.*, Preface to First Ed., p. 211.

[4] *Ibid.*, p. 221.

[5] *Ibid.*, p. 219.

iii. MARX AS A YOUNG HEGELIAN

After he had to flee Germany in the aftermath of the failed revolutions of 1848, and in exile had direct contact with international reform movements that were rooted in the several European national working classes, Marx saw the heart of the political problem more clearly: since Germany lacked a significant capitalist economy, with neither a defined bourgeoisie nor a proletariat, it enjoyed the luxury of criticisms that were idealist, that could stay aloft from the real movements for freedom. These real movements were necessarily rooted in the struggle between different classes, Marx concluded, a struggle that was ultimately for the emancipation of the proletariat.

Turning against those idealist conceptions was one way in which Marx and Engels reacted to the crushing defeats the revolutionary upheavals had met after insurgencies and the like swept across much of Europe in 1848. Major agitation and uprisings broke out in France, in all of Italy, in many German states and across most of the Hapsburg Empire, Switzerland, Spain, Denmark, and Rumania; more sporadically outbreaks occurred in Ireland, Greece, and Britain.[1] Ultimately they were all defeated.

The bitter dregs left in history's cup after all hope of victory had been drained by the subsequent period of reaction had the effect on Marx and Engels (as on many other radicals at the time) of causing them to repudiate all wishful thinking and analyses that were fuzzy or emotional. Contemptuous of a politics of good wishes and eschewing moral precepts on principle, Marx and Engels insisted that what was now absolutely necessary was to be hard-headed. Their sharpest barbs against critiques of capitalism or of the world order were aimed at those which betrayed soft origins or intentions. Disdainful of calls for socialism that appealed to peoples' senses of morality, the approach of the "utopian socialists," Engels and Marx contrasted the latter's own "scientific socialism," based as it was on researches in political economy that demonstrated the necessity for capitalism to lead to its own collapse.

Marx's materialist denial of spiritual entities and forces is arguably a consequence of the fact that by the early 1840s the few published works by Young Hegelians that articulated their still inchoate radical critique were all in works about religion.

The first of these, by David Frederick Strauss, was his *Life of Jesus* (1835), a daring examination of the historical figure of Jesus Christ and the creation of the myths associated with him by the early Christians; it was widely seen as an attack on Prussian religious beliefs and institutions. Bruno Bauer took the critique of Christianity further, questioning altogether the historical validity of the Gospels. In 1841 Ludwig Feuerbach's *Essence of*

---

[1] Eric Hobsbawm, *The Age of Revolution*, p. 112.

Christianity analyzed the human creation of religion as a process of the alienation of humans from their own destiny, which under the influence of religion, had been relocated to heaven and put under the domination of God. Only by destroying religious alienation could humanity hope to fulfill its destiny as a species, what Feurbach called its "species being."

With scathing sarcasm, Marx and Engels attacked the dominant tendency among the Young Hegelians to believe that to oppose an oppressive situation it was enough simply to argue against the *ideas* that gave rise to it, what the two critics referred to as the "innocent and childlike fancies [that] are the kernel of the modern Young-Hegelian philosophy," waging wars of "principles" and ideology "only against these illusions of the consciousness."[1] What these Young Hegelians utterly lacked, Marx and Engels concluded, was any inkling that their criticism should have a relation "to their own material conditions."

In the struggle against bourgeois society Marx believed the role of religion was merely a sideshow, diverting peoples' attention from the real issues of their day-to-day material existence. From Strauss, Bauer, and Feuerbach, Marx did take numerous insights into that society, but he insisted that their points were ultimately pointless, since they were aimed in the wrong direction — at the heavens, instead of where they were required, on Earth, and specifically on the struggle under capitalism between the different social classes.

Marx and Engels' critique of bourgeois society adopted from Hegelianism the notion, common to both the anti-mechanists of the 19th-century *Naturphilosophen* and the 17th-century enthusiasts,[2] that reality was determined by the playing out of the tensions and antagonisms between opposing polarities, what became known as "Marxist dialectics," not, as the simple mechanical model had it, where one force simply overcomes another. Whether it is the phenomena of colors or those of social classes, the clash of opposites is *the* force of transformation. In the *Holy Family* (1845), Marx and Engels wrote:

> Proletariat and Wealth are opposites. As such they form a whole. They are both formations of the world of private property. What concerns us here is to define the particular position they take with the opposition. It is not enough to state they are two sides of a whole.
>
> Private property as private property, as wealth, is forced to maintain its own existence and thereby the existence of its opposite, the proletariat.[3]

---

1 Karl Marx and Friedrich Engels, *The German Ideology* (Parts I & III) (New York: International Publishers, 1947), pp. 1, 3, 6.
2 See Part One, Chapter 4 (v), and Part Two, Chapters 5 and 6.
3 Quoted by R. Pascua, "Introduction," *German Ideology,* pp. xii–xiii.

iv. Marx on Nature; Consciousness as Determined by Life

In their break from the Young Hegelians, Marx and Engels attacked the lofty abstractions of Absolute Spirit and Freedom to insist that consciousness itself is only a consequence of the more fundamental *material* substratum within which it arose. Though they later qualified this formulation and conceived of the relationship less mechanistically than it is generally interpreted, still, in the main, the ideas of a given society, they asserted, are *determined by* its relations of production of the means of life. Rooting their philosophy of revolt in the actual working conditions of people reflected their desire to ground emancipatory programs and demands in the *real* world and in objective phenomena. As they saw it, as methods of production changed through history, peoples' conceptions about themselves and their world would also change. With such a methodological approach, Marx and Engels asserted, "In direct contrast to German [i.e,. Young Hegelian] philosophy which descends from heaven to earth, here we ascend from earth to heaven." As they succinctly formulated their new ontology, "Life is not determined by consciousness, but consciousness by life."

However, the disdain Marx felt towards the pious intellectualizing of the Young Hegelians ultimately served as well to push Marx considerably back into the camp of the very mechanists from whom, one can say, he had been trying to escape from the very onset of his political consciousness. Indeed, for his doctoral dissertation (University of Jena, 1841), Marx choose to write an analysis of the differences between the atomistic theory of the ancient Greek thinker, Democritus, in which simple mechanism determined all outcomes, and the later system of Epicurus, where random unpredictable deviations in the atomic motions "allowed freedom as well as determinism."[1] To the student Marx, this was a contradiction worth exploring.

After all, freedom, in its most simple terms, is the absence of necessity — and it is mechanism which is philosophically the most extreme embodiment of the ideology of necessity.

Yet, Marx (as are all of us) was inevitably caught in the ebbs and flows of the dialectic of history, and ultimately *it* would encourage the force of Marx's penetrating analysis to play out in some directions more than others. In the later part of the 19th century, when the idolatry of *res scientifica* was reaching the apogee of its newly established orbit in the skies of Western culture, mechanism was a powerful organizing principle, a kind of beacon for anyone at sea in the storm of contending ideologies that characterized those turbulent times.

It was mechanism, after all, that had (in the form of his theory of natural selection) enabled Darwin to succeed in 1859 in establishing *his* (and

---

[1] Dirk Struik, "Introduction," p. 14, Karl Marx, *The Economic and Philosophic Manuscripts of 1844* (New York: International Publishers, 1964).

Wallace's) theory of evolution after over two centuries of various evolutionary schemas had been proposed by a dozen or so generations of philosophers and writers, including Erasmus Darwin, Charles' grandfather.[1] Savants dating back at least to Robert Hooke, if not before,[2] had pondered the forms and features of the planet and its lifeforms and some had argued various schemes of evolution that frequently used cogent reasoning and fairly persuasive evidence. Yet none of these earlier evolutionists had a mechanism that could, in a comprehensible fashion, explain *how* evolution, so mysterious in its essence, could work — could work, moreover, without any kind of conscious intent, either by a creating deity or by a sentient nature herself. And under the sway of mechanistic principles, *that,* of course, would be the gravest of philosophical no-nos.

It was this purely mechanical explanation of the engine behind evolution, his theory of Natural Selection, that gave to Darwin's theory of evolution its unstoppable power. One of Darwin's admirers was Karl Marx, who took great inspiration from the English naturalist, who had made the study of living beings a true science, just as Newton had, with force, made physics a science. Marx wanted to do the same for the study of political economy. Admiringly, he offered, as mentioned earlier, to dedicate *Das Kapital* to Darwin.

If we could follow Marx's path as he was pulled hither and thither by the polar forces of mechanism *vs.* freedom, I believe it might reveal the centrality of this struggle for him, as over the years he sought to give form to the stirrings of plebian movements for liberation. Along this axis, I would argue, some of his most significant and painful inner struggles may have been waged, and ultimately — because Marx felt a deep conflict on the central questions involved — lost.

v. MARX & THE OCCULT

As he involved himself in the political and social struggles of his day, Marx associated with several agitators and thinkers who were (or later became) mystics or occultists. Though little known, this aspect of Marx's development has bearing on the larger question of the failures within Marxism to comprehend the profound class, race, gender, and structural relevance of ecological questions to capital.

For example, one of Marx's associates was the Abbé Constant, an early communist writer, who in the 1840s and '50s was increasingly drawn into

---

[1] In his poem, "Zoonomia."

[2] See Part Two, Chapter 13. Hooke, for example, had noted the changing nature of species indicated by fossils found, and he surmised that those of shellfish, found on top of mountains, implied massive forces had in times past torn up the Earth.

magic. Constant is credited (by Colin Wilson) for "having started [the modern] magical revival virtually single-handed" with his teachings and (under the name Éliphas Lévi), numerous occult texts. Joining Lévi in occult projects was Flora Tristan, who had been the author of *Workers' Union* (1842), the first work to advocate the formation of an international union by working men and women in order to obtain their emancipation. It was praised by Marx in the *Holy Family.*

A close friend of Marx, Mikhail Bakunin, studied the works of *magi,* alchemists, and other occultists. Though we do not know if the two radicals ever discussed such matters, we do know that Marx and Engels both expressed their high regard for Jakob Boehme, the 17th-century radical enthusiast and alchemist, glimpsing in him the fundamentals of dialectical logic.[1]

Undoubtedly, the most important figure in this regard is that of Moses Hess, one of the earliest 19th-century advocates for Zionism. Hess's religious mysticism was at the core of his social and political critiques. Like Marx a German Jew from the Rheinland, Hess played a singularly crucial role in the development of Marx's revolutionary outlook. It was Hess who pointed out the contradiction between private property and the ideal society,[2] winning over many of the Young Hegelians to the idea that the abolition of private property was a critical pillar for reform, and that the just society would necessarily be a socialist one.[3] Greatly influenced by Spinoza, Hess adopted a philosophical monism, in which a Creator God is immanent *in* the created world, as the basis of his "revolutionary pantheism."[4] In this spirit he set out to join the "struggle against the levelling encroachment of inanimate mechanism which deadens organic life and substitutes for it a uniform inorganic mechanism."[5] It was Hess, too, who in 1844 emphasized the need for *action* as a way of reaching both self-consciousness and the true essence of human existence. Hess showed how alienation was inherent in a society whose workers exist to make commodities. Defined as the producers of commodities, such workers in the end *become* products, commodities themselves. Money, the lifeblood of capitalist society, ended up, Hess argued, in enslaving humanity. Only in a communist society could it be different.

Two of Hess's converts to his vision were Engels and Marx. The former visited Hess in 1841 and reported, "My conversion to communism was definitely due to Hess. Hess was the first to make it plausible to me and my cir-

1 Rosemont, *op. cit.*

2 Struik, *op. cit.,* p. 15.

3 Mary Schulman, *Moses Hess, Prophet of Zionism* (New York: T. Yoseloff, 1963), p. 50.

4 John Weiss, *Moses Hess, Utopian Socialist* (Detroit, Wayne State Univ. Press, 1960), p. 72.

5 Quoted by Schulman, *op. cit.,* pp. 49–50.

cle."[1] It is widely accepted that a little later, Marx was similarly converted to communism by Hess. It was also Hess who first introduced Marx to the ideas and writings of the French socialists.

Though a modern writer has blanketly dismissed any notion that Hess's "mystical prophecies" could have had any influence on Marx, and Marx and Engels did come to hold Hess ("Rabbi Hess," they called him) in contempt, perhaps the matter of influences should be seen as more layered and complex, reflecting the tectonic forces at play in the working out of Marx's overall system.[2] One would certainly suspect that the one person responsible for introducing Marx and Engels to communism had a deeper impact on the younger men than a simple transfer of certain kernels of social theory.

Finally, of course, there was Hegel himself, the star of the philosophical firmament when Marx was obtaining his doctorate and a force with whom Marx necessarily had to come to terms. If the ultimate metaphysical duality of the time was that of mechanical materialism vs. idealism, who better than Hegel represented the latter? Marx was quite clear that he had taken Hegel's mighty insights and inverted them, so that they were embedded in the ground of human existence rather than in the clouds.[3]

Though it is unclear whether Marx really understood this, that Hegel's own sources for dialectics sprouted from the soil of popular and peasant magic, is apparent from a quick glance at his *Lectures on the History of Philosophy*, where philosophers now seen as part of the main tradition of Western thought such as Hobbes (four pages), Berkeley (five pages) or Locke (twenty pages) are often accorded less attention than central occult figures like Giordano Bruno (18 pages) or Jakob Boehme (29 pages).

Hegel is indebted to writers like them and other mystics, it is clear, for his understanding of what has been understood as "Hegelian dialectics." Valuable as their insights might have been, however, Hegel was markedly uncomfortable with the "excesses" these occult writers betrayed, their enthusiasm marking them as the enemies of order.[4] The 19th-century Junker philosopher was not happy with the passions these earlier dialecticians gave free rein to, and ultimately he was forced to repudiate them, afraid above all of what he saw as their "enthusiasm" — in this simply mirroring the reaction

---

[1] *Ibid.*, p. 56.

[2] Struik, "Introduction" to Marx, *Economic & Philosophical Manuscripts of 1844*, p. 15.

[3] Wilbur Applebaum, "Friedrich Engels and the History of Science," M.A. thesis, State University of New York at Buffalo, 1964, p. 55. Marx, *Capital* (1939 ed.), Preface to the Second Edition, p. xxx.

[4] Hegel, *Lectures on the History of Philosophy*, trans. E. S. Haldane and Frances H. Simson, M.A., in 3 vols. (London: Routledge and Kegan Paul, 1963), vol. 3, pp. 116–37, 189–93, 216.

of the propertied classes in the second half of the 17th century to the English revolution of the 1640s, discussed earlier.[1] Thus Marx got a version of dialectics after it had been "cleansed" of certain improprieties.

Finally there is the background to Marx and Engels' writing of the *Communist Manifesto* (1848). In the late-18th and early-19th centuries, radical politics and revolutionary agitation were frequently to be found in the various secretive Freemason lodges, whose members were drawn to these fonts of Enlightenment ideology and Freemason occultism, where class distinctions did not matter.[2] By the later 1830s and 1840s a shift in the class composition of some of these clandestine groups was underway, in some, the largely elite, mostly educated, membership becoming more composed of craftsmen and journeymen. This was true of the League of the Just, the core of which went on to form the Communist League. And it was the Communist League that was to call upon Karl Marx and Friedrich Engels to draft what became the *Communist Manifesto*.

vi. TAKING LEAVE OF HISTORY

The philosophies of Boehme, Bruno and Campanella, or later, of Winstanley, Coppe, or Earbery in the 16th and 17th centuries were, as we saw, expressions of the social and political upheavals going on during their lives, as early modern times confronted, among other matters, the huge migrant population of the marginalized created by the growth of private ownership of land. We can see this confrontation most clearly in mid-17th-century England.

Similar associations between movements of the oppressed and powerless and occult or mystical involvement have a much longer history. Many upheavals during the 14th-century Peasant Wars, for example, had religious mysticism and enthusiasm at their cores, so too in movements associated with the Albigensians in the early 13th century, as a century earlier the movement led by Joachim of Fiore.[3]

Wanting to close the door on this tradition was entirely in keeping with the conservative bent of Hegel's philosophy. Relying on Hegel and the other Young Hegelians for much of his own comprehension of dialectics, and as a determined materialist who railed against the *idealist* excesses that charac-

---

[1] Chapters 7 to 11.

[2] Hobsbawm, *Primitive Rebels: Studies in Archaic Forms of Social Movements in the 19th and 20th Centuries* (New York: Norton, 1965), pp. 162–63; cf. Han Suyin, *A Mortal Flower,* (n.p.: W.W. Norton), pp. 46, 128–29 for a Chinese playing out of the same pattern of associations.

[3] Ehrenreich, *Dancing in the Streets*; Evans, *Witchcraft and the Gay Counterculture*; Evans, *The God of Ecstasy*; and Gary Snyder, *Earth Household* have illuminating discussions of this tradition; also, Bailey, *op. cit.*

terized German activism, however, Marx may very well have been an unwitting heir, even a major source for transmitting Hegel's conservative aims. In turn, this partial blindness led, I believe, to other gross distortions.(We shall return to these speculations in my concluding chapter.)

Consider the profound difference between a self-professed movement for the liberation of the oppressed that claims as its own the rich history of earlier movements in the same general direction of its own, rooted deep within the soil, as they are, of human history, on the one hand — and a different kind of movement, on the other hand, that takes great pains to distance itself from those earlier struggles because they were *too* utopian; *too* Christian; *too* based on moral principles; *too* far from the direct path to modernity, which necessarily had to lead through the stage of capitalism before the true liberation of the working class could occur; or *too* attached to earlier social forms like collective ownership of land, guild protections, village economies held together by a web of familial, tribal, historical, or other complex organic ties that did not easily fit into the model of development towards Progress favored by Marx and Engels. For the most part, it is this second attitude towards earlier movements that is seen as communism matured as a movement.

Marx and Engels' movement thus uprooted itself from the soil of peoples' histories, from their real passions, real pains, real victories and defeats, and real goals.

Instead, we find a kind of historical arrogance, a wholesale repudiation of past efforts based on a superiority rooted in its correct, unsentimental, scientific analysis. In part this is a product of a mentality that eschews the softer, more human qualities, preferring only the hard, determinate, objects of science, and the need for objectified knowledge worn as a cloak to justify a kind of historical arrogance and a repudiation of whatever did not fit the model. It would seem that standards arguably appropriate to a mid-19th-century revolutionary movement, at whose center the proletariat is engaged in a struggle against Capital to recreate itself, have been imposed on earlier times, when Capital did not fully exist, and the proletariat was accordingly engaged in a different kind of struggle. This constitutes a rigidly mechanistic approach to social transformation. And does it not, additionally, really amount to an abandonment of the human history that Marx had wisely chosen as the matrix of his analysis? In this regard, Marx's enterprise was possibly doomed to failure.

Perhaps it might be thought unfair to expect Marx to have anticipated the way in which Darwinism ultimately became the foundation of many a socially conservative philosophy, or to have foreseen the specific playing off of "evolutionary" as opposed to "revolutionary" theories of change and the use of the former to demean radical activism. But a similar pattern would have been part of what Marx and Engels learned as they studied the Peasant

Wars, patterns seen in other contexts (like China) where "gradualist" or "catastrophic" theories of change have historically tended to have been favored by conservative or radical communities, respectively, offering either ideology, it would appear, a mirror in nature that reflects their preferred image of social transformation. And this social and intellectual polarization would surely have been noticed by Marx, writing his doctoral dissertation on Epicurus' critique of Democritus' atomism in Periclean Greece for its mechanistic determinism.

The above considerations suggest an alternative interpretation of the fact that from its inception as a dominant philosophy of working-class struggles, Marxism has been plagued by the problem of "mechanical Marxism," where the fluid and supple analysis Marx had pioneered degenerates so readily into a formulaic, dead, ultimately ponderous set of empty phrases only dimly related to realities. Why is it that time and again, as in Spain in the 1930s, when faced with the challenge of the open seas, mechanical Marxists (the Comintern) seriously misread the winds of change and simply steer the ship of Revolution "safely" onto the rocks?

Marx himself, seeing the deadening way in which his doctrines were being applied, announced that he himself was not a Marxist. But was not mechanical Marxism, in fact, but a drawing out from Marx what was already implicit? Faced with choosing a path of liberation into modern times, the Communist movement did not so much decide upon an alternative direction from that of the bourgeoisie, but rather promised that socialism was a truer, more efficient, and certainly more equitable way to reach the same general destination, only with a better use of science and technology and planning — including now an attempted "science" of human history.

We shall return to these questions in Part Three, and pursue this additional inquiry: whether it is this predilection towards mechanical Marxism that explains the nearly incomprehensible tendency of many contemporary revolutionary movements to bog down in swamps of dogma and revolutionary "purism," effectively isolating themselves both from the people whose lives such movements profess to be improving and from the larger currents of human history. Finally, we shall discuss why, despite Marx and Engels' beliefs in the historic role of the proletariat in bringing about socialism, "Marxist" revolutions, with the partial exception of Russia, have been made primarily in peasant-based societies lacking much of an industrialized base.

Before we have those discussions, however, two prior investigations must take place, in part so that they can embed our later considerations of these questions in a context enriched by these earlier inquiries. The first of these, in the "Interlude" that follows, will provide our first serious consideration of the critical question of just how catastrophic, how damaging, are the environmental disasters many believe to be imminent? Till now, I have skirted around that question, assuming a dire situation but never getting around to explaining why. Now I will make my case.

Part Three, following the Interlude, is our second extended investigation, where the historic critique of mechanism and of the way its prerogative reframed the way the world was understood and felt is now brought to bear on *modern* science and technologies, in particular by undertaking a close analysis of high-tech and biotech industries and cultures.

But first: just *how* bad is our environmental crisis? Are we in a state of general, system-wide collapse? Or are those who hold such beliefs simply the latest in a long line of Christian (or other) apocalyptics, who have simply abandoned their hairshirts for a more stylish REI Goretex?

Interlude

[Another geologist,] Charles Archambeau, told *The New York Times*, "You flood that thing [the proposed Yucca Mountain nuclear waste storage site in Nevada], and you could blow the top of the mountain. At the very least, the radioactive material would go into the ground water and spread to Death Valley, where there are hot springs all over the place, constantly bringing water up from great depths. It would be picked up by the birds, the animals, the plant life. It would start creeping out of Death Valley. You couldn't stop it. That's the nightmare. It could slowly spread to the whole biosphere. If you want to envision the end of the world, that's it." — Rebecca Solnit, *Savage Dreams: A Journey into the Landscape Wars of the American West* (1994)

I don't garden much anymore. I'm afraid to see what's going to come up. — Mary Osborn, who lives near Three Mile Island and has seen deformed flowers, trees, and vegetables growing in her neighborhood.

i. ALL POWERFUL NATURE

At last we can address the critical question: what *is* the magnitude of the present ecological threat? Are the rantings of the eco-calyptics, myself included, justified? Or do the various disaster stories told by all of our overwrought eco-alarmists turn out, upon a closer analysis, to be simply a story about age-old natural patterns, perhaps driven along new, more technologically-defined pathways, but not in any sense off the map altogether? Will not nature, all-powerful nature with her unfathomable urge towards life — that force that sends blades of grass to cut their way up through concrete, that enables a plant to grow out of bare rock and roots to take hold in next to nothing, or that permits a breath to persist under the most tenuous of conditions — ensure that life shall continue and flourish on our planet?

It may be reassuring to realize that, most likely, in some unimaginably-long term, the latter is more likely to be the case, that the planet's vitality, finite though it is, still overwhelmingly illuminates even the darkest of shadows that human intervention in the workings of nature might be able to cast. No human creation, it would seem, at an initial assessment, can be compared to the raw energies churned up by even one hurricane. Yes, I can believe the survival of life on Earth probably is not in question.

What *is* definitely in question, I shall argue, is the survival of the vast amounts, enormous diversity, and spectacular quality of the lifeforms that the planet, till recently, has been adorned with. That such incredible marvels wing through the air, burrow beneath the root-cleaved soil, and hunt and play in the shadows of the seas, and that such unlimited ranges of lichen, fungi, fauna, and flora are in evidence nearly everywhere demonstrates how very fecund the Earth can be, despite the innumerable visible signs of collapse, compared with yesteryears, that are claimed.

And yet, it is precisely this richness, this unfathomable beauty — the intricate strands that are spun into our vast web of lifeforms as a whole, and all that *rests* on this fecundity that is being radically diminished in our onrush of despeciation, our loss of former glories. The signs are everywhere. And they are overwhelming.[1]

While many of these tell-tale threats might be doubted, quibbled over (as I see it) with a factoid here or a conflicting statistic there, some of these devastating losses should be considered unassailable — except, as with the effects of, say, cigarette smoking, there will *always* be *some* scientists who throw up methodological roadblocks to cut off any avenues to clear and obvious conclusions.[2] Critics can always claim, as they do, that causal chains have not truly been established, as, indeed, they perhaps have not, for the model of causal demonstration by inductive logic and a plethora of examples so favored by Western science to establish cause-and-effect linkages is impossible to fully satisfy. In pursuit of the level of proof demanded by Sprat and the Royal Society's new experimental science, how can scientists isolate single causes out of the multitude of layers in which any one individual, any one act, is located, the extended and overlapping contexts of all things, especially living creatures?[3]

---

[1] A recent study found that currently mammals, birds and reptiles "are going extinct at a rate 100 times faster than normal...." Peter Femrite, "6th Mass Extinction in Progress."

[2] For example, a Dr. Alvan Feinstein wrote an editorial for the *Journal of Clinical Epidemiology* advocating for an "evidence-based" medicine, essentially pushing for criteria for proof that was next to impossible to meet. (Phone interview, Prof. Robert Proctor, March 8, 2013.) Feinstein was allied with tobacco interests.

[3] Hence the inevitable conclusion of all official studies that are carried out is that further studies are needed. For the nit-picking of scientists struggling

One can never really *prove* that an individual case of cancer, or even a cluster of such cases, were uniquely caused by a particular effluent from a nearby chemical firm or that the failure of salmon to spawn has anything to do with deforestation near their particular riverhead. Too many factors enter into an extremely complex playing-out of events, such as even any *one* life always is, let alone a whole complex ecosystem. And so, even as Thomas Sprat had promised, the very exacting demands for certainty that the new science laid down for the path of inquiry in the 17th century frequently establishes, in many instances, virtually insurmountable barriers to understanding. As we saw in Part Two, the work of Sprat, Wilkins, and others codified a "scientific method" *designed* to encourage challenging *any* conceivable theory of what *is* by presenting so many questions and posited lapses in logic that, in theory, no theories, *no* explanatory schema, truly could ever pass muster. Thus, once more, tobacco scientists can argue for decades what we all know is utter nonsense about the safety of smoking, and, more to the point, may even have some evidence and a small measure of methodological rectitude behind their claims. And scientists can readily question one another's statistics, for most of them know there is a fine art in constructing cohorts, age, location, or other criteria for inclusion/exclusion being used to camouflage or reveal egregious liabilities.

Yet, where critical political and economic interests are not involved (or sometimes precisely because they are involved, so that powerful individuals or institutions greatly desire the claims of a particular theory to be accepted), such exacting demands can be, and frequently are, relaxed, and glaring holes or inconsistencies can be ignored or forgiven without sufficient cause. In these ways, the ideological strictures laid down at the beginnings of modern science can continue to serve as gatekeepers to bar from the citadel of science conclusions that are unwelcome, sometimes on issues that cut to the heart of privilege and power in modern society. It is an imperfect process, and occasionally explosive matters manage to intrude into public consideration, but these are far fewer, and pack far less of a punch, than would otherwise occur.

In this Interlude, I want to concentrate on a handful of situations presently underway that I believe will clearly have catastrophic effects on some fundamental terrestrial processes of renewal, processes that are vital to the survival of humanity — and a huge swatch of the rest of the natural world, large arrays of species, habitats, and whole regional aquifers simply being wiped out along with most or all of humanity, if these threats are not beat back before we reach points of no return.

That I call these threats unassailable does not mean, as I discussed above and must emphasize again, that they are cavilproof. Reasonable questions

---

not to come to conclusions about environmental degradation having a harmful effect on forests, as a result of political pressures, see Charles E. Little, *The Dying of the Trees: The Pandemic in America's Forests* (New York: Viking, 1995), pp. 52–55.

can usually be raised even of the best of theories, and many of them have huge gaps and areas that are best not examined too carefully. Newton's Laws of Motion, the most successful of all theories, had basic flaws and a certain amount of circular reasoning,[1] as does one of the most successful of modern theories of quantum mechanics, the quantum electrodynamics that won Feynman, Schwinger, and Tomonaga their Nobel Prizes in 1965, where central mathematical absurdities in the theory were maneuvered around in order to save a theory that otherwise was very elegant, useful, and predictive. The most revered of theories often have troubles at infinitesimal distances or at boundaries, utterly failing as distances go to zero, i.e., at point-centers, or becoming useless as more than two or a few bodies are involved. We believe, nonetheless, in a great many cases, in ideas and theories that others quite reasonably might raise fundamental objections to, and we do so for a variety of reasons, many of them subconscious. Thus, science is rarely able to attain complete closure on any deep questions.

Before I begin my enumeration and descriptions of the most serious blows to the vitals of our overall terrestrial ecosystems, so as to assess the true magnitude of these threats, one last admission: similar devastations have happened before. Certainly the cataclysm that occurred about 63 million years ago when a large asteroid or comet appears to have hit the Earth just off the Yucatan Peninsula, in hand with massive volcanic eruptions, wiping out the dinosaurs and much of the planet's lifeforms by blotting out the sun for long after with atmospheric debris, was such a crisis — as well as a striking confirmation of parts of the Newtonian teaching about cometary impacts.

Out of this disaster, it is agreed, in the eclipsing of the great reptilian age, was actually born the advent of the great mammals and so (we like to believe) the stage was set for the coming of *homo sapiens*. It is, indeed, difficult to shake the sense that the deity could now finally rest, even if we are consciously trying to avoid such anthropomorphism or Old Testament cosmogony. There is some evidence, too, as Hooke speculated, of the Earth's having changed the angle with which its axis is tipped to the plane of its solar orbit, an event, as Hooke pointed out, that, if it were sudden, would have sent ferocious shudders down to the very foundations of the planet, possibly shattering continents and sending oceans sweeping across the lands. Ice Ages also have come and gone in fairly regular intervals, imposing their own harsh sentences on the biota of many hitherto thriving habitats.

Probably the most extreme example of these crises to Earth's lifeforms occurred about two billion years ago, in what Margulis and Sagan refer to as the "oxygen holocaust,"after microbes found they could utilize water as a source for hydrogen via photosynthesis, and so produced as a by-product

---

1 In his *The Science of Mechanics*, Ernst Mach subjected Newton's theories to a fundamental critique, which was instrumental in Einstein's development of his two theories of relativity.

vast amounts of the hitherto rare gas, oxygen, that was eventually to fill the atmosphere. This proved poisonous for nearly all life precisely because oxygen is so terribly bioactive. When the percentage of oxygen in the atmosphere on the early Earth shot up from the previous 0.0001% to 21%, it constituted an unprecedented crisis in the biosphere. The now defenseless microbial life had to undergo a profound transformation in order to survive. From that crisis came, biologists believe, the invention by microbes of a new metabolism that actually *required* oxygen, in effect taming the poison by making it the central actor in *respiration,* a newly-crafted process that generates such huge amounts of energy for those organisms using it. Evolution continued, now based on a vastly different kind of life; and the Earth was changed forever.[1]

Such vast transformations, when they occurred — and if some are still speculative, all are not — would they not have wreaked havoc of the magnitude and kind that the apocalyptics are crying doomsday over in our times?

Yes and no. In sheer numbers, perhaps, there *are* similarities in the degree of the collapses back then and the ones many anticipate in our near futures. But there is a more fundamental story.

ii. A Catastrophe of Inconceivable Magnitude

At a deeper level, some of the devastations now underway threaten the roots of life itself in a manner no mere comets, axial transformations, or a gaseous poisoning of the biosphere are capable. Perhaps the most terrifying of these catastrophes, already well under way, is the progressive dispersal of large quantities of plutonium into our environment. It is unclear whether DNA molecules — arguably one of nature's more ingenious inventions — could continue to function in the presence of significant amounts of plutonium. The true impact of plutonium dispersal throughout our living spaces, which has been going on for nearly eight decades, is unfathomable. We can only wait and try not to panic.

Plutonium is a man-made element — in the 2010s, with increasing numbers of women physicists, chemists, and technicians, man- and woman-made. It is quite simply the most toxic substance known. Prior to the Manhattan Project to build the world's first atomic weapons. plutonium did not exist on Earth except for the trace amounts synthesized experimentally a few years earlier. Here's how toxic it is: as little as one pound of it, experts agree, if distributed equally around the world, is able to induce lung cancer in every person on the planet — though since nearly everyone realizes that under the rule of capitalism, equal distribution of anything is anathema, our situation may not be quite *so* dire. Plutonium has been made by the crash programs to build and test nuclear weapons by the US, USSR, Britain, France, North Korea, South Africa, India, Pakistan, China and [Israel]..., and also by the feverish

---

[1] Margulis and Sagan, *op. cit.,* pp. 93–109.

construction of nuclear-power facilities across the globe. About 435 commercial reactors currently operate or are near operation on our planet. Some reactors can produce as much as *several hundred pounds* of plutonium *a year*. It has been estimated that some two and a half million pounds of plutonium have been produced in the past six decades.[1]

Plutonium emits alpha, gamma, and beta rays; it is the alpha rays, with a half-life of 24,500 years for Pu–239 (the heavier of the two main plutonium isotopes and used for making thermonuclear weapons and for fuel in most reactors) and a half-life of 88 years for Pu–238 (used as a power source by NASA for space missions) that are particularly damaging: absorbed through the lungs and bloodstream, combining with proteins in the blood and thereby transported to storage cells in the liver and bone marrow, there able to shoot out its random plutonian subatomic projectiles to work their dark magic against the chromosomes of any lifeforms that come in contact with it.

In humans, leukemias, bone and liver cancers and brain tumors are frequently the result. Plutonium also becomes concentrated in the sperm and ova, and can pass the placenta wall to effect fetuses. It can also enter a person through wounds or by being eaten. DNA and somatic tissues in general come under a terrific assault.

It takes 490,000 years (twenty half-lives) for a hypothetical one pound of Pu–239 to decay to the point where only 0. 0001% is still present as Pu–239, but 0.0001% of a pound is a whopping 0.000015 ounce, and given that a particle as small as 0.000000003 ounce is thought to constitute a lethal dose, is still extremely dangerous. To get to a level below 0.000000003 ounce takes another thirteen half-lives for Pu–239, a total of 808,500 years. No human society, and certainly no government, has existed for more than a few tens of thousands of years. Nor, needless to say, any structures. Yet many scientists and authorities believed it prudent to push full-speed ahead on plutonium tech.

Large amounts of plutonium, alas. have already been dispersed into the biosphere. The explosion of a NASA rocket in 1964 resulted in 2.1 pounds of Pu–238 that it carried in a SNAP–9A power source being vaporized in the atmosphere, carrying its plutonium to "all continents and… all latitudes."[2] In 1962 three US Thor missiles exploded on separate occasions, each explo-

---

[1] David Albright, Frans Berkhout, and William Walker, *Plutonium and Highly Enriched Uranium* (Oxford, England: Oxford Univ. Press, 1997), pp. 395, 396, and 480–83. Unfortunately, Albright *et al.* do not break down the amounts by isotopes, so these are estimates of total plutonium. Cf. Jeremy Bernstein, *Plutonium: A History of the World's Most Dangerous Element* (Washington, D.C., John Henry Press, 2007), pp. 169–70, where total plutonium, civilian and military, is estimated at approximately 1900 metric tons at the end of 2004.

[2] Karl Grossman, *The Wrong Stuff* (Monroe, Me.: Common Courage Press, 1997), quoting NASA, *Emergency Proc. for Nuclear Powered Satellites*, p. 12.

sion showering Johnson Island and its lagoon with plutonium. In fact, two thirds of the Thor missiles launched in nuclear tests performed so badly that command destruct orders had to be issued, scattering the plutonium in their warheads. A report by Sandia Labs indicated that between 1950 and 1968 about 1200 nuclear weapons, or 66 a year, were involved in accidents, including fires or being dropped during transfer. A Freedom of Information Act request produced "Accidents and Incidents Involving Nuclear Weapons" (Summer, 1957–Spring, 1967) that was 245 pages long. In 1984 it was estimated that 125 US thermonuclear weapons had been "damaged."[1]

Rocky Flats nuclear facility in Colorado, a major center for producing nuclear triggers (for thermonuclear bombs) for many years, has had multiple plutonium fires, and the government nuclear "plantations" at Savannah River and Hanford (where congenital nervous system defects have increased nearby) have leaked (often on purpose) or dumped huge amounts of radioactive waste, including large quantities of plutonium. Areas around Livermore National Laboratory, in the San Francisco Bay Area, where thermonuclear weapons are designed, are contaminated with plutonium.[2] In the former USSR, Lake Baikal has been similarly contaminated from a military complex there.

With plutonium remaining deadly for on the order of a million years, there simply can be no way to keep it *out* of our environment once it has been made. It cannot be isolated as waste. It is only a matter of time — and probably not that much time, at that. Given its huge energetics, plutonium quickly eats through any container it is put in. Using high quality stainless steel for "safe" containment at best buys a mere handful of years — surely, given the unbelievable toxicity of the substance, a worthy project, but in the context of nearly a million years, utterly insignificant. The plutonium has hundreds of thousands of years to wait: only a matter of time before earthquakes, floods, fires, volcanic activity, its own toxic emissions, or other natural (or human) disaster breaks into whatever "secure" container the plutonium is entrusted to and transforms the inevitable slow leaks from pipes, vents, gloveboxes, etc. into massive breaches.

---

[1] Charles Perrow, *Normal Accidents: Living with High-Risk Technologies* (New York: Basic Books, 1984), pp. 283–84. Officially the US government admitted to 27 such "broken arrows" (their code), but the International Peace Research Institute's count is nearly five times as many. On matters of fact I tend not to believe the Pentagon. Schlosser, *op. cit.*, pp. 327–28, 465, 309.

[2] Schlosser, *op. cit.*, pp. 309, 327, 465. John von Neumann, a major force in the Manhattan Project and a member of the Atomic Energy Commission (AEC), had written to Lewis Strauss, it's Chair, that "the sacrifice of human lives is an acceptable price to pay for technological progress." Steve J. Heims, *John von Neumann and Norbert Weiner: From Mathematics to the Technologies of Life and Death* (Cambridge, Mass.: MIT Press, 1980), p. 367, quoting a memo to Strauss of September, 1955 in Strauss, *Men & Decisions* (1962).

Given plutonium's extreme toxicity, it is hardly reassuring to learn how resistant US Air Force officers and weapons lab executives were to institute protective measures against accidental detonation of their thermonuclear weapons.[1]

The slow dispersal that began when plutonium was first synthesized by Glen Seaborg in 1940 and continued with atomic bomb explosions in the Trinity Test (July16, 1945) and over Hiroshima (August 6) and Nagasaki (August 8) and at least two thousand explosions since, as well as the contribution from the numerous "civilian" nuclear-power generators, has already had a dreadful effect. When tests were made of human breast milk and of human sperm, *all* samples had detectable levels of plutonium.

When energetic alpha particles shoot out from radioactive plutonium atoms, they easily pass through cell walls and can blast DNA molecules into pieces, thereby scrambling the life-replicating power with which that vital molecule is endowed when the pieces then reassemble, quite frequently sequenced in a different order. In short, plutonium dispersal *is* a catastrophe of inconceivable magnitude. In sufficiently high concentrations, it is possible it may act as a total dis-enabler of DNA function. This would, it goes without saying, put the planet's vitality to a severe test. Short of repealing the Periodic Table of Elements, there is simply no way to tame the ferocious toxicity of plutonium and its fellow α, β, and γ emitters.

iii. Felling the Tree of Life

The future of Earth's lifeforms rests, as well, on finding some thing or way to refill the hole in the planet's ozone shield, first noticed in 1985.[2] By now, many

---

[1] Schlosser, *op. cit.,* p. 440.

[2] Since they are sometimes confused, I should first explain the difference between this and another atmospheric degradation problem, global warming. In the short run, the latter will have disasterous consequences, including the melting of much of the planet's polar icecaps, a subsequent increase in sea level, and the disappearance of many low-lying coastal lands and cities and numerous islands with unique human populations and cultures. Average temperatures will reach significantly higher levels due to the trapping of the sun's energy inside the Earth's atmosphere as a result of the increased levels of "greenhouse" gases, primarily carbon dioxide and methane, mostly products of industrial use of fossil fuels and automobile emissions. But such increases and the havoc they will have created, would, I believe, possibly stabilize after a period of some decades or (more likely) centuries of widespread chaos, so that we would expect a new planetary ecology, one having transformed growth patterns due to the climactic variations, to emerge, one stable enough for farmers to begin to allieviate the predictable mass hunger that collapsing agricultural production would initially create. Information about the ozone and CFCs can be found in Bill McKibben's *The End of Nature* (New York: Random House, 1989), pp. 36ff.

are aware of the basic science involved in the crisis of the ozone. Since near the beginning of life on Earth, a layer in the upper atmosphere made of ozone — a form of oxygen in which three, instead of the usual two, atoms of oxygen bond together — has shielded the surface of the planet from the part of the ultraviolet spectrum from the sun that is very harmful to all living creatures.

In the mid-1980's ground measurements revealed that a substantial hole had developed in the shield over the Antarctic. During the years since, the hole has expanded and a second hole, somewhat smaller, has developed over the Arctic and Northern Europe. Scientists believe the holes are the result of a class of chemicals, the CFCs, that are used in refrigeration, in spray cans, and (for obvious reasons, seldom mentioned) in the use of rocket fuels by the US space shuttles and other rockets. Significantly, the largest source of CFCs actually came from computer production, though the fact that Silicon Valley was the world's largest contributor to ozone depletion, is, similarly, kept from the public.

Agreement has now been reached to stop the use and production of some of the top ozone-depleting chemicals. Rocket fuels, however, will not be regulated. We can only hope that previous patterns, where corporations frequently shifted production facilities out of the US in reaction to newly-established environmental regulations, especially with computer manufacturing increasingly being shifted to just such unprotected environments like Tijuana, San Juan, Manila, Singapore, etc., does not repeat itself. But a recent report by the *New York Times* reveals huge gaps in the Protocol and its enforcement.[1]

If the holes, Protocol, and shield alike are not closed, the predicted consequences will be devastating. Two ominous changes in particular, a greater incidence of fatal skin cancers and an increased rate of glaucoma, have been widely predicted; they are alarming enough, but they pale compared to the fact that a significant lessening of human (and other species') immune-system functioning is occurring as a result of the loss of the shield. Particularly vulnerable to the hitherto excluded harmful rays are the phytoplankton, the beginning of the oceanic food chain and hence at the very portal of the life process on our planet.

We have little to go on in anticipating the likely effects of a massive kill-off of the phytoplankton. It would be arrogant to predict. But it is certainly well within the range of possibilities that such a massive kill-off would be followed by similar collapses of sea populations (already, many of them, on the verge of disappearance), quite possibly including whales, who depend on phytoplankton for much of their diet.

Of the non-sea creatures, birds would be the most severely affected, along with particular human populations, as in Japan, that are heavily dependent on fish for their diet. But once started, there's really no telling how

---

[1] Elisabeth Rosenthal and Andrew W. Lehren, "Effort to Curb Dangerous Coolant Falters, Sometimes at Home," *New York Times*, November 23, 2012.

far the web of predator/prey would unravel before some species or other learned how to make do in some other manner, as happened in the "oxygen holocaust" some two billion years ago. It might happen fairly quickly and easily. Or it might not happen at all, and the die-off would be a telling blow against the Tree of Life itself, finally felling it and plunging the planet into an unmitigated darkness.[1]

iv. POINTS TO NO-RETURN

According to the analysis by Colborn, Dumanoski, and Myers, it is not plutonium, but certain synthetic hormone lookalikes, toxic chemicals like the PCBs, DES, and dioxins, that have been largely responsible for the catastrophic decline in human sperm production, motility, and function that has been found in several research studies over the past few decades. Repeated studies conducted in Europe, the US, India, Nigeria, Hong Kong, Thailand, Brazil, Libya, Peru. and Scandinavia have shown nearly a 50% drop in average sperm counts in humans from 1938 to 1990 — a period of about 50 years. The sperm that are found, too, are less vital, some swimming only with difficulty, as if in need of water wings. Testicles that fail to descend and incidents of testicular cancer are also increasing significantly. Nor is it human sperm only. Serious reproductive abnormalities have been widely noticed among panthers, alligators, frogs, earthworms, mink, and eagles, to name a few of the affected species. Colborn *et al.*, authors of *Our Stolen Future*, fault the process under way, largely since World War II, whereby some of the tens of thousands of new chemical compounds invented each year have been widely spread across the planet.

From the manner in which sperm concentrations have declined, it is clear that the effects stem from prenatal exposure to the toxic chemicals; the sperm count goes down systematically the later one's year of birth. It was a 1992 Danish study that led to widespread alarm, although earlier reports regarding decreased sperm vitality had been published. Reviewing scientific investigations of semen performed on "normal" men — meaning those who had not been treated at fertility clinics — conducted in North America, Europe, South America, Asia, Africa, and Australia, the Danish study concluded that counts of sperm fell from 113 million sperm per milliliter of semen to 66 million from approximately 1940 to 1990. The volume of ejaculate decreased as well, the net of the two effects amounting to a sperm decline of 50%. Though not part of this study, during the same fifty-year period, numbers of men with extremely low sperm counts increased from 6% to 18% of all men, and the percentage of men with high sperm counts (over 100 million/milliliter) had gone down significantly.

---

[1] In 2014 scientists reported that the ozone hole was beginning to shrink, but by the summer of 2015 it was again bigger then ever.

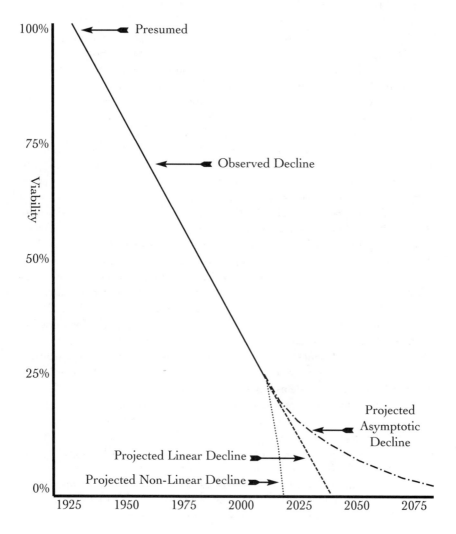

Graph Three
HUMAN SPERM VIABILITY DURING THE LAST PART
OF THE 20TH CENTURY AND PART OF THE 21ST

Because these results were so startling, there were immediate doubters. Indeed, the breakthrough 1992 study had been initiated by a physician who had been skeptical of earlier reports of decline in sperm viability that he had read. Three subsequent studies by others confirmed, as did his, the marked decline. In Belgium, research showed that over a sixteen-year period (1977 to 1993) the percentage of well-formed human sperm fell from approximately 40% to about 28%, and the percentage of sperm able to swim normally decreased from 53% to 33%.[1]

Two studies done in the US — one of which used a biased sampling method — did not agree with the steep declines others reported, but still recorded marked decreases in sperm count from different locales; in all other research, the data consistently indicated an approximate 50% decline in about half a century. Some later investigations have indicated the rate of decline might even be as high as 1.5% per year!

Several possible extrapolations might be made from the graph on the following page. Assuming that the linear 1% decrease per year holds into the future, viable human sperm essentially disappear by about 2040. Pessimists might wonder if at some point, due to some synergistic effect, a "point of no return" might be reached with a precipitous increase in the rate of decline, viability reaching a virtual vanishing point as early as 2020 or so. More likely is a gradual decrease in the rate of decline, viability never reaching absolute bottom but effectively disappearing by about 2100. In any of these cases, an absolute catastrophe for the species — differences between optimistic and pessimistic projections vary but by a century or so as to the point at which human reproduction simply stops[2] (a fate already fallen on numerous other species) or is relegated in its entirety to the test tubes. The overall tendency seems clear enough: worrisome human population growth ending in a precipitous population collapse. Not knowing whether optimistic or pessimistic projections are more likely to be correct, a prudent person — a prudent society — like Pascal, would err on the side of caution, since the stakes for being falsely optimistic are so unacceptably high, at least if we assume the human species has a will to survive!

Searching for answers in the late '90s new research replicated earlier results and scientists tried to determine if the declines varied from one country to another. A serious methodological roadblock intervened. Adequate laboratory facilities for this kind of investigation could not be found everywhere. Where fertility clinics, here an important source for data, could be found, mostly in industrialized countries, such as in Western Europe and in some US cities, the earlier dismal findings were again confirmed. At this point, worldwide tendencies, for lack of data, are not clear.[3]

---

1 Theo Colborn, Dianne Dumanoski, and John Peterson Myers, *Our Stolen Future* (New York: Dutton, 1996), pp. 174–75. Steve Connor, "Scientists Note Dramatic Decline in Sperm Count," *San Francisco Examiner,* (March 8, 1992).
2 Cf. the film, "The Children of Men."
3 I am extremely grateful for current information on this vexing problem from Shanna H. Swan, PhD, Professor and Vice Chair for Research and Mentoring, Department of Preventive Medicine, Icahn School of Medicine at Mount Sinai (telephone interview, August 14, 2013). Also, David H. Freedman, "Can Science Save the Human?" *Discover* (November, 2011).

Another study by Danish scientists found a marked geographical variation across the US. Lower sperm concentrations and worse vitality were found in areas with a greater use of agricultural pesticides.[1] Studies in Spain and Japan also found significantly low sperm counts, as was true for Finland, but in Denmark earlier spermatic declines appears, for no clear reason, to have levelled off. Relatedly, as early as the early 1990s, the *New England Journal of Medicine* reported a steady increase in the US in the incidence of 30 kinds of birth defects.[2] Most alarmingly, related fertility problems found in human females are worse in younger women.[3]

v. *Is* There a Way Out?

It astounds me that one can write such lines and not look out upon a concerted effort by governmental bodies and other authorities everywhere to get to the root of our spermatic crisis (I have little doubt that similar studies would reveal a parallel crisis as that of the sperm among human ova)[4] so as to end such overwhelming threats to all of our lives — for if these are not a common threat to all humanity, I cannot imagine whatever would be. Or, if readers would object (rightly so) that from all I have written so far, to expect governmental action on these matters is foolish, it astounds me that we cannot look upon a citizenry doing battle with all our resources against the forces responsible for such enormous dangers to our survival. It is one further measure of our numbing, of our sense of futility. Some people, of course, are doing battle, and polls, for whatever they are worth,[5] consistently show strong ecological concerns among people. But those doing more than worrying are a minority and what they are doing is

---

[1] Reuters, "A Special Reason to Avoid Pesticides," San Francisco *Chronicle* (June 10, 1994).

[2] Silicon Valley Toxic *Action*, vol. XII, no. 3 (Fall, 1994).

[3] Swan interview. Recent studies have also found a correlation between pesticide exposure and declines in bee sperm.

[4] Sperm are somewhat more vulnerable in that they lack a potential repair from a brother Y chromosome (responsible, of course, for making sperm). Two Y chromosomes, unlike 2 Xs, is a deal breaker as far as reproduction goes. Freedman, *op. cit.*

These problems in spermatic production are linked, a 2014 study at Stanford University found, to other health problems, such as high blood pressure, heart and vascular problems, skin diseases, endocrine disorders, cancer, and early death. Erin Allday, "Male Infertility Linked to Host of Health Maladies," San Francisco *Chronicle* (December 11, 2014).

[5] See Kubrin, "The Perils of Polling," *Propaganda Review* no. 4 (Spring, 1989) for how very little worth I generally give to polling results.

often something, like engaging in paper recycling, that while conceivably useful,[1] is at most a minor irritant to the power of the poisoners.

Why *is* it that government and corporate leaders can systematically rain poison down on habitats everywhere and not face universal outcries or in most places effective opposition? That a gigantic experiment is being conducted on the human (among others) gene pool for the past several decades should be obvious to just about everyone:

* radiation attacks from atomic testing (above ground until 1963 — and even after by China and others — and then underground until recently;

* assaults by pesticides and herbicides on food supplies and widespread food "additives" and hormone saturated meats;

* rainwater laced with acids and aquifers infiltrated by industrial solvents, many of which are known mutagens;

* the wide dispersal of PCBs, dioxins, and organo-phosphates, all closely related to the nerve gases developed for World War II;[2]

* the increasing occupation of every cubic inch of the biosphere by industrially-made microwave, ELF, and other portions of the electromagnetic spectrum, some of which appear to alter cell functioning.

In Los Angeles, a potent pesticide, malathion, is being sprayed over residential areas in an effort to suppress an undesirable fruitfly, just as in Vietnam Agent Orange was sprayed to get rid of strategically undesirable trees. In these and many other ways too many and too horrible to contemplate, we are being systematically poisoned, all by authorities who continually repeat the mantra of their class during the last half of the 20th century: *There is absolutely no danger to the public.*[2]

There are also the worrisome alarms that frequently sound, warning us that this species or that is endangered or already extinct. Red flags are pop-

---

[1] The major polluting engineering firms (Bechtel, PG&E, Exxon) are strong supporters of paper recycling. Some say industry actually profits from it.

[2] See some of the statistics on farm worker diseases and death just from the organo-chlorine pesticides in Tom Athanasiou, *Divided Planet: The Ecology of Rich and Poor* (Boston: Little, Brown and Co., 1996), p. 27. Argentinian doctors have reported "an apparent correlation between the arrival of intensive industrial agriculture and rising rates of cancer and birth defects in rural communities," based on data from hospital birth records, court records, peer-reviewed studies containing epidemiological surveys... and data from the government and pesticide industry. Associated Press, "Argentina: Monsanto Denies its Pesticides are Unsafe," San Francisco *Chronicle* (October 24, 2013).

ping up here, there, everywhere, ever more frequently. Frogs, an "indicator species," particularly sensitive to environmental stresses, are especially endangered nearly everywhere, a latter-day canary in the mine that is the Earth, showing the rest of us how terribly toxic our environments have already become anywhere we look. In some habitats frighteningly substantial percentages of existing plants or animal species are now considered endangered. Indeed, so many species are threatened, endangered, or already gone that numerous scientists and others have concluded that the Earth is undergoing its Sixth Great Extinction Crisis, akin to the oxygen holocaust or the Yucatecan cometary impact, but. now entirely human in origin.

Though sad to consider, I believe it is not too difficult to imagine an Earth in which human beings had become extinct. Given the role they play in the life of the soil, I find it next to impossible, however, to imagine an Earth without earthworms. Yet, in an area of the US Midwest, earthworm numbers have fallen to 3% of normal, an absolutely staggering collapse of population — with apocalyptic overtones. One hesitates to consider the implications such a drop-off can readily portend.[1]

All these dangers will be discussed in greater detail and with a finer eye to historical nuances in Part Three. There I try to examine the precise nature of modern technologies in order to grasp better their essence, their spirit. These newer technologies, many of which are particularly toxic, are widely perceived as completely surrounding us and associated with nearly everything we do and all that we are accustomed to. To the contrary, I hope to demonstrate that these procedures and techniques come to us from a particular direction, have a common history, and carry a shared intentionality. While a great deal of our modern world is associated with such toxic threats, an astonishingly wide range of our practices, institutions, and products are, by way of contrast, at least for the short run, relatively benign. On such a basis, using a process of environmental triage, Part Three's conclusion will offer a potential way out of the environmental cesspool into which, it is widely believed, the modern world is inexorably headed.

---

[1] The data on earthworm decline comes from Charles E. Little, *op. cit.*, p. 229. A science textbook widely used not so long ago in California middle schools gives a density of earthworms in deciduous forests as 225 per square meter, and of open fields as 95 per square meter. A decline to only 3% of the higher number would leave less than seven earthworms per square meter. *Holt Science* (New York: Holt, Rinehart and Winston, 1986).

Part Three

All in All, You're Just Another Brick in the Wall[1]

> "Imperialism's technologies, psychologies, and ideologies lunge like freeways towards the linear horizon, never knowing their place or purpose or end point, producing in their wake a disruption so massive it cannot be made sustainable." — Chellis Glendinning, *Off the Map: An Expedition Deep Into Empire and the Global Economy* (2002)

I've seen the best minds of my generation pondering formatting questions, unsure how to transfer a file from one platform to another

who ride herd on a swarm of numbed silicon crystals, rendered senseless from the first waft of arsine gas looking for an open Boulean gate to allow the downloading to proceed, already enough valued time wasted on the boot

who sit at their laptops, their eyes set in that 20-inch stare in a different kind of war, peering into some other world inside their necromantic monitor willing the two machines to exchange points-of-view in a frenzied data-flow — 1101110100110010110 oh Ohhh a digital stream-of-consciousness & an engineer's epiphany their awareness hostage to the rectangular array

who take meandering paths, staring intently at arms-length screens as they dowse for their next wifi fix

whose research ends up sponsored by hyperactive sidebars, spasmatic images of things to buy airline tickets shoes medications friends or mates chosen with a nod of their plastic rodent familiar (no longer feared), & now jacked by semiconductor voltage steps eager to execute closing a factory,

---

1 Pink Floyd (1979).

launching a missile's rain of fire, or attempting
to open a balky valve in an out-of-control nuclear reactor

who keep their hipster's beat by the frequency of their mouse clicks

who shuffle across streets as if dosed with a high-tech Thorozine™
in a daze of twitching thumbs key to key, engrossed in a binary caballa

who treat the present as future memory, obsessively documenting
each occasion, firm in their knowledge that History
is being made & must be minutely Recorded

who revel in a cybered connectivity to everyone & everything &
everywhere but are not so good at looking in eyes,
preferring Facebook™ to faces, texting to speaking

whose every thought & action presents on their screens,
aglow & frantic as the control panel on a bomber
its field of vision subdivided into domains of command & control
attending to take-offs & landings of data-sets
or menus to pick from (all preset) laid out as if a virtual mall
while the algorithms are covertly taking control

16

Mechanism & Ideology
In the 20th and 21st Centuries

As [Nils] Bohr learned more about the bomb, he gradually came to realize the true scale and scope of the Manhattan Project, discovering what historian Richard Rhodes called "a separate sovereignty linked to the public state through the person and by the sole authority of the President." The Manhattan Project had its own bureaucracies, its own Air Force, its own pilots, its own bombing ranges, its own factories, its own industrial workers, its own laws and police, even its own quasi-universities. At its height, the Manhattan Project employed over 130,000 people: It represented an industrial sector equal in size to the entire American auto industry. Bohr came to learn that the Manhattan Project was much, much more than a secret weapon. A secret geography and an attendant mode of sovereign governance had taken hold. In a conversation with Edward Teller, [Bohr said], "You see, I told you it couldn't be done without turning the whole country into a factory.... You have done just that." — Trevor Paglen, *Blank Spots on the Map* (2009)

i. THE "PUZZLE" OF LIFE: MAKEWORK FOR THE INTELLIGENTSIA

Part Three of *Marxism & Witchcraft* will extend the analysis of how we came to be walking down the devastating ecological path we seem to have chosen, continuing to focus on the essential antagonism between the worldview of "animism" and that of mechanism. Though not wholly new in the 17th century, mechanism emerged during the maturing of that watershed century's scientific revolution as the dominant framework for most of the leading thinkers (though philosophers like Spinoza, Lady Anne Conway, and Leibniz saw things differently).

Many people believe that contemporary thinking, particularly in an age of electronic communications, have for the most part left such naive mechanism behind, multiple links, windows, and multimedia on one's screen more web-like. Though such belief is not entirely baseless, Part Three will argue to the contrary, that despite its mystique as the "Information Age," at a deeper level, computers represent a technology not only of deliberate obfuscation, but one that remains thoroughly wedded to a mechanical model of how the world is constituted and works. John Wilkins' attempt (Part Two) to create a language altogether free of ambiguity is now embedded in the 1s and 0s of computer code, its binary vocabulary precluding in-betweens of any kind in every instruction and datum. We can also see the virtual apotheosis of the mechanical view, in what its followers refer to as "synthetic biology," as we will discuss in later chapters.

A central result of the 17th-century campaign by natural philosophers *against* enthusiasm and for the mechanical philosophy was that the phenomenon of life ceased being a mystery, becoming more of a puzzle. A most unusual kind of puzzle, one forever denied a solution, since the premise of the mechanical philosophy — a cosmos dead and indifferent and thoroughly predictable — is in direct conflict with the phenomena of life. The mechanical philosophy, willy-nilly, thus provided a basis for a cognitive world that intellectually, as well as emotionally, was necessarily sterile.

Put plainly, once death was split off from life, matter from spirit, objective from subjective, the community from the individual, inner from outer, facts from values, science from art, knowing from feeling — and, yes, good from bad, black from white, rich from poor, and man from woman (and all of these and more ultimately followed from the premises of the mechanical philosophy) — in a world such as this, there are few things that can be discussed with any real coherence.

Interpreting a world that is senseless is, of course, an endless Sisyphean task, and the official intelligentsia, mostly academics and media spokespeople, men and now women who accept the dominant cultural modes, perforce engage in a form of pretence, intellectual make-work that usually goes nowhere, attempting to explain what in essence is inexplicable. For on the basis of the overwhelmingly mechanical models, ethics, psychology, family dynamics, or the proper workings of society will resist clarification as the obvious divide between what really occurs in their respective domains and the restrictive categories provided by those models are ignored. These intellectual exercises in futility, although ultimately meaningless in terms of actual clarification of matters, are decidedly *not* unproductive, however, for the period in which the mechanical philosophy came to dominate official culture demanded of its universities and schools, its churches and journals of opinion ("high," "middle," and "low") that they serve to train burgeoning numbers of officials, lawyers, entrepreneurs, managers, bureaucrats, white-collar workers, and (though for different reasons) eventually manual work-ers. Part of the "higher" education some of those jobs demand is so that the officials who run affairs can be marinated in the vocabulary, assumptions, and implicit social grammar of the mechanical philosophy, which favors some possibilities over others at critical junctures. This process was well un-derway in the 18th and 19th centuries, as the worldview of Newtonianism came to dominate philosophy, politics,[1] psychology, religion, music, and eco-nomics, in addition to its taking over, one by one, the various sciences.

ii. LIVING IN UNREALITY: YOURTOWN, USA

From Part Two it should be clear that with the 17th-century victory of a particularly mechanistic scientific approach, and with its redefinition of matter, space, time, causality, life, death, health, language, ideas, thought, and everything else concerned with such concepts, "reality" as it was sup-posed to be understood became alienated from many people. No longer the sensuous world of fields and streams, seasons and cycles of growth experi-enced by humans for eons, this new "reality" increasingly allowed only some kind of perceptions of the world to be valid, while others were rejected, re-pressed, probably for many momentarily allowed to register before being discarded as invalid by a population being instructed as to what counted as perceptions and which ideas were acceptable.

Thus, though 17th- and 18th-century thinkers professed to want to lib-erate philosophy from clerical control, nonetheless most were hell-bent on demonstrating how a mechanical analysis was just the ticket to a deep com-prehension of the subject, *any* subject, giving us a society in Hobbes' *Leviathan* consisting of human atoms or, in the latter century de la Mettrie's *L'homme machine (Man a Machine)* (1747). In the French Enlightenment, this culminated in the *Encyclopedie* of Diderot and d'Alembert. The mechanical philosophy, with its notion of a world already dead, thus planted a perverse, ideological, seed, one whose horrific harvest we must face today — that grim conceit of Capital taking root and growing, becoming by now a formidable material force to be reckoned with, of a nature where death has an ontologic grip on everything and everyone.

This new reality has led us into our awful fix, the environmental crisis the planet faces today. In order to allow these terrible threats to our biosphere to have come to pass, the mechanical philosophy functioned as a profound ideolog-ical weapon in the battle for control. Mechanism proved to be an astonishingly powerful metaphor for manipulating people, as a result of the ruling circles in ef-

---

[1] An early example of this was *The Newtonian System of the World, The Best Model of Government: An Allegorical Poem* (London: 1728), published one year after Newton's death by one of his disciples, John-Theophilus Desaguliers.

fect being able to define the very categories into which thought and perception could flow. Indeed, when alternative ways of perceiving or feeling, of interpreting reality, could be labelled "insane," and official culture could insist that what some people perceived was only "hallucinations" or "visions" and not to be taken seriously, the modalities of control have been immeasurably ramped up.

I earlier suggested that the fact that asylums for the insane emerged as institutions in England and Europe precisely in the 17th and 18th centuries was a reflection of the controls (and most of all self-controls) that had to be put in place for the "Age of Reason" and of the Enlightenment to throw overboard as "superstition" traditional forms of knowing, many whose primary defect was that they were embedded in the cultures of the peoples then being colonized. The new science of the 17th and 18th centuries was fashioned into philosophic and ideological weapons both to cheer on the vigorous indictment against the beliefs of the indigenous and to serve as expert witnesses for the prosecution. The enthronement of mechanical science bestowed on it the power to decide what is real and thus a whole new dimension of socially-sanctioned coercion could be mobilized against deviation, not unlike the strictures provided earlier by the churches. In other words it was possible to tame nature in the 17th century only by putting at risk the sanity, overt or latent, of many who were forced to inhabit the resultant wastelands emerging around the mines or clear-cut forests. Mechanical "reality" was a powerful anti-elixir, effecting a vast numbing of the spirit, enabling most people to make an uneasy peace with this new civilization that denied what was so obvious. (As a century or two previously, the witchcraft wars had been an earlier and bloodier stage of the same process.)[1]

As science became the fundamental intellectual modality of the modern age, since the scientific revolution playing a decisive role in the formation of a new ideology, emerging triumphant at the tail end of an extended period, which we might date from the witch persecutions of the last quarter of the 15th century,[1] as the official codifier of the real. And what is *not* real, from now on, in total denial of the earlier widespread magical worldview, is the idea of nature being alive, the cosmos and the Earth having souls.

Unfortunately, this new reality that we have inhabited ever since is so firmly entrenched in our culture and our minds that it is virtually impossible for us to be aware of its workings or its presence, let alone consider what might be some of its limitations, for we have no neutral background against which to see its true shape and contours. By now its assumptions have permeated all of our ideas, our vocabulary, even our syntax. Nearly all of us are truly incapable of imagining the different forms our thoughts and feelings, our sensibilities,

---

[1] Like others, I am using the publication of Kramer and Sprenger's *Malleus Maleficarum* (1486) to date the war, but of course there had to be prior reasons that led to their malefic work.

could take if the rise of science had happened otherwise. I was reminded of this when on September 21, 2016, I attended a public lecture[1] where the speaker, in describing her work with the indigenous of Bolivia, showed us images of beautiful cloth bags, elaborately decorated, used to hold potatoes and other vegetables at their harvest festival. A shock went through the crowd when she explained that the decorations were on the *inside* of the bags, for the benefit of the vegetables, not the harvesters.

As a result, Part Two of *Marxism & Witchcraft* will inevitably fail — it too, in a way, an exercise in futility, for though many readers might finish reading it with their present senses of reality profoundly shaken, for the most part they will, alas, still be *intact*. That was not my aim at all.

iii. CURRENT TURF BATTLES IN THE WAR FOR IDEOLOGICAL HEGEMONY

Accordingly, as was my plan in Part Two, I need to demonstrate the often subtle ways in which our basic awarenesses are once again being re-defined by *current* scientific and technological developments so as to reinforce power imbalances threatening the life of our planet. That will be the aim of Part Three. Since we are only several decades into an intellectual/ideological shift in consciousness as profound as the 17th-century mechanical philoso-phy, many of us grew up to see this transformation begin and were probably captured by it. Though some of these newer forms of thinking will be famil-iar, it will be instructive to see how the new understanding of the world that came to dominate the last half of the 20th century took form. As we shall see, in many ways the contemporary transformation of comprehension and awareness is a continuation, and even an intensification, of the same pre-scriptions which the mechanical philosophy historically has stood for.

Like the changeover to the mechanical philosophy in the 17th century, the digitalization of society in the late-20th and early-21st centuries, as is ob-vious, is ushering in a total transformation of consciousness, virtually a new ideology that alters the whole of our culture and even our ways of perceiving. Inevitably relations of class, gender, race, ecology, the law, etc., etc. *ad infinitum et nauseum* will be affected. Because at the present time we still have our feet in both worlds, and those of us in our fifties or older — occupying two essen-tially different worldviews, two frameworks, two sets of vocabulary — have an unusual vantage point from which we can perceive the process of trans-formation and grasp the shape and textures of what is coming. Seeing these changes *as* they are taking place perhaps will enable us better to understand the magnitude of what is being lost, what gained, in the change from the old worldview to the new.

---

[1] By Silvia Rivera Cusicanci to the Anthropology and Social Change Depart-ment at San Francisco's California Institute of Integral Studies.

In pursuing such considerations, *Marxism & Witchcraft* will range far and wide in our explorations, but readers should keep in mind that the overall aim of such inquiries ultimately is simply to show how those different avenues reflect on our fight for survival and for viable habitat and the Earth's immense diversity of speciation.

17

An Opening By Way of Digital Watches... And Other Electronic Gizmos

When a Kogi shaman [in northern Colombia] builds a temple, he actually makes a model of his universe. The temple is, in fact, a loom on which the sun weaves the cyclic pattern of time and transforms its structure into organized space.... Through the year, as the sun moves north, south, and north again, it is said to spiral about the world spindle. It weaves the thread of life into an orderly fabric of existence, and the cyclical changes of the sun's daily path are transformed into a cloth of light on the temple floor.

Just as the daytime sun weaves in white thread, from west to east, its nighttime alter ego, traveling in the underworld from west to east, weaves a black thread th[r]ough the year's fabric between each pair of white threads. The female earth is the loom and provides the north-south warp of the cloth. The sun is male, and like the shuttle it penetrates the vertical threads of the warp. — E. C. Krupp, *Echoes of the Ancient Skies: The Astronomy of Lost Civilizations* (1983)

Right now, today, we who live on the Pine Ridge Reservation are living in what white society has designated a "National Sacrifice Area." What this means is that we have a lot of uranium deposits here, and white culture (not us) needs this uranium as energy production material. The cheapest, most efficient way for industry to extract and deal with the processing of this uranium is to dump the waste by-products right here at the digging sites. Right here where we live. This waste is radioactive and will make the entire region uninhabitable forever. This is considered by industry, and by the white society that created this industry, to be an "acceptable" price to pay for energy resource development. Along the way the:y also plan to drain the water table under this part of South Dakota as part of the industrial process, so the region becomes doubly uninhabitable. The same sort of thing is happening down in the land of the Navajo and Hopi, up in the land of the Northern Cheyenne and Crow, and elsewhere....

We are resisting being turned into a National Sacrifice Area. We are resisting being turned into a national sacrifice people. The costs of this industrial process are not acceptable to us. It is genocide to dig uranium here and drain the water table — no more, no less. — Russell Means, quoted in Peter Matthiessen, *In the Spirit of Crazy Horse* (1992)

i. STRAIGHTENING OUT THE CIRCLE OF TIME

Just as in the 17th-century reformulation of human consciousness, not only are the ways *we* perceive the world and reason about it in the process of being profoundly redefined, so too are our visceral connections to the world, our personal bite on it. Like the earlier transformation, there are a number of unexamined assumptions in the current reformulation with ominous intellectual, social, political, and economic ramifications. A whole new definition of the cosmos and all that pertains to us and it is emerging, and on its basis a new social reality is being erected, including new language, art, politics, ethics, sexuality, etc. This new understanding of the "real" and its numerous ramifications, especially as it bears on our environmental future, constitutes the focus of the remainder of *Marxism & Witchcraft*.

It is the world of computers and information-processing technology, of course, that is responsible for these changes. This chapter is an attempt to dig up deeper, often near-invisible meanings to the ways the information-processing industry is figuratively turning our world inside-out, using as our shovel a close examination of recent changes in how the concept of time is now being understood and measured. As our entrance to Part Three, this extended inquiry into the profound social and intellectual effects new notions of time are having on the various worlds we inhabit, will reveal their deep resonance with our ecological crisis, as we shall see.

The post-World War II technologies and sciences of war-making and of space exploration have led to a modern instrument for measuring out the units and flow of time that vast numbers of people use to connect themselves to temporality. *Digital* clocks and watches (at present, even more, cell-phone read-outs), in contrast to those that have a circular (or an analogue) format, provide ever more people with their fixes on "times" — especially if we count all the other digital-time displays surrounding us, from microwave ovens, automotive dashes, VCRs, computer screens, receipts and parking-lot vouchers, camera screens, and all the other household and workplace appliances and gizmos that continuously broadcast "time" into whatever space we occupy, reminding us everywhere we turn of its centrality. On the surface, this might seem a simple alteration, a mere change in form. On the contrary, I shall argue that it should be understood as a mutation, even an assault, on the very concept and shape of time.

As we shall see, this simple change in format can threaten to destroy traditional comprehensions of time as a concept. Given the many human domains in which time is the fundament on which rest our myths, personal transformations, our religion and ethics and history, not to mention our music, poetry, and sexuality, implications of the new digital forms are truly vast and, as we shall see, profoundly disturbing.

ii. Re: Cycling vs. Progress

Intellectually and spiritually, time for millennia has been the deepest of our mysteries: philosophically intractable, more impervious (especially in Einstein-time) than space to rational comprehension, understood as much emotionally, by way of mythology and poetry, as by science. And always (till now) time has been principally (and in principle) circular: through the eons, centuries, years, seasons, months, weeks, days, hours, minutes, seconds... the big and the small units of time; or through the harvests, rainy seasons, tides, migrations of the herds, seasons of the heart... cycles of time whose duration varies but where the phenomena, like the seasons, return over and over again, forming an endless chain of cycles, receding back and extending forward as far as thought can fly. Such is time, made manifest in archaic times everywhere in the world in the form of different kinds of calendars and sticks stuck into the ground to cast shadows; early in European history, time was embodied in mechanical instruments, clocks. Clocks and calendars are instruments built on the circle.[1]

Since the 14th century, clocks have consisted of hands that marked time's passage by sweeping out arcs of a circle "clockwise" — meaning sunwise, that is in the direction the sun appears to move through the skies as it defines our days — on the face of the clock. In earlier technology, the shadow passed in the same direction around the face of a sundial or on the ground. That the structure of time is circular has always been woven into

---

[1]As we saw in Part One, human cultures tens of thousands of years ago appear to have known about one critical cycle in the heavens, which takes around 26,000 years to return to the beqinning, called the "precession of the equinoxes," until de Santillana and von Dechend, thought to have only been discovered in Classical Greek times. They make a very plausible argument that the body of world mythology, including the story of Odysseus, is a coded narrative of that cycle.

the fabric, the mythology, of all non-industrial cultures. If in sone societies language and tenses indicated a sense of the "direction" of time's "arrow"; the stories nonetheless were all cyclical; rituals consciously strive to keep the circle or wheel of time turning.

Though Christianity, with its historically unique incarnation of Christ, seemingly introduced an inportant nodal point, as a critical qualification regarding the essential circularity of time, the promise of Christ's return at least stayed within the circular frame[1] and time in the West remained essentially *circular*, even *after* Isaac Newton in 1687 based his new physics on the *linear* flow of what he called "Absolute Time"; and time fundamentally retained its circularity even when industrial capitalism, with its inherent demand for a continually-increasing production of wealth, takes as its founding axiom a presumed inexhaustible store of natural "resources" that such production processes require, as well as a "sink," infinitely deep, into which the resultant wastes can be dumped. Even though linear thinking has been rapidly expanding its "sphere" of power from at least the 17th century on, partly as a result of Newton, as Part Two emphasized, knowledge of the circle of time could not be suppressed — at least until now.

It is my contention that widespread digitalization threatens to change all of this, that time portrayed now as a seemingly endless chain of Arabic numerals laid out in a line, moving forward from its "befores" to its ineluctable "afters" (only in the repetitive boring sequential build-up to its *faux* climactic transition from 9 to 0) will inevitably tear down cultural walls protecting the deepest stories of our being.

Once the visual dance of shadows or hands across a demarcated background is lost, replaced with the flashing alphanumeric dot patterns, the structure of time, of the circle of continuity embedded in it, starts to dissolve. I suggest that time progressively becomes more linear, male, and ultimately less comprehensible. Fundamental emotional and spiritual cores — well- springs of our very survival — are thereby covered over like creeks in a expanding urban center. We will find it harder to find our way to those truths, to that deep knowledge.

Having survived Christianity, Newton's postulate of linear inertia (and hence of Absolute Space and Time), and Henry Ford's conflating of Progress itself with the assembly line, the magic circle now has its back to the wall, for its embodiment in time's sphere, its last refuge in the linear stranglehold of Western civilization, is under attack, a consequence of recent developments in the economy and culture of the industrialized countries.

Digitalization of time breaks the circle — that circle of time, which is none other than the circle of life, that relentless passage of death into life and from life back into death, the dance of the cosmos and the source of all mystery.

In contrast to that endless dance, that continuous transformation, digitalized time underwrites passivity and inactivity, since the user of a digital time-

---

1 Although St. Augustine argued otherwise, claiming that Christ's incarnation negated cyclical time. (Dobbs, *Janus*, p. 73.)

piece is necessarily a mere observer in his or her perceptions of time. When we look at a circular clockface, we are forced to question it. The literal hands of time beg our interpretation and each of us must decide, according to our individual wishes, how much information we take from the instrument. If I have no pressing need to do something soon, glancing at my clock may simply inform me that it "is" about a quarter to six AM; if there is something I must do in a short while, I might want to know more accurately that it "is" just a little past ten to six; while, aware that my children are likely to get up at about eleven-thirty tomorrow morning (a concert the night before) and that I cannot function or be other than miserable on less than five hours sleep, and my desire to type another five pages prior to taking to my bed, a finer slicing of the time my instrument reveals might be chosen. On occasion I need to know how many fractions of minutes, or seconds, it "is." In the labs performed by my seventh-grade science students, I used to encourage them to estimate fractions of seconds.[1] The point is that we interact with our analogue instruments of time; they act as extensions of our senses and our consciousnesses.

With digitalization, on the other hand, I am compelled to be utterly passive, for it is the manufacturer of the instrument who has determined how fine or coarse my temporal gradations are (and, except for stopwatches, most manufacturers choose the same size slices), so that even if "about a quarter to six" suffices for my purposes, I have no choice but to read that it "is" 5:51:40, the numbers (or the ugly alphanumeric dot-patterns we have come to accept as numbers) flashing with a period of one-half second. Whatever the manufacturer's choice, I am stuck with it, for all time, since all I can do is press the button to obtain "the time," and the kind of time I get is determined, every time. I do not interact with my instrument, and *my senses and my consciousness in effect are extensions of it.*

iii. CLASS WARS ON THE BATTLEFIELDS OF TIME

I want to return to digitalization and to the machine language it forces our minds to speak later on, but first I want to point out some of the social consequences a transformation in the form of time that we carry can bring with it, consequences both profound and prosaic, cosmic and comic. In a brilliant article, the historian and peace activist E. P. Thompson illuminated the many transformations to Europe and to Europeans in the 18th and 19th centuries as a new "time-discipline" (as he aptly named it) was disseminated and enforced as a social prerequisite to the maturation of industrialization.[2]

---

[1] Some clockfaces, omitting numbers or even some of the minute marks, make the estimation of minutes necessary.

[2] My discussion comes from Thompson, "Time, Work-Discipline, and Industrial Capitalism," *Past & Present* no. 38 (1967): 56–97.

In non-industrial societies, work rhythms are determined by the tasks at hand and the weather. A farmer has to harvest a crop in response to sun and rain, a sailor puts out to sea according to tides and winds. These kinds of working rhythms in the West were, of course, transformed in the 18th and especially the 19th centuries (earlier in the case of mining) into the endlessly repetitive machine-driven rhythms of the factory: impervious, focused on the schedules of profit and loss, its whistles shrieking day and night in the mill towns spreading like blight across the land, as industrialism remade former agricultural or fishing communities into company towns and hundreds of thousands, ultimately millions, of men, women, and children were forced into waking, starting, stopping, eating, sleeping, and excreting in unison, in time with all of the others working the same shift. People had to learn a whole new sense and meaning to time.

Thompson draws upon an impressive range of material to show just how much the new factory time was resisted, how absenteeism, "unproductive" use of time on the job, and workers not coming to work on Mondays and Fridays have been major problems for the owners of capital since the beginning of industrial production. Indeed, just as the new time-discipline began to penetrate society, resistance to it was possibly at its highest.

In the Cameroons, for example, in response to recent efforts to industrialize his country, one worker asked: "How man fit work so, any day, any day, weh'e no take absen'? Ho be 'ego die?" (Thompson translates: "How could a man work like that, day after day, without being absent? Would he not die?") Under industrialism, time remains as a vitally important social and conceptual terrain where intense struggle continues to go on. After fifty years of faithful service to a firm, a white-collar worker's reward until recently, was, accordingly, a gold watch.

Capitalists were not always so free in sharing their time, however. At the beginning of the industrial revolution, it was just the opposite, time being closely rationed and kept behind locked doors. A worker from an early textile mill, for example, complained:

> I worked at Mr. Braid's mill.... There we worked as long as we could see in summer time, and I could not say at what hour it was that we stopped. There was nobody but the master and the master's son who had a watch, and we did not know the time. There was one man who had a watch.... It was taken from him and given into the master's custody because he had told the men the time of day.

Another worker reported that where he worked

> there were no regular hours: masters and managers did with us as they liked. The clocks at the factory were often

put forward in the morning and back at night, and instead
of being instruments for the measurement of time, they
were used as cloaks for cheatery and oppression. Though
this was known amongst the hands, all were afraid to speak,
and a workman then was afraid to carry a watch, as it was
not uncommon even to dismiss anyone who presumed to
know too much about the science of horology [clocks].

One factory owner ordered the warder of his mill to keep the factory
timepiece locked up so that none of the workers could change it, from which
we can conclude that, on occasion, workers too played with the hands of time.

It is clear, time could not be kept from the workers forever, for it is too
much the nub of the matter for the modern era. Even when industrialization
was in its infancy, schools were enlisted to teach the lower classes about time,
essential to bring about their submission to the cleansing discipline of work.
In the mid-18th century, complaints about the dangers posed by the idleness
of charity children were met by praises for schools that taught them "Order
and Regularity," partly by forcing the students "to observe Hours with great
Punctuality." In 1770 William Temple proposed sending poor children to
workhouses for employment in manufacturing when they reached four years
of age for twelve hours a day, with two hours given to schooling. One of his
contemporaries observed that by the "habit of industry" being instilled by
such schools, children by the age of six or seven will become "habituated, not
to say naturalized to Labour and Fatigue."

Yet it was only late in the 17th century that clocks commonly acquired
minute, as well as hour, hands, and that watches became at all trustworthy.
There is some evidence that a general diffusion of access to time, that is to
say, the spread of clocks and watches into the parlors and pockets of artisans
and workers in England occurred "at the exact moment when the industrial
revolution demanded a greater synchronization of labor" (entering working-class homes back then, I would imagine, just as television did in the US
in the 1950s).

Thompson sees the form of struggle over time changing dramatically
once industrialization has spread.

> The first generation of factory workers were taught by their
> masters the importance of time; the second generation
> formed their short-time committees in the ten-hour move-
> ment; the third generation struck for overtime or time-and-
> a-half. They had accepted the categories of their employers
> and learned to fight back with them. They had learned their
> lesson, that time is money, only too well.

In contrast to the time-discipline of industrial society, Thompson describes the notions of the Nuer, in southern Sudan, who "have no expression equivalent to 'time' in our language," leading Thompson to conclude that therefore they lack a sense of time as a thing that flows or that is capable of being wasted or saved. The unit measures of time for some non-industrial people frequently are some concrete activity that is socially shared: the time for rice to cook or for frying a locust in Madagascar, while in the culture of the Cross River natives, it is the time it takes maize to roast. In the Aran Islands, time's passage is in tandem with the shifting of winds; among the Benan, the measure is when sweat bees come out (two hours before dusk).[1]

Different cultures, obviously, experience time in a variety of ways, and early on in the West, the form and substance that time took emerged as an important battlefield where war could be waged over how society was to be organized and its fruits distributed: workers fighting just to be able to know the time; struggles for control of the movement of the hands of the clocks at workplaces; bitter strikes ranging for years over the accepted length of the workday; furious struggles to keep children from long (or heavy) labor; and measures to ensure that the working class be disciplined from an early age in the proper husbanding of their time. That the lessons went both ways is obvious from phenomenon of 19th-century revolutionaries aiming their guns at clock towers so as "to stop the day." In May, 1968 a clock at the Sorbonne was disabled, rebels writing below it, "Nous y mettrons le temps." (Alternatively translated by Duerr as "we'll take the time off," or "we will decide what time it is.")[2]

iv. THE COMMODIFICATION OF TEMPORALITY: FROM SUN TIME TO ATOMIC TIME

Given this broader framework of time's manifold identities, what can be discerned from the present digitalization? Though time's role in the earlier battles over work and play (see the following chapter, on dance) still occur, the stakes have dramatically been raised, for this remaking of time takes to an unprecedented level our culture's disconnect from the natural order of things. It is not exaggerating to suggest that we are witness to the circle of time being hammered straight — a reshaping that may well be catastrophic, since through its intimate connection with the dance of life, reflected everywhere in the cosmos, the circle of time is sacred. That circle has been at the

---

[1] Besides Thompson, "Time, Work-Discipline," see Wade Davis, *Shadows*, p. 30.
[2] Duerr, *op. cit.*, p. 117. Eric Hobsbawm, (*Primitive Rebels*, p. 167) reports on one revolutionary organization whose subunits were based on temporal divisions such as a week (6 men and a leader, Sunday), a month (4 weeks, July as leader), a season (3 months, led by Spring) and a year (4 seasons).

core of time's deeper meanings since it first emerged as a "concept" however many thousands of years ago that took place.[1]

If nature is to truly be understood mechanically, it arguably becomes crucial that its last remaining circle, the domain of time, finally be flattened out. Whereas the mechanization of the world picture of the 17th-century scientific revolution initiated a new shape for time (based on the mechanical clock as metaphor) it was unable fully to instill a linear hegemony, leaving it to electronic culture to finish the job.

Another profound change to time's meaning, it too masking itself as a minor technical adjustment, devoid of any larger meaning, has also developed in the past few decades. For tens, arguably hundreds of thousands of years the sun in the heavens has defined (along with the moon, etc.) time's passage. Days and years were paced out according to the apparent migrations of the sun across the daytime skies, and elaborate mythologies accounted for the complexities of differing day/night lengths as one moved from summer to fall, winter to spring, or traversed the latitudes. Early on the lengths of shadows cast by upright sticks from the apparently peripatetic sun, source of the Earth's light and heat and life, became time's measure (in league with lunar cycles) in every culture. Though many different ways existed for defining the length of the year, all of them nonetheless measured it according to the motion of the sun.

This is no longer the case, at least in the United States and other Western nations. In the US, the length of the year, as defined by the National Bureau of Standards is determined not by the sun at all, but with a "more accurate" clock based on energy transitions in atoms:

> For the first time in eight years, the earth is running on time, the National Bureau of Standards said yesterday. As a result, the bureau said, "leap seconds" will not be added to the world's atomic clocks to keep them precisely attuned to the earth's orbit around the sun. (1981)

It is the atomic clocks that are now time's true measure.[2]

To be sure, there are arenas and needs for which a sun-based measure of time might well be awkward, if not naively atavistic, even dangerous, say for space exploration by rockets, or for atomic physics. Yet, consider the steep price paid conceptually for this new measure, no matter how much

---

[1] Certainly time was one of the first domains of the natural world to be marked and measured, much sooner than land or weight of crops. It seems obvious that it was one of the first aspects of nature to be conceptualized philosophically — as well, of course, as mythopoetically.

[2] Gary Tauber, "A Clock More Perfect Than Time," *Discover*, vol. 17, no. 12 (Dec., 1996), pp. 68–77.

more "accurate" it is than the older one. Time will now be determined not directly, indeed, not even by a thing (sun or Earth) being counted, but by a *statistical average* of a huge set of events (transitions in the energy levels among trillions of electrons in certain isotopes of cesium atoms) far removed from most human experience and only statistically related to the traditional year, previously defined by the Earth's passage (post Copernicus) around the sun. The transitions of the Cs–133 atoms that the National Bureau of Standards dutifully keeps a measure of are connected neither causally nor logically to the motion of the sun across our skies.

The turning of the year, accordingly, is no longer an event, the return in the sky of the sun to the place it was exactly one year earlier,[1] but an *average of a vast number of individual events* as electrons shift from one energy level to another. However more "precise" or accurate this new measure is, something vital is undoubtedly lost in this change from the sun, which everyone *sees* and *feels*, to imperceptible energetic transitions inside a particular kind of atom as time's official container[2] — which cannot be directly detected by anyone not possessing the proper, expensive, instruments.

The above changes to the circle of time facilitate others, perhaps more prosaic but still shattering shifts in what is meant by temporality. In the first years of the Bay Area Rapid Transit in the San Francisco Bay Area, stations were run — in this Age of Information — without clocks, traditionally, for obvious reasons, a kind of centerpiece in transit stations since the building of the railroads. Instead a digital message board, used to announce where incoming trams were routed to and to run video commercials for banks, insurance companies, career-training schools, and the like, periodically also flashed "the time." Late to work, we would have to watch the screen attentively, if not obsessively, forced to read the advertisements that scrolled by extolling what were, in essence, the corporate sponsors of Time.[3]

At a deeper level, these many "assaults" on time that the previous pages described and the spirit underlying its digitalization amount to a profound attack by the forces in command (whether human, economic, spiritual, or metahistorical or, more likely, a subtle interweaving of them all) on this critical domain of nature, rendering it into a technological artefact, experienced only *through* representations of the measured and recorded data (here, of time, but similarly with space, mass, etc.), and ultimately it is the recording that we are allowed to see and feel. For if time can be reduced to an artefact of our technology, what part of the sensuous cosmos, what overarching concepts could withstand the pressure to follow it?

---

[1] This is one of three ways astronomers define a year.

[2] One wonders how the physicists got the monopoly on time's franchise? I seriously doubt the poets were ever consulted on the changes made.

[3] Currently, no ads on the screens and digital time is occasionally displayed between announcements about the trains.

v. Our Nanosecond Taskmasters

Atomic clocks measure the time in miniscule increments, trillionths of a second, and so do computers; for many of us, living in the first decades of the 21st century, the pace of life and the press on our time is ever more frantic, even terrifying. We watch events unfold, frequently as spectators, often as victims, as if passengers on a long train racing down the tracks out of control, continually accelerating, while we are powerless to do anything about it. The technological innovation of accounting for infinitesimally smaller units of time, I believe, can be directly tied to this experience of the breakneck pace at which our lives feel driven.

To be sure, much of this we experience as a result of Capital's continual attempt to squeeze increasing productivity out of each unit of a worker's time, something going on at least since capitalism learned how to add and subtract. But the crunch of time that we experience today seems almost as if an afterthought, since the real source of the temporal pressure is the result of the competition between different computer technologies over the speed of their computations. At the present time the very best computers can handle about 10^{18} floating point calculations a second, but intense research and development, tied to the continual battle for ever-greater miniaturization, is ongoing to increase that speed.[1] Thus the competition between the US and the Japanese or between IBM and Fujitsu is over the productivity to be squeezed out of less than a quintillionth of a second of computer time!

In the final analysis, human workers have to compete with these machines and allow their work rhythms to be driven by those electronic circuits, a result foreseen by Norbert Weiner, one of the three seminal theoreticians behind modern computer technology, who in the 1940s predicted that, if controlled by the corporations, computers would become slave-like competition for the human workforce, a dire forecast he shared with union leaders.[2]

What a far cry this is from the classic battle between workers and management as recently as the early 1970s, over four decades ago, in Lordstown, Ohio, where management at the Vega plant tried to increase production from slightly more than sixty cars a minute to more than a hundred a minute. The change would give workers only thirty-six seconds in which to perform a number of complex and often strenuous tasks, and a wildcat strike broke out over what the workers saw as an insane pace on the GM assembly line.

[1] It is noteworthy that the computer industry's continual drive for smaller and smaller (hence faster) components and for integrated circuits were the result of the US Air Force's demand for a "self-contained inertial guidance system." Indeed, by 1962 all the integrated circuits produced in the US were bought by the DoD. Schlosser, *op. cit.*, p. 224.

[2] Heims, *op. cit.*, p. 342.

They chose to take their stand and the longlasting strike was closely studied and seen as exemplary by both labor and management for many years.

Now, in contrast, it is a millionth-trillionth of a second where the war is waged!

That the significant fight for productivity is over the speed with which *machines* can work is fraught with alarming consequences for we humans who must work in tandem with them; we cannot help but be caught up in their frantic "inhuman" pace — if for no other reason than that the work we do will now be continually assessed by management, who asks whether it might not be done more "efficiently" using computer technology.[1] Douglas Rushkoff reported in 2011 that "[f]or the first time regular people are beginning to show the signs of stress and mental fatigue once exclusive to air-traffic controllers and 911 operators."[2] Hence the sense in recent times of onrushing, adrenalin-fueled frenzy, the runaway train mentioned earlier, the convulsive nature of these times, nearly everywhere a battlefield or potential battlefield, the mass migrations, job losses and marginalizations of more and more of us and for so many of our youth, descents into permanent joblessness, the shattered families, famines, and disasters falling from the sky like particulate matter from the smokestacks of Progress — and perhaps Chicken Little was onto something after all. Thus, too, an important reason for the widespread fears regarding a looming apocalypse, with numerous scenarios adopted by ecologists, Christian fundamentalists, New Agers, survivalists, and the rest of us, too confused to fit into any (one) camp, but alarmed nonetheless.

vi. HI-TECH'S MAKE-OVER OF REALITY

To summarize, digitalization of clocks' reporting of time is part of a broad array of transformations of how time is perceived and understood. Besides the new alphanumeric displays, official time is no longer something people experience directly, as before, through the warmth of the sun against our faces, our bodies drinking it in, for now time's measure is by means of a statistical average of a certain energy shift in atoms, which we cannot experience. We must trust the experts who will "experience" it and duly report to us. Meanwhile the size of our temporal units are being sliced, thanks to computerization, into ever-finer increments, now in the quintillionths of a second. Finally, in using these new timepieces, we no longer are active interrogators of our measuring instruments, our needs dictating the degree of approximation appropriate to report, accepting, rather, what the makers of

---

1 The question of efficiency, as we shall learn in Chapter Nineteen, is by no means a straightforward one.
2 Douglas Rushkoff, *Program or Be Programmed: Ten Commands for a Digital Age* (Berkeley: Soft Skull Press, 2011), p. 36.

the gadgets have chosen. Rather than our measuring devices being extensions *of us*, in effect we are becoming extensions *of them*.

As if to divert our attention from these deeper truths about time, the new technology brandishes the illusion that it is we who now finally control time, with our VCRs, TIVOs, DVRs, asynchronous chats and conference calls, and fast-forwards.[1]

Are these fundamental transformations in the measure, experience, meanings, and size of "time" simply the accidental by-products of aerospace and the military (where electronic technology began, and the font at which it so hugely was subsidized), or are we witnessing more fundamental changes taking place?

What follows is, of course, a mere sketch — difficult to adequately describe, let alone analyze, a cultural explosion in the moments after detonation. We are only a few decades into this particular historical convulsion. Yet, deeper patterns underlay these transformations to time that at least in broad outline can be described. Once more, as in Part Two, where we wanted to understand the 17th-century transformations of the meaning of concepts such as matter, space, time, change, etc., we should look at the movement of Capital as a guide. We saw that the emergence of capitalism in 16th- and 17th-century England, especially in mining, cloth manufacturing, and extensive deforestation, necessitated a new relationship of society to nature. Out of this was born the mechanical philosophy, with its belief in a world composed of brute, senseless, dead matter. In essence matter was redefined, so as to make impossible an earlier sense of the sacred immanent in the natural world, which, in the name of profits and Progress, had become a troublesome impediment to 17th- and 18th-century assaults on forests, streams, commons, and fens.

A similar process is underway to weave the new garment that time is now being cloaked in. There are new social realities that are either emerging or are being planned that require the divorce of time from the circle of birth and death, till now the events giving time its poignant and devastating power. Traditionally it has been *through time* that we have learned the great mysteries of life and death and *in time* that we experienced the unfolding patterns of our lives. These essentially sacred lessons, we shall see, have become embarrassing barricades holding back Progress in the last half of the 20th and the beginning of the 21st centuries, to be torn down once and for all, unnecessary romantic illusions (those in power appear to believe), leftovers from our former rural past.

These new social realities that are threatened by traditional notions of time are the product of the new technologies, of course, particularly those of "hi-tech," which have created new modes of production and a vast expansion of the domain where capitalism can impose its overpowering logic. Thus, as Rushkoff points out, hi-tech "is biased against time altogether."

---

[1] *Ibid.*, pp. 33–34.

George Dyson concurs that in the digital universe, "time as we know it does not exist."[1] In particular, the new field of bioengineering, based on the presumptions of Capital that the creation and destruction of new or old life-forms are a proper field for its operations and imperatives, is central to opening up the interiority of life to "the rules of the market."

Biotech won its critical conceptual and legal beachhead when the US Supreme Court ruled in 1980 that new forms of "life" created by genetic engineering may be patented! Eventually, it became legally possible to patent parts of already-existing species, simply by being the first to decode a particular part of its DNA in terms of its molecular sequencing. In such a manner, folk medicines used for thousands of years to heal a variety of ills have become the focus of "biopiracy," seeking to expropriate for profit traditional knowledge and practice in non-Western countries (this example is from India, the Neem tree), one of the newest forms of colonialism and of (information super-) highway robbery from a vast new expansion of the privatization of our knowledge commons. This makes explicit the social might wielded by scientific institutions in supplanting widely-shared cultural knowledge gleaned from millennia of peoples' experiences.[2]

Biotechnology should not be understood as an *extension* of earlier processes, particularly beginning in the early decades of the last century, whereby herbicidal and insecticidal assaults on numerous insects, "weeds," fungi and other species (some because they eat cash crops, others simply for being in the way in the eyes of the market) were carried out. Rather, as we shall see, biotech represents an *inversion*, its opposite. Offshoots of the nerve gases developed in the years leading up to World War II, such poisons began to be used systematically in agriculture as it was being transformed in the 1920s and after into agribusiness. Agribusiness declared war on many species, seeking *to eradicate* them in a kind of chemical final solution. Now, with biotech in control, the goal is *to create* brand-spanking new species.[3]

As a result of chemical-based agribusiness, monoculture and the progressive loss of topsoil worldwide have become the main crop. Increasing monopolization has led to a devastating decrease in seed variety across the globe, an alarming loss of genetic diversity, even as we realize how essential that diversity is to the continued health of farming.

Marxism & Witchcraft will suggest that this new social reality includes increasingly denatured lives that an ever-more urban world population must

---

[1] *Ibid.*, p. 28. George Dyson, *Turing's Cathedral: The Origins of the Digital Universe* (New York: Vintage Books, 2012), p. 301.

[2] There is a brief discussion of the patenting of the Neem by the Critical Art Ensemble in *The Molecular Invasion* (Brooklyn: Autonomedia, 2002), pp. 54–55.

[3] According to David Weir, less than 1% of the more than 1,250,000 species of insects, are harmful to crops. *The Bhopal Syndrome: Pesticides, Environment, and Health* (San Francisco: Sierra Books, 1987), p. 22.

now endure, nights illuminated more by the strobified flashes of emergency vehicles and digitalized screens beaming out news clips in bars, post offices, coffee shops, etc., than by moon and stars. Meanwhile, in response to the ever-finer slices of time, ever-more sufferers are driven to unprecedented levels of anxiety, record numbers on antidepressants and/or anti-anxiety meds at ever younger ages,[1] while meth labs spread across the land, and as our spirits falter or break trying to keep pace with the always-smaller pieces of time that our machines flaunt at us.

Most significantly and terrifyingly, these new social realities are the toxic spew of modern technology and the horrific waste areas being created by design or accident at the Love Canals, Time Beaches, Sevesos (Italy), Three Mile Islands, Gulf of Mexico, and Fukushimas (the list grows by the year) — cesspools of modern chemical and radiation industries, joined in recent decades by the industries of the Information Age, many of them now "zones of infertility," as I named them in Part One. As I shall argue at greater length in Chapter 34, a great many of the practices that are creating these zones of infertility and the arrogance that allows them to be created, date from not that long ago — a clue, perhaps, of how we might yet escape their deadly grip. We were able to get a glimpse of the actual planning of one such zone when a few decades ago the US National Academy of Science, the official government body for science, recommended that the US Southwest should be declared a "national sacrifice area" in order to ensure US energy and mineral self-reliance, thus sanctioning wholesale development of coal, uranium, and other mineral ores at the preposterous expense of that breathtaking terrain (among other treasures, including the Grand Canyon!) and the flora, fauna, including human, and other lifeforms living there.

The new social reality has a new priesthood, industrial society's guardians of the once-sacred gates between life and death; called "risk-assessment engineers," their job being to determine how many predicted deaths, maimings, cases of cancer, widows or orphans, or de-speciations are acceptable prices for this piece or that of Progress.

In the pages that follow, I will try to demonstrate a deep connection between the replacement of circular time by digital time and these new developments in production processes and in the need of Capital to extend its domains. The flattening of the "circle of time" at the present will be revealed, like the mechanical philosophy of the 17th century, as serving as an assault on traditional beliefs in order to exert greater power over nature, indeed, over all of our many commons.

---

[1] Given how such meds frequently affect users, this constitutes an astounding accomplishment, something previous rulers could only dream of: masses of their subjects/citizens *voluntarily* acting to control and suppress their sexuality.

These new forms of time help mask deeper patterns, a divorce of time from the cycle of life and death that till now has constituted the way humans, indeed, arguably, all living things, *experienced* time, a change related to certain high hopes riding on bioengineering.

In sum, time as a fundamental cognitive, experiential, emotional, and spiritual wellspring in our various cultures is being so thoroughly transmuted that we can truly conclude that time as a concept is being hollowed out.

vii. RHYTHMIC METHODS

The new social realities, most of them, based on new forms of technology, all demand that the circle of time be finally rendered flat. In the following chapters, I shall investigate in more detail the social, intellectual, political, and moral implications of these new social realities. For now, however, a more practical question may confront many of my readers. Am I proposing that everyone destroy his or her digital watch? I would not presume to make such decisions for others, though I would never wear one of those ugly instruments; and when, on occasion, I need to glance at one, it is with a certain measure of distaste. One thing, however, is that I would think it advisable that people should at least remove any such timepieces before masturbating.

Fundamentally, sex is a matter of rhythm, or of a medley of rhythms — and is not time the cultural container that holds *all* rhythms? Time measures out and contains, time carries within its currents, the life energy that manifests in the coupling (or tripling...) of our and most of the rest of the species that cavort sexually, partly for procreation, and partly for recreation. We can all too easily imagine how our present, fundamental remaking of time will inevitably affect *those* rhythms, and so be one more way our sexuality is undermined, another essential aspect of our being which must be tamed as a necessary part of the present assaults on life. And what part of living is so essentially unruly and so a threat to those who want to control the rest of us, if not our sexuality?

This shackling of our sexuality, we will see in the following chapters, is part of a more general assault on our bodies that has been part of Capital's agenda for quite some time.

18

Dances of Diminished Desires

In a world without Dionysus/Pan/Bacchus/Sabazios, nature would be dead, joy would be postponed to an afterlife, and the forests would no longer ring with the sound of pipes and flutes. — Barbara Ehrenreich, *Dancing in the Streets: A History of Collective Joy* (2006)

[L]ooking once more quite closely at history both East and West, some of us noticed the similarities in certain small but influential heretical and esoteric movements. These schools of thought and practice were usually suppressed, or diluted and made harmless, in whatever society they appeared. Peasant witchcraft in Europe, Tantrism in Bengal, Quakers in England, Tachikawa-ryu in Japan, Ch'an in China. These are all outcroppings of the Great Subculture which runs underground all through history. This is the tradition that runs without break from Paleo-Siberian Shamanism and Magdalenian cave-painting, through megaliths and Mysteries, astronomers, ritualists, alchemists and Albigensians; gnostics and vagrants, right down to Golden Gate Park [in 1967]....

It has taught that man's natural being is to be trusted and followed; that we need not look to a model or rule imposed from outside in searching for the center; and that in following the grain, one is being truly "moral." It has recognized that for one to "follow the grain" it is necessary to look exhaustively into the negative and demonic potentials of the Unconscious, and by recognizing these powers — symbolically acting them out — one releases himself from these forces. By this profound exorcism and ritual drama, the Great Subculture destroys the one credible claim of Church and State to a necessary function.

All this is subversive to civilization: for civilization is built on hierarchy and specialization. A ruling class, to survive, must propose a Law: a law to work must have a hook into the social psyche — and the most effective way to achieve this is to make people doubt their natural worth and instincts, especially sexual. To make "human nature" suspect is also to make Nature — the wilderness — the adversary. Hence the ecological crisis of today. — Gary Snyder, *Earth House Hold: Technical Notes & Queries To Fellow Dharma Revolutionaries* (1967)

Especially repellent to Europeans were the rituals of indigenous people, since these almost invariably featured dancing, singing, masking, and even the achievement of trance states. In large parts of Africa, for example, the identification between communal dance and music, on the one hand, and what Europeans might call "religion" on the other, was profound....

The anthropologist Jean Comaroff noted that of all the "native" customs and traditions in southern Africa, "collective song and dance were especially offensive to Christians."...Europeans tended to view such activities, wherever they found them, as "outbreaks of devil worship, lasciviousness, or, from a more 'scientific' perspective, hysteria." — Barbara Ehrenreich, *op. cit.*

On no account will Negroid excesses in tempo (so-called hot jazz) or in solo performances (so-called breaks) be tolerated; so-called jazz compositions may contain at most 10 percent syncopation; the remainder must consist of a natural legato movement devoid of the hysterical rhythmic reverses characteristic of the music of the barbarian races and conductive to dark instincts alien to the German people (so-called riffs). — Nazi strictures regarding music, quoted in Barbara Ehrenreich, *op. cit.*

i. WHO GOT RHYTHM?

Profound changes in worldview do not stay locked up in the tower of the mind. Willy-nilly they come down into the body and are expressed somatically, artistically. Let us see what this looks like by taking a cursory look at music and dance in the transition to modern times, a period which saw the adoption of the mechanical philosophy by the leading scientists. Consider, first, the music characteristic of non-industrialized people, which is driven and embodied in and by its rhythm instruments, indeed, often half a dozen or more drummers and a like number of other rhythm instruments playing at the same time as but one or two melodic instruments, perhaps a horn or reed, picking out a tune; the song, in effect, is buoyed up on and carried along by currents of the numerous rhythms.

Compare that with the music that began to dominate European higher culture with the coming of capitalism and industrialization from the 18th century on, the classical orchestra where one drum, tympani or kettle, sits all alone in a crowd of sometimes nearly a hundred musicians, the drums only occasionally brought in to play as accents (as in that epitome of this era's music, Beethoven's 9th [Choral] Symphony). This is so different as to be properly called an *inversion* of earlier musical traditions. In fact actually dictating the rhythm in orchestral settings has been transferred to a *conductor*, typically a man in a tuxedo and on a raised platform, and who plays no instrument but who orchestrates the instrumental comings and goings. Like the owner/foreman of the mills and mines and other industries in early modern times, the 18th-century conductor would set the pace and allot rewards (cash, bows).

Another, related transformation in most Western music that sets it apart from other societies is how one *becomes* a musician. In most cultures children, experiencing music at home or at festivals, swaying to its rhythms and captivated by its tonalities, in that way learn what is generally agreed is the "universal language" of music. In the West, in contrast, one must first be taught how to *read* music,[1] become literate in its keys, its time signatures, its rules of harmony, making one's way around the arcana of diminished thirds and augmented fifths. Only then is one allowed on stage.

Whereas in other cultures, learning music is like learning to *speak*, in the West it is more like learning to *read*, thereby requiring a teacher and making it more of a cerebral act.

Not that Western classical music, divorced as it is from primordial rhythms, is thereby entirely removed from the sexuality associated with them, simply that for a long time the only kind of dance — and it is dance where music plays out its inherent seductions — that was allowed in the concert hall was ballet, where despite its flagrant sexuality of both costume and touch, for a complex set of reasons (not the least of which is the dominant culture's homophobia), the "dangers" of intimate touch have been rendered not only sexually androgynous but (see below) literally in bondage.[2]

---

[1] Mara Sonya Kubrin, "The Origins of Language: The Multilanguage Theory," Spring, 2009, Seminar on Psycholinguistics, Columbia University.

[2] At about six years of age I saw my first ballet, shocked at how the dancers were clothed so that buttocks, breasts, and genitals were accentuated, and how they touched! But I felt guilty that I had seen this, and convinced myself that it was really only culture. I thus "matured."

DAVID KUBRIN

ii. LEAVING THE GROUND BEHIND

The process of how and why music as a whole had to be tamed in Europe in the period leading up to Mozart was described in some detail in Part Two, for more than any other human art, music had to be divorced from the states of rapture it traditionally had so readily induced and that were now seen as encouraging social, religious, sexual, and political enthusiasm. And so in the late-17th century, at the height of social turmoil, new harmonic rules were adopted that "tempered" the scale, making it possible for instruments to meld together their distinctive voices, but at the price of significantly undermining certain forms of harmony that had been based on pure tonality. To enable the different instruments to play the same composition, a modular octave, related to mechanism — indeed, much of this invented by Mersenne, the high priest of mechanism — was made the basic unit of harmony, with quantitative rules governing the selection of fundamental tones. Quantitative rules now informed musical technique and established norms for harmony.

The least purely contemplative and most embodied aspect of music, dance, provides a window through which we can see the temper of the times clearly. Looking at dance we may observe how the themes of Part Two continue to play out in the 18th and 19th centuries in Europe, particularly in the case of formal dance, ballet, for dance reflects physically the historical tensions of a society. As early as the 17th century, but finally realized only by the Romantic ballet in 1832, formal dance became obsessed with the desire to "take flight," leaving the ground (and hence, nature) behind. This mania for flight gathered force just as dance as an art form separated itself from the earlier traditions, wherein dancing occurred in a social setting, by the aristocracy or by the peasants, or, on occasion, both in the same place, people dancing mostly for pleasure.[1]

Renaissance dance *had* no leaps or jumps; its orientation was towards the ground or floor. For the aristocracy, heavy, bulky elaborate dance costumes were material barriers to flights off the ground. *Court* social dancing, with its elaborate codes of dress, etiquette, appearance, and so on, precluded spontaneous actions, as well as any real enjoyment of boundless movement. Self-control was used to squelch spontaneity, while cool restraint and elegance walked arm-in-arm with a measured tempo. At the same time, *peasant* social dancing, as depicted graphically by Breugel, was a rowdy affair.

> People jumped, juggled, shook, laughed, and tumbled. The feeling of vitality and movement in these works is unmistakable.

---

[1] My discussion of the development of formal dance here is based on Leonard Pitt's "The History of Flight," *Somatics Magazine: Journal of the Mind/Body Arts & Sciences*, vol.VII, no. 1 Autumn/Winter, 1988–89, pp. 24–35.

Cultural influences in social dancing during the Renaissance sometimes passed from the court to the peasants, who on occasion adopted styles of aristocratic dance to add a touch of elegance to their own. At the same time, nobles frequently copied

> the spontaneity and imagination of the peasants by taking their dances and dressing them up in order to make them acceptable to the courtiers. The minuet, originally a peasant dance, was picked up by the court in the early 1700s and cleansed of its "primitiveness."

And "primitiveness," we should realize, if not actually enthusiasm, must have been a very close cousin.

When formal "dance masters" first emerged in 15th-century Italy, a process of codification and dance choreography began. The writing down of dances developed. Separating dance from nature began with a vengeance during this period. For one thing, the beginning of "professionalism" in dance brought about a condemnation of peasant dancing; perhaps inevitably the two-way exchange between dancing styles, court and peasant, faded. One mid-15th-century Italian dancing master praised the dance of the nobility, while describing popular dance as vicious and artless, since it emerged from the

> common people who frequently, with corrupt spirits and depraved minds, turn it from a liberal art and virtuous science, into a vile and adulterous affair.

Once more, our practiced ears should hear the silent pejorative, "enthusiasm," behind a sentence like that, and a fear of sensuality. "Artifice" replaced the "natural" for men and women, directly expressed through a naked contempt for the body. Court dancing focused not on what the dancer *felt*, but on how he or she *appeared* to others.

It would be a mistake, however, simply to counterpose pre-modern times with what came after as the natural *vs.* mere artifice, as if it were that simple. By no means were the cultures and mores of the Renaissance or of classic Rome or Greece — or even of Neolithic society — simply "natural," for layers of assumptions and understandings were built into the actions, ceremonies, and stories, even in what we naively assume to be "simple" tribal peoples. So it is not a question, really, of earlier representations being more natural, at least not in the first telling, but rather that after the onset of modern times in the West all artifice, and virtually all of culture, bent toward an increasingly narrowly-defined end — to wit, the subjugation of the Earth and of all the creatures dwelling in the manifold of its innumerable niches.

To the end of that subjugation all else was subordinated, as to a single task, though so entwined was that one task with the whole that we can find reverberations of its imperatives pretty much everywhere we look. And since that task was the fettering of nature, the new artifices, those created in early modern times and thereafter, are cast in the mold of anti-nature. So though there are exceptions, they are progressively fewer and weaker, and more and more do we find artifice in general consciously and proudly dressing itself in the garb of something tamed.

From Italy, classical dance moved to France. In the space of the three decades ending in 1610, as many as 800 ballets were presented in France! Under Louis XIV, himself an accomplished dancer, ballet flourished, and found a base in the Dance Academy that Louis created. The Academy took over a performance space at the Palais Royale and, for the first time, because of its architectural layout, European ballet was able to take to the sky, emerging as "la danse verticale," seemingly in defiance of gravity.

It is not without irony that just as Newton was undertaking the "enthronement" of gravity as the first, basic, "force" in nature, dance was trying to transcend it. To defy nature in this and other ways, dancers focused their training on developing *self-control.*

> {To] dance elegantly, to walk gracefully, and to carry one-self nobly, it is imperative to reverse the order of things and force the limbs, by means of an exercise both long and painful, to take a totally different position from that which is natural to them.[1]

Thus claimed one dance master. By basing their craft on such an obvious divorce from nature, dance masters were, of course, simply playing their particular role in the general campaign to disconnect and distance people from the natural world, a necessity, as we saw in Part Two, if they were to make their peace with the wholesale assaults on the woods and glades, mountains and valleys, that occurred worldwide as European civilization began to dominate the globe. Pitt observes,

> The ballet body of the [Dance] Academy was the somatic expression of the emerging mechanistic world view. The dance's flight from corporeality and the cultural need to gain distance from nature were two aspects of the same historical trend.

---

[1] Georges Noverre, 1759, dance ideologue and theoretician, quoted in Pitt, *Ibid* Today, one of the obvious signs of a person's class is how s/he moves..

Indeed, after discussing parallel transformations (similarly in defiance of nature and the health of the body) new to 17th-century birthing practices, such as the increasing use of stirrup-bound supine birth positions and the utilization of forceps to drag babies *up* from the mother, *against* gravity, Pitt summarizes, "The age of Reason may have been a flowering for the European mind, but it was the beginning of the 'dark ages' for the body."

iii. PAS DE DEUX IN THE SMOKE-FILLED SKIES

In *La Sylphide* (1812), ballet literally was finally able to "take off" and to offer the illusion of flight on the part of the sylph, the conclusion of a 150-year-long artistic process, through the use of gliding leaps. Pitt brilliantly shows how the Romantic ballet of the 19th century reflected the bitter disappointment when the promise of betterment seemingly offered by the Industrial Revolution had proved to be an illusion, for Progress only ushered even *more* people off the land and into dark cities that were dominated by their huge smokestacks. In some cities the skies were thick with smoke, stench filled the air, and grime was everywhere. The underlying process of forced urbanization to create a work- (and non-work-) force, which we described in Part Two, had become more of a threat to the countryside by the 1830s, especially in England and France, and by the end of the first half of the 19th century, a huge rural depopulation had occurred. Again, as in the 16th and 17th centuries, the workers and would-be workers found in their new homes, the cities, only despair, this time based on

> crowded tenements, rampant disease, and an unrelenting
> rhythm that told them when to eat, sleep, work, and rest.

It was one more assault on the peoples' connectivity to nature, another brick in the wall. In England Thomas Carlyle wrote of his despair in 1829 as he faced this world

> all void of life, of Purpose, of Volition, even of Hostility...
> one huge, dead, unmeasurable, Steam-engine, rolling on, in
> its dead indifference to grind me limb from limb.

His words reflect the real deadening effect of teaching successive generations, through school, sermon, and popular literature and song, about the mechanical philosophy and the senseless motion of the underlying particles that constitute the real world.

Elsewhere Carlyle commented that "We war with rude nature, and by our resistless engines, come off always victorious and loaded with goods." Yet the protest *against* this *in dance,* by means of the Romantic ballet, offered only a too-brief glimpse of nature undefiled, itself based on toe dancing and other frequently painful contortions that amounted to an "abdication of the flesh." Thus even the protest against mechanism is premised on the impossibility of a real connection with nature. At the heart of the Romantic resistance, that is, the somatic self was redirected *away from* a natural being and sought not a true alternative, only its negation.

In contrast to Balinese, Japanese, and African cultures, where dancers' consciousnesses reside in low centers of gravity — in the lower body, an orientation that holds true for non-industrial cultures as a rule — the "danse verticale" of high European culture had acquired an other-worldly orientation. The shattering of consciousness attendant upon the West's declaration of war against nature, as Pitt makes clear, thus was clearly articulated in dance. Just as the decades following Newton witnessed the refashioning of written and spoken language, religion, philosophy, psychology, ethics, politics, education, and so on, all of which remade themselves in the image of the new science of inertia and motion, so too did formal dance (despite its attempt to escape gravity), where music was most embodied.

One result of all this is the strange spectacle provided by modern audiences of classical music, where, hearing performances of compositions often acclaimed as "moving," listeners sit virtually frozen into utter immobility, as they witness the most exalted creations of a Mozart, Beethoven, or St.-Saëns. Though the musicians can move somewhat freely, it is only as directed by the conductor. Members of the audience, on the other hand, almost never move; except when checking their program notes, until permitted finally to applaud. Here music has been dissociated from all movement, becoming, in effect, largely cerebral.

iv. POSTSCRIPTS, 1999/2011

Alas, perhaps the beat does not necessarily go on, for my discussion earlier about the primacy of rhythm in the indigenous music of nonindustrial cultures and the rhythm-deprived music of more thoroughly-industrialized societies was first written nearly three decades ago, and though already the drum machine had made its entrance, I was too distant from the musical domains where it pounded out its mechanical handclaps or more complex beats to take proper notice of it. When I finally a decade or more later (1999) incorporated rap or other drum machine-dominated genres into my analysis, in this work, it was mostly to denigrate them. Thus:

> Mechanical drumming crosses a critical line, I believe, or rather with the machines in charge of the rhythm, the line between vitality and non-vitality, between worship of life in its various forms, which dance and music at their heart

are, and worship of the machine, of anti-life, has been decisively blurred. Put still another way: in music we find a
complex and always shifting dialectic between the forces of
abandonment and freedom, on the one hand, and those of
structure and control, on the other, and once we have
passed over to the domain of mechanical "rhythm," there is
an unqualified victory for the "structure and control" pole.
Riding mechanical rhythms, dance can only go so far. Much
of the dance, in fact, is robotic. There are inevitable, if frequently hidden, limits. Not so dance based on people-cre-
ated beats, because, in principle, anything is possible.

And yet... in the past decade and more, in part, of course, under the prod-
ding of Rael, my then-teenage son, I listened to newer forms of hip-hop and
to the poetic voices of Bay Area youth, and I have repeatedly been astounded
by the intricate rhythmic play created by human voice, breath, instruments
and machines, beats laid side by side and layered and counterposed so imag-
inatively that I wept with sheer joy, my head and shoulders weaving here and
there, that I came belatedly to see that the dialectic I had so pessimistically
described in 1999 was, indeed, a dynamic one, and that the lifeforce that
drives on the best music cannot long be ignored or be minimized.[1]

v. ALTERNATIVES TO NATURE

Nineteenth century formal dance was based on the denial of the body, on
a repudiation of nature, dance consciously fulfilling the somatic mandate of
the mechanical philosophy by reducing the human body to an artefact —admittedly, in ballet, an exquisitely graceful artefact — in that sense, machinelike;

[1] Though my text recants the dire fears expressed in my 1999 fulminations,
the fears were not all that wrong-headed. Recent research has demonstrated
the emotional sterility associated with unvarying rhythms. A number of investigations have shown listeners (musicians and non-musicians alike) to be
less responsive to music that lacks the "subtle changes" in timing and tonality
good musicians (often instinctually) bring to their playing. Roxanne Cash
reported watching her son as he "was listening to stuff that was heavily auto-
tuned, with drum machines. It's got all feeling bred out of it...." Emotion in
music depends on human shading and imperfections, "bending notes in a
certain way," Ms. Cash said, "holding a note a little longer." Slight variations
in timing are "crucial" many musicians believe. "When everything is perfectly in time, the ear or mind tends to ignore it, much like a clock ticking in
your bedroom — after a while you don't hear it." (Pam Bulluck, "To Tug At
the Heart, Music First Must Tickle the Neurons," *New York Times: Science
Times* [April 19, 2011]).

as with 20th-century digital timekeeping, breaking the circle of time by constraining time's wanderings to the main highway of Western conceptions of linear, Progressive, history, going always from lesser to greater, rather than round and round, in its repudiation of the principles of living matter. Yet digitalization of time is also emblematic of something else, a larger, later systemic toxicity of 20th-century high technology.

We shall later examine in detail those toxic connections, using the preceding discussions of digitalization as an introduction to those broader questions of hi-tech and its relation to our present crisis. However, first, two prior discussions are in order — the first a closer look at the hi-tech world we now inhabit to see how it works, or — in quite alarming ways — does not. Following that, before discussing "toxicity" in its social or intellectual sense, we will examine a deeper chemical toxicity at the core of hi-tech.

19

What Do You Mean, They Don't Really Work?

The computer has thus begun to be an instrument for the destruction of history. For when society legitimates only those "data" that are "in one standard format" and that "can easily be told to the machine," then history, memory itself, is annihilated....

In the recent American war against Viet Nam, computers operated by officers who had not the slightest idea of what went on inside their machines effectively chose which hamlets were to be bombed and what zones had a sufficient density of VietCong to be "legitimately" declared free-fire zones.... Of course, only "machine readable" data, that is, largely targeting information coming from other computers, could enter these machines. And when the American President [Nixon] decided to bomb Cambodia and to keep that decision secret from the American Congress, the computers in the Pentagon were "fixed" to transform the genuine strike reports coming in from the field into the false reports to which government leaders were given access. George Orwell's Ministry of Truth had become mechanized. History was not merely destroyed, it was recreated. And the high government leaders who felt themselves privileged to be allowed to read the secret reports that actually emerged from the Pentagon's computers of course believed them. After all, the computer itself had spoken. They did not realize that they had become their computers' "slaves," to use Admiral Moorer's own word.... — Joseph Weizenbaum, *Computer Power and Human Reason: From Judgment to Calculation* (1976)

[T]he technologies that did emerge [since the 1950s] proved most conducive to surveillance, work discipline, and social control. Computers have opened up certain spaces of freedom, as we're constantly reminded, but instead of leading to the workless utopia Abbie Hoffman imagined, they have been employed in such a way as to produce the opposite effect. They have enabled a financialization of capital that has driven workers desperately into debt, and, at the same time, provided the means by which employers have created "flexible" work regimes that have both destroyed traditional job security and increased working hours for almost everyone. — David Graeber, "Of Flying Cars and the Declining Rate of Profit," *Baffler* no. 19 (2012)

Now or next year, sooner or later, by design, by hack, or by onslaught of complexity, it doesn't matter. One day someone will install ten new lines of assembler code, and it will all come down. — Ellen Ullman, *Close to the Machine: Technophilia and Its Discontents* (1997)

i. Some Naked Truths About Hi-Tech

Many and mighty are the questions raised by what has been called the "computer revolution," but I should clarify one matter early on, for though it might not be (compared, say, to the devastating ecological consequences of computer technology)[1] the most important thing to say about computerization, it situates all other things in a rather more intriguing context: in a fundamentally critical sense, *computers really do not work!*

Now, of course, on the face of it, that is a preposterous thing to say, for quite obviously, computers *do* work. My friends regale me with endless stories of things they can do that would be unthinkable without their "smart" phones or laptops. By some measures, the new computer technologies are quite competent, utterly impressive in their scope and depth, their ability to stitch together disparate realms of experience into a hodge-podge of a whole, the wide range of visual or aural or other effects available at the touch of a finger, the data easily accessed.

More significantly, for leftists the Internet has proved itself vital for things like WikiLeaks' release of texts and images showing, for example, the murder of unarmed civilians in Iraq by a US helicopter, and as tools used adroitly by the Zapatistas to stimulate dialogue with revolutionaries throughout the world.

Yet, critically, computers do *not* work the way it is claimed for them and they do *not* work the way they must in order to justify the pervasive and ever-widening role over essential matters they are being assigned by the institutions that rule our lives. There are, for example, many things computers simply cannot do that they pretend to do, functions society and programmers are increasingly mandating them to perform. The consequences of this profound mismatch between the critical jobs this technology is made to do and the fact that it is manifestly unsuitable for many of these tasks is on display in the utter

---

[1] About which, see Chapter 21.

dysfunctionality of so many of our essential institutions and the looming possibility of small glitches escalating into devastating collapses of vital services.

The increasing takeover of information-processing machines of a vast array of responsibilities from payroll to corporate planning and military war plans and healthcare and financial transactions and scheduling and inventory…. that virtually every major institution and many of the most fundamental processes of our society have been totally given into the keeping of computer technology can not be a compelling argument for the efficiency, let alone the functionality, of computers, given the sense of ongoing crisis that so many of these institutions and processes are experiencing.

In order to answer such questions about whether this new kind of machinery works or not, let us closely examine the two areas for which computers were *specifically* developed: the military and the business world.

ii. THE PERFECT SOLDIERS

One might think that its role in the military would be an obvious place where the effectiveness of information-processing technology can be easily demonstrated, but that is not the case. It was for military purposes, of course, that computing technology was conceived and developed in the aftermath of World War II, in response to enormous calculating demands for code-breaking, for predicting ballistics for artillery, and for designing the first thermonuclear bombs. It has been the Pentagon bankrolling the new technology from the git-go, deciding what gets made and taking control of the bridges of the digital Niñas, Pintas, and Santa Marias as they (with most of us in the hold) sail off to the New Worlds of cyberspace.

Perhaps the greatest success of much of this technology is singing its own praises, its gee-whiz stories of deering-do, where news, advertising, and marketing has, breathlessly, become as one. This was on full display during the Gulf War in 1991 and even more in Iraq and Afghanistan, in part due to a kind of electronic cheerleading carried on the backs of the "smart bombs." Significantly in the months and weeks leading to the first Gulf War, millions of Americans took to the street in protest of the coming war.[1] The media campaign about the wizardry of the US's weaponry, on their way to make their "surgical strikes," played a major role in pushing that opposition back into their living-room recliners to watch on TV just how nimble and clever this new weaponry was, humanely deployed so as to minimize any "collateral

---

[1] At one such demonstration in San Francisco months before the formal war began, my lover, Roz, asked plaintively, "Didn't we just do this?" in reference to the anti-war protests we had both been involved in with regard to Vietnam, Chile, El Salvador, Nicaragua, etc. over the previous decades; after conferring with our comrade, Starhawk, nearby, Roz returned and said, "Star says it's like doing dishes, you gotta keep on doing 'em."

damage," that loathsome, coy euphemism (also deployed for the first time in 1991). In many bars across the US, crowds cheered as they watched Patriot missiles on their way to "intercepting" incoming SCUD missiles, as if viewing their usual Sunday football games. For men, especially, the spectacle of the new weapons working so *efficiently* seems to have been particularly persuasive, changing the minds of a number of those who had previously marched to oppose the war.

Yet, an analysis by Theodore Postol, a physicist who was once a science advisor to the Pentagon, concluded that the Patriot missile. was an "almost total failure [in its] intercept[ion of] quite primitive attacking missiles." TV screens, indeed, did show incoming SCUDs disintegrating and US or Israeli-fired Patriots exploding, leading viewers to think that the former was caused by the latter.

According to Postol, the SCUDs actually tended to fall apart as they neared the ground, "fragmenting into many pieces and making their interdiction extremely difficult." Close examination of videotapes supposedly showing Patriots bringing down SCUDs "shows SCUD warheads streaking by unscathed." Levels of ground damage, Postal claims, support the conclusion that the Patriot attacks were unsuccessful. (Raytheon Corp., maker of the Patriot, has denied these charges, fearing for the billions of dollars in postwar orders for their missile that might be threatened.)

In the months following the Gulf War, we slowly found out how many of the claims about smart weapons in the early days of the war were primarily the product of a very successful PR campaign by the Pentagon and the war-making industries, their attempt, post-Vietnam, to fully control all media portrayals of their war-making, including its new practice of embedding approved reporters under tight controls of what they could see, show, and write in the Pentagon's battle against anti-war sentiments. The actual war was quite different from this antiseptic image conveyed by those "smart" weapons. Civilian casualties in Iraq were substantial, and predictable given the strategy followed by the US forces and their allies. The bulk of the bombs and shells used was not of the "smart" variety touted as minimizing civilian deaths, maimings, and injuries, and where it was necessary to admit to those, they were disarmingly referred to as "collateral damage," in the Pentagon's new depths of Orwellian language. As in all wars, most ordnance was fired and landed blindly. The US shooting that actually hit and killed allied troops, the so-called "friendly fire," was frequently from *automated* weaponry, which are rather prone to mistaken attacks, as in the shooting down of the Iranian airliner carrying hundreds of civilians by the USS Vincenne's missile defense system in 1988.[1]

---

1 San Francisco *Chronicle*, as quoted by Chris Hables Gray, *Postmodern War: The New Politics of Conflict* (New York: The Guilford Press, 1997), p. 46. I want to thank Gray for sharing his important work with me.

Israel's Patriots were able to hit 41 of the SCUDs they were fired at, but destroyed only 44% of their warheads and "may have caused more actual damage than [they] prevented."[1] The Falcon, a "smart" bomb, cost $2 billion to produce, but was only 7% effective, though in tests it succeeded 99% of the time.[2] In the US invasion of Panama, too, 300 civilians and 23 US servicemen were killed, nearly 40% of the latter (in a small sample) from "friendly" fire.[3]

This is ironic, because it is quite likely that computer-managed weapon systems were deployed in the first place in large measure to do away with an altogether different kind of "friendly fire": what was called "fragging" in the Vietnam War, where, beginning in the late '60s, increasing numbers of angry or revolutionary or scared US troops started turning their weapons on their officers in retaliation or in self-defense. Rebellion spread through the ranks, and the ability of the US military to fight was seriously sapped.[4]

Some years later I happened to be working as a technical drafter and designer. Among a variety of petrochemical, mining, chemical, scientific, and electronic projects I made drawings and designs for was one military job at GTE Sylvania. Military contracts typically are "cost plus," meaning that the more the corporation spends in making a particular product, the higher will be the profit they are allowed — a virtual guarantor of regular cost-overruns, of course. In my particular section, sometimes we had nothing to do for days at a time, unproductive but racking up costs and therefore profit. Our supervisors did not mind, but they wanted us to "look busy." I had noticed piles of military intelligence and technology trade magazines lying around and I whiled away my "idle" hours pouring over them, doing research for this book, I was shocked at what I saw, more in the advertisements accompanying the occasional article than in the articles themselves. All the weapon systems of note, according to these publications from the late 1970s, were being automated, reconfigured around computer technology, it appeared: planes, tanks, ships, anti-aircraft installations, all of it.

If the advertisements and editorials were to be believed, the drive towards computerization was so strong that it wouldn't be too long before each foot soldier had several microprocessors on his back — to aim his

---

[1] John A. Clusman, "Friendly Fire," San Francisco *Chronicle: Insight* (August 7, 2005) reports that Army historians "have estimated ground casualties from friendly fire in World War II, the Korean War, and the Vietnam War at approximately 2 percent, while they soared to 17% during the 1991 Gulf War." On the Iranian airline that was attacked, Gray, *op. cit.*, pp. 65–68.

[2] *Ibid.*, p. 68.

[3] *Ibid.*, p. 166.

[4] Stephen Kinzer, *Overthrow: America's Century of Regime Change from Hawaii to Iraq* (New York: Henry Holt and Company, 2006), p. 306

weapon, keep inventory of ammunition and K-rations (as they were then called), and deposit paychecks automatically in his bank.[1]

Initially, I was astounded. Had the fools in the US officer corps (who constituted the audience for this literature) learned *nothing* from the Vietnam War? Indeed they had, I finally realized, but not the same lessons that I, an antiwar organizer in the '60s and '70s, had. I thought they would have learned from the utter failure of "McNamara's Line," the "electronic battlefield" the US Secretary of Defense installed near the end of the war (at the suggestion of the Jason Group of liberal scientist consultants to the Pentagon) to enable the US — with minimal troop deployment, but automatically tripped ordnance — to interdict and destroy National Liberation Front and North Vietnamese troops. Heavy reliance was placed on sensors (said to be able to distinguish the smell of human urine from that of water buffalo), which would detect the "enemy" and then call in withering bombardment by US aircraft and long-range artillery. The electronic battlefield, however, was a miserable flop — the Vietnamese were known, for example, to hang bags of human urine in trees as a foil to the smell-sensors and they similarly befogged movement sensors — despite its advertised "cost-effectiveness."[2] Using software "models," computers were also used in Vietnam to analyze villages to determine which were "friendly" and which "hostile," so as to pick which villages to bomb. As a way of separating the Vietnamese into those who were for us and those who weren't, it, too, didn't provide useful guidance, though it ended up killing a great many villagers.

But if this was the lesson *I* learned from Vietnam, there was another, perhaps more important, lesson for the officer corps. However ineffective the electronic battlefield might have been, it at least had one sizeable advantage over live troops — electronically-controlled firepower does not "frag" its officers. For unquestioned, effective "command and control," electronic weaponry is obviously far preferable to live soldiers who can decide *where* to point their weapons or even whether to fire them. The US military was really in a tremendous bind, for while McNamara's line was full of huge holes, there was no question as to *who* controlled it. The same could simply not be said of the South Vietnamese and US forces, large numbers of whom in the late '60s and early '70s were refusing to fight, deserting, or rebelling.

---

1 Under the circumstances, it would have been unwise for me to be seen taking notes, so I am unable to cite specific journals, dates, or pages.

The paragraph in the text was first written in the mid-1980s; since then, most of this has, alas, come to pass.

2 For a good discussion of the inflated claims made, compared to the actual failure of Operation Igloo White, as it was called, see Paul N. Edwards, *The Closed World: Computers and the Politics of Discourse in Cold War America* (Cambridge, Mass.: MIT Press, 1996) pp. 3ff.

As militants from the black liberation and the anti-war movement in the late '60s were recruited or drafted into the US armed forces, this alarming insurgency rapidly spread. With mutiny afoot in its ranks, the officer corps learned a vital lesson. When some of these same officers, several years later, were working in the defense industry, they would have been inexorably drawn to the promises of automated weaponry, consistent with a well-established fetishization of technology in the US, especially by the military leadership. Officers and ex-officers, we can assume, would have been partial to weapons whose political loyalties were never in question, that would fire only when and at whom they were directed by their "superiors." At a time when the Pentagon was attempting to confront the dire possibilities of nuclear weapons launched by unauthorized personnel, the issue of command and control of weaponry was a particularly serious concern.[1]

It is clear that many of the officers, who had been frightened about themselves being fragged in Vietnam, ten years later when I was reading those intelligence magazines, would have decision-making responsibilities as lobbyists, consultants, or procurement officers (once again, categories that bleed into each other) in the Pentagon and its war-making industries. Even if only at an unconscious level, the appeal of automatically, rather than politically, discharged weapons must have been palpable. This is, I believe, one of the *two* major reasons pushing the Pentagon towards its fixation with computer-generated weaponry.

The second reason for the rush to embrace automated firepower predates the Vietnam War, and has to do with the profound contradictions that lie at the very heart of nuclear warfare. At the end of World War II, modern warfare entered an altogether unfamiliar realm, where the rate at which battle configurations unfold (supersonic speeds), the distance at which battles may be joined (scores or hundreds of miles away, with lock-on radar, or many thousands of miles with ICBMs) and the consequences of responding poorly or too slowly to an adversary's threats (nuclear annihilation) are *so* extreme that the military leadership of the US concluded that weaponry could no longer be left under the control of humans. Grave paradoxes, indeed, confronted military strategists in a nuclear and supersonic age. The way to resolve them involved a huge committment to finding ways to meld fighting men and machine-weapon into reliable battle-units.

The substitution of automated machinery for the traditional weapons of war was a gradual process, beginning in the years after World War II.

---

[1] A related reason for electronic weapons is that they allowed the officers to get around the very serious problem faced by the Pentagon of "the reluctance of soldiers to fire on targets that might include innocent civilians. Electronic-targeting techniques made the victims faceless." Lenny Siegel and John Markoff, *The High Cost of High Tech: The Dark Side of the Chip* (New York: Harper & Row, 1985), p. 83.

Both the US military and commercial airlines realized in the late 1940s that training pilots on actual airplanes was unwise. Too much of a monetary investment in planes and in the training of personnel could be lost in a single crash for military or corporate executives to put novice pilots in *real* airplanes. For training purposes, instead, flight simulators were used; these would pitch, roll, shake, and dive in response to pilots' manipulations of the controls. Thus was begun the creation of artificial environments for pilots.

Pilots in combat today face literally impossible tasks in battle. While having to fly their planes at supersonic speeds and to evade enemy fire, they must respond continually to data about their air speed, oil pressure, altitude, fuel, enemy radars, electronic countermeasures, and their own weapon systems, all while navigating. Such a pilot must fly

> a large quantity of high explosives at supersonic speeds,
> making life-and-death judgments in fractions of seconds,
> based on reports from radar screens, paying attention to a
> couple of dozen equally vital instrument displays, listening
> to system status reports and command communication, all
> at the same time.[1]

The kicker is that these same pilots are "only semi-conscious at times in supersonic combat due to the effect [in tight turns] of G-forces on the brain." Such semi-conscious beings, it bears emphasizing, in some cases have their fingers on triggers capable of launching the equivalent of Armageddon!

This insane situation is a major force behind the large investments in recent decades in a sub-discipline of computerization, Virtual Reality (VR), the creation of simulated spaces into which a person can be "immersed." We shall be considering VR in more detail below, but for now we want only to look ahead at US Air Force plans (and as the Gulf War and subsequent wars in Iraq, Afghanistan, Pakistan, etc. revealed, they are already partially in place) for the *simulation of reality*, once used primarily for training pilots on mock-ups, to *replace external reality* for pilots. Already, or in the near future, inside pilots' helmets video displays of a cartoon-like map of the terrain around them, created out of the computer memory in the plane of a "stored-terrain data base... [and] synchronized with real-time radar," no doubt, where appropriate, exhibiting on such "terrain" such seasonal variations as snow, trees in leaf, or water in the rivers. Instead of looking through cockpit windshields at an *actual* landscape, pilots will see mock-ups on screens in-

---

1 Howard Rheingold, *Virtual Reality* (New York: Simon & Schuster, 1991), p. 202. By now we should add a multitude of intelligence reports the pilot must monitor, as discussed below, pp. 375ff.

side their helmets that will change in response to their planes' *actual* (as interpreted by computers) paths. Flying "in" such artificial displays, pilots will be alerted as to changes in status of fuel, air speed, and so on, by alarm lights or sounds; whenever their radar system "verified a target... a symbol would pop up in the pilot's virtual field, and his own attentional mechanisms would zero in on it." The pilots would have learned instinctively how to look at any such symbol to learn what was "encoded in its shape, color, position, velocity, and by saying the appropriate word," such as "bang" or "zap" or any other designed word or sound, the pilot's nervous system would be directly pitted against the enemy, firing weapons without the mediation of a button or of stick manipulations.[1]

That the obscene play, plane-to-plane or plane-to-ground, of a weapons system bearing the makings of apocalypse is taking place with at least one of its key actors in a semi-conscious stupor some of the time and not actually looking *at* what he or she is shooting at is where any analysis should have ground to a halt decades ago. No military commander in his right mind, *unless* under the domination of an ideology so strong as to usher him past the most glaring of military absurdities and contradictions without being stopped short, would have gone along with such a semiconscious military weapons system — especially one carrying such devastating firepower. The ideology that can so blind a military commander, indeed, whole nations of military commanders, that they would opt for a semi-conscious fighter-pilot comes, of course, from several millennia of training the masses of foot soldiers, the grunts of war, precisely how to be (at best!) semi-conscious in the carrying out of their duties; and, from centuries of buying into the mechanistic analysis of reality.[2] In particular, if each phenomenon is to be studied, piecemeal, after it is broken down into its smallest components, as Descartes advised, then it is entirely possible for the dazzling speed and "penetrating power" of supersonic fighter jets to win the day in the final argument whether to build such awesome weapons, while the military absurdity of having such battle stations flying many times *without* conscious direction would have been someone else's responsibility for figuring out a "solution," as their "component" of the overall project. (Following this kind of logic, decisions must similarly have been made to go ahead and build a system of "civilian" nuclear-power generators that rested on the production each year of *tons* of the most toxic

---

1 Faith in the promised performance of electronic weapons is frequently far in excess of real-world conditions. The autonomous land-vehicle prototype, for example, was cancelled when it was realized that it had problems distinguishing shadows from objects or ditches from roads. Similarly, after spending $1.8 billion, the Divad air defense gun program was abandoned. (Gray, *op. cit.*, pp. 53, 60.)

2 Readers might recall that it was in military matters that the mechanical philosophy found one of its first explicit applications, when Frederick the Great in 1686 created the first military drill book.

poisons in existence, plutonium, with the expectation that somewhere else the problem of toxic storage would be dealt with.)[1]

The kinds of expensive and unwieldy high-tech weapon systems procured by the US military in recent decades have frequently been the product of what seemed like a slapstick comedy, but with alarming implications and of course astronomical ticket prices. Vying for the bucks of competing services (Air Force, Navy, Army, Marines, etc.), each wanting a plane with different capabilities in terms of tonnage carried, range, airspeed, maneuverability, weapons on board, and electronic countermeasures available, the armament companies end up pitching different *versions* of the *same* plane to the different services. Which plane, being oversold, overdesigned, but undermachined, ends up significantly overweight, years late in being deployed, with enormous cost overruns, and minimal reliability. Sometimes the same basic design is modified so that what is ordinarily a bomber can function as a transport plane or an electronics-warfare plane. Given its predictable excess weight, the plane's speed, altitude-capability, and maneuverability fall drastically short, while it uses far too much fuel, has therefore a much shorter range than required, and tends to crash at an alarming rate, so that a third or more of the fleet is soon grounded for long periods of time. Parts availability becoming increasingly problematic, many of the planes — or, in different versions of this same sorry story, tanks, destroyers, or missile systems — end up being cannibalized to enable others to stay in the air. Many of our major weapons, most notably of course the components of the SDI or starwars missile defense, are simply elaborate, frightfully expensive, oversold, duds.[2]

---

[1] At a NRC conference on reactor safety, influential scientists and academics argued that nuclear power was important for economic and political reasons and that in the future new technology "might" be developed to deal with the problems of radioactive waste, and so it was proper to proceed full-speed-ahead. (Perrow, *op. cit.*, p. 70.)

[2] Thus in the mid-'80s the US bombed Libya, but "in order to be sure there would be an absolute minimum of US losses, the Libyan operation had to be done at night with planes flying close to the sea; this meant that the whole flight had to be controlled by automated mechanisms. But this total dependence on machines forced a third of the bombers to return to base without discharging their bombs due to equipment failure." George Caffentzis, "Rambo on the Barbary Shore" in Midnight Notes Collective, *Midnight Oil: Work, Energy, War 1973–1992* (Brooklyn: Autonomedia, 1992), p. 299. Equipment breakdowns for the B-1 bomber decreased the numbers able to be on alert. (Gray, *op. cit.*, pp. 58, 60, 247.) During the late '70s, from one-half to two-thirds of F–15s were grounded on a typical day due to mchanical problems. (Schlosser, *op. cit.*, p. 347).

Wayne Biddle concluded that, "our weapons tests now use so much computer modeling and simulation that no one knows whether some new arms really work." Indeed, suggests Paul Edwards, for many in the military it was immaterial whether many major weapons or defense systems actually *worked*, since there were other, more fundamental purposes the systems served, for industry and for research funding, for example. Some war-making scenarios or systems, like SAGE, were only meant as "paper" exercises.[1]

Where it is vital that weapons or other systems based on hi-tech components work with a very high degree of reliability, as in the manned missions to the moon or the space shuttles, the US will install unusual back-up computers capable of substituting for one another, for the high visibility of such programs and the enormity of the role they play in the US's overall strategic plans justifies the extra weight, costs, etc.[2]

Precisely where the new technology is so adept, paradoxically is also where it is so dysfunctional. Take its use in military intelligence, for example, where computer technology, with its prodigious capacity for data, enables enormous amounts of information to be brought to a focal point, seemingly empowering its user, in this case, the military. Truly a vast number of sources can be marshalled to weigh in on a particular battlefield situation or a threat to a unit or to an individual soldier.

> Data is among the most potent weapons of the 21st century. Unprecedented amounts of raw information help the military determine what targets to hit and what to avoid.

Precisely how the veritable flood of data brought forth can prove to be a huge problem is the gist of a *New York Times* article, "In New Military, Data Overload Can Be Deadly. Your Brain On Computers. Wired Warriors,"[3] where Donald Rumsfeld's and the Project for a New American Century's "emerging revolution in military affairs" comes in for a rather devastating review.

The neocon vision set forth by the Project for a New American Century (PNAC)'s founding document, "Rebuilding America's Defenses: Strategy, Forces, and Resources for a New Century,"[4] is one of small, light, and highly mobile fighting units whose electronic wizardry enables the kind of military power that used to be dependent on heavy artillery and ponderous

---

1 Edwards, *op.cit.,* p. 110.

2 On redundancy in the space program, see Perrow, *op. cit.,* p. 274.

3 Thom Shanker and Matt Richtel, *New York Times* (Jan. 17, 2011).

4 "Rebuilding America's Defenses: Strategy, Forces, and Resources for a New Century" (A Report of the Project for the The New American Century, n.p., September, 2000), p. 62. My thanks to Marling Mast for providing me with a copy.

corps of tanks to be deployed. These new soldiers will be wired and able, by dint of their access to vast troves of intelligence data, to fight circles around a more numerous, but bewildered, more technologically primitive, foe, a 21st century version of Cortés vs. Montezuma. The eager cohort of PNAC military experts foresee the coming day when a unit of seven soldiers would be capable of dominat[ing] an area the size of the Gettysburg battlefield —where, in 1863, some 165,000 men fought."[1]

These new soldiers, projected from 2000, are partially realized in 2019 in Afghanistan, Iraq and elsewhere, though maybe not (yet?) with the capsulated "climate-controlled, powered fighting suits, laced with sensors, and boasting chameleon-like 'active' camouflage." These soldiers will be on skin-patch administered drugs to "help regulate fears, focus concentration and enhance endurance and strength."[2] Their helmets will include a video display allowing vision "around corners and over hills." These "information-intensive forces," according to PNAC, operating in small units, may well come to replace the present "clash of massive, combined-arms armed forces." In addition to the use of drones, the small units would carry "fleets of robots, some small enough to fit in soldiers' pockets."[3]

The realities of "information-intensive forces" is the focus of the *New York Times* article on data overload, zeroing in on an instance where 23 Afghani civilians were wiped out by an American helicopter assault. The attack was plotted at a Nevada Air Force base, where a drone operator's team was attempting to determine what was underway in a village where they spied a convoy forming.

The team continued to monitor visual shots from the drone while simultaneously engaging in dozens of instant messaging and radio exchanges with intelligence analysts and US soldiers in the area. Scads of data was being relayed back and forth as the gathering took shape. So much data, in fact, that "solid reports" that the gathering included children got lost "amid the swirl of data."

> [D]rone-based sensors have given rise to a new class of wired warriors who must filter the information sea. But sometimes they are drowning.[4]

The sheer volume of data renders it much more difficult to consider the reliability of an single datum. A crude quantitative calculus would be an

---

[1] *Ibid.*, p. 62.

[2] *Ibid.* As the Wehrmacht, the German army, was in the *blitzkrieg*, primarily methamphetamines. Norman Ohler, *Blitzed: Drugs in the Third Reich* (transl. Shawn Whiteside (Boston: Houghton Mifflin Harcourt, 2016); reviewed by Anthony Beevor, "The Very Drugged Nazis," *New York Review of Books*, March 9, 2017).

[3] *Ibid.*, p. 60.

[4] "In New Military, Data Overload Can Be Deadly," *New York Times*.

all-too-easy default rule of thumb, to wit, "*x* number of sources say *a* is happening, but *y* number say no, not *a*, but *b*; and since *y* is so much bigger than *x*, let's go with *b*."

Since September 11, which unleashed the dogs of war to try out PNAC and Rumsfeld's "revolution in military affairs," "the amount of intelligence gathered by surveillance technologies has risen 1,600 percent." Troops now commonly use "handheld devices" to communicate, establish bombing coordinates, receive directions. Jet plane screens now "can be so packed with data that some pilots call them 'drool buckets'" since they tend to get befuddled trying to decipher their multitude of messages.

Alarmed by this problem, the Pentagon, of course, is engaged in research on how to *go around* it, such as one study where subjects were fed a variety of intelligence data, including some from drones. As the quantity of data was increased, the subjects experienced levels of *theta* brain waves, an indicator of "extreme overload." Tests showed that soldiers operating a tank while monitoring a video feed frequently did not see targets right in front of them.

"Every day across the Air Force's $5 billion global surveillance network, cubicle warriors review 1000 hours of video, 1000 high altitude spy photos and hundreds of hours of 'signals intelligence' — usually cellphone calls." One junior officer is described in the *Times* article as working 12-hour shifts monitoring 10 TV screens, mostly from Afghanistan drones, while he uses an instant messaging system that involved as many as 30 different chats, including commanders of troops in combat zones and headquarters. Meanwhile the voice of a U-2 spy-plane pilot is fed into his ear and he may be talking to another pilot, while engaged with his own IM input.

Besides the two reasons I have described for the Pentagon's mad rush to electronic weapons systems — first, such weapons being under the control, more or less, of officers, less prone to restless rebellion, as in Vietnam; and, second, because their speed of operation and automatic nature make such systems seem capable of overcoming the difficulties of semi-conscious pilots and the supersonic speeds and complexity of operations that modern warmaking now entails — there lies a *third*, deeper reason for the Pentagon's wholesale embrace of digital weaponry. The US emerged from World War II already thinking of how it would wage World War III, confident of its presumed role as leader of international capitalism and therefore its need, in this new nuclear age, of being able to mount military action anywhere at any time. The lessons of the Manhattan Project were clear, as Nils Bohr (see epigraph, Chapter 16) understood. So too did the US Air Force Comptroller who saw "that efficiently coordinating the energies of whole nations in the event of a total war would require scientific programming techniques."[1] This would be possible only by using the capacities thought to be afforded by large computers.

---

1 Heims, *op. cit.*, pp. 314–315.

iii. COMMAND & CONTROL?

Although some of the problems with electronic warfare lies in its high rate of failure, devastating consequences can result from the systems functioning *precisely* as they were meant to. During the 1967 Middle East War, six urgent messages were sent to a US intelligence ship, the USS *Liberty*, to get out of the battle area, because US intelligence had determined that the ship was being targeted for attack by Israeli forces. Since it was critical for the ship to move quickly and discretely, the message was sent on a top-secret channel, but at the time no top-secret, secure, channels were available and the communication system, information-processing *in the way it had been programmed*, searched for a considerable time for communication relays with the necessary clearance. Finding none going to the Mediterranean, the system sent two of the messages to the Philippines, one to Germany, and another one — they were getting warmer — to Greece, one to Morocco, one to Maryland; one message was lost. After two days, the *Liberty* itself still had not received the critical warning. Staying in the battle zone, it was attacked, as predicted, by an Israeli gunboat and 34 US sailors were killed, with 164 wounded.[1]

One year later a more dangerous showdown occurred, again because of an information-processing system that worked as it had been programmed, again leading to disaster. This time it was the USS *Pueblo*, captured during a spying mission against North Korea in 1968. Here, too, warning messages to the ship had been sent by Pentagon intelligence analysts, but they were never received, in this instance, too, probably because the routing of the messages, for security reasons, was exceedingly circuitous. Consequently, the command for the ship to leave the area was lost. When capture seemed imminent, the *Pueblo* was unable to call upon the nearby US Seventh Fleet for protection, since, as a spy ship, it reported to obscure military agencies so as to mask its activities.[2]

---

[1] Given that it was Israel that killed the 34 sailors, the incident was quickly dropped; had it been the USSR, Syria, Iraq, or Cuba, of course, the US State Department and press would have kept the issue on the front pages for some time. Details are from Schlosser, *op. cit.*, p. 356 and Bracken, *op. cit.* In 1977, ten years later, the Pentagon relied on a system, WIMEX, a global network involving sensors, satellite feeds, and computer centers that tied together twenty-six major US command centers around the world. In a system-wide test, "over 60% of its messages failed." (Gray, *op. cit.*, pp. 62–63.)

[2] Communication seems not to be a Pentagon specialty. During the US invasion of Grenada, an Army officer was forced to call Fort Bragg from Grenada to ask it to relay a message to the Navy in Grenada. The Army's radio equipment was not compatible with the Navy's or the Marine's. (Schlosser, *op. cit.*, p. 448.)

Summarizing the instances of the USS *Liberty* and *Pueblo,* Paul Bracken, in *The Command and Control of Nuclear Weapons,* comments that if either incident had occurred during a full-blown crisis, with a condition of full alert, the traffic of messages flying back and forth in the tizzy of nuclear apprehension could have easily overwhelmed communication links so that an even greater breakdown in the system of command would have been likely.

Since military command has been the driving force behind computerization and of advances in telecommunications, defining industry priorities, it is highly instructive to look at the factors leading to the structural form that was created to carry out this essential mission.

> The trend towards vertical integration of warning and intelligence systems [in the US] with the nuclear forces began in the late 1950s.... Throughout the 1960s and 1970s, data from spy satellites, submarine and aircraft probes, communications and signals intelligence, and human agents were coordinated in interconnected data fusion centers. Information was passed from warning and intelligence sensor to force commander, permitting instantaneous status reports.[1]

Bracken comments that each incremental step in building the elaborate communications system, tying together warning and fighting, gave obvious advantages, increasing the warning time for an enemy attack, for example, or making US forces safer. To be sure,

> [t]he system that resulted from these changes must surely be the most technologically elaborate organizations ever constructed by man. But did it make any *overall* improvement in the responsiveness of the forces to changes in enemy activities? In its individual increments, improvements certainly occurred, yet its aggregate effect was to produce a total system that was tightly coupled and highly interdependent, one in which a small stimulus reverberated worldwide.... But it produced such strong internal overcompensation dynamics that layers of checks and balances, "fail-safe" procedures, and human interventions were necessary to dampen them. On the one hand, the instability of intense alerts *could reinforce the tendency to attack.* On the other, it *could compel* prudent leaders to *order de-alerts to avoid provocations or to keep from losing control* of events.... Both... exist in a crisis.[2]

---

[1] Bracken, *op. cit.,* p. 214.
[2] *Ibid.,* pp. 214–15. Emphasis mine.

In plain English, the system of command and control of our nuclear weapons, based on elaborate information-processing systems and telecommunication linkages, might very well encourage a war to escalate out of control during a crisis, actually hastening the outbreak of nuclear hostilities; *or* it might prove to be so resistant to going on the offensive that all provocations were ignored; and (for those who worry about such matters) perhaps might even not be capable of calling into play the nuclear forces when push comes to shove and they are "called for."

What an astounding admission! Were reason and logic in command at the Pentagon, Bracken's conclusions would be sufficient to cause an overhaul or even abandonment, of the architecture of post-World War II US national security, built out of the bricks of computer-based technologies. Indeed, an obvious question is whether information-processing mentalities should even be *banned* from the war-making apparatus? For, it bears repeating, Bracken, a highly-regarded Pentagon consultant, has demonstrated that the very complexity of the system the Pentagon has built in order to increase security will be prone to make some tense situations escalate out of control, possibly resulting in all-out nuclear firefight. Or, just as likely, the electronic layering of the system could result in a profound system-inertia that makes mobilization of the armed forces for a full-scale conflict nearly impossible to put into play.

In light of the strong inclination to downplay serious problems in their military plans or operations by the Pentagon and their advisors — especially, as Bracken's are, ones that go to the heart of their war-fighting capacity — it is hard to avoid concluding that the "military-industrial complex" for all its PhDs, has been built on the intellectual equivalent of landfill: prone to liquify if given a good shake.

These are not minor matters. Indeed, I hope I am not seen as churlish for pointing out that the US military began its heavy reliance on hi-tech weaponry sometime in the 1950s[1] and since then, with the exception of the Gulf War and Grenada, Panama, and the Kosovo conflict in the 1990s (in which the US had no ground troops) *none* of our wars since have ended in anything like victory. The new weaponry does in fact provide unprecedented power and control, but not the kind of control that really counts in the end. If lethality were the measure, surely these hi-tech weapons are enormously successful. But if instead we ask whether these systems and machinery are effective in political, diplomatic, or geopolitical terms, the answer is not the least bit clear.

---

[1] For example, electronic systems in a typical US Air Force fighter cost approximately $3000 in the period after World War II, but by about 1970 cost about $2.5 million. In the mid-'80s, electronic weapons constituted about 30% of all Pentagon purchasing; by 1990, it was expected to rise to 50%. (Siegel and Martoff, *op. cit.,* p. 30.)

Given this history, given the compelling evidence of system irrationality and instability, it is remarkable that nowhere along the way, no general or admiral said, "Wait a minute. Let us look more carefully at what we're doing. Does this make any sense?" — initiating an honest assessment of those irrationalities and instabilities. If any did, their voices would not have been heard, for a strong ideological commitment to mechanistic thinking would have made any such criticism appear senseless.

Instead, the computers were put in control of more and more of our war-making machinery. So much so that by the 1991 Gulf War, General H. Norman Schwarzkopf, the commander of Operations Desert Shield and Desert Storm, admitted to reporters in the days preceeding the onset of hostilities that because his battle plans were so computerized, he could not easily change them.[1]

iv. PROFITABILITY VS. CONTROL OF PRODUCTION

The Pentagon is probably not that surprised that its electronic gee-whiz weaponry is not pulling its weight. According to the historian David Noble, it is something that they've known for quite some time. One of the earliest examples of computer (analogue, pre-digital) use by industry is found in the turn to automatic machinery that came to dominate certain aspects of machine design, especially in aviation, from the 1950s on. Examining that turn reveals that the push for *automatic* machinery was for political more than economic or technical reasons.

Management at the time wanted to "build into the machines the skills of the machinists for certain operations, for a particular restricted set of movements," because they believed that a properly set-up machine could then "be operated by a relatively low-paid unskilled person who could, without much thought or ingenuity produce specified parts in high volume."[2] Though at first glance this reflects economic reasons for these changes in production methods, a closer analysis by Noble reveals a profoundly political basis for early computer-based machinery.

Though traditionally machinists controlled their machines (lathes, milling machines, drill presses, etc.), now the machines would control themselves — or rather, the engineers, off in another room, would control them, and thus the operators who worked them. That cost-cutting was not the real purpose is clear from managements' repeated reluctance to measure

---

[1] Gray, *op. cit.*, p. 46.

[2] That this first automated machinery ("Numerical Control," or N/C) was based on earlier analogue, not digital, computers does not, I believe, invalidate the analysis here, especially given that once the digital machines were on board, similar results were found. See below. David Noble, *Forces of Production: A Social History of Industrial Automation* (New York: Oxford Univ. Press, 1986), pp. 80–81.

how efficient the new machines actually were. Indeed, every time (under strong union pressure) they reluctantly did engage in such studies, they found that automated machinery *actually cost more*.[1] Nevertheless, this decline in profitability did not dissuade management from carrying forward in their project to automate production. This is because their motives lay much deeper, as we shall see.

Engineers tended to see this machinery as not needing skilled operators, as if apart from whoever operated the tool, "it had a life of its own."

> [F]rom here it was a simple step conceptually, to imagine machines without men, especially for engineers... who viewed the automation of machine tools as simply another fascinating challenge in the development of automatic control technology.[2]

Who controlled the machinery of production was a vital issue in aviation in the 1950s because during World War II there had been many conflicts between management and the workers. On the basis of the exceptional skills of master machinists, they had been able to exert considerable power in deciding appropriate production processes *and* the length of time they should take, sometimes, on critical issues of production, in defiance of management. For example, the metal stock the machinist used might vary in its composition, cutting edges might have slight flaws needing compensating for, etc. To management (and the US government, the aircraft industry's only real customer during World War II), *the* central matters for *management control* were precisely those two, how production should be carried out and how long it should take. The presumptions of the machinists, and the militant union their skills had allowed them to form, at many points during the war were galling to management and the US Air Force, as Noble has shown.

Indeed, even as early as the last decades of the 19th century, "scientific management... aimed to shift the locus of skill from the production floor to the toolroom." But

> however much the new tooling allowed management to employ less skilled and thus cheaper machine operators, it [the machine] was nevertheless very expensive to manufacture and store and lent to manufacturing a heavy burden of inflexibility — shortcomings which one Taylorite warned about as early as 1914. The cost savings that re-

---

[1] Management at the time was forthright about what it saw as the stakes, speaking of an "emancipation from human workers" and that automation was really a "philosophy of control." (*Ibid.*, pp. 235, 237–38.)

[2] *Ibid.*, p. 81.

sulted from the use of cheaper labor were thus partially offset by the expense of tooling.[1]

The unions were afraid of being perceived as anti-technology, as Luddites, or as against Progress, and after a number of strikes, acts of sabotage, and other forms of direct action had failed to stop the new procedures, decided not to fight the machines, hoping against hope that they would ultimately bring greater prosperity to labor. The union had learned that "data (however bogus) talks almost as well as money...."[2]

"Numerical control" technology, as the automated processes were known, was introduced into aviation production in the 1950s, partly to overcome these tooling costs (in addition to its effect on de-skilling of labor), but once more the extensive costs of the solution wiped out any savings brought by "efficiency." Noble found this to be a long-lasting pattern by looking at the US military's practices going back two centuries. In cases of war-production where costly technologies were brought in so as to enable hiring cheaper labor and to increase management's control over production, "the tab for the conversion was picked up by the State — the Ordnance Department in the early nineteenth century, the department of the Army and Navy around World War I.... There seems to be a pattern... in which the government *systematically shores up the position of management vis-a-vis labor* in the *interests of national security*."[3]

The economist Thomas Weiskopf of the University of Michigan investigated the relationship of capital investment in equipment and productivity, his results calling into question the presumed relationship between the two. From 1948 to 1978, as the ratio between capital and labor in the manufacturing industries nearly doubled, the average rate of annual growth in productivity declined by more than half. The business community, as well as the Pentagon, was keeping tabs. In 1983 the *Wall Street Journal* reported that automation of manufacturing had "mixed" results, concluding that "unsuitable machine's computerized equipment often doesn't work the way it's supposed to... the new equipment is more fragile than old-fashioned industrial equipment and problems with the software used to run the equipment are ever more prevalent." The same year, *Business Week* warned of other problems with the new technology: "The number of new jobs created by high technology will fall disappointingly short of those lost in manufacturing."[4]

---

[1] Taylorites (after Frederick Taylor) were early efficiency experts, who made elaborate "time-motion" studies of production processes as a way of implementing a radical speed-up for workers. *Ibid.*, p. 80.

[1] *Ibid.*, pp. 258–259, 304.

[2] *Ibid.*, p. 80; emphasis mine.

[3] *Ibid.*, pp. 341–43, 348.

v. The Embarrassing Productivity Gap

Next to the Pentagon, the biggest customer for computer systems has been business. The need to invest in the newest IT machines and software was taken for granted by the financial, commercial, and manufacturing giants in the days of the mainframes (1950s and '60s); as personal computers became available ('70s and '80s), virtually every organization and business rushed to put its affairs into digital hands, including eventually a great many small businesses and movement groups.

In every instance, the switch was driven by the belief that computerization would increase efficiency and therefore profitability. What happens if we search for that efficiency, to see just where it manifested itself in such a wide variety of enterprises?

The search, it turns out, is an arduous one, still on-going, for the alleged efficiencies (and the increases in productivity that would flow from such efficiencies) have not been the least bit eager to show their faces. As late as 1991, after decades of investments in hi-tech devices, John Sculley, the CEO of Apple Corp., commented on the till-then-missing increase in productivity that presumably should be credited to computerization:

> One of the most astounding comments on my industry is that there is no measurable productivity increase from all of these computers that have been bought by white-collar workers over the past 10 years — none.
> So billions of dollars of computers have been bought, and we can't point to any measurable productivity increase.

What an astounding admission, and, as we shall see, a not-uncommon one in regard to computers. The Emperor himself (or one of them) is admitting his nakedness. Of course, Sculley hastened to regain some decency, not to say respectability, by immediately kicking up dust around his words to mask the industry's nudity:

> It's not that the [computing] technology is bad. It's that we've mapped it on top of the old way of working. So business needs to look at new ways of behavior and working. Government needs to learn new ways of working with business.[1]

---

[1] Alas, in the more than two decades that have elapsed, I have misplaced the clipping from the San Francisco *Chronicle* where this is from, and so cannot provide the month and day. Sculley nearly a decade earlier pointed out to Steve Jobs that most executives "found computers more trouble than they were worth." Walter Isaacson, *Steve Jobs* (New York: Simon & Schuster, 2011), p. 150.

A number of articles in the business press spell out the grim statistics to which Sculley had alluded. Corporations in the US had been spending 5% to 10% of sales on computerization, but at the time had achieved only 1% increase in productivity, which could well be statistically insignificant. By the late '90s, one out of every two workers was likely to use a computer at work. The service sector of the US economy, responsible for 75% of private sector jobs and possessing over 85% of computer technology in the US in the period under study (to the mid-'90s) had not been able to reduce the ratio of regular workers to management. Stephen Roach, an economist with Morgan Stanley investments house, argued that "[i]f computers were truly making things more efficient that ratio would have fallen."

This matter of the "'productivity paradox" has puzzled a great many economists and information technology enthusiasts. Robert Solow, a Nobel laureate in Economics, commented that "you can see the computer age everywhere but in the productivity statistics." In fact, during the period since the early 1970s, when business has increased its investments in computers by over 30% a year, the rate of growth of productivity has fallen from 2.85% a year (1947 to 1973) to about 1.1% a year in later years.[1] Since it is an article of faith to the cheerleaders of information technology that these machines save labor, in the absence of evidence they focus now on writing about what the computer "revolution" *will bring* about at some point in the future. Some, like Sculley, assert that in the absence of evidence it is simply too early to see the real efficiencies that the new technology is bringing about; more time will demonstrate just what potential will inevitably be unleashed.

While waiting for the efficiencies to be found, of course, computers have been the tool for the massive offshoreing of jobs out of the US and the downsizing of the workforce. Though this downsizing itself was undertaken in order for the corporations to be more competitive, by reducing bureaucracy and unnecessary layers of management, in fact, the offices continued to fill up — the largest growth of jobs in the years before 1998 was for office workers, some 40% now of all workers in the US (1998 figures). Many more of today's office workers are professionals, having at least a bachelor's degree, including those who are management; communication experts; business consultants; lawyers; high-level sales people, like stock brokers or real estate agents; scientists and engineers having management responsibilities; financial experts; marketers; etc. Indeed, the niches multiply and the MBAs proliferate.[2]

---

[1] Computers did not cause the decrease, but nor did they alleviate it. See David McNally, *Global Slump: The Economics of Crisis and Resistance* (Oakland, PM Press, 2011) for a lucid analysis of the decline.

[2] Jeff Madrick, "Computers: Waiting for the Revolution," *New York Review of Books,* March 26, 1998.

In the late 1990s some analysts believed that they had finally found Sculley *et al.'s* Holy Grail of an increase in productivity due to computerization. In the last few years of the '90s, some claimed that the statistics demonstrated a growth in productivity that was "nothing short of a miracle."[1] Closer scrutiny, however, shows that those productivity increases were the product of fancy accounting tricks (in an era in which accountant chicanery has increasingly played a role in corporate obfuscation and fictitious "profits.") Misleading productivity claims are made easier by the ambiguity and confusion surrounding all suggested measures of what constitutes "productivity," it turns out. Jack Triplett showed that in the industries most heavily invested in computerization (finance, wholesale trade, business services, and communication) productivity "had either been increasing very slowly or declining" during this period. Commercial banking, another heavy investor in IT, also did quite poorly. Hi-tech manufacturing, in large part due to Moore's Law, did show increased productivity, but the use of information processing technology in other sectors did not affect theirs.

What might appear as an upswing in productivity does result from downsizing. Fewer workers now handle the workload. A survey in 2004 reported that 62% of American workers claimed that their workload "had increased in the previous six months." Over half said work left them feeling "overtired and overwhelmed."[2] A great deal of the work now being done is, for management, essentially free. Increasingly workers set up and clean up on their own time; unpaid internships are proliferating. University scientists are sometimes expected to raise their own salaries through grant applications; if successful, they must then administer them.

If the widespread (and enormously expensive) use of computer technology has to date not produced its promised increases in efficiency, productivity, and profit, I believe it is a fair question, as the title of this chapter indicates, whether computers "really work"? Similarly, the dysfunctionality of the weapons-systems based on computerization leads us to the same questions. For it turns out that "really working" is not really the issue.

vi. THE DIRTY SECRET OF MICROELECTRONICS

Rest assured, neither business nor the armed forces (private as well as public) will be abandoning electronic cash registers — they track inventory! — or digital drones — they allow targeted assassinations! — anytime soon, despite all of the evidence presented above. Many of the major decision-makers already know these things. For — let the dirty secret come out —

---

[1] Doug Henwood, *After the New Economy: The Binge... And the Hangover That Won't Go Away* (New York: The New Press, 2003/05), p. 46. I am grateful to Henwood for guiding me through some of the literature on these matters.
[2] *Ibid.*, p. 251.

whether they actually work — to produce more profit! to win more battles! — isn't, for them, the real issue. As I will argue later,[1] what really matters for both the business and military consumers of electronics is *control*. And *for control* — up to a point, but as my endless list of electronic failure modes testifies, not beyond it — *nothing beats digital*. For the binary straightjacket — a Boulean labyrinth for yes-and no-decision trees — appears able, without ambiguity, without gray areas, to assign each and every entity to its proper and unique place in the digital cosmos. What a fortuitous match for the minds of *managers*, whether of investments or of guided missiles, with their visions of a universe where ambiguity is, well, a class enemy. What a victory, finally, for the mechanical philosophy.

Since whether they work is not really the issue, at least for those who control this technology, we should not expect rational analysis, such as I might present, to threaten the quarterly reports for Raytheon or Oracle. For, of course, though the machines do not behave as promised, are not, in a word, *productive*, they are enormously *profitable* — if not to the banks or telecommunications,[2] which invest heavily in IT — to the makers of the chips and operating systems, whose money the banks will gladly invest for them.

We come to the final reason why "computers do not work," our chapter theme. They are, as most people who work with them are all too aware, an extremely vulnerable, fickle, kind of machine, prone to mysterious malfunctioning or total breakdowns — how often are we told "the system is down"? — easy to scam on, subject to viral attacks and hacking, liable to massive breeches of personal information, etc. Were these many vulnerabilities (which we will discuss in some detail in the following chapters) something encountered in, say, a department store's inventory, it might be considered a reasonable tradeoff, but in fact the vulnerabilities extend, as the use of computers do, to the most vital institutions and operations critical for the functioning of the whole of the developed world, from (most alarmingly) nuclear reactors, fuel refineries, government records, transportation networks, medical centers, payrolls, water treatment, national defense, finance, and so on, functions at the core of any viable society. Giving over such vital functions and institutions to the control of such exceptionally vulnerable systems is literally suicidal, especially when one considers just how *easily* and *frequently* breakdowns begin:

* Two Mariner spacecraft heading to Mars were lost as a result of programming errors, one because a "." was used instead of a "," in the code.

* In November, 1979, a massive Soviet attack appeared immanent as a result of a training tape simulating such an attack that had been mistakenly

---

1 Chapter 22.
2 *Ibid.*, p. 50–51.

loaded into a computer, which then transferred its data into the active on-line alert system; authorities discovered the mistake after six minutes, thankfully, before a counterattack could be launched. NORAD's out-of-date computers were malfunctioning; repair was often impossible due to lack of parts availability.[1]

 * Eight months later another alarm of a Soviet launched missile attack sent B-52 crews scrambling and starting their engines. Luckily before the planes could take off, a faulty 46¢ computer chip for a multiplexor was found, responsible for the erroneous display on the Strategic Air Command's map.

 * NORAD's computers, the linchpin in the US defense system against Soviet attacks, were actually obsolete when installed. But budgetary cuts and bureaucratic rigidity forced their purchase, despite complaints from NORAD's head that the computers lacked the processing power needed for crucial tasks. A major problem was lack of spare parts, many of which had not been manufactured by Honeywell for years.[2]

 * During routine maintenance, someone dropped a wrench, causing a fuel leak that led to the accidental launching of a Titan II missile that crashed and exploded a short distance away. It was carrying a nuclear warhead.[3]

Every week the breakdown of systems and linkages are reported. They have been there since the beginning of Information Technology, and as they became commonplace, we failed (and fail) to ask critical questions about how the working guts of our societal infrastructures actually function these days. Huge vulnerabilities are blown open by hackers, while the fragilities of the machinery continue to cause massive problems.[4] In 1983 computer errors cost Cleveland schools $4 million, when a clerk in the county auditor's office placed the "5100" code for residential buildings in front of the $.... 35,000 value of a couple's house, artificially boosting the local tax base by half a billion dollars. Ten years later failures in the Pentagon's accounting network were believed responsible for billions of dollars that were missing. In 1992 FAA glitches caused a major transportation breakdown; in 2009, they were still occurring, this time because one circuit board failed. In New York City and in the FBI

[1] Schlosser, *op. cit.*, pp. 366–67.
[2] *Ibid.*
[3] Perrow, *op. cit.*, pp. 286–87. Lenny Siegel and John Markoff, *op. cit.*, pp. 31–32. Schlosser, *op. cit.*, p. 392.
[4] Somini Sengupta, "Hacker Rattles Security Circles," *New York Times* (September 12, 2011); James Temple, "Internet Vulnerable to Sophisticated Attacks: Dot Commentary," San Francisco *Chronicle* (January 22, 2012).

and the California DMV and the Los Angeles school payroll system and many other places, attempts to upgrade computer systems lead to huge cost overruns, ongoing crises as the new machines fail to run adequately for many months or years, causing a partial paralysis in government agencies, often because "transferring the data from the old system did not go smoothly." In Los Angeles schools, the district in 2007 upgraded its accounting and payrolls with a $95 million computerized system. Chaos ensued, as thousands of payroll checks over- or under-paid teachers. In July, 2007, 30,000 faulty checks went out, sending desperate teachers to spend many hours at district offices trying to sort out their missing pay, desperate to pay for rent, food, healthcare, mortgages, etc. By September, still months shy of a hoped-for resolution, school officials plunked down another $50 million for a new fix and hired a consultant for another $10 million to advise them on how the problems might be solved. One of the major problems? Teachers commonly work a 10-month job, but are paid in each of the 12 calendrical months, a peculiarity easily reconciled by a clerk with a calculator but apparently too vexing for the new computer system, which "was not designed to… annualize" their salaries. As of Fall, 2014, *seven years* later, the new computer system was still dysfunctional. Similar mayhem hit CUNY when the New York City university installed CUNYfirst in Fall, 2014, throwing many colleges into chaos for much of the year.[1]

---

[1] "Cleveland Budgets Left a Mess By One Small Computer Goof," U.P. (June 24, 1983); Gilbert A. Lewthwaite, "'Pentagon Can't Keep Track of Its Money," San Francisco *Chronicle* (April 13, 1984); David Dietz, "Boxer Scolds FAA Over Air Traffic Snarl," San Francisco *Chronicle* (April 1, 1992); Harry Weber, "FAA Glitch Wreaks Havoc on Flights," San Francisco *Chronicle* (November 20, 2009); David W. Chen, "Housing Agency's Computer Woes Put Aid Recipients in Limbo," *New York Times* (February 26, 2011); Greg Lucas, "Computer Bumbling Costs State $1 Billion: Repeat Snafus in DMV, Other Agencies," San Francisco *Chronicle* (February 18, 1999); John Abell, "Computer Crashes Costing Corporate America Plenty: Study Puts Tab at $4 Billion a Year for Downtime," San Francisco *Examiner* (August 30, 1992); Steve Lopez, "Wanted — Payroll Mr. Fix-It for L.A. schools, Points West," Los Angeles *Times* (September 19, 2007); Joel Rubin, "Monitor to Oversee School Payroll Repair," latimes.com ('September 17, 2007). I am grateful to Fran Kubrin for providing me with copies of these last two references. Sasha Lilley, "Against the Grain," KPFA (October 31, 2014). The fiasco of the equally long-lasting FBI computer upgrade is briefly recounted in Betty Medsger, *The Burglary: The Discovery of J. Edgar Hoover's Secret FBI* (New York: Alfred A. Knopf, 2014), pp. 505–06, 508, 510. Shomial Ahmad and Peter Hogness, "CUNYfirst's Breakdown," *Clarion* (Newspaper of the Professional Staff Congress) October, 2014, and Peter Hogness, "A CUNY first upgrade is delayed," *Clarion*, January, 2015.

Or consider the utter mayhem that resulted when Pacific Gas & Electric, the major utility corporation in Northern California, transferred its records into electronic form, a pivotal act in 1993 that, according to a federal grand jury indictment of the corporation, 17 years later led to a disastrous explosion in a residential neighborhood in the town of San Bruno in the Bay Area. The explosion killed eight people and destroyed 38 homes.

The conversion of the company's paper records into digital form was "marked by disorganization that result[ed] in the loss of much information," according to a newspaper account of the indictment. The utility company was clearly aware that the new database consisted of "incomplete and erroneous information," the indictment charged. However, instead of seeking better documentation for its pipelines, PG&E turned its ignorance into a business opportunity to cut costs, adopting in 2004 a company policy directing its engineers "to make critical decisions about its pipelines based only on information that was readily available." If information was missing, as it was for hundreds of miles of PG&E pipelines, its engineers "didn"t have to consider it."[1]

The state of California has undertaken several projects to "modernize" record keeping, only to see their costs "spiralling out of control," for example, of medical files in its huge prison system (from $182 million to $386 million in three years), of case-management for the state's judiciary (from $260 million to $1.9 billion), and for the state Department of Veterans Affairs, the last effort called an expensive failure by the state auditor in June, 2016. Some officials are calling for the projects to be dropped or at least delayed.[2]

Massive data breaches in South Korea in 2014 launched an emergency plan to issue ID numbers to every Korean over age 17, at a cost of billions of dollars. The vulnerability of the all-important national identity card was especially pronounced as a result of "South Korea's enthusiasm for the Internet and information technology," including the government's providing fast Internet access to nearly all homes and businesses.[3]

In 1992, unplanned breakdowns were believed to be costing corporations $4 billion a year, this in addition to the billions spent on upgrades and the many billions on the Y2K fixings. Computer experts anticipate crises even greater than Y2K when, in the near future, US Social Security num-

[1] "PG&E Scrambles to Find Pipeline Data in Paper Trail," San Francisco *Chronicle* (March 5, 2011). Jason Van Derbeken, "Criminal Indictment of PG&E in Disaster," San Francisco *Chronicle* (April 2, 2014).

[2] AP and San Francisco *Chronicle*, "Cost to Modernize Prison Medical Record-keeping Doubles to $386 Million" (December 12, 2016); Kimberley Veklerov, "Fix Sought for Court's Inadequate Case System," San Francisco *Chronicle* (February 1, 2017).

[3] AP, "ID Thefts Force New Numbers to Citizens over 17," San Francisco *Chronicle* (October 15, 2014).

bers have to go beyond their present nine-number template because of population growth, or when the vast expansion in mobile phones necessitates an expansion of phone numbers in the US beyond their present ten-digit format. In such quite mundane adjustments to the way "information" is bundled, major breakdowns, as in Y2K, will periodically require massive rewritings of code worldwide to stave off disaster, at unimaginable costs.[1] And even so, as experts readily admit, the machinery is so fragile that a single individual could conceivably hack it to pieces. Indeed, top industry cyber-security experts expect that in the *near* future "a devastating cyberattack" that will take down banks, stock exchanges, power plants, food distribution networks and communications.[2] As if a dress rehearsal for the type of attack anticipated, one year later a distributed denial of service assault on a key Internet routing node took down the Internet across the US and in parts of Europe and Asia for much of a day.[3]

And with so many systems increasingly interlinked, with unexpected non-linear interactions that seem to come out of nowhere, alas, catastrophic breakdowns are only a matter of time, a topic we will explore In more depth in Chapter 22. Ellen Ullman, a software engineer, explains just how fragile matters are:

> We throw away old hardware… Only software gets to age. Too much time is invested in it, too much time will be needed to replace it. So, unlike the tossed-out hardware, software is tinkered with. It is mended and fixed, patched and reused....
>
> The preciousness of an old system [of software] is axiomatic. The longer the system has been running, the greater the number of programmers who have worked on it, the less any one person understands it. As years pass and untold numbers of programmers and analysts come and go, the system takes on a life of its own. It runs. That is its claim to existence: it does useful work. However badly, however buggy, however obsolete — it runs. And no individual completely understands how.

[1] Chris Allbritton (AP), "Future Glitches Make Y2K Seem Way 2EZ," San Francisco *Chronicle* (October 9, 1998).

[2] Thomas Lee, "Beware the Real Big One: An Online Security Earthquake," San Francisco *Chronicle* (July 21, 2015), where IT executives and academics predicted "cripple[d] banks, stock exchanges, power plants and coummunications" from a cyberattack in the next few years.

[3] Marissa Lang, "Attacks Put Huge Holes in Web," San Francisco *Chronicle* (October 22, 2016); Wendy Lee and Daniel DeMay, "Why the Web Went Down: DNS and DDoS Explained," San Francisco *Chronicle* (October 22, 2016).

Ullman recounts working on a mainframe computer system where the program she was working on

> was sixteen years old when I inherited it. According to the library logs, ninety-six programmers had worked on it before I had. I spent a year wandering its subroutines and service modules, but there were still mysterious places I did not dare touch. There were bugs on this system that no one had been able to fix for ten years.... My program was near the end of its "life cycle." It was close to death. Yet the system could not be thrown away.[1]

Artificial Intelligence guru Marvin Minsky concurs:

> When a program grows in power by an evolution of partially understood patches and fixes, the programmer begins to lose track of internal details, loses his ability to predict what will happen, begins to hope instead of know, and watches the results as though the program were an individual whose range of behavior is uncertain.
>
> This is already true in some big programs.... It will soon be much more acute.... large heuristic programs will be developed and modified by several programmers, each testing them on different examples from different [remotely located computer] consoles and inserting advise independently. The program will grow in effectiveness [meaning, range], but no one of the programmers will understand it all.[2]

Or, as MIT computer scientist Jospeh Weizenbaum explained, "the sprawling complexity of any computer system mean[s] that it cannot even in principle be understood by those who rely on it."[3]

Such considerations lead Ullman to dire conclusions:

> What worried me, though, was that the failure of the global electronic system will not need anything so dramatic as an earthquake, as diabolical as a revolutionary. In fact, the failure will be built into the system in the normal course of things. A

---

[1] Ellen Ullman, *Close to the Machine*, pp. 116–17; I have slightly altered the order of Ullman's paragraphs.

[2] Quoted by Joseph Weizenbaum, *Computer Power and Human Reason: From Judgment to Calculation* (New York: W.H. Freeman and Company, 1976), p, 235. The first bracket is in Weizenbaum, the second is mine.

[3] Corey Pein, "Blame the Computer," *Baffler*, no. 38 (Mar.–Apr. 2018), p. 34.

bug. Every system has a bug. The more complex the system, the more bugs. Transactions circling the earth passing through the computer systems of tens or hundreds of corporate entities, thousands of network switches, millions of lines of code, trillions of integrated-circuit logic gates. Somewhere there is a fault. Sometime the fault will be activated. Now or next year, sooner or later, by design, by hack, or by onslaught of complexity. It doesn't matter. One day someone will install ten new lines of assembler code, and it will all come down. [1]

We shall later (Chapter 22) address the obvious question: if computers "do not work" why are they relentlessly taking over our many institutions and corporations? If not to win wars or to rack up ever greater profitability, what is their real purpose?

But first, as promised, a close look at the central issue of the toxicity of hi-tech, examining its productive processes and the premises behind information-processing machinery.

---

[1] Ullman, *op. cit.,* pp. 31–32.

20

Technology & Toxics:
Some Preliminary Observations

That computer technology does not work as it is mandated to, failing at a high rate even as it is given increasing control over ever-wider aspects of society (banking, finance, national defense, insurance, air traffic control, the healthcare system, etc., etc.) is alarming enough, but its many failures and the devastating damage they can cause pale in comparison to the much greater physical and cultural toxicity of hi-tech. In this (more general) and the next (focusing specifically on hi-tech) chapters, we will look closely at questions of physical toxicity. Chapters 22 through 27 will examine forms of cultural toxicity in computer technology, analysing a process of colonization of human consciousness that is embedded in hi-tech and that affects how and what we learn and what we allow ourselves to believe.[1]

In order to undertake our investigation, a few general remarks, by way of warnings, clarifications, and qualifications may be useful:

* In no way do I consider this work to be anti-technology; nor is that my personal belief. I believe humans are inherently technological, that toolmaking has been part of who we are for as long as we have been on the planet. Many ingenious and wonderful technologies exist — some many thousands of years old. Such technologies built the Great Pyramids, for example. One of my favorite ancient technologies: the simple but profound way devised to connect stationary land with a water level that rises and falls with the tides, by the use of a sliding ramp, hinged at one end and unattached at the other, resting on a floating dock to allow goods and people easy access to water vessels. Another is the paddy for the growing of rice, whereby precipitation (frequently in monsoon-laced steep terrain) distrib-

---

[1] Rushkoff, *op. cit.*, p. 22.

utes precious water to the seedlings in the individual paddies, at a rate that mostly keeps intact the structural elements of the system involving some thousands of plots, as the water pours down the mountainsides. There are some wonderful technologies that are modern. I have the utmost respect for my typewriter and my hearing aids.

Yet, there has also been a decided tendency in recent times for technology to explore particularly troublesome kinds of techniques and materials, alarmingly more toxic and deadly, as will be discussed in this and the following chapter. At the same time the word "technology" has itself been restricted in popular usage to *electronic* devices and their uses, thus rendering most critics of such components and their manifold applications "anti-technology,"[1] thereby excluding any such critics from what is some circles must account for well over 90% of social interactions.

* Fear of technology in the US is pervasive — and also frequently masked. It is everywhere around us, even as it co-exists and partly merges with the profound faith that ultimately technology not only will save us, it is all we can look forward to, embodying *the only hopes we are allowed to have* for the future anymore. A glimpse into the profound and widespread apprehension about contemporary technology was apparent in the movie "Batman," where the titanic apocalyptic battle between Batman and the Joker takes place at the Chemical Works, with its steaming vats and tanks filled with noxious substances, obviously meant to constitute a Hell on Earth.

* Any analysis I might offer here of the "evils" of hi-tech is not meant to be a prescription that we abolish or severely restrict it. Those are separate issues and will be discussed in Chapters 30 and 34. I do not believe the *present* balance of forces would allow an aroused public to oppose and successfully banish the particular tools and technologies so beloved by the corporations, governments, and their militaries, not to mention the legions of the young. The economic, social, and cultural forces driving hi-tech are too overwhelming for people, even if armed with an analysis, facts, justice, and determination, to stop it.

However, the increasing prevalence of hi-tech machinery and processes, by virtue of its very pervasiveness, may create overwhelmingly dangerous conditions and problems that will force humanity to take a critical look at its technophiliac path, perhaps even to turn in a different direction. The chemical toxicity of hi-tech production processes, as we shall learn, means that there is a close connection of IT industries and zones of infertility. Sooner or later we may be forced to confront a situation where the question of whether we

---

1 Traditionally technology referred to practical applications of knowldge in a specific art, most commonly the industrial arts. Any tool, say, a scissors, counts.

should continue tolerating a devastating crapshoot with our genetic foundations has become a burning one for hundreds of millions of people.

Large numbers of people will already have come to question that same technology as they experience its profound power to destroy their jobs, for many of them without providing satisfactory (or any) substitutes. Both of these issues and what they might lead to will be discussed in Chapter 30. In the meantime, the time for that day of possible reckoning may well still be some years or decades in the future; or it could be rather soon.

* It is important to reply to the arguments of those who say that hi-tech is already here and it is therefore silly to debate whether it belongs or not. Once a technology becomes established, say these voices, it is impossible to reject it, "to put the genie back into the bottle."

Such arguments are quite common, though rather terrifying, reflecting imaginations unable to conceive of society making collective decisions to do things differently, *even if* the biosphere would be severely compromised unless those particular changes were put in place *and if* the abolition of a particular process, machinery, or toxin could conceivably make the difference in the survival of our and other species.

Indeed, if facing catastrophic ecological consequences, we fail as a society, as a species, to consider rejecting technological practices or ways of production that have been established as largely culpable in the crisis, then not only are we doomed, we are in violation of a presumed near-universal code that biological entities fight to survive when threatened.

We must take heed of the fact that there are powerful forces doing everything *they* can to make sure that we do not ever consider such questions, playing on our fears of being dismissed as fuzzy-minded, overly emotional, romantic, impractical, or any number of other bad things.

Some (mostly non-parents, I would think) misanthropically have concluded that the rest of nature would be much better off *without* humanity's presence and step forth to cheer on the prospect.[1] But if we allow humans to be driven into extinction, vast numbers of other species and countless habitats will go with us. *Species-suicide*, in other words, given our role in the world, is tantamount to *species-mass murder*; and in the absence of, as yet, clear evidence of non-terrestrial lifeforms, amounts to what can only be called a *cosmic* crime!

* Finally there is the cliché, particularly common on the left, that any particular technology or tool *per se* is neutral, that machines simply have no good or evil to them, nor any implicit values, ethics, or politics. According

---

[1] Earth First!, but not only them, are on it, as in "Voluntary Human Extinction: One Brick Shy of a Full Solution?" *These Exit Times* (Special Earth First! Journal Edition, 2000), a satirical take on this.

to this view, any value, positive or negative, that a given technological innovation has depends on *who* is using it and for *what* ends. Perhaps this cliché was once true, although I very much doubt it; it is manifestly false now, and has been since at least the development of nuclear power and weapons.

Anyone who argues that some form of nuclear power/weapons, given that the technology generates thousands of tons of toxics that never before existed on Earth (plutonium) and that remain extremely toxic for periods of hundreds of thousands, even millions of years, can be benign or even helpful is delusional. For even after over seventy years of intensive research on this vital issue, there is no known way to contain radioactive plutonium safely and extremely good reasons to believe that in principle *no* reliable method could ever be found, especially given the indisputable facts that no human culture has lasted longer than 40,000 years (Australian Aborigines) and that all machines inevitably fail at some point or other. With plutonium, *no* failure is allowable, not with a substance of such unprecedented toxicity. Generating high-level radioactive wastes that must be kept in total isolation from air, water, or soil and from contact with any life forms for what, in human terms, is forever, is absolute folly, a sure recipe for disaster and indicator of social insanity. Short of repealing Mendeleev's Periodic Table of the Elements, such isolation is a fool's quest (fitting for an age of manifest foolishness). No such technology could, in any sense of the word, be considered "neutral," capable of being used for good or evil according to the druthers of who is at its controls.

Public discussion of other radioactivity-based technologies is long overdue. Many of them send dangerous amounts of radioactivity into our environments, none as deadly as plutonium, but few are really safe. Making matters considerably worse is the US government's decision to classify much of the waste as ordinary scrap, so radioactive materials gets recycled in building materials, consumer products, *toys*. The widespread overuse of X-rays in medicine, diagnostically and possibly clinically, needs a careful examination. But that discussion lies beyond the scope of this book.

It is horrific to consider the uses since the early 1990s of "depleted" uranium artillery and missiles by the US, NATO, Israeli and who knows what other armed groups, the radiation from which is certainly not depleted, only somewhat diminished, these true weapons of mass destruction spreading their toxic dusts onto the streets and fields of Iraq, Afghanistan, Kosovo, Gaza and elsewhere, the malign harvest of which is an explosion of cancers, miscarriages, and malformed babies. Besides the Iraqis, etc., US soldiers live in such dust, in effect, Pentagon sacrifices.

ii. Are All Technologies Socially Neutral?

All it takes is one counterexample to disprove a generalization, such as the cliché that any technology *per se* is neutral and that it is a matter of whose hands are on the steering wheel that determines which direction it will go.[1] In our concluding chapters we shall consider the question of just which present-day technologies can be considered so dangerous that they are wrong to pursue under any circumstances and what criteria we can use in deciding such questions.

Nuclear power (and weapons) is one such counter-example, but with a little effort we can readily find others — where the effects of a technology as a whole are inherently negative. Agri-business, the wholesale replacement of biological principles and safeguards by "scientific" measures in growing of food and other crops, is another instance. No technology based on monoculture and that yearly robs the ground of its topsoil can *possibly* be up to any good. Even short-term, any good capitalist will explain, it is foolhardy to sell off one's capital equipment (soil) in order to meet day-to-day needs. But that is what agri-business does in regard to the topsoil. It is a measure of the success of the mechanical philosophy that so few realize that the topsoil is simply irreplacable capital for those who plant. Its conscious sacrifice is unconscionable and should compel a rejection of any form of factory farming.

Both the nuclear industry and agri-business, though in ways mere extensions of the principles and procedures of the past few hundred years, are characteristic of 20th-century ventures, both of them springing forth out of the perverse crucible of the 1930s, where the bloody travesties of European histories since the 16th century came to the unprecedented apotheosis of death that was World War II. Genocide was part of the military strategy of every combatant in that war, as we shall be discussing later.

For now, keeping this in mind, let us examine another World War II technology, microelectronics, specifically in terms of how exactly its various components are manufactured and how that might affect the locations where they are made — its airs, waters, and places — and the workers who toil to make them.

---

[1] See Jerry Mander, *op. cit.*, p. 43.

21

What's That Floating in Our Digital Sewer?

i. THE ECOLOGY OF INFORMATION

Among the many problems posed by hi-tech industries, foremost is that electronic production facilities have a devastating effect not only on the ecologies of localities where the components are made (and those where they are disposed of) but on the Earth as a whole.

At the beginning of the 21st century, with every place under some kind of toxic assault at the hands of our species, the effects on the biosphere of any recent technology must be closely investigated by a vigilant public.

Marxism & Witchcraft will describe a three-fold manner in which hi-tech undermines: *first,* our physical health, the *use* of computers taking its toll on vision, backs, wrists, and generating a range of nervous disorders, but most importantly the *manufacturing* of information-technology hardware, the chips and circuit boards, the iPads and smartphones, as we shall see, sabotages humans (for starters) healthy reproduction; *second,* our intellectual health, as knowledge and wisdom are reconceptualized in terms of "data" and its "processing," a digital redefinition with the noteworthy benefit that while *knowledge* is notoriously resistant to quantification, *data* readily lends itself to measure, thereby facilitating its packaging into commodities (like collateral default obligations) as part of a restructuring of markets Capital has undertaken in recent decades under neoliberalism; and *third,* our spiritual health, as communication increasingly is screen to screen, keypad to keypad, bypassing face-to-face and even voice-to-voice human interactions at an ever-accelerating rate.

The several following chapters will examine closely the intellectual and spiritual issues, as well as the ideological and epistemological implications of our emerging binary ontology. In this chapter we focus on the multitude of health and ecological issues.

Some of my analysis comes from what I observed in my recent 20-year stint as a science and math teacher in a San Francisco Unified School District inner-city middle school, but prior to that, the source of many of my examples and conclusions in these chapters came from what I saw, heard, ferreted out, and smelled at a series of jobs over a decade of employment, first as a drafter, then promoted to designer at a number of Bay Area hi-tech corporations and institutions — including Bechtel, Exxon, Pacific Gas & Electric, Stauffer Chemical, GTE–Sylvania, Varian, Fairchild Semicon-ductor, SOHIO, Raychem, Stanford Linear Accelerator Center, Cutter Labs, Fluor Mining and Metals, and on projects subcontracted for Hewlett-Packard, TRW, and Shell Oil. At those places I designed piping systems; plumbing; fire-alarm systems and sprinklers; alarm networks; machinery; chambers for high-energy physics experiments; instrumentation; platforms for chemical-storage tanks; heating, venting, and air conditioning systems (HVAC); and the like. In several of the jobs I helped design production fa-cilities for the manufacturing of computer components.

My major traumatic experience, a wake-up call regarding issues of the environment, came when I was hired by one of the largest electronic firms (yes, it is in the above list) in the early 1980s. My supervisor directed me to examine all the production areas in one of their sprawling, many-build-ings sites (one of several it had in the Bay Area) in order to track down likely sources of a chemical leak, which I later learned was an extremely toxic acid, HF, or hydrofluoric acid.

Finding these sources (or not, since their discovery could finger liability) was critical because two clusters of birth defects and miscarriages had ap-peared in the San Jose area and, after investigating, the EPA had a good idea they came from these labs. The firm, it was soon clear, had no real idea of just where, or how many, sinks there were to check. Years of continual shift-ing production processes and a repurposing of labs, recorded only haphaz-ardly — the "as built" drawings, frequently different from what was designed — over a long period of such retrofitting in a sector of the economy, with the dual prod of the wars in Central America and the space shuttle, in almost continual metamorphosis, had created a considerable amount of uncertainty.

My job was to document the many sinks, try to ascertain what chemi-cals were in use and where. Armed with clipboard, rough and generally out-of-date architectural drawings, safety glasses, white lab coat, and rub-ber gloves (little protection against HF, about which I was not warned, which in even small quantities can maim or even kill), I was sent forth with my flashlight to find and examine all sinks and drains, taking note of their sizes and what other pipes were in their vicinity, as well as the sizes, mate-rials made of, and likely content of any such piping in their maze of plumb-ing and piping manifolds. I was hardly an expert on any of this —my work as a piping designer had been to draw *on paper* the routes by which the pipes would bring the right stuff to the proper places. Though I knew how to specify on a schedule what a given pipeline should be made of, all of my knowledge of materials came from catalogues. I might well fail in the field distinguishing iron from zinc, seeing a pipe in the flesh, so to speak. From the nebulous and gigantic responsibilities thrust on me by my supervisor, I surmised that I was probably the first person given the enormous and essential task of locating the leaks, all of them.

Sinks and pipes were everywhere. Given a score or more like me and many months to investigate, along with someone to correlate our findings, it might have been possible to give at least a preliminary accounting; but working by myself, the task was simply overwhelming. While on my short time on this job I was unable to give the firm more than a cursory guidance on where to look, my job took me from lab to lab, where I was allowed to sniff around.[1]

I got a literal noseful. What I smelled truly alarmed me. Earlier work designing piping at a chemical refinery had given me, I believed, a nose for carcinogens, for the gene-dissolving solvents and other malevolent brews industrial chemists have been devising in an ever-expanding array since at least the late 19th century, and especially since World War II. In the production facilities where the stench was so appalling, I was painfully aware of how minimal my in-and-out exposure was compared to the (mostly) women who were embedded in such gut-retching odors for hours, weeks, months.

In other jobs, I designed production facilities for electronics, responsible for routing the pipes to bring the requisite liquids and gases in appropriate quantities to, and removing gaseous/liquid wastes from, each workbench where the microchips or other components would be made. Though most of my jobs were short-term (often I was a temp designer) and my responsibilities pretty small, with all the important decisions being made by the engineers who told me what they wanted designed, I had already made the decision that I would collect the dirt on the industrial practices I observed. Hi-tech in particular had induced a kind of foreboding ever since I had taken an elementary programming course at Caltech (no such course was part of the curriculum in 1960, but an eager graduate student offered it for no credit, and I was curious) and got a whiff, this time metaphorically, of the dumbing down of communication that was sure to result if all discourse had to submit to the binary ontology.[2] In 1960 I intuitively knew that there would be vast realms of intelligence that would not, could not, truncate themselves and so would be left out. Now, in the early 1980s, I vowed to take note of what I saw, and I perused documents that I happened upon.

My discussion of the toxicity of hi-tech industries must be prefaced by two important cautionary notes: first, electronic-production processes are hidden behind corporate proprietary screens, trade-secrets that boards of

---

[1] We shall return to the critical question of how electronic production appears to interfere with healthy reproduction below and in subsequent chapters. By 1992 there was a three-fold increase in birth defects in the vicinity of the leak. (Silicon Valley Toxic *News* vol. 10, no. 1 [Winter, 1992] and Silicon Valley Toxic *Action*, vol. XVII, no. 1 [Spring, 1999].

[2] More on this dumbing down in the following chapters.

directors resolutely fight to defend. The law allows the corporate need to protect its profit-margins to trump the public's need to protect its safety. Accordingly, though there is much we do know about production of hi-tech components, there are many particulars where we are in the dark.

A second cautionary note has to do with the basis on which my analysis is made: by the late '80s, I was working as a middle-school teacher, and so my direct observations of industry practices and access to company documents ended. Production today, over three decades later, has fundamentally changed in at least two particulars. Much more of the work is done by robots. And most of the physical manufacturing occurs in China, Manila, Singapore, San Juan, and other offshore facilities. As I have continued, now from afar, to follow the industry, it seems not all that much has changed in terms of worker protections, except now most manufacturing occurs in countries with minimal environmental protections. I am convinced that my critique in these pages is still, in the main, true, a conclusion suggested by the recent reports about conditions at Foxconn and the situation of over a hundred workers at one of the subcontractors for Apple's iPhone who are suffering from sore limbs, extreme weakness, dizziness, severe headaches, and numbness as a result of their exposures to n–hexane, a solvent. Some are so crippled they can no longer climb stairs or button shirts. Both Apple and the subcontractor make public statements of their concern for the workers and their intentions to take future precautions, but in practice little has changed.[1]

ii. Java's In & Dirt's Out!

Connections between ecological issues and hi-tech production are a critical and timely topic, given how many people in the environmental and technical communities believe that the *way out* of our present environmental nightmare is precisely *through the use of high technology.* If such views win out, as we shall see, the social forces that got us into our environmental stew would simply be allowed to continue adding new ingredients to the pot and stirring vigorously. (That I believe this might in the first place be a recipe for disaster should be no surprise to those who have read this far.)

Computer production has largely managed to acquire an image as a relatively "clean" industry, in contrast to the "rustbelt" or "smokestack" factories, whose visible pollution can be seen exiting the chimneys and fouling adjacent streams with foul, toxic effluents. The cleanliness of hi-tech is implied by the photographs of tech workers in their white coats, booties, hair coverings, and face masks. Though computer technology is responsible for a whole new army of gadgets that regularly grate on our ears with electron-

---

[1] Casey Newton, "Apple Tackles Labor Issues," *San Francisco Chronicle* (January 14, 2012); David Barboza, "Workers Poisoned at Chinese Factory Wait for Apple to Fulfill a Pledge," *New York Times* (February 23, 2011).

ically-created sounds, including car alarms and the maddening *ostenato* of the back-up warning that trucks now broadcast, the plants where components are made are mostly quiet, compared to older technologies, augmenting their "clean" aura. Being the industrial core of something so high-minded as an "age of information" certainly further polishes the image of the industry to a higher gloss; "campus"-like facilities (for management and software development) completes this picture. That the industry is known to be so fanatical about keeping production facilities fastidiously clean, as well as the strict monitoring of "clean rooms," to an ill-informed public once more suggests that hi-tech is all spit-and-polish. To feed this understanding, the reception rooms, hallways, and lobbies of hi-tech firms sport giant photos of glaciers calving or wild rivers running freely down a craggy mountain ravine, or egrets or herons hunting for fish or grubs on a back-lit wetlands, while all stationary will prominently note its provenance in recycling.

Yet, hi-tech production is a reckless abuser and overuser of the planet's already dwindling sources of fresh water that those fish swim in, something visitors to the Monterey Aquarium (built with Hewlett-Packard money), now the foremost marine "museum" in the US, are unfortunately not told.[1] Extensive damage to groundwater in the US comes from computer plants, for example, in a number of communities in California where wells used for drinking water have been contaminated with numerous solvents (toluene, benzene, acetone, methyl ethyl ketone, methylene chloride, trichloroethylene, xylene, TCA, among others).

Most alarmingly, in *every* instance of hi-tech manufacturing where investigations were conducted, a range of reproductive abnormalities was apparent, starting with the Fairchild leak noticed in 1982, but including plants in Massachusetts, Japan, Scotland, Taiwan, Russia, and Mexico, where researchers found increased likelihoods of miscarriage, stillbirths, infant mortality, birth defects, menstrual irregularities, early menopause, and so on among women workers. Some studies found miscarriage rates 40% above that of other women employed.

---

[1] The Monterey Bay Aquarium applied for and received an exemption from a state law banning dumping of wastewater into a protected marine zone, a ruling based on trading off the benefits of the "public outreach and education on the marine environment" it offers versus "any danger posed by the millions of gallons of treated fish, bird, and animal waste it dumps" into Monterey Bay. Susan Rust, "Aquarium Can Dump Wastewater: State Regulators Exempt Monterey Bay Aquarium From a State Ban…," *East Bay Express* (November, 2–8, 2011). The Silicon Valley Toxics Coalition has followed the issue of water use closely. See, for example, Silicon Valley Toxics *Action* (vol. xv, no. 2, Summer, 1997) on "massive water pollution and water resource depletion" by hi-tech industries. Water use by hi-tech is "among the highest of all industrial sectors." (*Ibid.* vol. xiv, no. 21, Summer, 1996). One electronic facility in Arizona was reported using 1.6 billion gallons of water a year.

Not surprisingly, given these problems, ovarian, cervical, uterine, and breast cancers in excess of normal are also connected with workers in electronic production. Electronic workers also experience greater difficulty in conceiving. Women who worked at computer monitors during their pregnancy also appear to be vulnerable, with half of them experiencing abnormal outcomes.[1] One engineer in a Scottish computer firm reported that when the firm was "working against a production deadline," chemical alarms were turned off and "there were women vomiting all over the place."[2] Women workers at an RCA plant in Taiwan all reported having had one or two miscarriages. A number of them were using Chinese herbs to try to increase their chances of pregnancy. A study of the Digital Equipment Corporation in Massachusetts showed over a 75% increase in miscarriages for photo-lithographic workers, and over 118% increase for diffusion workers. An industry-sponsored study at UC Davis revealed clear reproductive risks.

It is also true that these studies were preliminary, for example, some dealing with exposures *in utero*, some for exposures that pre-existed the pregnancy. In *every* instance, though, the necessity for further research to pin down key chemicals or processes responsible was obvious, but in *every* instance industry refused to cooperate, would no longer release data or documents, and sometimes tried to smear or intimidate investigators.[3]

---

[1] "6000 Complaints Flood New Hot Line on VDT," *San Francisco Chronicle* (February 12, 1984); Silicon Valley Toxics *News* (vol. 10, no. 1, Winter, 1992) and vol. II, no. 1, March, 1984; Silicon Valley Toxics *Action* (vol. XVI, no. 1, Spring, 1998). Also, *Challenging the Chip: Labor Rights and Environmental Justice in the Global Electronics Industry,* (ed.) Ted Smith, David A. Sonnenfeld, and David Naguib Pellow (Philadelphia: Temple Univ. Press, 2006): Andrew Watterson, "Out of the Shadows and Into the Gloom? Worker and Community Health in and Around Central and Eastern Europe's Semiconductor Plants," p. 98 for Russia; James McCourt, "Worker Health at National Semiconductor, Greenock (Scotland): Freedom to Kill?," pp. 140, 146; Connie Garcia and Amelia Simpson, "Community-Based Organizing for Labor Rights, Health, and the Environment: Television Manufacturing on the Mexico–U.S. Border," p. 156; Yu-Ling Ku, "Human Lives Valued Less Than Dirt: Former RCA Workers Contaminated by Pollution Fighting Worldwide for Justice (Taiwan)," pp. 182, 184; and especially Joseph LaDou, "Occupational Health in the Semiconductor Industry," pp. 34–35 and 39. *Global Electronics*, Issue No. 117 (December, 1992).

[2] *Ibid.*, pp. 142–43.

[3] *Ibid.*, p. 147. Silicon Valley Toxics *News* (Vol. 10, no. 1, Winter, 1992; vol. II, no. 1, March, 1984); Silicon Valley Toxics *Action* (Vol. XVI, no. 1, Spring, 1998) and *Challenging the Chip*, pp. 112, 34, 35, 39.

TABLE TWO
CHEMICALS USED IN THE MANUFACTURE OF COMPUTERS[1]

ORGANIC SOLVENTS & LIQUIDS
acetone
alkyl aryl polyether alcohol
amyl acetate
aniline
benzene
2-butoxyethanol
n-butyl acetate
carbon tetrachloride
carbon tetrafluoride
chlorobenzene
chloroform
chloromethane
dichlorobenzene
1,1-dichloroethene
diethylene glycol monobutyl
    ether acetate
di-2-ethylhexyl phthalate
dimethylformamide
diphenylmethane diisocyanate
ethanol
ethanolamine
2-ethoxyethanol
2-ethoxyethyl acetate
ethyl acetate
ethylene glycol
ethylene glycol monobutyl ether
ethylene glycol monoethyl ether
ethylene glycol monoethyl
    ether acetate
ethylene glycol monomethyl
    ether
fluorocarbons
formaldehyde
isopropanol
isopropyl biphenyl
methanol
2-methoxyethyl acetate
methyl n-butyl ketone
methyl ethyl ketone
methyl isobutyl ketone
methylene chloride
petroleum naphtha
perchloroethylene
phenol
polybutene
polymethylene polyphenyl
    isocyanate
propanol
propylene glycol
silicone

styrene
ter-butyl-anthraquinone
tetrachloroethylene
1, 1, 1-trichloroethane
1, 1,2-trichloroethane
trichloroethylene
1,2,4-trichlorobenzene
toluene
toluene diisocyanate
trifluoroethylene
tritetrachloronaphthalene
xylene

OTHER ORGANIC COMPOUNDS
acrylic lacquer
acetonitrile
aliphatic diepoxide
amino resins
aminoethyl-ethanolamine
allyl glycidyl ether
bisphenol A
butyl glycidyl ether
cresol
diethylene triamine
3.,3-diaminodipropylamine
dibutyl phthalate
diethyl amine
diethyl triamine
3-dimethylamino-propylamine
epichlorohydrin
ethylene diamine
isodecane
parylene dimer
phenol glycidyl ether
phenolic resin furanes
phthalic acid anhydride
polyacrylate
polyamines
polycarbonate
polyethylene
polyamides
polyimide
polyisoprene
polybrominated
    diphenylethers
polybrominated biphenyls
polyglycidyl ethers of
    phenolformaldehyde or
    cresol formaldehyde
    resins
polyolefin

polypropylene
polysulfide liquid-polymers
polyurethane
silicone rubber
stilbene
styrene oxide
tetraethylene pentamine
    tributyl phosphate
tricresyl phosphate
triethylenetetramine
trimellitic anhydride

ACIDS
abietic acid
acetic acid
boric acid
chromic acid
citric acid
dichromic acid
fluroboric acid
hydrobromic acid
hydrochloric acid
hydrofluoric acid
meta-nitrobenzene
sulfonic acid
nitric acid
perchloric acid
phosphoric acid
sulfamic acid
sulfuric acid

ALKALIS AND OXIDIZERS
ammonia
ammonium hydroxide
calcium hydroxide
hydrogen peroxide
ozone
potassium hydroxide
sodium hydroxide
tetramethyl ammonium
    hydroxide

POISON GASES
arsine
boron tribromide
boron trichloride
chlorosilane
diborane
dichlorosilane
gemane
hexamethyl disilizane

---

[1] From "No Place To Hide," Vol. 2, no. 4 (September, 2000).

hydrogen cyanide
nitric oxide
nitrogen dioxide
nitrous oxide
phosgene
phosphine
silane
sulfur dioxide
trichlorosilane

OTHER GASES
(ASPHYXIANTS)
acetylene
argon
butane
carbon dioxide
carbon monoxide
cyclopropane
ethane
ethylene
helium
n-hexane
hydrogen
isobutane
krypton
methane
neon
nitrogen
propane
sulfur hexafluoride
xenon

METALS & METALLIC COM-
POUNDS
aluminum
aluminum etch solution
aluminum cobalt
aluminum oxide
aluminum silicate
aluminum acetate
ammonium pentaborate
antimony
antimony trioxide
arsenic
arsenic trioxide
arsenic trichloride
barium
barium carbonate
barium oxide
beryllium
beryllium oxide
bismuth
boron
boron carbide
boron nitride
boron oxide

boron trichloride
boron tribromide
boron trifluoride
cadmium
cadmium sulfate
calcium
calcium carbonate
chromium
chromium oxide
chromium salts
cobalt
copper
copper nitrate
diethylttelluride
europium
ferric chloride
gallium
gallium arsenide
gallium phosphide
gallium arsenic phosphide
gallium chloride
gallium oxide
germanium
gold
gold potassium cyanide
indium
indium antimonide
iron
iron oxide
lead
lead oxide
magnesium
manganese
manganese dioxide
manganese nitrate
manganese oxide
mercury
molybdenum
nickel
nickel chloride
nickel carbonyl
nickel fluoborate
nickel strike
niobium
palladium
platinum
platinum salts
potassium dichromate
potassium chromate
rhenium
rhodium
ruthenium
selenium
silver
silver cyanide
sodium dichromate

strontium carbonate
tantalum
tantalum compounds.
terblum
tellurium
tin
titanium
trimethyl gallium
tungsten
vanadium
yttrium
yttrium oxide
yttrium sulfide
zinc
zinc chloride
zinc cadmium
zinc sulfide
zirconium
zirconium oxide

OTHER CHEMICALS
Fluoride Compounds:
ammonium fluoride
ammonium bifluoride
hydrogen fluoride
sulfur hexafluoride
Phosphorus Compounds:
phosphorus
phosphorus oxychloride
phosphorus pentoxide
phosphorus tribromide
Chlorine Compounds:
hydrogen chloride
calcium hypochloride
chlorine
ammonium chloride
sodium chlorite
Silicon Compounds:
silicon
silicon nitride
silicon dioxide
silicon carbide
potassium silicate
Iodine compounds
iodine
potassium iodide
potassium cyanide
ammonium persulfate
ceric ammonium nitrate
naphthalene and paraffin
    mineral oils
petroleum distillates

High incidences of birth defects in several communities besides San Jose, California (see above) appear to be from the chemicals leaking from electronic waste-storage facilities into groundwater, especially since some of the chemicals, like the glycol ethers, are known reproductive toxins.

A March, 2000 report of the Russian Institute of General Genetics, announced that close proximity to computers itself interfered with reproduction in mammals, fish, and amphibians, the creatures exhibiting a number of different reproductive (and other) abnormalities, including greatly deformed embryos and atrophy of their gonads.[1]

Absolutely critical to the manufacturing of computer components are extremely toxic solvents and "doping" gases, a number of them also identified as damaging to reproductive processes. Doping gases are what makes silicon crystals *into* semiconductors, sometimes carrying a current, sometimes stopping it. One commonly used doping gas is arsine, "one of the most toxic gases known," with a toxicity threshhold of five parts per hundred million, that is "exceeded by few chemicals."[2] Arsine is toxic to every mammalian organ whose response was studied. Exposure to it quickly destroys a victim's central nervous system, like the nerve gases from which arsine was derived. The only cure, once arsine is inhaled, even in tiny amounts, is the replacement of all of the victim's blood! Phosphine, slightly less toxic, is another such doping gas. Like arsine, it too is related to the nerve gases developed for World War II. An explosion of one of the standard nine-inch cylinders of arsine gas could, within a few seconds, create above-toxic levels in a volume of air approximately 200 million cubic feet, the equivalent of a one-story building about two-thirds of a square mile in area! Virtually everyone working in that area, should there be such an explosion, would be killed.[3]

In addition, electronic-manufacturing facilities frequently use, and continually discharge, acid wastes, cyanide, heavy metal — ions (such as chromium, arsenic, copper, nickel, platinum, boron, lead, silver, and gold) and solvents (including n–butyl acetate, sylene, TCE, methyl chloroform, PCE, ethylene glycol, toluene, and hexamethyldisilazane, among others) — most of which are extremely dangerous to water and the humans, animals, plants, and micro-organisms that consume or live in it. Enormous amounts of ozone-depleting CFCs were used, until the 1993 Protocol of Montreal banned them.[4]

---

[1] As excerpted in *No Place To Hide*, vol. 2, no. 3 (March, 2000), p. 21. It was the mice and fish that experienced decreased size of gonads, up to five times smaller for the latter.

[2] Carlos D. Abraham, "Chemical Handling Problems and Solutions for Semiconductor Plants," *Electronic Packaging and Production* (July, 1976).

[3] *Ibid.*

[4] As was discussed in this book's Interlude, there are huge holes in this treaty that was supposed to plug up the hole in the ozone shield.

By 2000, well before iPhones and Facebook and the rest of it, 406 out of 2500 electronic manufacturers in the US self-reported that they discharged into the air, water, and land 117 million pounds of toxic chemicals a year. If all 406 and the remaining 2094 non-reporting firms can be assumed to be roughly equal in size, that would amount to roughly 700 million pounds of toxic emissions a year, over a decade ago.

Most electronic firms simply and inadequately "pre-treat" their wastes, which are then sent to public wastewater treatment plants, where they mix with rain runoff and sewer water. When chip production was still concentrated in Silicon Valley, such firms released an estimated 3,500,000 pounds of toxins into the South San Francisco Bay every year, including heavy metals, cyanides, solvents, acids and God knows what else. (There it joined the devastating amounts of mercury and cyanide leftovers from the 1849 Gold Rush.) The ecology of the San Francisco Bay is in serious trouble as a result.[1]

iii. WAGING THE WAR AGAINST DIRT

Management insists that a full-scale "war... must be waged against dirt" in factories making digital equipment, as a trade publication explains, necessitating specialists in "contamination management." But the coveralls, gloves, hair coverings, headmasks, shoe-covers, and high-velocity air "showers" that all electronic-production workers must use are not for *their* benefit, but to protect the silicon wafers being manufactured *from* the workers. For the production of reliable chips, all the more so with each successive stage in the miniaturization of components, rigid controls have to be established over temperature, humidity, ambient vibrations, and especially dirt.

Where ordinary air contains approximately five million particles with diameters larger than a millionth of a meter per cubic foot, for the purposes of many critical manufacturing stages, micro-electronic firms have to reduce that figure to less than ten (or sometimes even down to only one). Typically, to minimize dust, air in the designated clean rooms is continually filtered and recirculated, resulting sometimes in even higher concentrations of fumes from solvents, acids, etc. In such environments, enforced with tight controls, the bodies of the workers, according to one former leading designer of electronic-production facilities, are "the single greatest source of... contamination," "the worst dirt generator in... the process..." a mere "cloud of dirt," as well as an "enemy of the clean system and high-yield product."[2] To minimize

---

[1] "Silicon Hell," *San Francisco Bay Guardian* (April 26, 2000); Bill Soiffer, "New Study Says Toxic Chemicals Ruining the Bay," *San Francisco Chronicle* (December 8, 1983). See also Astra Taylor, *The People's Program: Taking Back Power and Culture in the Digital Age* (New York: Picador Metropolitan, 2014), pp. 180–81.
[2] Carlos Abraham, "In Sterile Workplaces, Every Move Counts," *San Francisco Chronicle* (July 17, 1985).

the bad effects of this human cloud of dirt, computer-production managers are advised to keep the production workers' bodies, if not absolutely stationary, at least restricted to a minimum of motion. In practice this leads to hiring policies that weed out applicants who bite their nails, scratch, have dandruff, chew gum, talk unnecessarily, or whistle. Applicants cannot wear makeup or scent, sneeze, touch their face, drum with their fingers or have dirty nails: all of those unnecessarily add to the ambient dirt.

Indeed, work conditions, as much as possible, must reach towards the "ideal (but impractical) conditions [where] each operator would work in an individual, closed chamber." Since the necessity for ultraclean conditions results from the drive towards miniaturization, primarily driven by the Pentagon's need to devise ever-smaller payloads for their missiles, even more restrictions can be anticipated as components continue in their anorexic obsessions. In order to produce chips with high reliability, the consultant to industry advises, the very best worker would be a robot rather than the "large, cumbersome, human operators" who presently compromise the product. Indeed, this is the solution the industry has increasingly turned to.

In the absence of sufficient levels of robotic technology, management is advised to monitor and reward or punish each individual worker's performance, to minimize the inevitable dirt. Typically these production workers are non-white, and in the firms where I worked overwhelmingly they were women, mostly Latina, Asian, and African-American.

Those women (and a few men, mostly in supervisory capacity) sat or stood at their workbenches, breathing the acid and solvent fumes, some of them at machines using ionizing radiation to implant circuitry on the components. The high-efficiency air-conditioning systems use powerful HEPA filters for the rapid and thorough removal of dust, not toxic fumes, so stench in the "wet rooms" remains sickening. In the '80s in Silicon Valley, women, many of them recent immigrants from Southeast Asia, were hired as subcontractors to take components home to clean on a piece-work basis, heating volatile and dangerous solvents on kitchen stoves, in many instances with young children playing at their feet. After such practices were ended in Silicon Valley, they continued in places like the Philippines and China.

To the limited degree that the production facility's high-capacity air-conditioning can remove some of the hazardous chemicals from production areas, it is only to disperse them into the surrounding atmosphere and water supply. Given a certain amount of government pressure, efforts are under way to diminish some of this pollution, but arguments about the expense involved ensures that some of the work is done only as profits and other considerations allow; arsine and phosphine cannot be "scrubbed" from the air exhausted from the facilities, so "dilution of these gases must be depended upon to render them harmless," our design expert, Abraham, advises, as if dilution makes any sense for a substance that is toxic in such miniscule concentrations and is considered "one of the most toxic gases known." A major complication is that many of the pollutants are highly corrosive, and so the pipes, vents, valves, or drains meant to carry them safely away themselves also begin to leak their contents into the land, groundwater and air.[1]

Given all of the above, it should surprise no one that Santa Clara (Silicon) Valley, the center of digital manufacturing, has more Superfund National Priority Sites (29, of which 23 are from electronic manufacturing) than any other county in the US.[2]

iv. WHOSE SET OF PLANS?

Though scares about groundwater poisoning have resulted in government efforts to monitor and control effluents, how effective the reforms are is another matter. The Environmental Protection Agency (EPA) in the US has never been inclined to ride herd on the chemical industry, even less so after being essentially gutted by Presidents Reagan and Bush the elder; son of a Bush set out to nullify one environmental protection after another.[3] Though Presidents Clinton and Obama have been rhetorically more favorable to issues of the environment, in practice ecological questions are shoved aside when they seem to unduly interfere with profits, as Obama demonstrated in relation to nuclear power and oil extraction. And with Trump, all bets are off.

Chemicals routinely used in semiconductor production, the solvents, heavy metals, doping gases, etchants (HF acid), and highly corrosive acid, together or alone, can do intense damage to workers when they inhale, touch, or are otherwise exposed to them. As a result of all their exposures, worker-illness rates among electronic-production workers are three times

---

[1] Similar considerations of corrosion apply to nuclear installations, with more alarming hazards (especially for the bioactive isotopes), because of the radiation bombardment the pipes, seals, valves, etc. are subject to.

[2] For the much-heralded Superfund sites (those posing extraordinary danger from toxic materials), the EPA has done not much besides spending its billions of dollars to identify which sites *should* be priorities for clean-up and drawing up plans, mostly only on paper, for how it *should* proceed, "bogged down in bureaucracy, delay and toothless enforcement." (San Francisco *Chronicle*, May 1, 1983). The toxic dumps, etc., still remain toxic, and continue to produce birth defects in babies born to mothers living in their proximity. (Silicon Valley Toxics *Action*, vol. XV, no. 3, Fall, 1997).

[3] John M. Broder, "Bashing E.P.A. Is New Theme in G.O.P. Race," *New York Times* (August 18, 2011). "The EPA Index," Silicon Valley Toxics *Action* (vol. XIII, no. 2, Summer, 1995). For example, to inspect some 15,000 facilities that generate hazardous wastes, the EPA deployed a staff of 8 (out of 17,000 employees). The EPA focuses its efforts (80%) at relatively low-risk polluters and in effect gives a pass to pesticide makers and users, routineley granting "emergency" exceptions.

that found in other manufacturing industries.[1] The workers risk chemical skinburns, blindness, and pulmonary edema, the latter possibly from exposure to diborane, an extremely reactive gas. At many firms workers have experienced persistent nausea, vomiting, damage to their kidneys and livers, bone damage, itching, oozing skin rashes, chloracne (a chief symptom of Agent Orange poisoning), eye irritation, swelling of the eyes, dizziness, headaches, migraine, various brain and nervous disorders, neck and facial paralysis, holes or deep ulcers eaten into the nose, coronary problems, high blood-pressure, extreme stress, emphysema, coughing spasms, back problems, and aching muscles. Most alarming are the high rates of miscarriage, offspring with birth defects, and other reproductive disorders that are all too common.

In addition, various forms of ionizing radiation are used in the production of electronic components, as is microwave radiation; the latter form of radiation is also emitted from many electronic devices used in homes. Both ionizing and microwave radiation can be toxic, although much more is known at the present time about the devastating effects of the former. Slight, but accumulative, low levels of exposure are always a danger around such equipment, where gamma radiation, which can induce mutations and cancers, might readily be absorbed.[2]

And then there are the cancers, lots of different kinds of cancers and lots of cases. Especially prevalent in remarkable numbers are brain cancers, 149 deaths from primary brain cancer at IBM from 1975 to 1989, or ten a year; but there are also cancers of the lungs, intestines, pancreas, kidneys, testes, thyroid, central nervous system (CNS), lymphatic tissues, melanomas, and hematopaictic tissue (IBM men) and lungs, bronchus, breasts, other female organs, CNS, lymphatic tissues and hematopaictic tissues (IBM women); liver, lung, colon, stomach, bones, nasopharyngeal, lymphatic, breast, and other tumors (Taiwan RCA facility). Residents living near the latter plant had cancer rates of three per thousand; normally one out of every ten thousand or less would be expected.

IBM kept a corporate mortality file of deaths among its workers, 25,000 of them from 1975 to 1989. It was found during discovery in a lawsuit. An astounding 8,000 of the 25,000 died from cancer, according to attorney

---

[1] LaDou, "Occupational Health in the Semiconductor Industry," in *Challenging the Chip*, pp. 32–33. I am very grateful to Prof. LaDue for his seminal work, as well as for his help in directing me through the literature on these vital matters.

[2] Charles Petit, "Weak Microwaves May Alter Cells," San Francisco *Chronicle* (January 8, 1980). See also Paul Broder, *The Great Power-Line Cover-Up: How the Utilities and the Government Are Trying to Hide the Cancer Hazards Posed by Electromagnetic Fields* (Boston: Little Brown and Company, 1993).

Amanda Hawes, who represented IBM workers suing the firm for their work-related diseases.[1]

One electronics worker, a 30-year-old woman, was in good health when she first began employment with National Semiconductor, where she was exposed at work to arsine, ammonium fluoride, hydrochloric acid, trichlorethylene (a solvent), and sulfuric acid. After a few years on the job she began to suffer from numb extremities, coldness, breathing difficulties, loosening of her teeth, anemia, kidney problems, and skin ulcerations. Soon she was "in a wheelchair and [with] mittens on," totally disabled. After five years at work, she died of complications of scleroderma, a disease that destroys both the skin and the connective tissues of the body.[1]

The wide range of potential sicknesses and diseases faced by computer workers (and the communities in which such production facilities are located) totally belies the popular notion of semiconductor industries as clean, indeed, antiseptic, with images of visually clean conditions under which some of the production processes are conducted and the "campus-like" appearance their headquarters affect encouraging such false notions.

To our list of ills, of course, we must add Carpal Tunnel Syndrome or Repetitive Stress Injury (RSI) that many people who work *on* computers get by word processing or operating a bar-code reader, or the numerous eye and nervous conditions people working at their terminals commonly experience. Troublesome transient magnetic fields can exist behind screens, too, that seem implicated in various kinds of dysfunction of their body's cells.[2]

It is impossible for these forms of toxic-laced production to occur in a community without its airs and waters being affected. Leaks can, at best, be minimized; never do they go away. Pipes, valves, cleanouts, safety valves — all of them leak at times. It is in the nature of all technology that the equipment can never be fool proof. Any process carried on with those pipes and valves not infrequently will result in whatever is supposed to be *in the pipes* ending up *on the floor,* or if the contents are under pressure, spurting out to contaminate an extended area, perhaps coating the skin of any nearby workers.

In communities where micro-electronic components are being produced or assembled, we should expect roadway leaks of chemicals being delivered, toxic permeation of the land at dumpsites or under leaking tanks; seepage into the local aquifer (as has happened in San Jose and Mountain View, California); releases into the atmosphere (daily and according to plan), of toxic gases, including arsine ("one of the most toxic gases known") and phosphine (close behind it), which are simply vented through tall smokestacks. Those

---

1 "Suit Over a Chemical Linked to Death: Santa Clara Firm Accused," San Francisco *Chronicle,* (January 12, 1984).

2 "Magnetic Fields Linked to Illness," San Francisco *Chronicle* (September 20, 1982); Broder, *op. cit.* See also Silicon Valley Toxics *Action* vol. XII, no. 3 (Fall, 1994).

gases and the solvents, etc. are some of the meanest chemicals made. That is what communities seeking to snag their share of computer-production jobs for their locality should realize is part of the Faustian bargain they will be forced to make. Since 1981, over 100 known toxic spills have occurred in Silicon Valley. One design firm I worked for was reported to prepare two different sets of plans, one real (for our client, an electronic firm, the other (to obtain government approvals) specifying the use of less toxic chemicals.

In addition to these many environmental assaults by hi-tech industries, the ratio of waste to product for electronic manufacturing is much higher for the computer industry than for all other forms of manufacturing. So for each pound of component or software sold, there are many more pounds of trash and toxic by-product to dispose of than in other forms of industry.[1]

v. The Price of Convenience

When issues of safety (or battery life, for that matter) are raised regarding the new technologies, users are quick to tout how much easier they make matters, how many things their devices allow them to do: maps to just where they have to go, calling all the turns, at the touch of a finger or voice prompts; finding friends on a crowded beach (or at a demonstration); instant communication; facts delivered on their screens within seconds on virtually anu subject! It is clear that hardly anyone can imagine life without their conveniences.

We might wish to take a serious look at the price we pay for such "conveniences," for they are considerable. Two key aspects of hi-tech's toxicity shout out for our immediate attention, particularly so in a book seeking to comprehend our species' apparent descent into self-destruction. The first of these is the malign effect the production of information-technology hardware (and presumably, as studies suggest, the mere use of such machines) has on human (and other species') reproduction. The many problems stand out in bold relief and in near consistency in study after study, plant after plant, as well as in the grim experiences of people and their babies who live in proximity to such production, or who work inside the factories where semiconductor components are fabricated; at their workbenches sit an overwhelmingly female workforce, nearly all women of color. That was true when production was in Silicon Valley; it is still true now that electronic production is largely off-shore.

There is a long history under colonialism of attacks against reproduction by women of color, from medical experimentation-cum-torture (the first hysterectomy was performed, "as an experiment," on an American slave with a perfectly healthy uterus); the transformation of sex into one more means of

---

1 Interview with Ted Smith, former Executive Director, Silicon Valley Toxics Coalition, August, 2012. E-waste accumulates three times faster than regular waste. (Astra Taylor, *op. cit.*, p. 181.)

producing (slave baby) commodities; forced sterilization; and, of course, the many rapes and other forms of sexual degradation. The word for reproductive crimes against women of color (or any ethnicity) is "genocide." Given the mass of evidence pointing to IT's undermining of healthy reproduction among women of color, it should be absolutely clear that this is a *genocidal* technology.

The second issue is more ethereal, though nonetheless real. Readers may recall from Chapter 1 the fuzzy boundaries between living and non-living. Various definitions to find the dividing line fall short, and there is no agreed-upon biological criteria for life, as I learned in Sophomore biology.

In the realm of the in-between lie crystals. They can grow, they repro-duce, they respond to stimuli(the first radios were crystal-based). Influential theories of the origin of life on Earth claim it emerged out of a crystalline stratum. The reactivity of crystals, to some, suggest a form of awareness.

That semiconductor production begins with treating silicon dioxide (SiO_2) crystals to a whiff of a nerve-gas derivative should, at the very least, set off some deafening metaphysical klaxons. Nerve gases were developed for World War II by the Germans and the Allies; they incapacitate the nerv-ous system; death is nasty and quick. Surely there is something rather strange that this new technology, based on an agent like this, should purport to be building the infrastructure for all our future thinking! Later chapters will explore the ramifications of these questions.

The devastating effects of information-technology ecological assaults on our lands and waters is nicely deflected by a widespread focus on how all of this activity is in preparation for the present "Age of Information," conjuring up images of disembodied ideas and Humanities 101, rather than the nasty conditions under which the actual microchips are made. Indeed, to hear many of the acolytes speak of it, the computer "revolution" is more of a spir-itual than a physical overturning, for in their mind, they are creating a world where at long last ideas will be truly valued, becoming, in fact, the new em-bodiment of modern Capital, and freeing up humanity for a vast leap in evo-lutionary development. In the next chapter, we focus on these ideas, more specifically, on the "information" that is said to be the foundation of this new digital world we are entering.

22

The Ideology of Information

...everything was an effect in the bloodless constructions Bernie and his peers were churning out. He worked tirelessly, feverishly, to get things right, to stay on top, make songs that people would love and buy and download as ring tones (and steal, of course) — above all, to satisfy the multinational crude-oil extractors he'd sold his label five years ago. But Bernie knew that what he was bringing into the world was shit. Too clear, too clean. The problem was precision, perfection; the problem was *digitalization*, which sucked the life out of everything.... Film, photography, music: dead. *An aesthetic holocaust!* — Jennifer Egan, *A Visit From the Goon Squad* (2010).

i. HARD DATA

Everywhere schools are embedding more and more of their curricula in digital form: simulated science "labs" on DVDs; data that students might collect with a digital probe, software automatically graphing results that students enter into their laptops or SmartBoards; texts found online, as well as homework support sites. In addition lessons and exams arrive via e-mail. Teachers in middle and high school receive elaborate spreadsheets describing what each of their students had "mastered" or not, based on a computer analysis of their computer-scored assessment tests that are administered on a regular basis. And so on. In for-profit colleges, most of the instruction is on computer, a practice that is increasing and spreading.

In this chapter we shall examine some of the *subtext* of this momentous change in education and the implicit philosophical lessons about the world and about themselves that students using these new information-processing technologies are absorbing as well. Far-reaching social, economic, and political agendas can be found in the very architecture of the machines that constitute the infrastructure of the "Information Age." Indeed, what we are witnessing is the advent of robotic-pedagogy,' much of it already in place, preparing these students for a purported "21st-century knowledge economy."

That such changes are occurring with hardly any public discussion is scandalous. In the absence of these discussions all we hear are the cheerleaders, gee-whizzing in union magazines or daily newspapers about the wonders-to-come, tips on how to incorporate one's teaching in this new modality, the latest chapter in the ongoing faith in technology to solve educational and social problems that in the US goes back into the 19th century. Educators write with great enthusiasm of what they foresee happening with sufficient computing power. But serious questions why and whether and at what cost are hardly ever raised, or if they are, as I experienced in the San Francisco Unified School District, administrative harassment and retaliation can be expected. Since educational resources are always scarce, especially in recent times, the huge chunk these machines and their networking and tech-support takes out of the budget is ruinous to other school needs — like teachers, librarians, nurses, counsellors, and paraprofessionals.

In attempting to open such an overdue discussion here,[1] I hope the kinds of critical questions such an extensive (indeed, totalizing) takeover of our educational institutions should raise may begin to be explored. Here we will look at the unexamined (by most of us) premises, at that *subtext,* of the digitalized curriculum; the next chapter will return to the particulars of electronic "schooling."

I shall argue that "information" as a newly-defined conceptual entity (see Chapter 24 for its origin) serves in the late 20th and early 21st centuries, just as the notion of the "inert body" did in the late 17th, as an ideological weapon for undermining the shrinking domain of the *living,* bringing it under ever greater control. And just as the widespread inculcation of the truisms of the mechanical philosophy in the 17th 18th, and 19th centuries helped drill successive generations of hard-nosed leaders and bureaucrats so that they might be ready to shoulder the awesome responsibilities and burdens of organizing and running the emerging world empire (and we should have no doubt that, as we saw in Part Two, on some levels and at critical times, this was a conscious enterprise),[2] so too today people are being bombarded with a new understanding of "reality," now based on "information," to prepare them for the tasks they must carry out as leaders, managers, employees,

---

[1] I am aware of and have benefitted from a number of other critics of the digital mania that has swept across culture, such as Clifford Stoll (*Silicon Snake Oil*), Nicholas Carr (*The Shallows*), Jerry Mander (*Four Arguments for the Elimination of Television*), Sven Birkerts (*Gutenberg Ellegies*), Neil Postman (*Technopoly*), Todd Oppenheimer ("The Computer Illusion," *Atlantic*), Jaron Lanier (various articles).

[2] See especially Chapter 8 on the Royal Society and Chapter 11 on Robert Boyle's writings from the 1650s about science, religious reform, commerce, and empire. In Chapters 28 and 29 we will return to the question of how conscious or not these considerations were/are.

and citizens of the political/technological/economic order now being consolidated by Capital, a world where, among other things, the "production" of new kinds of "organisms," as in bio-tech, is normalized.

To see how this preparation occurs, let us return to the digitalization of time. In Chapter 17 we examined two important modalities of this process: first, that the *circle* of time was being hammered flat, so that in a critical way the endless *cycle* of time in the world, that bedrock of human consciousness and emblem of life itself, digitally is bereft of any grounding; second, that our eyes and consciousnesses, instead of interacting with a visual representation of time's progression in the clock's hands sweep, sunlike, across a circular clockface standing in for the sky, experience only alphanumeric readouts in digital timepieces. Consecutive numbers flashing on and off replace the carefully orchestrated ratios established by the movement of second-, minute-, and hour-hands in the clocks we have known since the 14th century, where the circle of time had been choreographed into the instrument itself.[1]

To show that those transformations in our experience of time are part of a much larger picture, consider other instruments being digitalized. Though less emotionally traumatic than the digitalization of time, the use of binary instruments to assess length, mass, volume, or temperature raises additional fundamental questions about — and, more critically, significantly remakes — our world.

When I read a measuring instrument, a great deal of the time I want to read not "*on* the lines," but *between* or *among* them. Using an alcohol- or mercury-based analogue thermometer, for example, I might only want to see if my daughter's temperature is still above normal or not, or whether it is still slowly inching up or has, alternatively, stabilized. Analogue instrumentation such as clocks with faces or dials with pointers to display pressure or volume or lines on a scale for temperature, allow interpretations. They also allow "seat of the pants" assessments, where one can notice that something is closer to a foot in length than a yard or that it weighs a bit less than a pound. Digital devices, however, allow no role for the observer's intent; the degree of information delivered never varies, no matter what its user wants to know. Typically, the instruments measure to some decimal of a unit (of mass, length, degree Centigrade, etc.); many of the instruments carry on a constant electronic "chatter" as the last figure shifts back and forth: 4, 3, 4, 3, 2, 3, 4, 5,..., as if from a nervous tic in the circuitry itself. If I don't give a damn about the thousandth of a pound of chunky peanut butter I am buying, the chatter is a distraction, senselessly drawing my attention, like a drunk making a scene at a concert. It is an example of data clutter, of "information" that is useless but *commands* our attention anyway, in the sense that it is hard to tune out.

---

[1] Only gradually were minute and second hands adopted.

ii. Issues of Control: the Preferred Stock of Machine Thinking

Despite certain clear advantages of instruments with dials or other ways of visually "showing" a model of what you are trying to measure, *industry* needs to utilize instruments that can be "understood" and directly read by *machines*. To be fed a picture of a dial with the big hand just after the 2 and the little hand a little before the 4 simply cannot nourish a machine; its electronic controls, however, can readily digest that it is 15:18:08. However, though a person easily understands the implications of a scale whose needle points to the extreme right, nearly off-scale, a machine can only be made automatically to react to a reading of, say, 10,001 pounds per square inch (psi) in a particular holding tank by activating an alarm, since it can be set to react whenever the pressure exceeds 10,000 psi (or wherever the supervisor or engineer decides to set it), but that instrument is incapable of noticing the critical differences between 10,001, 10,006, or 100,000 psi. A slight increase over the predetermined limit is in essence the same, as far as digital instrumentation is concerned, as a huge surge that should command instant attention by workers and supervisors. Digital instruments lack the capability to make judgments, but they create the illusion that they can, and so are made to "decide" to shift to particular subroutines on the basis of certain data readings that pass through the Central Processing Unit. On the basis of that illusion, managers and engineers entrust data-processing machinery with enormous powers over increasingly large domains of our lives: patient treatments, gas pipeline transmissions, decisions as to who should be targeted for assassinations by drone missiles, etc. Not only do digital instruments allow no possibility for the exercise of judgments (analogue machines do not either), but they make it more difficult for any humans, who somewhere down the line are monitoring the data stream, to reach critical decisions. Analogue instruments, on the other hand, facilitate human reactions, for a needle arcing to the extreme right on a dial is an instant and obvious indicator of major problems.

Nonetheless, the movement is towards automatic production based on digital instrumentation. As I learned when working as a piping designer for a major chemical firm, readings of various instruments in process facilities are critical in deciding when the various pumps become activated, or a particular heat exchanger, safety valve, backup vessel, or a complex manifold is brought into play. Scores of interlocks — and interlocks pegged to other interlocks — are tied to one another, so that different temperatures, pressures, pHs, flow rates, concentrations, etc. (all assessed through readings by the instruments) can open or close particular valves, creating wholly different flow conditions in production.

Under the best of circumstances, this is a highly problematic technology; not too surprisingly, industrial plants experience massive leaks in tanks or pipelines, breakdowns, explosions, and other accidents. A few hours perusing the trade catalogues for valves, heat exchangers, pipes, instruments, tanks, etc., — all extolling for potential buyers a particular product in unstinting and nearly identical praise for reliability of welds and seals and the long, leak-free performance it will give — should be enough to convince anyone that such components of these process systems must normally leak with alarming regularity, all the more so to the degree that what is carried in the pipes, etc. is frequently corrosive, as well as toxic.

Given the incidence of accidents involving piping components, the move towards digitalized controls and instrumentation, in an effort to better manage the increasing complexities of the production process, has the exact opposite effect, allowing critical breakdowns to last longer and wreak more havoc than in the days when people were expected to respond to problems, large and small. Writing about the explosion and collapse of the Deepwater Horizon in the Gulf of Mexico on April 20, 2010, the *New York Times* reports, for example, that the crew of the Horizon "were frozen by the sheer complexity of the Horizon's defenses.... One emergency system alone was controlled by 30 buttons."[1] The greater complexities of these kind of facilities result in the different components and systems interacting in unexpected ways, so that the emergencies that unfold usually had never been anticipated.[2]

At Three Mile Island, too, computerized information misled operators and engineers in terms of what they needed to know and to do for a matter of *hours* as the machinery of the nuclear facility careened and bounced, out of control, heading towards a full-scale meltdown, coming within a half-hour of such a dreaded catastrophe.[3] The data-processing system, however, was incapable of keeping up with the unfolding crisis, at times getting hours behind in its ongoing status reports of pumps, flow conditions, temperatures, pressures, and the like, reports that were supposed to control pumps, valves, electrical switches, etc. and could, in theory, direct the technicians how to

---

[1] "Deepwater Horizon's Final Hours: Missed Signals, Indecision, Failed Defenses, Acts of Valor," December 26, 2010.

[2] David Weir (*op. cit.*, p. 33) argues that if Union Carbide's plant in Bhopal, India, like its sister plant in West Virginia, had automatic, computer-controlled safety systems in place it would have limited the severity of the Bhopal disaster. I disagree, more sympathetic to the view of Charles Perrow (*op. cit.*) that such centralized systems, all of which create unpredictable loops and unforeseen interactions among components, are inherently more unstable, introducing the potential for accidents that are more catastrophic. As Perrow also notes (p. 73), adding redundant components to a system as a defense against disasters, a common strategy, has "also... served as 'the main source of... failures,'" quoting E.W. Hagen's study of common mode failures.

[3] Perrow, *op. cit.*, pp. 17ff.

bring the reactor under control of some kind. Instead, the operators, super-visors, engineers, and experts were led every which way by an absolute sur-feit of miscellaneous data, *most of which lacked context or relationships.* Context or relationships are *precisely* what this new technology fails to provide, how-ever. In emergencies, especially, it is the most vital thing to know.

Chaos reigned in the control room at Three Mile Island, as klaxons loudly interrupted all conversations and every thought about once a second, over 100 different alarms with no way to suppress any of them so as to focus on the most critical ones, the operators trying to gain some control over a complex system that had been put together in a typically hodge-podge way so that no overview or schema existed to explain much of anything. And the accident, as is usual with such events, happened in a way that no one had anticipated in a technology so new and so massified. We shall return to this incident and the role of computerization as tools designed for control, but that frequently create chaos and make resolution nearly impossible.[1]

iii. PRIVATIZED REALITIES

But all of these so far are nothing compared with the even-further-reach-ing implications for the formation of modern consciousness that emerge from other forms of digitalization. The Voyager planetary mission took beautiful photographs of the rings of Saturn; when they were broadcast on TV and printed in books, NASA admitted that the pictures had been "computer-en-hanced." In other words, the bare data received from instruments aboard the space vessel had been doctored, as photographers will sometimes retouch a portrait to hide a pimple or make a chin look less prominent in a wedding portrait, so that features of Saturn's rings could be made more discernable.

While in part I was tickled pink to see in such stunning detail the rings that for hundreds of years — since their discovery by Galileo using his new telescope in 1610 — have haunted the world by their profound beauty and what they invite by way of thinking about the mysteries of our worlds, still I could not let go of a disquiet about this "enhancement" by computers of what we are shown.

Who decides what gets enhanced and by what process? What features does the program that controls the balances of light or dark and assigns the spectral values to the various pixels set out to look for, and what things does

---

[1] Chapter 29. To be sure, digital instrumentation does foster some kind of control. For example SmartMeters, touted for their use in energy savings, allow utility companies to shut off service of customers delinquent in pay-ment of bills, without having to send a crew to do so. Using SmartMeters, P.G. and E. expected to increase the number of such shut-offs from 37% (2005) to 85% by 2011. "SmartMeters Likely to Boost Shut-offs," San Fran-cisco *Chronicle* (January 26, 2010).

it try to minimize? Such are not trivial questions, and when something presumably less identified with the cosmos as a whole as that great crowned sixth planet, undoubted queen of the solar system, the potential for a grave misuse of power to control our very perceptions cannot idly be dismissed. Movies today routinely engage in such distortions, but those, at least, we see as "entertainment" (however much that category and advertising and education are encroaching on one another) and so we might not worry too much about the deeper implications of "Forest Gump" in terms of the meaning of "perception." But if scientists can "doctor" their data — scientists! those who first convinced us to accept and then gave us the apotheosis of data! — if *they* can doctor their data, how will we feel when a US Secretary of Defense shows "computer-enhanced" satellite photographs showing that the Russians, Iraqis, or drug cartels have deployed a certain weapon and so are in violation of some treaty, principle, or strategic interest of the US? When the Bank of America uses "computer-enhancing" to clarify video images picked up during a robbery so as to make identification of a suspect easier? Or to "bring out" his or her "race," as *Newsweek* did in its cover photograph of O.J. Simpson shortly after the murders of Nicole Simpson and Ron Goldman? Or when DAs play "computer-enhanced" recordings of a bugged conversation, so we can make out the garbled words, said to have been said, more clearly? When a mining corporation "computer-enhances" satellite pictures to support its case to the public, its investors, or to government officials that digging for a particular mineral in some threatened terrain is really a good idea?

As is well known, film and video technology has the capability today to fake any image, as with "Forest Gump," so henceforth, photographic evidence no longer can be trustworthy, even as to elementary questions. Objects or people can be taken out or inserted at will into photographed scenes;[1] can be shown in relation to others as an editor (or FBI director) so chooses; weapons can be made to appear. Not only are we as a culture and, at least in the past century or more, as a species, used to using our eyes as the primary way we learn about the world — "seeing is believing" is not an empty homily — over a century of photography has taught people in the industrialized societies to accept the reality of photographic images. Though subject to tampering, through retouching, that work generally left tell-tale marks and could be detected by experts — as, for example, when critics of the government's version of the John Kennedy assassination revealed that the historic photograph in *Life* magazine of Lee Harvey Oswald, Kennedy's official "lone assassin," "holding" a copy of the US Trotskyite newspaper, the *Militant,* in his one hand, while "brandishing" a rifle manacingly in the other, was a fake. The head of Oswald had clearly been inserted on the shoulders of another man. Shadows did not match and angles were awry.

---

[1]As with the photo of John Kerry doctored to make it appear as if he were speaking at an antiwar event where Jane Fonda spoke also.

Digital manipulations, on the contrary, leave no such evidence. Shadows can be changed to match a season, hour, or type of illumination. It is nearly impossible to tell an original from a derived image. If "Forest Gump" showed that perceptions could not be trusted, the film "Wag the Dog" showed how these new powers provide political authorities with unprecedented means of undermining democratic process.

If now, when such digital doctorings, say by a TV station, are not always being acknowledged, or are acknowledged but without providing any explanation of how the data was processed to allow a critical viewer to consider whether the information thus provided should be deemed credible, then what should we expect five, ten, or a hundred years down the road, when such modified information would presumably have become an everyday thing? In the absence of the necessary explanations, we are laid open to the worst forms of manipulations by those who control the images.

In ways such as these, computerization is giving us not simply a *different way of interpreting* "reality," but rather a *different meaning to* "reality." The most alarming example comes, not surprisingly, from the nuclear industry. In nuclear-power technology the single most critical part of a reactor is its cooling system, for if that fails to take away the massive amounts of heat energy continually generated by the radioactive decay of the concentrated nuclear fuel, the reactor quickly goes out of control, threatening a meltdown. As nuclear-power installations began to be constructed in the US and anxiety over potential "accidents" intensified among the public, the reassurances issued by the Atomic Energy Commission (AEC) were based on a "back-up" safety system, (the Emergency Core Cooling System, or ECCS), which in 1966 it began requiring on all nuclear reactors. An early report commissioned by the AEC had predicted as many as 3,400 deaths as a result of a major accident at a nuclear facility. In 1957 the report (WASH–740) forecast some $7 billion in damage from such an accident. Seven years later, a new report put projected damages at $280 billion, a forty-fold increase (1964 dollars), and 45,000 deaths. The Price-Anderson Act, which provided government subsidies to insurance companies if a nuclear accident occurred, was scheduled to expire in 1967, so the AEC pushed for a new study that would downplay potential dangers — in the words of one official, in regard to the issue of nuclear waste, potentially scary information should be "word-engineered" before being released to the public — in order to justify the AEC's prior decisions to permit numerous reactors and to justify the Act's renewal.[1]

---

[1] Daniel Ford, *Meltdown: The Secret Papers of the Atomic Energy Commission* (New York: Simon & Schuster, Inc., 1986), pp. 68ff. Stephen Hilgartner, Richard C. Bell, and Rory O'Connor, *Nukespeak: The Selling of Nuclear Technology in America* (San Francisco: Sierra Club Books, 1982), p. 119. The higher figures were in part because WASH–740 assumed a 150 megawatt plant, but by 1964, 1900 megawatts was a more realistic estimate.

The ECCS would make a catastrophic meltdown categorically impossible, the AEC promised, because any incident that removed the "primary" coolant from the reactor would automatically trigger a flood of water into the reactor core. On what basis were such reassurances issued? Not, to be sure, on a test of this critical equipment. The test was only computer simulations put together by engineers to predict how an ECCS *might* behave during whatever emergencies the AEC scripted for the test! But computer simulations are programmed on the basis of certain pre-picked variables and a number of assumptions about how all the variables will affect one another, as well as other assumptions about how the variables *not* picked are largely inconsequential anyway.

Typically an engineer will try to imagine the ways the components of any system might interact with one another, including possible feedback, assigning numerical weights to the various interactions. Such a methodology, it goes without saying, is fraught with arbitrary quantitative data, and assumptions, little more, about possible causal pathways, and can frequently fail. Should other variables turn out to have, under some circumstances, a major role to play — hypothetically, the outdoor temperature during an extended heat wave lowering the point at which common industrial materials might catch fire — or should. some interaction assumed to be minor actually turn out to be of some consequence, a simulation creates illusions that we know what, in actuality, we do not.

In fact, the particular simulation of the ECCS was especially irresponsible, because the computer simulation used was incapable of handling the three-dimensional geometry of the actual core, and so its calculations were made using only one-dimensional (linear) analysis. That limitation precluded *any* consideration of the very real likelihood that the tremendous pressures, heat, and possible explosions to be expected in any significant reactor emergency could very well change the sizes, integrity, and siting of the very pipes required to carry the emergency cooling water into the reactor core, making blockages exceedingly likely. Accordingly the analysts simply *assumed* that there would be no problem in the water reaching and remedying any emergency. Worse, scientists working on the update of WASH–740 were told by their AEC sponsors, blanching at the $280 billion figure, to claim in their summary that the chances of a nuclear accident "were exceedingly unlikely."[1]

Even more damningly, when in 1970 an actual test of ECCS was run (even then, not with an actual nuclear generator of the size commercial plants then in operation were, but with a miniature, nine-inch simulated re-

---

[1] Ford, *Meltdown*, pp. 101–02, 110; Daniel Ford. *The Cult of the Atom: The Secret Papers of the Atomic Energy Commission* (New York: Simon & Schuster, 1984), p. 71. John G. Fuller, *The Day We Bombed Utah: America's Most Lethal Secret* (New York: Signet Books, 1985), pp. 122ff.

actor), the ECCS completely failed. Despite this less-than-reassuring record, the AEC persisted in continuing to promise that the ECCS was completely reliable and that the public's fears were groundless, its safety assured.

Thus the critical distinction between a test of *how equipment actually works* and a test of *how a computer models the equipment's predicted behavior* (based on what the engineers — in many cases, the very people who designed the system in the first place — think might occur) was obliterated by the AEC. Since we might assume that the engineers who programmed the simulation knew the answer the AEC would want about the reliability of the ECCS, we should question whether the results were not simply built into the model they designed? Any failures of their simulated ECCS, they would realize, would be subject to particularly close scrutiny by the AEC, which throughout the process was prescribing the results they wanted the study's authors to reach. Some of the engineers' inclinations to ignore certain failure modes need not even have been conscious. Sometimes, however, it will be, as when the Office of Management and Budget of the White House "asked the EPA to use a new computer modelling approach" in calculating the risks of perchlorate in an effort to justify levels 15 times higher than before.[1]

So, on a question of species survival, or, less hyperbolically, of the death, maiming, and disease of potentially millions of people — an area the size of Pennsylvania was the unit of contamination put forth in WASH–740 — our very definition of reality has been transformed: and all with "virtually" no discussion of the matter and its ominous ramifications.

iv. THE COLONIZATION OF CONSCIOUSNESS

That a dramatic shift in our interpretation of our world and in the meaning of "reality" is taking place should by now be clear. Only a few decades into what seems more accurately to be a computer "coup d'etat" than a "revolution," such transformations are occurring with almost perfunctory notice, one more "disruption" we are meant to. The corollary of industrialization was its effective (sometimes, as with Scottish miners, actual) chaining of workers to the machinery at which they toiled, so that, as in Charlie Chaplin's "Modern Times," worker and tool, for all practical purposes, simply merge: the worker *becomes* the machine. Yet that worker thinks, gets bored, plans ways to get rich or get laid, questions the meaning of his or her work, and frequently yearns for the beauty, purpose, and joy in work that fewer and fewer can find. With digital technology, this all changes, for the worker will less and less be allowed to think or imagine autonomously — rather, his or her consciousness becomes bound to the screen's prompts, kept within the boundaries set by his or her software or operating system, and especially

[1]Juliet Elperin, "EPA Decides Not to Limit Perchlorate," San Francisco *Chronicle* (September 22, 2008).

its programmers, at which s/he works. The kinds and magnitude of the problems such a colonization of consciousness will inevitably bring about are hinted at by our feelings when forced to respond to someone's or an institution's computerized voice mail — the categories offered rarely apply to the things we need to do, ask, or know, and we listen in mounting frustration and rage as this becomes obvious.

If the industrial revolution can be said to have colonized our bodies, the on-rush of computer technology represents the same process in relation to our minds and souls. Reality is what our digital machinery registers. Our language, indeed, our sense impressions, must be recast so that they better "interface" with electronic reality; increasingly they are being redefined by it.

Though the mechanical philosophy of the 17th century taught people that what they tasted or saw or heard were really "based on" the more fundamental movement of hypothesized submicroscopic particles of whatever it is they were eating, looking at, or hearing, thus helping to reconceptualize the world as a machine, still the five recognized human senses maintained their inherent integrity. To be sure, they needed to be *interpreted*, but it was not by alteration, not by changing their very nature. Rather, the "laws of nature" were based on the "data" those senses (sometimes with the help of such new instruments as microscopes, telescopes, thermometers, etc.) provided. That is now all changing. The epistemology of 21st-century microelectronics assumes that perceptions exist only *after* they have been processed through a program, so that a computer can rectify them, showing us what we "need to know," to use the chilling phrase of the Manhattan Project. And the obvious question, with ominous implications, is: who gets to decide how to program the computer that makes such decisions? About how images, or sounds, or taste, or feeling will be "enhanced" electronically? What criteria will they use?

In effect, then, the military and business, the two major forces in setting the agenda for computer research and development, are carrying out what is really a theft of our consciousness. This is an epochal cultural revolution, one that will make earlier transformations in the way humanity interpreted our world that occurred (for the West) in Classical Greece, in the Italian Renaissance, or during the scientific revolution, look like small episodes in the history of human consciousness; yet it remains largely hidden from us under clouds of obfuscation and a downpour of hype about "information." And where those earlier stages in the development of Western culture emerged out of a huge outpouring of books, treatises, correspondence, manuscripts, speeches, sermons, letters, and countless conversations over tea or beer, some negative, some offering differing perspectives on the new ways of seeing and understanding the way things were, so that each of these stages was a product of widespread public (at least the literate public) debate, these new changes, to the contrary, are happening with barely any open discussion. What is talked about is mostly the minutiae, the how-tos of what kind of network and baud width. Profound philosophical, social, and political changes to our world are slipping by "virtually" unnoticed. In our ignorance we are rendered helpless — particularly so since open debate is stifled by the pieties and promises and mystifications of our supposed Information Age.

Let us take note, however, that simultaneous with this Age of Information we find an ushering in of a systematic drive at all levels to proletarianization of those most responsible for transmitting information: teachers. At the primary and secondary levels, this can be seen in the push for charter schools, in the demonization of teachers' unions, and strict supervision of lesson plans, sequencing, and teaching strategies, frequently including scripts from which teachers are told to teach. At the university level, we find the spread of adjunct instructors, a drive to curtail faculty powers, and MOOCS, classes of as many as 500,000 students. We will explore many of these issues in the following chapters.

23

Failures of Public Education: Or, Will an Apple iPad a Day Keep the Crisis at Bay?

> [W]hoever determines what technologies
> mean will control not merely the technol-
> ogy markets... but thought itself.
> — Douglas D. Noble, "Mental Materiel:
> The Militarization of Learning and
> Intelligence in US Education"

i. THE FIVE-SIDED PEDAGOGUE

As a middle-school science-and-math teacher in the last decade of the 20th and the first decade of the 21st centuries, I received an increasing amount of promotional material for DVDs or other electronic educational materials that would promise to teach my students the wonders of plant cells, of the solar system, or of the laws of optics, many of them embedding their lessons in simulated laboratory "experiments." Sadly, I realized how a principal on a strained budget might be tempted to opt for an $89.95 DVD that purported to engage students in lab work compared to the expense of glassware, safety glasses, and working sinks needed for a real (that is, physical) lab.[1] A real lab, where water may spill, glassware will be broken, and sometimes (if the lab is chemical) unpleasant smells might be part of the lesson.

Yet the push to do "experiments" on an electronic platform speaks to deeper issues than mere economics and a squeamishness about wet floors.

[1] In all likelihood, that principal will not compare the costs of said glassware, goggles, chemicals, etc. against the expenses of buying the computers, networking, DVD players, and the tech support required to keep it all working. Not only principals. The physicist Stanislaw Ulam commented that "It's infinitely cheaper to imitate a physical process in a computer and make experiments on paper, as it were, rather than reality." (Dyson, *op. cit.*, p. 192). Ulam was referring to altogether different kinds of "experiments" than the ones offered in DVD lesssons.

We can get a sense of what these issues are if we listen in to what the people behind such technology say to one another at their conferences. In 1984, for example, the organizer of the Institute of Transferring Technology to Education told a conference that the system of "doing experiments" on computers "would use the approach the Army has used for the past five years to teach personnel how to operate some of the most complicated tasks, without even touching the expensive machinery."[1]

If we examine the boast in the epigraph to this chapter, and what it rests on, we find alarming undercurrents. Beneath the overwhelming push to get children hooked into a computerized curriculum, a vast experiment, involving everyone who becomes a student these days, is being conducted to better engineer the connectivities between machines and people, a research endeavor born of the Cold War and the drive to automate the machines of war. Since World War II, as the military began to emphasize automatic weaponry, it has focused on vexing questions about how people interact with the machines with which they work. Though its ultimate goal was, and is, to replace humans in warfare, the Pentagon has put massive efforts into understanding, in the interim, just how humans perform their battlefield tasks in relation to their increasingly complicated and rapidly operating machines. From World War II, it was clear to the Pentagon that the human was the "loose cannon" in the "man/machine system": inefficient, slow to react, even slower to learn.

Pentagon Research-and-Development millions — and then billions — flooded into projects to clarify the learning process. It went hand-in-hand with the development of computerization, the specialized field (of which more below) of Artificial Intelligence (AI), and a new science of human cognitive processes. Increasingly, the new cognitive sciences (including among others, biologists, psychologists, and engineers) insisted on conflating human and machine-thinking, using Norbert Weiner's cybernetics as a model for both. In this view, when humans "thought," they were essentially merely "information-processing." Thus, under the spur of military priorities, the human mind in the "man/machine system" was reduced to something that engaged in a "'form of complex decision-making,'" or, as it is usually termed in schools today, "problem solving."

It is highly instructive in this context to look at what the two men most critical in the development of modern computers in the 1940s and '50s thought they were doing, for both Norbert Weiner, the MIT mathematician and originator of cybernetics, and John von Neumann, the legendary mathematician (and alleged model for the figure of Dr. Strangelove in Kubrick's

---

1 Sandy Stone, interview, "Sex & Death Among the Cyborgs," *Wired* (May, 1996). Douglas D. Noble, "Mental Materiel: The Militarization of Learning and Intelligence in US Education," in *Cyborg Worlds: The Military Information Society*, (ed.) Les Levidow and Kevin Robins (London: Free Association Books, 1989), pp. 19–20.

movie of that name), thought deeply about such matters in relation to human thinking. Weiner realized in the mid '40s that on the basis of what was understood about *matter*, things like life, organisms, and mind were fundamentally unexplainable. Using *immaterial* concepts like message, feedback, and control, however, Weiner believed "it will in principle be possible to give a fully scientific description of an organism." Such a substitution allowed his models to bypass "life" and "mind" altogether.[1]

Von Neumann (instrumental in the design of thermonuclear weapons, for which he invented one of the first US computers in 1952, and an eager booster of nuclear power)[2] also realized that too little was known of neurophysiology to develop a formal-logical description of the human brain. Using concepts like "inputs" and "outputs," however, it was possible to reason mathematically and logically, store information, act on general instructions, and recognize patterns with photo-receptors. This, von Newmann believed, would *roughly be equivalent* to the actions of a brain.

Thus, for both of the men who first developed computers, it was clear that their machines were not "thinking," as that concept is understood. Instead, they were *bypassing* thinking, replacing it with what they believed would be a rough approximation. Those who have followed Weiner and von Neumann on these matters have not shared their modesty at all. Thus, Weiner and von Neumann's distinctions have been lost over the years.[3] To many of today's information technology savants, the machines are, in principle, thinking; and it is only a matter of time, perhaps within a decade or so, before "they" are more intelligent than us, many claim, their hopes riding on a "Singularity," when humankind is essentially given a Pink Slip. More on that later.

Like the computer, the lion's share of what is considered educational tech-

---

1 My discussion of Weiner and von Neumann comes from Heims, *op. cit.*, especially pp. 209–19.

2 Von Neumann calmly accepted that the development of new technology might well necessitate sacrifice of many human lives. (*Ibid.*, p. 367). His memorandum to Lewis Strauss to this effect is found in Strauss, *Men and Decisions* (New York: Popular Library, 1962), pp. 451–53 from September, 1955. Approaching his own death, von Neumann, according to his daughter, Marina, was "very upset" when she observed to him that he could "contemplate with equanimity eliminating millions of people, yet you cannot deal with your own death," and he replied, "that's entirely different." *Dyson, Turing's Cathedral, op. cit.*, p. 272).

3 Alan Turing similarly believed that computers acted "without understanding what they were doing, but in later years fudged his position, willing to consider the machines intelligent.... Turing was the British mathematician whose writings theoretically laid out the criteria for the new logical machines. (Andrew Hodges, *Alan Turing: The Enigma* (New York: Simon & Schuster, Inc., 1983), pp. 327, 358–59.

nology today was first developed by and for the military, including standard-ized testing, overhead projectors, training by video discs, and computer-aided instruction. In their quest to obtain a better grasp of human "problem solv-ing," however, researchers increasingly ran aground on the shoals of igno-rance regarding how learning actually occurred. The problem was that human decisions in practice were, despite human inefficiency, arrived at ob-viously far more quickly than *any* machine protocol could lead to, as one lead-ing theorist of AI recognized, admitting that programmed learning in real-life situations readily necessitates "an unmanageable number of instructions steps" in its program.[1]

Computerized automated weapons are one major reason for the massive funding that flowed through the academic "cognitive" disciplines involved. Another crucial reason was, paradoxically, the awesome challenge of serv-icing the exceedingly complex war machines that resulted from the first. A fire controlman for the AEGIS cruiser (a missile-defense system), for ex-ample, requires over two years of training to perform his or her tasks. Var-ious publications to instruct recruits in maintenance of the Navy's F–14 interceptor add up to about 300,000 pages. For both these ends, the military urgently needed to *re-create* human thinking in order to make it more "ma-chine-friendly."

For these reasons, AI and cognitive science soon merged into "cognitive engineering," the realization that computer models for human thinking were critical, *not because they were necessarily accurate models of how people actually think*, but *because they enabled the military to use such models* "to improve human learn-ing and performance." This was recognized by some as early as the first half of the 1960s. Computer models were thus to function as a way "to enhance human cognitive performance," to gear it up, so to speak, so as to mesh with the cogs of war. "If we are really simulating people with computers, then the only way to improve people is to understand the procedures that the com-puter goes through and attempt to *teach... people like we... teach computers.*" Em-phasis is on re-designing human functioning to allow it to better function within its environment of complex computer systems. Herbert Simon, one of the leading AI researchers, was impatient with human learning and de-manded that the priority should be to speed it up. "I find it terribly frustrat-ing trying to transfer my knowledge and skill to another human head. I'd like to open the lid and stuff the program in," he confessed.[2]

Much of the terminology in education circles today, such as the need to teach "higher-order thinking skills," the mandate to have "task-specific" goals and measures of "on-task" performances and "performance outcomes," as

---

1 Douglas Noble, *op. cit.*, p. 22.

2 Douglas Noble, *op. cit.*, p. 22–24, 28, 29. Emphasis mine. I doubt if even Descartes and Gassendi could have been comfortable with such a level of mechanistic reductionism.

well as the search for "learning strategies" specific to a lesson and the attention given to "metacognition" as a means by which humans can learn to control their own learning — all comes out of this military emphasis on cognitive studies and engineering.

A very real danger in these approaches to teaching and learning is that a soldier — or student — who can through metacognition learn control of his/her own learning process will be much more capable of being controlled by superiors. "The more transparent is the [black] box [of human learning], the more efficient can be the control of its processes." As another early researcher in man/machine symbiosis put it in 1967, as society moves towards "computer-service cultures," education "is likely to take on attributes of real-time control systems."

To make their vision come true, however, the cognitive engineers needed to be able to put their ideas into practice so as to refine their methods and clarify their models. But, as another of the pioneers in this arena complained, as early as 1959,

> The final difficulty that... must be faced in the attempt
> to integrate the science of learning and the technology of
> education is that of gaining access to children of school age
> for... experimental investigations.[1]

This problem might be overcome, however, if, in F. Reif's view, education is thought of as a "component of cognitive engineering, with schools serving as laboratories for empirical research by cognitive engineers."[2]

In effect, our schools thus became laboratories where our young can be subjected to what amounts to a "militarized redefinition of mind, intellect, thinking and learning," as Douglas Noble warns us.

ii. THE CARTESIAN MENU

How this military redefinition of mind, etc. operates can be seen in most of the computer software, where, for all its self-proclaimed multimedia capabilities, ostensibly to combat linearity and simplistic thinking, there is an absolute hegemony of linear thinking. Computers — which utterly lack any capacity to *judge*, except for matters of lesser or greater — are, according to their enthusiasts, the tool *par excellence* for teaching "critical thinking." Yet virtually every time students log on to cyber-space, they will encounter a "menu," a list of options from which they are to pick. A series of menus from which one chooses options as a format to represent thinking or teaching is as simplistic a model of the real complexity of the way we think as a

---

[1] *Ibid.*, pp. 29, 28, 25, 29–30, 31.
[2] *Ibid.*, p. 33.

stick figure is of an actual person. It is Cartesian methodology and mechanistic analysis now *axiomized*, since it is structured into the technology and
its circuitry. All entities, all problems, are first atomized into a number of
subparts (menu choices), each of which in turn....

Again, as if we are in a world where illogic rules, these sequential menu
choices by students are what are considered "interactive." If choosing from a
menu at McDonalds is considered "interactive dining," I might allow that the
menus offered up by various software could be considered "interactive learning." More importantly, as we shall see, it represents a whole new level of
"dumbing down," as if one were to teach cooking by having students work
as interns with "chefs" at their corner McDonalds, in effect, giving the students prepackaged, very nearly predigested, nuggets of something that was
once meant to be vital and health-giving.

In wonder and despair I watched my students at the Lawrence Hall of
Science, a popular Berkeley teaching resource, flock to the computers next
to the exhibits, rather than to the exhibits themselves, there to choose from
such menus.

Let us look more closely at how science labs in electronic media teach lessons different from what are claimed for them. First let us examine some of
the questionable assumptions and ideology such labs appear to reflect. In, say,
a hypothetical simulated chemistry lab, a student might be instructed to "add"
certain amounts of "hydrochloric acid" to different "solutions" of "metal salts,"
generating on the computer screens some indication of resultant color changes,
precipitates, effervescences, temperature changes, or gases that presumably
resulted from the different manipulations of the variables. Besides some icon
to represent liquid, solid, gas, heat, etc., changing colors, and a cartoon-like
sound track that might accompany the different transitions, all a student actually *experiences* in a simulation like this is the sight of their screen where our
three-dimensional world has been rendered into two, and the sound from the
speakers, usually little electronic ditties, melodic clichés; the student will feel
the keyboard or mouse at his or her fingertips and will experience having to
manipulate either or both of those plastic surfaces with fingertips.

It is quite remarkable that such ersatz "experiences," confined to a
quasi-rectangular screen about a foot-and-a-half in front of the student's
hypnotized eyes, is commonly referred to in education as a "hands-on" lesson! But the hands here, we must emphasize, are on nothing but an artefact, a device (named after science's favored experimental animal) used for
transforming what is seen on that screen and opening "windows" from it
to different "worlds."

What are the worlds offered in my hypothetical chemistry lab? In no
sense of the word is it an *experiment* that such a "lab" guides the students
through, for *nothing happens* through the lab software *that has not already been
programmed* to happen by an engineer or programmer who wrote code for

the software. The students are simply entering a series of closed loops, simulations based on an assumption of which variables are important, and which can be safely ignored.[1]

What will *not* happen in such a lab are the kinds of things that happen all the time in real labs: real labs often do not unfold as the book/lab manual say they will. The teacher and students then have to huddle for a few seconds to several minutes, depending on class sizes and deportment, to figure things out a bit: to redo something, plot a new line of attack, get fresh chemicals to try a step over, and/or re-interpret what to make of the book/manual's expectations. Here is where the real kernel of (science) teaching, in my opinion, occurs, one teacher (or aid) to three or four students troubleshooting what they've done, figuring out, for example, how to change slightly the experimental conditions, or tighten an electrical connection, or, perhaps adapting a piece of equipment that's not quite right for what they are trying to do, but happens to be all that is available at the time. Significantly, both students and teacher/aid are in the dark during such a process, not really sure what is going on, matters ripe for discovery.

In simulated labs, indeed, things also go wrong, but not because of the ambiguities built into the world of reagents and beakers, electrodes and bunsen burners; no, *those* all do as they are programmed, thanks to the software, but things go wrong because of some problem in the software program or how the particular computer works the software or has trouble connecting to the printer/Internet/probe. In other words, what troubleshooting students and teachers in such labs "access" each other over is the quirky circuitry, format issues, and programs, and not over the recalcitrance of real matter (with the exception of the doped and etched silicon chips). Students really interact not with the chemical reality the simulation is supposed to be about and presumably concerning which it is supposed to teach the students, but with the computer. *The tool has become the lesson!*

Science and engineering students frequently speak snidely of labs that are simplistic, probably capable of being performed by automata, all rote with no real substance or much interest to them, contemptuously called "cookbook" labs. Today's computer-simulations are the worst form of cookbook "labs," all the more dangerous because they have successfully been packaged as their opposite, as truly "interactive" experiences for the students. No, these labs, it is worth repeating, are perfectly-closed loops; students can only experience from among a number (sometimes, given the computers' *forté*, a *very* large number) of pathways and outcomes programmers thought to provide. Only the degrees of each variable truly change. No surprises are possible. As Theodore Roszak argues about such "experi-

---

[1] These simulated "experiments" for students are not to be confused with numerical simulations based on hypothetical modelling, which to a degree can be open-ended.

ments" where everything comes out right, they eliminate the inherent *risk* of all real experiments. "Higher-order thinking skills" are what is in bold print on their packages, but this is really a very sophisticated form of "dummying down" of the curriculum. It is *pre-packaged* knowledge, to use my earlier metaphor, the fast-food of the educational system, providing little of substance, for there is nothing really to chew on.

In real chemistry labs, things go differently. Water may spill, getting tables, books, and papers wet. A test tube or beaker may break. Sometimes there are unpleasant smells. There may be some chaos, but it is the chaos of creation. The colors of the natural world, rather than those that are chosen by the software for their laptop for each of the pixels, are seen. Nothing can be more *tactile* than this. It is learning through *all* of the senses. Students have to pay attention to instructions about safely handling materials, for there are real consequences attached to their actions. Compare that to the simulated lab, where for the most part students are reduced to "clicking on" from a sequence of "menus" offered them, in each case being asked to choose between two, three, or perhaps a dozen choices, in every instance, the choices allowed made up by the programmer.

In a simulated "lab," "lenses" can only be used for optical "experiments"; it is simply impossible for a curious student to take one of the "lenses" and on her own try to see if lenses affect magnetism, or the reverse. "Magnetism" would be in a different program, probably on a different disc. If you are lucky, the school owns it, and, even luckier, the same computer can, though at different times, of course, run both of the programmed "labs."

iii. AN ERSATZ SCIENTIFIC INVESTIGATION

Another lab that ends up teaching the exact opposite of what science education should aim at, was not so long ago part of the "Science Olympiad" the San Francisco Unified School District held one Saturday each year, for competition among middle-school students. In this lab, computers were central to the effort to hoodwink students into believing that they were doing real science in a "lab" that was really a creative form of pure obfuscation. Students were asked to build paper airplanes from a standard kind and size of paper. Several possible designs were provided for students to copy, and they were encouraged to experiment with designs of their own. When the planes were finished, the students flew them in a set location and measurements were made of time aloft and length of flight for each plane. Winners were given awards.

The flim-flam occurred when the individual planes were then measured as to length and width and perhaps one or two other things and that data, together with the plane's performance statistics, was entered into a computer program. From this information, the computer then spit out "optimal" designs for the several variables.

In fact, no such ideal design parameters are possible. Whatever the computer comes up with is a sham. The airplane trials had at least a dozen or more variables, besides the crafts' lengths, widths, etc., none of them "controlled," acknowledged, or measured. What about the height of the person launching the plane, the angle of throw, the force with which the plane is sent aloft, the width and height of the hallway (assuming the plane was thrown inside) and any air currents from temperature gradients or breezes? What is the shape of the plane and angle of the craft's wings in relation to its body, for that matter? Its total surface area? Conceivably, one could generate many more aspects of this experiment that are unaccounted for and for which, in this lab, *no* controls whatsoever exist. To pretend to students that sense can be made from the hodgepodge of differing trials, based on their arbitrarily-chosen data, is to teach them *very* bad science. Yet, with computers, fake labs such as this are easy to imagine and tempting to implement.

Following the language and tropes of electronic machines, educators and students are increasingly encouraged to think of their own minds as fleshy things that in essence are like computers with so much of their "memory" filled already with data and with a number of "programs" already learned. Implied or stated outright is the reduction of thinking/learning to filling up more "memory" or changing one "program" for another.[1]

What is particularly alarming here is how deftly the goals of education have been redirected, again, virtually without discussion or debate, though again there has been a trainload of cheerleading pieces breathlessly describing what computers will bring into our lives only a handful of years from now. Books, articles, lectures, and advertisements bombard us with the belief that the computers open up to students a virtually unlimited amount of "information," as if, indeed, information is what students need, what education is all about. To the contrary, students, as we all do, have a surfeit of information, for we are surrounded by it, bombarded by TVs and *People* and Twitter, and what we miss one place we pretty well pick up at another. What students (as do the rest of us) need is *context*, we need to know how to *judge* between alternative and sometimes conflicting information. Which is precisely what computers cannot give.[2]

This information-besotted ideology of education is all new and carries considerable baggage. While alien to the traditional concepts of education, with the exception of some technical fields, *information* has distinct hidden

[1] Nicholas Carr makes the important point that, unlike computers, the brain is continually reworking our memories. "Biological memory is alive, computer memory is not," *The Shallows: What the Internet Is Doing to Our Brains* (New York: W.W. Norton & Company, 2010), p. 191.

[2] Michiko Kakutani, "Texts Without Contexts," *New York Times* (March 21, 2010).

advantages over knowledge or ideas. Since *ideas* are notoriously difficult to turn into commodities, unless they be for specific inventions, *data* or *information,* as mentioned before, is the virtual coin of the realm in our new digital kingdom. No surprise, then, that in recent years education, including the astronomical debt-load carried by most graduates, has become big business, its administrators routinely commanding princely salaries.

Previously, schools were understood to exist for education or training, and that meant mastering certain "bodies of knowledge." Whether algebra, English, US history, PE, physics, shop, art, or music, each subject had not only its own way (or methodology) of viewing/interacting with the world we inhabit, it also had certain skills it conveyed to students — how to treat variables, finding past perfect tenses, the role of the Bill of Rights in criminal law, for examples — *and* a set of frameworks that contained a whole range of a given subject's content — say, what the real numbers are, grammar, rendering textures with line strokes, or the laws of motion, etc. Lessons always occurred *within a context,* it was their bedding, the foundation of their significances.

Students need to learn different approaches to making sense of their world, not, as today's ideologues claim, "information." It is the contextualization that creates order out of the chaos of facticity, not simply *more* facts. Without context, information is simply "trivia," an obsession of popular culture in recent years. Students need to learn *how to make judgments,* need to learn *how to relate one thing to another.* Computers, wherein "information" comes via a series of menu choices, have decided weaknesses in regard to judgments, or, except in a numerical way, establishing relationships between things.

Computer education, then, frequently means a mere plucking of factoids out of an unseen cyberspace or data base, where they have little context other than the particular menu in which they are embedded.[1] To be sure, the factoids may come in a multimediated format. But the topics are atomized, cut off from any larger meanings, no matter how many "links" a website might provide to other categorical islands of atomized data in the cybersea of the Internet. In theory, the *students* make those meanings, find their individual patterns, often by means of project-based work where a particular topic is studied simultaneously through two or more subjects, like social

---

[1] Or as Carr (*ibid.,* p. 91) notes, a search engine will generally find snippets of text that might be germane to the key words used, but one gets the trees (or only the twigs and branches), not the whole forest. One English teacher said she could easily tell if students' essays were written on computers, because "[t]hey don't link ideas. They just write one thing, and then they write another one, and they don't seem to see or develop the relationship between them." (Joel Oppenheimer, "The Computer Illusion," *Atlantic Monthly* (July, 1997). Or, as a senior geological research advisor for Mobil pointed out, "you can't simultaneously get an overview and detail with a computer. It's linear. It gives you tunnel vision." (*Ibid.*)

studies, math, language arts, and art. But in practice, even here topics lack context, a history, a comparative framework.

On what basis are menu choices given? Who makes up the possible choices? At the conference "Computers in Education: A Critical Look" (UC Berkeley, June 3–5, 1995), one participant related a story of her use of the software simulation, SimFarm. While running the program, she was notified on the screen that her "crops" had been infected with "insects." As she searched her menu for an ecologically-balanced approach to the problem, she was dismayed to find neither Integrated Pest Management nor any other pesticide-avoiding treatments were given as possible strategies. Only some form of chemical attack on her "fields" could stave off disaster. She had been disturbed earlier when she similarly realized that the same program did not provide contour plowing among the options for how she might "till" her land.[1]

Similarly, other programs — many of them highly thought of as "creative," "educational," or even "ecological" — include choices and premises that have been arrived at on the basis of unstated logics, values, and goals of the engineers and the corporations who have hired them to construct the software. Who decides? And on what basis are the choices made? For most users, the range of options in their various menus will not appear as a contentious issue, for they will be presented as the "obvious choices." So they will appear to casual users.

In like manner we might wonder, on what grounds do the various web-browsers currently contending for market shares for search-engines help web-users get to the most relevant sites, make connections? How is their range of motion, their degrees of freedom, the breadth of category overlap, or the "bleeding" from one topic to another, controlled? Is it possible that some topics are purposely, or even unconsciously, marginalized, slighted when topic associations are linked for would-be web-surfers?

Chilling answers to these kinds of questions emerged in recent studies, the first a 2011 investigation by the *New York Times*, which asked an expert on on-line search to look into J.C. Penney's absolute dominance in search results, for a period of several months, as the first site listed for "dresses," "carpeting," "bedding," "rugs," "tablecloths," and a huge number of other categories, many of them not at all Penneyish in character. The *Times* report takes us into bizarre commerce involving "search-engine consulting firms" that for a fee help increase the on-line "visibility" of your web-site. Behind the scenes there is massive gaming of whose site is on top by means of purchasing "links" to your site from other sites — a major criteria, it turns out, for Google's ranking algorithm. The *Times* investigation revealed that the gaming is being done by some major retailers — BMW as well as Penney

---

[1] "Computers in Education: A Critical Look," *Transcript of Presentations and Discussions* (Berkeley Center for Ecoliteracy, [1995]) p. 33.

(the latter discovered engaged in wholesale buying of links on four separate occasions), as well as that Google has a curious hands-off and laid-back attitude to what was, in the *Times'* view, "a large, sustained effort to snooker" Google. A key Google manager in charge of the matter explained in New Age blather that Google "strives not to act out of anger," though he did admit to feeling personally "offended" by the actions that were bad for Google users.

As to how Google actually decides which sites rise to the top, which sink into oblivion, that is the responsibility of their algorithm, which Google will not divulge, claiming it is proprietary information. Using similar methods British Petroleum (BP) was able to position *its* news and analyses of the 2010 Deepwater Horizon explosion in the top ten in Google searches on the gigantic spill.[1]

The *Times* report raises the ominous question near its end, admitting it was merely speculation at this point, for which proof was elusive, whether Google's lackadaisical response to J.C. Penney's repeated successes in campaigns to dominate web-searches might be tied to the fact that J.C. Penney was also one of Google's top advertisers. Google hotly denied the very idea! But of course they would. And it is that question which is actively being investigated by the European Union. Microsoft has gone further, charging that Google "manipulates its search results to favor its friends and punish its enemies."[2] The *Times* article credits the claim of a man who is himself a major link-seller that Google searches fall into two categories, "information" and "commercial," the latter badly polluted by corporate jockeying, but the former not. Not only is this a violation of the first axiom of the Information Age, that information is the key "product" of our times, but the distinction totally falls apart as soon as one thinks of "information" searches involving the geology of oil-bearing rocks or genomic-based pharmaceutical products.

In the fractious and highly competitive world of bio-tech, what is to prevent an eager start-up from hiring its own search-engine consulting firm in order to get its own genomic tinkerings and the theories they embody to the top of any germane (or, as in the J.C. Penney example, not-so-germane) web-search?[3]

---

1 David Segal, "The Dirty Little Secrets of Search: Why One Retailer Kept Popping Up as No. 1," *New York Times* (February 13, 2011). Nick Hoppe, "Putting Their Best Socks Forward," San Francisco *Chronicle* (July 12, 2016). Astra Taylor, *op. cit.*, p. 106.

2 James Gleick, "How Google Dominates Us," *New York Review of Books* (April 18, 2011).

3 Apparently these techniques of market manipulation can work off-line, as well, as mayonaise maker Hampton Creek realized, sending out teams of "shoppers" to purchase large amounts of their product, "Just Mayo," and bombarding grocery stores with phone calls requesting it, so that their inflated sales figures would attract venture-capitalist investment. Olivia Zalecky, "Helping Just Mayo Sales Cut the Mustard." San Francisco *Chronicle* (August 7, 2016).

This is all rather astounding. Even more astonishing is the equanimity with which this chicanery seems to have been received. Fairly common knowledge that search engines can be manipulated has in no way resulted in a stampede to abandon the Google Kingdom. In what amounts to a collective shrug, Google remains the search tool used by most academics, scientists, journalists, students, officials, and by taxi drivers, sales reps and baristas.

This is as if, in the days when library card catalogues were where most research began, certain private interests had been able to privatize some of those Dewey decimals, as if Andrew Carnegie had claimed the right to control some of the drawers in the early card catalogue and was allowed to get away with it. Search engines, privately owned enterprises, thus are able to control what knowledge is readily accessible, which harder to find. One more beach-head for neoliberalism, with its drive to shrink the public domain.

Someone has taken the necessary and obvious step to study the feasibility of gaming Google searches in order to sway election results. The study's conclusions: no evidence that it has happened yet, but all-too-easy for insiders at Google or some other search-engine to wield such "surefire and undetectable way[s]" to manipulate election results. One commentator, a professor of computer science at Yale University, admits, "We don't have any way of knowing what biases, if any, the search engines we currently use have." Since Google already "tweaks" the selections made by its proprietary algorithm to editorially structure news reports, doing something similar for political issues would be easy, enabling them in theory to "covertly pick members of Congress and even the president," the author of the study (published in *Psychology Today*) concluded, lamenting that it wouldn't even be illegal to do so.[1] Silicon Valley has clearly demonstrated its pronounced political agendas: strongly libertarian; relying heavily on aerospace contracts and the military; anti-regulation, particularly on environmental issues (e.g. Facebook's support for Keystone X–L); and pushing a type of immigration reform that would enable it to hire low-waged foreign tech workers so as to avoid hiring the many well-qualified but more expensive US tech unemployed. It is no stretch to conjure up motives for pulling off such political manipulations via algorithmic shenanigans.

As private corporations the Facebooks, Googles, or Microsofts are able to carry on as they will, treating their algorithms or coding as proprietary matters. With no accountability for its choices, Facebook took down photographs of nursing mothers, but allows photos of women being violently attacked to remain up.[2] As the Googles, Facebooks, Twitters, and the rest of them come to occupy the key nodal points for our economic, educational, social, and po-

[1] Evan Leatherwood, "For a Public Search Engine," *The Nation* (May 6, 2013).

[2] KPFA, "Evening News" (June 9, 2013, 6:28PM). "Is Policy Out of Focus? San Francisco *Chronicle* (July 23, 2014).

litical interactions, technocratic elites have been, in effect, handed the keys to the kingdom. Keep this in mind as we proceed in our analysis of hi-tech.

So, in terms of how links are made or how the menu is determined, there may be hidden biases. Sometimes, the limits are the result of the particular data available on-line. The notable physicist, Philip Morrison, tells a story of watching as a programmed lesson explained plate-tectonic theory by lighting up appropriate pixels on a screen map of the Earth wherever earthquakes contained in the Internet database had occurred, thus tracing the tectonic plates. Marvelling at the ease with which the program illustrated the actual subterranean plates, the quakes delineating the boundaries between them, Morrison relates that nonetheless he was conscious of the lesson's distortions, since only earthquakes occurring after 1961 (when such data had first been entered into the standard format of computer-speak) had been used in generating the tectonic map. Such historically-epochal earthquakes as New Madrid, Missouri in 1811, Alaska (1964), San Francisco (1906), Lisbon (1755) and Naples (1538) were not even represented. As Joseph Weizenbaum comments, "The computer has thus begun to be an instrument for the destruction of history. For when society legitimates only those 'data' that are 'in one standard format' and that 'can easily be told to the machine,' then history, memory itself, is annihilated," and he wondered about the long-range implications of a "data bank" being constructed by the *New York Times* of current events that similarly will include only that data that had originally been made by typesetting machines, this by the US's newspaper of record, and posing "how long will it be before what counts as fact is determined by the system, before all other knowledge, all memory, is simply declared illegitimate?"[1]

In other words, here and (as we shall see) elsewhere the "Age of Information" is premised on the *de facto* truncating of what is actually known, dazzling displays of information-*transfer* achieved, it would appear, by engaging in a significant measure of information-*suppression*.

Were Internet databases offered merely as supplementary to the often more substantial pen-and-ink or cuneiform records, in some areas going back millennia, the damage done might not be so extreme; but time and again older records are quietly purged and the expurgated digital database substituted. So it happened with the rebuilt San Francisco Main Library, where the new librarian, Kenneth Dowling, "one of the nation's leading advocates for the high-tech library of the future,"[2] was brought in at the height of the dot-com. bubble and proceeded to destroy the old card catalogue once the considerably more limited on-line catalogue was available. He then had scores of thousands of volumes thrown away that he deemed outdated.

---

1 Joseph Weizenbaum, *op. cit.* pp. 237–38.
2 San Francisco Public Library web-site.

Given San Francisco's role as an outpost of hi-tech industry, his moves were closely watched.

The mass conversion to on-line catalogues and the discarding of card catalogues has, in fact, been catastrophic, what the historian Helen Parish has compared to the burning of the library of Alexandria in 34 B.C.E. The transfer of all the particulars that cards contained to a digital format, including publishing information, physical description, subject categories the work was relevant to, etc., as well as being generally incomplete, is expensive: 60¢ to $6 a card. Errors in the process are common: 1.4 errors per discarded card, according to one study, and even if recognized, many errors are never corrected, as it would be far too expensive. The University of Chicago conducted a one-time overall correction; it cost $150,000.[1]

The electronic records also are ham-fisted in terms of a person's identity. Marriage, the winning of honors (e.g., Isaac Newton becoming Sir Isaac Newton), even an author dying, so that William Faulkner (1897–) becomes William Faulkner (1897–1962) or Mao Tse-tung becoming Mao Zedong seem to gum up the interstices of electronic memory. In one electronic catalogue, Thomas Maucauley's works were separately catalogued under eight different versions of his name. Worse, the electronic records are much more elusive, not answering the beck and calls of reasonable searches. A study of fourth, sixth, and eighth graders (at Downers Grove Public Library in Illinois) found that card-catalogue searches were successful 65% of the time; once the system went on-line, that figure dropped to 18%. Adults at Northwestern University had a 39.5% failure rate using on-line catalogues.

Subject searches in electronic catalogues are notoriously problematic. "Labor" brought up a mixture of entries regarding the AFL–CIO and birth. "Traffic control, Alexandria, Virginia," directed a reader to works about the destroyed library in Alexandria, Egypt.

Cards in trays are easily subdivided, so that organized labor can be readily distinguished from Lamaze classes. The amount of listings in a single catalogue drawer, about 1000 cards, are far more quickly flipped through and glanced at than a similar number of electronic listings in a data-base can be scrolled. Sometimes subject searches (as on the UC Melvyn) dredge up so many listings that the would-be reader is simply advised to check back later, not during peak hours, as in "Rome–History," "Censorship," "Air Pollution," and a host of others. On Hollis, the system used at Harvard, "Textile" drew a blank, "Textiles," on the other hand, directed the reader to numerous holdings. Card catalogues encourage judgments to get around ambiguities like singular vs. plural; not so with on-line listings.

As increasing proportions of libraries' budgets are allocated to their electronic-technology needs (on average, 30% in 1992), there are fewer resources,

---

[1] Nicholson Baker, "Discards" in *The Size of Thoughts: Essays and Other Lumber* (New York: Random House, 1996). San Francisco Pubic Library web-site.

as in San Francisco, for purchasing books, magazines, movies, or records, or for hiring librarians or extending hours of operation. Most databases only go back a set number of years, as if earlier publications are of no value.[1]

All of which constitutes implicit censorship. Critical works, published only a handful of years previously, are screened out, as are works by minor publishers or those published in the wrong places. While all libraries have to limit their acquisitions, they carried catalogues of those libraries that, as official national libraries, did not — the Library of Congress for the US, British Museum for Britain, Bibliotheque nationale for France, etc.[2]

The hidden alleys of cyberspace that the 0s and 1s must traverse in their breathless run from one cell to another, whether in the form of instructions, data, etc., must be explicitly spelled out in thick, turgid tech manuals (now on-line, as they've become too bulky to print) that must accompany any new system, attempting to show users how to meld machine, networks, and applications to their varied purposes. Compounding matters considerably, proprietary-based deadends are purposely erected by firms like Microsoft, Apple, or Facebook, trying to prevent users of Windows from wandering "off the farm" into the browser/operating system of rival firms like Netscape. Steve Jobs was notorious for building a virtual moat around Apple, insisting his products could not work with the digital *hoi poloi* of Microsoft, IBM, etc.[3]

Once more, though the rhetoric is about "globalization" effacing borders in our new "Information Age," the actualities more resemble the parcelling out of knowledge into competing guilds and secretive craft traditions, Apple carefully picking which apps it will allow its phones to run in a kind of neofeudal locking-up of knowledge, inside the keep of this castle or that of hi-tech.

iv. Modularized Imaginings

As is clearly the case with television, there are good reasons to believe that working on computers actually saps students' imaginations. Multimedia can make it worse, for in an effort to work through a few of the senses at the same time, multimedia programs for secondary students are apt to include a stored library of drawings, "clip art," an all-too-convenient repository of generic images, like a visual muzak, which leaves still less for students to do themselves. The computer does most of the synthesizing. In many classes,

---

1 *Ibid.*

2 When I tried to obtain the standard catalogue for the British Museum (now Library) at the San Francisco Public Library, most of the librarians had never heard of this standard reference work. Persisting, I finally found that it was in storage and could be ordered, a couple of volumes (out of dozens) at a time, a day before I needed them; in effect this major research tool had been rendered nearly useless. There was no online version at the library.

3 Isaacson, *op. cit.*, p. 237.

students no longer even have to make graphs of their findings, for now it is done for them by their computers, by passing the tactile matching of abscissas to ordinates that embodies the lessons of what graphs *are*.

For their use, the computer will have libraries of sounds, images, symbols, etc. Creating their "art" from the stored images, students will be able to choose some colors, can shrink or enlarge the images, and pick from a set number of possibilities where to put them on the pages. Clip art is quick, it allows students to gussy up their presentations, and it is a lazy way to learn, akin to supplying students with a variety of muzak tape-loops and telling them they can each be a musician with such tools as their "instruments." Especially with younger children, whose lack of fine motor controls but vivid imaginations often leads to wonderful representations emerging out of the ends of their pencils or crayons, the use of clip art will be very appealing since they will be convinced that such efforts looks more realistic, hence "better" than their own freely imagined drawings. This is a point made forcefully by the child psychologist Joseph Chilton Pearce in remarks at "Computers in Education" after one such program had been demonstrated to participants.

Whereas schools traditionally put students to making big banner-like signs to advertise back-to-school nights, dances, and the like on butcher paper that got hung across hallways, now the signs tend to consist of computer-generated big block letters and stock images, perhaps of a one-room schoolhouse or pencils and erasers or a computer, clichéd icons to remind students of the educational nature of the event; yet one might wonder whether the earlier signs, made by students kneeling on the floor with their bottles of tempera and brushes, were not an important part of how students came to learn literacy? We might wonder, as well, what such works composed on their screens from a palette of preselected colors, a collection of stock images, and often canned chimes or tonal phrases might do to students' aesthetics as they go digital? What will happen to motor skills as fewer and fewer students draw or use real paintbrushes (not simulated brushes)?

Student electronic presentations for their portfolios collect together several such menus for administrators, teachers, or parents to examine and to click through; depending on their choices, they will be shown a multimediated package, perhaps announced by a chime and showing a short video clip while they read a couple or three sentences about the topic. For a report on Egypt, they might choose "pyramids," and would read a little snippet of information, more likely than not an unattributed direct quotation from the text- or library book. Any number of inherently fascinating Egyptian topics, mummies, Cleopatra, the Rosetta stone, the library of Alexandria and its burning, the yearly flooding of the Nile, Egyptian religion, their pharonic succession are thus reduced to "augmented" sound bites. Once again, this is an alarming dumbing down of the curriculum, garbed in the finery of hi-tech to make it look impressive, but it should fool no one. Indeed, what is really being taught the students is how they can and should *package* their learning, but what they learn or how deeply they delve into it is of secondary importance.

v. Hitting the Mainline: Connecting Through the Modem

If any of the above points regarding the failings of computers for education are raised with most administrators or teachers, they frequently reply that computers "are just a tool," to be used or misused as with any other. But computers in schools are not only tools. They are a program, an ideology, a re-making not only of the means of education, but of its ends, and frequently they become *the* ends that in the US were first articulated by the military. One need only see how much money in very limited education budgets, and the changing proportions of those budgets, are being spent on the various digital doodads. Or look at any publication, be it trade journal, newspaper, union periodical, popular magazine, etc.: if there is an article having anything to do with education, it will necessarily have a photo or graphic of students, teachers, or visiting politicians standing in front of the ubiquitous computer monitor, all eyes on the screen. In a short time, computers have, indeed, become *the* icon of education, supplanting pencils, blackboards, apples, and mortarboards. Increasing proportions of grants, of workshops, of parental-school programs, are structured around this mere "tool." Computers are not, as some critics of electronic education are saying, merely the latest in a long line of technological fixes that periodically come along to promise to right education's wrongs, for the film strip, video, and typewriter, much as they may have promised to transform educational processes, never packed the totalizing, even colonial, claims that computers do.

Indeed, for those pushing what is oddly called a movement for "educational reform," an onslaught of more computers and greater Wi-Fi access has become the magical tools that will heal all of our educational ills, pushed by Arne Duncan (the first of Obama's Secretaries of Education), Jeb Bush, Bill Gates, the Koch brothers, and Marc Benioff (CEO of Salesforce). On-line virtual schools and/or donations of iPads will bring our beleaguered schools "into the future," Duncan promised, clearly favoring the machines over the several flesh-and-blood teachers who had to be fired in order to purchase the machines demonstrated at the press conference where Duncan and school officials celebrated this transition.[1]

---

[1] Jill Tucker, "High-grade gift to schools. Tech titan donates $2.7 million, tells SF officials to think big when they seek support," San Francisco *Chronicle* (October 7, 2013). Jill Tucker, "Strike up the bandwidth. 3-year project brings cutting-edge technology to SF schools," San Francisco *Chronicle* (June 16, 2011). Neil J. Reley, "Education chief pushing for more tech in classroom," San Francisco *Chronicle* (September 13, 2012.)

As in the increase in productivity from computers that keeps eluding financial analysts, so too with the efficacy of educational technology. How the tethering of students to keyboards or SmartBoards improves students' learning has yet to be demonstrated, but no matter. School districts unwilling to budget to keep elementary classes under thirty students or to provide counsellors, nurses, art, P.E., or music have few qualms about coughing up the bucks in order to provide all their students with iPads or increasing network capacity, confident that it will make a difference, for the siren song of the hi-tech future renders actual evidence superfluous. "We have SmartBoards in every classroom but not enough money to buy copy paper, pencils, and hand-sanitizers," the co-president of the Parent Teacher Organization at an elementary school in Kyrene, Arizona complained. One article summarized, "In a nutshell: schools are spending billions on technology, even as they cut budgets and lay off teachers, with little proof that this approach is improving basic learning," and quotes the former director for education at the Bill and Melinda Gates Foundation (which energetically promotes the electronic classroom), who in 2011 admitted "The data is pretty weak. It's very difficult when we're pressed to come up with convincing data." In fact, the OECD reported in 2016 that "students who use computers frequently at school do a lot worse in most learning outcomes."[2] No matter, the technophiles propose "putting technology at the center of the classroom and building the teaching around it." In other words, in relation to the mere "tool" that is virtually synonymous with data, *actual* data is no longer necessary.

I am not claiming that hi-tech tools do not have distinct educational advantages. When grading a math test I had just given my seventh-graders, I was confronted with the results of an obviously organized cell-phone swapping not only of answers but of the wrong-headed step-by-step process by which the foolish results had been obtained. In a 2009 survey, over a third of teenagers admitted to plagiarizing from the Internet. Transmitting photos of tests by first-period students to those in subsequent classes are routine.

A "crisis in higher education," one more of our fundamental institutions in a state of turmoil, is the subject of many an editorial or position paper, given the huge enrollments but abysmally low graduation rates; skyrocketing tuitions; students typically exiting colleges with bone-crushing college-loan burdens for the rest of their lives, making them in effect indentured servants, forced to take any job available; the lack of actual jobs in their areas of study to be had by many exiting graduates, hence exacerbating their financial precariousness; instruction delivered in many institutions by armies of "adjunct" instructors, educational piecework where PhDs (usually) are hired by the course, working without benefits or even office space to confer with students, barely surviving by teaching at three or four area colleges, so taking

---

[1] Bill McKibben, "Pause! We Can Go Back!," *New York Review of Books* (February 9, 2017).

on huge commute times and expenses; and the increasing corporatization of the major colleges and universities, with managers and MBAs rather than educators as Presidents or Deans, while football and basketball and biotech spinoffs bring in massive amounts of funds.

Not surprisingly, salvation from these overlapping crises is on offer to these Deans, right on their monitors![1] The latest hi-tech nostrum, MOOCs (for Massive Open On-line Courses) are being offered at even the elite universities (Stanford, MIT, Harvard, UC Berkeley, Princeton, Caltech) in order, they say, that higher education be made available for free to anyone who wants it, through no-cost enrollment in on-line courses, taught by topline professors at those august institutions. The "massive" is no hyperbole — some of the MOOC courses have enrollments of 500,000 students!

Indeed, within four years of being instituted, MOOCs were dubbed the "Most Important Education Technology in 200 Years" in an *MIT Technology Review* headline. Standing in the way of what one author refers to as a "MOOC mania," however, are two massive problems, one financial, the other pedagogical. The first is how this "free" educational opportunity will find "a revenue model that satisfies investors," for just like Facebook, Twitter, Google, and the rest of the on-line sites, Coursera and Udacity (two of the major sources of MOOCs) are expected to be "marketable." Other than by running ads on their web pages, how for-profit MOOCs might earn their ways is not clear, however.

The second barrier to the march of MOOCs across the educational landscape is the quality of the instruction frequently offered and the dismal records of student achievement. In terms of the former, one author investigating a Coursera MOOC found it to consist merely of a semi-audible video of one or another professor lecturing to a hall of students at their elite university. Instead of being able to raise questions of the two professors who "offered" the course, students "were encouraged to ask each other" on on-line forums; students would then "vote" what the "best answers were." In another MOOC, student writing assignments were read and graded by other students in the course. Quizzes on the videos students watched frequently "didn't recognize [their] correct answers," to which the course coordinator replied that "the trick to getting the computer to recognize your answers as 'correct' is to recycle the same terminology you hear in the lecture video." Understandably, the students complained that they were being told to parrot back their lessons.

---

[1] The following discussion relies largely on Nathan Heller, "Laptop U.: Has the Future of College Moved Online?" *New Yorker,* May 30, 2013; David L. Kirp, "Tech Mania Goes to College: Are Massive Open Online Courses the Utopia of Higher Ed — Or Just the Latest Fad? *The Nation* (September 23, 2013); and Jon Wiener, "Inside the Coursera Hype Machine," *The Nation* (September 23, 2013).

The dismal results such "education" delivers should be no surprise. Despite great fanfare at a rollout of MOOC courses in three math classes at San Jose State University by Governor Jerry Brown and Sebastian Thrun, a Brown advisor who co-founded Udacity, only 29% of students enrolled passed the remedial math class, compared to 80% in a face-to-face setting. The gap was slightly less in an algebra class. And in a MOOC on statistics, 51% passed, as opposed to 74% who passed a classroom-based version. It turns out that students at community colleges, frequently from poorer families or families of color, lack the learned discipline to sit for hours in front of lessons on their monitors. Dropout rates were considerably higher than in classroom courses.[1]

It should also not surprise us that faced with the tendency for students' attentions to wander away from their laptops, particularly given all the on-line "disrupters," someone has devised a technical fix: web cams monitor students' facial expressions while they look at their screens and if a student appears bored, the lesson can be tweaked, say by temporarily cutting to some supplementary material. An instance — in the following chapters we shall meet many more — where the hi-tech solution to a problem only ends up compounding difficulties.

It would be tempting to use the metaphor of a virus in regard to computers taking over our school — multiplying rapidly within the host, taking over more and more of the normal functioning — except that an even more telling metaphor, that of addiction, lies closer at hand. Early on, Silicon Valley firms, particularly Apple Corp., donated computers to schools, particularly in certain urban areas. "Just try it out, see what it feels like," was their come-on. Of course, free computers could not last.[2] Once schools became interested in the machines (or cowed into thinking they had better not be left out while others pursued them), the machines had to be purchased; but grants were made available and free software and trouble-shooting was often thrown in. Now, some years down the line, it's cash up-front, and the initial machines no longer seem to get us off. They're too slow, lack networking capabilities, have small memories or crude graphics, won't run the latest games or formats. The school needs to "upgrade" — sometimes in a mere handful of years after the initial machines were bought. And it isn't just the computers themselves. As more and more electronics is added to the curriculum, and web downloading of graphics and Internetting and multimedia are needed, electrical service from the utility company must be vastly increased and the school needs to be rewired to allow networking and Internet access. New programs and operating systems demand more memory, greater speed, different modalities of carrying signals from there to here. Computers, operating systems, software, cables — their continual transformations render

---

[1] McKibben, "Pause!,"*op. cit.*

[2] Cathy Castillo, "Computers in California Schools," *San Francisco Examiner*, This World (April 29, 1984).

yesterday's digital tools nearly irrelevant and a fix is soon needed again, most always one that will cost even more than the last.

vi. SACRIFICING OUR YOUNG

Not only do computers undermine the futures, environmentally and economically,[1] that our students face, it is clear that their using them (at school and at home) poses serous threats to their health. Working at the keyboard/monitor for a substantial percentage of their required educational committment, however, raises profoundly disturbing questions.

For years now, evidence has accumulated about probable health problems related to computer use. Both government and industry groups have been understandably loathe to press for research on these matters, hoping the issue will quietly disappear. Insurance companies, similarly, are afraid to acknowledge the extremely serious health issues resulting from use of digital technology. From the terminals, three potential health hazards have been identified. The first of these, ionizing radiation, might be fairly easy to remedy given the time and resources; with proper shielding — assuming employers are willing to buy it and that parents find out what to do and can afford it, and assuming that the shielding reliably stays in place after installation — ionizing radiation can be guarded against (ignoring, for now, the issue of "permissible levels" of exposure and how such guidelines are established). The second problem is the transient electromagnetic fields that are found in proximity to the terminals. As a result of these fields, according to one hypothesis, health problems, including increases of cancer, leukemia, birth defects, etc., have been identified. Such fields would be much more difficult to shield against. The third medical problem, damage to vision, associated with "'extensive" use of computers, has been widely reported. If a serious research program into this latter problem were implemented, it is possible that a cause might be pinned down and eventually remedied; but my own guess would be that the roots of the interference with vision will lie deep, a result of extensive visual fixation on screen imagery; it may well be fairly intractable.

However "extensive" is defined, it is likely that for increasing numbers of youth health problems are now simply part of their curriculum, issues that may in time become serious or even debilitating. In a school sufficiently computerized, a student working on his or her portfolio and on a few course-related projects could well be spending enough hours a week at the computer to trigger some of these more serious pathologies. Repetitive Stress Injury (RSI) is one of the most epidemic of injuries in the US, with an increase in *reported* instances of about 1250% in the decade from 1982 to 1992. A coali-

---

[1] See Chapter 30.

tion of concerned unions have cited research, however, showing that instances of these injuries may actually be 50 to 100 times greater than what is being reported.[1]

And these may well be getting off easy. For besides the numbness or weakness in the wrists that are common knowledge, other computer users who fall victim to RSI are experiencing strong, recurrent pain or serious motor impairment.[2] A study noted that RSIs are not fatal, but that they "can be just as disabling" as black lung, brown lung, or asbestosis, and it pointed out that by the year 2000, an estimated 75% of all workers will be at risk for this often crippling injury.

Given that scattered bits of information about these dangers of work at computers have been aired occasionally, the fact that schools, whose charge is to nurture and protect children, should without acknowledging or addressing these health issues, devote increasing amounts of instructional time — especially so if we take seriously future projections — to students from pre-kindergarten on, working at these machines injurious to many, indicates the degree to which education today has lost its bearings, if not, indeed, its soul.

Now work itself is often a threat to one's health and safety. Especially with the coming of industrialization has this been so, but even earlier, in mining, sea or land transportation, working with horses, cattle, or pigs or other farm labor, for a long time workers have had to worry about accidents and job-related diseases; there have been maimings and killed workers for millennia. With the steam engine and the other machinery of industry, the frequency and severity of deaths and crippling injuries surely increased.

Schools, once they no longer used corporal punishment to rein in defiant and disobedient students, were different. There were bullies, sure, but they were not part of the school structure. There were also P.E. and shop classes that introduced students to the use of potentially dangerous machinery, and of course there might in some school be injuries from hazing or team sports. With the exception, perhaps, of football and hazing, rules that render such school activities reasonably safe can be enforced and necessary precautions incorporated.

This is not the case with regular school work on the computer; for some of the dangers, such as the widely reported instances of eye damage, it is unclear what could be done to "shield" users. Placing students in front of their consoles on a regular basis, we are exposing all of them to threats to their health. Where is the morality of such a pedagogy? What are the legal ramifications, for that matter, especially since schools are already hard-pressed to pay for the rest of their educational program? In all probability, not all students will experience serious eye damage from computer use; but some

[1] David Diamond, M.D.,"RSI: How to Protect Yourself," *Clarion* (March, 2012).

[2] *Ibid.*, p. 176.

will, and a proportion of those will have started using in their schools, some because computers were a required course. If are rightly furious at tobacco companies for knowingly addicting our school children to their sickening cigarettes, even though such companies are *not* charged with the protection of youth, what should we make of their schools, which are so charged, and yet, unthinkingly (though not unknowingly) put their students in front of machinery that threatens their health?[1]

Nor are these mere theoretical musings. In San Francisco, students at Lowell High School reported that 67% of a surveyed population of students had at least one physical health problem arising from their use of computers, especially eyestrain (40%) and pain of hands, wrists, and back. Emotional problems arising from their computer use were reported as well.[2] Only months after Napa, California began a New Technology High School, where every desk was outfitted with a computer, used in every academic class, students were complaining of sore eyes, wrist pain, and headaches.[3]

As discussed in Chapter 21, a number of studies explored early correlations between working at terminals by women and adverse outcomes of any pregnancies, as well as adverse effects on ova of various species placed in proximity to computer monitors. Further studies are attempting to pin down the particularities of terminal work plus exposure to Extremely Low Frequency (ELF) electric fields or the influence of at-home exposures to waterbed heaters or hair-dryers, etc., finding some positive correlations, discarding others. Enough is known, however, to be wary of exposure for the time being.

Any cellular pathology introduced by transient magnetic fields would understandably act more powerfully on fetal tissues, since they are undergoing extremely rapid cellular duplication for their development and growth. But the cells of pubescent youths or of six-year-olds are probably not that far behind those of a fetus in terms of vulnerability. Yet students at these ages are placed in front of computers on a regular basis. So inured have we become, by the end of that most toxic of centuries, the 20th, to the spread of poisons and disease in our many environments!

In the meantime, not only are computers now emerging as a preferred platform for (virtual) "field" trips, but younger and younger children are

---

[1] In California courts have ruled that K-12 public schools are "legally obligated to protect students from foreseeable dangers, unlike public colleges and universities." Bob Egelko, "Public Colleges Not Liable for Violence, Court Rules," San Francisco *Chronicle* (October 12, 2015). Also Naomi Wise, "Is Your PC Killing You? Tips, Advice and Products for Pain-free Computing," Bay Area *Computer Currents* (June 1–June 12, 1995).

[2] Melisa Olmos, "Study Finds Computer-Related Student Health Problems," *The Lowell* (February 14, 2003).

[3] Oppenheimer, *op. cit.*

being hooked up; iPhones have supplanted TVs as the babysitter of choice, parents glad to see their children get a "head-start" in the use of electronic tools ("it'll definitely give him [her son] the advantage over children" who learn to navigate cyberspace only in middle school, one mother concluded.)[1] Experiments to determine the efficacy of iPads as a platform for the teaching of children even younger are underway. Kids and even infants' software is a booming market. "Many parents eager to give their kids the right start are placing computer mice in their babies' chubby little hands almost before they can hold a fork or spoon."[2]

Thus these "mere tools" are destroying skilled jobs and replacing them, if at all, with low-skill and low-pay alternatives; in manufacturing these mere tools, grave damage to the planetary environment is inflicted; and working at their school keyboards additionally subjects students to serious threats to their own health.

In all of these we present youth with a "catch-22" of gargantuan proportions. Just what *is* this world for which they are being groomed? The following chapters will attempt to refine further our comprehension of the emerging digital culture.

---

[1] California Teachers Association *Action* (December, 1994).

[2] Laura Evenson, "At Home With Reader Rabbit," San Francisco *Chronicle* (April 25, 1994); Laura Evenson, "Booming Market for New Kidware," *Ibid.*; Dawn Chmielewski, "*Cat in the Hat* or Mouse in the House," San Francisco *Examiner* (November 22, 1998). Hanna Rosin, "The Touch-Screen Generation," *Atlantic Monthly*, vol. 311, no. 3 (April, 2013). Wendy Lee, "Kids Learn How To Code," San Francisco *Chronicle* (July 31, 2016) for San Francisco's United School District's decision to teach computer science in pre-school, hoping to "foster computational thinking."

24

In Which We Diss Information Theory

> The United States has a strategy based on arithmetic. They question the computers, add and subtract, extract square roots, and then go into action. The arithmetical strategy doesn't work here [Vietnam]. If it did, they'd have already exterminated us with their planes. — General Vo Nguyen Giap (1970), quoted in Gray, *op. cit.*

> Natural languages… are able to express an unlimited profusion of ideas with a limited vocabulary because the same word may have different meanings, depending on context. Words do multiple duty. In English, the word *set* and *run* each have about 140 possible alternative meanings. Such economy makes language ambiguous by its very nature, and an unsuitable vehicle for logic. — Jeremy Campbell, *The Improbable Machine: What the Upheavals in Artificial Intelligence Research Reveal About How the Mind Really Works* (1989)

i. Reality in Black & White

If "information" is indeed our new ontology and epistemology, as well as an increasing driver of our economy — and to many of the visionaries of the digital movement, our ethics and morality to boot — let us examine what "information" actually means. What is the deeper reality behind our binary ontology? What will we find if we dig down to the foundations of this digital New Age that is taking possession of the general culture? At the birth of the Information Age, a new theory of information emerged out of Bell Labs to shape it, guide it, and ultimately to justify it, a theory we shall now examine.

World War II had produced a glut of messages of all kinds, radio, cables, wireless, eventually radar, microwave transmissions, mostly coded, going near and far. This vast expansion of messages criss-crossing nearly every land brought communication engineers to an acute awareness of certain theoretical questions. Similar concerns emerged as Norbert Weiner, at the center of the invention of the modern computer, used the experiences of artillery systems in World War II to develop his theory of feedback loops, called "cybernetics." Signal processing and cybernetics brought to a focus attempts to clarify what messages were all about.

If I were to write that the signal received by a radar detector had an anomaly, most readers, possibly after a moment or two of confusion, would figure out that there had been an apparent "typo," the "t" having been left out of the fifth word of this sentence: "write." Part of every "signal" consists of a certain amount of redundancy, like that unnecessary "t," and some is "noise," parts that are either meaningless or countersignal, masking what is being sent. How much noise can there be before a signal itself is rendered indecipherable? In World War II, this was a burning question. Orders issued in the din of battle or heard in a cockpit over staticky airwaves above the drone of a bomber's engines and possibly anti-aircraft explosions were frequently garbled. How much redundancy exists in a given message? Are there kinds of redundancy of which we are not aware? Do some kinds of messages tend to have a greater degree of redundancy? When we view an image of a loved one or something we are very familiar with, how much of the image could be hidden or masked before we lose our ability to identify him, her, or it? How much ambiguity exists that context alone can clarify as to meaning?

The Cybernetic Theory of Information emerged in 1948, out of a paper by Claude Shannon, an engineer at Bell Laboratory in New Jersey, that sought to answer on both theoretical and practical grounds these and other related questions. It was necessary, Shannon believed, to focus these questions very narrowly, and his paper was presented as a "mathematical theory of the capacity of communication channels to transmit data."

Frequently lost in the present reification of "information" is the signal fact that as a subject of analysis, "information" was defined by Shannon and his co-workers *independent of* any *meaning*. Indeed, as far as Information Theory is concerned, "information" could consist of a copy of the King James Bible or it could be the random sequence, rbxtnpil, a "word" (so far as I am aware) totally devoid of meaning in any language.

From the point of view of Information Theory, however, both, except for length, are considered equivalent. As Warren Weaver commented regarding Shannon's paper, "In particular, *information* [his emphasis] must not be confused with *meaning*." [my emphasis] Since what was at stake for Shannon and Bell Laboratory was the issue of transmission of signals — how to do it more efficiently and for less money — there was no reason for "information" to have any relationship to human meaning.

However, so defined, "information" opens up a whole new world of *commodification* of *data*, within decades the virtual meal ticket within the burgeoning Infosphere constituted in the late-20th and early-21st centuries by the intertwined bureaucracies instituted by governments, drunk on the omniscient potentialities of surveillance of *every*one, in league with the Lords of Capital, equally besotted by their new algorithmic marketing tools able to mine the minutia of *every*one's thoughts and actions in order to reach into the motherload of bank accounts — or for those without, the servitude of long-term debt.

A new world opened for Capital by Bell Laboratory's and Shannon's canonization of Information in the shadow of World War II; if with the onset of the Cold War, that world was rapidly populated, by now its real-life manifestation in servers and data-warehouses and playrooms for the coders is fueling construction frenzies in dataopolises like San Francisco, Austin and Bombay.

For the purposes of efficiency and (in theory at least) in order to get rid of any ambiguity in the information, what gets "processed" in this Age of Information has all been encoded digitally. That means that all communication, as is generally known, occurs in the "binary alphabet" consisting of only "1" and "0". These correspond in the circuitry to an electronic switch or gate being closed or open. Electronic signals are routed through *semiconductors* that, depending on the electrical voltage differences, either conduct or don't.[1] Every "word" entered into a computer, whether it is data or instructions, must be in this binary form, which means that computers contain only mathematical values; moreover, considered a datum at a time, there can only be two possible forms each signal might take. Words in English or other spoken languages that are in the computers as general instructions or as part of an individual program are encoded digitally; numbers, too. All a computer does —can do — using such inputs is to take a code of "1" or "0" and either *pass it on* or *invert it* (changing 0's to 1's and *vice versa*). That's *it*. On the basis wholly of those two kinds of responses, wired in to the labyrinthine circuitry of countless microchips, a computer can add, subtract, compare numbers to one another to determine which is larger, store them, or move them from one place to another in its memory. Again, that's *all* a computer does. By iterative processes, however, complicated mathematical functions can be performed

---

[1] A silicon wafer is made into a semiconductor by being "doped" by arsine, phosphine, or one of several other gases, whose extreme toxicity was treated in Chapter 21, pp. 409.

— but only as a string of elaborations on those five elementary operations. Kris Meidling, a geological researcher for Mobil, explains, "[w] hat they do well is what can be calculated over and over," adding, "[w] hat they can't do is innovation."[1] According to the visionaries of computerization, forms of "thinking" and "reasoning" and something called Artificial Intelligence will emerge from these strings of rote number transfers and signal manipulations.

Binary can be cumbersome. Our "10" is binary's "1010," our "2018," binary's "11111100010." Cumbersome, but simplicity itself. At each step the signal can be — can do — only one of two possible things. Middle possibilities are ruled out by definition. Thereby, the *demon* of ambiguity, the enemy incarnate of many technical minds, is supposed to be exorcised. No greys, no mediations, no ambiguities, no on-the-one-hands and on-the-others. The "words," instructions, and data put into computers, and what the computer itself puts out, are confined to those two possibilities, 0 or 1, at each step of the way. Believers in computers being used to schedule, inform, educate, diagnose illnesses, plan buildings, play, invest, create art or music, prove theorems, recognize patterns, or tell an incoming missile from a passing airplane's toilet's effluvia have to convince themselves that in each of those activities *all parts and processes and all descriptions of situations can be reasonably broken down into series of yes/no decision branches.*[2] And, inexorably, the wired among us are being taught to think more or less in just those ways. Thus is a fundamentally binary consciousness implanted deep within all of us.

ii. MACHINE QUESTIONS; BANISHING AMBIGUITY

It will be helpful to briefly remind readers of earlier discussions in Parts One and Two about the difference between our ordinary Aristotelian logic, used by the dominant culture, and an alternative, "dialectical" logic, according to which there are no absolute distinctions between categories of opposites, so that the interactions and mutual overlappings of love and hate, hot and cold or bitter and sweet are recognized and form the basis of all discourse and analysis. In such a logic, as in the now famous yin/yang circle icon, polar opposites are always in the process of becoming their inverse. This dynamic is inherent in things, in situations.

Since each entity in a dialectical logic has "aspects" of both extremes of a given category (e.g. has aspects of both wet and dry), change is paramount. This approach, which is commonly found in the thinking of nonindustrial societies, is opposed by Aristotelian logic, the basis of our dominant culture. Here a law of identity and contradiction is the starting point of all discourse.

---

1 Oppenheimer, *op. cit.*

2 Orwell believed an important aspect of State control would result from shrinking human languages, so as to make it more difficult to express, or ultimately even conceive of, alternative realities. (Markoff, *op. cit.,* p. xvi.)

A thing either is or is not "A" — "A" being some quality, moral category, aspect, or anything else. Identity is not a matter to be trifled with, according to Aristotelian logic; things have to be clearly identified as to their essence.

Searching for certitude, Aristotelian logic has circumscribed ambiguity, as well as contradiction, making it harder to conceive of change, though in his many scientific writings Aristotle sought the secret of transformation. Binary logic, the language that computers "talk" among them-"selves," is a much more decisive articulation of Aristotelian logic, only now it is embedded in the very matrix of computer code, and hence of computer ontology. How, indeed, even think about grays when only a 1 or a 0 can occupy any single element, any cell? According to one of the fundamental principles of mechanistic thinking, the whole is no greater than the sum of its parts. When middle grounds simply do not exist among the elements of this new reality it is more difficult later for them to emerge. Because the new Theory of Information holds that for the purpose of sending and receiving of signals, it is essential to preclude ambiguity, the new binary numerology is forced to use indirect ways to represent middle states.

Consider how such a two-toned ontology is played out in music, with the use of modern, digitalized recording technologies. Music played by a jazz ensemble, for example, will be recorded digitally by periodically "sampling" the music being played. Thus the original sinesoidal wave-form of any particular sound wave is transformed into an approximation, a step-function, as follows:

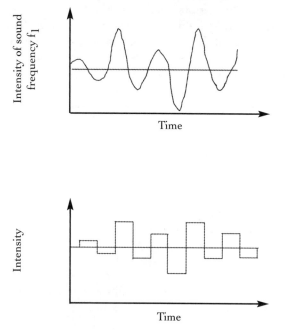

Digitalized sound wave, after sampling. Here only one frequency, f_1, is sampled; in practice, a range of frequencies is so treated.

The "gray areas" where the sinesoidal wave moves diagonally up or diagonally down, have been truncated in the step-function, becoming a series of either vertical or horizontal lines, the approximation based on an averaging and sampling technique made on the original wave. At certain time intervals and in certain clumps of tonal ranges, readings of what frequencies or tones are present, and at what intensities or volumes, are taken. This then becomes the basis for the CD, MP–3, iPod or other vehicle for the music being manufactured.

"The [analogue phonograph] record has as much fidelity as the materials will allow. The CD has as much fidelity *as the people programming its creation thought to allow.*" At present, the music is sampled 48,000 times a second, that supposedly being a fine enough division to catch the essentials of any musical offering. Using exceptionally refined analogue equipment, however, people with sensitive ears find that the losses to the music from digitalization are considerable. Subtle phrasing gets lost, as do nuances of transitions and delicate shadings. Some listeners report that digital recordings sound "dead" or "cold" to them, mechanism having finally succeeded in the "taming" of music. With CDs "one loses the sense of musical gesture, of delicately shaped phrasing, of communication between players."[1] As signals are further reduced for the purpose of transferring them to an iPod or some other platform where speed or signal compression is pushed, even more degradation of the sound takes place. Once more, important "information" is being purposely jettisoned.[2] Our world is not discretely ordered. Even the dividing lines between living and dead are fuzzy. This is not the case when using computers. As Rushkoff, a digital enthusiast, explains, in the digital world "everything is made into a choice. The medium is biased towards the discrete [and]... forces choices when none need to be made." But, he continues, "[E]very translation of a real thing to this symbolic realm of the digital requires that such decisions be made.

> The digital realm is biased towards choices because everything must be expressed in the term of a discrete, yes-or-no, symbolic language, ... forc[ing] choices on humans operating within the digital sphere.

---

1 "The Quest for Perfect Sound," San Francisco *Examiner, This World* (March 9, 1986). Rushkoff, *op. cit.*, p. 53. Emphasis mine.
2 This simplifies a more layered story. The binary truncation I discuss is significant becasue unlike other distortions of recorded sound, both analogue and digital (from overload, wow, flutter, inconstancy of power source, etc.) this is *purposeful* suppression of musical data. See "Audio system measurement" and "Comparisions of analogue and digital recording," *Wikipedia* (Thanks to Brook Schoenfeld for help on this.)

[I]n that sphere, programmers "pick the categories that matter, and at the granularity that matters to his or her employer's purpose.[1]

Digitalized sound does sound "cleaner," as its advocates boast, since the sound is clearly *under control.* The older technology's recordings are nosier. Scratches, equipment hum, and so on are present. But the music is also more present. Of course there were distortions, since the process of transferring the sound waves into a groove on a wax disk would be an imperfect one. But nuances of transitions were not snipped away to fit into the "binary absolutism," as it has been called by Burt Alpert.[2]

What, if anything, is lost in these money-saving binary "adjustments?" Quite a lot, according to Rushkoff, who recounts that early on tests showed that music "played on a CD format had much less of a positive impact on depressed patients" than the same music played on analogue records. Identical music played through identical speakers revealed that the CD format actually moved the air molecules in the room "significantly differently" than with analogue recordings. Studies in Germany of youth used to listening on MP–3 players demonstrated that they were unable to distinguish between "several hundred thousand notes" readily detected by their parents.[3]

iii. THE DIGITAL IRON MAIDEN

In the sampling technique used in the digital recording of music, at every interval each tonal clump will be registered as being either present or absent. It is either "A" or "not-A," either with or without tone. A new musical reality emerges as a harmony of empty and full tonal boxes, Aristotelian logic actually coded into the foundations of the electronic language. As such, all questions by definition must be resolvable into 0 *or* 1, on *or* off, yes *or* no.

To be sure, some questions lend themselves to such answers. A very large number, and by far the more interesting ones at that, I would argue, do not. Yet this is the only language the machine uses, for all electronic communication — whether for information transfer, program instructions, spacecraft guidance instructions, or what is called computer "art" — occurs in the same binary alphabet. And at *every* step — in defining the task, writing the program, entering data, and providing answers or protocols — there must be a reduction into this truncated reality, yes or no, 0 or 1 — or in an emotional context, to "friend" or not. Reality shoehorned into yes/no modalities, into a machine-logic that has been imposed as an ideological constraint in accord, I would argue, with a new political economy of turn-of-the-century Capital.

---

[1] Rushkoff, *op. cit.*, pp. 53, 55.
[2] Burt Alpert, *Inversions: A Study of Warped Consciousness* (Ann Arbor: privately printed, 1973), p. 192.
[3] Rushkoff, *op. cit.*, pp. 54, 70–71.

What happens to the ambiguities, the grays, that so obviously are part of reality when a particular part of the world gets translated into its equivalent "information?"[1] What happens to poetry, to emotions, to nuanced shifts from one state to another in all its complexities? Well, they can still be represented in our written languages and of course those will be, for inputting into the maws of hi-tech, translated into binary code, the language of the machine itself, which is, as it must be, totally without ambiguity: the marching orders of the software can call out only for a right *or* a left. Jumps are not recognized, nor hops, no sliding or flying after a particularly challenging leap.

Joseph Weizenbaum pointed out that "every computer permits the asking of only certain kinds of questions," compounding matters by accept[ing] only certain 'kinds' of data." More bluntly, "A computing system has effectively closed many doors that were open before it was installed."[2]

Some of the in-betweens become irretrievably lost. One problem with a "sampling" technology for music, particularly in the case of jazz (as with much of African music) is that it is common for performers to "bend" their notes, approaching a tonal value from above or below and "sliding" into or through it. A sampling technology that clumps tonal values, time intervals, and volumes, is likely to miss many of the subtleties of the music as performed. (I would expect to see something similar in digital photography.)

Since the goal of the digital *avant garde* is the translation of all knowledge into computer memory and programs, this would constitute a giant leap forward in fulfilling the program set forth by many of the leading Royal Society philosophers in the later phase of the 17th-century scientific revolution, as described in Part Two: to eliminate from human discourse all ambiguity, all nuance, all that *might be* confusing. So, they mandated that all language should provide one word for each thing and that for each word there should be one and only one referent.

Such a world would not only be devastatingly dull and wrongheaded, it is dangerous. It achieves certitude and order only by hacking away all that cannot be squeezed neatly into its arbitrarily established (these days, binary) boxes.

iv. Projecting Language onto a Flat Surface; From SDS to XDS–940

Let us remember that the campaign for language reform in the 17th century stemmed in large part from the desire on the part of the propertied classes and their supporters to eliminate *enthusiasm*, which erupted when men and women got "carried away" by the force of some orator's eloquence

---

1 In *Close to the Machine*, p. 22n, Ellen Ullman explains that though computers might use a "fuzzy logic," for situations where some conditions are not well-defined, "at the level of code, the logic is not fuzzy." Programmers will instruct the computer in a "logically determinant manner."

2 Pein, *op. cit.*, p. 34.

(more often than not a lay preacher, women as well as men) calling for justice and liberation, quite possibly not deferring sufficiently to the prerogatives of property and class. To put an end to such "excesses," the forces of order in England decided they needed a mechanical language to beat back the forces of unreason, one that banished ambiguity, that repudiated different levels of meaning (as with metaphors, similes, etc.), and they advocated cutting freely at what was seen as a certain flabbiness in the English language. People had been carried away. That had to be curtailed. Even metaphors were thought to incite the passions; a language with a "manly spirit" was needed to tame them. John Wilkins, a major figure both in the establishment of the Royal Society and in the campaign for language reform in 17th-century England, advocated a style of speaking and writing "as near the Mathematical plainness" as possible, and was known for his boring discourses. Such a reformed language, it was hoped, would be incompatible with revolt — or even with imagination, for the former was seen as stemming from the latter.

Theodore Roszak has been able to peer into the turbulent waters of the '60s radical upheavals and counterculture to identify two, somewhat distinct, core philosophical currents belonging, on the one hand, to the "reversionists," and on the other, to the "technophiliacs." Both tendencies saw the present industrial world order as sinking into a cesspool of its own making, but the reversionists saw *the way out* as *going back*.

> If the raggle-taggle youth of the sixties had any guiding star before them, I think it was the hobo Taoist saints and shabby Zen masters, civilization's original anarchist philosophers who taught the art of living lightly on the Earth. Young and raw as the counterculture may have been, there were those in its ranks who recognized the relevence of that tradition to the needs of a culture sunk over its eyes in an obsessive struggle to conquer nature, to obliterate all traditional wisdom in the name of "progress," to transform the planet into an industrial artifact. They perceived the nuclear death wish that lies at the core of that Promethean obsession and, accordingly, they proposed a more becoming human alternative.[1]

The other current, the technophiliac, was also strongly present in the '60s, reflected in the huge following for the doctrines of Marshall McLuhan and Buckminster Fuller, as well as the near-universal drive to know about the latest sound system Acoustic Research was producing. Out of this second current eventually

---

[1] Theodore Roszak, *From Satori to Silicon Valley* (San Francisco: Don't Call It Frisco Press, 1986), p. 12.

emerged the doctrine popularized by the *Whole Earth Catalogue* and its successors (*Co-Evolution Quarterly* and *Whole Earth Review*), edited by Stewart Brand, that computers were simply one more ingenious tool. For the technophiliacs,

> the cure for our industrial ills will not be found in things past, but in Things to Come. Indeed, it will be found at the climax of the industrial process. What is required, therefore, is not squeamish reversion, but brave perseverence. We must adapt resourcefully to industrialism as a necessary stage of social evolution, monitoring the process with a cunning eye for its life-saving potentialities. As we approach the crisis that threatens calamity, we must grasp these opportunities as they emerge and use them to redeem the system from within. The way out of our dilemma is to tunnel fearlessly through until we do reach daylight.[1]

Janus-like, to get through what was felt by many in the '60s as the coming breakdown of society and/or a revolutionary upheaval, many currents in the movements looked in both directions, backwards towards the Golden Age of Native Americans and forward to the Brave New Worlds of electronic wizardry. Significantly, the seeds for what became the personal computer movement, the belief that the diffusion of computing technology will provide a basis for solving all manner of the country-wide social, economic, political, organizational, and intellectual problems, first sprouted in soil upturned by the social turmoil that erupted in the US during the Cambodian crisis in the spring of 1970.

When President Nixon suddenly expanded the highly unpopular Indochina war by sending US troops into Cambodia, it precipitated a severe domestic reaction. Troops in Cambodia, it turned out, necessitated troops on college campuses to contain the instant student rebellion everywhere. The killings of unarmed students at Kent State and then, a few days later, at Jackson State University (a black college, hence with less media attention), by National Guard and state troopers lit a fuse that exploded across the country's campuses. Some universities and colleges leaped into the fray, hoping thereby to direct this upsurge of outrage into safer, more controllable, channels. Thus at Yale University, where a huge May Day rally of insurgent youth gathered to protest the New Haven murder trial of Black Panther leader Bobby Seale, and called for a student strike there, Yale President Kingman Brewster issued a public statement expressing doubts that a black revolutionary could receive

---

[1] *Ibid.*, pp. 25–26. There is, perhaps, a curious parallel here to the traditional Marxist notion of slavery and industrial capitalism being "necessary stages" in the economic development that leads, inevitably, to the eventual proletarian creation of communism.

a fair trial in the country, seeming to throw his prestige and that of Yale onto the side of black liberation.

At Dartmouth College, where I was on leave, when students responded to the crisis by calling for a strike, newly appointed President Kemeny (a logician whose expertise centered on computer language), tried to get in front of the rebellion by calling off classes for the rest of the school year, while students were encouraged to lobby for peace; presidents at other colleges acted similarly.

On the West Coast, however, a different pattern emerged. There, idealist hackers, a great many of whom were dropouts, antiwar activists, and former SDS agitators, took the initiative to build a new vehicle for organizing for social change. These hackers wanted to use computers for *radical* ends and to subvert the corporate State. They formed a group called Resource One,

> the creation of a group of Berkeley computer folks who had come together during the Cambodian crisis.... Distressed at the near monopoly of computer power by the government and the major corporations, this small band of disgruntled computer scientists set about building a people's information service. By 1971 they had managed to acquire a retired XDS–940 time-share computer from the Transamerica Corporation, and had quartered it in the Project One warehouse community... in San Francisco, where they hoped it might be used by political activists to compile mailing lists, coordinate voter surveys, and serve as an all-purpose social-economic database.[1]

Resource One, never much of a success, eventually became the basis for something called Community Memory, whereby access to a computer terminal was to be opened up to the "community" in the form of a "people's electronic bulletin board." Peoples' Computer Company (a radical hacker newspaper which began later, in 1972) expressed the ideology of these digital-activists:

> Computers are mostly used against people instead of for people, and to control people instead of to free them. Time to change all that.

Their motto was "Computer power to the people."[2] Some of the same energy and same people later set up the Peacenet computer network of left activists.

---

[1] *Ibid.*, pp. 35–36. John Markoff, *Machines of Loving Grace: The Quest for Common Ground Between Humans and Robots* (New York: HarperCollins, 2015), p. 100.
[2] Isaacson, *op. cit.*, p. 59.

It was out of this ferment, as Roszak notes, that the informal meetings of the hackers and designers involved in conceiving and inventing the personal computer first emerged. Groups like the Homebrew Computer Club (out of which emerged Apple Corp.), Kentucky Fried Computers, and the Itty Bitty Machine (a play on "IBM") Company met in their by-now-legendary garages and basements to discuss technical, philosophical, and political issues. Their vision was one of the awesome power of computers being made accessible to individuals and communities, instead of being locked up in the expensive mainframes of established institutions and corporations. Their work reflected the same democratizing ethos as that of Resource One and involved some of the same people.[1]

iv. FLIGHTS FROM THE BODY

Just as John Wilkins, Thomas Sprat, and others in the 17th century stepped out of the chaos of the English revolution and Civil War to argue for a new way to re-establish order and the rule of property, so too, out of the radical insurgencies of the 1960s and '70s a radical binary culture crystalized to propose putting the pieces of social and cultural reality — tossed this way and that during the recent turmoil of riots, assassinations, an out-of-control war, and a demoralized citizenry — back into a new order, one that made sense for its technocratic advocates, themselves a product of the vast expansion of the scientific and technical sectors that had been generated by first the Cold and then the Indochinese War.

Confused by their own technophiliac orientations and caught up in the recurrent American utopian technocratic infatuations that fervently believe that technical fixes are possible for what are essentially intractable political and social dilemmas, the technophiliac reformers of the 1970s and '80s ended up establishing a strange binary reordering which somehow merged war-making, massive corporations, and Liberation into one very heady potion.

It is clear that a cult of technomania emerged in the early '70s as a safe alternative to the chaos of the '60s, roiling societies and terrifying authorities everywhere, an alternative especially necessary after the wake-up call of 1968 when, in the wake of the Tet Offensive in Vietnam, rebellion and insurrections spread worldwide, and the even ruder wake-up call of Kent and Jackson States two years later. If actually changing the social world of imperialist war, racism, misogyny, a runaway attack on rivers and forests and of indigenous cultures was too dangerous, at times tumultuous, even deadly, the virtual world would be a substitute terrain where a higher form of change could be effected — a virtual world, ironically, forged out of the electronic wizardry that was being perfected in that very same war, where the mightiest military in history was

---

[1] Roszak, *From Satori to Silicon Valley*, pp. 38–39.

pitted against an army of peasants, at the beginning armed only with the very crudest of weapons, fighting against F-14s and other electronic platforms.

The "electronic frontier," as one digital visionary named it in 1996, offered an alternative arena for effecting change, cyberspace, which opened up whole new dimensions, where escape from the turmoil of the '60s was on offer and where worlds could be created, limited only by one's imagination.[1] And once computers were in the hands of the masses, the possibilities for transformation could be virtually limitless, and voyagers into cyberspace could be *in control* of reality, even to the point of choosing whole new identities. No longer tightly linked to a physical body, in the world of 0s and 1s one can pick one's sex, age, even one's species (while, in the physical world, real biological species were disappearing at a devastating rate).

Blazing the trail in the '70s was Stewart Brand, whose *Whole Earth Catalogue* perfectly captured many of the values, tendencies, and questions generated by the movements of the '60s and later. In an interview in 1984, Brand admitted, "This generation absolutely swallowed computers whole, just like dope."[2] One computer visionary, Danny Hillis, a leading Artificial Intelligence researcher, in fact told Brand that he gave him "credit for making the counterculture decide that computers were okay when on their side." It could have gone, Hillis admitted, either way.

Around the *Whole Earth Catalogue* and its various successor publications and offshoots (*Co-Evolution Quarterly, Whole Earth Review,* the WELL,[3] and the Global Business Network [GBN]) Brand has articulated a distinctly accommodationist ideology. Through high technology, particularly with the spread of personal computers, the liberatory aims of the '60s would be realized. These aims, now tied to a powerful locomotive of networked cyberactivists, would give rise to liberated individuals, through their modems exercising vast power to remake the world.

To be sure, the raging passions of the '60s have been cleaned up, recast. Now government, war, racism, corporations, US imperialism, the issues that mobilized millions of Americans as the war in Indochina dragged on and on have dropped out of sight. The overthrow of oppressive political or economic structures no longer entered into the vision of liberation. Rather, liberation now meant seeing government as irrelevant, as a source of bureaucratic barriers to creativity. Through the creative use of these new electronic tools, "outlaw zones" could be established for visionaries to put their ideas into practice. These new tools opened up a whole new age of information, of ideas. As with LSD,

---

[1] John Markoff, *Machines of Loving Grace,* p. 173.

[2] Roszak, *From Satori,* p. 47.

[3] Many who became members of the WELL were filled with utopian hopes for real *social* change. For a summary of such visions, see Jon Carroll, "Modest do-gooders finding a place on Net," San Francisco *Chronicle* (June 15, 2014).

so too with Virtual Reality, (see next chapter); these visionaries will be able to experience states of pure being, for all intents and purposes, disembodied.[1]

Brand at times bemoaned the linearity of traditional thinking, and believed, just as his mentor, Norbert Weiner, had, that through cybernetics, feedback theory, and the like, new levels of complexity would be opened to serious analysis; but in fact Weiner's cybernetics, and the "systems theory" based on it, has a thoroughly mechanical basis — where humans were likened to servomechanisms.[2]

Combatting such crude models was supposed to be fixed by what is called "systems theory," but as Lilienfeld explains,

> Systems theory is the latest attempt to create a world myth based on the prestige of science. The basic thought forms of systems theory remain classical positivism and behaviorism. As epistemology it leaves philosophy no further along in resolving the Cartesian dualism; it attempts to resolve this dualism by mechanizing thought and perception,[3] or rather by constructing mechanical models of thought and perception.

Once more, behind the perhaps-more-modern vocabulary, we find the principles and elements of mechanistic thinking.

Stewart Brand's own personal odyssey in growing up, his fascination with the world of intelligence and his infatuation with Ayn Rand, may have shaped the peculiar brand of liberation politics and the resultant collaborations he and his Global Business Network entered into with the corporations and the military over the years, such as Royal Dutch/Shell, Volvo, Texaco, AT&T, IBM, the Pentagon, the Joint Chiefs of Staff, and Herman Kahn, the Rand Corp. theorist of how to wage nuclear war. Brand even suggested the

---

1 Ullman, *op. cit.*, p. 29, reports how the global network became a substitute revolution, with a "withering away"(!) of former beliefs in social transformation, a common path for many of the formerly radical digital visionaries. Thus the prevalence in Silicon Valley of libertarian politics, the merging of free-market ideology with a faith in technology to solve all manner of problems. Ironic in an industry that from its inception has been so dependant on government subsidies. On Brand see also Lee Worden, "Counter-culture, Cyberculture, and the Third Culture: Reinventing Civilization, Then and Now," *West of Eden: Communes and Utopia in Northern California*, (ed.) Iain Boal, Janferie Stone, Michael Watts and Cal Winslow (Oakland: PM Press/Retort, 2012).

2 Fred Turner, *From Counterculture to Cyberculture: Stewart Brand, The Whole Earth Network, and the Rise of Digital Utopianism* (Chicago: Univ. of Chicago Press, 2006), pp. 21–22.

3 R. Lilienfeld, *The Rise of System Theory* (Wiley, 1979), pp. 249–250, as quoted in Grey, *Posthumous War*, p. 139.

deployment of the US armed forces for the long-term protection of the global eco-structure, as if the Pentagon and Greenpeace could be merged.[1]

Indeed, something strange has happened to the rage that once sent protesters against the Cambodian invasion into the streets and now redirects them to their laptops. And as in the 1650s, a new language has been developed to codify this transformation.

If Stewart Brand was the prophet of this new cybertopia, Steve Jobs was its avatar, or at least the exemplar of the "new man" born of this new alt.politics, where effecting change in virtual worlds was deftly substituted for the social rebellions of the '60s in a slick PR bait'n'switch. Again and again and still again Jobs identified with revolt, explaining that "The idealistic winds of the sixties are still at our back." At the launch of his Lisa computer in 1983 Jobs frequently extolled how "revolutionary" it was. The same year he told John Sculley, in respect to keeping the price of the Macintosh relatively low, "I want to make this a revolution."

So too his work at Pixar and Apple, his iPhone and iPod, the launching of the Apple stores, he stressed, were all "revolutionary." His "Think Different" massive ad campaign used photographs of Einstein, Martin Luther King, Jr., and Bob Dylan to indelibly link Apple with the rebels, the trouble-makers. By working on an Apple platform, Jobs made clear, one was fighting the big corporations, personified by IBM's Big Brother. The launch of the iPad, he said, was "revolutionizing the world"; accordingly, its advertising "needs to be a manifesto." Advertisements repeated its "revolutionary" intent. In case people weren't getting the message, the March 2, 2011 launch of the iPad 2 had Beatles' music on the sound system, finishing with "You Say You Want a Revolution." He was our new Mario Savio and, suitable for this new age of Information, a consummate huckster.[2]

Not that the NGOs and all manner of political activists did not use those very same electronic tools to effect social change on the physical planet: mailing lists were made into databases (and thereby made easier for the FBI to obtain); listserves established; Kickstarter campaigns created to fund projects in minority communities; cell phones activated to coordinate affinity-group actions in demonstrations, and so on. But the remove of cyberspace from the physical world had its price, as the ease of creating electronic communities for the most part displaced the critical work of *actual* organizing, the tedious but crucial door-to-door, person-to-person, eye-to-eye, and voice-to-voice contact whereby strangers can be woven into communities of activists. The cyber-activists, of course, having to avert *their* eyes from the spectacle of the workers in China who produce those tools and work under horrific conditions, numbers of them jumping to their deaths in despair, so that

[1] Stewart Brand, "Army Green," *Whole Earth Review*, no. 72 (Fall, 1992), pp. 58–59.

[2] Walter Isaacson, *op. cit.*, pp. 107, 150, 157, 230, 332, 499–500.

workers must now sign a pledge stating that they will not try to kill themselves but if they do, their families will not seek damages; where three people died and fifteen were injured when dust exploded; where 137 people exposed to a toxic chemical suffered nerve damage; where Apple offers injured workers no recompense; where workers, some as young as thirteen, according to an article in the *New York Times*, typically put in seventy-two-hour weeks, sometimes more, with minimal compensation, few breaks, and little food.[1]

And Jobs, the self-proclaimed revolutionary, ultimately responsible for this state of affairs, had a cult of personality during his life and after his death that easily equaled that of Josef Stalin.

In cyberspace, made possible by Pentagon R&D, free from the meddling hands of clumsy government authorities, a true anarchy was really possible, claim the cybertopians, where their visions might be freely pursued in a rarified atmosphere, far removed from the CS gas and Mace that were increasingly deployed against activists in the late '60s.

Deja-vu, indeed, for is this not strikingly parallel to the efforts back in the mid-17th century by men like Thomas Sprat, John Wilkins, and Robert Boyle to lead savants and artisans of the time into pursuits and comprehensions more in keeping with the designs and prerogatives of property and the Crown, including the pursuit of profits in the North American colonies, through a careful pruning and redefining of language in general and the particular descriptions of the natural world, in order to preclude the kinds of radical utopian visions advocated by seers like Campanella, Comenius, or Winstanley? In other words, a similar ideological counter-revolution to that, at whose core lies the cold heart of mechanism, is again at hand. Indeed, we *have* been here before.

And Silicon Valley today represents a thoroughly schizophrenic ideological construct, an industry the most subsidized in US history,[2] that both decries government interference and provides those same governments with the very tools and weapons needed to repress their increasingly marginalized populations.

That Brand and his virtual comrades were able to successfully proselytize for a whole new kind of liberation has allowed our old friend, the mechanical philosophy — now reshaped, occasionally gussied up in the clothes of "systems analysis" so as to pretend to nonreductionist thinking — to continue to shape our visions, in order to serve the needs of late 20th- and early

---

1 Sue Halpern, "Who Was Steve Jobs?" *New York Review of Books* (January 12, 2012).

2 The US government spent hundreds of billions of dollars to develop the Internet alone, let alone military and aerospace (Astra Taylor, *op. cit.*, p. 223).

21st-century Capital — just as the original 17th-century mechanical philosophy stepped forth to give shape to the social debate that greeted early capitalism's (especially the mines's) despoilations of the natural landscape. The vocabulary and concepts of the Information Age simply take the debate about life and death in (and to) the cosmos to a whole other level.

Thus it is true that ours is the "Age of Information," but this is precisely because Capital in the late-20th and early-21st centuries has set its sights on the transformation of *knowledge* into the ontological status of the *commodity*, the capitalists' holy-of-holies. As such, as is true of commodities as a rule of Capital, pressure is on to *standardize* knowledge, to *speed up* its production, as well as *deskilling* those who produce it, a proletarianization of its producers going hand-in-hand with a mechanization of how it is to be produced. We see this in the proliferation of multiple-choice tests, MOOCS, attacks on teachers' unions, attempts to abolish tenure, the spread of "adjunct" professorships, the Common Core standards, and "Value Added" compensation schemas for the remuneration of teachers.

But we see the same dynamic in biopiracy, the explosive growth of "intellectual property" law, indeed its emergence at the core of the various "free-trade" agreements like NAFTA, GATT, and the like, pushed under neoliberalism by the WTO and US financial circles under both Democratic and Republican administrations. Facebook's harvesting of its vast crop of "Likes" and processing them through its algorithms to bring them to market, or Google with its crop of keystroke analyses, are only the more obvious manifestations of this reconfiguration of knowledge into a product through its reconfiguration as data.

In his novel *Bugs*, Roszak captures some of the new mentality well:

> What nonsense! No wonder these men [the technicians of the Information Age] placed such faith in machines, told the world that machines were superior to people. They were machines. They had already mechanized themselves. None of them knew the true depth of their lives, the wisdom of their bodies. None of them knew the earth, its patient and insistent power.

Later:

> Heller's work, Gable's work, her former husband's work — it was all fleshless, abstraction, bound up with matters of state. There was nothing here that touched the senses, nothing that made the imagination dance.[1]

Heller, the main character of *Bugs*, is responsible for creating the National Center for Data Control, to be built in Washington, D.C. and housed

---

[1]Theodore Roszak, *Bugs* (Garden City, New York: Doubleday, 1981), p. 260.

in one of the world's largest geodesic domes, with its marble facing looking as if it "brooded over the city like a vast, disembodied cerebrum."[1] Heller ran the center and argued on its behalf against the doubters. There was a

> hidden agenda behind Heller's public relations campaign. It was not simply a matter of winning friendly opinions for the Brain [as the Data Center was called] but of teaching a new conception of life and mind to a species that was the old, failing order of life and mind.[2]

This new conception of life and mind will be examined in Chapter 26. But first let us take a look at this new technology's presumptions of its totalizing power, such that it confidently contests even what "reality" consists of. Indeed some of the more far-seeing digital savants — intoxicated possibly by the string theorists' positing of multi-universes — believe that in Virtual Reality they can simulate a world as valid as the one the rest of us — deprived of special gloves, helmets, or other sensor-laden devices — must continue to live in.

[1] *Ibid.*, p. 1.
[2] *Ibid.*, p. 15.

25

One Click Makes You Smaller... Virtualizing Reality

> Having failed to create computers capable of equaling human beings, they've set out to impoverish human experience to the point where life is no more attractive than its digital modeling. Can one picture the human desert that had to be created to make existence on the social media seem desirable? — The Invisible Committee, *To Our Friends* (2015)

i. An All-Improved Reality, Where You're the Boss

Once again the field of Virtual Reality (VR) is being promoted for a hoped-for mass market. What wonders will be afoot when VR "infonauts," as users of VR have been termed by one enthusiast, venture forth for adventures in their simulated environments? VR has additionally been presented as having potential usefulness for architects, pharmaceutical scientists, and athletes. Yet, VR also starkly demonstrates some of the more alarming examples of the undermining of human perceptions and comprehension created by the new technologies.

As with the rest of hi-tech, most of the original push for VR came from the Pentagon. Especially important was the US Air Force's need by the end of World War II to build increasingly realistic fake environments that pilots-in-training could be immersed in, as described earlier. More than two decades later Pentagon analysts were impressed with the training undergone by Israeli commandos, who rescued the hostages taken at Entebbe in 1973 after having practiced their mission at a mock-up of that airport. US Department of Defense money backed one legendary early VR project, the Aspen Movie Map (1978), where one could "tour" the "town" of Aspen on screen, stopping to "linger" at interesting "locations" or choosing to "go" straight, "turn" left or right at "corners," and even "enter" selected "buildings" in order to "examine" their "interiors." Ultimately, the Pentagon explained, it would like to have libraries holding detailed electronic maps of key installations in any potential enemy's territory to use for training missions based on simulations, just as the Israelis had done. Today, more and more of the military's war-game exercises, which used to consist of real troops, real tanks, real guns (shooting mostly fake ammunition), real weather, real tasteless food, and real mud occur entirely on-line.[1]

Besides for military applications, VR systems offer new approaches to traditional problems. Architects, designers, or potential renters can "experience" entering a building undergoing design; chemists can construct VR models of molecules or viruses to experience "tactilely" the way one molecule or virus might interlock with another.[2]

In addition to the Pentagon, the adventure and entertainment industries provided the motivation and research money in Japan, England, and the US. Disney, Atari, Fujitsu, and Toshiba pushed the fledging efforts to re-create reality. Howard Rheingold, a notable hi-tech promoter, calls the VR voyagers "infonauts," who head deep into cyberspace, a head-mounted device creating the whole of their fields of vision and hearing and with a glove, also crammed with sensors and controls, helping them negotiate their simulated spaces. VR can be as prosaic as a three-dimensional video game. Graphics are generally crude, even cartoon-like. Instead of wrestling molecules side-by-side to see if there is any chemistry between them, participants might "slay" "dragons" or have other adventures. While inside their simulated experience, the infonauts interact with the creatures or elements inside their VR fields, and so experience the game as a "lived" experience.

VR has been defined as

> an environment in which the brain is coupled so tightly with the computer that the awareness of the computer user seems to be moving around inside the computer-created world the way people move around the natural environment.[3]

To learn how to create such artificial environment, NASA funded research to assemble "a body of knowledge about the ways the human senses can be fooled into accepting virtual versions of the physical world."[4] (Had the technology been sufficiently perfected by 2010, imagine how useful it would have been for BP in the aftermath of the Deepwater Horizon disaster in the Gulf of Mexico to show the public and the government what was "really" going on.)

---

[1] Howard Rheingold, *Virtual Reality* (New York: Simon & Schuster, 1991), pp. 16f, 100f.
[2] *Ibid.*, p. 29.
[3] *Ibid.*, p. 79.
[4] *Ibid.*, pp. 45, 207.

As Frederick Brooks, an academic pioneer in VR, has observed, "The danger of more and more realism [in VR] is that if you don't have corresponding truthfulness, you teach people things that are not so."[1]

To say the least there are disturbing, even nightmarish aspects of VR, as well as numerous philosophical and political questions that demand to be asked. For starters, what is the significance of the emergence of a new consumer entertainment industry that promises to provide everyone with devices for creating "realities" over which they can exercise absolute control *just when* people around the world are becoming alarmed about toxic assaults on the cities, the airs, waters, and lands? How convenient to have access to new "places" whose aquifers are not permeated with cancerous and mutagenic solvents; where habitats and species are not rapidly disappearing while Progress paves over the countryside.

Rheingold makes this quite explicit, projecting a future having "a world of tens of billions of people, [where] perhaps cyberspace is a better place to keep most of the population relatively happy, most of the time."[2] In other words, a further chapter in the ongoing numbing of our capacity for outrage.

One of the early enthusiasts for VR was the late Timothy Leary, who also spoke eagerly of leaving Earth to head for "greener" pastures in space, abandoning the planet while she stewed in her poisoned juices. Of course, along with the polluted Earth, he would be leaving behind the innumerable lifeforms — animals, plants, fungi, etc., who live here and will not be able to leave, including nearly every one of the several billion humans, most of whom are too poor, too dark-skinned, too female, or too mindful of not reviving the discredited colonial patterns of our past, to benefit from Leary's and others' plans for cosmic colonization. For Leary *et al.* the white man's burden has taken on truly celestial dimensions.

But no alternative reality, as VR and its proponents offer it up, nor any other planet or moon can be allowed, even for a moment, to allow us to escape the grim realities of our degenerating biosphere, and we cannot confuse "control" over what transpires on a video monitor a foot-and-a-half in front of us with actual control over the conditions that determine our real lives. I would hope that by now we would be a mite suspicious of such ploys. No, our need is to act to save ourselves, *all* of ourselves.

Howard Rheingold in his study of VR was apprehensive — not enough, however, to dampen to any degree his awe-struck enthusiasm for the whole thing. He expressed wonder, however, about what will happen (as he foresees coming to pass) when "reality itself might become a manufactured and metered commodity?"[3] Indeed! Metered, presumably, requiring a payment,

---

[1] *Ibid.*, p. 45. A lesson, I am sure, of considerable interest to President Trump.
[2] *Ibid.*, p. 352.
[3] *Ibid.*, p. 17.

and so undoubtedly off-limits to the poor, in effect prisoners inside a machine-constructed world; unmediated sunsets and ocean vistas reserved for a privileged few?

ii. BLURRING THE LINES; ANIMATING CARTOON REALITIES

In this reality that is virtual — visually, audibly, and tactilely — one is able to change what s/he experiences, including transforming his or her own body or face. This "is bound to have a deep psychological effect, soon calling into question just what" — I would hope we could still stay with "who" — "you consider yourself to be," one commentator has noted.[1] However, as with Artificial-Intelligence (AI), the related but different discipline within the computational community that we shall explore in the next chapter, the forecasts VR designers make of what their craft will soon be able to create are likely vastly inflated, if not downright delusional, a recurring pattern, as we shall see, in much of computer culture. There are reasons to question whether the "reality" so created in VR can ever be other than "cartoon-like," as in the projected VR screens for fighter pilots. Since it is likely that VR graphics will retain a cartoon-like appearance (see below), a gap between its simulated environments and our physical worlds will undoubtedly still exist. On the other hand, if for ten or more hours a day one is peering into a screen or screens, the gap might not be all that noticeable.

No matter how big a memory a particular computer can stuff into its electronic circuitry, VR technology has an especially prodigious appetite. If manufacturers decide to create VR environments, for example, that instantaneously (in "real time") respond to changes in the VR user's gaze, finger positions, or other such controls, so that the representation of the infonaut inside the virtual scene moves at the same time as the controls are manipulated, then the *number* of elements of the scene that can be modeled or represented in the virtual scene will necessarily be limited; accordingly, details — shadows, '"superfluous" objects, three-dimensionality, gradation of coloration, minor parts, etc. — will simply be ignored. *Or* the VR manufacturers can program their environments to present a more realistic picture of things as they actually are in our physical world, including shadows and details and the like, but thereby their simulation will be incapable (because of the inevitable limits on memory in depicting such a complex "world") of matching changes of the controls with changes of the virtual elements *as they occur.* Things will be delayed for some moments and nothing will take place in "real time." Some such tradeoff is inherent in the technology itself, rather than disappearing as memory capacities continue to expand, for the *need* for ca-

---

[1] *Ibid.*, p. 191, quoting Eric Gullichsen. One might reasonably also wonder whether the rush to alternative on-line "identities" is not opening a door to socially-sanctioned schizophrenia?

pacity will also grow, exponentially as it turns out, as a picture takes on more complexity and realism. Early VR experiments were often only crude out-lines of geometrical shapes, for example. Though the objects depicted in cy-berspace now have more body to them, and even sometimes shadows, they are still crude, belying Rheingold's confident assumption that computers "are only beginning to approach the point where people might confuse simula-tions with reality."[1]

Some years ago a colleague pointed out a popular simulated marine en-vironment screensaver on a new Macintosh computer our school had re-cently purchased. I admired its range and subtlety of hues, staring at its "fish" and "crabs" moving across the screen. Every few moments some of the "creatures" depicted were shown moving. After a few seconds watching, the jerkiness of their movements became grating. Movement only occurred at certain defined intervals, and when it took place, several of the "creatures" moved at the same time and did so in small jumps. I mentioned my experi-ence to my computer-scientist friend, who pointed out that as memory ex-pands and programmers become more ambitious, we can expect manufacturers to attempt *to create continuously moving "fish,"* but all the screen-creatures will still be restricted to *either* horizontal *or* vertical motions. Later improvements in technology might take on that challenge, sending some of the "critters" off on seeming *diagonals*, but a close look at their paths will re-veal them as consisting of combinations of horizontal and vertical movement so as to *look* diagonal; the individual creatures would still *lack any interactions*, plus the *motions would still be in straight lines*. His point was that no matter how far computers can extend their memories, software designers will never be able to incorporate in their screen depictions (including the screens making up visual fields of infonauts) more than a tiny fraction of the innumerable ways, big and small, that the natural world unfolds all around us. The VR renderings will forever retain some of their crudeness, mere shadows (as in Plato's cave) of the complicated cosmos we actually inhabit.

On the other hand, an experiment done at Stanford University revealed that at least half of the subjects couldn't tell the difference between things they had done and things they had done only in a computer simulation. In-deed, the inventor of Second Life, Philip Rosedale, claimed that by 2020 his online world would be indistinguishable from real life.[2]

A startling instance of this may well be pilots, who, after considerable time training with crude graphics purposely substituted for the physical re-ality of the villages and people they are meant to bomb, may cease to differ-entiate between the two. Cartoon-like and crude thought the VR images may be, for the Pentagon they apparently do the trick. For a pilot "steering a large quantity of high explosives at supersonic speeds, making life-and-death

---

[1] *Ibid.*, pp. 34, 145, 186, 204.
[2] Rushkoff, *op. cit.*, p. 69.

judgments in fractions of seconds," *and* doing this "only semiconscious at times...," such crude representations may be more than adequate.[1] Indeed, by the time of the Gulf War visual fields of symbols which had been used in training exercises began to be used on the real battlefield. Rheingold foresees a time not so far in the future where we shall live "in computer-created worlds for huge portions of our waking hours," especially as "reality" disappears behind a screen and that screen wraps itself around the whole of one's visual field.[2]

Nonetheless, VR enthusiasts like Rheingold have little doubt that the simulations will soon become real enough to be indistinguishable from our ordinary reality; and when that occurs, Rheingold warns, "we are in for major changes."[3]

What about the other organs of the national security state? How might they choose to utilize this new dimension of reality? Prosecutors or police might be delighted with the opportunity of immersing suspects involuntarily inside VR simulations of the crimes to which they were being trained to confess. Deprived of sleep and food, possibly with other forms of torture accompanying their interrogation, and run through the "crime" in VR repeatedly so that they actually "experience" doing the very things the confession is about, how many suspects might get confused as to just what *did* happen, what they *might* have done? VR experiences, of course, leave no tell-tale black-and-blue marks, nor any sign of having taken place. A defense attorney would be hard put to prove that his or her client had been subjected to such an injected "experience." Other interrogation/torture possibilities came to mind, too, when I read Rheingold's descriptions of the plan to use laser microscanners to implant, rod by rod and cone by cone, a total visual picture in a (potentially involuntary) infonaut's retina. If the eyes are indeed the windows to the soul, what would such total control over a person's visual world enable interrogators to do? I could not be sure, but the question sends chills up my spine.

In the Winter, 1992, issue of *Whole Earth Review*, Rheingold, the author of one of the earliest books on VR, wrote that he was in the unique position for a reviewer (of four books, including his own, on VR) of knowing what the author of *his* book would say differently if he were writing the book one year later.

---

1 Rheingold, *op. cit.*, p. 202.

2 *Ibid.*, p. 345ff. Besides a heartfelt sympathy for Rheingold's sexual partners, past and future, what are we to make of his speculation that through "teledildonics," the "sharing of data structure[s] of your innermost self representation[s]," may soon be seen as more intimate than "the physical commingling of genital secretions?"

3 *Ibid.*, p. 388.

The Gulf War and the way it was presented in the media, crystallized some of my thinking about the ethics of VR weaponry. In *Virtual Reality* I traced the origins of head-mounted displays through 23 years of development for the USAF Supercockpit project; described what I saw of Simnet, the armed warfare simulator network for tank crews, jet pilots and helicopter pilots; and provided a glimpse at a teleoperated humvee wielding a .50 caliber machine gun. But I did not foresee the marriage of simulation-as-training-tool to simulator-as-propaganda-weapon. The Gulf War showed how military leaders accomplished the virtualization of journalism by restricting the world's view of the combat to a few spectacular glimpses of video-game-like direct hits. Undoubtedly, the pilots and tank commanders in the Gulf War had trained in sophisticated computer graphic simulators that translated Defense Intelligence Agency maps of Kuwait and Iraq into virtual battlefields where planned maneuvers could be rehearsed electronically. The Gulf [War] was the first virtual war.

The question that arises now concerns the potential effects of blurring the line between war and video games.[1]

VR takes us on its magic journeys into a strange space that is no place and which harbors more than its share of *cul-de-sacs,* dimensional *non sequiters,* and deep metaphysical holes whose depth is unknown. The famous "cyberspace," a mathematical abstraction, has come to have a life of its own, an opaque void in which the binary 0s and 1s take their places as so directed, there to encode operating systems, memory, and instructions, the better to order our multitudinous affairs in the new world order that their military and business sponsors of information technology have constructed with their algorithms.

---

[1] Howard Rheingold, "Hands-Off Technology: Four Books on Virtual Reality," *Whole Earth Review,* no. 73 (Winter, 1992), pp. 88–89.

26
Capital's Final Solution?

Consciousness is an over-rated concept. — AI expert Marvin Minsky, quoted in Gray, *op. cit.*

"Cells are constantly making decisions about what to do, where to go or when to divide. Many of these decisions are hard-wired in our DNA or strictly controlled by external signals and stimuli. Others, though, seem to be made autonomously by individual cells."

It took science until 2012 to officially acknowledge that nonhuman animals possess feelings and consciousness. It may take a bit longer for biology to admit that the cells in our bodies are not simply automata, that they possess, if not consciousness, at least some sort of agency. — Barbara Ehrenreich, "Terror Cells: Ain't no cure for dystopian biology," *Baffler*, no. 26 (2014). (The first paragraph is a quotation, in her article, from a science news site.)

By the middle of this [20th] century, mankind had acquired the power to extinguish life on Earth. By the end of the century, he will be able to create it. Of the two, it is hard to say which places the larger burden of responsibility on our shoulders. — Chris Langton, "Towards Artificial Life," *Whole Earth Review*, no. 58 (Spring, 1988)

i. DISA & DATA

Since it is the twin phenomena of thought and consciousness that most glaringly contradict machine theories of life, it has fallen to the ideology of the Information Age to finally put them in their place, by demonstrating that thought and consciousness, whatever they are, can be modeled on the basis of machine logic. In this view, thought and mind are simply complex iterations of sophisticated algorithms and the like. At the same time as new, even more presumptuous machine theories and machine metaphors to account for thought and life have become popularized, especially among scientists and academics, Capital worldwide is waging a ferocious war for its "right" to commodify life itself.

Patents on component parts of human DNA, on bio-engineered "creatures," even on parts of individual people's genetic code, and on key components of the planetary heritage of seeds for medicines, edible fruits, and vegetables are being forcefully pursued by biotech and agribusiness. When in 1980 the US Supreme Court in *Diamond vs. Chakrabarty* ruled that an individual "species," "invented" through the then-emerging field of gene-splicing, could be patented, the terrain on which Capital could exercise its logic and imperium was vastly expanded. Now it was not just that forest or this river that inexorably appeared to flow into the seemingly insatiable bellies of Capital (as with the enclosures that began in the 16th century and are still with us today, especially in Africa), but the central processes and seedstock of Life in general was at risk of being swallowed whole.

In 1992 the legal battle over "owning" life reached a new depth when one group of scientists sought to patent individual segments of the human genetic code that they had isolated as parts of the Human Genome Project — even though they had no idea whatsoever what function the segments presumably played in ordering human life. Their claim was (temporarily?) denied, but the university-affiliated scientists involved vowed to continue their efforts to patent parts of the human genetic structure that the Genome Project reveals.

Since a new ontology demands a new epistemology, as 17th-century proponents of the mechanical philosophy understood, the Age of Information comes with new theories of what learning is, and feverish attempts to build machines that can "learn," can "think." In the new language of hi-tech, the categories of wisdom and of its distant cousin, knowledge, have been made matters of Information, and then debased further to "databases" and to "big data." These are, however, manifestly not the same things, not even the same *kinds* of things.

Much of the data that passes before us is but of ephemeral interest, particulars about a given variable, like aspects of the weather, stock values, output, pictures posted of a man's nuts covered with peanut butter, baseball scores, or "opinion," whose changing measures are tracked by the forecasters (the soothsayers of our times, plying their printouts as if they were animal entrails). Currency speculators, pundits, sportswriters, etc., analyze these in what is often excruciating detail. To the experts and historians, this is all very important stuff, but for the rest of us, the value of yesterday's — or for the currency traders, yestermicrosecond's — variables is of passing significance.

Emphasizing how quickly technology, and by extension science, seems to be continually changing not only our world, but how we comprehend its workings, apparently rendering last year's knowledge outmoded and irrelevant, the Age of Information wants to treat "out-dated" data dismissively, as we discussed earlier (p. 430) in regard to the computer-generated map of tectonic plates, at times extending this contempt even to books more than a handful of years old.[1] So too knowledge and wisdom are equated with quantities of data. "Database" does, however, accurately reflect the earliest (and truest) meaning of computers, machines that store and manipulate huge chunks of numbers; in essence they do nothing more.

ii. THE MINDS OF THEIR CHILDREN...

Schoolchildren are being taught that their minds or brains (the distinction tends to get lost) are essentially composed of memory cells that operate according to certain programs or software, those programs alternatively being things taught us by parents or religious institutions (psychological or spiritual), the stuff we learn in school (educational), things common to people in a particular nation or language grouping (cultural), or aspects we share as humans (biological). Learning is only a matter of filling our memory "banks" and thinking is having clear programs or procedures, free from ambiguity (which could lead to conflict), to reach significant conclusions. Not only is thinking compared with computing, increasingly it is simply identified with it. Some adults who should know better push such an understanding. Scientists, given the history of mechanical thinking, are more prone to this kind of reductionism. For example, John Lilly (one would have hoped that the dolphins would have put him right) engages in such mechanical identifications of thinking with computing.

Let me remind readers that the two men most responsible for creating the first computer, Norbert Weiner and John von Neumann, both realized that human thinking was far too complex to produce with their new machines. Instead, they opted to bypass altogether the messiness of actual thinking, reducing it to Weiner's categories of messages, control, feedback, etc., or to von Neumann's inputs, outputs, pattern recognition, use of formal logic, and ability to act on instructions, in order to come up with a rough equivalent of how a human brain actually works.[2]

---

[1] Thus, being disciplined in 2008 as a teacher vocally challenging the San Francisco Unified School District's fevered embrace of a pedagogy of test-accountability, with the glut of new standardized tests it was trying to impose on my classroom, I was removed from my teaching duties and school and assigned to a series of grammar and high school libraries to "weed them" of outmoded books. My supervisor instructed me that outmoded meant *anything* published before 1997! I had to argue to get books like Malcolm X's autobiography saved; most of my advocacy went for naught, unfortunately.

[2] See pp. 430–31.

Lilly and others appear to have jettisoned Weiner's and von Neumann's limited claims for what their computers could do. Indeed, perhaps the dominant metaphor of the Age of Information is the thinking machine, a conflation of wisdom with data (transfer). Such changes in the language and conceptualization of consciousness rest on a number of quite dubious assumptions about thinking and the glib conflation of epistemology with comparing one number to another. Upon examination, these assumptions prove quite untenable.

Such claims about the world and what thought is can be found best exemplified in numerous labs working on what is called "Artificial Intelligence" or AI, the drive — at the present getting a second wind of sorts, after suffering from a couple of decades of embarrassing failures to deliver — to produce machines capable of taking over that last alleged domain of the human. Once more Pentagon money has been heavily deployed, priorities have been mapped, and weapons (such as drones) are being developed centered on AI. For decades, work in AI was regularly used as a basis for projections of startling breakthroughs to be expected in the very near future, computers that would be capable of carrying out "intelligent" tasks, able to make a complex translation of a text from one real (everyday) language to another, for example, or of proving mathematical theorems. And yet, the breakthroughs always are elusive, forever receding into a promised next decade or so.

At the very first academic conference on AI in 1956 (at Dartmouth College), a statement coming out of the conference clearly articulated the fundamental axiom of AI: "every aspect of learning or any other feature of intelligence can in principle be so precisely described that a machine can be made to simulate it." Note the rather typical overreach, "every aspect" of learning.[1] Note, too, the Weiner-and-von Neumann-like hedge, "can in principle."

In his critique of AI,[2] Hubert Dreyfus examines the several areas where intelligent machines have been promised, including some overconfident predictions dating back almost forty years. He found similar patterns, consisting of greatly inflated initial claims followed by slow partial retractions, in the following areas: machine-based language translation; pattern recognition; game-playing; and theorem-proving, the four main domains in which AI has staked its claims to future motherlodes. In all four areas, the initial "promising" successes were quickly followed by seemingly insurmountable walls, as fruitless attempts were made to extend the early "breakthroughs" (that, in all instances, had been made on the basis of quite simplified systems) to more complex situations. As complexity was allowed into the picture, demands

---

[1] Markoff, *op. cit.*, pp. 105ff.

[2] My debt to Dreyfus is huge, for in-forming my inchoate misgivings. (Dreyfus, *What Computers Can't Do: The Limits of Artificial Intellgence* (New York: Harper & Row, 1979), and Dreyfus, *What Computers Still Can't Do: A Critique of Artificial Reason* (Cambridge, Mass.: MIT Press, 1992).

on the machines' performances tended to grow exponentially. Added complexity translated into a qualitative difference in the need for both an extended memory and faster speeds of computation.

A partial exception to this is pattern recognition, still not solved, but side-stepped, an "as if" capability achieved by means of statistical sampling.[1]

The problem in mechanizing human thinking is that the real thing has a profound ability to deal simultaneously with various *levels* of meaning, having ambiguities and nuances, indeed, even contradictions, and a certain fuzziness "around the edges" of the objects and situations that it cogitates about, in a way that no machine is, or ever will be, capable of.

By definition, in any search for *general* rules about thinking, machines must strive for "context-free" precision, procedures they can *universally* apply. But inevitably the real effect of such searches is to drain the computer's capacities, necessitating endless trial-and-error subroutines to discover for themselves the elusive context.

Time after time AI software has shown itself simply incapable of coming up with *any general rules* that do not implicitly preselect out of a particular complex situation precisely those elements specifically important to it. In other words, no *general* framework has been created that does not covertly utilize prior *human* intelligence that steers the supposed general rules to an application already tailored to the specifics of a *given* situation.

Dreyfus zeros in on two particulars of thinking that damn all efforts to "mass produce" it on machines. Human perceptions, he points out, are generally of "things" inside a "field" that is not-them, like a pencil sitting on the "field" of my desk. While the *things* are usually perceived rather specifically and in great detail, the *field* around them necessarily seems to fade into a certain obscure featurelessness, a "mere" background against which the objectness of the thing can stand out.

In human (and presumably other) thinking, as situations or purposes change, the boundaries between a thing and the field around it can shift *as directed by the will* of the person (or other creature) perceiving and judging. For example, I may be looking at an insect, in which case the "field" might be the bush the bug is crawling on. If I become interested in the creature's wing, the insect itself other than its wings becomes the "field." Or, intrigued by the way it has camouflaged itself on the bush, my focus might shift to the leaves or bark of the bush and the play of light and shadow and coloration. Any details of the bug's body structure that are not part of its hiding strategy will accordingly fade into the "field" for me. In other words, we pick out in any given instance just what is significant at that time; as significances change, so too do our attentions. Such mental or perceptual gymnastics, however, can change from moment to moment and are beyond the capabilities of the literal-circuitry of the muscle-bound information-processing ma-

---

[1] Markoff, *op. cit.*, pp. 153–57.

chines, programmed to carry out their instructions without ambiguity — no matter how prodigious their memories, how many numbers they can crunch per second, or how numerous their parallel processors are. Dreyfus is convinced that what enables people unconsciously and (largely) effortlessly to handle the transitions and ambiguities of real perception and thinking is that our perceptions and thoughts are products of *embodied* beings.[1]

As creatures with bodies, humans are capable of finding the relevant "facts" for a given problem out of an undifferentiated pattern, according to the purposes we need them for. To get a machine to "think," it would be necessary to select which "facts" it will operate on, or give it general principles so that the machine can find those "facts" itself. No such general principles, however — for the reasons outlined above — are possible.

AI is based on a set of three interlocking presumptions, each of which Dreyfus refutes:

a) For any situation, there is a set of facts that are each logically independent of one another, and unique to that situation.

b) at some level in the thinking process — frequently thought to be in the neurons in the brain — the brain must process signals in discrete steps, biologically either "turning on" or "turning off." In other words, the brain is a digital device.

c) All knowledge of the world is capable of being formalized, or stated as a series of formal propositions.

Dreyfus readily admits that AI and computer technology, in a certain sense, is itself the "embodiment" of long-lasting (but now, in some circles at least, quite discredited) philosophical traditions, in the West dating back at least to Greek antiquity, that teach that to account for human behavior people can be analyzed according to certain scientific principles *as objects* which act in response to other objects, as in a *physical system.*

Despite the insurmountable barriers that emerge in AI when, for example, attempts are made reliably to translate one real language, say in conversation, with its innumerable context-related clues, like intonation, body language, facial expression, gestures, and the myriad meanings of specific words, into another real language, without the need for human direction, AI proponents until recently have remained steadfast in their optimism; they inflated the limited advances that initially greeted their efforts when vastly simplified tasks for AI were addressed to imply that real thinking machines were still just a couple of years or so away. Progress was ever being forged, according to the AI community. Its failures were seen as minor, not fundamental. Announcements of successes were constructed so as to minimize the extreme limitations of the particular result. Taking seriously the definition of progress in AI offered by two of its proponents as being movement "towards an ultimate goal," Dreyfus notes that the "first

---

[1] Thus, a contradiction of the mind/body duality.

man to climb a tree could [have similarly] claim[ed] tangible progress towards reaching the moon."[1]

Most ominously, AI enthusiasts have succeeded in getting others (like the media) to join them in cheerleading an "intelligence" that is both *dis-em-bodie*d and lacking *consciousness* — if it's okay for a pilot at the controls of a plane carrying thermonuclear weapons at times to be unconscious, as in tight G-turns, why not for the algorithms that ride herd on our Google searches, or the iPhones that can find where our friends are having dinner nearby, or the "instructional" DVD that our child is hooked up to in his elementary school? The late Marvin Minsky, inventor of the widely used LEGO educational software, certainly seemed to think there is no need. "Consciousness is an over-rated concept," he believed.

Perhaps consciousness is merely an atavism for romantics who insist that thinking is something different from information-processing.

iii. "Not the Animal Thing" (1992)

When I was finishing an early draft of this work, the latest *Whole Earth Review* (successor to the *Whole Earth Catalogue*) appeared on the stands, its theme that of artificial "life," or "a-life:" self-evolving software entities on the computer screen as the newest "cutting-edge" technology. Programmed both to "evolve" and to withstand efforts to wipe them out, such a-life entities were being designed at several installations by technophiliacs obsessed with creating a simulated evolution of human-created computer-based "life-forms." At some point, probably such a-life could be joined to a structure of many silicon microprocessors, in a way that allows "evolution" of different programs to affect the actual form, size, and functioning of the microprocessors. In a perverse poetics, the major center for such work initially was the Los Alamos National Lab, until recently specializing only in the design of nuclear weapons — the implied inversion should fool no one.

Just as do their peers in AI, proponents of a-life — forms they see as capable of "reproducing" and "mutating," as biological forms do in the natural world — alternated between extremely confident predictions regarding their power to create "silicon life forms" four or five decades from now and confident statements of "fact" that implied that such creation, in principle, had already taken place.

A-life proponents created programs with built-in mechanisms that "cause their actual program to randomly be changed," just as they believed is the case in biological mutation, and to have some of the programs "survive" and make (sometimes "mutated") copies of themselves, while others fail and so "die." In this way, a-life researchers professed to be constructing, within

---

[1] Rachel King, "What's next? Chips that think," San Francisco *Chronicle* (November 7, 2011).

their doped-silicon world, the essence of life. One of the leading a-life investigators, Tom Ray, in describing his rush into a field that was "obsessing me... the thing that kept me awake at night," explained his reasoning:

> I would consider a system to be living if it is self-replicating, and capable of open-ended evolution.... Artificial selection [as in animal and plant breeding] can never be as creative as natural selection.... Freely evolving [computer] creatures will discover means of mutual exploitation and associated implicit fitness functions that we would never think of.[1]

Some of these projected silicon "creatures" exist only in cyberspace, software programmed to change itself ("evolve") at intervals, perhaps increasing their endowments of the highly sought after "fitness functions." Other such creatures, as mentioned above, will presumably encase their a-life program within a metal and plastic "body," the "physiology" of which will be controlled by the changing program so that it, too, evolves, functioning as robots of sorts, existing in our three-dimensional space.

As Kevin Kelly describe in considerable detail in this *WER*, Darwin's theory of natural selection leaves lots of holes and makes promises of explanations that never are provided. Kelly portrays neo-Darwinian and non-Darwinian theories that try to fill in the holes in Darwin's theory of evolution, or to replace it with an altogether different theory of how evolution proceeds.[2]

According to Kelly, natural selection, and evolution itself, since we have but the single example of their alleged partnership, and that of phenomena that mostly occurred over the course of the previous few billions of years, is impossible to prove, or, as some philosophers of science demand of any real scientific theory, incapable of being falsified, of being refuted by any conceivable negative evidence. Using computer models of life, however, a-life researchers hope to provide the missing crucial tests.

> Biologists will fight it, but in the end persuasive proof or disproof of darwinism, and a second example of life, will both come from this unlikely abiological [computer] source.[3]

Tom Ray had few doubts that "forms of "life" virtually are "out there, waiting for us to create [electronic] environments for [them] to evolve into."[1]

---

1 Steven Levy, "Artificial Life: The Quest for a New Creation," *Whole Earth Review*, no. 76 (Fall, 1992), p. 23.

2 Kevin Kelly, "Deep Evolution: The Emergence of Postdarwinism," *Whole Earth Review*, no. 76 (Fall, 1992), pp. 4–21. In a later chapter (Chapter 31, pp. 547–52) we shall discuss these critiques of Darwin.

3 *Ibid.*, p. 7.

The fascination with a-life, significantly, in a number of its researchers comes paired with a profound antipathy to their *own* lives, or at least for the bodies in which their lives are unfortunately embedded, something found as well among many of the VR researchers. In contrast to Dreyfus's conclusion that *embodiment* is a critical basis for all thought (and life), leading AI and a-life scientists *are fundamentally alienated from their own human bodies* — as was also the case with the advocates of the mechanical philosophy in the 17th century, men who were also afraid of the human body and of the passions it was capable of generating, extending the traditional Christian alienation from and hostility to this world to a new ideological plateau. That turn away from the body has now found its "natural" vehicle in computers.

For example, one pioneer of AI, Danny Hillis, explained that humans are

> a symbiotic relationship between two essentially different kinds of things. We're the metabolic thing, which is the monkey that walks around and we're the intelligent thing, which is a set of ideas and culture. And those two things have coevolved together, because they helped each other. But they're fundamentally different things. What's valuable about us, what's good about humans, is the idea thing. It's not the animal things.[2]

Hillis also explained his wish to be able to "have one of my machines be... a friend."[3] A profound darkness of the soul is hinted at by this flight from the body, as well as a not-so-hidden misanthropy.

iv. THESE NEW GODS DO NOT PLAY (2013)

The drive to transcend the limits of biological life picked up a head of steam from the Human Genome Project and the new technologies it (and similar attempts to read the genome of a number of other species) spawned. New ways were devised to speed up, even to automate, critical chemical reactions in the replication of DNA. Out of this ferment emerged the field that calls itself "synthetic biology," wherein the quest to build new forms of life has devised a way of using the computer mouse in a quite different manner than in the earlier push to develop a-life. Now the awe-inspiring crunching power of computers are to be used to read and rapidly replicate huge quantities of DNA, thus facilitating the manufacturing of life, it is said.

The proponents of synthetic biology see one path to artificial life in the mass production of the "building blocks" of life, "codons," lengths of DNA that specify a particular amino acid to be made (there are 64 codons). One

---

[1] Levy, *op. cit.*, p. 22.
[2] Steven Levy, "A-Life Nightmare," *Whole Earth Review*, no. 76 (Fall, 1992), p. 39.
[3] *Ibid.*, p. 40.

of its visionaries likens these building blocks to Legos and calls them Bio-Bricks, mass-producing and making available to researchers these standard-ized biological parts (sort of a Kragans for living systems). There were 1500 different BioBricks available in 2008.[1]

The academic scientists/entrepreneurs —that new hybrid born in Silicon Valley and exemplified by bio-tech — foresee the creation of new "organ-isms," ones they will design as part of an industrialization of life itself, churn-ing out by the millions on bacterial-factory platforms the creatures they plan to create. Besides providing codons on demand, new amino acids will be de-signed and produced, then new codons for *their* manufacture. Out of this, al-together new creatures can be made.

J. Craig Venter, a major investor, researcher, lobbyist, and ideologist for synthetic biology, proposes using bacterial cells, whose genetic material has been largely sucked out, replaced by synthetic genes designed by his firm, as factories. Asked whether in creating new life forms these synthetic biologists were not playing God, one of Venter's associates, a scientist named Hamilton Smith, replied, "We don't play."

Drew Endy of Stanford, the inventor of BioBricks, explains that

> We would like to be able to routinely assemble systems from pieces that are well described and well-behaved…. That way, if in the future someone asks me to make an organism that, say, counts to 3,000 and then turns left, I can grab the parts off the shelf, hook them together and predict how they will perform.[2]

Synthetic biologists "imagine nature as a manufacturing platform: all liv-ing things are just crates of generic cogs; we should be able to spill all those cogs out on the floor and rig them into whatever new machinery we want." Instead of making planks from a felled tree to make a bookcase, Endy thinks you could program the DNA in the tree so that it grows into a bookshelf."[3] This strikes me as akin to an apotheosis of reductionism. It is as if nothing has been learned since Descartes, who likened the screams of animals being tortured to the grinding of ungreased gears and cogs.

---

[1] As of 2010 there were over 5000 BioBricks listed for sale, over three times more than at the start of 2008. Bernadette Tansy, "Leaving MIT For Stanford, Assistant Professor Emphasizes Collaboration in Synthetic Biology," San Francisco *Chronicle* (December 26, 2007); Jon Mooallem, "Do-It-Yourself Ge-netic Engineering: In the Burgeoning Field of Synthetic Biology Even Ama-teurs Are Building Life Forms," *New York Times Magazine* (February 14, 2010).
[2] Andrew Pollack, "His Corporate Strategy: The Scientific Method," *New York Times* (September 5, 2010); etc. group, *Extreme Genetic Engineering: An Introduc-tion to Synthetic Biology* (Canada, 2007), p. 15.
[3] *Ibid.*, p. 16; Mooallem, *op. cit.*

In articles in the popular press, the industrial production of life-saving medicines and of alternatives to fossil fuels are touted, but with Pentagon money again financing much of this work, bioweapons are more likely to emerge, that and a whole new level of malpractice by Big Pharma.

Synthetic biology, taken on its own terms (that is, ignoring the many reasons it probably is not feasible) raises some very serious questions. It astounds me that a little more than fifty years after the structure of the DNA molecule was first determined, many scientists believe it is sufficiently understood to begin making new models, new forms of it. After all, even now DNA is so little known that a considerable portion of the life-defining molecule is dismissed by biologists as "junk DNA," i.e., worthless, masking their ignorance by this glib denigration. To say the least, this betrays no small measure of scientific hubris.

Second, the belief by the synthetic biologists that they might string together snippets of DNA already existing or newly designed ignores what reluctantly many biotech scientists have come to realize, that single genes do not have single expressions of their behavior. Just like words, each with a variety of meanings, genes turn out to have multiple functions, different ways of being used. "I 'ran' the press all night long" is an altogether different "ran" than the "ran" that competed in races or the "ran" undertaken by the previous governor. So too genes express themselves, as biologists have been discovering, in a multiplicity of ways according to time, place, and present physiological needs. For both natural language and for biological organisms, their inherent ambiguity of expression is why neither translate well into the ambiguity-phobic binary language of hi-tech.

Thus, tinkering with living organisms is not the same, despite the synthetic biologists' deeply ingrained mechanism, as putting a larger air-intake valve in a carburator to boost performance. The hot rod reference is apt, for though some of the synthetic biologists acknowledge the need for precautions in work of the kind they propose, others betray a more lackadaisical attitude, foreseeing eager high-school sophomores designing new creatures for a Science Fair project — and true to the libertarian proclivities of much of hi-tech, what right does government or anyone else have to tell them what is or isn't permissable?[1]

The two US centers of synthetic biology are Boston (Harvard, MIT, etc.) and the Bay Area (Stanford, UC Berkeley, UCSF, etc.). It is fair to ask how those

---

[1] For a terrifying account of how most governments are refusing, despite claims to the contrary, to monitor or even to test the safety of genetically modified organisms, see Steven M. Druker, *Altered Genes, Twisted Truth* (Salt Lake City: Clear River Press, 2015). The push into molecular biology, firmly based on physics and chemistry rather than biological principles, was heavily promoted by the Rockefeller Foundation starting in the 1930s. By now, the White House and the FDA are extremely supportive of biotech, suppressing large amounts of their own negative scientific findings. Writing about the Reagan, first Bush, and Clinton administrations, the *New York Times* observed, "What Monsanto wished for from Washington, Monsanto — and by extension the biotechnology industry — got" (pp. 18, 138).

locales will fare when, inevitably, a breech allows the release into the environment of their fancied new organisms? For starters, all existing biological entities on our planet have predators, creatures that eat them or their eggs so that they are unable to reproduce without limit. What about these new, presently on the drawing table, critters? Are we to believe that they will always be manufactured in tandem with other creatures able to keep their numbers in check? And if not, what assurances do we have that superbacteria, superweeds or superfungi will not, as in some cheap Hollywood thriller, march or swim roughshod over the land and (both syn-bio centers are on the ocean) through the seas?

v. PROMISES, PROMISES

There are excellent reasons to believe that, like AI and VR, a-life and synthetic biology, too, should be seen as little more than fantasies by their technophiliac proponents that will never come close to the reality they so confidently promise us and their financiers. With AI we saw the inherent structural reasons why, once the complexities of the real world begin to be introduced into their models, the limited successes reported on very simple problems can never be extended to establish the kinds of capabilities required if true "intelligence" can be manufactured. So too in the VR world, where when the infonaut repositions his/her gaze or fingers, the resultant on-screen transformations will become less and less synchronized with those motions as the figures themselves take on more real three-dimensionality, shadows, perspective, and other complexities, beyond the pretty much cartoon-like worlds the VRers and garners have produced to date. As mentioned earlier, the inherent limitations of computers, including the severe truncations from their binary ontology, will render forms of a-life or synthetic biology singularly unconvincing — having, for most of us, still used to the genuine three-dimensional creatures of nature, perhaps as much verisimilitude as plastic flowers.

Nonetheless, I think it is important for us to take the claims of the AI, VR, and synthetic biology visionaries very seriously, to assume, if only for the sake of argument, that they will one day be able to accomplish the many things they see as their mission, as if acting on an ontological Manifest Destiny, creating machines able to think better than people; virtual "realities" more convincing (or at least *as* convincing) than our material, present world; and life-forms indistinguishable in principle from biologically-rooted life.

What if they can do what they promise, if not today, then a decade, a century, or a millennium from now? What would it mean? And just why this push? Now? Let's look at some of the hidden agendas behind all these attempts to push through to a different understanding of life.

27

Constructing an Ideology of Species Suicide: Humans as Anachronisms

i. FLESH THINGS & MACHINE THINGS

The hidden agenda behind computerization and the pretenses of its "cutting-edge" frontiers (VR, AI, and synthetic biology) are not hard to discern if we dare look. In a word, computerization/simulations of *reality*, of *intelligence*, and of *life* itself finally complete the flight away from the body (and from our humanity) that the mechanical philosophy of the 17th century had initiated, but complete it on a profoundly different basis than was conceived of by the 17th-century visionaries. That earlier flight, again, was no real beginning, only a furthering and a deepening of the alienation from the flesh so central to Christianity and to Western culture going back at least to Plato and to monotheism.

Computers were invented to serve the military requirements revealed by World War II and its aftermath:[1] to carry out the massive calculations needed to know where artillery should be aimed to hit moving targets, to crack enemy-coded messages, and to develop the thermonuclear bomb. After the war, business came to be the next biggest investor in and user of the new information technologies. In both cases, military and business, the purposes of computers clearly has been "to enhance the power of those who possessed them...." From the beginning, questions of power were central in the design of the machines and their operating systems. The special talents of computers lies in how they enhance power. As Michael Shallis, originally trained as an astrophysicist, but now an investigator into questions concerning technology, explained:

> The three reasons behind computer design — efficiency, power, and to compete with human thought processes — all have one thing in common: the desire to replace and re-

---

[1] *Aka* the War after the War to End all Wars.

duced the role of human beings in a social structure. It can be argued that *the computer is an anti-human technology.*

Indeed, this is the conclusion that computer inventor Norbert Weiner had reached. For management this attempt to transcend humans, this preference for machine-substitutes, quite simply is because "[r]obots and computers do not get sick, do not need holidays and do not go on strike."[1]

Those who must work with and in computers suffer from a range of disorders, some of them from what might well be seen as sicknesses of the soul. If the workers are at data centers or the remaining mainframes, they will work in totally artificial environments, in rooms lacking windows or any other connection with the outside weather or rhythms of night and day — indeed, the equivalent of the miners cited in Part Two, except these "mines" go deeper, further, into the marrow of our humanity, as we have seen. Given the finicky nature of computers, temperature and humidity are rigidly controlled. If the machines are a major part of the workplace, light from outside is, as a rule, banished, both because of glare and to allow the heating, ventilating, and air conditioning systems to work, without having to contend with the harsh reality of things like the sun.[2] In her work on the interactions of people with computers, Sherry Turkle quotes one programmer, who seems quite at home in such spaces:

> I think of the world as divided between flesh things and machine things. The flesh things have feelings, need you to know how to love them, to take risks, to let yourself go. You never know what to expect of them. And all the things that I was into when I was growing up, well they were not those kinds of things. Chemistry, you could get exactly the right values when you did your experiments. No risks. I guess I like perfection, I stay away from the flesh things. I think this makes me a kind of nonperson. I often don't feel like a flesh thing myself. I hang around machines.[3]

One hacker explained, "You can create your own universe, and you can do whatever you want within that. You don't have to deal with people...."

---

[1]Michael Shallis, *The Electric Shock Book* (London: Souvenir Press, 1988), pp. 223, 225. No sick days, but a considerable amount, as it turns out, of "down time," for the technology crashes frequently and is notoriously fickle, as we have seen and will discuss further in the pages that follow.

[2] *Ibid.*, pp. 226–27.

[3] *Ibid.*, p. 226–27, quoting Sherry Turkle, *The Second Self.* Some of this may be common in technical fields. I vividly remember as an undergraduate physics major feeling akin to the billiard balls whose impact we had to study to learn about momentum and Newton's Laws. Like them I felt hard and unyielding on the outside and with little interior (emotional) life.

He relished the power to create "a self-contained fantasy world of exact logic, predictable parameters, selected data points."

A theoretician of cyberculture admits, "For many people who tended to be socially inept and quite shy anyway, the quasi-intelligent character of the machine [computer] has replaced human social interaction."[1] Not only does Silicon Valley in California have the most Superfund sites and some of the worst air and water pollution in the US, but its rates of divorce, broken homes, drug and alcohol addiction, and children raised without fathers are also the highest.[2] People who work as programmers often find it difficult to leave their machines. It takes them typically a whole weekend to recover from their work at their computers, where they have become cut-off, with glazed-over eyes. Physically they change. Even at home they acquire an aversion to natural lighting. Appetites decline and they suffer from high levels of adrenaline, nausea, and various nervous disorders.

The humans who work/play with the new technologies manifest a number of strange behaviors and attitudes, attested to by a steady stream of articles in the press about this pathology or that, including a cover story in the late *Newsweek*, "iCrazy: Panic, Depression, Psychosis. How Connection Addiction Is Rewiring Our Brains" (July 18, 2012). Most commonly are found obsessive behavior; bad sleep; memory and mood problems; sexual dysfunction; hypertension; cardiovascular disease; withering attention spans; and extreme addictions, akin to heroin, according to some physicians who treat users needing their next e-mail fix.[3] A study of Southern Californian users of "smart phones" found, for owners under 50, that most of the respondents checked their e-mail, texts, and social networks every 15 minutes![4] When a mother tried to take her son's video game and he fought her, she described him as being "possessed" (a concern we shall explore in the next chapter). Another young man, told by his mother to log off, continued on-line for some time, paying for it with his mother's credit card after he had bludgeoned her to death. A couple carefully took care and "nourished" their on-line virtual baby, while ignoring their real child, who died of neglect. At least ten people logged on, forgot to move, and died of blood clots.[5]

In social situations, including dates, people will be working their screens or keyboards and conversation, should there be any, more often than not is in reference to a screen into which all are looking, rather than at each other. Screen interactions with other people are preferred by many, especially

---

[1] Sandy Stone, *op. cit.*, p. 136.

[2] Shallis, *op. cit.*, p. 230.

[3] Lindsey Tanner, "Addiction to Video Games Should Be a Disorder, AMA Says," San Francisco *Chronicle* (June 22, 2007). Brian Awehali, "Slow Type," East Bay *Express* (May 7–13, 2014).

[4] "iCrazy," p. 28.

[5] *Ibid.*, pp. 27–28; "Addiction to Video Games."

among the young,[1] over live presence, partly because of an apotheosis of *control,* since e-contacts can always be terminated — or "unfriended," that tortuous redefinition of that culturally critical word, "friend," now, as with electronics in general, reduced to a yes/no status, the grays or nuances of friendship banished.

Consistent research findings suggest a serious impairment in memory functions and other kinds of mental performance and cognition from Internet use. Structural changes show up in the prefrontal cortex with as little as *five* hours on the Web! Alarmingly, in a Stanford University study in 2005, frequent multitaskers did worse than non-multitaskers in a test that required task-jumping, suggesting that one's ability to attend to many things at once *decreases* with practice. For people under 35, 35% check their Facebook or Twitter after sex, about the same number during dates, and while driving, 40%; for people over 35, the percentages (in late 2009) were around 9%.

The length of time people are tethered to their electronics is rapidly increasing — an over 25% increase between 2005 and 2010, in one Kaiser study. At work and at play, staring at the ubiquitous screens is what people *do.* In the US over a third of smart-phone users get on-line before leaving their beds. An average person deals with about 400 texts a month, four times more than in 2007. For teenagers, it is 3700 a month, or 125 texts a day, or allowing 6 hours for sleep, about 7 an hour. Children lament parents who are "present and yet not there at all," absorbed in their iPads, e-mail, or Facebook, according to MIT researcher Sherry Turkle. Mothers reflexively reach for their cell phones when spending time with their kids, even when nursing, absenting themselves. In kitchens or living rooms, the families sit, each in his/her own digital cocoon.[2]

Numerous articles in the popular press describe anguished parents watching their kids disappear into the maw of video games, Facebook, obsessive texting, etc., but powerless to break their sons' or daughters' fixations, trying to establish "reasonable" limits on cell phone or Facebook times, despite a realization that any such limits would likely just be ignored, or banishing devices at dinner.

"This is the parenting issue of our time," said a doctor and creator of the documentary "Screenagers: Growing Up in the Digital Age." "Parents are pulling their hair out and feeling scared, and kids… also feel hijacked by it," said a family therapist.

Grown-ups too attempt to establish certain hours or days when they will not use their devices, or go to events where their phones must be sur-

---

[1]Thus a shy teenager prefers approaching a boy she has a crush on "by text, where I feel more me." (Jeanne Phillips, "Dear Abby," San Francisco *Chronicle* (March 31, 2017). "It is as though they all have some signs of being on an Asperger's spectrum," a teacher at a private middle school observes of her students. (Jacob Weinberg, "We Are Hopelessly Hooked," *New York Review of Books*, February 25, 2016.)

[2] "iCrazy, Addiction to Video Games," pp. 27–28.

rendered. Valiant efforts, but hard to be optimistic about their efficacy against compulsions this powerful.[1] As of the end of 2006 US parents were daily spending an average of nine-and-a-half hours tied to screens.

Some 30% of teenagers are Internet-addicted in China, Korea, and Taiwan, a sickness that is now included in the official mental health diagnostic manual. Data suggests similar figures for the US as for Asia. Internet addicts have brains showing marked deterioration (including 10–20% shrinkage) of the area of the brain responsible for memory, speech processing, emotions, sensory information, and motor control. Their brains look like those of alcohol or drug addicts. A college student in the Midwest who maintains tabs on four avatars reported that his real self "is just another window… usually not my best one."[2]

Researchers believe Internet usage is creating "a whole new mental environment," one that is causing serious depression, anxiety, loneliness, obsessive-compulsive behavior, attention-deficit disorder, and outright psychosis. One UCLA scientist, the Director of the Semel Institute for Neuroscience and Human Behavior, likened computers to "electronic cocaine," while a Stanford scientist is engaged in studying whether the multiple digital selves adopted on-line might constitute "legitimate, pathological" selves akin to those with multiple-personality disorders.[3]

Under the onslaught of the new technology, workers in 1998 reported an average of 190 messages a day, many requiring a response — fax, e-mail, Twitter, Facebook (even Post-Its). People complained of being "treated like they are machines that are on all the time,"[4] the worm of the mechanical philosophy boring still deeper into our psyches. The corollaries of this mania for connectivity are time that is wasted and a lack of clarity. Not to mention the destruction of real (person-to-person) connections. And these machines that are touted as making work more efficient, as we all know, frequently create "dead" time for workers who must suffer frequent service interruptions, wait-times for booting-up or for programs to run, on-hold to tech support, riding herd on format issues, not to mention "fatal" cyber-viruses.

The complexities that computers have been brought in to tame, since people have devised new ways of doing things that no human can under-

[1] Emily Listfield, "Generation Wired," (*Parade*, San Francisco *Chronicle*, October 9, 2011); Leah Garchik, "How to kick back, unplug and forget it," (San Francisco *Chronicle*, March 8, 2017), among many others. Marissa Langs, "Reducing screen time," San Francisco *Chronicle*, (February 5, 2016).
[2] "The High Cost of High Tech — Gadget Gorge May Drain Brain," San Francisco *Chronicle* (April 17, 2011); "Quality Time, Redefined," *New York Times* (May 1, 2011); "iCrazy."
[3] "iCrazy."
[4] Kirstin Downey Grimsley, "Workers Face a Daily Deluge of Messages, Study Shows," San Franciscso *Chronicle* (May 21, 1998)..

stand any more, in fact flunk the assignment. Sometimes they are equal to the task. But only sometimes, which for things like air-traffic control, military-weapons systems, nuclear-power plants, or keeping cities stocked with adequate supplies of food, is not nearly enough.

Nicholas Negroponte, the author of *Being Digital* and the hero of Stewart Brand's celebration of the MIT-based Media Lab, where Negroponte is director, and where digitalization has become a technical challenge, an art form, and a theology, confesses to being bullied by an ugly digital watch that he owns. Though disliking the instrument and preferring another, knowing how difficult it would be for him to transfer all the data its chips contain, he keeps on wearing it. Once he allowed its battery to die and lost a great deal of vital data, becoming "information crippled for weeks."[1] If Negroponte, a key player in the AI and VR fields, is baffled by digital demands, it's a good bet that the rest of us might have strong grounds for feeling befuddled by binary.

An editor for *MacWorld* commented in 1995, "Back in the old days when I toiled on a typewriter, I never spent a whole morning installing a new ribbon. Nor did I subscribe to *Remington World* and *IBM Selectric User.* I did not attend the Smith Corona Expo two times a year."[2]

ii. COMPLEXITY BY DESIGN

A number of chapters ago I pointed to the US military and business in the US as the twin driving forces behind the computerization that began in the late 1940s and '50s. A third force was the belief that modern matters were now so complex that human beings could no longer keep track or make sense of all the moving parts. Of course the Manhattan Project exemplified this and, more generally, World War II. The rest of society, alas, quickly followed along the pathway blazed by that mammoth enterprise to pulverize the two Japanese cities in August, 1945: insurance, banking, transportation, DMVs, the machinery of State and finance, of agriculture and chemical manufacturing. Bring on the computers, it was thought, because they will enable us humans to survive this onslaught of complexification.

With the solution (computers) in sight, the job of surrendering to these complexities proceeded, based on a blind faith, nothing more, that the machines in fact were equal to that task. That, it turns out, was dead wrong. Three Mile Island, the Deepwater Horizon, repeated FAA or FBI snafus, reveal this new machinery's inability to track complexity when it counts. So too a myriad of other stories, as we have seen.

---

1 Negroponte, *Being Digital* (New York: Knopf, 1995).
2 "iCrazy."

So, the machines cannot and do not with sufficient regularities handle those complexities; more often than not they compound them, and tech support has to ride in to the rescue.

Knowing this, at present, does us no good. It is too late. Once you have given over inventory, routing, payroll, logistics, targeting, transportation, property-ownership records, or education into the keeping of the 0s and 1s, there is no going back. One knows people who give up their cars. Giving up e-mail, cell phone, iPod, etc.? I can think of very few, certainly no institutions. There are only upgrades.

In part, the machines are unequal to the task of sorting through the layers of complexity because their very birth was from an amniotic sac of intended obfuscation. The Manhattan Project was built on two contradictory impulses. The first, the need to plan and execute an unprecedented scientific, technical, political, and industrial enterprise, necessitating untold numbers of wheels turning simultaneously under the watchful eyes of General Groves and J. Robert Oppenheimer. But the second goal, in utter contradiction to the first, was to channel all information into the labyrinthine corridors of "need to know" criteria as to just what each of the scientists, accountants, technicians, shipping clerks, and machinists was allowed to learn about what they were doing. Most of the personnel, even higher-ups, were privy to small pieces of the overall plan, aware only that it was "something big."[1] The component pieces of the elaborate research and development undertaken were split up among several laboratories and within those, among many subgroups. Within the small work-groups (true to the workings of dialectics) the same logic was followed, so that people working side by side had to carefully guard their discussions. Thus when computers were in place in the early '50s, ratcheting up to the task of building thermonuclear bombs, using nuclear fusion instead of fission, the machines were burdened with enormous amounts of data *as well as protocols to keep most of it hidden.* From the Nazis, then from the Communists, but ultimately from the US public.

The early drive to get computers to do their work thus arose out of a context that had the two complementary, though contradictory, functions: to handle massive quantities of information *and* to control very rigidly all access to it. Mystification and obfuscation were thus at the very core of computer development.

Computer technology, additionally, was uniquely able to satisfy the security needs created by nuclear technology. Conveniently, in developing nuclear technology, military and "civilian" alike, the governments in question had to engineer a data-processing technology that, with some modifications, was capable of being utilized for encoding, surveillance, detection, alarm-

---

[1] Of the more than 130,000 people working on the Manhattan Project, including the scientists, only a dozen were aware of what its purpose was. (*Cyborg Worlds*, p. 73.)

tripping, and the like, vital parts of any national security state relying on nuclear weapons or power. True to its beginnings, data-processing technology is a machinery of control: control of workers at their work-stations; control of the flow of information; but more basically, control of our consciousness.

At the dawn of the Information Age, mystification and obfuscation were therefore structured into the circuitry, the language, and the architecture that made computers able to handle the massive amounts of data and compartmentalize it. To a considerable degree, this is still the case. Explaining why end-to-end encryption (of e-mails, medical records, etc.), despite widespread concerns about confidentiality and cybersecurity, a designer of such systems stressed the "contradiction of usability and security." Another expert on cybersecurity pointed out that "the tools [for end-to-end encryption] are far too sophisticated and difficult for the average person to use.... Even security pros find them tedious." Such encryption also presents barriers to key-word searches and to targeting advertisements, which might account for much of the industry's recalcitrance.[1]

In this Age of Information, more often than not what we are served is information *glut*, an excess of news and gossip and updates and reports and currency conversion rates, and most of it is difficult to sort out. Behind this seeming paradox there is another, more worrisome than the first: computers are "necessary," even vital to our society, we are told, precisely because we have developed these tremendously complex systems where information flow is too voluminous and too complex for humans to follow, so that without computers, it would be impossible to have... well, things like nuclear-power facilities and the vast banking and insurance companies and systems, or gargantuan companies like BP or Bechtel, with their multi-billion dollar projects for refineries, dams, airports, cities, and mines nearly any place in the world. Nor could we have the national-security defense organizations — and thousands of other kinds of organizations and processes we have all become used to. Generating such a list, if we dare admit it, at least suggests the possibility that much (I would think nearly all) of what computers make possible are things most of us feel oppressed by and that we are clearly better off without, from ecological, social, and simply human perspectives. Yes, it is true, there are so many people now in the world — but not enough to make a qualitative difference from what it was in 1935, before the locomotive of World War II built its head of steam and roared out of the station, inside its caboose carrying, as it turned out, the computer, beacon of wondrous futures sure to come.

To their more impassioned advocates, on the other hand, those monstrously complex systems, defying human comprehension and so requiring computer networks to make them (marginally, as it turns out) functional, are a new kind of natural selection, giving evolution a hand by favoring the

---

1 Wendy Lee, "End-to-end email encryption still a struggle," *San Francisco Chronicle* (January 22, 2017).

survival of only those "minds" capable of monitoring such modern systems. As it turns out, though, those nimble minds must be non-human, for these complex systems will inevitably encourage the evolution of some "new species," one better suited to the scale and pace of the industrial (and informational) future than humans conceivably could ever be.

But, as we have seen, this is surely a gigantic self-deception. Those gargantuan systems that computers are needed to run do not, in fact, become functional simply by being put under digital supervision and control. We have been conned into thinking that these impossibly complicated networks and systems (like the cockpit of a jet fighter flying at Mach 2 and armed with nuclear missiles), once put within a computer's dominion, in fact, become manageable. It manifestly is not so.

As these megasystems fail us, under the tutelage of their computer systems — whether it is the Pentagon's budgetary supervision, the FBI, the FAA, 911 emergency services in the Bay Area, air-traffic control at the nation's airports, etc.: in each instance we are reassured that it is only a matter of time before the problem of the compatibility of the old computers with the new ones can be worked out, or that they must get rid of certain bugs, or rewrite the overall program, etc. or coordinate this agency with that, and everything will work fine. By now we should know better than to believe such assurances, and instead of averting our eyes from the larger pattern, admit what is going on, and the degree to which the many crises of our institutions and social systems are in large part a result of the blind rush to be integrated into digital information-processing control systems. Besides their responsibilities for the crises, one of the main functions of the computers may well be to hide from us precisely how out of control things truly are.

I was once hired to do minor design work on piping and mechanical systems for part of the development of Alaska's oil fields. My company's responsibility was to design sea transport, to bring all that was needed to Alaska for this enormously complex, massive project so as to get the necessary housing built for workers; roads constructed to bring in materials and machinery; workers imported, fed, and bedded; machinery manufactured, transported, and installed; harbors enlarged and so on. Our project group, part of a construction corporation that was itself a subsidiary of one of the major oil companies, had designed a fleet of barges to carry equipment and supplies up the west coast of the US and Canada to Alaska.

A modular design had been developed for the barges, with numerous individual variations from the base design specified for particular barges, in line with the nature of how it would be used. Each barge had four or five levels. At each of those levels, separate drawings were needed to show details of either the architectural, structural, electrical, mechanical, piping; plumbing, heating, ventilation, and air conditioning; or instrumentation designs — and numerous specifications and other drawings spelled out the materials to be used, furniture installed, paint, budgets, "manpower" projections, schedules, etc. Several major engineering and construction corporations located up and down the west coast were involved in the undertaking, in a joint venture, as is increasingly the rule on large projects, and so the drawings for the modules I was helping design, not surprisingly, were not located *at* my firm. Instead we had microfilms of the many drawings, updated periodically, and an elaborate coded system for obtaining a copy of any one — I would guess out of hundreds of thousands — of them. To know how to route a given pipeline down a wall or bulkhead, I would need to check the electrical or mechanical drawings for the same level in order to avoid sending a conduit through a space already occupied, or, to follow routings, I had to consult drawings from other levels or other modules to see how a particular problem was handled elsewhere. On each barge there were also distinctions between left and right (port and starboard) to consider. A coded sequence of about a dozen or so letters and numbers would in theory fetch the drawings I needed.

My supervisor, I was given to believe, had developed the code by which our drawings were located. Yet as he helped me my first few days on the job to call needed drawings up from our microfilm library, I got used to seeing him looking puzzled as he stared at a print he had just requested. Not quite what he wanted, it appeared, but just *why* it wasn't often seemed to elude him. He would stare and stare. And *he* had helped develop the code by which we indicated which drawing we wanted. We ended up with prints of the wrong module, or the correct module but the left instead of the right side, the fourth level instead of the second, the electrical instead of the instrumentation, and so on. The sheer volume of separate pieces of information and the elaborate systems built to put each piece in its proper box had produced a labyrinthine hall or mirrors in which it was all too easy to get lost... as did my supervisor on a regular basis.

This was in the early 1980s, around the time of the famous design flaw revealed at the Diablo Canyon nuclear facility, where at the last minute it was discovered that the piping supports, so critical in an area of earthquake faults, as Diablo Canyon is, had been installed backwards, right and left having been reversed. The complexity of the project and the tendency for critical distinctions to get lost in the overwhelming flood of "information," each piece requiring a slight modification of the "modularized" coded "address," and subtle variations, such as a space where one was not specified, that sends the computer off on the wrong tangent — all of these acting as layers of fog to make misunderstandings inevitable. I wondered whether something similar happened in the case of the mirror image reversal of the pipe supports at Diablo Canyon.

On the basis of all this, I propose the following: information-processing technology, far from offering us "access" to a treasure trove of "information," quite often serves *to hide or mask it,* and is thus *a tool of administration, commonly used to build a technical fortification, from behind which bureaucracy, and hence power, can be better defended.*

Like radiation, electronic messages cannot readily be "seen" or "tasted," "smelled," or otherwise perceived, except electronically, with instruments. The bytes leave little trace — and hence can be easily misrouted, as we saw in the case of the emergency messages to the two US spy ships, the USS Liberty and the USS Pueblo, that never reached them, leading to the fatal military engagement with Israel for one and capture for the other, disasters facilitated by the national-security safety measures structured into the electronic infrastructure of the military command and control apparatus, so as to ensure secrecy. Within computer "memories," texts linger in shadowy states, stored in obscure backwaters that are sometimes forgotten, as Oliver North found out when records he had kept on-line and thought he had erased in his cover-up began to emerge in the investigation of the Iran-Contra conspiracy.

When a technical writer I know, editing text for a major engineering firm, submitted a third version of a project to the firm's word processors, he was surprised to receive back a hard copy that somehow had incorporated his latest corrections into the first version of the text, which he thought he had already deleted. A number of corrections he previously had incorporated into version two had seemingly snuck back into their original form. For a day or so he and the word processors were confused as to how his several texts had so melded. Eventually they realized that the initial set of changes had been entered into one disc, while the second set (the third version of the text) had been put into another, uncorrected, disc that contained the same file. In the press of work, losing track of which disc is the active file and which an earlier version or a backup is all too easy.

As Jonathan Franzen found, to his dismay, when US publishers used the file of an earlier draft of his novel, *Freedom,* not the one he had finally submitted. Like Toyota, the author had to issue an embarrassed recall.[1]

Thus spurious memories, which should have been erased but weren't *everywhere* in memory where they were located, have the resourcefulness of the Jesse James gang in eluding capture. Mysteriously appearing from time to time they continue to do their damage and then quickly withdraw into the mountainous terrain of "memory" — and so false arrests are made on the basis of superseded warrants;[2] bills demand payment not once but over and over

---

[1] So far as I am aware, there were no fatalities from Franzen's defective product.

[2] Warren Siegel, "Computer error could land you in jail," San Francisco *Chronicle* (April 18, 1984). Rachel Swan, "Software blamed in wrongful arrests," San Francisco *Chronicle* (n.d., 2016?). The opposite also occurs, computer "glitches" leading to wrongful prisoner releases "at jails and prisons across the U.S." in the thousands. In Washington state, more than 3,000, a problem that wasn't corrected for 13 years, though it was discovered in 10. (Rick Anderson, "Inmates freed too early, for years," *Los Angeles Times* (April 16, 2016).

again as if a new form of tribute were being extracted as the price of our electronic thralldom; or the Pentagon goes on alert because of a malfunctioning 46¢ chip in a multiplexer in its vast control system for destroying our planet.

Interactions with banks, utilities, stores, insurance companies, and the organs of the state changed dramatically upon the transition to electronic record-keeping or payments,[1] the new forms and nomenclature frequently defying the logic and common sense that formerly enabled one to negotiate earlier bills, determining what to pay and why. Statements sprouted arcane sequences of letters and numbers, data conjoined with a ciphered code whose purpose we could not glean. Numbers easy to relate to what is owed melded into ones of little apparent significance, critical threads got lost in the internal codes of the software used. Sometimes seemingly identical (or worse, near-identical) data is entered in two different columns with no clue as to how the columns differ or why.

Another example of clarity for machines coming at the expense of obfuscation for most humans is the use of only bar codes for pricing; patrons have no way of knowing what something costs, and few bother to ask a worker or hunt for a scanner.

Digital technology proves to be especially maladroit in its handling of identity, of names. Many computer systems responsible for vital functions regularly choke on data-entries for names that are "unusual." Apostrophes are particularly troublesome: many an O'Connor, D'Angelo, or O'Dowd find themselves facing adamantine digital walls (reinforced by typical bureaucratic reification of "rules") when they attempt such simple but essential tasks as booking a flight, registering to vote, enrolling in school, or gaining access to their medical records. Dutch surnames with a "van" or spaces between letters (say, van de Kamp), alas, regularly befuddle our computers; so too Arabic names like al-Hussein, using dashes, especially since once a name has been "stored in the database… a hyphen or apostrophe is often mistaken for a piece of computer code, corrupting the system." So too for an increasing number of African-American names, such as "D'Andre."

In the case of voter registration, many thousands lost their right to vote in the 2004 Michigan caucus, due to such marks in their names, an egregious example of ethnic-based, binary voter suppression. Alas, many of the people who experience this new form of Ellis-Island renaming end up ditching the apostrophe or dash just so they can get the damn ticket or whatever they are being denied. Thus, Niali O'Dowd (editor of *Irish Voice* newspaper!) chose to fly as ODowd, Lima Al-Athari became Alathari, and Erin Carney D'Angelo has truncated her official name (for all forms) to Dangelo. In effect they have, for the sake of convenience, of fitting into the binary choices provided,

---

1 "As Benefits Go Paperless, Check-Day Rituals Vanish," *New York Times* (January 29, 2011).

acquiesced in a form of self-identity theft, aided and abetted by our new "information" technologies.[1]

Languages like Polish, Russian and Romanian are similarly losing their diacritical marks, crucial for both pronunciation and for part of the meaning of words, under IT pressure.[2]

A different form of identity theft befuddled me as a middle-school teacher at the beginning of each school year. Many of the students appearing in class the first day had been on a pre-enrollment printout I was given just before school began, listing the assigned students for my five classes. The students' names were also frequently truncated on the pale green sheets the San Francisco school district's information-processing office had delivered to our school, since only so many letters for first and last names were allotted.

A sizable number of my mostly Latino, African-American, or Asian-American students, commonly with names a mite in excess of what was provided, ran afoul of the cut-off line, making calling the roll awkward the first week, since I could not tell from what I had been given whether I was looking for a boy or girl, as the Robertas or Robertos became "Robert"s, the Angelas "Angel"s, the Josephines, "Jose"s, etc. As well, cultural signifiers were thus lost by the "information" machinery.

If a few days of gender or ethnic ambiguity seems like a small price to pay for the wonders and "efficiencies" of hi-tech, consider the breakdown at Three Mile Island when operators lost control of the plant, in large measure because so much was going on that the computers fell *hours* behind in their print-outs. Similar confusion characterized the Deepwater Horizon explosion and fire.

Repeatedly we find this same pattern, instance after instance of information — the holy-of-holies of the Digital Age — being consciously altered or dropped in order to speed further the transmission of the data that *is* retained. We can no more assume that our Age of Information is an era of homage to information *per se* than we can accept that George W. Bush's "Clean Air Act" was an attempt to clean up our skies.

iii. The Demons Inside Your TV

Of course, much of the person-to-machine interface centers on the screen, an extension — a massive one, as it turns out — of the earlier screen of television that entered the mass market in the 1950s. Those earlier screens and what lay behind them certainly played havoc with those who were their first consumers, so much so that structural neurological changes were found by German researchers in the brains of children who grew up in the decades after TV began.

[1] Sean ODriscoll [NB], AP, "Names with an apostrophe do not compute," San Francisco *Chronicle* (February 22, 2008).

[2] Associated Press, "Campaign sets out to save Poland's complex alphabet," San Francisco *Chronicle* (February 22, 2013).

A profound critique of TV and its baleful effects was written by Jerry Mander, a former partner in an advertising firm that produced many ads for television. What follows is my extension of Mander's critique of TV to a more general "screen culture," as I shall refer to the shared or overlapping characteristics of computers, TVs, digital watches, cell phones and the like — devices that essentially reduce the affective/effective world to two dimensions, to a rectangular shape usually framed in plastic.[1]

Watching TV, viewers' internal organs slow down their metabolism; for example, the heartbeat slows, pulse rates tend to even out. A slow, steady rhythm takes over brain-wave patterns. While sitting around the sets in generally darkened rooms, the visual field is sharply reduced into a small window of light. Of the other four acknowledged senses, only sound is engaged, a condition of serious sensory deprivation.[2] Meanwhile, TV zaps its patterns at a viewer's retinas, at a rate and in a configuration (fluorescent dot patterns flashing on and off) such that the conscious mind is simply overwhelmed. Under such conditions, in the earlier television sets, a variety of messages (none more insistent, however, than the "buy me") rode as passengers on board a continual transfer of substantial amounts of electronically-defined light energy from the set *into* the viewer.[3]

The state of zombification described by a great many TV viewers, from young kids to adults, certainly is a vivid demonstration of how awfully effective a tool TV has proven to be — not least as a tool for the entrapment of consciousness. Once a set is turned on, brain waves slow down, until there are a predominance of alpha and delta waves. These slow synchronous brainwaves are encouraged by the lack of eye movement, since the screen beams images into the eyes so effectively that, unlike what occurs in nearly all other instances of seeing, a viewer's eyes do not have to actively scan a

---

[1] I exclude movies from my characterization of screen culture for a number of reasons, some of them technical: we watch movies as reflections of light off of screens, whereas TV and computer images are literally shot *into us*. Other differences include the rhythm of the flicker, resolution; etc.

[2] (2013): Since this was written, TV has reformulated itself, flat screens (that, with their new technology, last about a fifth as long before their pixels begin to give out, compared to their cathode-ray predecessors) delivering their light via liquid crystals and the like rather than a directed beam of photons shot out from the cathode towards one's retinas. (Computer monitors still fire photons into their users' eyes, however.) Simultaneously, many people now watch wall-filling screens, while perhaps a greater number watch on cell-phone screens, both extremes a far cry from the standard 19-inch sets of yore. To some extent, as a result, my analysis here is dated, but overall I believe its conclusions are sound.

[3] Jerry Mander, *op. cit.*, pp. 165, 167–68, 171, 201.

scene, *seeking* information. Such visual fixation is associated with a lack of definition.[1] In such a state, organized thought is rendered much more difficult. The experience is thoroughly passive.

The particular flicker of the TV (perversely very close to the rate of flicker of a fireplace or hearth, for millennia the universal sensual experience of humanity's evenings); the nature of the spectrum it emits; the coarseness of the TV or video resolution of images — all these help in zombification. In effect the eyes — the "windows to the soul" — are taken captive. Mander spoke to a number of experts on hypnosis who confirmed that the experience of watching TV screens was akin to a classic hypnotic induction.

Some of the reasons for these reported experiences with TV (and now computers) are technical in nature, a consequence of the very kind of technology screen culture is built around. But watchers of TV commonly report the following states of being: hypnotized; their energy sucked away; brainwashed; addicted; mind turned to mush; unable not to watch if a TV is on; mesmerized; zombified; their mind colonized.[2] Parents, too, report their kids looking like zombies when viewing TV, or of walking, after watching, as if in a dream. Some parents wondered how they might get "my kids off it and back into life." Mander's own son, Kai, told him that the TV "makes me watch it."

Mander described his own being possessed by the images "even after the set was off, like a [visual] aftertaste. Against my will, I'd find them returning to my awareness hours later." In addition to the more well-known belief that kids who watch TV are much more violent in their play, it is clear that TV has turned "a generation of children into passive, uncommunicative 'zombies' who couldn't play, couldn't create, and couldn't even think very clearly."[3]

I once assigned my 7th and 8th grade students to submit reports about the major cycles in their lives. I had in mind their eating, breathing, heartbeats, sleeping, eliminating, rhythms of play, celebration, and ritual. But the logs they handed in astounded me for what they revealed about television rhythms —though that may be an inappropriate word to use for a device that is as much a part of their time awake as vision itself. For many of them turning the set on is the first thing they do upon awakening, and turning it off (if they do) is the last thing they will do at night; in between, they watch the tube before, during, and after breakfast (if they eat any) and they watch it as soon as they return from school.

Reflecting on the widespread experience that "people are watching television for four hours every day [Mander's 1978 figures] and they say they can't stop it, and also claim that it seems to be programming them in some way, and they are seeing their kids go dead...," Mander concludes: "really,

---

[1] *Ibid.*, p. 168.

[2] *Ibid.*, pp. 157f.

[3] *Ibid.*, p. 163.

I deeply feel there is no need to study television [further]. The evidence is [already] what lawyers call 'prima facie' proof."[1]

The various forms of "passive-ication" that the technology of TV (and the screen in general) imposes independent of its subject matter (whether it's "Jeopardy" or "Sesame Street") accounts for the quality of life in front of the screen. Mander also depicts TV's emotional sterility, for sensitive emotional changes cannot be portrayed on the TV screen, owing to its technical crudity. That accounts for TV's programming focus on the melodramatic, the stereotypical, and the violent, more generally, on extremes.

There is also what amounts to a hyperactivity of the medium itself, including its heavy reliance on continual shifts in camera angle, distance, and perspective, so as to keep viewers glued to their screens, despite these limitations, based on such pseudo-actions. TV is forced to use *technical transitions to hold viewers' attentions*, because it is *incapable of using feelings or aesthetics* to do so. According to Mander, television's avoidance of depth is because, technically, it has no choice.[2]

TV (along with movies) also developed an homogenized global culture, as US-based shows are beamed worldwide, bouncing off the ubiquitous satellites, from Montenegro to Soweto, transmitting US experiences, values, jokes, mannerisms, and commodity fantasies to audiences the world over, and taking over, within a given culture or country, the forms of interaction between people, as TV images, fashions, color schemes, and snippets of dialogue become the currency of peoples' social contacts and standard greetings, expressions.

iv. Vampires of the Will?

Of course it is well known that computers are a much more powerful technology than TVs, owing to their "interactivity," and that their users are in a continual dialogue with the machine, or rather its program, having to respond to the machine's prompts in everything they do, whether sending an e-mail or researching an article. Yet, according to Michael Shallis, it is this very interactivity that is so troublesome.

> The computer engages not only our attention but also our will…. It is very difficult to turn off the computer, especially

---

1 In an interview (March 20, 2013) Mander said he thought such matters have stayed about the same, except, of course, by now many more hours will be spent on computers, phones, video games, and the like. A 2015 study concluded that teenagers spent almost seven hours a day in front of TV, video games, social networking sites, etc. (Benny Evangelista, "Teens, screens spend lots of time together," San Francisco *Chronicle*, November 3, 2015.)
2 *Ibid.*, pp. 302ff.

when programming. The machine draws you into it, engages you at a deep interior level... your eyes become remote....[1]

Programmers mostly lose the battle of wills they continually must fight with their screens and keyboards. Shallis reports that working at their consoles, the hearts of programmers actually become cold, a result, he believes, of their wills being drawn from them and of their taking on the heartlessness of their machines. Shallis finds this struggle over will most ominous:

> It is as if there is an entity in the computer that is more than an anthropomorphized projection of the human mind... as if there is a beast trying to get out, or at least trying to suck us in. People working with computers tell about how the machine pulls them into it. Children talk about being *in there, in the machine itself.* Wherever you look in the computer world you find a subversion of the human will, whether it be in the displacement of the worker by the machine, by the control the machine has over its users or the way the computer cools the heart of the programmer.[2]

One programmer told Tracy Kidder that he experienced an unpleasant sensation "of being locked up inside the machine [that] lingered three days" if he managed to tear himself away from the basement where he wrote code. An engineer told her that "[s]ilicon-based life would have a lot of advantages over carbon-based life."

> He said he believed in a time when the machines would "take over." He snapped his fingers and said, "Just like that." He seemed immensely pleased with that thought.[3]

○ ○ ○

Machines traditionally have no "rights," since they are created by people who then control them; it is their "nature." So if the mass of people can be persuaded, first, that life is essentially machine-like; and second, that they themselves similarly are simply machines, how much easier is it to quell any spirit of rebellion born of the plenitude of outrages and injustices in the world? Such an outlook would ensure that any such revolt will be stillborn, unable to draw even a single breath. This is the other side of the passivification, the other side of reductionism.

---

[1] Shallis, *op. cit.*, p. 228.
[2] *Ibid.*, p. 233. My emphasis.
[3] Tracy Kidder, *op. cit.*, pp. 128, 241.

Since people commonly do enter trance-like states working at their monitors or watching TV, we might want to take a closer look at the process. Into what kind of world does one get taken? Is there "something" "in there," waiting for us?

Before we can answer this admittedly creepy query, an important digression is necessary. For the obvious question arises, and we need to address it first: just how conscious is any of this? Aren't I really advocating an elaborate — and highly unlikely — conspiracy theory?

28

To Think That All This Time
They Have Been Making Fools of Us!

> The computer, one might well conclude, was con-
> ceived in sin. Its birth helped ratchet up, by several
> orders of magnitude, the destructive force available
> to the superpowers during the cold war.... As
> George Dyson writes... "The digital universe and
> the hydrogen bomb were brought into existence at
> the same time." Von Neumann had seemingly
> made a deal with the devil. — Jim Holt, "How the
> Computers Exploded," *New York Review of Books*,
> June 7, 2012

i. THE MASKS OF IDEOLOGY

There are several side questions that till now *Marxism & Witchcraft* has
glibly side-stepped that the next four chapters will attempt to address.
One of these is essential to our inquiry: how conscious have the ruling
classes been in any of the modalities by which mechanism was — and is —
being promulgated? Was there in the 17th century a gigantic conspiracy to
"put one over" on us (and on the Earth, by the way)? Was Isaac Newton
conscious of how he was helping the mine-owners and emerging forces of
mercantile capital when he adapted Descartes' theory of inertia? For that
matter, how conscious is the present ruling class of the profound implications
of the remaking of the world in a digital form that we have been exploring
in the previous chapters? Are they aware at all of the issues as I have presented them here?

These are important questions and I hope it will not be thought evasive
when my answer is that the ruling class in 17th-century England both *was*
and *was not* conscious of what it was doing in mechanizing the world-picture.
I believe the same is true now, that ruling elites *both* grasp the larger issues
and are blinded to them. Both consciousness and unawareness exist(ed)

about the underlying motives for the ideological campaign that is/was waged, but they exist in different ways, in different parts of the elites' compartmentalized minds. By understanding both modalities and how they coexist I hope we may begin to comprehend how this ideology really operates.

Here I can do no more than conjecture about how such a split consciousness might work. My hypothetical model was suggested by a startling essay by Henry Kissinger, kingpin of the Nixon administration, in turn and concurrently Secretary of State and National Security Advisor. Since his undergraduate days at Harvard, Kissinger had betrayed an acute sensitivity to the needs of elites — including the Rockefeller family, which patronized him. In promoting himself for the eventual role he played in trying to extricate US forces from the political, military, and moral morass of Vietnam into which they had sunk, a startling defeat of the Empire's most advanced fighting machine ever by a "primitive" colonial subject, Kissinger wrote *American Foreign Policy: Three Essays,* in 1969.

Given its timing, I believe these essays should be seen as the equivalent of Kissingers c.v. in his bid for becoming the central figure of the Nixon administration.

It is at the conclusion of the lead essay in that book that Kissinger ventures onto our terrain, with rather shocking revelations. There he examined what he saw as the philosophical basis of world power and the differing perspectives key players bring to the struggle for stability. He lamented that the fundamental barriers to world peace only incidently had to do with the variety of political structures he had focused on in his essay. More basic, Kissinger suggested, is what he called "two styles of policy and two philosophical perspectives" that are found in the world. These he defines as the "political as against the revolutionary approach to order" or as the alternative paths taken by what he calls "the statesman and the prophet."[1]

The political approach to order is followed by "statesmen," presumably men like Nixon, Kissinger, Adenauer, de Gaulle, etc., men who "manipulate[s] reality," with a goal mainly to survive, aware at all times, given the frailty of human nature, of the vast potential for ill-conceived courses of action to lead to disasters. Under the guidance of the statesman, therefore, "gradualism is the essence of stability." This salutary point of view predominated in European history, Kissinger says, between the end of the 17th century and the beginnings of the French Revolution (*i.e.,* right after the Restoration intellectual counter-revolution detailed in Part Two had consolidated its hold over "respectable" opinion), and then again from the Congress of Vienna (1815) that ended the era of the French Revolution to the beginning of World War I.

In contrast, the social unrest convulsing many European countries in the 16th and 17th centuries and after the French Revolution (until Napoleon's

---

[1] Henry A. Kissinger, *American Foreign Policy: Three Essays* (New York: W.W. Norton & Co., 1969), p. 46.

downfall) and again following World War I, including the "contemporary uprisings in major parts of the world,"[1] are guided by "the prophet," men (and women) presumably like Winstanley, Robespierre, Kropotkin, Lenin, Ho Chi Minh, Harriet Tubman, Emma Goldman, Malcolm X or Fred Hampton, someone not so much interested in "manipulating" reality as with creating it; less concerned with what is possible and more with what is right; less focused on means and more on ends; and who, because of his or her belief in the perfectibility of human nature, seeks for total solutions to social wrongs, embodied in timeless remedies independent of particular circumstances. The prophet is willing to "risk everything" and is contemptuous of those who fail the test of History. Though the prophet "represents an era of exaltation, of great upheavals, [and] of vast accomplishments," his or her efforts to transform the social world leads to "enormous disasters."[2] Where the statesman, according to Kissinger, is interested in permanent structures and mainly tries to ascertain the *utility* of any new idea, the prophet pursues a vision of a new order and is concerned with the *truth* of new ideas.

It is when Kissinger comes to define the differences in philosophical perspectives between these two kinds of international and political visions in today's world that his remarks directly bear on our questions of consciousness by ruling elites. Kissinger points out, much to my surprise, almost as if he had been given an advance copy of *Marxism & Witchcraft*, that the two polarities he had characterized really represent

> the divergence of... two lines of thought which since the Renaissance have distinguished the West from the part of the world now called underdeveloped (with Russia occupying an intermediary position). The West is deeply committed to the notion that the real world is external to the observer, that knowledge consists of recording and classifying data — the more accurately the better. *Cultures which escaped the early impact of Newtonian thinking have retained the*

---

[1] References, we might surmise, to Indochina, Cuba, southern Africa, and anywhere else where the passion for liberation had reached a state of smoldering or open flames, which in 1969 would have included nearly every impoverished country in the world where peasants and workers were struggling in some measure, carefully monitored, we can be sure, by the CIA and duly reported to Kissinger. (*Ibid.*, pp. 47–48.)

[2] Kissinger would come to know first-hand how such "enormous disasters" can result from some of the "great upheavals" *he* was largely responsible for, as in the coup he helped engineer in Chile to replace the elected President Salvador Allende by the murderous General Augusto Pinochet in 1973, and Chile's descent into fascism that ensued.

essentially pre-Newtonian view that the real world is almost completely internal to the observer.[1] [my emphasis]

While the domination of a non-Western, non-Newtonian point of view in their societies may in the past have prevented successful adoption of Western technology and the spread of consumer goods so common in the West, still the pre-Newtonian perspective common in the Third World

> *offers great flexibility with respect to the contemporary revolutionary turmoil.* It enables the societies which do not share our cultural mode to alter reality by influencing the perspective of the observer—a process which we [in the West] are largely unprepared to handle or even to perceive.[2] [my emphasis]

Kissinger laments that in today's world non-Western societies have not only been able to utilize modern technology, but that it has been available to them essentially "as a gift," since they can incorporate its products without having had to take on "the philosophical committment that their discovery imposed on the West."

> Empirical reality has a much different significance for many of the new countries than for the West because in a certain sense they never went through the process of discovering it (with Russia again occupying an intermediary position). At the same time, the difference in philosophical perspective may cause us to seem cold, supercilious, lacking compassion.

Not fair that in a mere handful of pages, Kissinger has managed to sum up a chunk of the argument that it has taken me several hundred (so far) to develop! As much as I, he seems to be well aware of the role Newtonian thinking played and plays in the dampening of the hopes for alternative social realities, by its avowed objectification (and mechanization) of all that is outside our consciousness (and now, with computerization, the seeming mechanization of consciousness, too). He also recognizes, it would seem, that their refusal to atomize and deaden "reality," as is axiomatic in the West, gives

---

1 *Ibid.*, pp. 47–49. Kissinger's insights seem to provide a fruitful framework for understanding the historic failure of Marxism for postulating that the industrial proletariat would uniquely be the class equal to the historic task of ending capitalism, while, as has occurred in the 20th century, in nearly every instance ("with Russia [again] occupying an intermediary position") socialist revolutions to date have largely occurred in societies dominated by the peasantry (i.e., non-Newtonian). We shall discuss this further in our concluding chapter.

2 *Ibid.*

Third World people added power to manifest the reality they come to choose. In other words, Kissinger appears to acknowledge the social force that magic (pre-Newtonian consciousness or animism) can wield in the world.

Given Kissinger's history of articulating the point of view of ruling elites, perhaps I may be permitted to use his comments here as indicative of a degree to which ruling circles *are* conscious of the advantages they gain from the vast changes the scientific revolution of the 17th century ushered in. The awesome responsibility of ruling an empire, of damning a river or felling a forest, can rest only on the shoulders of a Newtonian-educated administrator/executive. For anyone retaining a significant remnant of animist consciousness, such masterly exploitations of the natural world were not readily imaginable. Only a mechanist would be able to give the orders that tear down mountains, or crush lives in a mine cave-in, or to rationalize in the short run the loss of numbers of workers (or soldiers, residents, etc.) as an acceptable cost for the potential horn of plenty the idea of Progress perpetually dangles just in front of us, as the promise for the long run, as our soon-to-be-reached reward if today we continue to opt for "rational" methods of organizing society and nature. Only a person whose education has served to kill off passion ("enthusiasm") can seriously consider destroying Eden in an effort at promoting happiness ("life, liberty, and the pursuit of property").

And yet matters, taken less superficially, are not as one-sided as the above suggests. The kind of simple-minded conspiracy theory that would follow from the previous paragraph fails to fully grasp matters, and may actually keep us from appreciating the deeper paradoxes concerning ruling-class awareness. From other remarks that Kissinger makes in the same essay, it is clear that he doesn't *really* understand the implications of his own words, as much as we (who *have* patiently read these many pages) hopefully do. Though he lauds the mechanistic philosophical background that has produced all that the West has accomplished and that has provided the statesman with his invaluable wisdom, perspective, and caution, elsewhere Kissinger reveals his *lack* of awareness of many of the central implications of mechanism.

Previously in this work, Kissinger had complained at great length about how modern states, and especially those in the West, are often incapable of facing the overwhelming problems of our times. He admits this is an era when more than ever an intuitive understanding of the movement of world history is essential, given that vast and complicated forces at play have led to obvious disintegration of the old order and the emergence of what was (in 1969) a still unclear new framework.

Yet intuition, according to Kissinger, is all but impossible for today's leaders. This is so, he observes, precisely because of a vast bureaucratic political and social machinery carefully constructed in the West. The problem, Kissinger claims, is that this bureaucracy has "introduced an element of rigidity" that permeates the whole administrative apparatus and precludes any real grasp of either the problems or their solutions.

He seems to understand that this rigidity and the paralysis it causes is the flip side of the built-in Newtonian and Cartesian hedges that only a few pages on Kissinger praises for their pragmatic damping of the passions, yet it is also clear that much of the ideology, which elsewhere he describes as if from the outside, that is to say, *consciously,* so thoroughly shapes and defines his own perceptions and thinking that he, too, falls victim to its purposeful distortions, *unconsciously* swept along with its mystifications. For example, he complains that all too often in bureaucracies the

> quest for "objectivity" — while desirable theoretically — involves the danger that means and ends are confused.... Attention tends to be diverted from the act of choice... to the accumulation of facts.

Precisely so, since methodological diversions were a central part of the plan by which mechanistic thinking, according to spokespeople like Thomas Sprat and John Wilkins, was able to offer tangible assistance to the men of property and order at the Restoration. Of this, however, the good Doctor Kissinger is oblivious. In fact, he argues that the kind of leadership that prevails in the West

> is more concerned with method than with judgment; or rather it seeks to reduce judgment to methodology and value to knowledge.

The machinery of state has become horribly fragmented. Problems are first

> segmented into constitutent [*sic*] elements, each of which is dealt with by experts in the special difficulty it involves. There is little emphasis or concern for their interrelationship.

The fact that modern bureaucracies, in their "quest for objectivity and calculability often lead to impasses," Kissinger insists on seeing as "paradoxical."

> Research often becomes a means to buy time and to assuage consciences. Studying a problem can turn into an escape from coming to grips with it.[1]

Precisely so, precisely so.

---

[1] *Ibid*, pp. 18, 30, 29, 21.

Kissinger shouldn't be able to have it both ways. Clearly, if "gradual change and slow construction" are the statesmen's goals, it is essential to put a brake on the pace of social transformation, a brake against upheaval that can be controlled from above. That is the major reason bureaucracies were instituted in the first place, following upon the promises of Sprat and the Royal Society, and the reason why a mechanical division of each problem into its constituent parts for their ponderous individual deliberations is imposed as an all-powerful methodological social tool. It is a mode of operation almost guaranteeing paralysis of the public will — and thus allowing for the free play of the private. Far from the "fragmentation" and rigidity being paradoxical developments in the history of Western society, as Kissinger claims, they are *essential parts* of an elaborate machinery whose underlying purpose is to ensure that far-reaching solutions to problems have virtually no chance even to be considered, let alone to be instituted. Yet it is painfully clear that Kissinger sees hardly any of this.

So, if on the one hand, at times a Henry Kissinger is able to pierce through the veil of ideological obfuscation and realize the role in social pacification played by Newtonian consciousness, on the other hand, to a considerable degree he is also a prisoner of that same ideology. And to him the world really *is* as Newton described it.[1]

It would add too many more pages to an already long book and overtax my modest research skills were I to explore fully this model of how social elites seek to control our comprehension, while at the same time these manipulations frequently ensnare their perpetrators, and so becloud their own understanding. Historically some kind of dialectical relationship is at play between a conscious ruling elite and an elite that is captured by its own false consciousness, one that they or their representatives (in schools, churches, op-ed pieces, think-tanks, etc.) propagate.

---

[1] In this regard, we might remember AI expert Joseph Weizenbaum's comment on the purposely falsified strike reports fed into the Pentagon's system so as to hide Nixon's secret bombing of Cambodia from the public, reports which were then shown to Congressional leaders, pleased to be let in on the know.

> [T]he high government leaders who felt themselves privileged to be allowed to read the secret reports that actually emerged from the Pentagon's computers of course believed them. After all, the computer itself had spoken. They did not realize that they had become their computer's "slaves," to use Admiral Moorer's own word, until the lies they instructed their computers to tell others ensnarled them, the instructors, themselves. (Weizenbaum, *op. cit.*, pp. 238–39).

ii. Lies & Damn Lies

To see solely or primarily a ruling class conspiracy to fool us down through the ages misses this central drama: that the ruling class and its opinion-makers fall prey to their own ideological manipulations — for lies told often enough eventually must begin to convince their own tellers, except perhaps for a small minority. If the natural philosopher who transferred his allegiance in 1655 from animist modes of explanation and embraced the new mechanical philosophy did so while conscious of how his shift fit into an overall campaign against the political and philosophical "enthusiasm" made necessary by the chaos generated in the English Civil War and revolution; or if the bishop who in 1670 proposed that Parliament outlaw sermons that used "fulsome and lushious Metaphors" was similarly aware of the use of poetic flights of the imagination by the enemies of order during the previous decades' insurgencies: still, within a generation or less, I believe, the assumptions behind these cultural transformations would have become nearly axiomatic, perceived dimly if at all, essentially submerged beneath the surface of daily consciousness.

Certain things are simply taken for granted during normal times. Yet when, some time later, conditions change, as they inevitably do, and once more a left or some other kind of threat becomes a credible force and the framework of society is fundamentally challenged, so that a renewed justification of things as-they-are is required among the elite, awareness of those matters and of the critical reasons why some answers rather than others are allowable to the critical questions emerges anew.

iii. A Demonology of Empire

It is perhaps possible to go deeper into this intriguing question of conspiracy, at least if readers are willing to follow me in some creative speculation. We might get a glimpse at one level on which a conspiracy "once upon a time" was quite possibly initiated that would help explain how we got into our present fix. What follows is quite different from all that I have presented so far, not only in what is even for me the outlandish nature of my claims, but also in its being unabashedly speculative, for critical parts based more on supposition than on a trail of documentable evidence. There is a good chance my speculation is not true — but another, conceivably better, chance that it is. Suggestive evidence exists to make my speculations quite plausible. As long as the preceding qualifications are kept in mind, it is worth exploring the shape and historic ramifications of this "once upon a time."

First some background. The conspiracy I shall outline might help explain some aspects of the advent of the modern world empire, and its astounding tenacity for over four centuries, in defiance of both logic and good taste (as well as justice).

The conspiracy was one based on magic, and involved the English Renaissance mathematician and *magus*, John Dee, a figure instrumental in the rise of Rosicrucian philosophy in Europe, in which connection he was discussed at some length in Chapter 6. Dee was a figure shrouded in mystery and legend, one of the foremost *magi* in European history, his reputation suggesting a parallel with Merlin himself (of whom we have little concrete historical evidence). Significantly, Dee was unquestionably both the architect and chief visionary behind the creation of the English Empire, which began during the reign of Elizabeth I, as discussed earlier.

Readers may recall that then-Protestant England had been at war with Catholic Spain, the navies, merchant ships, and pirates of both nations (categories more separate in theory than in actual historical practice) vying for control of the "new" world across the sea, which was both the booty and a weapon in their extended economic, political, religious, philosophical, and military conflict.

John Dee and his longtime associate, the shadowy Edward Kelley, established a milestone in Renaissance magic, cabala, and alchemy. As recounted earlier, both men were numerous times at the center of intrigue or sometimes shut up in prison. Contemporaries charged Dee with necromancy, magic involving the dead. It is clear the two men did invoke demonic spirits in their work. If readers accept my conclusions in Part Two that alchemists in the 17th century did succeed in creating gold out of "'lesser'" materials by a form of magic, then Dee and Kelley are prime candidates on a short list of those thought to have been able to do so. Kelley was a powerful medium, which Dee was not.

As a team, the two *magi* travelled to important power spots in the cosmic terrain of magic. Their material-plane travels to Prague, where the alchemically-inclined Rudolf II was Holy Roman Emperor, was described earlier as a pathbreaking tour, at once a secret diplomatic mission on behalf of Elizabeth I and a spiritual mission which, Yates claims, had enormous import for the spread of popular and academic magic in early 17th-century Germany during her reign, as discussed earlier. The involvement of the English crown over the centuries in occult practices and traditions rooted in earlier pagan customs and beliefs has appreciable evidence for it.[1]

As discussed earlier, Dee was a quite influential figure at the Elizabethan court, an author, the most eminent mathematician of his time, and a man with a vision of the world as it should (and did) become. Against the reactionary Catholic Counter-reformation, centered in the Hapsburg Court, of which

---

[1] For a literary treatment of this tradition, see Katherine Kurtz's intriguing novel, *Lammas Night* (New York: Ballantine Books, 1983). This has continued into modern times; witches and other occultists performed spells in World War II to forestall a German invasion. (Caroline Casey, "The Visionary Activist," KPFA, March 2, 2017.)

Spain was a center, stood England, already physically separated from the continent. England possessed strengths and traditions "dating" back to Arthurian times, according to Dee, that he made the basis for his impassioned and extensive efforts to promote an English Empire to rule the world. Protestant England, led by Elizabeth, came to signify to many of her subjects the defense of religious liberties, in large measure due to Dee's extensive propaganda. His activities on behalf of an imperial greater England were persistent — and in these endeavors, Dee obviously had the ear of Elizabeth.

As far back as 1570, Dee had outlined a plan to "MAKE THIS KINGDOME FOURISHING, TRIUMPHANT, FAMOUS AND BLESSED." His scheme included having England acting internationally as the ruler of commercial exchanges, and he prescribed for particular areas of the economy, such as the cloth trade and tin production. Dee believed in the colonization of "Atlantis" (the "new" world) which was on the way to the East, where occult lore was more of an established touchstone. Dee thought the occult would play a significant role in the millennium, which, for many influential 17th-century thinkers, was eagerly anticipated.

In Dee's vision, England's role in the world would be at once economic, political, and above all, religious. With Elizabeth as Empress, England as an Empire would lead a worldwide reformation. Dee contributed significantly to the technical foundation on which this empire was to be built, publishing his *General and Rare Memorials pertayning to the Perfect Arte of Navigation* (1577).

Dee also planned a more general work on the philosophy and history of navigation. The navigational tables for Elizabethan mariners that he planned were never printed and did not survive. Part of this work was purposely burned, possibly, Dee's biographer suggests, because it was politically dangerous. Dee was a forceful advocate for a powerful navy and is cited as "the literary pioneer of the claims to sovereignty of the sea which was put forth by England in the seventeenth century."[2] Some claim that Dee was the major influence behind Sir Francis Drake's voyage to explore North America and he was close friends with all of those promoting the expedition.

To push for the territorial expansion an imperial England must rest on, Dee presented Elizabeth with a map of America, on the back outlining the Queen's "Tital Royall to... foreyn Regions." Much of his claim was based on the conquering of Iceland, Greenland, the northen isles, "encompassing unto Russia, But even unto the North Pole (in manner)" that King Arthur was credited with.

A colony somewhere near Terra Florida, was established, according to Dee, by Lord Madoc, "Sonne to Owen Gwynedd Prynce of Northwales." On the basis of such claims (and Dee's biographer, French, points out that this document was written around the time of Drake's return from North America, in 1580), Dee established his legal claims for world empire. It has been suggested that it was because of Dee's imperialist propaganda that a revival of Arthurian themes occurred during the reign of Elizabeth.

---

1 Yates, *op. cit.*, p. 183, n. 1.

"Through conversations with Elizabeth and such ministers as Burghley, Walsingham, Leicester, and Hatton, as well as with men like Rogers, the older Hakluyt, and Dyer, the expansionist ideas of Dee spread."[1] He had frequent access both to Elizabeth and to her key ministers, as well as to the center of the intellectual ferment brought to a head in Renaissance England. Dee's ideas were extremely influential, as well as being perceived by some contemporaries as fundamentally dangerous.

The frontispiece of Dee's *General and Rare Memorials*, his technical work on navigation, is remarkably revealing of Dee's use of magic. It portrays Elizabeth at the helm of a ship named "Europa," its rudder emblazoned with the arms of England. The plate is heavily laden with emblems indicating the fullness of Dee's vision. Elizabeth is portrayed being offered a laurel crown and a number of Hermetic symbols speak to the occult dimensions of the challenge facing her at this time of widespread turmoil across late-16th-century Europe and England itself. The moon and stars in the frontispiece are placed so as to imply a favorable disposition of the elements towards the fulfillment of Elizabeth's challenge, and there are signs, too, of the great troubles she will face if she does not follow her obvious destiny. The Hebrew sacred four-letter name of God and the archangel Michael are placed so as to empower and protect the whole enterprise proposed by Dee.

All of these constitute an occult "spell" to ensure success in the accomplishment of this grand design.

> The mixture of favourable religious and astrological portents
> implies that Elizabeth has a sacred obligation to implement
> Britannia's entreaties [in the frontispiece] and that no forces
> on earth can thwart her if she undertakes the task.

Clearly, the Queen must act to strengthen her monarchy in order to save the "foundering ship of Christiandom."[2]

That someone with Dee's reputed powers as a *magus* should introduce his major work on navigation swaddled in such magical vestments suggests that we take a closer look at his magic. It is here that *Marxism & Witchcraft* soars into the realm of wanton speculation. Speculative though the following might be, it explains a great deal that otherwise remains incomprehensible.

---

[1] French, *op. cit.,* p. 198. Sir Walter Raleigh, wanting Elizabeth's approval for an English colony to be established in Virginia, argued that it would "increase her dominion, enrich her coffers, and reduce any [indigenous] pagans to the father of Christ." (Ronald, *op. cit.,* p. 360). Dee seems also to have had ties to members of the Familists, discussed in Chapter 7. (Woolley, *The Queen's Conjuror,* pp. 63, 186, and 306, n. 8.)

[2] French, *op. cit.,* pp. 184–85.

If we suppose, as I have argued in Parts One and Two, that magical work can effectively impinge on the unfolding of day-to-day events, and at times even lubricate the hinges on which historical development is apt to turn, and if we remember Dee's reputation, these speculations might prove rewarding.

Dee's graphical spell in the frontispiece, by itself or, more likely in conjunction with other magical workings Dee might have undertaken, obviously seeks to protect the Empire he was promoting and to breathe life into it. A man like Dee would not, on a matter this central to his visions, leave matters half-done. No doubt he would have utilized whatever powers he could muster.

What might Dee's imperial magic have consisted of?

In conjunction with our anti-nuclear organizing work in the early '80s, and later in movements opposing US warfare in El Salvador and supporting Nicaragua against far-right oligarchs, my coven/affinity group of about ten witches had incorporated magic into our ongoing political work.[1] By the end of the '80s, after nearly a decade of such work, our group found itself focusing on some kind of root that grew in what might be called a spiritual plane and that seemed to have blossomed into the inter-related oppressions that we, as good activists, were daily confronting and thinking about — apartheid, AIDS, racism, patriarchy, housing, and of course capitalism... the list was endless, and where did all of them come from? And in trance work that was part of our practice we seemed to detect a strange "entity" in our visions, there at the beginning of modern times and which continues feeding on energy so as to sustain the structures of domination and power-lessness that had come to allow these many oppressions to flourish and grow so prolifically, towering over so many of our lives. In a number of trances we encountered this "entity" and noticed more about it — at least did those of us who were better mediums than I. (In all honesty, I thought my work in the group was helpful, but my visions were considerably more fuzzy than some of the others in the coven.) One of our members had a dream about a painting in Madrid's Prado Museum of Spain's Philip II, Elizabeth's Catholic rival and sometime suitor; it appeared to bear on what we were feeling, and indirectly pointed to John Dee. What we saw looked like an empowering magical spell that had been cast back when the framework for these many oppressions and forms of domination was put in place. If Dee were involved, as the dream seemed to suggest, then my speculation is that perhaps we were looking at the magical spell Dee cast for the victory of the undertaking that became the British Empire.

That Empire did essentially come to control the world by the 19th century. It has proven to be enormously rewarding for some, but exceedingly horrific for most under its dominion. Not that that Empire was the beginning; obviously it was not. But it was a critical moment in the ultimate victory of colonialism and all that followed in its wake, all that was congruent with it.

---

[1] See Chapter 32 for a fuller discussion.

The mine, the plantation, the leveled forest were emblematic, and they spread far and wide as the Empire took shape and extended its domains, draining wetlands, dredging estuaries, and creating monocultures. And while the Empire changed and diversified, it never really ended, by the 1950s having simply ceded its mace of power onto the United States after the two world wars, And by the last half of the 20th century multinational corporations— whose minions in the institutions of finance and global commerce, like the World Bank, the International Monetary Fund, and so on give special attentions to their interests — are able to carry out their designs beyond the reach of mere nations.

Has the astounding success of that Empire over a period of several centuries and through some shape-shifting here and there been the result of some kind of magical empowerment, a spell whose very successes at the beginning and ever after kept on empowering the original magic, somehow allowing it to feed on its victories? Once the idea suggested itself, crazy though it certainly appears/ed, it was difficult to shake it off, knowing just who Dee was and what his interests, connections, and powers were. Dee as both ideologue for the English Empire and the spymaster at its heart, as the man who designed its espionage network.[1] Additionally, our coven's trance-visions resonated with such a supposition.

Yet keep in mind, as stated at the beginning of this discussion, this part of the story is speculation, a series of what-ifs. What is not the least bit speculative, however, is Dee's involvement with matters of magic *and* his ceaseless activities on behalf of an English global dominion.

Some four centuries later, by the late-20th and early-21st centuries, supposing there were such spells by Dee, what might it mean now? An obvious question is how is it so powerful that it has maintained its power, even increasing it, over those 400 years? But what if this spell for the victory of the Empire that Dee cast had incorporated an aspect by which it was regularly re-empowered — just like the repetitious sound each time a mantra is pronounced re-energizes its power, or like a Tibetan prayer is "sounded" by each wind-driven flap of a prayer flag in the Himalayas —so that over the years and centuries its vitality remained strong or even intensified? Suppose such an arrangement, for example, was able to trance-form each victory of the British navy into a magical re-invoking of the entities and powers originally conjured up by Dee (and any associates) in the first place? And what if, generalized beyond the British navy so that success by any agency of Empire, from the colonial medical administration to quasi-governmental entities such as the New England Trading Company (with which Robert Boyle was closely tied in the 17th century) or the International Monetary Fund in the 20th and 2st, continues, in varying ways, to feed the original spell; and what if victories by any Western country (except, of course, by Europe's own colonies, places

---

[1] See Chapter 6.

like Ireland) over the rest of the world are nearly as good as a victory for Britannia itself, for Britannia had passed on the scepter of power?

If all these are supposed, then we have a very formidable magical entity, conceivably even one able to operate without continued human intervention or consciousness since Dee's time. And if human hands *are* needed, why, Opus Dei or the like might be imagined for those foolhardy enough to entertain such paranoid (though maybe true) fantasies.

By the 1990s, the Empire had indeed changed, England having been joined at the feeding trough by most of the other European powers, the US, and Third World countries like Japan, which decided to join in the plunder and to adopt the logic of domination; and colonialism having yielded to neo-colonialism, as the titans of the Empire realized that a few dark-skinned proxies might be beneficial, brought in to play critical roles in mediating between the demands of the corporations and the destinies of the subject populations in places like Chile, Indonesia, Mexico, the Philippines, Kenya, and countless other nominally independent countries; Leninism proving, as in the USSR and China, also a strong basis for imperial reach; and multinational corporations having emerged, entities with vanishingly fewer ties to specific national bases, that are instead sited in a number of continents and able nearly overnight to shift operations from one locale to another in the endless search for the least constraints on their doings.

As always, that Empire was commodity-oriented, Malaysia and other colonies' forests being felled at dizzying speeds, for example, to become the lumber to build houses, chairs, bowls, and cooking utensils to be bought and sold; but increasingly in the 1980s and '90s the Empire was one of capital running amok and chasing itself as moneys were laundered in the scores of billions of dollars by spy agencies, drug cartels, banks, developers, the Vatican, and financial snake-oil entrepreneurs — and again, these categories in practice turn out to overlap a great deal — and as they began to sell new forms of indebtedness, junk bonds, touted as the answer to a number of corporate needs, in a process aided and abetted by computerization. Spates of mergers resulted, and the junk bonds became a major force behind the frenzy of "downsizing" of workforces, and the feelings of panic surging through the working populations. Those bonds also sent corporations in a mad scramble to latch onto whatever they could find by way of assets to convert to cash, including the attempt by the Maxxam Corporation to clearcut the largest privately owned grove of redwood trees in North America, in Mendocino County, California in the 1980s.

All this was, however, but a prelude to the dizzying array of toxic mortgages and "derivative" investments, harder and harder even for experts involved in this cabala of a run-amok finance industry, to comprehend, which as we now so painfully know, exploded into our still-unresolved worldwide financial crisis of 2008 — and on and on.

Indeed, as Rushkoff points out, in the information-centered digital world there exists an ongoing and increasingly powerful impetus towards abstractions.

Not coincidentally, the push towards abstractions fit to a "T" the structural changes in the financial industry in the latter part of the 20th century.

> Once the financial world came to understand that its own medium — central currency — was biased in the interests of the lender and not the producer, every business attempted to get out of the business it was actually in, and scale up to become a holding company, Thus, great industrial companies like General Electric shed their factories and got involved in capital leasing, banking, and commercial credit. Meanwhile, those who were already involved in banking and credit moved up one level of abstraction as well, opening hedge funds and creating derivatives instruments that won or lost money based on the movements of economic activity occurring one level below. Even craftier speculators began writing derivatives of derivatives, and so on, and so on.[1]

Rushkoff goes on to connect this digital drive for abstraction with the strange new economy we now live and work in (or don't).

> The existing bias of business towards abstraction combined with the net's new emphasis on success through scale yielded a digital economy with *almost no basis in actual commerce, the law of supply and demand, or the creation of value.* [Emphasis mine.] It's not capitalism in the traditional sense, but an abstracted hyper-capitalism utterly divorced from getting anything done. In fact, the closer to the creation of value you get under this scheme, the farther you are from the money.[2]

This is a characterization that might be truer with each passing day.

A host of theoreticians has rushed in to explain this strange new economics, using models from fractal theory and mechanisms adapted from slime-mold behavior in a vain effort to predict where it is all going, but all are vested in the axiom that everything can and should be abstracted from everything else.[3]

---

[1] Rushkoff, *op.cit.*, p. 76.
[2] *Ibid*.
[3] *Ibid*.

So the Goldman Sachs and the Bear Sterns put together, and wildly prolif-
erated, portfolios of these abstractions and abstractions of abstractions, in a kind
of metastasis of financial entities no one really much understands, except that
they generate spectacular profits and offer numerous opportunities for chicanery.

And Capital, lo and behold, might it be able to use this financial Philosopher's Stone to "multiply to infinity" the very nature of commodities, thereby
creating the new markets it must constantly find if capitalism is to survive,
while the pundits ponder their statistical derivations in a vain effort to explain the accelerating gap in incomes between rich and poor?

Returning to the series of "what ifs" in regard to the magic spell I am
suggesting might have been cast by Dee, what might be its impact on the
world empire I have described? How might it be manifest today? In addition
to the obvious ones of legal documents that originally established land claims
and asserted sovereignty, written by Europeans over the past several centuries, papers that would, of course, bring into play as necessary corollaries
a whole infrastructure of institutions, including armies, prisons, hospitals,
schools, banks, lines of credit, courts, and perhaps constitutions, would Dee's
spell take on physical trappings? Trappings that might even evolve over time?

By now the social system those relations of property have established
and the institutions that form the backbone of that system rest firmly on the
electronic networks linking together the varied component parts and levels.
IT is a tool exceptionally empowering to the increasing centrality of finance
as the driver of the capitalist economy in the 21st century, CPUs everywhere
calling out the pace of production like ubiquitous AI foremen.

As Elizabeth I set out both to root out nests of Catholic opposition to
her reign and (as Dee forcefully advocated) to forge an English Empire to
rule the world, Dee was one of two men responsible for putting in place a
vast network of spies and informants essential to both ends. (Already torture was seen as a crucial tool for their system of surveillance.) Dee used
his profound knowledge about mathematics as well as his immersion in ca-
belistic studies to devise the ciphers and codes needed to communicate with
far-flung informants and agents.

Here I will venture another outlandish, but conceivably true speculation,
suggesting the possibility that not only is IT technology and the computers
at its heart the current embodiment taken by Dee's spell, but that his repeated work with various demons in his magical work with Kelley has lent
a decided demonic cast to what these new technologies have made manifest.
Such a conjecture, outlandish as it certainly is, might prove useful in our
being able to understand many of the IT-related social and cultural pathologies discussed in Chapter 27 and elsewhere in this work. There is some evidence to support this conjecture.

---

1 *Ibid.*

2 *Ibid.*, p. 76.

Besides the epigraph at the head of this chapter, consider the observation made by a Lecturer in Literature at Brunel University — an institution heavily involved with hi-tech studies, that played a significant role in the development of computer technologies — that there are increasing numbers of references to diabolical themes or entities in hi-tech culture. Readers may recall that I raised the question at the end of the last chapter as to what, if anything, waited for those who felt themselves sucked or absorbed into the screen of their TV or computer, but that I deferred that question until we could first explore the matter of possible conspiratorial intent in the spread of mechanistic theories and the like.

Let us now examine that question of who or what lies on the other side of the screen. I shall suggest the possibility of specifically diabolical aspects in the strange screen world that has so many of us fixated on it for so many hours of our days. There is more than a little evidence to suggest something malefic is going on, as we saw in the previous chapter, especially.

At the highest level of computer programming, the Brunel Lecturer pointed out, experts tend to name their programs (*i.e.*, the word that "invokes" the program to emerge out of the machine's memory, so that it can be run) by names taken from the occult, with an emphasis on the malefic side of magic, including such "PANDEMONIUM," "MAD," "MANIAC,"[1] "STANDARD DEMONS," "SATAN,"[2] "INFERNO," etc. In "LOGO," a much-applauded program to teach young children about computers created by one of the leaders of AI, there are a number of commands that are referred to as demons. To run these, the computer "user is asked to summon up the demon required," Shallis observes, continuing, "Such an act has more than a ring of blasphemy about it, and yet it seems innocuous and normal in the context of this technology." He suggests that those who create the programs

> are acting like agents for the propagation of an unnatural, subterranean, cold and dark world, whose spread, in the name of efficiency, enhances the dangers of the electronic web around us and which we see taking firmer grip on our society day by day.[3]

---

[1] In 1951 John von Neumann invented a new, more versatile and powerful computer for the Atomic Energy Commission, specifically to work on problems involved with the design of the first thermonuclear weapons and and named it **M**athematical **A**nalyzer, **N**umerical **I**ntegrator **a**nd **C**omputer. Officials did not notice the acronym until later. See Shallis, *op. cit.*, p. 234. Jim Holt, "How the Computers Exploded," *New York Review of Books* (January 7, 2012).

[2] Paulina Borsook, *Cyberselfish: A Critical Romp through the Terribly Libertarian Culture of High-Tech* (New York: Public Affairs, 2000), p. 107.

[3] Shallis, *op. cit.*, pp. 234–35.

But how could this *possibly* be? To suggest demonic forces behind the creation, say, of Apple Corp., sounds like madness, a level of paranoia almost stratospheric. Was it not described earlier[1] how the personal computer movement emerged in part from currents set in motion out of the opposi- tional tide that surged forth in reaction to the US invasion of Cambodia in Spring, 1970? Surely to argue that demonic influences were at play is to muddy the waters of political analysis and irresponsibly, irrationally, and needlessly to underplay the very real economic, social, and cultural streams that flowed into the surge of computerization in recent decades.

iv. The Simulation of Heart

And yet let us, nonetheless, tentatively pursue Shallis' inferences (re- jecting, I hope, at least for a few moments, any impetus to toss this book onto a shelf, never to be read again). If the screen into which more and more of us disappear delivers us over to a trance-like state, into what kind of world do we cybertravellers get taken? What is found on the other end of the elec- tronic cables, so to speak, and to what purposes? What is possibly gained by invoking demonic influences?

What *are* demons? They are commonly thought of as forms of super- human intelligence, acting somehow so as to affect our human world, as Shallis points out. Traditionally, they are sometimes thought of as acting to steal a person's will, as taking over one's consciousness, and as having a coldness about them.[2] Sometimes they are said to have a strange flicker in their eyes.

In Japan computerized robots have begun killing (an earlier draft called it "murdering") people. Also in Japan a leading hi-tech and science city, Tsukuba, constructed on the site of a demolished village, has a "slight aura of creepiness" about it, according to Japanese popular opinion. It also has the highest suicide rate in Japan.[3] It was whatever was behind a TV, rather than computer, screen, that sent hundreds of Japanese children watching cartoons into seizures, spasms, and induced nausea in 1997. Over 700 were hospitalized in two separate waves in reaction to the show. One scene that featured a "vividly colored explosion mixed with a few seconds of flashing bursts of blue, red and white light, each about one-thirtieth of a second long, was particularly implicated. A writer for such TV programs claimed that

---

[1] Chapter 24.

[2] *Ibid.*, p. 234, and this work.

[3] "Japanese TV Yanks Dangerous Cartoon Show Off the Air," San Fran- cisco *Chronicle* (December 18, 1997); Associated Press, "Japanese TV Leaves Hundreds of Viewers in Hospital. Shocking cartoon gives kids seizures," San Francisco *Chronicle* (December 17, 1999).

they are purposely crafted so that viewers "can't take [their] eyes off it without missing crucial visual clues about the meaning of the action." A father watched in horror as his daughter lost consciousness. "She started to breathe only when I hit her on the back."[1]

The alien "intelligences" on microchips serve as enablers for the emergence of the transnationals, disembodied corporate entities which have dramatically remade our world, in a mere handful of years succeeding in establishing a considerable independence from any one nation, no longer rooted in a national soil or culture or language, as mentioned earlier. With the microchips on line, there is little to tie any corporation to this rather than that spot, and their ability to employ or not ultimately gives the multinationals the upper hand in any negotiations with governments or regulators.

Besides being the original basis for intercontinental missiles and thermonuclear bombs, the chips now make possible the immiseration of increasing number of people worldwide. Discussing the changes to the world economy from the 1970s on, the historian Eric Hobsbawm points out that the countless millions once driven off their land by the growth of capitalism and industrialism from the 16th century on for the most part could eventually be absorbed, even if, at the introduction of waged labor, it was reluctantly, into the workforce; whereas those now being laid off due to computer-based automation have a quite different future to anticipate. In today's economy (this was written in 1994) the

> number of workers diminished relatively, absolutely, and, in any case, rapidly. The rising unemployment of these decades [after 1970] was not merely cyclical but structural. The jobs lost in bad times would never come back when times improved: they would never come back.[2]

Experts and laypeople agree. A September 2013 study by Oxford University professors predicted about 47% of jobs in the US could disappear in the near future because of the work being computerized. In Japan, the estimate is 49% of jobs will be done by robots or computers in the next 10 to 20 years.[3]

All of these together, then, would provide the scaffolding from which would hang my possibly paranoid — or, better, my decidedly paranoid, but perhaps also true — fantasies about demons lurking in the binary alleys of cyberspace: hypnotic, even addicting, "entities," possibly creatures which

---

[1] *Ibid.*

[2] Eric Hobsbawm, *Age of Extremes: A History of the World, 1914–1991* (New York: Vintage, 1996), p. 413.

[3] Carl Frey and Michael Osborne, "The Future of Employment: How Susceptible are Jobs to Computerization?" (September 2013), www.oxford-martin.ox.ca.uk. My thanks to Alison Bryant for her assistance.

were originally invoked by a spell cast by John Dee (a man *known* for invoking demons in his magical workings with Edward Kelley) and a spymaster for the nascent Empire; which drain peoples' wills; entrap their consciousness; decrease their mental faculties and narrow the terrain of their perceptions. Encounters with these inhuman forms of alien "intelligence" end up rendering more and more of the human population superfluous. And this technology is made possible only by the initial step of dousing the silicon crystals (to some thinkers, a form of proto-life) with a nerve-gas derivative, such as arsine.

In the Age of Information, capital has finally succeeded, after a fashion, in creating a simulation of mind and life at the center of the machine. But these are creatures of some nether, un-Earthly realm. Many of us, alas, can no longer tell the difference, for by now the psychic numbing that the mechanical philosophy has carried out has done its work in the deepest recesses of our souls. These entities, whatever they might be, that drain the will of the person at his or her monitor, entrancing them in its electronic glare, may simply be the demonic aspect of capitalism itself, with its continual choosing of the dead over the living in the ontologies of matter, language, music, religion, and culture.[1]

A varied population occupies the etheric realms, different kinds of demons, and there are a number of diverse perspectives, including Buddhist, Native American, fundamentalist Christian, Jewish, Taoist, pagan, etc. on who these spirits are and what they might mean. I do not think this is the place to try to "flesh out" my speculation by trying to pin down Shallis' and my conjectures as to the ultimate nature of these "cold intelligences" that have suddenly appeared at the helm nearly everywhere. Just what kind of entities might these creatures be in terms of those varied denizens of the spirit world, the traditional elementals, gnomes, devas, incubi, djinn, sprites, etc.? Who knows? There are times, and I think this is one of them, where it suffices to raise a new set of questions without attempting an answer, content to let them marinate a while in the juices of our myriad consciousnesses before attempting to cook up tasty food for our thoughts. In the end, perhaps the questions will yield nothing, revealing themselves as little more than idle speculation.

---

[1] I am not claiming such spirit entities like demons, sprites, djinns, incubi, etc. are always malefic. Not all are, as the fairy tales attest. But these denizens of the tales are all tricky.

In the case of John Dee, his occult enterprise, according to Yates, a vital underpinning of Rosicrucianism in the 17th century, came wrapped in the odious arms of an aggressive assault on the non-Europeans of the world, given Dee's forceful advocacy of the English Empire that eventually did subjugate much of the world. My own political prejudices lead me to presume that such an enterprise of course was the construct of a malign enitity. In Chapter 33 we will take a closer look at magic used for malefic ends. See Benjamin Woolley, *The Queen's Conjuror.*

But I doubt it. And certainly, as we reach the 100th-year anniversary of a series of world and local wars that have unleashed weapons of mass destruction[1] across the globe and, in the ebb of the Cold War, is witness to so many armed conflicts on virtually every continent that they almost blur into one another (under the onslaught of TV-ization), in an ongoing maelstrom of suffering and atrocities, it becomes clear that we need help for our beleaguered imaginations as we ponder how we ended up in this unfathomable mess? Engaged in ongoing mass slaughter of people, beasts, habitat. Like the miners in Bolivia feeling the weight of the recently imposed deadly labor in the bowels of the Earth, we all might well wonder if, indeed, malefic spirits have been running central parts of the show for some time now?

How else, indeed, are we to account for Los Alamos Laboratory, maker of the Bomb, becoming the center for research into "a-life," a sacrilege of almost cosmic dimensions.[2]

iv. INPUTS/OUTPUTS & YOU!

Both in popular and learned media, many articles and books decry (or in some technical circles, applaud) that our machines may soon be our bosses, electronics and robotized actors increasingly taking over more and more domains in military, economic, educational, and medical functions. But what if those writings and widespread concerns are, in fact, only smoke-screens that divert our attentions from a deeper — and far more ominous — present, not future, truth: that in our public and domestic lives, at work and in play, we humans are increasingly *being robotized*. The evidence is overwhelming, though its very ubiquity renders it hardly noticeable. Consider:

* for most of their days (and nights), through work responsibilities, social media, entertainment, communication, etc., etc., more and more people are spending the bulk of their awake (for some, sleeping, too) hours tethered to one or more electronic ombilici;

* for most of that time, their eyes will be trained on a screen (with the older, CRT technology, electronic pulses of photons projected onto their retinas) and using their fingers to manipulate the screen and to respond to its prompts;

* when engaged with digital doodads, people will experience many lapses of time when the machine is engaged — booting up, transferring files,

---

[1] I mean this in the sense the term was used in the run-up to the Iraq invasion, referring specifically to radioactive, chemical, or bacteriological weapons; lately US officials are using the term to refer to ordinary explosives, as in the Boston Marathon.

[2] See Chapter 26.

etc. — but *not with them*; during this "down time," people are generally passive, simply waiting for the machine to activate them. In effect, they have been put "on hold," or "turned off";

* people are increasingly experiencing withdrawal problems with their machines, the gaps between connectivity growing shorter and shorter as the platforms of engagement — iPad, laptops, Twitter, iPhone, Facebook, Instagram, games, the multitude of apps — proliferate;

* mines introduced the three-shift workday; email has made the *whole day* into one extended shift;

* each input to the machine — typing key words for a search, clicking a mouse to pick from a menu — elicits only requests for additional inputs. One's consciousness is enmeshed with the circuitry of his or her machine, in step with its rhythms, its will; always the need to choose;

* on their machines, people respond to menu choices; what those choices are, however, is generally someone else's decision — an engineer's, a CEO's, a general's;

* thinking is thus axiomized as a process of choosing; in effect, one is consuming "ideas";

* tracking what we choose, the machine knows better what choices to offer us next time; we have incorporated the machine's logic inside us;[1]

* in the 1950s and after, Pentagon planners, in response to the new war-making platforms, found it necessary to integrate weapons and soldiers at a deeper level than the traditional eye-to-sight, finger-to-trigger loop; supersonic jets avoiding heat-seeking missiles require pilots who can think like machines, since many of their responsibilities and choices have already been given over to the machine. Through its overwhelming role in setting agendas for the information technology industries, the Pentagon consciously set out to teach people to think like machines. Getting the schools awash in computers in the 1980s and after was a critical first step;

* down hallways and sidewalks, on trains and buses, people's eyes seek out their screens, not other people, generally not the surroundings;

---

1 As Rushkoff explains, "the more we learn to conform to the allowable choices, the more predictable and machine-like we become ourselves. In other words, we are training ourselves to stay within the lines." (Rushkoff, *op. cit.*, p. 59. The popularity of the cliché *to think outside the box* just as most thinking was literally being shoved into electronic boxes.

* social gatherings increasingly center on people's screens — for prior arrangements, experiencing, sharing, documenting, and broadcasting to others in a screen-to-screen intimacy, a reaching-out; so too on dates;

* the last thing before sleep, the first upon waking: checking the screen;

*the screen as a validator of one's import.

Compare the above with what we think about robots: machine-like entities that act repetitively, lacking affect, under automatic controls, according to the will of another, faithfully carrying out his, her, or its wishes: the similarities are alarming. In the space of a mere handful of years, a deep trance has captured much of what passes for conscious thought.

Growing up in the 1950s, when the US was engaged in war in Korea, I watched newsreels and read papers filled with scare stories about the enemy "brainwashing" GIs they had captured. The word has lost its potency over the decades since as it was degraded with over-usage, but in its original coinage it conveyed a fearful picture of the evil Communist enemy, replacing our thoughts and beliefs with one imposed from without by coercion. Once again, the parallels are unnerving.

There is, indeed, a deep pathology here, a fantasy world being built by men and women profoundly at war with their own humanity, working energetically on the mechanical brain that will inevitably supplant us, the assumption that silicon-based "life" would have distinct advantages over carbon-based "wetware" with all its animalistic messiness. As one AI researcher explained, in the future we shall all be living "in the interstices of an electronic network, incomprehensible to us, as fleas live on the back of a dog." A common trope among hi-tech visionaries and followers is the equating of them*selves* to their *brains* — as if it were that simple — a vivid example of the flight from nature. That brain, they believe, is something that soon will be downloadable onto a chip, achieving thereby a profound form of immortality. Not a few of them hope for the day, sometime soon, where "in the end we will not need physical bodies at all, for we will be able to reconstruct ourselves totally in cyberspace." Indeed, to some, "the illusion of incarnation will be indistinguishable from the real material thing."[1] Assuming backup copies were kept off-line in case of a massive systems-crash, a person could "live" forever once "an active copy made from the tape has resumed your life."[2]

[1] For an account of such "transhumanist" thinking, see Sam Frank, "Come With Us If You Want To Live: Among the Apocalyptic Libertarians of Silicon Valley," *Harper's Magazine* (January, 2015). Also, Anne Brice, "The Immortality Machine," *East Bay Express* (November 7–13, 2012.)

[2] Kidder, *op. cit.*, p. 241; Shallis, *op. cit.*, pp. 231–32; Borsook, *op. cit.*, p. 104; Margaret Wertheim, *The Pearly Gates of Cyberspace: A History of Space from Dante to the Internet* (New York: W.W. Norton & Co., 1999), pp. 254, 259, 262, 265.

For what is our modern mania for truncated communication — the Tweets, the LOLs, OMGs, and DoDs, emoji-strewn texts, and the jettisoning of spaces between words — but a dramatic manifestation of a profound drive to cut language "down to size," (less and less of it actually *spoken*) that comes out of that initial binary 0/1 duality? How such a strange drive could gain traction is a mystery, for really it represents no less than an attempt to escape from our very humanity — until we remember John Wilkins, Sprat, and the Royal Society's efforts to "reform" the English language by scrubbing it of ambiguity, "fulsome Metaphors," figurative language, and the feminine expressions, their solution to the "excesses" of the Civil War by the cobblers, apothecaries, printers, armies of apprentices, and farm laborers leading the revolutionary masses in taking down the Monarchy and challenging private property (the source of "original sin" according to many of them, like Winstanley) in their quest to build an English republic.

And now, once again authorities' reaction to rebellion — the '60s — and economic crisis — the '70s— is to clamp down on language, on *expression*. In their terms, not an inappropriate strategy.

Alas, for many of the young, escape into cyber-fantasies is the only relief they can find from a world that is unbelievably bleak. Josh, a regular user of multi-user domains, explained: "I live in a terrible part of town [in] a rat hole of an apartment, I see a dead-end job, I see AIDS." His cybered world is where Josh can see an "alternative" to that depressing reality, even if it is constituted entirely of 0s and 1s.[1]

---

[1] *Ibid.*, pp. 289–90.

29

On the Lam in Silicon Valley

i. MORAL RESPONSIBILITY IN AN AGE OF CYBORGS

Any efforts to resist demonic possession or robotization at the hands of our digital devices may leave little energy for anything else. However, so long as we are human, it is difficult not to be concerned with questions of right or wrong, of how to live an ethical life. With unrelenting cultural pressures to make us all believe we are nothing but machines, ethical questions take on, to say the least, a rather perplexing incoherence.

One night about 2 AM a few decades ago, a close high-school friend, finishing a book he was writing on a famous pair of serial sexual murderers in Los Angeles, called me and got right to the point: Where did I think evil came from? He was obviously intoxicated. It had been well over a year since the two of us had last talked. When he posed his question, I have to confess to being at a total loss. I probably mumbled a few clichéd pieties, fished out of a sea of platitudes I on occasion swam in. I am sure my friend considered the call a waste of his time. Besides lacking the clear theological foundations provided by my friend's recent rediscovery of his boyhood Catholicism (in high school we had shared a love for the iconoclastic essays of H.L. Mencken), evil was a problem I had so far avoided.

Partly it was denial by me, partly naivete, but mostly it was growing up in relative privilege, as the child of sort-of-white parents,[1] of, by adolescence at least, comfortable means, my parents able to benefit by the prosperity of the decades after World War II. The source of evil? I had no idea! I had had too little personal experience of it even to give me material to chew on. A little bit of bullying in school, a slight brush with antisemitism, authoritarian school administrators, etc. At that point, my enemies were mostly political — and distant, those who waged illicit wars, the perpetrators of horrific treatment of blacks, Jews, Latinos, women, or any of an army of the downtrodden, starting with the native people

---

[1] As a Jew, I have taken to calling myself "off-white," which I believe better captured the social ambiguities of Jews in the US in the last half of the 20th century as I grew into adulthood, and now, in the 21st, with a resurgent fascism.

who had once enjoyed the bountiful land in which I lived, and endured horrific military subjugation and political, economic, and cultural oppression.

But these were abstract wrongdoers. I found it difficult to conceive of them as truly evil — even the cops who had arrested me at demonstrations, even the White Citizen Council-connected thugs who were aghast at our "outside agitation" and subjected us to late-night high-speed chases in Tennessee and Mississippi in the mid-'60s. I was able to see the twisted logic behind their actions and see how they actually could believe in what they were doing. Lyndon Johnson and Richard Nixon too, I tended to see as men driven by agendas set by forces far beyond their personal control. At worst, they too seemed agents of someone or something else.

There were, of course, the Nazis, whose cesspool of civilized depravity had served in my youth, as it still does, to frame all moral questions for many of us, but in the '50s as I grew up they too were far enough away in time and space to represent only an abstract measure.

No, I did not know evil.

More recently evil things have been done to me and I have had many long hours to ponder them, to wonder at the circumstances that might have given birth to these acts, and to guess as the nature of the people who commit them. Some of these people have at one time been quite close to me. As I pondered, I thought back to the late-night telephone call.

What must such people think as they do things that grievously hurt or abuse others, perhaps someone they once loved? How do they see their own actions? What are their thoughts, feelings, passions? "Surely they must see that...." But, no, the more I saw evil things done close at hand, the more was I struck by how large a role in encouraging destructive acts is played by delusion and self-deception. People are capable of the most heroic mental gymnastics to avoid seeing or hearing what, to us, on the outside (or other side), is so incredibly obvious. Such a mentality, surely, particularly when coupled with the cultural instincts — thanks to mechanism — of compartmentalizing the different "components" of our lives, must be what allows a Lyndon Johnson to have ordered mass-bombing runs on peasant villagers during the day and at night presumably to be a "good" father to his daughters. So too I used to think of the McGeorge Bundys, Robert McNamaras, and the other architects of the Indochinese War, the defining evil-doers of the political education I obtained in my activist youth; and so, too, now that evil has been done closer to home, do I see the same pattern of self-deception and delusion.

I saw the same in my family when growing up, the men who wielded awesome (and wrongful) controls over others at work emerging into the shadows of twilight as my decent, loving father and brothers: humorous, compassionate, moral — and racist. In no way could I deny the evil nature of many of their actions in the world where they, the owners of a small business, had to be "responsible" — responsible to business, for my family, or for national security for the McGeorge Bundys. "Surely they have to understand that…" we think, but just as surely they do not, for they cannot; they see and hear and are able to acknowledge only what makes sense in their self-referential world, or so it seemed to me.

I doubt if this really answers my friend's question about the origins of evil, for he was staring into the metaphorical face of men who not only murdered, but tortured and enjoyed the anguished and desperate pleas and screams of their victims, and there are surely those who consciously feel that they, freely or under some kind of compulsion, must ally themselves with evil, who choose that path as their destiny.

One reason may well be demonic. The look in Charlie Manson's face as he was displayed to the press in 1969 was of a man possessed by someone or something. In magic we learn that a thought-form can become enlivened simply on the basis of powerful mental concentration, so that even if the Devil is a Christian invention, as many witches believe, centuries of focus on him by millions of people have made his powers real. And there are those who, whatever their reasons, feel their true allegeances lie there, with demonic evil that is set against the world of humanity.

Such people have no need to believe in the righteousness of their actions, no need for an elaborate chain of self-deception to lead them down the destructive paths they take. And yet, I think such people are a minority among those who commit truly evil deeds.

Only in such a way, I believe, is the empire able to survive — only by making the carrying-out of evil, in Hannah Arendt's words, "banal," was it possible for all the pernicious things that actually had to be done so the empire could be built and continue to survive. Only by a series of actions and inactions that each, in and of itself, was relatively insignificant, and, looked at in a certain way, can seem "reasonable," could something so monstrous be constructed. And, of course, by "empire," now, I mean all of it: Europe versus the rest of the world, but also men against women, people against nature, whites against people of color, straights against… etc., etc.

ii. SELF-DECEPTION, THE FUEL OF POWER-OVER[1]

Self-deception and delusion, then, are the psychological tools that eviscerate the body of truly heinous acts, rendering most of them flat and unspectacular, for delusion enables a person to justify all manner of crimes and sets into motion the engine of self-righteousness — a thousand times more destructive to the world, conceivably, than fossil fuel-based internal-combustion engines.

At the beginning of Empire, at least the modern "beginning," the critical 16th- and 17th-century watershed that this study has focused on, the *original* delusion was the false image of nature, consciously and carefully crafted as

---

[1] See Chapter 1.

an ideological construct to fight the upsurge of social enthusiasm; and precisely at the time when the propertied classes were engaged in the remaking of the social and economic order, and resistance was mounting among the plebians, nature was reconceptualized as a dead thing. It was taught that all of reality was to be understood by taking things apart into their component parts and subparts. Thus it was hoped that enthusiasm in Europe might be rendered impotent and that the "savages" in the Americas could be brought in line with European designs. Those who could not adapt to the new "reality" were often simply labelled "mad" and locked up — a sobering lesson not lost on the rest of us, who therefore vowed to maintain a connection with the arbitrary shape of things officially acknowledged as "reality," so as not to lose contact with the bulk of the population who seemed to believe it.[1]

In the name of rationality, open-mindedness, Progress, and what came to be identified as the modern, people were pressured into denying the reality of basic experiences of their day-to-day lives, as was discussed in Part Two, and hence was the ground broken for just about any form of delusion and self-deception to take root and propagate. That first lie, that nature is simply a machine made of dead matter, is the truly monstrous one. Once accepted, however, all other falsehoods have an easier time blossoming.

iii. TURBULENCE IN THE WATERS OF CONSCIOUSNESS

In our time the basis for widespread delusions and self-deceptions is less from distortions of the original mechanical philosophy with its dead material substrate, now taken as a given, and more from our Information Age's silicon-based reality, in what amounts to a kind of slight-of-hand: a silly con, if you will. The data stream that goes through the chips' Boulean gates, where the 0s and 1s pass to and fro, we shall see, is frequently discarded, lost, misplaced, degraded, made easier to alter surreptitiously or otherwise distorted on a regular basis. Binary logic may, indeed, insist on only allowing an on-or-off state, but the ambiguity thereby banished has an uncanny way of sneaking back in, sometimes riding in on the back of voltage surges.

Most glaringly, in this Information Age, data in electronic form has a marked tendency to "wear out." Simply put, after a certain number of years, records are no longer reliable. Data stored magnetically will degenerate over time, and not a very long time at that. If not copied onto paper or transferred to another file, the data becomes unreliable or lost. Some of NASA's data from earlier missions are by now irretrievable. Disks wear out after only a few years' time, and at any rate unless "read" *on the very same computer and with the very same software with which they had originally been made* — this in a technology in which upgrades of equipment and operating systems take place every few years —

---

1 As discussed earlier, see George Rosen, "Irrationality and Madness in Seventeenth and Eighteenth Century Europe," pp. 162–67.

all that will be discerned is a meaningless chain of 0s and 1s, no clue as to what they might have once meant.[1] According to Jeff Rothenberg, a senior computer scientist at the RAND Corporation, "It is only slightly facetious to say that digital information lasts forever — or five years, whichever comes first." In contrast to analogue tapes, which "remain playable for many years," data on digital magnetic tape, according to "conservative estimates," "should be copied once a year...." Citing the near-loss of data from the 1960 US Census; the Department of Health and Social Services; the Public Land Law Review Commission; herbicide information necessary for analyzing the impact of Agent Orange; and files containing P.O.W. and M.I.A. records from the Vietnam War; among others, Rothenberg points out the danger that "the chronicle of our entire period [is] in jeopardy" since digital files are "far more fragile than paper."[2]

It is estimated that the electronic catalogs that libraries have will perhaps have degenerated in about fifty years. Before then, presumably, the information will all have been copied, but in our age of perennially shrinking budgets, especially for social niceties like libraries, it is hard to be optimistic. More likely, as with bureaucracies everywhere, library staffs will be forced three decades from now to pick and choose which of their records they can afford to recopy. In effect, many library holdings will be erased from memory, effectively thrown away. Similar horror stories will no doubt exist for federal, state, and local government records, for commissions, for medical and insurance files, for financial data. The mind boggles at the implications, short and long term, of all those critical records being transferred to an electronic basis that is fundamentally impermanent.

In sum, the files themselves degrade and in any case, reading them becomes increasingly problematic as a result of how often hi-tech reinvents itself with ever-newer operating systems, platforms, software, and computers — like snakes on meth in perpetual molt.

Readers who have trouble believing me, with my obvious prejudices on this, might be more open to the late Steve Jobs' confessions. In 2010 the *New York Times* tech editor, David Pogue, recounted a disturbing phone call from Jobs. A year-and-a-half earlier Pogue had written about his objections when Apple removed a particular jack from its latest laptops, a portal he had been intending to use to edit 100 MiniDV tapes he had made on a camcorder, tapes of children growing up, appearances on TV, family trips, etc. Without the jack, he feared his tapes would have to go unedited. The tech editor felt as if Apple, which till then had included a video-editing program on every Mac, "was yanking the rug out from under us."

[1] "Time and Technology Threaten Digital Archives," *New York Times* (April 7, 1998); Jeff Rothenberg, "Ensuring the Longevity of Digital Documents," *Scientific American* (January, 1995).
[2] Rothenberg, *ibid.*, pp. 42, 45. Patricia Cohen, "Fending Off Digital Decay, Bit by Bit," *New York Times* (March 16, 2010).

Apple's CEO replied to the *Times* column by phoning Pogue. Presumptuously, but maddeningly accurately, Jobs insisted that the tech editor would *never* edit his tapes. He asked when Pogue thought he would get to the project. "Maybe when I retire," the editor replied, to which Jobs objected, "You know what? By the time you retire there won't be a camcorder left that can play them. Ten years from now there won't be a camera left that can play them."[1]

This is the dirty secret of our new digital reality. Jobs was discussing camcorders, but his remarks apply across the broad spectrum of electronic technology, for it is the proud boast of information technology that it is continually devising new ways to move the 0s and 1s, and that means new gadgets and new software. And so, once connected, it takes an enormous effort and continual investments of time and money *to stay* connected with the ever-more megabytes needed to keep up with the newer functions and with our digital Joneses. And all those files one has made... unless continually copied and recopied format to format, platform to platform, they will migrate to realms beyond reach in a region of cyberspace forever closed off. While our Information overlords, in exchange for cash, help us keep making our connections to an increasingly circumscribed reality we identify as freedom.

iv. In Remembrance of Whose Past?

History has frequently been viewed as a dangerous subject, for parallels can be drawn, trajectories plotted, promises redeemed. It is taught less and less in US public schools these days, squeezed into a curricular corner by being incorporated into the social "sciences" like economics, geography, social studies, and now downgraded further, along with the other subjects not on the standardized tests that presently define what students get to study. With the most important documents that daily define our present being formatted now into a medium that after a handful of years or decades will be unreliable, the very basis for history, for all written group memory, is in effect wiped out. Up until recently, the written record that was the basis for history itself had a history, and documents could be examined in minute detail decades, centuries, sometimes even millennia after the fact, in order to ask ever-newer questions about defining moments in the unfolding of our common lives over the millennia, starting with cuneiform and slashes made in sticks to record the moon on her cycles many thousands of years ago.

Examination of the written record or mark was crucial to ensure accuracy, for forgeries and fraud are always possible and subtle clues not always immediately noticed. With physical record-keeping, one may find a different

---

[1] David Pogue, "The Past, From Tape To Drive," *New York Times* (April 15, 2010).

hand, paper used, typeface, ink, placement,[1] or, not so long ago, the use of white-out to indicate later changes. But since, in principle, one electronic open switch is identical with any other, electronic records have a less-accessible history and fraud is "virtually" undetectable.[2] In this way, too, history will, under current trends, be effectively abolished.

Erasure of records, of course, is not new, but for the most part it was by authorities or other interested parties whose suppression of evidence (of a loan, a deed, a promise, a love affair , etc.) could often be detected. But not here. And except for floods, fires, and the like, erasures were not random, nor, as is the case with digital amnesia, was the loss of records system-wide, so that potentially all the records (of a firm, a CIA operation, a network) are affected.

Of course, history will still be made, and within the severe limits posed by this disappearing act on the part of key components of the record, of how we in literate societies have always learned from the past, there will be those of us who still are driven to continue writing history, for only thus can we pretend to understand the way things are at the present. Alas, the ease and time-savings some historians claim their word-processors give them or the ease with which they can at present Google some article or find some record will be more than outweighed by the sad reality that the raw material for our craft is being irretrievably smashed to bitts.

v. Data Glut & Data Sluts

Once in the system, information is out of sight and maybe out of mind, but it may still be doing work, perhaps being acted on by someone not "authorized" to do so. Unauthorized entrants can alter data, transpose it, distribute it, copy it, erase it, or some combination of these, and because their surreptitious entry is by way of the migrations of innumerable elusive electrons, it is generally quite difficult to discover that any of it is going on or who did it. Newspaper accounts focus on teenagers or the Chinese "accessing" Pentagon-linked computer installations, raising a number of "national security" questions, or hackers who mess with financial records or implant computer "viruses." But I would bet far more common are FBI- or National Security Agency-initiated raids to fetch mailing lists, budgets, names of contributors, or other information from the computers

---

[1] Thus, as noted on p. 278, in my first scholarly publication, I was able to use as an important piece of evidence a slighting comment Newton was reported to have made regarding Fatio's theory of gravitation, that it was clearly a later addendum to the document, written off to the side and in a different ink. The printed versions of the document did. not reflect these discrepancies. (Kubrin, "Newton and the Cyclical Cosmos," p. 338 n. 52).

[2] Wertheim, *op. cit.*, p. 298 on the ease of digital criminal enterprise.

[3] See the revelations of Edward Snowden.

of unsuspecting left-leaning organizations or individuals, or one corporation spying on another.[3] The electronic umbilici with which those organizations "network" with like-minded groups or people are really two-way highways, with only loose controls over who chooses to travel them, or in what direction.

Some of the revolutionary organizations in which I worked in the 1960s and '70s made a point of never keeping our sensitive files or records in our offices, to guard against FBI raids; but today, if an organization is on-line, it is a good bet where to find critical membership lists, drafts of internal documents, and the like.

> For the snoops, the sneaks, the meddlers, data glut is a feast. It gives them exactly what their survival requires. They exist to reduce people to statistical skeletons for rapid assessment, name, social security number, bank balance, debts, credit rating, salary, welfare payments, taxes, number of arrests, outstanding warrants. No ambiguities, no subtleties, no complexity. The information that data banks hold is life stripped down to the bare necessities required for a quick commercial or legal decision. *Do or don't give the loan. Do or don't rent the property. Do or don't hire. Do or don't arrest.* This is human existence neatly adapted to the level of binary numbers: off/on, yes/no.[1]

vi. ENSLAVED TO LEISURE

In the meantime, a profound technophobia — the flip side of a characteristic national technophilia in the US that has been especially strong the past few decades — grips sizable segments of American society. Partly this is generational, the younger crowd raised on MTV, Nintendos, video arcades, answering machines, and cell phones being at home with the info-technological infrastructure, and wanting only more of it, while older people find themselves incapable of making heads or tails of how even to operate things like VCRs, PCs, or answering machines with remote access — this issue rather than hair length, dope, musical tastes, or politics being the basis of current intergenerational conflicts, according to the article. Only now it is the parents doing the "rebelling." Another article tells readers that if they feel their gadgets are "running you instead of you them," they "are in good company." Long hours of people's "leisure time" are now given over to purchasing, learning how to use, setting up, updating, servicing, connecting one component to the others, and replacing these "time-saving" devices.[2]

---

1 Theodore Roszak, *The Cult of Information: The Folklore of Computers and the True Art of Thinking* (New York: Pantheon, 1986), p. 20.

2 For example, James Coates, "Machinery Strikes Fear," *San Francisco Examiner* (August 8, 1993).

Most of these new gadgets are harder to fix and require frequent replacement; in the case of automobiles, now festooned with numerous microprocessors and all manner of hi-tech goodies, dozens of trips to the mechanics are sometimes needed to deal with their quirks.[1] An automobile dealer claimed that after the microchips began being inserted into cars, it was not uncommon to have one repeatedly be brought in for repairs, as many as thirty times, prompting the passage of the "lemon" law.

> Another problem that consumers increasingly confront is dealing with computers, rather than people. As impersonal, inscrutable and error-prone machines replace clerks, straightening out errors in bills and other product service deficiencies can become an interminable and infuriating process. Intelligent people, folks who have no problem with math, who know perfectly well how to set alarm clocks and who normally have impeccable manners are becoming ranting, blithering idiots when it comes to dealing with the high technology that has taken over so much of their lives.[2]

Many a sophisticated digital gizmo remains in its box, its owner befuddled by arcane and frequently contradictory language describing the many wonderful options the piece of equipment affords them. Several years ago, an estimated 80% of VCR owners were incapable of programming them.

vii. BEARING TO THE RIGHT

When our major institutions are so large and complex that human beings can no longer manage their running and feel they must turn that responsibility over to digital logic machines, then we must question at a fundamental level the direction Western society has taken, the particular pathway picked among the welter of possibilities. Alas, more than three hundred years of allegiance to the mechanical model have so blinded us to all the potential branches off the historic path actually taken, some of which offshoots once loomed as real historical options, places where a different direction might have been chosen, that what now appears, looking back, as a more-or-less straight path, was more like a series of turns chosen over the years and the centuries.

But with the mechanical philosophy so engrained in the fiber of our cultural consciousness, by the 18th-century Age of Enlightenment that path was not

---

[1] See Ray Magliozzi and Doug Berman, "CarTalk," San Francisco *Chronicle* (August 13, 2016).

[2] A. Kent MacDougall, "The Gadgets That Run Our Lives," Los Angeles *Times* (n.d.) for the first quotation, Ben Fong-Torres, "The Heartbreak of High-Tech Anxiety," San Francisco *Chronicle* (February 15, 1984) for the second.

only seemingly a straight line, it already carried a considerable amount of philosophical momentum with it, in that certain branches were almost inevitably chosen, indeed they presented themselves as the embodiment of Reason itself. This momentum, let's be clear, is what accounts for widespread feelings of impotence in addressing the profound yearning for social transformation today.

For all intents and purposes, mechanical logic, structurally integrated into the innards of silicon crystals with the help of chemical "doping" gases, now run the essentials of our society. In being situated for their tasks, these AI programs, operating systems, algorithms, and recursive routines in effect "dumb down" the world in which we still live, simplifying real-world complex interactions into a radically truncated version so as to squeeze that world into the preconceived categories, like a size-eleven foot into a size-seven shoe, trying to ignore the places where social "blisters" painfully erupt, including students who cannot read, large numbers of whom are prescribed antidepressants and antianxiety drugs,[1] a normalization of genocide, etc.

viii. THE SOURCE OF EVIL?

Alas, my friend's inquiries regarding the source of evil is still unanswered. Self-deception can explain quite a lot but it cannot account for all the perversities of the human spirit, for those who truly delight in hurting others. I don't think my friend ever answered his question about the men whose heinous crimes he was researching.

[1] According to Hilary Rose and Steven Rose in *Genes, Cells, and Brains: The Promethean Promises of the New Biology* (London: Verso, 2012), what amounts to an avalanche of mental disease has materialized in recent years:
* The WHO declared that there is a pandemic of depressive illness around the world. By 2011, mental and nervous system disorders made up 13% of global disease, according to the WHO;
* What once was considered a rare disease, binary disorder, now affects 1 out of every 40 Americans;
* While ADHD in the 1980s affected about 1 out of every 500 children in Britain, the rate is now 1 out of every 20;
* Prescriptions for ADHD shot up like Jack's legendary beanstalk, a nearly 30,000% increase in a little less than 20 years (2010 figures) in Britain;
* Prescriptions for antidepressants increased 28% in the UK between 2008 and 2011, likely due to the financial collapse that hit;
* The European Brain Council declared that in Europe each year some 38% of the population would develop some kind of mental illness, much of it going unrecognized and/or untreated. (*Ibid.*, pp. 248–49).
"Just say no," except, of course, to the nostrums proferred by the pharmaceutical firms to smooth away the disfunctionalities of modern society for its beleaguered denizens.

30

Hi-Tech Gets Ready To Administer the Coup de Grâce

i. Should We Just Get Rid of the Damn Things?

Given the sum total of all the charges I have brought against computers and digital technologies — that they inherently mystify, confine, and hide; that in critical ways they do not work; that they enable inherently damaging social institutions to flourish and maintain power; that they are extremely toxic to human health and our environment; that they destroy our history and our spirit — am I proposing, therefore, that such technologies be *abolished?*

How could we *not* consider ridding ourselves of any particular technology that hs been reliably identified as an unprecedented threat to humans and countless other species? But note the operative verb: "consider." As it stands, the topic is dismissed out-of-hand, too outlandish even to discuss, as if assuming that anything that is technologically feasible not only *can* be, but *should* be done. Such assumed inevitabilities need to be challenged. I have tried to demonstrate that the new information technologies, at whose center are computers, are such threats, not only largely responsible for destroying the ozone layer, but in other ways undermining the ova that are our essential contributions to the future (bereft of those, there *is* no future, at least not in terms of the human race.)[1] That, as an abstract proposition, abolition in such a situation is not already an agreed-upon option speaks volumes about the degree to which we have lost touch with the thread of life.

Yet, as a concrete proposition, in relation specifically to information technologies, the notion of whether I advocate getting rid of those particular technologies is too complicated to elicit a straightforward *yes* or *no*. First, what *would* advocating in these pages the abolition of computer technology *mean?*

---

[1] Strictly speaking, extremely probable causes, since strict causality in situations involving scores, if not hundreds, of independent factors can rarely be proven beyond question, just as Thomas Sprat promised.

To be sure, if I had my druthers, then... — but (and this is crucial) I don't and (thankfully) never will have such power, so even though the rest of the above sentence might have read that... I would advocate abolishing, or at least severely limiting, digital technology, such that... in the absence of any *practical* meaning to the question of my advocacy of abolishing such a well-entrenched machinery, I feel compelled to ignore it, especially because it focuses attention and energy in the wrong places.[1] Answering it wouldn't do much more than allow me to feel superior, maybe even smug. Such a reply would not only be a thoroughly academic and formal exercise, it would also encourage the wrong kind of traditional elitist political thinking, the "wise man" telling others how to think and what to do.

A much better question, I believe, is the following: is it conceivable that there would arise *social* forces that mobilize countless people across the globe who *choose* to escape the electronic web that more and more of us are effectively caught in?

It is this latter question that I now intend to answer. It should be obvious that the dominant institutions of society will continue to maintain their commitment to the "command and control" of information-processing technology, as well as its promised (though undelivered) economies; accordingly they will ignore its very real drawbacks, even in their own terms — memory loss of vital data; lack of real return on invested capital; seeming inability to increase productivity as promised; heightened vulnerability to massive manipulation and theft; the potential of introducing catastrophic system-threatening instabilities; the military unreliability of such weaponry; etc. — that should, *if* those institutions had a *shred* of sense, scare them off.

The issue of cost-savings with the new technologies is, as we have seen, problematic. Money *is* to be made, but not, as advertised, because of efficiency or increases in productivity through the use of automation. Those are simply not found.

In *Labor and Monopoly Capital*, Harry Braverman, a former machinist, demonstrates how much industrial capitalism brings machines into the production process *not* because of efficiency or profitability, but because, in many cases, the machines gave management considerably more *control over*

---

[1] Despite the extreme destructiveness of these technologies, I think it would be mean-spirited to deny their use as aids to prosthetics for those whose disabilities might thus be helped. Though I have reason to believe that the use of computers in this regard is often overdone (i.e., education for learning disabled), the example of the late Stephen Hawking eloquently argues for some small instances where the benefits strongly demand toleration and a degree of co-existence. Similarly, children suffering the excruciating pain that comes from sickle cell disease seem to obtain enormous relief from the use of VR distractors, so too burn victims. Erin Allday, "Virtual reality offers children a welcome respite from pain," San Francisco *Chronicle* (August 22, 2016).

production.[1] We saw earlier[2] that this was the case with the introduction of automated machinery in the aircraft industry in the 1950s. In the latter case, management strenuously resisted efforts to evaluate the new automated processes to see if actual cost-cutting had occurred. When finally forced to make such a study, in part, due to pressure from the union, the results showed efficiency was not improved, nor were costs cut. What moneys were saved in one way were more than spent in unforeseen costs from the new methods. I suspect this is the case in a great many new methods of production that are introduced, and that Capital will knowingly (though with attempts to hide it from others) accept *costlier* procedures if thereby management *retains control* over what really matters to them.

Describing the decisions of executives at GE, Noble explains:

> In opting for control, GE management thus knowingly and, it must be assumed, willingly, sacrificed profitable production[,]... illustrat[ing] the ultimate management priority of power over both production and profit within the firm.... The goal [of capitalism] has always been domination (and the power and privileges that go with it) and the preservation of domination.[3]

However, computer technology is a cash cow in other ways. Capital has powerful reasons for continuing to lust after more and more hi-tech, for *despite* its many problems, described in detail above, and no matter how serious and alarming some of their consequences, multi-national corporations, on the basis of information-processing technology, have been able to carry out fundamental structural transformations to the world economy. It is on the basis of this new technology that the various parts and location of global production can be more solidly linked together, such that the division of labor, at the core of capitalism's profitability, is now considered for the planet as a whole, so that a given product might be a composite of parts manufactured in half-a-dozen different countries. An even greater transformation has occurred at the level of *finance,* with huge surpluses of US dollars accumulating in non-US banks abroad during the 1960s and especially the '70s from OPEC profits and growing US military spending, not to mention the increased amounts of US foreign investment, to the degree that, in the form of eurodollars, a new and totally uncontrolled commodity emerged that lent itself to massive speculation. As dollars, yen, francs, pounds, marks, and then euros and renminbi were traded back and forth, along with rupees, pesos, and the rest of them in

[1] Braverman, *Labor and Monopoly Capital: The Degradation of Work in the Twentieth Century* (New York: Monthly Review Press, 1974).
[2] Chapter 19, pp. 381–83.
[3] Noble, *Forces of Production,* pp. 320–21.

the frantic search for quicker profits, national governments eventually came to lose all control over exchange rates and the world money supply.[1] None of this could have occurred without information-processing technology.

And so, as governments and banks, employers and schools, continue to centralize information and attempt to erect higher, ever-more impenetrable bureaucratic walls atop their respective data-bases, while mining and selling the data gleaned from every one of our keystrokes or mouseclicks, our searches and "likes," it is unclear how much our individual decisions to buy computers or not could significantly divert such overwhelming technological currents. To be sure, individual decisions whether or not to turn the affairs of one's life and mind over to the PCs or iPads might affect his or her well-being, and even allow a certain integrity to be maintained against the extraordinary centralizing pressures — and given the tremendously addictive power of the information technologies, might be wise, indeed. And parents should consider resisting the silicon mania at school-board meetings, and the use of schools for Pentagon-guided experimentation. At the present it is not clear that much more can be done by individuals.

Our actions take place within contexts, in particular social settings, however, and *those* can play decisive roles in bringing certain historical possibilities to the fore or suppressing the likelihood of others. Without presuming to don the august robes of a "futurologist," I want to identify three areas where it is not unthinkable that overwhelming historical forces, even in the foreseeable future, could starkly pose the questions of whether continuing our present deification of information and the setting up of virtual shrines for its worship? It is not unrealistic that overwhelmingly people might choose to turn around: relinquishing certain technological directions taken, in particular an approach to issues of technology that goes back to around the run-up to World War II, as I shall explain shortly.

In my vision, three such historical forces, perhaps akin to giant waves that from time to time come crashing down on societies, forcing them to a stern accounting, and a profound restructuring of the beliefs and practices could evoke such a renunciation of the profound techno-spirituality that has taken hold of the whole of our institutions and abolished or thoroughly recast age-old customs everywhere.

ii. COMING DIGITAL TSUNAMIS?

The first such wave, for obvious reasons, is unemployment. In both long and short runs, digital technology creates huge amounts of unemployment. If that was a debatable proposition in the 1960s when the upsurge of automation was just hitting and when some public discussion of its implications occurred in journals of opinion, in today's world, with such woeful and in-

---

1 Hobsbawm, *Age of Extremes*, pp. 362–64, 277–78.

tractable unemployment everywhere, it no longer should be. Not only are there fewer jobs, both relatively and absolutely, due to "downsizing," what jobs *are* left are anxiety-filled both because for each worker, with downsizing, there is more s/he must do, and due to the vastly increased instabilities in the labor market. From the beginning this outcome was foreseen by some, including Norbert Weiner, with his prediction mentioned earlier, that vast numbers of both white- and blue-collar jobs would be taken over by automatic machinery. Weiner knew very well that management, left unchecked, would create levels of unemployment dwarfing even that of the Depression of the 1930s. Weiner also knew that the destruction or de-skilling of jobs was the *purpose* of the new technology, was one of the things they would do very well, and he warned the trade unions to anticipate a time soon where human workers, fearful of being replaced by robot workers, in effect would be competing against slave labor.[1]

Most ominously, in a never-published paper, Weiner pointed out in 1947 that "rather than being used to replace human energy and power," the "tendency of these new machines is *to replace human judgments* on all levels but a fairly high one."[2]

Thus, increasingly, large circles of people in industrial and non-industrial countries, urban and rural, among old and young, men and women, are cut off from the flow of commodities and labor which is the lifeblood of our several different kinds of society in the modern era, many rendered marginal specifically by digital technologies. How large that mass of marginal people must be before they choose to act out their inevitable rage against the social and technological fabric that has done this to them, I do not know. No one knows. But I believe it well within the range of imaginable trajectories opening up to the future.

It is, of is, of course, a classic Marxist fantasy that masses of unemployed rise up to overthrow the system that so oppresses them, a fantasy having only a partial resemblance to how history has actually played itself out in societies undergoing severe economic crises; but here I am less concerned with predicting what will happen and more interested in creating in our imaginations an appreciation of the forces conceivably unleashed by the blind rush to electronic enthrallment undertaken by institutions everywhere. I can imagine the numbers of un- under-, and never-employed reaching a critical mass, so to speak, after which, for this and other reasons, a collapse

---

[1] Hodges, *op. cit.*, p. 404. Benjamin M. Friedman, "Brave New Capitalists' Paradise: The Jobs?," *New York Review of Books*, (November 7, 2013). Nigel Cameron, "Open Forum, Where will people work when robots take the jobs?" San Francisco *Chronicle*, (December 2, 2014). Weiner's warning to union leader Walter Reuther and its aftermath is described in John Markoff, *Machines of Loving Grace*, pp. 68ff.

[2] *Ibid.*, pp. 71–72.

or a revolution (and hopefully the distinction between the two will be clear at the time) will confront a newly-reconstituted society with a clear choice and a serious debate whether it is possible to continue the digitalizing mania that has gripped the society, or, indeed, whether such technologies should be seriously curtailed or even done away with?

A second wave capable of shattering the digital framework to pieces might well be the consequence of the kind of system-collapsing cyber-attack or (as Ul;man predicted) a cyber-collapse that dramatizes the devastating vulnerabilities of networked infrastructures of State, finance, transport, defense, healthcare, and so on.

The third issue that I see as possessing an enormous power, conceivably even to the point of constituting another social tsunami that could lead to a confrontation with the Information Age, is that of its inherent toxicity, and especially its clear connection to human reproductive failures, which was discussed in Chapter 21. As at Love Canal, technological threats to their children can mobilize powerful movements of mothers and their allies.

Environmental nightmares have become our daily news, and the names of the more heinous "accidents" become part of our nascent, expanding, specialized vocabulary — Times Beach, Love Canal, Three Mile Island, Hanford, Rocky Flats, Chernobyl, Bhopal, Exxon Valdez, Semipalatinsk Polygon, Lake Baikal, Deepwater Horizon, Fukushima... by now, the list, growing by the month, in a litany familiar to my readers, testifying that the advanced technology our society is built around creates ever-larger "zones of infertility" that leave generation after generation of the maimed and dying, like the millions of Vietnamese upon whom Agent Orange was sprayed and those US and other soldiers who did the spraying or helped transport the materials. They live in our midst, as the victims of Hiroshima and Nagasaki have lived among the Japanese, outcast people, scarred, their genes under a dark cloud of suspicion. Have we already come to accept the normality of these zones (and these zonal outcasts) among us, terrain and creatures hostile to the continuation of non-toxic life for hundreds of thousands, even millions of years in some places? If a serious nuclear breakdown at a power facility goes out of control, as Three Mile Island came within half-an-hour of doing, such zones (which, at any rate, can never be isolated from food, water, and predator/prey chains) can be as big as "an area the size of Pennsylvania." It is as if the globe is being mutilated in front of our very eyes, one by one its habitats and creatures disappearing as differentiation gives way to uniformity and a grey shroud descends here and there across the lands.

From the farce of the Superfund for hazardous waste sites and the ineffectiveness of the Environmental Protection Agency, it is clear that the institutions of government and management and, to a lesser degree, perhaps, labor and education, have so lost sight of priorities that for them the spectre of living in a world with such spreading zones of infertility is not nearly as frightening as the instabilities that might result if private property were allowed to suffer any real limitations as to its deployment by capital in its quest for profits, even if the favorable quarterly statements sent out by the corporations are fashioned out of the lifeblood of future generations and if the price of Progress is the loss of another score or more of species from our planet.

So long as the dominant powers in our societies remain in control, we can only expect more such zones of infertility, spreading and linking up (like the small towns around Los Angeles and our other major metropolitan areas), acquiring rankings in terms of what horrors emanate from them and for how long they will be lethal. Nor are all such zones necessarily land-bound. The world's oceans harbor "over four hundred 'dead zones,' where the lack of oxygen precludes marine life."[1] We can unfortunately expect more homogenization, and increasingly more serious ecological disasters as water, weather, and crops are thrown more and more out of balance, not least from global warming; epidemics will inevitably follow. They have already begun, alas, for AIDS, lupus, Epstein-Barr, and, most alarmingly, what is called environmental illness, are crises arguably caused by or contributed to by the severe breakdowns ravaging our many environments.

But for many of us, the lessons of Love Canal, Chernobyl, and the like have not been lost. That our water, air, and, not least, the health of our unborn are the sacrifices demanded by the demonic gods of modern technology, capitalist and state socialist alike, and of the modern industrial system in general is becoming increasingly clear, and simple survival instincts — and *what else*, after all, *can* we rely on? — will require that computer technologies in particular, because they are deeply implicated in the attack on our future, may very well be called into question. Their continued dominion may well become a burning question for our children and grandchildren, if not for us. And so, perhaps the growing mass of victims ground under by the seemingly inexorable wheels of Progress might finally prove to be too much — like the mass of the unemployed who finally act, a number that is wholly unpredictable — and those wheels will grind to a halt. Surrounded by our maimed, our task of organizing a new society will in every sense be an act of healing (see Chapter 34 for more on this) and we shall find our way to some blend of old and new in a society altogether different from anything it is likely we could imagine now.

iii. Can't We Get The Genies Back Into Their Damn Bottles?
A Rebirthing For the Modern World

But it is surely too late at this point to go back(wards) technologically and socially, many will argue, for by now we are simply ensnared in our

---

[1]Lee Balinger, "From Sea to Dying Sea," *CounterPunch*, Vol. 24, No. 2 (2017); Thomas M. Kostigen, "Garbage Patch: How the Pacific Ocean Became the World's Largest Dump," *Discover* (July, 2008).

present civilization and its beguiling appurtenances. So far enmeshed in a tangle of misguided visions and poisonous technologies are we that no conceivable way exists to get out and back, they insist.

Yet our situation may not be so bleak as it seems. To be sure, we are alarmingly greatly entangled, and some of the knots, as I have implied, were first tied five thousand or more years ago, through times of patriarchal usurpations, the construction of large-scale irrigation systems by centralized political entities, and the arming of the Mediterranean region, according to differing interpretations, where the woof of what would eventually become the mechanical tradition was first laid down. And it is true that the emergence of mechanism as a dominant ideology goes back a good three or four centuries — how to untangle our destinies from the legacy of *that* convoluted history?

Simply because these are such fateful times, life hanging in the balance, trying to imagine such a gargantuan social undertaking, such an unimaginable turn, is clearly called for. When the five-hundredth anniversary of colonial domination came in 1992, it elicited elaborate plans and celebrations by those who had followed in the footsteps of Columbus and the Conquerors. In North, Central, and South America the anniversary also evoked a chorus of indigenous voices shouting in condemnation. Indians of the Americas gathered, joined by victims of colonialism from the Pacific Islands, South Africa, and elsewhere, along with white supporters, to demand an accounting for the many crimes of those five centuries of imperial rule.

Such an accounting is especially called for, for the war against the Earth that has been our focus here and the war against the indigenous turn out at bottom to be the very same war. The accounting is necessary particularly since the crimes against the indigenous peoples continues apace — as with the Western Shoshone, whose lands until recently were used for nuclear bomb tests, the Mayans in Guatemala, the Amazonia Yanomana. Such monstrosities cannot be allowed to continue. But they do. It is what extractive industries, which gird the planet, are all about, whether it is for ore or wood, oil or water. The time is, indeed, ripe for deep thinking on such matters — probing with a relentless honesty into the planning and practices underlying the colonial project, shining our light as deep as possible into long-forgotten recesses, for they might be concealing important State secrets.

More significantly, an analysis of the kinds and degrees of assaults on the biosphere reveals a crucial fact: as will be detailed in Chapter 34, the central processes and ingredients of our present ecological disaster have come to play significant roles only in the past eighty years or so — and eight decades is not a very long time ago, not a very long way to look back and reassess. It is to a time within living memory.[1] Of course, eventually we shall

---

[1] Some reviewers of a Freudian bent might notice how close this is to my own age, and they may make of that what they will. I insist, however, that the critical reason for this kind of historical framing is because it was then that, in the course of World War II, genocide started to become ubiquitous, practiced by practically every combatant in that conflict, as discussed in the last chapter of this book.

have to look at all of it, to retrace a great many of our steps, in our minds at least, and to undo quite a lot of what we have wrought for the past five thousand years or so. Our very logic will need refashioning, our definitions of health, of the relation between past and future, our sense of work and play. We shall have to examine our underlying mythologies, our creation stories, our idea of growth.

But — and this is critical — we don't have to do it all at once. We not only can, we *must* choose priorities and find reasonable grounds on which to stand while attempting to escape the flood of poisonous realities that are rising all around us. Such grounds are important. Without them too many feel only despair and resignation. All this will be discussed in more detail in Chapter 34.

Though one can point to earlier battles which partly revealed some of the West's maniacal and genocidal agenda (including, of course, the Conquest), World War II took that logic to a much higher plane and invested it with technologies actually equal to the task of wiping out hundreds of thousands of people in an instant, as well as factories of death. As we shall discuss in some detail later, this constituted an epochal transformation in social and technological practice, as manufacturing in general normalized production processes specifically associated with carcinogenic and mutagenic agents, as in the production of plastics and the vast array of poisons demanded by agribusiness. These particular technologies are the ones that shall have to be severely curtailed, if not outright abandoned, for survival of countless habitats and species, as we shall discuss.

A special look at the issues posed by the technologies of food production and of bioengineering must be a priority. I believe that biotech, beginning with the splicing of genes from one species to another; should be seen as simply the most recent techno-ideological assault on life, the latest chapter in the war against the living that Capital necessarily wages in its necrophiliac lust to control. (Where its assumed mechanical interpretation of reality is now injected into living cells, the "interchangeable parts" of life now able to be ordered from a warehouse.) "Necessary" because without the premise of infinite resources to tap, capitalism cannot expand, as it *must*, and the need for corporations continually to enlarge their markets precludes in principle any real rapprochement between the needs of Capital and those of the creatures of the Earth.[1] Part Two revealed how the early exponents of mechanical thinking were well aware of the larger environmental and economic issues on which a mechanical model of the world would bear: enthusiasm as

---

1 Some digital visionaries claim manufacturing in coming years will play a greatly diminished role compared to "information" economically, but I see only more trucks on the roads and ships at sea, carrying material goods to markets. The "promises" of nanotechnology seem just that, promises, one more utopian technofantasy.

a threat to the social order, the economic and political role of women, hierarchies of power and wealth, and especially land-use questions having to do with the commons and the protection of rivers and woods. All those were very much in the foreground in the 17th century, as were the many mines newly brought into play that dug deeply into the flanks of the planet in a mad search for coal, precious metals, or the metals of war, and fouling the waters and filling the air with smoke and noxious fumes in the process.

The stakes today are higher, for the legal monstrosity of patentable forms of life has eased the way for agri-business's tendency to put such overwhelming emphasis on a mere handful of (inevitably hybrid, hence sterile) seed varieties,[2] so that an incredibly rich legacy of plant genetics is rapidly disappearing worldwide, and it has provided the motivation for the gene splicers to get busy with their "scissors and tape." Robotized factories are built even as multi-nationals export their production facilities to countries where wages, environmental concerns, and safety measures are minimal. Indeed, a new spectrum of labor is emerging, from the purely robotic machine on the one end to the disembodied AI program "who" engages in "intellectual" labor at the other end — and off to one side stand the cowed, real human workers, who, against a foreground of increasing unemployment, must compete with such "creatures," able to do so only by increasingly mimicking their most regressive features, as Norbert Weiner foretold.

All these damaging aspects of high technology must lead us to focus again on the question of science in Western culture, as the next chapter will, for since its emergence as the dominant force in that culture some four or so centuries ago, science has been a celebrant of the subjugation of nature — and hence, in a very real sense, a willing participant and chief enabler of the valuation of death over life. Indeed, ultimately, only that which is dead can be objectified, and that above all was the project science took on for itself. Nature dead was a premise, it was a banner to march behind, and it was a weapon in a war (as most wars are) to the death — only this time, should ultimate victory fall to that worldview, a war to the death against nature herself.

---

1 I refer here to true hybrids, that is, offspring of parents of different species; there are plant varieties which are called hybrids but come from parents that are different varieties of the same species.

31

A Kaleidoscope of Truths

i. A Reformist After All?

I have shown the many ways in which the rise of Western science in the 17th century, by virtue of the mechanical principles which constituted its central narrative, served as an ideological beachhead for the imposition of long-term disastrous conditions on nature — and on the people and animals, plants and micro-organisms who in all cultures of necessity are of and work in that nature, transforming and being transformed by it; now I must address the obvious question: am I proposing (supposing it were even possible) an abandonment of Western science? Certainly the sum of all I have discussed so far might seem to point at such a conclusion.

The answer must be a simple and emphatic *no*. Such an abolition is neither desirable nor possible. For one thing, who could possibly invest hope or belief in any credo that calls on us to turn our backs on knowledge, no matter how problematic that knowledge may be, or at what price it has been gained? What is done, with different knowledge, *behavior* or *doing* can be changed, negated, or even better, transformed, however.

What is needed is not to *forget* or *repress* what has been learned over the past few centuries of scientific inquiry, not to mention all that was determined over tens of thousands of years since Neolithic times (if not before) from close observations, study and meditation on flora and fauna and of the stars and planets, but rather to put that knowledge into new contexts. It will turn out that some of these are not new at all, but old. One of the premises of the scientific revolution, enunciated clearly and emphatically by Thomas Sprat in his influential *History of the Royal Society*, was that scientific investigation was to be performed *out* of context, in isolation, especially in experiments, where "preconceived" ideas were forbidden to the researcher.

A battlecry of the new science, especially after Descartes' errors were "exposed" by the victory of Newtonianism, proclaimed that overall world-views were to be shunned, for they could only prejudice free inquiry. System builders were repudiated.

Actual scientific practice during and after the 17th-century revolution in natural philosophy was quite different from this positivistic credo. Not least, the "matter and motion" was, in the mature scientific revolution, simply taken for granted. Contexts certainly did exist for scientific research, for it is within frameworks of provisional understanding or hunches that models are built and experiments devised, after all; increasingly the practice was that these were left unstated or alluded to elliptically. On certain critical topics, concepts were taken for granted — like the axiomatic (by the 18th century) "matter and motion" as the core of all explanations — even as they might sometimes be explicitly denied by scientists consciously operating within their parameters, as was the case, as we saw, with Newton.

But it was true as well of Faraday and Ampère, and of many, many more. That larger-than-life exemplar of the scientific revolution, Newton, led the way in his denials, building his optical and kinematic analyses on the basis of a theory of matter and of a variety of forces, attractive and repulsive, including vital energies circulating throughout the cosmos to nourish the planets and stars, but once his theories came under criticism, he withdrew into emphasizing the reality of the phenomenon, and, except for his Queries to the *Opticks*, avoiding models. Eventually he orchestrated critical publications by his disciples where they might hint at what he dared not, sometimes even dictating their words for them, as in Samuel Clarke's replies to Leibniz in their famous debate over what the latter considered deficiencies of Newton's watchmaker-God.

The tragic result of this kind of subterfuge is the historical phenomenon of Newton's being the intellectual author of a worldview, mechanism, that he privately had critical objections to, a phenomenon that I have argued lies at the very root of mother Gaia's present dis-eases.

Making explicit where possible, some of the implicit worldviews that have generally been so carefully hidden is what I mean in calling for our accumulated scientific heritage not to be discarded, only (re)contextualized.

Let us go beneath the historical surfaces, to learn what the Newtons, Faradays, and Ampères thought they were doing when they were doing it — for, I suspect, we shall find that those hidden premises are the rule rather than the exception in science, at least in good science, and it was only adherence, by Newton and others who came after him, to a false ideology, which hides rather than clarifies actual historical practice, that barred us from learning about these premises in the first place.

This is what historians of science do, mining correspondences, memoirs, lab books, and the like to get a larger picture of scientific work. Surely we can only benefit from learning the inner thoughts and preconceptions of such men, or of scientists like Antoine Lavoisier, Charles Lyell, Marie Curie, Linus Pauling, or Lynn Margulis. For though these implicit notions are the seedbed for what grows in the gardens of their minds, these crucial hunches, premises and models almost never make it into what is published. Hence we get to see the flowers, but not the compost, mulch, or even companion plant-ing that helped them grow, for those things are kept buried.

For past scientists, this is a challenge carried on by historians. My pre-scription is that present and future science take pains to situate research within such frameworks, making broader claims, while still free to keep some-what separate empirical results that can stand independently of models. Such a proposal does not shrink from speculation. Nor would any such broad the-ory-mongering exceed by much the kinds of scientific work done at the pres-ent time in the name of string theory and multi-universes, immense systems erected that have scant means of empirical verification.[1]

ii. THE THREE CONTEXTS FOR A NEO-*NOVUM ORGANUM*; A MULTITUDE OF TRUTHS

Recovering or stating baldly such premises or overviews from the inner visions of past or future scientists will constitute the *first* of three specific contexts that I advocate as the basis for a new and reformed science.

The *second* context I think essential for any future science will surely be denounced, since it is the inversion of the premises of the mechanical phi-losophy. Where that 17th-century worldview posited a cosmos made of mat-ter that was, in essence, dead, thus ushering us, I have argued, into a reality where we are surrounding ourselves with a variety and staggering amount of lethal technologies, so that the dead matter once posited as a premise be-comes a reality for countless habitats, I would propose a science where the inertness of all matter is not a given, where instead there is an acknowledge-ment that all matter in the cosmos is *essentially* (as Newton wanted to believe) capable of self-organization and responsiveness. Other attributes we com-monly associate with life can be found diffused through matter in greater or lesser degrees. *How* this is so may, indeed, still be a mystery, but at least a premise of a vitality to all of matter renders life's shocking existence less of a violation of the cosmic order, less of a surprise.

Such an assumption avoids the dead-end questions of how life could possibly have emerged from non-living beginnings, that greatest of myster-ies, virtually impossible to account for except by a lot of arm-waving and fancy footwork that begs many of the most important questions. The premise of a self-organizing nature simply renders superfluous either "miraculous" explanations of life, or alternatively, explanations relying on purposeless, soul-less, blind mechanical interactions to account for the totality of reality, including life.

---

[1] See random issues of *Discover*, for example, or *Scientific American* in recent decades where the mysteries of dark matter and the recently revealed repul-sive force behind the expansion of the universe spin off centrifugally dazzling speculations as to underlying structures and processes afoot.

A *third* context I would propose for a reformed science will be a difficult challenge to existing epistemologies, as it proclaims that science is not *the* truth, it is *a* truth. A truth that is profound, but not monarchical. Science, to be sure, is a particular kind of truth with very great strengths, but as readers of Part Two will remember, having some potentially devastating weaknesses, profound blindnesses, as well, its penchant for simplistic cause-and-effect linear models, its recurring avatars of the reductionistic credo.

Indeed, this is true of Western culture more generally, although along with religion, science in particular has been most zealous in its pursuit of a single-layered "reality," which it alone could define. In order to hold in check the historic *intolerance* by science for the many other realities, there must be a recognition that there can be many truths, many angles from which to look at the mysterious world we are privileged to inhabit.

Science is certainly a fascinating, illustrative, marvellously stimulating and often extremely useful way to look at the world. But historically it has also proved to be capable of arrogance, self-righteousness, contempt for any competitors, and with a disposition for great cruelty towards any would-be alternative voices[1] — gross violations of the "spirit of free inquiry" that science also prides itself for, but inevitable, I suspect, in any quest that believes truth to be so one-dimensional that a single description could ever do it justice.

An admission that the stimulation and great explanatory value of science might need to be balanced by — or at least co-exist with — truths that are purely aesthetic, ethical, or poetic in nature can only be healing, not only of the breech between scientific and artistic worldviews, but healing to science itself. Indeed, infused more explicitly with the kinds of insights that come from other than scientific (or academic) modalities, science might well find itself acquiring more of a multidimensional shape, may find, in fact, that it can speak its truths in more poetic forms than previously and thereby become in a sense more accessible — and conceivably more powerful.

Put more simply, the truths of science are particularly wonderful gems in a crown of wisdom, consisting of many jewels. Without the sciences that crown would lose much of its glory, would glow with a noticeably dimmer, less brilliant, light; but dull indeed would a crown be that had only that one kind, one color, of jewel adorning it.[2]

---

1 As, for example, with Wilhelm Reich, or the untold billions of animals over the centuries tortured to death by scientists who had been assured by Descartes that their agonized screams could be ignored since "mere machines," as all animals are, are incapable of feeling, likening their shrieks to a set of gears badly in need of oil.

2 Some of these issues are discussed illuminatingly by Sheldrake, *Science Set Free*, concluding chapter. See also his *The Presence of the Past: Morphic Resonance and the Habits of Nature* (New York: Times Books, 1988) and *The Rebirth of Nature: The Greening of Science and God* (London: Century, 1990). See also Paul

iii. DARWIN & THE GODSEND OF BLIND MECHANISM

The three contexts that I advocate for a reformed science, of course, raise other issues. For example, the question of mechanistic versus animated theories of life lies at the heart of the misunderstood controversies surrounding "evolution." As the battle over evolution is presented in educated circles and in the media, believers in science as a form of inquiry into the ways of nature are pictured as fighting heroically on behalf of rationalism against an ignorant rabble who see in evolution mainly an assault on religion, and in particular a denial of the account of Creation given in *Genesis* of the Old Testament. Stated thus it is easy to take sides; the know-nothings are simply misled, even refusing to look at the evidence, just like the yokels in Tennessee in the Scopes trial.

In fact the conflict is much more complex, for much of it takes place in little-noticed rhetorical stratagems and falsely-posed oppositions. Once brought into the light of day, some of this hidden discourse reveals other aspects of the confrontation and points to deeper issues at the core of the contentious debate.

Let us begin at the first rhetorical sleight-of-hand, for that is what it amounts to. The sides posed are "evolution" versus some version of theological orthodoxy that looks to the Bible for its understanding. But it turns out that "evolution" stands not just for the notion that since the beginnings of life on our planet some three-and-a-half or more billion years ago, its various forms have come and gone, moving through time in the direction of greater biological diversity and complexity. No, "evolution" also means, specifically *Charles Darwin's* theory of evolution, first put forth in his seminal *Origin of the Species by Means of Natural Selection* (1859). With that work, it is said, biology as a subject took the leap into a true science, just as physics did with Isaac Newton's *Principia* (1687) and *Opticks* (1704) and chemistry with Antoine Lavoisier's *Traité élémentaire de chemie* (1789).

This jump from *evolution* to *Darwinian evolution* is understandable, given Darwin's role in convincing the scientific community and many others of the reality of evolution, but is nonetheless problematic insofar as no mention is made of other theories of evolution. For theories of evolution of the species have been, as we have seen, around for some time, predating Darwin. In classical Greek times, for example, are to be found evolutionary notions among some of the Pythagoreans, also in the 6th century BCE philosopher, Anaximander, including notions of a progression of species. Charles Darwin's grandfather: Erasmus Darwin, wrote a work on evolution, *Zoonomia*, in 1794–96. So too on the basis of his careful study of fossils, did Newton's contemporary and nemesis, Robert Hooke, as recounted in Chapter 13. In our times, Lynn Margulis presents a compelling alternative to Darwin.[1] Right or wrong, these other theories of evolution at least deserve a mention. Ideally they might even enrich the controversy over evolution, reveal new facets of the doctrine.

In particular, by not mentioning other theories of evolution, the public is led to uncritically accept as a given the specific notion that set Darwin's theory of evolution apart from the others, his theory of Natural Selection as the mechanism that could account for the perceived strong evidence, fossils in particular, that species do evolve. The question, for Darwin and others, was *how*, and to that Darwin seemed to provide a definitive answer: natural selection. Darwin's natural selection established a theoretical *mechanism* by which, without *volition* or *sentience* on the part of the causal agents, how species change over time was rationally accounted for, establishing a proposed motor that drove the process forward.

Darwin believed that just as human breeders were able through volition to select which seeds are to be planted or which bitches are to be bred with which sires so as to guide the development of specialized varieties of flowers or dogs, so too nature, *without volition*, could "choose" for certain characteristics to survive or not. The differential survivability is what established evolution.

Darwin's natural selection assumed, as had recently been established by Charles Lyell, the British geologist, that life existed on a very old Earth, so evolution could operate over vast spans of time. Second, Darwin accepted, as argued in 1798 by Thomas Malthus, that population pressures inevitably caused shortages of food and shelter, in addition to suitable mates for all species on a regular basis. With such pressures, it is clear, crises will erupt repeatedly, and many will die, while others live. Darwin's natural selection, thirdly, took account of how around any of a species' characteristics — the color of a wing, length of forepaw, sharpness of beak, swiftness, etc. — variations of quantity and quality were generally found. Natural selection then assumed these variations were somehow inheritable from parent to offspring (though nothing was theorized at the time about genes or chromosomes or DNA or mutations.)

Under conditions of dearth — of food, shelter, and/or mates — on a planet regularly facing changing environmental transformations (a basin over eons becoming a mountain, say) just what is needed to survive itself changes, and some of those inheritable variations might under particular stressors be just what could do the trick, to ensure, in particular, survival — to sexual maturity, especially — and the ability to propagate its fortuitous variation(s) unto new generations. Thus some seemingly random variations become keys to what drives evolution onward. And it is done without planning by anyone. It is "natural."

[1] Dick Teresi, "Lynn Margulis," *Discover* (April, 2011), pp. 66–71.

At this point it is important to point out that in mid-19th-century Europe the leading philosophers and intelligentsia were increasingly under the sway of materialism, a post-Enlightenment confidence born partly of the startling transformations, seen everywhere, especially in the explosive rise of industry, its factories and railroads, steamships and electricity, the new mastery over chemical combinations. Those not gravitating in materialism's direction otherwise were engaged in trying to refute it, marshalling counter-evidence and logics to escape its pull. Materialism was certainly a powerful current as well among the agitators and enthusiasts in the revolutionary struggles that erupted into insurrections in 1830, 1848, and 1871 and in the growing and influential labor and socialist movements.

Darwin's theory fell on such fertile philosophical soil, in other words, inspiring *both* the capitalist class in 19th-century Europe, who were wont to point to the dog-eat-dog of natural selection as naturalizing the fight-to-the-finish social milieu of industrial capitalism with its rampant child labor, and a workforce driven to malnourished exhaustion as a matter of course; *and*, as well, the movements to plot the overthrow of that capitalist order, to fight for a shortened workday, safer production methods, and social security. So impressed was Karl Marx with Darwin's work that he sought to dedicate *Das Kapital* (1867–95) to the resistant scientist.

In other words, natural selection carries considerable social and political baggage in its train. At a time when much of the scientific community *wanted* to banish the long-established belief that some special vital powers existed that enliven living organisms, Darwin's natural selection, based on his teaching that blind mechanism would suffice to somehow make brute matter live, was, so to speak, a godsend.[1]

But was it *true?* Does natural selection, in fact, account, as Darwin's book is entitled, for the *Origin of the* Species? Does it explain how an Earth teeming everywhere with bacteria and other micro-organisms could some eons later become populated by an overwhelmingly diverse Tree of Life, currently consisting, it is estimated of perhaps as many as 20 to 50 million different species?

Here is where the public discourse of evolution-as-the-only-rational-belief *versus* the dull-witted fundamentalists amounts to little more than a cartoon version of the controversy. For serious questions can be (and among biologists, are) raised regarding the adequacies of natural selection as an explanation of the vast biological diversity that speciation on the planet hath wrought.

To begin with, Darwin himself engaged in a bit of sleight-of-hand. His central examples of natural-selection-in-action refer primarily to how *variations* of one kind are "selected" over others. But having a slightly more elongated beak is one thing, becoming a whole new *species* something else.

---

[1] But see Sheldrake, *Presence of the Past,* pp. 272–74 for Darwin's own ambiguous beliefs on the matter, his own attraction to vitalistic powers in living creatures.

How do these come about? In other words, does the selection of longer-necked giraffes (as the hypothetical fruit grows higher off the ground over time) for countless generations of proto-giraffes, each with a slightly longer neck than its parents, or of increasingly darker-winged moths (as London's skies got darker from industrial soot) in time give rise to a new kind of animal or insect, unable to mate with its ancestor species? Just as the dog breeder is able to bring out numerous refinements of dogs, specialized breeds of a dazzling variety, but never create a brand-new creature that is not-dog, natural selection is capable of accounting for the more resplendent tail of a peacock, but *can* it explain how *Archaeopteryx* (fl. circa 160,000,000 years ago) gave rise to peacocks? (Here's where Lyell's millions of years came in handy — in enough time, anything in theory becomes possible.) But it is not clear that natural selection is up to that job. As some Neo-Darwinians like to point out, "extrapolating the gradual transitions of microevolution (red rose to yellow rose) could not explain macroevolution (worm to snakes)."[1]

To make speciation from natural selection more plausible, the principle of geological isolation is invoked: populations that are cut off by a new river or mountain range or where a peninsula becomes an island, and so are forced to evolve independently. All well and good, once life has come up onto the land, but what about earlier, when for the first few billion years of life on Earth it was only found in shallow seas where such isolation is harder to come by. How then did speciation occur? For it did, even if to a much less extent.

Explaining speciation is made considerably harder by the virtual lack of instances *per se* actually found in the fossil record. Fossils of different species are found in abundance; fossils of intermediaries, of what interceded between any two distinct species — missing in action. According to Ernst Mayr, the noted evolutionist, there exists "no clear evidence of any change of a species into a different species or for the gradual origin of any evolutionary novelty."[2] Most species, Stephen Jay Gould points out, far from showing "directional change" while on Earth, "appear in the fossil record looking much the same as when they disappear...." Species do not "arise gradually by the steady transformation" of ancestors, Gould observes, but "appear all at once and 'fully formed'." In other words, speciation is apparent in the successive layers of strata that can usually be dated, so *befores* and *afters* can be established. But how the befores *became* the afters, that is still, despite Darwin, rather a mystery.

---

[1] Kevin Kelly, "Deep Evolution," *Whole Earth Review*, no. 76 (Fall, 1992), p. 14.
[2] Jeremy Narby, *Ibid.*, p. 142. I am grateful to Chris Carlsson for bringing me to this important book.

Even within species, classic problems have dogged Darwinian evolution since its inception, such as the leaps required to believe that natural selection alone can account for some of the more outrageous of life's enormous feats. It is one thing to account for the giraffe's longer neck after countless generations of almost-giraffe ancestors, but something altogether different trying to understand how such gradual processes could lead to the evolution of sexual reproduction, warm-blooded metabolism, or web-building, where small incremental variations would presumably have *no* selective advantage until they were pretty well fully functional. Fitting these under the principles of natural selection stretch the theorizing of the Darwinians to the breaking point.

Another major problem with natural selection as an explanation of evolution is that it fails one of the major tests that, according to an influential theory of scientific inquiry, are critical for any theory to be considered scientific. Sir Karl Popper, the eminent British philosopher of science, has articulated the critical provision that any theory that purports to be *scientific* must *in principle* be refutable. That is, to count as science, it must be theoretically possible to disprove that theory by presenting contrary evidence, something altogether different, even contradictory to, what the theory predicts. One would be hard put to refute natural selection in such a manner. For *any* species that has established itself successfully in a given habitat has, by definition, demonstrated that it has the "right stuff," for it *has* survived. There are many plausible hypotheses, like the melanin that in humans comes with darker skin offering advantages *vis à vis* the scourge of malaria in Africa, but plausible hypotheses, even a great many of them, do not, particularly in Popper's terms, establish a scientific theory.

Thus natural selection emerges as something other than it has been made out to be. For one, it does not explain speciation, but rather, variation; two, we are at a loss to imagine any creature, no matter how outlandish, whose confirmed existence (now or in the distant past) does not demonstrate that its biological characteristics could be *assumed* to have provided it advantageous adaptability to its environment. So evolution by means of natural selection acts less as a theory and more, as Popper himself suggested, as a kind of heuristic or a metaphysical principle, a kind of finger pointing out directions in which to look to find how organisms might have adapted to their habitat, how complex the myriad of ways of being able to thrive, as creatures are wont to do. As a finger, invaluable; as a scientific theory in the P(r)opper sense, maybe not.

Does natural selection, then, actually describe how the natural order operates? In other words, leaving aside the possible tautological nature of natural selection, as well as the question of whether, properly speaking, natural selection is a way of understanding not speciation as much as individual characteristics, leaving those aside: is the purported mechanism of natural selection, how nature "blindly" diverges in one direction rather than another actually descriptive? Do the variations arise at random, and do some prevail because they provide greater success rates in continuity of ova and sperm unto successive generations? In a word, does nature, at the level of living creatures, operate by blind mechanism? For that is what Darwin is proposing, what natural selection was triumphantly declaring.

And here the Creationists might well have a point. To call *evolution* a mere hypothesis is to ignore substantial evidence of its existence — but insisting on natural selection as its sole motor force is more of a leap of faith, on the whole lacking substantial evidence to confirm it, and ignoring some striking counter-evidence.

The mutations which we now believe are the basis of any new variations emerging have been theorized as purely random, despite the fact that overwhelmingly, mutations (mistakes in copying the DNA or broken chromosomes) tend to be *damaging* to organisms. Moreover, experimental evidence exists of the opposite, that is, organisms that appear to have acquired certain mutations *purposefully*!

A strain of *E. Coli* in 1988 was deprived of food but put on a medium with a sugar the bacteria were biologically unable to metabolize, mutations then took place that provided the enzyme needed to be able to digest it, a result that was statistically extremely unlikely. "This experiment," the three scientists reported, "suggests that populations of bacteria... have some way of producing (or selectively retaining) only the most appropriate mutations."[1] In the same issue of *Nature,* another scientist commented that their work could support "the iconoclastic view that bacteria have mechanisms [NB] for making just those mutations that adapt the cell to an available energy source."[2] The mutation was at a rate about 100 million times greater than would be statistically expected if it came about by chance. Why *that* particular mutation would appear at *that* moment is not something natural selection can explain. Debates regarding the adequacy of natural selection do occur among biologists. Such discourses need to become more public.

In physics, (the powerful arbiter of what-is-real), Bell's Theorem and its experimental confirmation,[3] the phenomenon of quantum entanglement, have effectively demonstrated what Einstein considered "spooky actions at a dis-

---

1 John Cairns, Julie Overbaugh, and Stephen Miller, "The Origin of Mutants," *Nature* 335 (8 September 1988), pp. 142–45; Rupert Sheldrake, *The Rebirth of Nature: The Greening of Science and God.*

2 Franklin W. Stahl, "Bacterial Genetics: A Unicorn in the Garden," *Nature,* no. 335 (8 September 1988), pp. 112. Barry G. Hall, "Adaptive Evolution That Requires Multiple Spontaneous Mutations," *Genetics,* (December, 1988), pp. 887–97.

3 Kaiser, *op. cit.*

tance,"[1] instances of non-local causation; Newton's bugaboo, too, was it not? Effects and causes, separated by vast distances, appear, however, to act instantly — monstrous to most scientists because it might imply a kind of sentience in nature. Weird though such notions might appear, their oddity pales compared to the bizarre nature of so much of quantum mechanics and relativity theory — travel between two places that occurs without a trajectory! Time that ceases to exist at the center of a black hole! Fluids that "climb" out of containers near 0°K! Or the mystery of the Big Bang itself, the strangeness of it all, koans of creation! It is time for the scientific community to face up to considerable evidence for this most-feared notion, that nature is not a mere automata of cams and gears, or of causal chains in space and in time whereby one thing becomes another,[2] but is at times and in ways we do not understand a self-actualizing being into the bargain — whatever that might mean.

But of course to say this is to understand our relationship with nature in an altogether different way, as indeed we must if we are to survive. It is to attempt learning and using the language of the natural world, her fauna and flora, her rocks and rivers, her great moving masses of roiling clouds travelling on ferocious winds as a different kind of presence, as agent rather than object. This, of course, is what the shamans have been saying all along.[3] It is this story that modern societies, after centuries of purposely banning it, need to heed, even as we continue to go on figuring out what it all means, but armed in our times with the Erlenmeyer flasks and our electron microscopes to enable deeper insights into this fearsome universe we have the adventure to participate in.

iv. EARTHEN LUNGS, EARTHEN SPINE?

At any rate, the Earth's being alive most probably has more than a metaphorical significance, and there might be distinct terrestrial "physiologies" that should be considered, maybe even protected. For instance, it has been suggested that there are (as Newton as a young man surmised, though in a different form) elaborate "breathing mechanisms" whereby huge amounts of air are "inhaled" and then "exhaled" on a daily basis in the vast cavern system of the Colorado plateau, and that, along with their diametrically opposite Tibetan counterparts, these play vital roles in planetary weather patterns.[4] Had those caverns become the primary repository of the US's radioactive wastes, as was

---

[1] *Ibid.*, p. 30.

[2] Jim Holt, "Something Faster Than Light? What Is It?" *New York Review of Books* (Novmeber 10, 2016). It might be wise to lead all classical imagery, with its mechanistic underpinnings, to a long-overdue retirement home, to be kept alive in textbooks as object-lessons in arrogance and in shortsighted priorities.

[3] Abram, *op. cit.*

[4] At the conference "Is the Earth a Living Organism?" (Amherst College, August, 1985).

once the plan by the US government, how might that have affected such a Gaian respiratory system?

Or consider the Mid-Ocean Ridge structure (M.O.R.), a 40,000-mile-long series of underwater volcanic vents at the bottom and centers of most of the Earth's oceans, that winds around the globe, ending up somewhere in the Aleutians, not very far from where it begins in the seas of Siberia. Arguably, the M.O.R. can be seen as the "backbone" or seam of our "vertebrate" planet, a nerve center responsible, as it so strikingly is, for virtually the whole of Gaian dynamics. For the M.O.R. is where a continual creation of new ocean floor, out of the recycled magma of subducted ocean crust, pushes the tectonic plates, their movement, in turn, responsible for continental drift and earthquakes, while the subduction feeds volcanic mountain formation, for starters. And it has been suggested by many scientists that the M.O.R. might even be where life on Earth originally began.[1] How will such hypothetical terrestrial "physiologies" or any others still to be found fare under the various assaults on nature under way?

At any rate, the monstrous notion that nonlife is the essence of matter everywhere, as we have seen, has historically been used to inflict all manner of abuse and suffering on the various inhabitants of the planet — from the microbes in the soil to the human toilers deep within her mines.

Some scientists, especially lately, are beginning to voice hesitant support for something like this second of the contexts I am proposing, returning to earlier *panspermic* notions that forms of life exist everywhere in nature. Indeed, complex organic molecules *are* found deep in outer space and some scientists now propose that the "seeds" of life may have come to the primitive Earth initially (as Newton seems to have believed) on the comets that over an extended period frequently bombarded the infant Earth. And forms of

---

1 Elsewhere I have described the M.O.R. as a terrestrial dragon, for charted across the sea floors, it does look like one, even having what looks like two short legs that go north and northwest on its one side and southwest on the other (the Cape of Good Hope dividing them). After passing Australia and New Zealand, the M.O.R. heads across the South Pacific Ocean and then abruptly turns towards the coast of South America, reaching land somewhere in Baja California and forming the San Andreas fault system and then the Ring of Fire *just where* the dragon's "tail" would be. In Chinese culture, "dragon currents" are seen as carrying specific terrestrial energies and are the basis of *Feng shui*. The only place the M.O.R. rises above the ocean floor is on an island off of Iceland, called, interestingly, "Dragon's Head Island." (Kubrin, "The Dragon Tracked to His Lair?" *W.I.S.E. Newsletter*, Autumn; 1986; this is an expanded version of an article originally published in *The Ley Hunter* and in *Reclaiming Newsletter* in 1986. See also William M. Kaula, "The Earth as a Planet" for the M.O.R. as a dragon (*Geophysical Monograph* 60, IOGG vol. 10, 1990), though wholly in a metaphoric sense.

life have recently been found in places, such as deep beneath the surface of the continents, that are completely unexpected in traditional biology. A jump to the view that matter is pregnant with life, as Newton held, may not, in times like these, be much of a leap at all.

v. SCIENCE & ITS COLONIALIST PAST

Allowing for a kaleidoscope-like multiplicity of truths might actually serve the historic role of allowing the scientific community to make amends for some grave lapses committed as it struggled centuries ago to be born. At the birth of classical Western science in early modern times, it was, overwhelmingly, an enterprise of males and nearly altogether European. Partly this was for social reasons, a matter of what kinds of people were given the *privilege* of being admitted to the *doing* of science. It was in part also for theoretical or ideological reasons, because both women and people of color would presumably be reluctant to abandon their beliefs (which at one point were nearly universally held) that nature was alive. Those who held such views certainly could not be allowed to enter the Temple of Science, they would only sully it.

In recent decades the old exclusion has loosened considerably, for if one goes to the science departments of major US universities or museums, research labs, certain technical industries, or the foundations that increasingly fund the above, women and people of color are certainly allowed to participate, if not in equal numbers or necessarily having tenure or full professorships (or even an office) in the extended institutions that make up the larger scientific community. Though permitted entrance into that community, for the most part they have not been granted the privilege of being there on the basis of the animist principles on which, historically, their cultures had been based, for admission to the citadels of science, has to be on the basis of the reductionistic principles of mechanical science. *If* those newcomers were able to pass the catechism regarding those matters and the inert cosmos they would be trained to study, they could be allowed in, the scientific elites, like elites elsewhere, conceded from the 1970s on. Those historically excluded from science thus won the *privilege of participating,* but *not* the principle of *doing so on their own methodological and conceptual grounds.*

Some might argue that the rationale for the exclusion of certain principles, the insistence on a number of "givens" regarding objective, passive matter, for example, was because only in this way was Western science able to establish itself. That is certainly true of science after the Restoration. In the 16th and earlier 17th century, however, such was not the case. Magical ideas can be found in many of the seminal thinkers; Newton was not alone in this regard. And unlike Western science, alchemy was pursued by women as well as men.[1] One of the ancient seers of the alchemical craft was said to be Maria the Jewess, for example, and Helvetius' astounding transmutation was performed by him and his wife, herself knowledgeable about the craft. Also, the Rosicrucian movement was quite explicit about establishing its reform of all knowledge on the basis of cabala, alchemy, and the teachings ot the East.

Moreover, it is clear that in the case of the indigenous people of New England, scientists such as Robert Boyle (and I think we may safely assume others) played up the role Western science could play in their subjugation. The new science was for Boyle a weapon to use in England's plan to profit from the resources and the labor of the "savage Indians" in New England. To this end Boyle promoted ridding the minds of Native Americans "of their ridiculous Notions about the workings of nature and of the fond and superstitious practices these Errors engaged them to."[2] "Passive" matter, as I have argued all along, was the emblem behind which those who set out to "tame" the land — whether it was through mining, deforestation, fen-draining, or establishing plantations — had marched. It was to get access to those lands that subjugation of the indigenous people was necessary in the first place.

Thus, to exclude from scientific investigation the cultural principles of the women and people of color who have finally been given the privilege to enter is to continue that same battle on different grounds. It is to prevent any notion of an animated world from being seriously considered, so as to keep intact the 400-year-old walls, erected to enable science to enclose off its unique domains, where certain inquiries about the world could be made, where it could be assumed that nature would willingly lay supine on the lab table and wouldn't squirm, would not *be active.*

Tear down those walls, some will fear, and science itself might disappear. Keep them up, others (myself included) will argue, and the crimes of racism and sexism, as well as justification for subjugation of the land, are perpetuated.

How to resolve this tension will not be easy, for in defining just what could be in and what had to be excluded, Western science from the middle of the 17th century on carved out a preserve from which magic would be excluded. In large measure, this was the purpose of the walls. It was important to delineate how Western knowledge about nature was superior to native notions that believed such nonsense as that trees could talk or nature spirits convey power. It was important, too, as Part Two showed, because the experience of the English Civil War and revolution had demonstrated how magic and imagination could both whip up the flames of insurgency and draw forth an understanding of how things might be made different, so that, as the Rosicrucians insisted,

---

1 See Chapter 11. Also, Meridith K. Ray, *Daughters of Alchemy: Women and Scientific Culture in Early Modern Italy* (Cambridge, Mass.: Harvard University Press, 2015).

2 J.R. Jacob, "The New England Company, the Royal Society and the Indians," *Notes and Letters* (n.d.), p. 453.

everyone, and not just the already privileged, *through* science, would be healed of their illnesses, share in the reform of knowledge, and benefit from the wealth newly generated on the basis of the new learning.

There is one more aspect of this matter of mechanism vs. animism to consider. In the early 1990s I attended a lecture by a Native American physicist at the Bay Area science museum, the Exploratorium, where the scientist, Eric Jolly, wove a basket in the traditional manner, just as his grandmother had taught him, while explaining the many mathematical and scientific principles implicit in his grandmother's (and his tribe's) teachings. That this was so I did not doubt, but I also knew there was a fundamental difference between traditional teachings and what he would have learned as a professional physicist: Native American traditional knowledge (as among the indigenous people of the world, in general, whether in the Americas, Oceania, Africa, or, indeed, at one time, Europe) was always pursued within a *sacred* context, while in the West, since the suppression of the Rosicrucians (and in a related way the pilloring, then apotheosis, of Galileo), scientific knowledge has taken pains precisely to establish its independence of any such context, to stand seemingly above everything but the "truth" of nature — though, as we saw in Part Two, that was often not the case and a context, religious, social, political, philosophical, etc. — was implictly present. In the case of the indigenous peoples, the sacred context was mostly of some form of magic.

Accordingly, Western science really stands at a crossroads. One path leads, as before, away from questions such as these about the lifefulness of things and into an impassioned denial, *in principle,* that such powers of an animate world *could conceivably* exist. It is not an empirical question, really.[1] Any example can be denied, if not on one basis, then on another. (Thus, in recent years, one of the scientists associated with the camp of the scoffers, when presented with unassailable evidence of a pronounced, statistically significant, tendency for results indicating a form of ESP had occurred in a controlled experiment, told the press that it meant *nothing* because the researchers had not explained *how* the effect worked — as if, in fact, science purported to explain how gravity worked, or quantum mechanics, or relativity or any of the rest of it, as if Newton had not successfully claimed, in the end, that he did not have to explain *how* gravitation worked, it was sufficient simply to demonstrate its effects.) People of non-European cultures will, no doubt, still be admitted into the fields of science, but only if they agree to play by the traditional rules along this path.

Another path, a radical path, would proceed on the basis of a realization of the need, given the historical moment, to change directions, to seek some

---

[1] The noted 19th-century physiologist Hermann von Helmholtz proclaimed that "[n]either the testimony of all the fellows of the Royal Society nor even the evidence of my own sense, would lead me to believe in the transmission of thought from one person to another [telepathy].... It is clearly impossible." Sheldrake, *Science Set Free,* p. 232.

kind of rapprochement with non-Western points of view, with the magic that historically has animated the cultures that stood in the way of the Western project to subjugate those lands and peoples. Such a radical path is obviously not without dangers, and running battles have been fought within organizations such as the American Association for the Advancement of Science (AAAS) against its moves in the early 1970s to allow unorthodox forms of "science" into its annual meetings. Yet, it is also true that the old path is racially and culturally specific and has been complicit in the attacks on the lifefulness of the world. To stay on that path is to be out of phase with the rest of humanity. Accordingly, it presents dangers of another kind.

vi. Uncocking the Rifle of Species-Suicide

The adoption of the three contexts or premises that I outlined above (first that we be made privy to scientists' inner musings; second that the matter of the cosmos, indeed, the cosmos itself, is lifelike or at least pregnant with life; and third that science shows us only one of several facets of the universe, which is knowable in more ways than one) are essential if we are to utilize science, and its cousin, technology, without being enslaved to them — as culturally and socially, we are at the present. Yet these propositions, as I have indicated, will strike many in the scientific community, because of its history, as recipes for disaster. That is because these propositions utterly defy fundamentally important conventions adopted at the very beginnings of science's ascent to the dominant position it presently occupies in the intellectual cosmology of our culture.

To enable science to function as it has for the past four to five hundred years, its practitioners came to think that it was necessary to abstract physical reality into passive, law-abiding, component parts, and for these to make sense, all vitality had to be removed from physical matter, all sentience; passive matter can, indeed, act in a law-like manner, as, of course, can passive people, the ultimate target of this doctrine. Passive matter, in turn, turned every thing, every process even, into *objects*, which allowed scientific methodology to march behind the much-waved flag of objectivity. To bring into question, nay, deny the premise of passive matter now will be to court disasters, some will fear, striking at the very foundations of science itself.

Secondly, to pose the question whether science should occupy the only stage in the theater of our knowledge might appear to undermine a major historical claim at the core of Western culture — that, being "objective," science alone among all of the ways of viewing the world could offer *the* truth, could provide us with certainty, discovering lessons that everyone had to accept, unless, of course, they had "taken leave of their senses." To now relinquish that claim, to be satisfied with putting science on the same footing, say, as a pretty poem, to recognize the "truth" good art is able to convey, might appear as essentially abandoning the search for knowledge itself.

In other words, such resistance to my three contexts, though certainly unfortunate, would be perfectly understandable, for these premises, necessary though they might be, will inevitably transform the very nature of scientific inquiry — and therefore, almost everything else. Precisely so, since it has been the argument of this study that it was the particular forms taken by Western science that have rendered us potential witnesses of our own extinction. We are like the proverbial condemned prisoner hearing the rifles being cocked — except, to a certain extent, it has been we, collectively, who do the cocking. Radical changes *are* needed if science and technics are truly to serve the cause of the continuity of life on the planet, rather than the cause of death. We *must* uncock the rifle. We *have* no alternative plan. By agreeing to a multifaceted vision of what is *real,* a new science will be accepting that at bottom much of existence is a mystery, as it is. We may inquire as we will, some of what we want to know may forever elude us. It is foolish to counterpose such mystery to knowledge, as if they were opposites or sworn enemies, for we should realize that at the center of knowledge there is true mystery, just as at the center of mystery there is true knowledge. It is foolish to radically separate them.

Lest this be construed as an apology for obscurantism, let me point out that in virtually every field of inquiry — economics, law, music, government, education, and physics, for examples — central actors in their respective learned or aesthetic discourses are fundamentally surrounded by shrouds of uncertainty as to their core meanings: respectively, "money," "tort," "harmony," State, "learning," and "time," for starters, so that discussions of economics, law, music, etc. rest on essentially perilous foundations. Economic debates unclear about what money really *is,* for instance — or any of the myriad of other foundational concepts in any number of topics — will necessarily yield comprehensions that must coexist with a core measure of uncertainty, and are accordingly mysterious; contrarily, I believe, many of these mysteries are rooted in a profound measure of understanding, if not of the answers, at least of what the major questions should be. Indeed, we might recognize a subtle dialectics that relates mystery to that which is knowable. Knowledge as such would be respected, but, in keeping with our second premise, it would be the explicit goal of that knowledge to honor and serve the continuation of the Earth as a planet where the rich dance of life can go on and on.

vii. VALUE-FREE INVESTMENTS

Knowledge is not, as we have been led to believe, some disembodied entity that emerges from the purported "value-free inquiries" engaged in by creative and free spirits. Instead of trying to mask the real interests and committments of those engaging in inquiry of some kind or other, we should coax them out into the open, demand that the inquiry be honest and not simply answer the easy and obvious questions. Implicit values as well as institutional ties and aspirations of investigators should be acknowledged and articulated, the better to enable others to evaluate the merits of their work. Articulating one's intentions should not excuse slanted presentation or skewed evidence. Rather, it is hoped that it would make an altogether illusory "objectivity" a tad more substantial by embedding it within an acknowledged subjectivity. Admittedly this notion of an embedded objectivity is utterly utopian, but it is also, in the present circumstances, utterly necessary, for notions of "objectivity" have effectively been put through the corporate shredders, now that the venture capitalists are in the labs as well as the conference rooms, and tens of millions of dollars of investments are riding on what the data is said to show.

In the face of Monsanto, Cargill, Genentech, and Big Pharma, in league to carve up the genomic terrain, their claims now staked into our collective flesh, a brand new scientific world is gestating on the basis especially of biotech. Indeed, a new historical figure has emerged, the scientist/entrepreneur (spawned first in Silicon Valley and along Route 128 around Boston in the '50s and after with the seeding of electronic spinoffs from the Stanfords and MITs), now firmly embedded in the culture of biotech, these men and women equally comfortable in lab coats or pin-striped suits, are purveying their genomic wares; the "better ones" may spin off three or more corporate entities like "in real life" avatars to market his or her breakthrough discoveries.[1] The universities want their shares, as well, the increasingly corporatized institutions of "higher" education making sure that their interests are well-represented by the armies of lawyers negotiating these shameless selling of our bodies, insisting on their proprietary rights to "their" ideas, so they can capitalize directly from the biotech products and processes devised by their professorial or research staffs.

Thus, the "truth" — which has been the preserve of universities, their historic mandate, as they have seen it in the West for some time — now comes obviously encumbered in huge financial gains/losses that will accrue to one party or the other as this theory or that one proves to win the day (and the patent rights). Any pretense of "objectivity" or of "value-free" inquiry under such circumstances is preposterous. The litigation we can look forward to as patents, priorities, or applications are inevitably contested, along with the march of PhDs to testify on both sides, should, however, be rather entertaining, courtroom melodramas in academic mufti (and ripe for the picking by Reality TV).

Under conditions of the production of knowledge like these it is clear that notions of "peer review" for publication of journal articles or awarding of tenure[2] or fellowships, when a number of the parties involved have sub-

---

1 These doings are nicely described in Hilary Rose and Steven Rose, *op. cit.*
2 The contested tenure fight of Prof. Ignacio Chapela at UC Berkeley in 2004 is a vivid example of what is involved. Chapela had a unanimous tenure

stantial financial interests in the outcome, are ludicrous. Indeed, when different universities (or even factions within a department) have proprietary interests in alternative visions of the genomic realms, department meetings might well become like a subspecies of proxy fights at yearly corporate stockholders' meetings!

If, as has been the case for the past 350 years or so, the methods of science become, willy-nilly, the methods of nearly everyone else, then we can look forward to seeing these dynamics, at present mostly concentrated in microbiology departments, taking over academic debate in general, and we can ponder individual corporate sponsorship of contending social, political, or philosophical views — indeed, many corporations are *already* stepping up to name professorships of this or that in the name of their enterprises. Sponsored "research" can conjure up the answers wanted, as was discovered of two Harvard professors in the mid-1960s who under sugar-industry funding challenged the notion that sugar consumption might lead to cardiovascular disease by "demonstrating" the supposed far-greater threat posed by cholesterol, initiating a major shift away from butter to margarine and other polyunsaturated fats and various "non-fat"nostrums. The scientists, one of whom was Chair of the Nutrition Department at Harvard, wrote to sugar-industry representatives "We are well aware of your particular interest — and will cover this as well as we can," before delivering a paper in the 1967 *New England Journal of Medicine* that critiqued reputed links between sugar consumption and heart problems.[1]

Under such conditions, an embedded "objectivity" might work by providing the impetus for presentations that place an extra burden of proof on "favored" theories. Such signposts, I believe, will be critical if we are to find a path enabling us to make our way into a viable future.[2]

viii. WHY WAS IT AN APPLE?

Frequently, political activists on the left counterpose "symbolic" protests or actions to "real" ones, believing that these actually lie at two different

---

recommendation from his *department,* but in a highly unusual turn, the tenure committee of the *university,* headed by a professor whose professional interests were hurt by Chapela's researches critical of the claims by biotech firms as to the safety of their experimental plantings, denied tenure. After a lengthy political and legal battle, Chapela prevailed.

[1] Victoria Colliver, "Efforts to shift science on sugar," San Francisco *Chronicle* (September 13, 2016). Editorial: "Science is soured by sugar dollars," San Francisco *Chronicle* (September 14, 2016).

[2] On a conceptual terrain where multiple "truths" are allowed to cohabit, some criteria are necessary to be able to distinguish beliefs that are defensible from ones that can be rejected out-of-hand. Feyerabend in *Science in a Free Society* offers some guidance.

poles. They believe symbolic actions make merely formal statements about the matters being protested, perhaps by "symbolically" interfering with particular kinds of business-as-usual operations. Nothing "real" actually gets changed. For example, the historic 1967 blockade of the Pentagon by opponents of the Indochinese War, because it occurred on the weekend, when most Pentagon workers were not there, was criticized by some at the time as "only" symbolic.

This polarization between *real* and *symbolic,* I hope to show, is false, because at a very deep political and magical level, reality *is* symbolic. Among the rulers of our society, the symbolic nature of reality is intuitively grasped, as we saw in Chapter 28 above in the case of Henry Kissinger, no doubt learned at their prep schools and in their training to be debutantes, if not, indeed, at their nannies' chests. Their actions and priorities, when they grow up and assume their "rightful" responsibilities, continually demonstrate this.

Let us look at some of those actions to illustrate what I mean. The Paris Peace Talks that were announced by President Lyndon B. Johnson in the speech he gave (after the Tet Offensive) in April, 1968, in which he also declared his decision not to run for re-election, demonstrates this with remarkable clarity. Many Americans were extremely optimistic at first that at long last the horrendous war in Southeast Asia might be over, but they saw their hopes get knotted up in what was obviously bureaucratic muddleheadedness, as the negotiations bogged down for months in what seemed to be utterly senseless squabbling over the *shape* of the table for the negotiations (should the opposing sides ever get around to *that*). Endless quibbling over the table's desired shape was the source of much anger and countless jokes and editorial cartoons as the public and the press incredulously saw their elected leaders haggle over what was obviously a minor detail, nothing getting accomplished while dead bodies, US, Vietnamese, and others, continued to pile up.

Yet, the arguments over the shape *were* the negotiations, and rightfully so, for the shape of the table would embody the very matters the negotiations had to resolve. The war began, many will remember, when the US moved to direct and then take over the military response to what had begun as an indigenous rebellion in the southern part of Vietnam against the corrupt, landlord-backed, US-sponsored "national" leadership, essentially picked in New York City. The US had moved to make permanent the 1954 temporary division of Vietnam into southern and northern parts, which were to be reunited in the elections in 1956 that the '54 Indochinese Peace Accords had mandated. Because all parties realized that Ho Chi Minh would win any such elections, the US refused to allow them, then blamed the resultant rebellion that broke out in the now-angry southern provinces on its usual menace of "outside agitators" — these, it turned out, from the northern provinces. Thus, to the US government, the war *was* two-sided, North against the South, and the National Liberation Front (the "Viet Cong"), based in the South, was a mere front for the North, a different country altogether. The US was simply assisting the legitimate government of South Vietnam in defending itself and in "nation-building." For the US, this "reality" was central to its political and diplomatic, as well as its military, strategy, especially when its military effort to make this "reality" a *fait accompli* was buried in the Tet Offensive. A rectangular table would reflect the US-reality, one end for the South (which would include its ally, the US) and another for the "North," those outsiders who had dared to invade their own country, including their fraudulent "National Liberation Front."

For the National Liberation Front, who began the rebellion in the first place, reality was altogether different. From the beginning they had insisted that their efforts were indigenous to the southern part of the country, and that the aid they got from the northern part was merely supportive of what were, or at least began as, essentially local efforts. Moreover, since the division of Vietnam by the 1954 Accords was temporary, aid from the northern half in no way transformed the civil war in Vietnam into anything like the international conflict the US insisted it was. The only real "outsiders" in the war were the US (and Korean, Australian, and other allied) troops. It was the US which had imported from the outside a puppet government subservient to its own Cold War obsessions about falling dominoes. For the National Liberation Front and North Vietnamese, a circular table would reflect the political realities of the war, which *de facto* had several "sides," including the National Liberation Front, the South Vietnamese puppet government, the North Vietnamese, and the outsiders, the US. All should sit *around* the table and negotiate.

Thus for the negotiators arguments about the shape of the table, far from being a side show, were the *kernel* of the affair, for it was necessary to clarify the central *political* question the war had failed to resolve before other matters could be considered. Accordingly, spending months on this thorny issue of shape was justifiable. On January 17, 1969, nearly a year after Tet, 1968, "both" sides finally agreed to expand the initial negotiations, which had begun between the US and North Vietnam, to include now both the South Vietnamese government and the National Liberation Front, all parties to sit, though without flags or nameplates, at a *round* table.

We can also see the deep understanding of the powers of symbols by ruling circles in the rituals designed around the first construction of a civilian nuclear power facility in the US, in Shippingport, Pennsylvania. On national TV, President Eisenhower in a Denver studio touched a "magic wand" with a radioactive tip to a sensor, thereby activating an automated power shovel 1,300 miles away (in Shippingport) that dug the first symbolic shovelful of dirt.[1] At that ritualized moment in our culture, when in initiating any new edifice to Progress, power traditionally celebrates itself, Eisenhower's actions

---

[1] Hilgartner, Bell, and O'Connor, *Nukespeak*, pp. 44–45.

were consciously designed to say it all: automation, the apotheosis of the new medium, TV, remote sensing, the national implications of the new power of the atom, all put in motion by a military hero, the winner of World War II. Indeed, the magic of it all!

Corporate, political, and military leaders generally have sure instincts when it comes to picking the right time and place for initiating policy so that a precise symbolic message is clearly sent. On more than one occasion, President Johnson chose to escalate the air war against North Vietnam exactly at the moment when foreign delegations were in Hanoi, hoping to facilitate the setting up of negotiations, negating Johnson's *public* proclamation of his willingness to negotiate an end to hostilities. His words, repeated dutifully by the press, said one thing, his actions, aimed at the Vietnamese and foreign governments, who are practiced in this kind of "conversation," clearly conveyed the opposite meaning, that of his fundamental opposition to a cessation of the war on any grounds except that of a total US victory.

Other politicians similarly are astute at using symbolic language. Chairnan Gorbachev picked the same town in Missouri, Fulton, where Winston Churchill in 1947 announced the onset of the "Cold War," to inform the world that it had finally ended. Bill Clinton chose the very morning when a Los Angeles jury found Los Angeles police officers guilty in the second Rodney King trial to have the White House articulate his sympathy for victims of crime and to repeat his campaign call for 100,000 more cops on the streets. Ronald Reagan's campaign for president was kicked off with a speech in Philadelphia, Mississippi, for most observers an arbitrary choice, but an obvious statement of his solidarity with Southern racists, since in 1964 Philadelphia was where the KKK had brutally lynched James Chaney, Michael Schwerner, and Andrew Goodman, CORE members in the Mississippi Freedom Summer Project to struggle for voting rights for the black population.

At times popular forces seem to grasp the reality of the fight over symbols, unapologetically striking their blows and taking their stands in a kind of theater of insurgency, as in several episodes during the 1968 revolt in Paris — or in Paris, 1789, for that matter; as with many of the Yippie! actions in the US in the '60s or in San Francisco the work of the Diggers, as well as the original Diggers in the late 1640s; or the dramatic use of giant puppets for street theater that was a vital part of the Seattle anti-WTO blockade in 1999 and in other anti-globalization mobilizations since. Frequently a symbolic theme is built into the core of actions, as, say, when activists march from one symbol of State oppression to another, making indelible the frequently mystified connection between the two.

More common, I am afraid, is a timidity, a fear that the creative use of the imagination might distract from the "real" struggle, and so a reluctance to develop an art (and hence a magic) of insurgency. A major reason for such timidity, I believe, is the spiritual void in much of left culture, a void that in itself is testimony to the oppositional forces allying themselves long ago (in the case of the Marxist left, more firmly and with fewer reservations than Capital, it sometimes appears) with mechanical science and an apotheosis of Progress — and so an aversion to matters of the spirit, at least in their metaphysics.

On questions regarding the use of political symbolism, magic, not unexpectedly, has important things to say, for at the core of magic is the truism that reality has a symbolic kernel with which one can creatively engage. This is where my work as a witch in the West Coast anti-nuclear movement in the 1980s might be able to illuminate alternative approaches to political opposition and organizing, the subject of the next chapter.

32

Spells Against the Empire

i. Catching a Broomstick to the Insurrection

As mentioned earlier, about a decade after becoming aware of the role of magic in the English Civil War and revolution, I was invited to join an affinity group that would use magic as part of our political struggle against the threats of nuclear weapons and power. Just what does it mean that I agreed? That we would "use magic" in pursuit of what we considered justice and an end to imperialist wars?

I had come to believe that returning to an ancient animist belief rooted in the living energies of the biosphere is an important step in treating those deeply-ingrained beliefs and practices that sicken our culture, producing devastating imbalances that threaten all of life. But what would that mean politically? How could those archaic notions about vital forces in nature strengthen opposition to the social forces molding our many lives to their market-driven contours, as those notions must if magic is to have any significance whatsoever? What could magic help bring to pass in our struggles for liberation, for an end to this oppression or that — or for all of them? I have recounted how throughout history many shamans, witches and midwives at times had political and social agendas: since our predicament demands a protracted struggle against those at the controls, for they are clearly steering in the wrong directions, what would our agendas look like and what could an animist perspective lend to these struggles? In short, does a philosophical commitment to magic help in one's political organizing? Does it affect one's will to resist? One's strategy or tactics? What might witches, specifically, do to foment revolution?

In 1981, in connection with a planned blockade of the Diablo Canyon nuclear power plant under construction, several witches formed Matrix, an affinity group[1] and later a coven. In the more than eight years of Matrix's

---

[1] A unit of political organization first used in the Spanish Civil War of the '30s, affinity groups were adapted for use in the US by the New Left in the early '70s.

operation, we explored the forms political magic might take in the fight against the dominant political and economic powers in US society, and the worldwide capitalist system for which they stood. Since it was in this group that most of my work of this kind was carried out, our experiences necessarily will serve to guide my discussion.

It is important that I not be understood as pointing to witchcraft for doctrinal reasons, implying that our path, or the path of paganism in general, represents *the* path. Such is not my intent. For a variety of reasons, it happened to be the way for me. So I simply know it better. But I have no doubt there are other, equally valid, paths, ones guided by kindred spirits.

There is a deeper problem. Written from the point of view of what I experienced, particularly in our campaign against nuclear power and weapons, my discussion comes out all wrong, screaming me! me! in every paragraph. Inasmuch as I was able to experience and do some extraordinary things, because of our magic, such me!s may be somewhat inevitable. Bear in mind that my magical powers are rather pedestrian. Yet, when it is critical, like when loved ones are seriously ill, or in the political campaign this chapter will focus on, when I was pushed to do far more than I am normally capable of, I have often surprised myself. Which is to say that there were important things to be done, no one else to do them, and with the help of a lot of others, I was able to make myself a vehicle to bring magical power to a focus.

Matrix did our organizing within the cauldron of a partially successful anti-nuclear movement in California (and elsewhere) in the '80s. Often working with other affinity groups or individuals, from the beginning we engaged in magical rituals in the hills overlooking the Diablo Canyon construction site, frequently as an offshoot of mass protest by thousands who had come for a weekend of rallying and civil disobedience. Getting into the hills for our rituals involved dodging surveillance from mounted security forces and helicopters, hiking on moonless nights in the back country, guides to help us try to avoid the many patches of poison oak.

Whenever we did magic about the nuclear plant, first and foremost we built safeguards in psychic space to prevent the facility from ever running amok, as nuclear power is prone to do; even more, we tried to ensure that the plant would never run. One such hex was done a few days before the famous discovery that the blueprints used in the construction had a right-to-left reversal for the piping supports, an absolutely critical component in the earthquake-ridden country where Diablo Canyon was ridiculously sited. That discovery gave opponents of the facility a three-year reprieve before a license would (alas) eventually be issued.

It would be a mistake to think this discovery was *because* of the magic we did; it would also be a mistake to discount the magic. Many thousands of us had been mobilized on all kinds of levels to oppose this ecological monstrosity being built in our midst. Marches, petitions, appeals to politicians, speeches, letters to editors, civil disobedience, etc. amounted to a considerable social force. As I have pointed out, magic can act like a metaphysical WD–40, loosening up the joints of history so they can move more easily. But without that social force, motion is less likely. It is helpful to see magic as perhaps helping to facilitate certain outcomes over others, using energy to nudge the playing out of reality in certain directions.

In a variety of ways, at the Diablo construction site, in jail after being arrested for civil disobedience, or back in the Bay Area afterwards, Matrix led or helped in rituals and group trances, cast spells as protections from the nuclear perils, especially but not exclusively focusing our imagery on the Diablo installation. After actions, such as those at Diablo, or at Vandenberg Air Force Base where the Minuteman II missiles were then being tested, or at Lawrence Livermore National Laboratory, the facility whose expertise, as we saw it,[1] lay in designing ever-more-horrific forms of nuclear Armageddon, it became our practice if incarcerated to conduct rituals and workshops on magic in the jails — particularly in the women's jails, where in numbers and experience Matrix members were stronger. In fact, some of our best magic was done inside the jails.

During one fifteen-day incarceration after a blockade of Livermore Lab, I was pretty much pushed into what was, for me, an unprecedented level of magical work, serving as some kind of vessel for powers that I apparently had in Matrix, learned how to tap into. Nearly a thousand of us, more women than men, were arrested on June 21 and 22, 1983. The authorities put us in nearby Santa Rita jail. Not all of us were in for the whole fifteen days, but most of us were. The day of the action and our initial arrests was Summer Solstice,[2] a day of power that the anti-nuclear movement organizations had planned the action around.

My extended description of our incarceration and what happened should help answer the questions this chapter started with — how might a belief in magic be relevant to, or even compatible with, a politics of resistance or revolution? In a sense, Santa Rita was where I truly began to function as a witch.

Much to our continuing amusement, since it played into the ongoing politics, theater, and utterly surreal edge of our non-violent war against the war machine, the authorities had decided to incarcerate us 1,000 prisoners in circus tents they rented for the occasion, two for the men and one for the

---

[1] After reading Eric Schlosser's masterful *Command and Control* (2014), I learned that at least a few of the bomb designers were trying, mostly unsuccessfully, to make the thermonuclear warheads less prone to accidental detonations. Assurances issued by officials that such accidents are impossible is mere PR.

[2] Many antinuclear actions at the time were scheduled on solstices or equinoxes, the holy days of the pagan year.

women, about 200 yards away from ours, space in the regular jail was either not available or deemed politically unwise.

Since it was Solstice, once we were all in custody and had been issued our single blanket and given a baloney sandwich dinner, several of us witches led rituals in both the men's and women's tents the first evening. In the men's quarters, it was planned mainly by Roy, another member of Matrix, with a little help from me — and Wally and Luis joined in to take parts in the ritual when we conducted it. All of us had pagan backgrounds and Wally was a witch from a different tradition than ours. In jail all of us had agreed to be part, along with about ten other men, of the same "cluster."[1] About 80 men (out of approximately 450) showed up the first night in detention to participate in a ritual of empowerment and a victory in our campaign against nuclear threat, as well as making contact with one another, that we had planned; for most of them. I would think it was the first time they had been part of a rite that was not part of one of the mainstream religions or State-sponsored.

Our ritual came right after a Jewish sabbath that had begun to conjure up the spirits, and preceded a Sufi worship, a powerful one-two-three punch for the various divinities we were calling on that night. The dancing, singing, and chanting, once we began our invocations, very quickly and easily became ecstatic. Feelings of joyous release, celebration, and of our own power were thus released on the first night of our arrests; as the night wore on bonds of friendship and committment were renewed or established with old friends and new.

During the days and nights that followed, the jail/circus developed a remarkable "organic" politics and culture. As will be discussed shortly, we discovered that we could exert a very real political power even when incarcerated. That fueled feelings of joy — and trust. Meetings and nightly talent shows were scheduled, and about a dozen or more workshops were held daily on topics like non-violence, the nature of thermonuclear weapons (this one led by Dan Ellsberg), international law, anarchist theory, etc. I presented on about half-a-dozen afternoons a workshop,

---

[1] All of those arrested were encouraged to organize themselves into affinity groups, a handful of individuals who presumably knew each other, some of which, like Matrix, had been together a couple of years or more. Several affinity groups, in turn, were supposed to organize themselves, ideally along the linkages of shared interests or values, into "clusters." For our cluster, much of the grouping had occurred in the weeks leading up to June 21. Spokescouncil meetings, designed so that each cluster would send one rotating representative, were the organizing and debating forum for the tents, as they had been leading up to the action. Some individuals in the tents were not in affinity groups and thus tended to be isolated; efforts were made to help them get organized into existing or new affinity groups.

"Marxism & Witchcraft," an earlier (and much abbreviated) version of this book.[1]

ii. WHO'S IN CHARGE HERE?

By the end of our first week in jail, a strikingly unusual political situation had developed. In the non-violence trainings that everyone planning to join the protest had been asked to attend, activists had held ongoing discussions about a strategy of "Jail Solidarity," meaning that after our arrests we would demand that *all of us* arrested had to be treated absolutely the same by authorities. We would not allow the singling out for harsher treatment of "leaders" or "troublemakers," as was the constant practice of penal authorities in our previous actions. The State (of California, in this instance) and behind it, the federal government that insisted on its inherent right to deploy nuclear weapons across the face of the planet, had precisely the opposite strategy, as the inheritor, through its traditions, of the old rule of oppressors everywhere to divide and conquer. Intimidation through special treatment of select, strategically placed, activists was their stock behavior, as it had presumably been since the powerful first separated off from the powerless.

Making our protest especially important to us was Livermore Lab's historic role as the main designer and chief advocate for the US arsenal of thermonuclear weapons. Originally the lab had been founded, with Edward Teller's strong advocacy, as a foil to Los Alamos Laboratory, where the atomic bomb had first been designed and made, since Los Alamos scientists were under the influence of former director J. Robert Oppenheimer, who had been reluctant to develop the H-bomb, Teller's baby. If you were against nuclear weapons, Livermore was clearly an abomination, spewing out its toxins and radioactivity into the Bay Area.

Rendering the legal authorities relatively powerless in our particular situation was that most of us had decided as part of Jail Solidarity to be arrested "anonymously," refusing to divulge our names when arrested or giving obviously false names such as "John Wayne," "Karen Silkwood," or "Ban D. Bomb." (My arrest name, a pun understood by virtually no one, was "Sue Donim.") Faced with nearly a thousand John and Jane Does, the criminal justice system, at least in that California county,[2] all too easily breaks down.

---

[1] About eight to ten men attended each time, except near our release, now housed in regular jail barracks in greatly reduced numbers, when Daniel Ellsberg and I gave a joint workshop on "The Theory [me] and Practice [Dan] of Genocide" that was attended by about 30 men.

[2] Yet this was a county that as far back as the Free Speech Movement in 1964 (when Edwin Meese II, by 1983 the Attorney General of the US under Pres. Reagan, had been DA) had a long history of dealing with mass arrests of protesters.

The thousand of us who were practicing non-cooperation soon realized that thereby we possessed a considerable power.

This was obvious when the Sheriff's Department arrived the Monday following our arrests to take us in groups before the judge for our arraignments. Both the women and the men in their respective tents decided in impromptu meetings (by consensus) not to cooperate, not to go. In consultations with our lawyers, we had been told of the sentences the judge had said he would give those pleading either guilty or *nolo contendre* ("I admit nothing," in essence allowing the State to enter a guilty plea for you). Two aspects of his planned sentences were unacceptable. The first and most important of these was a direct negation of our Jail Solidarity, the premise that repeat offenders, those arrested who had earlier convictions for civil disobedience, would get harsher sentences than the rest of us. Second, all of our sentences would likely include a period of probation, so that if we again engaged in civil disobedience during its duration, jail time would be probable.

Both of these reflected the basic political strategy of the State — to discourage by selective prosecution any continuation or escalation of our struggle. We wanted to have nothing to do with such sentences. (A third part of the planned sentences that were unacceptable to many of us was a fine for our "crime," since it would fall disproportionately on those not working, having low-paying jobs, high medical expenses, or large families.) What made our particular situation so remarkable, we soon realized, was that not only did we dislike the judge's announced sentences, unlike prisoners everywhere else we actually might be able to change it! A thousand of us, acting in unison, could do what one or a mere dozen could not.

So when the sheriff and his deputies came to the tents that Monday and ordered us to line up to go to our arraignments, after an impromptu meeting, the 450 or so of us simply said no. We would not go! We would stay put-until we got assurances that our sentence would not include the two objectionable components. We communicated with the women in their tent and they had reached the same conclusion. The deputies who had been present during our discussion about not cooperating, actually then left, bringing great relief because of the possibility that they might have decided to drag us forcefully to arraignment.

And there things stayed for the balance of that first week — and beyond. Our judge, probably hand-picked especially for the task, was not the least sympathetic to our cause. A conservative who seemed to value law 'n' order more than air 'n' water, he was obviously outraged by our insubordination. So were many others, even some of our friends. Since when did prisoners dictate their own sentencing? The very idea ran counter to every principle of government.

Precisely so, when that government deployed and threatened to use nuclear weapons. We knew that if we held out, close to a thousand anonymous defendants, we just might be able to name our own punishment and thus re-define the nature of our "crime." We refused to go to arraignment again on Tuesday. And Wednesday....

By Friday, a week after our arrests and with most of us still in the tents, things had noticeably escalated. A whole society and culture had sponta-neously emerged in the tents to accompany and feed our resistance. When, after several days of standoff, the local National Guard arrived at the men's tents with portable showers and spare G.I.-issue clothes — since all of us had been arrested without any spare underwear, socks, etc. — I was de-lighted to see some men immediately cut letters out of cardboard with makeshift tools so that, in true government fashion, our "names," "DOE," could be stencilled onto our G.I. shirts with marking pens — a pun, since Livermore Labs was run by the Department of Energy.

Message centers and bulletin boards were established; sculptures, as-sembled of discarded materials, hung; forums instituted for political debate, along with the classes, workshops, and nightly talent shows. Wally, of our cluster, who had previously done time, showed dozens of us how to fashion an almost-warm parka out of the single thin wool blanket we had all been issued the first night, which helped give us a little protection from the dev-astating night winds of the Livermore Valley that had kept all of us sleepless and miserable, and had laid about a third of us low with colds within a couple of nights.

iii. SICK IN THE SLAMMER

I had learned that, like most magical practitioners, witches are healers. During our fifteen days in Santa Rita, I participated in and was witness to instances of extraordinary healing. Some of it vastly increased my power as a political actor in the tents, as I shall explain. Instances of healing for me and for Roy, that might seem misplaced from Chapter 11 (where I discussed the healings attributed to the Irish Stroker), particularly stand out.

I had confessed in a Matrix meeting some weeks prior to our action my anxiety over being arrested, owing to my severely limited hearing. Ever since my early thirties I had had hearing losses in both ears, a condition I shared with several members of my immediate family, in which the middle ear be-comes calcified, its parts less mobile, vibrations dampened. Meetings, rituals, lectures, dinners with friends, indeed, all large-group settings and many small ones were ongoing torment as I hung on the pain of every word not heard, every joke I could not follow but knew that I was probably the butt of, every decision I agreed to not really knowing exactly what it was or how we had come to it. Rituals and trances were especially troublesome, since spiritual people seem to think that the more their utterances are clothed in a barely audible but oracular murmur, the more they were able to evoke a tangible spiritual presence. One-on-one conversations were also difficult, but there it was easier to ask "what?" — though I hardly every did.

The fact that heavy scenes can quickly develop in jail among anarchist activists, prone to spontaneous confrontations with the authorities for this reason or that, did not escape me, and having to react to those without being able to hear the threats issued by the guards (or the other prisoners) frightened me, though I was still determined to be arrested. When I told them of my fears, members of Matrix assured me that they would do magic to help me. Though I expressed gratitude, it was *pro forma* — I was partly deaf, the goddamn stapes bone in my middle ear was almost fused in place, and what in the world did they think they could do about *that*? It was sweet that they offered, and I tried to focus on their kind wishes.

Shortly after our arrest, I was taken to the bus that eventually carted about 30 or 40 of us to the tents. As the bus filled, it wasn't long before political discussion began. For one thing, we had to figure out how to react if the cops made an issue of the fact that a couple of the men had been able to slip out of their plastic handcuffs and were proceeding to help others out of theirs. I was astounded to notice how well I was following the conversations! I even could hear men's comments from the back of the bus. I was torn, both wanting to believe my ears, but also afraid of belief, worried that my naive faith that I was actually hearing would only inflate a bubble of happiness that would inevitably burst later on.

I, of course, kept on testing my new hearing, trying to compare sounds I could now decipher with how loud I thought they "really" were, meaning how well I would have been able to hear them a week earlier. Normally buses I was on were in motion. I had: to wait till the bus filled up and started driving us wherever they would take us before I could really do a proper comparison: and it was true, something had changed in my hearing — at least on the bus!

Upon reaching a large field upon which several circus tents were erected, we were taken off the buses and each issued our sheet, pillow, and a single thin blanket. I found a place to sit and wait. I also continued to assess my ears. Conversations sprang up everywhere, rumors, arrest stories, numbers, "do you know that comrade?", and the ever-present conjectures about our processing and probable sentences. I was hearing in dozens of new situations, single speakers and groups, close to the speaker and across a space. The conclusion was inescapable. The tents themselves were terribly noisy. In the constant winds of Livermore Valley, they flapped interminably, an ever~present snap of canvas against air as the skirts of the tents lurched first one way and then the other, straining against the restraints of their peg-and-rope tethering. As the tents filled with more and more arrestees, with the rising din of scores, then hundreds of men talking and settling in, adding to the cacophony, in the middle of all that, I was hearing!

Accordingly, in the tents I was able to participate actively in meetings in a way I hadn't been able for over a decade. No longer did I have to suffer in my isolated silences and I could now eagerly take my turns going to spokescouncil for the first time, confident in my ability to report back accurately the gist of what had been said and decided and on what questions feedback from clusters was requested. To be sure, I had to work for my new hearing. I energetically spun the volume control of my hearing aid to tune in mumblers, strategically placed myself near the physical or aural center of any discussion, and cupped my better ear — but I had *always* done those things and they had never helped enough. Now, it was clear, I was hearing, under quite trying circumstances, almost as well as *anyone* in the tents. There were still some things I could not make out, but that was true, I realized, for most of the people there at one time or another. What I could not hear now seemed the exception, not the rule; more importantly, I learned not to worry about it, trusting what I *could* hear to fill in any blanks. Being able to hear, in turn, gave me the confidence to read situations as they developed.

My magic teacher and lover, I am convinced, was largely responsible for this astounding transformation. She later told me she had created a silent chant that allowed her constantly to energize the spell she had done to help my hearing. She could not explain it, except she alluded to "going inside your ear and fixing something."

Before we had become lovers, I had awoken one night to sense a bird flying past my head and across my bedroom. My first thought was that my cockatiel had got out of the aviary I had in my kitchen, but then I realized that the bird in my room had a different size, flying style, and color, and possibly more to the point, didn't even seem to have a solid body, was not really material! After many years of pondering the matter, the best way I can understand it is that it was some kind of energy form, a bird that was not a bird of our world. I had no doubt at the time that if it wasn't my cockatiel, it had to be my teacher. What form she might have taken when, a year or more later while I was in the tents and she flew into my ears there, I do not know. I did not doubt that all the while I was incarcerated she had literally made it her 24-hour-a-day project, asleep and awake. Most importantly, her magic actually worked, fused stapes bone or no.

Alas, a couple of hours after our release from jail on July 4, 1983, I realized my hearing had begun to revert to its earlier, marginally functional state. I was quite upset, though not really surprised, and remain deeply grateful for the gift of my hearing during those critical 15 days, as well as in awe of the generosity and gifts of my teacher.

Even more striking was the healing done for Roy, for it is possible that it saved his life. Roy was a wonderful though ornery comrade, a member of Matrix in his thirties who precociously displayed many of the hallmarks of a curmudgeon. He nearly always bitched about the quality of our magic and our politics, but I don't think I had ever heard him complain about personal matters. By the second or third night in jail, however, Roy was in the throes of agony. He thought it might have been a reaction to a very difficult Spokescouncil he had been in for our cluster, or perhaps, he later speculated, the weird fish dinner we had been given. But something was terribly wrong in his gut. He had a severe pain near his groin and he vomited repeatedly. His pains were obviously excruciating. He was doubled over, as if in the grip of a gigantic, tight fist, and his cries grew louder, more desperate, finally becoming screams, which he no longer even tied to muffle. We were terribly scared and did not know what to do, for nothing we tried lessened Roy's agony and the anguish of his cries tore at us.

When Roy went to the infirmary, they only offered him aspirin, which he knew was not medically appropriate for his symptoms. One of the medics did speculate that Roy might be having appendix problems. We notified our comrades on the outside and in the women's tent, so they could send him healing from a distance, but even though such work had returned my hearing, I found it difficult to believe they would be able to help Roy out as he lay there, writhing in his misery. About eleven o'clock that night, he lay thrashing about continuously; his agony palpable. Without telling us, he later left the area where our cluster slept to go near the tent's entrance, the better to negotiate his frequent vomit sorties.

An hour or so later, Wally came to our cots to get Luis and me, He had decided on something that might help Roy. Wally led us to where our friend lay and put his hands on the small of Roy's back. He soon told us he had found a blockage inside Roy — some "knot" of "energy." Wally directed Luis and me to ground ourselves, a traditional magical exercise done as a preliminary for all work, and for both of us literally to "pump" the Earth's energy (magically accessible through grounding) from the ground into him, so that he could channel it into Roy.

I visualized the energy coming out of the ground and into my body, as I had many times before, in response to my breath; my tension, fear, and will that our comrade's sufferings be eased made the image more vivid. The tension and fear I willed into the ground on my expirations; kept inside they would only inhibit any help I could provide. I felt the energy rising into me; carried on my breath, it flowed through my hands, which were on his lower leg, into Wally. Luis did the same. He and I were mere conduits of Earth's healing powers, playing a passive role (though I remembered to visualize Roy in radiant health and to surround this mental image with a white, healing, light). It was Wally who was using, shaping, and directing whatever energy the three of us could conjure up to carry Roy's pain out of his body and back into the ground.

I could not tell if Roy was alert enough to participate with us. For a few minutes I had little idea how Wally's work was proceeding, and again tried to ground my fears that Roy might be dying. But his moans grew less frequent, less agonized, and his agitation noticeably diminished. Within ten minutes he was fast asleep! I could hardly believe the difference.

After the three of us thoroughly grounded again, so that nothing we had taken from Roy stayed in us, Wally explained that he had no idea what kind of blockage was in Roy's gut, but it had sometimes felt like a snake tied up in a knot;[1] at any rate, he had felt it move during our work. Roy slept soundly until quite late the next morning, not even moving. His face, earlier contorted by his pains, was at peace.

The next day Roy's nausea was gone, though his stomach was bloated. He did not want breakfast. Otherwise, he had no discomfort. He used the portashower, then lay around. He felt weak. That evening he was able, again, to sleep.

At around three A.M. however, Roy awoke in excruciating pain again. His suffering only got worse. Once again, Wally gathered Luis and me around Roy and once more we proceeded to try to ease his pains. Again I grounded, though with trepidation, and tried to visualize energy flowing from the ground into me and from me into Wally. Was I less focused or was there more difficulty tonight? I wasn't sure, but I fought feelings of despair. After a short time, Wally reported, "I can't do it, whatever it is is tied up tight tonight," he confessed. (I do not claim to remember his words exactly.. This is *what* I remember, but it was first written down a couple of years afterwards.) "I can't get anything to move at all."

Wally's announcement was gruesome news, though not entirely a surprise, as we had all seen Roy's lack of response that second night. Wally thought Roy should be hospitalized, but when Roy tried to get to the infirmary, a guard told him it was closed until the next day. When Roy, who had reached the guard only with great difficulty, heard this, he collapsed onto the damaged tarmac and groaned. The guard "nudged me with his boot and urged me again to return to my bunk [actually, cot]."[2] Somehow Roy managed to get back to the tent and alerted us.

Soon we and a number of others were awake, eventually a large number of the men, demanding that Roy be treated, chanting for his hospitalization. Eventually a van did materialize. Thinking it was an ambulance, we helped Roy get in.

As soon as the doors closed, Roy realized "we had been duped, for it was a prison van, not an ambulance." Roy was taken to the main prison, strip-searched, given prison coveralls, and put into a steel cell with steel bunk and no blanket against the bitter cold.

Roy's appendix burst near dawn. His cries for medical help went unheeded. Some time later a medic came, took Roy's temperature and left. Much later, after dark, he was escorted about half a mile to the infirmary and given an EKG.

---

[1] This was before the full moon and the snake dances performed there. See below.
[2] Letter from Roy.

While there he was interrogated for a long time by guards. He asked for a drink of water, only to have one of them reply, "Give him some radioactive water." The guards told Roy he might be charged with inciting a riot (because of the many of us demanding he be allowed to see a medic). At last he was asked to piss in a cup. When his pee came out bright red, the guards finally sent for an ambulance.

When Roy got to the hospital in Oakland at 8:30 that night, one of the members of Matrix, a dear friend of Roy's and a nurse by profession, was waiting in the emergency room. Though it was not a hospital she worked at, by acting like the nurse she was, she was able to fool the other medical workers into thinking she belonged — as indeed, she surely did.

Even then, though the intern had suspected appendicitis, it was another two days of being observed in a locked prison ward, moving around only in leg irons — Roy's "crime," let us remember, the charges most of us ended up serving 15 days for, was "jaywalking"; we had blocked an access road, obstructing traffic — before he was finally operated on.

The delay in surgery came because Roy's symptoms, as is common in his family's history of appendicitis, were atypical. When the doctors, still not sure what was going on, finally operated a couple of days later, they found Roy's ruptured appendix, surrounded by a lot of pus. Strangely, the pus had not spread. There was no peritonitis, which puzzled the doctors and nurses. Roy was later to learn that appendix problems ran in his family, but his relatives' burst appendices all resulted in peritonitis. Through our comrade, the nurse, and other Matrix members we were able to follow Roy's progress from afar, and I conducted a healing ritual with several dozen men on the eve of his surgery, as he began his very slow and painful way back to his health.

This was the first, but I later led several other healing rituals, basically "shaping" and transmitting an intended healing energy, as our incarceration lengthened and our health — or that of family or friends outside — deteriorated in the harsh environment.

iv. A DRAGON IN THE LAND

As it happened, that second Friday night was to enjoy a full moon, plus a partial lunar eclipse. As a witch I knew another ritual under such special circumstances could be powerful. Roy, who had planned the first ritual, was now in the hospital and it appeared no one else was planning a ceremony. If there was to be any pagan rite, I concluded, I would have to arrange it. I called for a gathering at sundown on what was called the "phone plaza," the level tarmac outside the larger of our two tents and adjacent to the row of pay phones we had been lucky to have at hand and that made our incarceration much more tolerable.

While I had been in Matrix, an affinity group of witches, for a couple of years, so far I had seen myself as deferring to others do the "real" magic; I still tended to think of myself primarily as an historian, not a practitioner, of magic. I did not trust my psychic powers and felt too inexperienced, too prone to make mistakes with the forces I might conjure up. My magic teacher continually chided me for my timidity, my lack of trust in myself. It had only been one year since, with great trepidation, I had stepped forth to take my first public role at a large Summer Solstice ritual (at the Livermore Labs, in fact), invoking into the magic circle we cast the direction, West, and the spirit of water associated with it. I had also helped Roy plan and then enact the celebration the previous week, the night of our arrests.

Prior to the Livermore action I had attended a Holly Near benefit concert where someone from the women's encampment at Greenham Common in England had spoken. Greenham was a key US Air Force base where the new Cruise missile was going to be deployed, and women in England had set up an encampment where for 18 years a vigil and civil disobedience took place.[1] Of course what those women were doing was part of our direct action at Livermore. The speaker had discussed the ritual magic the women at Greenham Common had done, where they I used the image of a dragon as part of their focus.

I was aware of the magic dragons embodied both from work in Matrix, as well as from my initial forays into magic undertaken during my year in London for further research into Newton. Without quite realizing what we were doing, an artist friend and I, both curious about such matters, fell into an impromptu seminar, where we taught ourselves about magical literature and ideas. My friend was in close contact with John Michell, one of the seminal figures in the revival, under the name of "Earth mysteries," of the study of geomantic principles and structures; I probably learned indirectly from my friend of Michell's *View Over Atlantis*, then being finished, about dragons and dragon currents.

Accordingly, I knew that the dragon (or sometimes a snake) in many cultures, including the magical traditions of the West, was associated with terrestrial energies — as the Chinese in their *Feng shui*, or geomancy, noted with their "dragon currents."[2] Linking the Greenham Commons anti-nuclear struggle with ours made perfect sense; it would only make both

---

[1] Many critics pointed out that the Cruise missile was designed as part of an overall "first strike" US nuclear strategy.

[2] See above, Chapter 31, p. 566, n.1. My work on the Mid-Ocean Ridge and the dragon came later. The myth of the serpent in *Genesis* and of St. Patrick's ridding Ireland of snakes take on different meanings in this regard. A glance at any map where there are rivers shows in the meander pattern why snakes and terrestrial forces were associated.

stronger. I set out to do this magically by using the image of the dragon as part of our ritual.[1]

Mount Diablo, as its name suggests, is a mountain on the edge of Livermore Valley with a long history of magical associations, a sacred place for Native Americans and hence automatically assumed by the Spanish to be associated with the devil. From times I had spent on the mountain and from tradition, I was aware that the mountain had a certain "male" energy, as opposed to Mt. Tamalpais, another local mountain holy to Native Americans, about 35 miles to the west on the other side of the San Francisco Bay that was reportedly "female." Those two mountains, along with the moon, would serve as our male and female "deities" in the ritual I planned.

Matrix tried to walk a fuzzy line between being true to the forms of traditional magic and avoiding dogmatism in having things "just so." Many activists who might come to our rituals either had some other religion or were militant atheists, easily alienated if pushed to dance or chant invocations to some "god" or "goddess"; but to the sun or moon, to a mountain or a dragon, traditional emblems of nature and myth, and for us concrete embodiments of the sacred energies that pagans revered, many activists could enthusiastically respond.

In the days leading up to our ritual, I consulted frequently with Wally, Luis, and Kelly — the latter himself rather new to paganism. Kelly nervously bombarded me with questions as to how he could participate in the making of our ritual, even as I was bombarding my teacher back in San Francisco, whom I spoke to by phone nearly nightly. She, in turn, was in daily phone contact with our comrades in the women's tent. Using her as a conduit, sounding board, and consultant, the women in the tents and I arranged to use common themes in our respective full-moon rituals. I admitted to Kelly my own neophyte status, but I was confident and reassuring as I explained parts in which he could help. Matrix saw rituals as living forms that would change according to the circumstances; we could not worry about doing things by the book.

v. ECLIPSING THE NUCLEAR THREAT

About a hundred or more men showed up around sunset to pay homage to the full, and later, with the eclipse, the not-so-full moon. I briefly explained the structure of our rite — a fairly standard form I had only recently learned — and taught a few of the chants we planned to use in our magic. We breathed together to ground, then poetically invoked the four directions, East, South, West, and North, along with the elements those directions em-

---

1 At the time I did not think of Wally's finding of a "snake" blocking up Roy's gut.

bodied in our tradition, air, fire, water, and earth. Thus we created a sacred circle and our magic could proceed. Through our invocations, chantings, and dancing we interwove the two sacred mountains, as well as the moon, into our work. A few days earlier, Kelly had found a man's hairnet blowing across the phone plaza, and using that as a "web," we invoked Spiderwoman, the weaver, an African and Native American deity we knew about from our working with Santeria priestesses. Using those spiritual forms and people's individual prayers we built to a series of ecstatic peaks, using yarn we brought to tie the moon, mountains, and dragon, and we weavers and the women of Greenham into a powerful symbolic web, working for our cause: our opposition to the nuclear/national security apparatus; our determination to see our struggle through to victory in our fight for solidarity on the issue of how we would be sentenced; and for many of us, our fight against a host of other issues and oppressions that were inextricably linked to the nuclear threat and the nation-states/empires that relied on it, comfortable in their striking terror into the hearts of billions of people around the world.

The moon waxing full that night was the culmination of our eventual victory, as her eclipse and later passing over to her waning represented the beginnings of the end to the nuclear terror we all lived under. The mountains and dragon tied all of it, and us too, to age-old symbols for the Earth's energies upon which our magic was grounded. All this was done not intellectually, but viscerally and musically, *through* and *in* our bodies. Madly we danced and gave voice to our passions and our visions. The ecstasies experienced *en mass* made the ritual of the previous Friday night a mere warming up.

As the ritual created peak after peak of ecstatic release, I consciously remained not wholly part of the ecstasy, partially standing apart, a vessel for the energies, a conduit monitoring and teasing the flow, helping to shape it and at times with my voice to slightly change its course. From my many rituals done with my coven, I had tried learning to "feel" the energy of a ritual, of the dancing, chanting, or other form of focusing of our energies, and how to aid in bringing it to a peak when appropriate, how to allow it to "ground" when that seemed best, and how to avoid having the collective energy we created become dissipated. I mentally directed the energy emerging out of the scores of men so that it wove together with the women's ritual at their tent a few hundred yards away and with the magic of the women in England, and more broadly to the vision of a world without nuclear weapons we knew was shared by so many billions around the planet.

All of us were astounded at the sense of liberation and of power we felt that night. The intensity and joy were unparalleled for most of us. Afterwards many men (not merely those who had been at the ritual) in and out of the tents milled around, talking, singing, telling stories, sharing feelings of joy — and experiencing a sense of our own power. It was a warm night and people stayed up late. Veterans of the Abraham Lincoln Brigade taught some of the men songs from their struggle, though perhaps some of them singing had not even known who Franco was. Everything that night had a sparkle, an aura, was numinous.

vi. Retreat Into Pathos

The contrast in mood the next day, Saturday, could not have been more stark. It was our second weekend in the slammer. We were all beginning to feel our loneliness. I missed my lover, and felt bad being away from my ten-year-old son, Yarrow, diagnosed after I was jailed, with mononucleosis. Being cut off fed all our doubts, and for the first time disappointment became one of the dominant feelings. It was palpable that Saturday. As it turned out, that morning it was my turn on behalf of my cluster to attend the daily Spokescouncil meeting, the rotating "leadership" body for our ongoing protest. From the beginning the meeting was an utter disaster.

For a week we had held out, refusing to go to arraignment and thereby able to stymie the criminal-justice system, and we had felt stronger each day. We had felt a near-total unity, all of us John and Jane Does. And now, that morning, sitting in the circle of about 30 men, it was clear that it would have been difficult for us to come to a common agreement on what *year* it was. Our meeting dragged and was pathetic — and scary. We could not have stood up to the most egregious injustice that day, no matter how arbitrary, how onerous,. At least that is how it felt.

Helping to shape our mood, some of us realized, were two very real problems that had emerged in our ranks. One, surprisingly, was dietary. A number of men had decided when arrested to fast as a continuation of our protest. As our incarceration continued, they tried to organize the rest of us to join them. And their numbers did grow. Their strong action posed a couple of serious difficulties to the group, however. While some of the men fasted out of Gandhian principles, others had different agendas — protesting treatment in the tents; or that there were no vegetarian foods available; or because of the judge's likely sentences; or to emphasize the repugnance of the Lab's work. Under such circumstances, it was impossible for the large numbers refusing to eat to make a clear statement to the public as to why they were not eating — though in a series of meetings of the fasters, they made a concerted effort to do so.

Their attempts to articulate what their "cause" was did not go very far. They were not eating because … with a "menu" of five or so reasons and yes, more than one "dish" could be ordered.

This gastronomical division in our ranks should not have been much of a problem. The real difficulty with the fasters was that a week of not eating had made many of them dreamy. Spacy. At times, edgy, not to be trifled with. And above all, tired. Many of them seemed to have real trouble finishing a sentence or otherwise focusing.

In itself, this too might not have been so bad had not some of those fasting insisted on continuing to play leadership roles in our Spokescouncil meetings. Some whole clusters, it appeared, were fasting, and they continued to send representatives (as was not only their right, but their obligation) to the Spokescouncil meetings. Other fasting men simply took their turns representing clusters where some were eating. These men came to meetings, they spoke... and spoke. And often rambled. Some seemed to hear God speaking to them about what our legal or political strategy should be — and perhaps He or She was. And who was *I* to judge? But I could see how it made reaching decisions difficult. To me and others the faster's lack of grounding definitely was affecting our ability to hold productive (meaning we could reach agreement on important issues) Spokescouncils. Our cluster (and I believe some others) had discussed this problem a day or so earlier. It was a difficult issue because the fasters did not want to be disempowered simply because of their lack of caloric intake — indeed, many of them felt more spiritual, more prophetic, because of it. And the Spokescouncil *was* the important focus of whatever power we had. Attempts to discuss this problem at the Spokescouncil that Saturday morning ran aground in a morass of confusion and bad feelings.

On a second divisive issue, I thought discussion was more fruitful, though it did not noticeably improve our dispirited mood. As that first week had drawn to a close, more and more women and men were wrestling with their personal need to get out and back to their daily lives. Most of us had been arrested expecting to spend a day or two in jail until being released with some kind of suspended sentence. Only a few, with an eye on the increasingly harsh sentences being given over the previous couple of months to non-violent anti-nuclear protesters, had anticipated the possibility of longer jail time, especially once we decided on jail solidarity, and made contingency plans. Those who felt the most need to get out had jobs, families, schools, or other commitments that could be denied only at great personal costs. Yet many of them felt wretched about abandoning us in what was still the middle of our protest. Solidarity was our political strategy, our ideology, *and* our strength. We knew if we held firm to our demands for equal treatment for all and probation for none, before we would allow ourselves to be taken to arraignment, we might actually win! People leaving jail by agreeing to give their real names and allowing themselves to be arraigned would thus, it was feared, sap our strength and undermine our chance of victory. A few men and women had already left during the first week. Any others would possibly be seen, some thought, perhaps correctly, as spoilers.

Luckily, by late in the first week this second division had also become apparent to me. In an earlier Spokescouncil I had proposed that a straw poll be taken in all of the clusters to see how *many* men (and in their tent, women) *had* to leave, how many could hang on for another several days? For a week?

A month? Or even longer, if need be? By Saturday enough of those results were in to see that there *were* enough of us to stick it out, continuing our fight. We could easily lose one or even two hundred Johns and Janes and still continue as a massive administrative, juridical, financial, and ideological headache for the county (and national) government. Out of the roughly 425 men left in the tents, less than a hundred, if my memory serves me, felt a strong need to get back outside in the near future. At least three hundred would hold on for at least another week, and some of us, if necessary, were prepared to stay longer. On the women's side a similar inquiry was made, and despite what were undoubtedly perceived as greater family obligations, we were even stronger. In other words, the second source of division in our ranks should not have been difficult to resolve.

This happy discovery of our ability to willingly say farewell to comrades who had to "cite out" (as their legal exit was called) while secure in our capacity to maintain what was in effect a boycott of the criminal-justice system, was a topic of discussion at that hapless Saturday morning Spokescouncil. We concluded that we could gladly see our numbers diminish and still feel, as nearly six or seven hundred Does, that we could continue holding to our two demands for jail solidarity. These conclusions should have been cause for rejoicing and celebration, but in that pool of stagnant energy that was Saturday's meeting, no rock, no matter how weighty or significant, could make much of a splash.

Having just helped lead the ecstatic ritual of the night before, having seen and felt the tremendous power we had created, and having put the topic of our projected ability to maintain significantly high numbers in jail on the agenda for this meeting, I was especially bewildered by the palpable stagnation. How had all of our enthusiasm of the previous night disappeared so quickly? And to where? The whole of the tents, not simply those who had come to our ritual, had lit up. You could see it in the faces of those still awake late into the night. How could twelve hours make such a striking difference?

But it had. The meeting could only be described as a swamp of bad process and worse feelings. I became profoundly depressed, even though I was well aware that what was behind our paralysis were those problems of a rotating leadership body with perhaps a quarter of its members (after a week of not eating) subject to periodic hallucinations; and the mutual fears and unspoken guilt by those who needed to leave jail, and any resentment against them by others, for their breaking of solidarity. My understanding of the roots of our sad malaise, alas, did not seem to give me any noticeable means of changing it.

My despair only deepened when I attended, right after Spokescouncil and lunch, a "Hands Around the Tent" demonstration. Our supporters on the outside had organized a rally in solidarity with those of us in jail that Saturday, calling for a bold attempt to ring the huge nuclear-weapons facility with people holding hands in a human chain, cardboard cutouts to take the place of the 1,000 of us in the line. Their action was called "Hands Around the Lab." We had no idea in jail how much support we had, for we only saw local newspapers, in which we were troublemakers and devils incarnate, while we spoke mostly to family, affinity-group members in our support network, or other loved ones, for many of whom we were angels.

That morning the guards had taunted us by claiming that only 30 people had shown up for Hands Around the Lab, which was about an hour's drive from San Francisco and nearly as far from Oakland or Berkeley; we had no way of knowing whether, as was probable, the guards were lying. In our despair, believing them was the path of least resistance.

In the case of both the Lab and the tents, authorities made it physically impossible for actual encirclement, erecting barriers, probably knowing instinctively that in addition to questions of security, our surrounding them would be very powerful magic. Our own mirror-image demonstration, Hands Around the Tent, was the saddest demonstration I had ever gone to in over a quarter-century of activism. (Another three decades later, it is still true.) Though on the men's side a score or more had shown up, our energy was nonexistent. It felt as if *no one* had come. At the previous Monday's impromptu after-lunch meeting, songs had rung out for what seemed like hours, verse after verse. As one song died away, another was begun immediately. Our spirit had been indomitable. At "Hands Around the Tent," on the other hand, a song was exceptional if it got through even *one* of its verses. Hardly anyone sang, and those who did had little voice, their words struggling to get past the wads of self-doubt and fear stuck in their throats. Where had our power, our spirit, gone? Soon I could not sing, either — even once when, in a vain effort to overcome my crashing defeatism, I took the initiative to begin a new song at the vigil, abandoning my effort after a few sad bars, when hardly anyone had joined me. None of us had an ounce of conviction, it was obvious. There was no focus here, only dispersal and dissipation.

The longer we stood in the hot sun on the tarmac, on the very spot where the previous night's ritual had unleashed levels of ecstasy in scores of us, the more pathetic we became.

vii. THE WAKING OF THE DRAGON

My cluster had scheduled a meeting for after Hands Around the Tent. I was reporting back about the horrible Spokescouncil meeting. Almost all of the other members had experienced the equally dismal afternoon vigil. As we mulled over the depressing state of our once-strong movement, something occurred that instantly turned our world upside down and which to me clearly reflected the workings of magic.

While in our cluster meeting we were discussing our obvious fall into despair-drenched radical torpor, a legal worker from the left-wing law collective that worked on our behalf approached the edge of the tent; as a legal worker he had access to us. Reaching the tent, he cupped his hands and dramatically yelled out, "Hands Around the Lab had over 10,000 people!"

The news hit us like a stroke of lightning! I do not know what other people's expectations were, but at the depths of my afternoon despair, I had easily imagined a mere handful of supporters showing up, buying the gist of the guards' purposeful rumor. Figures of a couple of hundred people, or even only 50, would have surely saddened, but not necessarily shocked, me — especially as I experienced our own effete efforts to our cause.[1]

Ten thousand! These were numbers beyond our greatest hopes, and showed the massive amount of support outside for the campaign against nuclear weapons and for what amounted to our blockade of the courts.[2] This support provided the spark that rekindled our own will to resist.

I do not know *how* it happened, but within a second of the announcement of the ten thousand, our cluster leaped up from our meeting, and someone (Wally thought it was me, I was sure that it was him) spontaneously rang out the simplistic, but at the time catchy chant, "Stand fast! Hold tight! Everything is gonna be all right!"

And Wally was in front, beginning a snake (or was it a dragon?) dance down the aisle between the cots in the tent. The rest of our cluster joined in behind, and then others behind us. Within a few seconds, there were scores who had become part of our dance around the tent, as suddenly the dragon we had invoked the previous night, the dragon of the women at Greenham Common and the dragon inside Mounts Diablo and Tamalpais, now became embodied in us, alive in our dance of, by now, hundreds of us! The celebration encircled the tent, first inside, then, as earlier we could not (and again, imperfectly, given the barriers) outside, with the mass of men repeatedly chanting, "Stand fast! Hold tight! Everything is gonna be all right!"

---

1 Kelly later told me of his impassioned plea to members of his affinity group on the outside to drum up support. They organized a well-attended demonstration at the county courthouse, voicing our demands, and wearing hand lettered tee shirts declaring "Free the Livermore 1000!" Afterwards, still wearing their shirts, the organizers went to see the newly-released, anti-nuclear movie, "War Games," in Oakland and were approached by people in the audience eager to talk about our action and our demands. Clearly support did exist.

2 We needed support for legal, spiritual, and material reasons — people to take care of pets, vehicles, apartments, or jobs. People to send us sweaters, underwear, or medications, like the friends of one man, with cerebral palsy, whose motorized wheelchair had stopped working the very day of his spontaneous decision at the blockade to undergo arrest. With great effort his friends got replacement batteries to him. A fundamentalist Christian, he had come to both our rituals.

Just as the dragon, we were alive again, our bodies jumping with a joy that just minutes before had been unthinkable. Soon a makeshift band sprang up to begin the party that lasted far into the night. Empty plastic five-gallon water bottles, as usual, became drums, along with all manner of other objects used to beat our ecstatic, rhythmic victory, and someone had a penny whistle that I could wail away on. Our joyous frenzy, it seemed to us, carried out from the tent to the lab, wound around it, and then went out to the world beyond, there to make solidarity with all of its creatures. A group of men playing music left to walk to the barbed-wire fence separating the men's from the women's compound and there we sang to the women. Those with better ears than mine could hear the women singing back. We traded songs and chants for awhile, in our empowered state even moving the barbed wire back several feet so as to get closer to our women comrades, once more taking charge of defining how we were to be "kept."

Having agonized over the depths of our despair that morning and afternoon, I was dumbstruck by the sudden and total reversal, even as I thought I understood what had happened. What occurred not only *felt* magical, it made the most sense if the wild swings of our spirits and bodies were analyzed in magical terms, using categories I was, through magic, becoming attuned to. The dragon, especially, who is known for his strategic rests, where he gathers his strength, had revealed himself. No one in our cluster had *thought* of what we were doing when we began leading the men in the tent in a snake dance, where ultimately almost everyone there was behind us. But having done a similar dance to honor and bless the dragon the night before, there was no need to think. We had invoked the dragon and he had appeared, both on Friday night and now, after a brief snooze, at that critical moment late Saturday afternoon. The dragon stood for terrestrial energies in archaic cultures and in Matrix we tried always to ground our magic in those energies. The exuberance of our dance drew from those terrestrial energies, at least that is how I understood it. The fight against nuclear weapons, against the instrumentality of Armaggedon marshalled by the superpowers, was a fight ultimately for the sanctity of the land, a defense of mountains and rivers and savannahs.

Of course, it is absolutely true that the news of the ten thousand would have injected new life into our defeatist ranks under any circumstances, but the form it took, the precise way in which that new life became manifest — there I clearly saw the signature of magic, of the collective spell we had cast the night before. And it is my firm belief that the degree of power that was unleashed was partially because of that magic. It is not something I could "prove," nor do I want to.

From that Saturday on, nothing of substance could block the free flow of our political will in the tents. To a considerable. degree, we ran the tents, in our numbers and solidarity, as well as our anonymity, we had a considerable degree of autonomy and power.

The guards were all-too-aware of the stakes involved. Oppression over the centuries had created its own perverse logic, and they knew as if by instinct that our drumming Saturday night was an implicit threat to their pretended, and real, powers. That too was magic. While normally one or more guards patrolled the tents every ten minutes or so, the night of our victory they stayed away. The tents — at least that night — were ours! Our spiritual victory was manifested in how we were incarcerated.

Our second week in the tents was, accordingly, highly charged. In groups of threes, ten, or a dozen, men left to go back to their outside lives, to carry our struggle there. I conducted short but moving rituals nearly every day as they left, held so the we who remained could bid them goodbye, even while binding our lives together politically and spiritually, represented by the piece of yarn that I tied around their wrists and ours, connecting them to us as they took their leaves; nearly all the men participated in these goodbyes and many spoke. We sang. We knew we were not weakened by the departures, and those who left could go without guilt and with a clear mandate to organize in their outside communities on behalf of our fears and demands.

All these gatherings were celebratory. I was taken aback when a reporter with the Pacifica station, KPFA, who had smuggled a small tape recorder in when arrested, arranged to interview me and a Methodist minister in the tents and realized that I was, indeed, functioning there as a pagan priest.

Visiting the tent one night, Paul, the legal worker from the law collective, turned to me and said, "This must be what it is like being in Gdansk," at the time the scene of the heroic struggles and victories by Solidarnösc. I wish I could report that I retained a modicum of (at least public) humility and disallowed his hyperbole, but my memory sadly reports that I merely nodded as if I indeed now knew what Gdansk must be like. The feelings in the tents were very heady, indeed. We felt free, we *were* free, at least freer than we were in our outside lives. Incarcerated, my every movement monitored and restricted, watched for infractions of dress codes (conceivably, as an identified leader, under special surveillance) I was nonetheless as strong as I have ever been in my life. We would stay until our demands were met, and though the nuclear weapons would no doubt remain and the Lab continue for some time to do its baleful work, we would strike a telling blow against the weapons and the mentality that produced them.

We felt our power in the tents. We had a whole county criminal-justice system tied up because of that power. Jail solidarity was apparently working. We knew how costly, in money, political legitimacy, and power our continued incarceration was to the authorities, and most of us were aware of the national implications ot our holdout. I wrote a two-page essay, "Why We Are Here," an attempt to explain our refusal to go to our arraignment and "published" it by posting it on the central bulletin board, using the *nom de guerre* I had adopted for the Livermore blockade of "Sue Donim." Numbers of men copied it by hand for themselves, family, or comrades in the women's tent and the KPFA reporter had me record it for broadcasting.

On the critical issue of solidarity and not accepting sentences of probation or greater penalties for second offenders, for the bulk of the protesters, we actually won! It applied to all those who on those terms went willingly to arraignment on the morning of July 4, 1983, gave their legal names, and were sentenced to time already served. Two other groups, those who had individually "cited out" during the two weeks in the tents, and a group of several dozen who chose not to plead *nolo* at their arraignment but to come back later for a "mass trial," we could not negotiate into being part of our sentence. Nonetheless, it had been a tremendous victory for us and a resounding defeat for the government and the national-security apparatus and ideology that underpins it. Henceforth, the State acted as if it wanted to avoid the morass of mass arrests, mindful of the judicial, financial, and especially the political nightmare of the nearly 1000 John and Jane Does fed, housed, clothed, and endured for all the time we refused to participate in the criminal-justice system. To the State, it had to have been a major political defeat and a humiliation, that only by it agreeing to our sentencing demands did we finally allow ourselves to proceed through the machinery of the State's justice.[1]

viii. INNER & OUTER PATHWAYS

Roy's nearly dying and his extended recovery scared Matrix and raised serious questions about our work. Our Summer Solstice rituals, when the sun reaches the peak of his power in the northern hemisphere and begins a slow decline into the cold embrace of winter six months later, focuses on the theme

---

[1] It is less clear why the movement, too, drew back. In part I suspect it was the result of a pronounced tendency in US movement circles not to acknowledge our real victories, to see them as defeats. As a possible example, the disappointment in 1964, when the Mississippi Freedom Democratic Party delegates were not seated at the Democratic Party convention in Atlantic City, a critical defeat but a defeat wrapped in the (to me) even larger *victory* of critically breaking down the structure of Jim Crow in that pariah state, pretty much in the course of a single summer's campaign, an unimaginable achievement. Perhaps, too, the two weeks in jail was too much of a "sacrifice" for many of us. A follow-up meeting where we tried to reach consensus about the meaning of our action bogged down in bickering and had trouble agreeing about common goals. No doubt the Reagan counter-insurgency wars in El Salvador and Nicaragua drew much of our attention away from nuclear weapons *per se* and focused us more on the concrete war-related issues at hand. Civil disobedience was still a valued tactic, but now mostly of handfuls, not hundreds. The hundreds or more still came, but they were now more inclined to observe legal lines in the sand.

of the sun's self-sacrifice and later rebirth, a mythic theme mirrored in Greek mythology with the story of Persephone's descent into Hades and Demeter's desperate search for her. The Solstice ritual in the men's tents, which Roy had largely led, had focused on the theme of our own individual self-sacrifice. Each man was asked to reflect on his own sacrifice in committing himself to the movement against nuclear weapons, especially in being arrested.

The question had been generated, prior to the Santa Rita tents, within Matrix, and irked Roy, who felt that he had personally given up very little. "What the fuck have I really sacrificed?" he demanded in his North Carolina drawl when the two of us were alone. "A few god damn days in jail. Big deal!" In effect, he yearned to sacrifice more, and in magic, and life, as we often painfully learn, we often get exactly what we ask for. There were other possible ways "bleeding" had occurred from mythic realms into Roy's flesh-and-blood reality that had to be considered.

The sun is commonly portrayed mythologically as the king, and Roy, whose last name was King, was accordingly a monarch twice over, thrice if you included his being a Leo. A fourth "crown" would accrue to him in some magical traditions because at the time he and Starhawk were lovers, and even though our anarchist principles repudiated "leaders," Star had begun the group and played a dominant role in our work. As the myth of the dying sun was ritualized in our solstice rites, both as we were being arrested on the morning of the solstice and that night in our ceremony, it is possible we failed to shield ourselves from other pagan tropes, such as that every seventh year royal blood must be spilled so that the kingdom itself can survive:

> [T]hou knowest the law. For this was I chosen long ago. The cycle must be observed. The succession shall pass in orderly fashion.... all that the prince was saying was as true in the here and now as it had been ... before. A sacred king was observing the sacred cycle, a willing sacrifice to ensure the survival of the land.
>
> (Katherine Kurtz, *Lammas Night*, p. 423)

That our anarchist politics mitigated against our conceptualizing Starhawk as our leader or queen, or Roy, as her consort, our king, for that matter, may have been irrelevant, as was the fact that we certainly did not believe in blood sacrifice. Perhaps in calling for sacrifice, we had asked for more than we bargained. We could not know for sure, but it would be foolhardy to reject such notions out-of-hand.

Matrix continued to participate in mass protests and in civil disobedience, but the 1983 Livermore action was a watershed for the movement and future civil disobedience became more focused. The fifteen-day sentences that most of us drew was probably a factor for both the movement and the State. Nevertheless, it is clear that the anti-nuclear movement in the '70s and beyond ac-complished a great deal, if not in the "eclipse" of the nuclear threat, at least its considerable occlusion. Mostly as a result of the Three Mile Island near-melt-down, the nuclear-power industry in the US was dealt a body blow from which it took President Obama, with his push for nuclear power, to try to heal. No new plants were constructed after Three Mile Island, though Diablo and others were allowed to go on-line once construction was finished. Militarily our vic-tories were several. Many nuclear weapons were cut back or abandoned during the Reagan years and after, in the face of widespread opposition worldwide. The Cruise missile was deployed in severely reduced numbers. The MX and Pershing missiles were similarly cut way back. Not least a ban on the testing of nuclear bombs was finally achieved, though with the usual loopholes.[1]

As early as 1982, George Kennan, the US Ambassador to the USSR who famously enunciated the policy of "containment" of the "Soviet threat" in the late '40s, had written around the time of our ongoing actions at Liv-ermore that the current antinuclear movement, being the "expression of a deep instinctual insistence... on sheer survival," is "too powerful, too elemen-tary, too deeply embedded in the natural human instinct for self-preserva-tion" for the authorities to brush it aside.[2]

Matrix's political focus broadened as we confronted a range of related issues looming large in the Reaganite '80s: Central America, *apartheid*, AIDS, needle exchange, Palestine/Israel, homelessness, etc. At the same time, our magic seemed to deepen.

This perhaps resulted from rectifying an earlier mistake, for we had un-thinkingly taken to calling the "place" we went when we engaged in trance work by the same name as our affinity group/coven, which was public knowledge. Upon return from the tents, I realized it had been careless, mak-ing it easy for anyone trying to gain access to our magical work. Indeed, in our trances, we felt as if we were being "watched."[3]

Accordingly, we decided we should "move" to a new trance spot. At the new location we imagined, our magic qualitatively changed. For one thing, we felt a much-closer connection to our personal and spiritual ancestors[4] — the source of power for witches, as for many traditional or animist religions. That connection, it appeared to us, allowed us to tap more readily into the

---

[1] Interview with Bill Simpich, March 30, 2013.

[2] "On Nuclear War," *New York Review of Books* (January 21,1982), as quoted in George Katsiaficas, "Eros and Revolution."

[3] Both the Pentagon and the CIA are known to have engaged in occult re-search. (William J. Broad, "Pentagon Reportedly Spent Millions on ESP," San Francisco *Chronicle* (January 11, 1984).

[4] What in animist traditions is a reverence for one's ancestors becomes, through the lens of Christianity, "necromancy," or working with the spirits of the dead, hence demons.

major political wellsprings, both at the present and in the distant past, that sustained the propertied classes in their inordinate power.

As discussed in Chapter 28, we did especially powerful trance work from our new, more secure, site. We discerned something that we surmised that had been part of powerful spell work done hundreds of years earlier, by John Dee, we conjectured, at the beginnings of the drive for English global hegemony to ensure the victory of that Empire.

There were images, too, of the place on the magical plane where the virus of oppression had first bored into a cell of the body politic, a hint that there was a place we could effectively ply our craft to try to bring back balance in the dance we call life.

For the next five years we worked our magic against Star Wars, the wars in Central America, South African *apartheid*, AIDS, etc. Even as we honed our magical tools for use in the struggle in the streets against current US efforts to topple the Sandinistas, for example, we tried to grasp at those elusive wisps of historical threads that seemed to connect the US Contra war in Nicaragua back to the expansion of Elizabethan England into the "new" world at the end of the 16th century.

On several occasions, we felt our workings resonate within larger patterns of energy, which were rearranging the structures of global security, as if we had found a kind of node from which we could play some role in helping shape the emerging map of global conflict. Perhaps it was mere illusion. Such matters can never be proved, nor is the interaction one of cause and effect, as I hope I have adequately emphasized. I can only report how it felt as we witnessed the unfolding of world politics.[1]

Perhaps we reached further than we were capable. At any rate, just when our work felt most successful, most linked to the real world of virulent deadly pandemics, mass starvation of children, international nuclear-armed missiles, and the proverbial pork-belly futures of capitalist markets, perhaps glimpsing the fruits of our labors manifesting themselves in the newspapers, Matrix fell apart. Various inadequate explanations of what happened have been given, but in fact we don't know what occurred (and if we did, this would not be the place to hash such matters out), except this: personal differences developed within the group that we should have been readily able to resolve, but instead feelings degenerated, and abuses of trust (by me, specifically) and power erupted among us. As a result our coven had a raucous falling-out.

ix. TRANCE FORMATIONS & THE POLITICS OF ECOLOGICAL REVOLUTION

It would be too depressing and mean-spirited to leave it like this, not to say misleading, so let me briefly review what we *had* been able to accomplish in our seven years together. First I should acknowledge that though Matrix

---

1 For reasons of security, I must be suitably vague.

as such ceased to exist in the late '80s, most of us remained active with one another, as in the 1999 demonstrations that stopped the World Trade Organization (WTO) in Seattle, when we were in an extended affinity group for the action. In Seattle many of the key organizers behind creating that vehicle that shut Seattle down, preventing the trade meeting and exposing its many crimes against the planet, were ex-members or close associates of Matrix and of the larger cluster within which we had worked.

I must emphasize that I have detailed our work in Matrix not as the model, but as a means to show how animist, Earth-centered spiritual committments that amount to a magical orientation to the world might have powerful and practical implications in the politics and culture of resistance and revolution. Secondarily, our work in conjunction with many other activists and groups shines a light on aspects of an oppositional movement in the 1980s that is frequently ignored in discussions of the sweeping victories, politically and ideologically, wrought by Reaganism.[1]

Our initial assessment of Matrix's purpose, to demonstrate to fellow activists the relevance and power of magical work in political actions was easily accomplished even before our first year had passed, at least in the West Coast anti-nuclear movement. This was not because of our work, as because what we were doing was itself resonating with what many other groups and individuals were themselves concluding. The political issues, particularly those relating to the environment, pointed the way towards the Earth, even as the Earth herself called out to us, especially to those who identified as feminists. Or so we claimed, and it would take a willful denial of the severity of our environmental degradation to conclude that those calls were "merely" our hallucinations. Others obviously heard her plaintive calls for help as well.

No doubt Matrix was more public in what we did than most of the other groups or individuals, but they were there. We felt them, and in one place or another ran into them. Some of the individuals were still alive, others were

---

[1] This is not the place to do it, but an argument could be made that the anti-nuclear movement domestically and internationally played a major role in the ending of the Cold War. Particularly remarkable was the way in which the US anti-nuclear movement served as an inspiration for the growing Soviet movement against nuclear weapons, which centered near Semipalatinsk in the Soviet Republic of Kazakhstan (where the USSR tested its thermonuclear weapons). Naming itself the "Nevada-Semipalatinsk Movment" after the place where in the late 80s the major anti-muclear mobilizations were concentrated in the US (where it tested *its* weapons), 10,000 Soviet copper miners in 1989 struck, demanding an end to nuclear testing. In the last days of the moribund Soviet state, their demands resonated with broader circles in the USSR, including those affected by the catastrophic 1986 Chernobyl nuclear power plant in the Ukraine. (Personal communication, Jackie Cabaso, Executive Director, Western States Legal Foundation, March 2017.)

able to walk only in the spirit world. Rituals we led in this world were well and enthusiastically attended. We were obviously tapping into something far deeper than our own limited vision. In jail or before actions, we regularly initiated rituals that proved to be remarkably powerful. People came because they could *feel,* even at a distance of a hundred yards, that power, enjoy it, want to be part of it, draw from it for their own physical, psychological, and political strength in jail, under conditions of enforced confinement.

The Seventh Day Adventist (I remember him through a veil of nearly three decades, as "Robert") who on the spur of the moment decided to get arrested at Livermore, obviously felt it since once jailed he came to our witchcraft rituals and danced — not allowed in his religion — with me, the identified "witch" (for my part it being the first time I had danced with a partner in a motorized wheelchair, let alone one whose battery was unfortunately very dead).

One could also feel continuity between the images used in these rituals of "empowerment," as we termed those, held before major actions, and the free and creative politics played out later at Vandenberg Air Force Base, Livermore Laboratory, the Concord Naval Weapons Base, or the streets of San Francisco and Seattle.

It definitely seemed that these magic spells had had a marked effect on the realities of what we called the "material plane." I have already discussed the rituals overlooking the Diablo Canyon construction site that was closely followed by the discovery of the reversed pipe-support blueprints. Similar "coincidences" occurred at other installations we had targeted in our actions and our magic. We saw repeated instances of the energy magic can conjure. After a powerful dawn Summer Solstice ritual in 1982, we blocked access to Livermore Laboratory for a bus carrying lab employees by stretching a fifteen-foot magical web across the road, made at the ritual out of yarn and charged objects and spells (drawings, feathers, photographs, beads, herbs, etc.), embodying our intentions. When three California Highway Patrolmen, running interference for the bus, did a hasty U-turn on their motorcycles and rammed into our magic web held by about eight of us Matrix members, it stood fast, and I was surprised to see the charged web hold and the three patrolmen crash to the ground.[1]

---

[1] Though I only learned this later as I wasn't present for part of the charging of the web, the spell placed on the web specified that still greater power would be released if it were to be physically torn apart. Police were puzzled when, some time after our arrest, our supporters cheered them as they were forced to cut the web into a number of pieces in order to remove it from the security fence where, feigning that I was tying my shoes, I had surreptitiously tied it while waiting my turn to be cuffed. An especially loud hurrah greeted their throwing the several pieces of the now-dismembered web, after some effort, over the perimeter fence surrounding the Lab, so that the web and its just-liberated spells were physically *inside* the weapons facility! I

In our magical work we continually (re-)discovered extremely powerful techniques. One group, including several members of Matrix, in the middle of a ritual overlooking Diablo Canyon one night was discovered by mounted security guards; it was able to mask an extended political debate, including important legal matters, such as who would stay to be arrested, who fade into the surrounding woods, by chanting, singing, or dancing their "discussion." In such forms, the discussion apparently went right over the guards' heads and escape was facilitated.

Not least, the healing work we did, alone or with others, such as the two-week return of my hearing and our temporary relief for Roy's appendicitis and possible prevention of peritonitis, offers striking evidence of the real power our magic could raise and bring to bear on real problems of health and survival, such as will unfortunately loom ever larger as environmental and social realities continue to deteriorate on our planet. Though they felt as if they had some effect, perhaps those rituals which we did to help "heal" the Earth were mere theater, whose only effect was to make us feel better about ourselves. The same could not be said of healings we did for individuals who were sick, for there it was possible to see more concrete results.

Ultimately history is created by masses of people, moved this way or that by the proverbial winds of change. We saw our job in Matrix as working with those winds, through our magic imagining the air currents flowing in accord with our visions, which we hoped would resonate with the desires of masses of people needed for systemic change, for what might truly come to be the revolution society needs to uproot the Tree of Capital, simply because it has for so long so thoroughly blocked off all light that the Tree of Life has been withering. That our political work was rooted in our magic gave that work a depth and a spiritual connection that I believe is vital to all real and lasting change, especially given the stakes now. Similarly, it provided a direct connection to physical and political reality for our spiritual work.

As our breakup eloquently testified, those connections did not suffice, did not allow us to solve all the problems of the world or of the left. The group had numerous failings. But those connections did allow our politics to be grounded in the natural world, in the airs, waters, and places of our planet, and it was clear to us that we drew inordinate power from that link to our world. Sinking psychic roots into the ground beneath us every time we did magic or politics was more than a metaphor — it seemed to me that

doubt that they ever bothered to remove the remnants as it was in an area of the Lab's extensive grounds that was not landscaped.

After our arrests, handcuffed in a van, Matrix members alternated between discussing our fears that we could be charged with felony assault on the motorcycle officers and trying to decide who should have the movie rights for what had just occurred.

it made that ground an active participant in all we did, rather than simply a neutral place our feet touched as we stood or walked.

Yet the Duponts, Mellons and Kochs and the class they represent also use the "tool" of magic, as do the organs of the national security state. Magic can convey malevolent as well as benevolent intentions. The next chapter addresses the crucial issue of malevolent magic in Germany during the first several decades of the 20th century.

33

Magic & the Nazis

Hitler speaking before a large audience is a man possessed, comparable to a primitive medicine man, or shaman. — Henry Morgan, "The Analysis of the Personality of Adolf Hitler, with Predictions of his Future Behavior and Suggestions for Dealing with Him Now and After Germany's Surrender," a report to the OSS[1]

Hitler is one of our pupils. You will one day experience that he, and through him we, will one day be victorious and develop a movement that makes the world tremble. — Jörg Lanz von Liebenfels, in a letter of 1932 to a fellow occultist

i. An Aryan Ecology

My description and partial advocacy in the previous chapter of some form of neopagan spirituality and politics skirted one extremely critical problem: is not such neopagan ideation shockingly similar to that of the German youth movements of the 1920s and '30s that fed significantly into fascism? Does it not resemble key aspects even of Himmler's SS, which functioned very much like a magical brotherhood and even had a network of organic farms to grow medicinal herbs for them, including one at Dachau?[2] The affinities between fascism and ecology, for that matter, are also quite disturbing. These matters need to be carefully scrutinized. This chapter attempts to further such an examination.

---

[1] Morve Emca, "Hitler ENTJ," *Baffler* no. 41 (September–October, 2018), p. 33.

[2] Robert Proctor interview by Sasha Lilley, "Against the Grain," KPFA, February 4, 2013.

Indeed, many of the top leaders of the Nazi Party, including Heinrich Himmler, Rudolf Hess, Alfred Rosenberg, and William Darré (Minister of Agriculture and Reich Peasant Leader from 1933 until 1942), and especially Hitler himself were keen students of the occult.[1] Jung thought Hitler ruled more through magic than through political power, calling him a "medicine man," and claimed that "Hitler's power is not political; it is magic."[2] Top Nazis took deep draughts from the well of animistic metaphysics; nourished thus, environmental concerns, sensitivities, and commitment grew strong, at least until 1939, when Germany went to war and a more "rational" — or at least anti-occult — outlook came to dominate top circles in the Nazi Party, led by Goebbels, Bormann, and, Göring.

In fact, deep contradictions rent the body of fascism on the matter of nature. Singing their paeans to wild, unfettered nature, the Nazis proceeded above all to erect the epitome of the machine-State, based on the industrialization of death itself, a regime whose very name conjures up images of row upon row of dead victims, like crops growing in their sacred German soil, richly composted with their ideological filth.

[1] As might be expected, a number of books explore this topic, their levels of scholarship varying. Because occult teachings are often not written down, but are passed on orally, the goal of scholarly authentication may be altogether unattainable, but different authors negotiate this problematic terrain differently. See for example, Peter Viereck, *Metapolitics: The Roots of the Nazi Mind* (New York: Capricorn Books, 1961); Nicholas Goodrich-Clarke, *The Occult Roots of Nazism: Secret Aryan Cults and Their Influence on Nazi Ideology. The Ariosophists of Austria and Germany, 1890–1935* (New York: New York University Press, 1992); Dusty Sklar, *The Nazis and the Occult* (New York: Dorset Press, 1977); and Michael Baigent, Richard Leigh, and Henry Lincoln, *Holy Blood, Holy Grail* (New York: Dell Books, 1983).

One of the central figures in the occult background of National Socialism was a man named Jörg Lanz von Liebenfels, who called for the incineration of racial inferiors as a sacrifice to the god Frauja (an Aryanized Jesus), which might require our reexamining what we think we know about the Final Solution, and the wholesale killings of homosexuals, Jews, Roma, the mentally ill, etc., given Hitler's seeking out Lanz (1909) and the latter's claim in 1932: "Hitler is one of our pupils. You will one day experience that he, and through him we, will one day be victorious and develop a movement that makes the world tremble," (in a letter to another occultist). (Goodrick-Clarke, *op. cit.*, pp. 90, 97, 192; Sklar, *op. cit.*, p. 20). The import of Lanz von Liebenfels is questioned by John Lukacs, *The Hitler of History* (New York: Alfred A. Knopf, 1997), p. 62.

[2] David Talbot, *The Devil's Chessboard: Allen Dulles, the CIA, and the Rise of America's Secret Government* (New York: HarperCollins, 2015), p. 230; Lukacs, *op. cit.*, p. 266n.

Both Himmler and Hitler had their soft spots, but in both men it was expressed in relation to animals rather than people. Hitler, who did not flinch watching films of men being tortured, could not endure looking at a movie that showed the sufferings of animals. Himmler, a vegetarian for "moral" reasons, had his treasured copy of *Mein Kampf* bound in human skin. Towards non-Aryans, he, like Hitler, expressed his utter contempt.

Pagan outlooks, worship, and cultural affinities are not particularly German. In every culture I am aware of, the ground cover is pagan, on top of which we find later growth, usually in the form of organized religions, but all indications point to a spiritual kinship among humans to the natural world as far back as we know and can surmise, especially where, as was universally the case everywhere until about a century ago, nearly all people got food through hunting, fishing, gathering, or agriculture, instead of at a WalMart or 7–11. Pagan subculture can even now be found across the English and other countrysides and has become urban. In Germany it became (and remains, according to the Social ecologists), the ground upon which National Socialism easily implanted its heinous ideology.

Naziism included condemnations of the destruction of the whales, protests against deforestation projects, the utmost attention given to ecological considerations in the construction of the autobahns, opposition to wetlands draining — truly visionary, some of them, as well as a recognition of the eclipse of nature that was both the premise and the conclusion of modern industrial society, along with a program to resist it. In fact, some of my railings against modern rationality and the dull, uniform world it produces might seem to echo the rantings of Hitler himself, who saw bourgeois mechanical science as a trap, whose effect was the deadening of the sensibilities of modern man. Am I not essentially saying the same things? How can I seriously try to repackage such detestable garbage?

Indeed, all the resemblances are there, for fascism, as well as witchcraft (at least on the surface), is an *organic* rebellion against the deadening of the spirit — though, in the case of fascism, it was a rebellion that came in an inextricable weave of racism, antisemitism, eugenics, authoritarianism, and male supremacy.

From the early 20th century there had been a German ecological theory of the modern alienation of humanity from both nature at large and from one's own, personal nature, that came wrapped in odious racist ideology. It was upon this that Hitler and the National Socialists built. The *volkische* leaders of this early ecological movement believed that what had been lost was the *German* connectedness, the loss suffered by a race uniquely situated to liberate mankind from the evils of cosmopolitanism, Christianity, mechanical science, and Jewish conniving — uniquely suitable, as *Germans*, for re-establishing (some) humans as part of the natural realm.

According to the analysis by Murray Bookchin and the Social ecologists, the ecological appeal to occult schemas in early-20th-century Germany, rather than to an assessment based on rationality and an analysis of social conditions, doomed their critique to serving, as it ultimately did, to justify the elimination of "inferior" races. To Social ecologists it is but a small step from nature worship to *führer* worship.[1] Indeed, one Nazi enthusiast *did* write:

> This striving towards connectedness with the totality of life, with nature, a nature into which we are born, this is the deepest meaning and the essence of National Socialist thought.[2]

On the contrary, said Bookchin, social conditions and humanity must be at the center of any analysis. Any ecological vision, as with "Deep Ecology," which does not put people at the apex of the system, so that a specifically human lens is used to refract their perspective on things, is unacceptable, at best misanthropic and at least potentially fascistic. Humanity's interests must be paramount.

Social ecology's blame of reverence for nature and a turning away from science and rationality for early-20th-century German ecologists being recruited to genocidal ends is a convenient and ultimately simplistic answer to the many burning questions that the first half of the 20th century has bequeathed to all of us who come after.

Of course, having argued throughout *Marxism & Witchcraft* that mechanical science, instrumentalist reason, and brutalizing technologies are at the roots of our ecological crisis, I am loathe to follow the thread of Social ecology's reasoning. Other than not wanting to believe that I am proposing a path even remotely connected to the one that led to the Third Reich, however, where do I think Social ecology's analysis goes astray?

Naziism did grow in the soil of a German worship of nature, as the Social ecologists emphasize. So, too, however, did Marxism. As discussed at the end of Part Two, the Left Hegelian circles in the 1830s and '40s in which the young Karl Marx first emerged as an articulate social theorist were, like the Germany of a century later, awash in critiques of mechanical science that were philosophies *of nature,* written by the *Naturphilosophen,* as they called themselves; and some of the men and women Marx and Engels associated with would go on to become leading figures in occult circles in the 1850s. The Social ecologists misinterpret the complex history of social struggles rooted in articulated spiritual sentiment (as, for example, in the Diggers, Seekers, Ranters, etc. in the English Civil War, and revolution). Because of their profound wariness towards matters of the spirit, they simply ignore this background to Marx.

---

[1] Janet Biehl and Peter Staudenmaier, *Ecofascism: Lessons from the German Experience* (San Francisco: AK Press, 1995), p 9.

[2] Ernst Lehmann, "Biologischer Wille. Wege und Ziele biologischer Arbeit in neuen Reich," (1934) quoted in *Ibid.,* p. 4.

Between Marx's time and the early-20th-century German *volkische* movement, out of which Naziism arose, massive industry, later in coming to Germany than elsewhere in Europe, by the late 19th century had subjugated city and country alike to its iron will and filled both with the dark smoke of Progress. Thus

> ...industrial development [in Germany] went ahead at a tumultuous pace.... German steel production, roughly equivalent to that of France in 1880, exceeded its closest rival by almost four to one by 1910. Germany's coal output increased seven times over between 1870 and 1913, a period in which British coal production increased less than two and a half times.[1]

Indeed, "[b]etween 1860 and 1910 Germany's industrial output per head outstripped that of Britain, France, and the U.S. In just 12 years (to 1907) machine production increased by 160 percent, mining by 69 percent and metallurgy by 59 percent." Thus were rails and mills, steel and chemicals laying in place the material and intellectual infrastructure that would eventually make possible the horrific trench warfare of World War I, followed by Germany's devastating defeat. This wealth of experience obviously molded the shape of the youth movement that created the back-to-nature ideology in the 1920s and '30s, as did something else: the emergence in late 19th century Germany of a virulent nationalism and anti-semitism. As a consequence, *volkische* ideology in the 20th century was not simply a return to pagan roots, it was a celebration of a specifically German paganism, rooted in *German* soil.

Such a particularized paganism is missing a critical perspective *of the whole*, so essential to any real ecological vision, any real dialectics. Indeed, in order for the Nazis to create the *lebensraum* (living space) for an expansionist Germanic race, it was necessary to cause other races to inhabit *tod-raum*, or spaces of death. Ultimately, of course, in pursuit of empire, the German soil itself was reduced to a charnel house.

That the Social ecologists accept as a given the marriage of a critique of mechanization and a yearning for a spiritual connection to nature with racist ultranationalism rests, then, on a refusal to look at the real historical record in all of its complexity and its contradictions. Rather, according to their axioms about social change, human reason is what must always drive our analysis. Appeals to feelings or to spirits induce in the Social ecologists profound anxiety. It is this, I believe, that leads them to ignore the philosophical critique of Enlightenment mechanization which was found not only among the Left

---

[1]Donny Gluckstein, *The Nazis, Capitalism, and the Working Class* (Chicago: Haymarket Books, 1999), pp. 5–6, quoting W. Kendall.

Hegelians, but in Blake, Wordsworth, members of the Frankfurt School, and other critics of modernization. The Social ecologists surely know of these voices. Including them in their analysis of fascism, however, would necessitate questioning whether the bonds that Social ecology sees between a sacred reverence for nature and German imperial ideology are really that solid.

The constellation of pagan/racism/antiscience/imperialism that the Social ecologists take as a single entity can thus be disassembled into discrete parts that can (and did) stand alone. That they formed a coherent pattern in the 1920s, '30s, and '40s in Germany and elsewhere does not mean that they always do so or that any time you find one of them you will be likely to find the others.

Underneath the sincere pagan anti-mechanistic sentiments, as an element of early Naziism, we find primarily the concrete foundation of mechanism, as the death camps finally revealed to those who had missed this reality up to then. Indeed, the Nazi ideologue Ernst Jünger extolled the ability to regard one's own body as a machine beyond pleasure, pain, and emotion.[1] The magic that is at the core of fascist ideology is what we used to call "black magic," but which is probably best termed "malefic magic," — magic designed to harm, to destroy, to spill blood, to humiliate, to dominate, magic whose lineage is overwhelmingly patriarchal.

At the present time of a resurgent fascist movement in the US and across the world, a recrudescence, as well, of forms of *volkisch* or white nationalist paganism is taking place. Woton, Odin, and other Germanic war gods or goddesses are again part of skinhead, white supremacist, and neonazi rituals.

Indeed, as Shane Burley shows, within the broader pagan movement opposition is building against nativist paganism.[2] What *can* prevent a modern neopagan movement from degenerating into neofascism?

I believe a kind of ideological vaccination can conceivably provide some form of protection against such a degeneration. First a healthy neopaganism should embrace a feminist ideology. What exactly that means will, of course, be subject to discussion and debate, but it should be a given that patriarchal ideas and practices are anathema. Aryan paganism that was the backbone of the Nazis, on the other hand, was thoroughly patriarchal.

Even more than in the bourgeois culture, for which the Nazis expressed such disdain, were women seen by the fascists wholly in terms of their submission to men. Nazi virtues were *male* virtues, and women's job was primarily to breed ever stronger, ever blonder, ever more manly Aryan heroes. The Nazi movement, for all of its male swaggering, was also strongly asexual or antisexual, at least in its ideology. Sex was really depraved; the real threat of the "lower" races such as Jews and blacks was their sexual degeneracy

---

[1] Jeffrey Herf, *Reactionary Modernism: Technology, Culture and Politics in Weimar and the Third Reich* (Cambridge, UK: Cambridge University Press, 1984), p. 78.
[2] Burley, *ibid.*

and how they sought to drag good Aryan women down into their lust-be-sotted bestiality. For the purpose of the right kind of breeding, however, promiscuity was encouraged, and young German girls were directed in this regard to be serviced by the men of the SS. Sex, then, was a duty, while sex as pleasure, let alone as a sacrament, was merely a cover for filth.

In contrast, neopaganism of the kind I have been describing is generally (even in a time of AIDS) celebratory of sexuality. *Feeling good* is an act of worship, ecstasy a sacred obligation.

Second, an Earth-centric spirituality could never ally itself with nationalist or racist ideology. The pagan gods and goddesses need no passports or visas to wander the planet, with Yemaya found in Brooklyn kitchens and Spiderwoman in a Mongolian yurt. The German paganism of the 1920s, in contrast, was bound together with racist ideology and to a fetishization of blood purity.

Third, a neopaganism that speaks to the Earth, to my mind, would eschew any formal hierarchies, as opposed to the core Nazi virtues of hierarchy and blind, unthinking *obedience*, the infamous *Führer* principle that was the backbone of fascism. If so ordered, an SS officer knew he had to be capable of carrying out the most heinous of acts utterly without feeling. Far from encouraging ecstasy, the Nazi elite sought to be in absolute *control* of all their feelings. To feel was to be human, and the fascists wished to transcend humanity, as they believed they could transcend the world.

The neopaganism I have participated in, to the contrary, *celebrates* its humanity — as well as its animality. Eating, breathing, lovemaking, working, sleeping, thinking, sweating, excreting — they are, all of them, holy in their own right. And there is a deeply ethical caveat that must be taken into account in all of one's actions, according to pagan code: "And [if] it hurt no one, do as thou wilt is the whole of the Law." If an act does hurt someone, then simply following one's own inclinations or pleasures is not acceptable, and is apt to lead to unpleasant consequences for the doer.

❋ ❋ ❋

Not wanting to demean Deep Ecology in general or Arne Naess, the radical Norwegian philosopher behind its formation, I must acknowledge that Social ecology's wariness in regard to Deep Ecology is not altogether without merit, as I sadly observed in 1998 at "Green and Gold," a conference at the University of California Santa Cruz on the devastating ecological impact of the 1849 California Gold Rush. There, two of the main US spokesmen for Deep Ecology, Bill Duvall and George Sessions, anchored an afternoon forum. In his presentation, Duvall aggressively attacked the issue of "invasive species," but early on in his crude attack it became clear that what he was really after were the hordes of Latinos pouring into the US. He actually began his talk with an idyllic portrayal of California in 1775, "before the first Mexican gangs invaded my California" to do "what gangs of Mexicans always do, rape, pillage, burn, and murder." A little later he made sure to mention that the CEO of the notorious Maxxam Corporation, then threatening to log a critical redwood forest, was "a criminal Jewish capitalist." In the face of population pressures, both Duvall and Sessions said what was needed was strong, authoritarian governments, citing as an example a Japanese dictatorship from 1615 that over more than two centuries had succeeded in stabilizing Japan's population. Only thus can we be protected "against the invading hordes," and combat the central issue of environmentalists, population growth. In the face of so many people, all other problems fade into insignificance, Sessions claimed, using that as a reason why the movement should ignore "side" issues like social justice, which only distract us. Duvall pledged his allegiance specifically to "the soil of Turtle Island" — i.e., America —and ended by prophesying the burning of cities, as a necessary form of purification.

In 1998, it was clear, this could readily lend itself to an American fascism,[1] and in 2019 it increasingly looks like a mass base for fascism has been put in place.

ii. DRINKING BUDDIES

Confronting the many disparate claims on one's identity, particularly in an age when so many of us have left ancestral homes and live far from motherlands or families, often in what are polyglottal ghettos, is no easy task. Language, class, religion, sports team, family, occupations, gender, even, now, whether one has an Apple or a PC, the radio station one listens to, and, in the new market-defined world of our youth, of course, the brand of one's athletic shoes, jeans, warm-up jacket, etc. — each and every thing pulls at our splintering selves, each demanding to be our "main squeeze," often pulling in opposite directions these many pieces of that self.

Against such splintering, however, stands the interests of the State. In the histories of all countries one finds massive use of physical violence in order to mold the different regions, peoples, languages, religions, and cultures into one sovereign State, with its one army, one language (with a common orthography, hence the first dictionaries), one currency, and one set of laws.

How, on what basis, *should* allegiance *today* be formed in our various lands? Are there any bonds that should be primary? Or is it an anarchy of self-identities, a wild smorgasbord of disparate and possibly conflicting loyalties? Onto this heavily-mined field of contention, the group Planet Drum has ventured, offering a perspective rooted in their ecologically-defined politics. In light of the massive coercion needed to constitute the modern nation-state, Planet Drum argues that we should consider distinctive regional commonalities that are generally found to include dialect, transportation, in-

---

[1] I treated these issues in "Toxic Ideologies," *Reclaiming Quarterly* (Summer, 1999).

dustry, energy sources, crops, ecological communities, and, not least, weather and rainfall. Such commonalities have the potential to bind a people together as a community, according to Planet Drum's "bioregional" principles. In practice, it often turns out that people organize *around their common watersheds*.[1] This, to me, seems like a good starting point.

There is both a terrifying beauty in this perspective, as well as a possible guide to escape from our multitude of messes. Terrifying because when you come down to it, though there are damn few things worth going to war over, water is arguably one of them. The need for water is the ultimate non-negotiable issue, a worrisome notion in a world in which overdroughts on water sources have been ratcheting up by orders of magnitude everywhere under the escalating demands by agribusiness, resource extraction industries, electronics, and, of course, the military, all known for their inordinate thirsts. All of them also dump toxic wastes into rivers and streams.

This is why the struggle at Standing Rock over the proposed Dakota Access Pipeline threatening the water has resonated with wide segments of US society. "Water is life" could not be clearer.

Beyond the anxiety that a recognition of the horrible overdroughts and who the biggest drinkers are justifiably evokes, there lies at least a source of hope, a slight one, to be sure. In a world increasingly chaotic, might not the common need for water, especially potable water, and for working out the competing interests for it help ground our political entities and inevitably direct their attentions, as they must, to those who overuse and abuse that water? At present, of course, water usage for the most part in the US is regulated by various governmental bodies thoroughly controlled by industrial interests and situated within a governmental structure overwhelmingly acting as a superpower, exercising its nuclear dominion over the planet. There should be no illusions that this would be an easy fight to wage by people dedicated to the ecological health of the planet. Yet since our survival so obviously is at stake, fight it we must.

A bioregionally-defined politics would have at least a basis for developing principles and goals able to transcend boundaries along tribal, linguistic, gender, racial, class, species, or national lines. The danger is that competing loyalties could serve as flash points,[2] but they might also, under the desperation (hence, the opportunity) given us by the magnitude of our crisis, serve to help us work out mutually satisfactory solutions, first for water, and perhaps later to a host of non-water issues.

There is a compelling democratic logic to a riparian politics, too, for there is no one who is not directly affected by the way issues come to be resolved. In no sense would bioregional deliberations be about things that people felt did not affect them directly, not in a world where the evidence of bad water is seen in the hospital wards and in the babies born to compromised bodies, as in Flint, Michigan.

---

[1] Interview with Judy Berg, Director, Planet Drum (September 18, 2014).
[2] Especially competing interests between upstream and downstream.

The wonderful thing about water, too, is that ultimately it is all the same water. When the skies weep with acid rain, the water cycle itself is severely compromised; in no sense could riparian politics today or in any conceivable, enduring, future, become the basis for a real withdrawal into narrow regional interests or identities. Our watershed is affected by what occurs in the adjacent river valleys, and, indeed, truly downstream, as they flow into the sea, they are *all* joined. Does not this universal branching pattern of rivers offer us the hope of a true politics *and* a culture that can do honor and pay homage at one and the same time to the general *and* the particular, that can see in the particular all the glories and tensions contained in the overall sum of things? Perhaps in this we return, as in the Taoists, and as in Thales, the Presocratic philosopher, to the profound understanding of water as the mother of us all, including Gaia herself.[1]

iii. THE ONE-SIDED TUG OF WAR IN THE RUHR VALLEY

Wilhelm Reich, the German disciple of Sigmund Freud, had broken over Freud's siding with the repressive forces he thought were necessary to enable "civilization" to emerge. Under the sponsorship of the German Communist Party (KDP), Reich went on to establish enormously successful networks of "Sex-Pol" clinics in the Ruhr Valley in the early 1930s, educating working class Germans about issues of sexual health. These clinics taught about birth control, abortion, acknowledged the sexual needs of teenagers, provided psychological counselling, and raised issues of the availability of privacy for working-class people.

Reich remarked on the very large numbers of men and women he had seen at his Sex-Pol clinic or events or occasions presented by other Party organs whom he later saw at Nazi rallies or presentations. After the Nazis had already come to power in Germany, Reich raised the question why had it been the Nazis, but not the Communists (who in the 1920s and early 1930s had massive support) who were victorious — not in bringing the disaffected to their door in the first place (for both sides did that), but in keeping them inside once they'd entered?[2]

Of course, a thousand criticisms might be made of the crude lines of the Stalin-led Third International and the ridiculous policies it imposed on the KDP (as with many other national parties) in their ongoing struggle with the growing Nazi movement.[1] But against the Nazis, one imagines, crudity alone might not have been much of a liability. Something deeper must have

---

[1] I cannot forego mentioning that the water, it is now believed, was brought to the young Earth by cometary impacts.

[2] A number of Reich's illuminating writings from the mid-1930s were published as Wilhelm Reich and Karl Teschitz, *Selected Sexpol Writings: 1934–37* (London: Socialist Reproduction, 1973). See also Reich, *Sex-Pol Essays, 1929–1934*, ed. Lee Baxandall, trans. Anna Bostock, Tom DuBose and Lee Baxandall (New York: Vintage Books, 1972).

taken place. Reich went on to present an analysis in terms of what he saw as a "mass psychology of fascism," a mind-set born of desperation, eager to be told what to do and whom to do it to, as well as what to believe in a time of soul-searching social chaos. But is it prewritten that desperate men and women will turn to an ideology based on hatred and contempt for humanity as a way out of their misery? In the disintegration of the Weimar Republic, Nazis and Communists battled daily over a period of many years, vying for the loyalties of the despondent masses. The Nazis prevailed. Communists ended up killed, in exile, in the concentration camps created by a politics based on the hunt, centered on hatred. Why did they, rather than the Communists, win?

Might a partial, but perhaps central, answer lie in the recognition by the Nazis of the need for a spiritual revolt against all the things that were wrong in their world — that in acknowledging and even empowering that spiritual hunger, the Nazis, alas, won over the souls of the German people, indeed, won them in a battle that was *never even waged*, for to the Communists there simply *was no useful role* for spirituality. It was something to be denied altogether, a mere diversion. Ernst Bloch argued that German Marxism was so committed to capitalist development that it left the field of cultural revolution and appeals to myth and emotion to the Right.[2] Contemporaries remarked on how readily the Nazis took over allegiances that the German peasants had formerly given both to their increasingly abandoned Catholic Church and to many of the Protestant denominations. In the pre-Christian pagan traditions, still alive in Germany, the Nazis found the embodiment of a spirituality centered around the life forces. It was the demonic nature of their enterprise that enabled the Nazis to *invert* that life force (even as they reversed the direction of the swastika) so that in their hands it became part of the great instrumentality of mass murder. Those lost, demoralized Germans, many of them, chose the Nazis. I would suggest that their choice came in good measure because the Nazis recognized, indeed, to a degree shared, the spiritual hunger among the German people, but that how, and in what direction, they mobilized those spiritual aspirations was their own diabolic invention.

iv. PATHS WITH ROOTS

For all my use in this chapter and the last of the specific example of paganism, let me repeat that I am not advocating a narrow spiritual pathway, singling out witchcraft or neopaganism as the sole or primary outlook by

---

[1] Not least the stongly-pushed notion, this at a time of growing electoral gains by the Nazis, that an even bigger enemy for the KDP was the German Socialist Party, the SPD. (Gluckstein, *op. cit.*, p. 109f.) See the next chapter for more on this.

[2] Herf, *op. cit.*, p. 41.

which our liberatory goals should be advanced. Witchcraft, or more gener-ally, the shamanic arts, is only one of several possible paths. What is impor-tant, I believe, is that whatever spiritual pathway is taken, it must be rooted in our planet, Earth, in her rhythms and lifecycles, at least as much if not more than any orientation towards skyforces, however important those latter may be. In a real sense, on such an Earth, each step is an act of connection, a form of prayer, if you will. Another way of saying this, and something else as well, is that our spiritual path should not be one of continual ascent, away from the human and the animal and the planet, and towards so-called more angelic and ascetic characteristics. Only if we are connected, Earth *and* sky, can the trap of enforced spiritual hierarchies, be they of the Christian priest, Jewish rabbi, Muslim iman, or the Eastern guru variety, be avoided, I be-lieve, another key condition a viable path should offer. Eastern philosophers have no monopoly on spiritual insights, any more than Western religions have on spiritual obfuscation. Hindu teachings, for example, with their rigid notions of caste and hierarchy, lend themselves as readily as orthodox Catholicism to terrestrial as well as cosmic forms of oppression.[1]

I would also hope the path is one of celebration, joy, even ecstasy for the gift of life and the planet that makes that possible, with music and dance, with all the arts to express this.

No viable spiritual path in the early 21st century could ally itself with or ignore any tendency to maintain, let alone intensify, the industrial rape of our planet. That the Earth is under attack from the forces of "develop-ment" and industry should, I would hope, be obvious by now to almost everyone. The evidence is there for those willing to look, to question, and to try imagining alternatives to what is. Any path, any magic grounded in *that* Earth, I believe, unless fraudulent, will feel that reality, and its priorities, strategies, and values will, in the real context of the world today, sort them-selves out accordingly. All who take seriously the need to preserve as much as is possible of the biotic diversity and wondrous beauty that exists on our planet would find compromise with those destructive forces impossible. Our historical moment has narrowed our options and our choice of paths, so that, at least in this regard, the way out should become clearer.

As should be obvious, our larger task as a society is to find and keep to that direction, that path (or paths). Lacking it, we are lost, and more to the point, we surrender all hopes that our children and grandchildren might have a life other than a living nightmare. I assume the path we are looking for must be one to the left, for without a conscious and resolute opposition

---

1 When, as the Indochina War grew more heated, in the middle of the de-bates some hippie would suggest an explanation of napalmed Vietnamese babies on the basis of their alleged karma, I had to repress fantasies of bury-ing my fist in the smug face mouthing such obscene spiritual pieties and ex-plaining that such was obviously *his* karma.

to the ways social and political power has been and remains a weapon in the exclusive hands of the men and women of property and without a dedication to resist the desecrations and pain, the death and humiliation, that result from their ownership, we can go nowhere worthwhile. Since that power flows from and is a reflection of their property, it is necessary to challenge the sanctity with which private property has been vested for some 400 years and more. A man or woman's possession of a piece of paper saying (s)he owns so many acres or square miles does not, by any stretch of a healthy imagination, allocate the right to destroy the river flowing through it, to tear down the mountain that sits astride it, or to foul the airs over it. Not in a world in which we hope to survive.

Therefore, my concluding remarks to this book are addressed to such an opposition, if you will a revolutionary movement, one that respects human needs, the needs of all living creatures, not Capital and *its* needs. A revolutionary movement has to know, to begin with, how historically people have been lured in the opposite direction, towards powerlessness, despair, entrapment, and surrender. How in the world did we allow our current crisis to fester as it has, for such a long time? The answers, as we shall see in the next chapter, are in large measure bound up with ideology and self-delusion.

The obvious difficulty in what follows in the final chapter is that for the most part such an opposition or revolutionary movement simply does not exist at the present time. To be sure, there are powerful, and even strong, local struggles, oppositional tides surging against this bulwark of privilege or that, most recently with the Occupy Wall Street and Black Lives Matter movements. Yet, taken as a whole, the left as a credible force is largely on the margins of things, particularly in 2019, as the forces of reaction have taken power.

Accordingly, in the concluding chapter, I shall indulge in a little hyperbole and write as if there has been a decisive demise everywhere of the leftwing movement. Yet, we instinctively realize that, as always, phoenix-like, such movements will rise again out of the ashes of defeat to confront anew the ever-growing threats to the planet's many inhabitants. What should such movements, be they single-issue or general, local, national, or international, bear in mind as they dry their feathers and look around for means of sustenance in preparation for taking on the long flight of liberation that awaits them? What lessons from a long line of humiliations and failed strategies might they heed?

34

The Mire of Left-Wing Dogmatism.
Who Can Heal the Earth? Conclusions

"Pessimism of the intellect, optimism of the
will." — Antonio Gramsci, *Prison Notebooks*

i. Draining the Bogs of Dogmatism

W e have traced the ideological sources of our mad rush into species-suicide, as well as discussing how the left, especially the Marxist left, has until recently been reluctant to perceive the true depths of this unprecedented world crisis. I have argues that in part this can be traced to a form of mechanical Marxism that became a dominant voice as the revolutionary left too often was mired in a bog of confused perceptions and unfocused visions. Over more than a century and a half, alas, the marsh has become choked with the decaying remnants of those many years of sterile, dogmatic debates and corrupted ideas. Far too many revolutionary organizations and movements found it difficult to maneuver through what has become a proverbial swamp.

Why does the left find it so easy to become stuck in a politics and analysis that are nearly as laughable in their pretense as they are tragic in their consequences? Especially when oppressions other than those based on class are raised on the left, the convoluted arguments of the ideologues can become the most dogmatic and ludicrous. For example, the Soviet Union's principled position of strong support for the liberation of African Americans in the US in the 1930s and after, a position followed by the Communist Party in the US, even as both of them denounced jazz music, a vital and absolutely integral expression of black culture, as a form of "bourgeois decadence." Examples, unfortunately, are easy to find. Perhaps one of the oddest was offered by the Communist Labor Party in the US, one of the many splinters resulting from the breaking up of the New Left in the early '70s, deciding a solution was at hand if only all the residents of a handful of Southern states in the US, no matter what their skin color or parentage, were to be considered "Negroes," just as the residents of all the other states, again independent of skin or parentage, would be considered "whites." Tidy, yes, but also embarrassingly absurd.

By all appearances, the marsh in which left-wing dogma grows must be an exceptionally fertile one, given the profusion of instances historically where the growth of dogma has choked off all possibility of a healthy blossoming of the political left. Certainly the notion, common until the past few decades on the Marxist left — that *as* a left should have known better — that ecological issues were of little importance to the "real working class," given our present predicament, must rank as a blunder of the first order, an egregious instance of such dogma. As I have argued, much of this reflects our sizable capacity for self-delusion and for alienation from our own culture that are at once both the roots and the fruits of dogma. This particular dogma arose from a false representation of the spiritual realm that was a consequence of the severe limits of Marx and Engels' analysis of religions in Germany, confined to Mediterranean-based, patriarchal religions, which they, and even more their followers, extended as a critique of spirituality in general. This extension has unfortunately made for some serious troubles:

a) if it is true, as *Marxism & Witchcraft* has argued, that a vital energy pervades the cosmos, the source of the Earth's overwhelming fecundity, then an honoring of that vitality is not only justifiable, it can even be seen, for those who choose to act this way, as an act of prudence. For a revolutionary movement to disdainfully refuse even to consider the *possibility* of such a living force is a dangerous arrogance. Under hundreds of names and permuted and sometimes debased into all kinds of forms and rituals, *some* of them hierarchical and historically agents of plunder, conquest, and murder, that vital power is the basis of virtually all of the world's religions;

b) clearly the hearts and souls of huge numbers of people worldwide have living and personal connections to this source, whatever it is. However we might feel about a particular institutionalization the spirituality of others might take, it is the height of folly to deny that a valid basis might exist for such feelings, visions, and desires;

c) a look at the history of the past several hundred years reveals large numbers of liberation movements that were specifically rooted in religious communities, for example, the anti-slavery and later the civil rights movement in the US.[1] So too Liberation Theology in Latin America. While some

---

[1] Stokely Carmichael, Chairman of SNCC in the late '60s, for example, was wary of adhering to a Marxist analysis of society "that seemd to reject [blacks']… religious and cultural groundings in favor of a purely economic understanding of social injustice." Peniel E. Joseph, *Stokely: A Life* (New York: Basic Civitas, 2014), p. 242.

of these were no doubt patriarchal, and tied to rigid hierarchies of class, many were not—and a blanket condemnation of all religion that fails to perceive these important differences. on this *central* aspect of culture the world over, readily opens itself up to all manner of foolishness.

In addition to the critical weakness in his overall worldview that emerged from his very partial critique of religion, I have argued that a second problem arose from Marx's dialectical logic and method resulting from his study of Hegel, since Hegel had purposefully toned-down that logic to sever it from its roots in popular magic.[1] This too weakened Marx's argument. In such a manner I suggest he exposed his doctrines to delusional spores of false consciousness — and it is the rapid spread of such delusions that prepares the ground for dogma to take root. Hegel had to prune his dialectical sources of their earlier associations with enthusiasm, for they were too threatening to Property and to religious authorities — indeed, these loosely-related insurrectionary and popular magic themes weave in and out of the European social terrain dating back at least to the apocalyptic visionary, Joachim of Fiore, in the 12th century, and arguable even as far back as the Bronze Age. A pruning, for Hegel, was essential.

This Hegel did in his *Lectures on the History of Philosophy,* where he repudiated the Campanellas, Brunos, Boehmes, and others for their *enthusiasm,* even as he adopted and formalized their logic for the foundation of his own system, writing of one such philosopher's "crazy and demented" behavior and of "the wild vehemence of his nature." Of Bruno, Hegel claimed that his attempt to "introduce order" was really based "in the wildest disorder." He similarly charged that "no method or order" could be found in Boehme's "barbarous" system. Indeed, despite his many fundamental disagreements with Cartesian rationalism, Hegel went on to declare that only with Descartes does the long voyage across the "tempestuous seas" of philosophy finally allow one to "hail the sight of land," in contrast to the "wild and uncontrolled" ideas of a Campanella, Bruno, or the others.[2] In other words, Hegel tamed dialectics, sheering off its insurrectionary history and thus essentially transformed the dialectics of popular imagination into an academic discipline.

And so the dialectic, in the hands of this conservative German apologist for the Junker class[3] was tamed, its "excesses" trimmed to make it accomodate existing relations of power. In Hegel there is no question of that dialectic acting to help the plebian orders call existing social hierarchies into question. In using *this* model of the dialectic for their social analysis, even turning Hegel's version upside down as Marx claimed he had done, to give it a material rather than a spiritual foundation, did Marx and Engels unknowingly cut some of the roots that could have linked their revolutionary theories and

---

[1] See the discussion in Chapter 15.

[2] Hegel, *op. cit.,* Vol. III, pp. 117–18, 137, 192 and 216.

[3] The Prussian landed aristocracy.

the movement itself to the rich history of popular upheavals that had convulsed Europe for centuries before them? In the absence of real history, alas, left-wing fables can too easily be spun.

ii. SCIENCE VS. THE SAVAGES

Despite some acute observations made by Engels in his discussion of the role of the Anabaptists in the German Peasant Wars, the major tendencies within Marxist and other radical social movements has been outright hostility to all religions, which are perceived as obfuscatory at best (indeed, as enemies of science and Progress), and at worst, in league with privilege and property. Marx and Engels were themselves militant atheists. Because of this, many social movements having recognizable bases in religion are viewed suspiciously, their social critique seen as backward or reactionary, even if (as is sometimes acknowledged) their hearts are in the right place. Especially do we find this suspicion of spiritual movements rooted in the land, where the mystical bonds evoked are by now thoroughly alien to the (generallly urban) revolutionary critic.

The other side of the notion of science as the domain of all that could truly be known was a disconnect from any sense of the sacred. Their own socialism, so Engels especially emphasized, was "scientific," not moral, in contrast to those that had gone before, that Marx and Engels disdainfully dismissed as "utopian." In the context of 19th century Europe, in which this was articulated, "scientific" stood for all that was true, objective, hard-edged, and in accord with Progress and the material and cultural gifts of civilization — which is to say, it stood for the world the colonial powers were building. Nineteenth-century writers, if not Marx himself, commonly counterposed science to the beliefs of non-European "savages," which were mere superstition, and so used science as a partial rationale and a major justification for colonialism, and the necessary social reconstruction it stood for. This too became gospel for the Communist movement. In the hands of Stalin, and interwoven with the national interests of the Soviet state, this Marxist claim to "scientific" canons of accuracy and predictability would be repackaged as "the science of Marxism-Leninism," and sold as if it alone offered the means of making correct prognoses about the unfolding of world history and of knowing exactly what positions revolutionaries should agitate in favor of. And so the sorry spectacle, in the 1970s especially, of several such Marxist-Leninist parties in any one country, as in India, each at odds with all the others and yet each proclaiming its ability to speak with the uniquely objective voice bestowed by its "scientific" method regarding what should be done.

iii. *WHICH* CLASS?

From its outset the Comintern, as the Third International was called, suffered from an egregious failure in regard to doctrines and programs for the liberation of the oppressed of the colonized world. It was simply assumed that revolution in colonized and dependent countries could only follow a revolutionary victory by the Western proletariat. That premise was roundly criticized for its Eurocentrism by India's M.N. Roy, Nguyen Ai Quoc (Ho Chi Minh), and others, at successive Congresses of the Comintern, where debate on this question occurred. At the Third Congress (1921), the topic of revolution in India was limited to five minutes, after a year in which "a wave of meetings [in India], demonstrations, and large-scale strikes... shook the entire country," according to a Soviet historian. Boycotts of the courts and schools, work stoppages in governmental offices, and the burning of British goods, involving millions of workers, resulted in "the colonial administration [being] practically paralyzed" in many places.[1] Roy used the five minutes to attack the incredible bias such a limit conveyed.

Similar movements were afoot in parts of Turkey, Persia, China, and Indonesia.

One factor reinforcing a Western slant in the concerns of the Third International was that increasingly its policies and actions were dictated more by the needs of the new socialist State, the USSR, than by what best served the *international* proletariat, that bedrock principle of communist ideology. Under attack from its outset, the new revolutionary government found itself compelled to seek support from some nationalist leaders held in great disdain because of their reformism, like Mustafa Kemal in Turkey and Chiang Kai-shek in China, in the former case allying itself with the Kemalists a mere month and a half after they had arrested 42 of the leading Communists in Turkey, slaughtering 15 of them outright and putting the rest on trial for "high treason." Similarly, in China the Comintern in effect sided with the party of the landlords and bankers by backing Chiang after he had slaughtered thousands of Communist leaders and militants.[2]

A second source for the Eurocentrism was the scant ranks of the assumed agent of Marxist revolutionary change in places like India, Burma, and Algeria, where as Roy himself admitted, "the proletariat hardly existed." Even where some industrial development *had* occurred, as in China, India, and the Dutch East Indies, the percentage of workers was tiny. Because of this, lead-

---

[1] My discussion of these matters is greatly indebted to Fernando Claudin, *The Communist Movement: From Comintern to Cominform*, trans. Brian Pearce and Francis MacDonagh (Middlesex, England: Penguin Books, 1975). The quotations are from p. 250. See also pp. 247–49.

[2] *Ibid.*, pp. 251, 272–73, 279.

ership in anticolonial struggles was likely to be by the intelligentsia and the middle class. According to Lenin's and the Comintern's analysis, movements in the colonized world would therefore invariably be nationalist and reformist ("bourgeois democratic") rather than internationalist and revolutionary.

Thus, in the colonized areas of the world, deprived of the key ingredient, the industrial proletariat, that according to Marx (speaking primarily of Europe) was the critical agent of revolutionary transformation, the many Communist parties that had formed in the aftermath of the 1917 Bolshevik revolution dogmatically advised the dark-skinned of the world: *to be patient!* Conditions were not yet "ripe."

And yet those oppressed masses in the colonies were hardly cut off from mass struggles, as mentioned above. Strikes, agrarian rebellions, anticolonial movements, and small insurrections were taking place in a number of colonies. During the late 1920s and after, both Stalin and his arch-enemy, Trotsky, held rigidly and mechanically to the same formulaic leadership of the proletariat, even in a country like China, involved in a drawn-out revolutionary struggle centered in agrarian areas, Trotsky claimed that an agrarian revolution could be conceived "only on the condition that there will be a new mounting wave of the proletarian movement..." in the face (after 1927) of clear evidence in China of the opposite. Like Stalin and the Comintern, Trotsky too "underestimated the revolutionary potentialities of the peasant masses in the colonies...."[1] Having a vibrant peasant movement but weak urban organizing in China, the Comintern tried to retard the progress of the former until the latter could be strengthened. Even with weakened and spotty Communist and labor organizing in the towns, Comintern theory was "so clouded by the idea of proletarian hegemony" that it called for strikes and armed insurrections in critical cities, resulting in "a complete fiasco," the small and weak Communist and union enclaves easily crushed.[2]

Because the mass struggles in places like India, Algeria and elsewhere were of the *wrong* class, Communist parties everywhere, through the leadership of the Comintern, were simply incapable of taking seriously the heaps of tinder (the universally oppressed peasantry) and the flint (the educated middle class) poised to ignite it throughout the colonial and dependent world. (The exception, of course, was China, which eventually, under Mao, acted in defiance of Comintern dictates.)[3]

---

[1] *Ibid.*, p. 287.

[2] *Ibid.*, pp. 291–92.

[3] The Comintern might also have been uncomfortable with Mao's argument that "the dialectical world outlook emerged in ancient times both in China and in Europe," as well as his criticism of 19th-century "vulgar evolutionism" that was used as an ideological weapon against Marxism, given Marx's own admiration of Darwin. Mao Tse-Tung, "On Contradiction," (August, 1937), in *Selected Readings From the Works of...* (Peking: Foreign Languages Press, 1967), pp. 74, 71.

At a deeper level, this profound disconnect between the worldwide organization seemingly dedicated to the liberation of oppressed and exploited
people of the world and the actual struggle for their liberation in places like
the Dutch East Indies, China, Latin America, Africa, and the Middle East is
but a reflection of the presumed intellectual superiority of the Western proletariat over its largely peasant colonial brothers and sisters, with their burden
of "superstitious" beliefs and "extremely low cultural level." Or, in the formation of Henry Kissinger, the peasants belaboring under the "pre-Newtonian view that the world is almost completely internal to the observer." Of
course, the Western proletariat, and through them, the Western Communist
parties, had learned well those Newtonian lessons. Their mechanical Marxism proved to be a powerful pillar holding up their ingrained Eurocentrism.

To the Comintern, as Claudin observed, "the socialist transformation of
the world meant its Europeanization."[1]

The Communist International's mechanical theory of successive "stages"
of the revolution led it to "miss the revolutionary boat" in Europe as well, as
it initially downplayed the very real proletariat revolution underway in
Spain, insisting against evidence that it was simply a "bourgeois-democratic"
revolution, maintaining down to 1934 that this bourgeois-democratic revolution had to be completed before it could advance to socialist goals. In 1936,
a mass movement in Spain exploded that, according to one historian,

> released political prisoners... compelled employers to re-
> engage workers they had dismissed for political reasons,
> and... began in March 1936, to take over the land. In the
> middle of the same month began a wave of strikes...
> [which] grew from month to month. Factories and work-
> shops, mines and building-sites were paralyzed, businesses
> closed down...

winning in a six-month period 95 percent of the strikes. In the face of enormous support for measures to destroy capitalism, the Spanish Communist
Party (PCE) and the Comintern emphatically insisted on mechanically limiting the aims and actions of the masses, rigidly adhering to the model of
1917 Russia. By 1936 Soviet foreign policy began to play a major role as the
PCE's and Comintern's advisers "set themselves with all the zeal at their
command" to carry out a program of "pushing the proletarian revolution
back within the bourgeois-democratic bounds from which it 'should' never
have escaped." This was at a time when

> Local authority [had] passed, in practice, into the hands of the
> armed proletariat. Also into their hands, and to a lesser extent

---

[1] *Ibid.*, p. 245.

into those of the peasants, passed all the instruments and means of production belonging to the capitalists and landowners.[1]

As if to demonstrate the stratospheric heights mechanical Marxism could aspire to, these doctrinal twists were but a prelude to the epochal, devastating alliance Stalin, and the Comintern, made with Hitler's Germany in August, 1939, just as Hitler's armies set out on their murderous march across Europe, imprisoning and executing Communists as they went. This afforded Nazi Germany an Eastern rear that would cause it no trouble (providing Germany "a calm feeling of assurance in the East," Molotov, the Soviet Commissar for Foreign Affairs, boasted.) Tortured justification by Stalin and other Comintern leaders suddenly, with smoke from the *blitzkreig* rising into the skies of Denmark, Norway, France, the Netherlands, Belgium, and Poland, now cast English, French and American imperialism as the chief enemy of the proletariat worldwide — an act of ideological acrobatics that was to stun Communist militants around the world, catapulting hordes of them into the sloughs of deep despair, as well, of course, as cutting the ground out from under the incipient Allied war effort, which Molotov derided even as he justified German's destruction of Poland. This dire situation persisted until Wehrmacht tanks roared into the USSR on Summer Solstice, 1941.

In mobilizing China's peasantry, Mao Tse-Tung broke from the dominant Comintern model, but he too was a prisoner of a mechanistic revolutionary practice. Thus, after the Communists defeated Chiang Kai-Shek and took power in 1949, campaigns against feudalism were launched in a China that lacked a feudal system such as characterized pre-modern Europe. Similarly, many peasants who owned land were not comparable to the Russian serf-owning gentry or to the English aristocracy, but politically were treated as if they were.[2]

In distancing itself from the "superstition" (i.e., the culture) of the colonized people, the orthodox Western revolutionary tradition severed the rich dialectic that might have woven the oppressed classes of both the colonial powers and the colonies into a common tapestry of struggle. This sundering of cultural realities between colonizer society and the colonized in itself makes the growth of dogma inevitable. For the task of the left, especially in the centers of Western power, must be to confront the historic phenomenon of the European colonization of the rest of the world. If the left is prevented by its ideological blinders from making an honest assessment of this situation, perforce it will invent a dishonest one.

1 *Ibid.*, pp. 166–242 for the Spanish policy. The quotations are from pp. 216 and 224.
2 Ian Buruma, "China: Reeducation Through Horror," *New York Review of Books* (January 9, 2014). Many essentially poor peasants thus became class enemies and were executed.

Thus were the doors opened ever wider for the demons of dogmatism to enter the meeting halls of the left. And having come in, they have fed on the excess energy that has had to be continually generated to maintain the fabrication, the lies, the tearing asunder. And, inevitably that original tear in the fabric of radical analysis proceeds to fray, and what had begun as a single tear leads to a general unravelling. This is compounded by a willful aversion to admitting it own mistakes; fearing that "fallibility undermines authority, [t]he left's typical method has been to brazen out errors…" explains China Miéville.[1] Especially this is the case when obviously ineffective organizing projects are celebrated as models to emulate. If success is essentially inevitable, acknowledged failures can be seen as "defeatist." In too many instances fading numbers, easily observed by the rank and file, are hailed as signs of progress.Once that first lie is accepted, in other words, others become progressively easier.

iv. AWAY WITH ALL DUALISMS!
(OR, RATHER, CURTAIL THEM CONSIDERABLY)

As we have seen in Part One, if we undertake a *class* (that is to say, a *materialist*) analysis of early forms of human spirituality, say in the Americas on the eve of the Conquest, what we find comes full circle, revealing a quite rich symbolic and practical connection between that spirituality and the mundane aspects of *production* (of food, shelter, and the making of health), that holy-of-holies in the Marxist pantheon. Historically, survival in the broadest sense was mediated by the shaman, divining where or when to hunt, gather, or plant, seeking a particular kind of balance through communication with the spirits of their place, thus tied to the minutiae of how to feed, heal, and reproduce a people and their culture.

Yet the matters of religion or of magic are essentially not material and at times can be understood in terms of a certain (for want of a better term) "spiritual energy." As I have argued in *Marxism & Witchcraft*, those two categories, the spiritual and the material, are not really polar opposites, as in Marx (as well as Descartes), nor is it true that the one can generally be explained "on the basis of" the other.

In other words, as a result of my *materialist* critique of the Marxist critique of religion, I must question that fundamental axiom of Marxism: that an understanding of the social movements of history must necessarily ride on the back of a specifically materialist analysis of a particular society. On the contrary, it is clear that there are at least some instances, institutions, and historical developments where ideas or concepts ("spiritual," "immaterial," or "metaphysical" categories in classical Marxist terms) should play a primary role in a comprehensive appreciation and analysis of world history.

---

[1] Miéville, *October: The Story of the Russian Revoution* (London: Verso, 2017), p. 152.

DAVID KUBRIN

As a young academic Marx believed that any critique of 19th-century German society must begin with a critique of its *religion*. Today, in contrast, any critique of late-20th and early-21st century advanced capitalist societies must begin, as we have attempted in these pages, with a critique of its *science*. That is indeed where the contemporary locus of ideological power lies. Accordingly, *Marxism & Witchcraft* has continually raised questions regarding the social and political roles of science, an examination, that is, of the very weapon Marx used in his critique of religion. Thus, this critique too has come full circle.

v. ALL BASE, ALL SUPERSTRUCTURE

In fact, the materialist analysis that is so fundamental to Marxist dialectic runs aground at this serious challenge: how to understand the relations between the material "base" of a society and the thoughts that society has about itself and its world? A long-running debate in Marxist circles has centered on the relationship between consciousness and its objects — in an effort to clarify what Engels meant when he said (presumably speaking for Marx as well) that though a society's material base both influenced culture or "superstructure" (the law, religion, art, science, etc.) and in turn is influenced by them, "in the final analysis" the causative influence always runs from "base" to "superstructure." It is here that Marxist history and analysis finds itself confronted with seemingly insoluble problems. Some of the best Marxist revolutionary leaders, philosophers, and historians have wrestled with this question, including Mao Tse-tung, Georg Lukacs, Antonio Gramsci, E.P. Thompson, Christopher Hill, and Eugene Genovese. Yet, despite brilliant contributions from all of these to the ongoing dialectic, Marxism as a mode of discourse has yet to resolve the thorny questions relating consciousness to its objects, and the relations between base and superstructure remain murky.

Readers who have come this far will recognize that a solution to these problems is unlikely within a debate that renders objects, as does bourgeois and Marxist culture alike, as objective, senseless *things* that exist only passively and inertly. In other words, the debate has occurred on the basis of false categories, with base and superstructure static antitheses more suited for a mechanical than a dialectical view.

I maintain that the relationship between consciousness and its "objects" lies at the core of the phenomenon of dogmatism, for dogma can be understood as the concretized shells left behind by words and ideas that once bore life, but have since ossified under the weight of having to tell so many lies and negotiate so many evasions.

vi. THE (NOT-SO) FINAL CONFLICT

Because our society is built on the negation of life, life as a phenomenon on Earth hangs in the balance. Something very radical — meaning going to the root of issues — is surely necessary to address such a sorry state. Social formations and ways of operating that have brought us to this possible dead-end must be called to account and torn down in favor of institutions and practices that are premised on a celebration — not in words and pious platitudes, but in actions — of life, actions that seek to nourish and preserve it.

These are not abstractions. Whole species *are* dying at alarming rates at our collective hands. Strange and terrifying disease patterns *have* emerged in humans and other species in recent decades. Whole habitats — some absolutely crucial to planetary life cycles — *are* being laid waste. Poisons like dioxin, PCBs, and plutonium, capable of subverting the birth of healthy offspring, are loose in the biosphere, breaking and entering ova and sperm of would-be parents. Human sperm viability worldwide is in astonishing decline.[1]

It is simply astonishing that those in power in our societies are openly poisoning us, without much more of an outraged reaction from the public. Over the past decades, the toxic effects of several agricultural, industrial, and electronic practices and substances have become public knowledge. Tens of thousands of unknown chemical inventions are released at large each year without investigating their possible toxicities, radiation technologies are given ever-wider scope, and various forms and frequencies of industry-produced electromagnetic waves fill our living and work spaces in ever-increasing densities, ratcheted up by many orders of magnitude by the massive deployment of so-called SmartMeters to monitor our electrical usage, as well as ubiquitous satellites for WiFi access *everywhere*.[2]

Authorities readily admit their casual and regular use of such practices and substances and acquiesce in their spread, in vain claiming to an increasingly aware population that, in the amounts used, these toxic substances and practices are harmless. Officials in Southern California, for example, combatted the potential spread of Med-flies by regularly spraying malathion, which is toxic to flies *and* humans and is thought to be mutagenic, over urban populations in greater Los Angeles. Public discussion in the major newspapers barely hinted at what should be the real issue: the regular poisoning of its inhabitants by their government.[3]

---

[1] See Interlude.

[2] In Europe, a "Precautionary Principle" requires tests for toxicity *before* usage.

[3] Mark Wheeler, "Fly Wars," *Discover* vol. 14: 2 (February, 1993).

Our challenge is all the greater, since though a ruling class is still in power, it is clearly out-of-control. Unfortunately, those rulers, capitalist or not, have only the barest glimmerings of the real problems and are by definition incapable of admitting the existence of the kinds of solutions that might conceivably help, for those cut to the core of capitalism's fundamental axiom about the sanctity of private property.[1] As a result, ruling circles rush in with paper-thin responses to the most fundamental of crises. What else *can* they do? But we, who do not have as our mandate the denial of the problems, and who can thus comprehend the depths of our predicament and the formidable (yet, shaky) foundations on which their power is grounded can, and indeed must, proceed differently.

If a left existed equal to the mammoth tasks and responsibilities at hand, how *might* it differ from what we have now? In the developed world, a left exists, but in most places it is marginally visible, even under a President Trump, except at times of crisis, which are usually fleeting. In the Global South, undergoing massive urbanization, however, a more vibrant left is apparent. In places like India, Ecuador, Nigeria, and Brazil indigenous voices articulating a "green" perspective on their continuing anticolonial struggles have emerged, offering new and intriguing models of organizing to pursue.[2]

I think a successful revolutionary movement today must be fundamentally centered around the problems this essay has addressed at such length: the survival of humanity, and of the countless other life-forms that by now depend on us for *their* well-being. Over and above (but *not* independent of *or* superior to) questions of class, race, gender, sexual orientation, hierarchy, or the myriad of other "issues" legitimately spawned by the revolutionary and radical movements

---

1 Perhaps this is not quite accurate, for ruling circles *are* aware that the environmental crisis has the potential to sink the ship of Capital. For example, two of the central figures in the Koch brothers' campaign to undermine democracy and shore up the edifice of "property rights" noted in 1998 that the "biggest threat" to free enterprise was the environmental movement, with its drive for "[e]xcessive governmental regulation of business," necessitating a forceful attempt to "defam[e]" its "hidden agenda." The previous year, Citizens for a Sound Economy, a Koch front group, warned that 76 percent of Americans "thought of themselves as environmentlists," and 65 percent were polled as not trusting business "to take action against pollution...." Nancy MacLean, *Democracy in Chains: The Deep History of the Radical Right's Stealth Plan for America* (New York: Penguin Books, 2017), pp. 195, 216. Some elected officials, like former President Obama, do profess to see some of the most egregious problems, but they tend to be long on rhetoric and short on any solutions that might impinge on the prerogative of property.

2 For example, ther successful fight against Bechtel's attempt to privatize water in Bolivia and the incorporation of the rights of Pachamama (Mother Earth) in the Constitution of Ecuador.

of the past decades and centuries, questions of our survival are paramount. How could it be otherwise? Without solving that problem, it is obvious, solutions to any of the others are simply irrelevant. Yet it will be impossible to solve the problem of survival without at the same time paying serious heed to the other forms of oppression that are also barriers to survival; indeed, as I hope *Marxism & Witchcraft* has helped explicate, colonialism and patriarchy and racism and hierarchy all emerge out of the same configuration (though all of these, in embryonic form, have long histories that can be traced to prehistory), so that a fight against one is a fight against them all; no more than the *yin* can be separated from the *yang* in their representation can these issues be treated separately. They can, however, be brought into greater or lesser focus, approached from this angle or that, as an occasion or crisis calls for.

It is probably the height of human arrogance (admittedly, the competition is fierce) to speak of "healing" the Earth, as many do these days, for her powers and her range are far too vast, but even if our forces are too puny to bring real health (or real death for that matter) to the mysterious creature, Gaia, that is our planet, it seems well within our capabilities to apply balm to her many local wounds: to restore a habitat here, clean up a river there, to push back development and stop the use of toxic poisons that have no business even being manufactured, let alone dispersed.

And there are creatures to be healed or treated, many of them human, some of them very likely in our immediate circles of family, friends, workmates, neighbors, and comrades.

The canaries in the mine this time are our neighbors, as well as the frogs, the corals, the snow leopards, etc. etc. AIDS is only one of several recent epidemic immune disorders, not all of them restricted to humans.[1] That diseases of the immune system, *the* disease-fighting faculty, should emerge now, in light of all the devastation we have visited upon the biosphere, is terrifying, the proverbial "wake-up call" for our species. There has been a vast increase of people suffering from allergies, including especially asthma. Particularly alarming are the growing numbers who cannot live in any environment having any of the vast number of modern invented chemical compounds that are at the core of our industrial society, and so they must spend their lives off in the rural woods in buildings of un-painted and un-stained lumber in near-total isolation, surrounding themselves with cotton and vinegar rather than vinyl, polyester, and Pledge.

The further weakening of immune systems, so that the body is attacking itself, is one of the expected consequences of the thinning ozone shield that has, until a few decades ago, protected us from the more harmful rays of the sun.

---

[1] Several years back tens of thousands of dead seals washed up from the North Sea onto English shores, thought to have died from immune deficiencies. That we see fewer reports of this kind at present does not, I believe, reflect a lessening of the problem, rather, it is more that by now the media accept it as normal.

All of these are, to say the least, exceedingly ominous signs. Meanwhile, at our Three Mile Islands, Lake Baikals, Chernobyls, Rocky Flats, Love Canals, and Fukushimas, we generate new "zones of infertility," extensive areas in which we can expect very high incidences of gross malformations in human and animal births and the plants that grow, probably for hundreds of thousands of years or longer.

Consequently, as the illnesses and those born to only partially functioning bodies and minds increase and spread, a revolutionary movement laying claim to universality and to dealing with the many needs of the planet must consciously think of itself as a movement of healers. For many of us that will mean learning to administer one of several life-saving or life-enhancing techniques to some of us who might fall, whether it be giving CPR, herbal, or yogic treatments for serious illnesses, or offering massages to one another at meetings—and at games, in the parks, in our workplaces, or in bed. Sometimes such treatments will be necessary because doctors (or clinics) are unavailable, as in many conditions of imprisonment or rural isolation; are in disarray, as under conditions of social breakdown, disaster, or war; serve as an oppressive force, as is often the case for women or people of color; are prohibitively expensive, as indeed, in the US, they often are; or are more damaging and intrusive, with a lower success rate, than the alternative, and far cheaper, therapies available. Whatever form it takes, however, a revolutionary left will necessarily pay attention to the critical need to heal ourselves — including, it is to be hoped, any creatures we live with in symbiosis, as companions or as sources of milk, eggs or meat — and will consciously think of itself in terms of a healing mission befitting the nature of our times and of the forces against which we contend.

At another level, the totality of our efforts to transform society can be seen as a form of healing. This is the case even if our work is seemingly in totally unrelated areas, like a strike in a particular industry where bread-and-butter issues are what appears to be most important. For we can assume that under early-21st-century capitalism, there are few workplaces where due attention (or any) really has been paid to the safety and health of the workforce, or where some kind of toxic substances are not being used or produced. Additionally, the conflict between labor and capital itself can be seen as a dis-ease, the result of practices and assumptions made thousands of years ago as privilege and class began to intrude into the relations between people, practices, and assumptions codified hundreds of years ago in the new laws regarding property.

As much as any pathogen, those laws, giving the owners of capital only marginally-regulated powers of life and death over their workers and their families, over rivers and valleys, *cause* disease, be it black or white lung, maimings, high blood pressure, or the cancers, asthma and ADHC striking down the children of migrant farm workers in the Central Valley and Salinas

Valley of California and elsewhere.[1] Science, as well as the law, helped establish this new rule of property in part by its teachings about the nature of "things" and its "objectification" of the cosmos, and by standards of proof on questions of causality in regards to toxics that are virtually unattainable. Among other topics, people learning the implications of the 17th-century scientific revolution saw that it was normal to block out any "subjective" feelings they might have had about the assault on nature, since that assault was but one of the prerogatives of property. Once again, learning to blind ourselves to this first outrage made it easier each additional time it was necessary to avert our eyes. So our healing movement must work on the psyche, as well as the body, to heal as well the breach in consciousness that occurred when people learned to accept as a given their divorce from nature and professed a desire to "rise above" it. How else can our movement think of ourselves, under such circumstances, except as healers?

Our world is dangerously out of balance. The craft of the ancient healers, witches, and shamans was principally to recognize when unbalance had created disease, and to carry out the necessary steps to restore balance. The sources of our dis-ease patterns are as much social as natural. The steps we must take are many, and the path is long and tortuous, but it is clear that it need take us into (among others) the social arena, where we must subvert the power of those who live only for property and are prepared to poison the rest of us (and themselves too) to keep and extend it. New sickness that is traceable, as in Lyme's disease, to a specific parasite, exists, but far more ominous for our times are the institutions whose daily functioning inevitably produces corpses by the tens of thousands such as the International Monetary Fund in the 1980s and '90s and beyond. That is when the IMF introduced those "modern devils," mandatory austerity measures called "structural adjustment programs," forced on developing countries to make them eligible for new loans — refinancing their high level of debt by imposing still more debt — and so decreeing the deaths of untold numbers of children from malnutrition, shuttered clinics, or drinking water that no longer coud be treated. Similarly, in San Francisco's Bayview district, historically a predominantly African-American community, which has 4% of the city's population but a full third of its hazardous waste sites, including the notorious Hunter's Point shipyard, where purposely irradiated warships (from thermonuclear bomb tests in the Pacific) were scrapped and on-going radiation experiments were conducted by the Navy's nuclear warfare research lab from 1946 to 1969.

---

[1] Thomas H. Maugh II, "UC study links ADHC, pesticides," San Francisco *Chronicle* (October 20, 2010). Kevin Schultz, "Pesticide tied to drop in child lung function," San Francisco *Chronicle* (n.d., but after 2013). Peter Femrite, "Chemicals, pollutants found in newborns, study finds," San Francisco *Chronicle* (December 3, 2009).

Slated for housing and other development once the US Navy abandoned the area, it was declared safe in 2004 and construction could begin. Out of 10,500 planned residences at one site, more than 300 have already been built. Unfortunately, it has repeatedly been shown that cleanup results were faked, with as much as 97% of data possibly falsified, while cover-ups by the Navy, California Department of Public Health, San Francisco Department of Public Health, and the EPA downplaying residents' obvious alarms.[1] A 1991–92 study revealed that the Bayview had four times the state average of hospitalizations from chronic diseases (asthma, congestive heart failure, diabetes, emphysema, and hypertension); and 138 hospitalizations per ten thousand, compared to the state's average of 37 per ten thousand. At Dr. George Washington Carver Elementary School in the Bayview, 80 out of 280 students have been diagnosed with asthma, more than 28%.[2]

Our imbalances are global and they are rooted in social realities. There are far too many in dire poverty while a few surround themselves in obscene displays of their (essentially stolen) wealth, sleeping under $15,000 bedspreads[3] and driving cars costing over $1,000,000. What else but a profound reflection of imbalance is this?

People for some time to come will get sicker and sicker. And the only revolutionary movement that can have anything worth saying in such a situation is one that takes on the full range of our oppressions — not as acts of charity, but as what is necessary for survival, for rebellion, and the deep recognition that an injury to one is, indeed, an injury to us all. For we have come too far and the stakes are much too high for us to think that solving our monumental problems with partial solutions or with half-answers is all that we can do. Specific reforms, quick fixes, will always be worth a fight, but we cannot ever lose sight of the whole or the need to transform all of an ailing world.

In terms of what needs to be done in the here and now, that will become apparent in the doing, in the playing out of our creative energies as we there and here collectively confront grievous, near-insurmountable problems — that, nonetheless must be surmounted. Successes there will inspire new visions and new trials here, and these can neither be predicted nor prescribed, only, as they unexpectedly win victories, marvelled at.

---

[1] Ida Mojadad and Laura Waxmann, "Toxic Relationship," *SF Weekly*, vol. 37, no. 95 (August 23, 2018), and J.K. Dineen, "Flawed Shipyard Cleanup Blasted," San Francisco *Chronicle* (August 16, 2018).

[2] Aurelio Rojas, "High Rates of Disease In Bayview: Study Lends Weight to Pollution Fears," San Francisco *Chronicle* (June 9, 1997)

[3] As featured some years back in the San Francisco *Chronicle*. Such are the seductive powers of late capitalism that by the time I had finished the article, I kind of wanted to possess such a bedspread.

vii. CONCLUSIONS: A TRIAGE FOR OUR ENVIRONMENTAL WOUNDS. DREAMING OUR WAY OUT OF ECOPALYPSE

Marxism & Witchcraft has — realistically, I believe — emphasized how bleak are our prospects as we face the terrifying reality of oceans, coral reefs, forests, wetlands, estuaries, and arable land nearly everywhere under tremendous assault. How is it even possible to imagine fighting on so many fronts at once? Where should we, as a kind of imaginary movement of all those affected by the disappearance and destruction of habitat, put *our* resources? On behalf of or against which species, what toxin, which river valley do we mobilize?

Here I want to suggest a strategic framework for a practice of ecological triage, a way to pick which battles must be fought (and won) now and which can wait. Under such a strategy, truly catastrophic habitat collapse could be immediately addressed, conceivably to be stopped and even, sometimes, reversed. Thereby we might just have a decent chance of avoiding spectacular global collapses of populations.

For the moment, let us assume what now seems preposterous, that the political and social will had materialized to confront our environmental crisis once and for all — realizing, of course, that such would not be possible without our simultaneously tackling a host of other fundamental social issues. To make our discussion simpler, let us further assume that legalities, "property rights," and the availability of the resources necessary to "do the job" are not issues, though, of course, in reality, they inevitably will be. But those are all questions that will have to be resolved in the course of the revolutionary struggle that will have brought society to this imaginary point.[1]

I will propose fairly clear ways to decide questions of environmental priorities. For in the absence of an understanding of priorities, too many would-be activists fall into a defeatism predicated on the false assumption that it is too late, essentially giving up. Establishing a practice of triage for ecological survival will allow us to steer clear of such an "all or nothing" approach.

Before we can discuss those ways, a brief excursion into the history of technology is needed, one that focuses on how production techniques have changed in recent times and how some of these changes have interfered with natural systems, with the airs, waters, and places. A cursory look at this his-

---

[1] According to the political writings of Thomas Hobbes and John Locke — the theoretical bases of much of both the US Declaration of Independence and Constitution — people willingly surrender a measure of their freedom to the sovereignty of the State, in exchange for the State's obligation to protect them. That social contract, in terms of environmental dangers, has clearly been broken by the US (and the many state) governments. Hence the justification for revolution.

tory reveals a startling fact, a clearly defined watershed moment where what went before and what after were altogether different. And that moment, that historical turning point, significantly, lies close to the edge of living memory.

Although the onset of colonialism and the vast social, economic, and cultural upheaval that followed, wreaked havoc on terrain, people, and communities, for the most part the baneful ecological effects of the newer practices and technologies were felt by those who worked on and or lived in immediate proximity to them. For the most part, dangers were somewhat localized. Miners suffered, so too their families and animals who breathed the dust brought back on their clothing. Similarly there was localized overcutting of trees, destruction of wetlands, and the monoculture of plantation agriculture. But even with the Industrial Revolution two or three centuries later, and the introduction of steam engines, *regional* or *global* environmental effects are mostly absent, for the blight of mass industrialization had not yet metastasized across the land. Toxic wastes fouled rivers, to be sure, but not whole aquifers.[1]

Such was the impact, for example, of early mining technology in the 16th and 17th centuries, although some mining and smelting operations used toxins like cyanide and arsenic, concentrated acids, or mercury (their toxicities might be diluted downstream. The steam engine of the 18th century and the automatic looms and railroads of the 19th similarly polluted particular locales, not whole regions. Each of the technologies, as it developed during this extended period, exacted its toll from the waters, from the land, and from the people and creatures who toiled with its tools, but systematic poisoning had not yet entered the picture.

This began to change in the last half of the 19th century, particularly in developments by the German chemical industry. It was the search for synthetic dyes, pharmaceuticals, and a way to fix nitrogen (largely, for agriculture) that led to the formation of enterprises which eventually became, in a kind of baleful dark alchemy, the German chemical cartel, IG Farben, a key player in the rise to power of the Nazis in Germany, and the producer of Zyklon B.

What IG Farben was in Germany, Dow Chemical and Dupont were in the US, though, particularly in the beginning, they were a step or two behind their German competitor.[2] Fierce rivalries pitted Dow against Farben and Dow against Dupont; but some of the negotiations that were part of their legal and commercial wrangling ended with rivals holding percentage inter-

---

1 As Paul Virilio observed, "Today the new technologies convey a certain type of accident, one that is no longer local and precisely situated, like the sinking of the Titanic or the derailment of a train, but general, an accident that immediately affects the entire world." Critical Art Ensemble, *The Molecular Invasion* (Brooklyn: Autonomedia, 2002), p. 76.

2 Diarmuid Jeffreys, *Hell's Cartel: IG Farben and the Making of Hitler's War Machine* (London: Bloomsbury, 2008.)

ests in each other, so that ownership was intertwined and frequently hard to disentangle. Significantly, some of the US chemical firms, like Dow, were known for Nazi sympathies before and during World War II.

Worldwide the chemical industry worked assiduously on warfare: how to supply it, how to organize and transport it, how to make it more deadly, and above all, how to justify it by the competition for key minerals, the fights among countries to obtain monopolies over tin, rubber, or bauxite ores. For World War I, the chemical industry produced the agents for the infamous gas warfare in the trenches and bombs explicitly designed for targeting *civilians*, in contravention of till-then respected laws of warfare among European powers.

In the 1930s run-up to World War II, the chemical industries, led by IG Farben, were especially busy. Besides long-lasting projects to free Germany from dependence on key foreign strategic materials — a critical bottleneck for Germany in World War I — by producing synthetic fuel and synthetic rubber, Zyklon B was made in great quantities as part of an industrialization of murder. So too the notorious nerve gas, sarin (the US developed its own version.)

In fact, World War II and its preparations represents in environmental terms a dramatic *watershed*. The scope of hostilities in that conflict, of course, was unprecedented, but more to the point *all* of the major actors in the war engaged in policies that were genocidal. The Germans and Japanese, of course, who were prosecuted for their notorious war crimes; but they were tried, obviously, by the victors, who themselves had engaged in widespread carpet-bombing runs over civilian areas of Dresden and Tokyo, among more than one hundred other cities,[1] and the one-two punch of Hiroshima and Nagasaki. British and US leaders should also have been in the criminal dock, So too with the USSR, which also killed for ethnic and other reasons in the hundreds of thousands and then millions.

As the conflict drove US, Britain, Japan, Germany, and the USSR to war policies that were explicitly genocidal, a parallel development was unfolding industrially. In part, not surprisingly, this was a direct consequence of developing the *means* of pursuing such a war, like the new fuels necessary for the V-2 rocket or the explosives for higher-yield bombs. But at a deeper level, there had been some kind of conceptual shift as well, a new way of looking at just what should be made and done. Technologies were now pursued that intrinsically were far more toxic than their 17th-, 18th-, or 19th-century predecessors. Plastics, for example, introducing a Pandora's box of carcinogenic chemical compounds in the manufacturing, use, and disposal of — such as the huge amounts of dioxins released when plastic trash is incinerated. Both world wars also required gargantuan amounts of food shipped in time and in the right amounts to ever-shifting (well, in World War II they shifted) battlefields, and from that logistical nightmare were

---

[1] Sasha Lilley, "Against the Grain," KPFA (October 21, 2014.)

eventually born agribusiness, packaged foods, supermarkets, and the production of our food by means of a perpetual I.V. drip of organo-phosphates into the harrowed lands, toxins, closely related to the nerve gases, being ladled onto our plates along with the chicken and corn, in the process inflicting untold numbers of cancers and early deaths onto farmworkers and their children working those lands. The topsoil, too, the very basis for growing food, is thereby degraded, its former vitality replaced by ever-larger doses of petroleum-based chemical fertilizers. And, as if to flaunt how far agribusiness can separate itself from the natural world, livestock today are fed what amounts to cannibalistic diets.[1]

In other words, concommitant with the genocidal war policies of Axis and Allies alike, in the factories and fields of the world, critical lines were breeched. Once more the chemical firms were in the forefront, with explosives, agrichemicals, and plastics all parts of a much larger agenda, in what really amounted to an apotheosis of the mechanical comprehension of nature, including a drive by the chemical industries to invent ever-newer molecules with virtually no thought given to questions of toxicity. Better living through chemistry, and no questions asked. Hand-in-hand, the radioactive industries, nuclear power and weapons production and testing, and the dispersal of radioactive medicine nearly everywhere generated widespread problems of transport, spillage, waste, much of it, like plutonium, extremely toxic for hundreds of thousands, conceivably even millions, of years.

In the years right after World War II, two ominous patterns became clear. First, some of the newer technologies were especially harmful to human and other species' abilities to reproduce. Of radiation technologies, this is obviously true, but many of the agricultural chemicals caused related genetic damages and infertility, as well as being carcinogenic. So, too, the chemicals, like the glycol ethers, used in computer production. Newer and more powerful solvents had been developed in the same decades and it soon became alarmingly clear that among the many things the newer solvents could dissolve was the still-only-partially-understood DNA molecule. And so many more malformed babies, stillbirths, women incapable of bearing, men with ever-diminishing sperm counts as a worldwide phenomenon, reproduction abnormalities shared among a great many species.[2]

The second ominous pattern is that, like the world war that brought to life these new technologies of the '30s, '40s, and '50s, the new forms and materials of production were creating ecological impacts that were regional,

---

1 Interestingly, the Hon. Mike Lord (U.S. District Court for Minnesota) remarked in 1978 that it was the government's role to warn the public of possible dangers, but by "about the end of World War II... it more or less threw up it[s] hands." *Silicon Valley Toxics Action*, vol. XII, no. 3 (Fall, 1994).

2 See Graph, p. 325. Also Erin Allday, "Problems with sperm linked to death risk," San Francisco *Chronicle* (May 16, n.y.)

not merely local, in many instances even global. Whole aquifers were drained or polluted. Coal-burning power plants in China spread toxic mercury to the US, and US deforestation brought on desertification in North Africa. Climate change is an example of this. Though explosive uses of fossil fuel (trees and coal initially) date back to the 16th and 17th centuries, the real impact in the form of climate change only came about in the late-20th century, following World War II.

The World War II watershed, then, consisted of a war-making apparatus of a number of nation-states that incorporated genocidal aims and methods into their battle plans *and* the development of new technologies that, by virtue of their interruption of normal reproduction, were also at least potentially, and often actually, genocidal,[1] particularly since the toxins nearly universally end up dumped, in the US, in communities where black, Latino, Asians, and poor whites, historically "surplus" populations, live, or end up exported to poor countries where the waste is pored over by human scavengers. The toxic effects of many of the new technologies are felt regionally or globally.

In short I have argued that some modern technologies go considerably beyond the mostly limited environmental damages of early industry, in recent years even becoming planetary (if we include the recent tendencies of NASA and European and Japanese space agencies to crash missiles onto the moon and onto comets), and even celestial, (dispatching rockets fueled by plutonium reactors throughout the solar system and beyond). This understanding is critical if we have any hope of finding an escape from our crisis. That key modern technologies actively undermine reproduction in numerous species worldwide (in a pattern seen from the second quarter of the 20th century on) is particularly ominous.

It is, however, also a particularly hopeful sign: since most of these truly catastrophic dangers are of relatively recent origin, a plausible scale of ecological priorities suggests itself. Because it is particularly the newer technologies that are most lethal and that pose such a clear and immediate danger, it is there we should start. This would involve re-examining the many industrial practices developed during the past eight decades, about the lifespan of many people today, particularly in the developed world.

In our imaginary world, dead-set on getting its environmental affairs in order, people will still work. At what, for how long, and so forth are not our concern here, though a few observations might be helpful. In an ecologically balanced society, all production will be because things are needed for *use*, not to make a commodity for *selling*, so considerably fewer things will be made, at least in the richer countries. Some goods will continue to be produced. The obvious questions are what *kinds* of production would be favored in this world? Which ones not? What is to be manufactured, and how, obviously will be central questions. Which of the many technologies with which

---

[1] See discussion in Chapter 21.

our lives have been nearly inextricably entwined must we disentangle ourselves from because they are too damaging?

There will be some instances, like nuclear power, that should have been stopped long ago and that will now have to cease say, within a year. While some critical habitat destruction can conceivably be stopped, debate on impacts that are less urgent, more long-range, could be afforded the extended study and discussion required for society to find clarity on how to proceed. This will, I believe, avoid the paralysis induced by the sheer multitude of environmental disasters in the air, water, and land, meeting our eyes nearly every place we look, unsure where to focus our resistance.

Some technologies, ways of doing and materials used, we will be unclear about. They may possibly be harmful, but not in a way that is catastrophic. Some of these might have been around for a century or so, perhaps, and another century might be okay—while a careful investigation is conducted to look at concrete impacts, research what alternatives might exist in terms of materials used, and assess whether any negative impacts are genetic or global.[1]

With healthy reproduction under serious attack, as our long-suffering spermatozoa, etc. are, any technique or material that undercuts ours and other species ability to reproduce, as basic a life-function as there is, must be stopped immediately.[2] So too with modalities of production that have detrimental global impacts that are genocidal, or that are or will pollute, deplete, or degrade regional aquifers. These are where critical lines must be drawn. Thus will we establish the working framework for a strategic system of environmental triage.

There should be no need (or justification) for "careful investigations" in regard to toxic impacts on marginalized communities, racial or tribal minorites, women, gendered-others, etc. In most instances multiple studies will have already been done. The need now will be for systemic action.

What sort of manufacturing might exist into a short (say, 50 years) future while our imaginary world, where the focus is on escaping ecopalyptic endtimes, figures out how to get to a sustainable future?

All production and all materials used in any manufacturing would be immediately judged on a chronological scale. Any materials used that were developed since the 1930s, especially by the chemical industry, will be immediately suspect, the question of their continued uses matters of the highest priority. Many of the commodities manufactured with toxic effects today were, not so long ago, made differently and with much more benign impacts. Those older methods would be recovered — as Cuba successfully did in the 1990s

---

1 Though generally not well known, a great deal of such research has been going on for decades by alternative technologists.

2 Given the understandable worries about worldwide population *growth*, it is important that we heed the clear implications of a pending population *collapse* of Graph Three.

after the collapse of the USSR, forced a return to agricultural production no longer dependent on chemical inputs. Here it will be the responsibility of our elders to teach, based on their collective memories, some of these older ways.

In many instances, a hold might be put on making certain things until older methods, pre-1930s, could be found and substituted. Printers inks might have to be immediately reformulated using earlier materials. Manufacturing of most plastics would be stopped immediately, the rest as soon as possible. So too the pernicious chemicals of agribusiness; anything that ruins topsoil cannot be tolerated any longer.

But a whole lot of things would be allowed, at least for a while, let us say fifty years, maybe even a century, while society debates long-term goals and how they might be reached. Will agriculture remain the primary source for food?[1] How much international trade? What mix will there be between modern and traditional forms of healing? How politically, ecologically, and economically, will regions be constituted? How might transportation be used to define such regions? How are youth to be taught and to what ends? These and a host of other questions will demand attention. In the meantime, contingent on not relying on any of the newer chemicals developed by the IG Farbens, transportation industries are likely to continue into the next fifty years or more, with a powerful emphasis on mass transportation,[2] but otherwise relatively similar except on the matter of scale, particularly for fuel-hungry carriers like airplanes, whose flights would diminish considerably. Fuels would have to be reformulated. Of necessity, and thankfully, it will be a slower world. Transformation will be occurring everywhere, but at a human, not Capital's, tempo.

Thus roads will be repaired, railroads laid and maintained; trains will be produced and run. For some time, again with different fuels, the internal combustion engine might still have a reduced role to play. Machinists will ply their craft, for machines of different kinds will have to be made and eventually be fixed by mechanics.

For climate change, or, perhaps better, "climate mayhem," a probable agency, greenhouse gases, has been identified, and the case is highly plausible.

---

[1] See Spencer Wells, *op. cit.*, who argues (p. 90) that modern diseases have their roots in the mismatch between human biology and our largely agricultural diet.

[2] Real mass transit — widely available, frequent, and cheap — will, of course, require massive allocation of resources. In the US a good source for these might be a special tax (or expropriation) from the oil and automotive industries which conspired, as is well-documented, to buy up and then purposely destroy many mass transit systems in a number of cities in order to force the public to buy cars and gasoline. Such a tax, justifiably, would be huge. The squeeze should be put on Big Oil. They can afford it. See Iain A. Boal, "A City for Idiots," in Chris Carlsson (ed.), *The Political Edge* (San Francisco: City Lights, 2004), p. 203.

The shrinking of the polar ice caps and worldwide retreat of glaciers are all we need to compel action. Since most of the claims about specifically human causation behind the climate crisis, are based on *computer simulations* (a mathematical analytical treatment of real weather patterns, given dozens if not hundreds of independent variables, would be too complex to carry out), in my eyes at least, it is not *irrefutably* proven and possibly never could be, still it would be foolhardy to delay action combatting increases in greenhouse gases while "further research" is done. We can no longer follow Thomas Sprat's and the Royal Society's recipe for delaying reaching conclusions and taking action until "every rubb is… to be smooth'd: every scrupple to be plained: everything to be foreseen…" for it is time to recognize that attitude for what it was, a way of deflecting responsibility. "Certitude" will probably have to be jettisoned as an impossible standard, and probabilities used to guide decisions when assessing all such questions of agency and toxicity.[1] (An added benefit is that this will provide socially useful work for armies of lawyers, for such redefined legal standards will raise all manner of legal and philosophical, not to mention scientific, issues.)

When the time to act is now, to demand *proof* that human agency is responsible before an all-out effort is made to reverse the build-up of heat-capturing molecules would be suicidal. Besides, curtailing the sources of greenhouse gases will inevitably curtail mass production, reducing the compulsive making of commodities under capitalism, a worthy environmental goal in its own right, though anathema from the perspective of a capitalist imperium to either expand or die.

Industrialization's mass production as a model for how goods are made will have to be carefully reconsidered. I have doubts it will survive even a cursory scrutiny, for the industrial model is premised on an *endless source* of the "stuff" out of which manufacture is possible, all of it, one way or another, taken *out* of our planet, as well as an *infinite sink* into which, without significant consequences, all the resultant wastes (from the making and the discarding) can be dumped, now *into* the planet. Both assumptions are demonstrably false and dangerous.

Though mines for extracting minerals are generally devastating to their communities, at a much smaller scale the taking of ores from the Earth may be considered acceptable into the immediate future. Scale will be important too for things like tanneries, smelting plants, mills, the production of both AC and DC electricity. More and smaller units of production will be used, scattered around so that if (temporarily) something having toxic effects is thought necessary, everyone will share in its toxic burdens, and to diminish the amount of transportation needed. All this will be made easier in the absence of capitalism's relentless pursuit of "efficiency," its unstated synonym for higher profits.

---

1 See the film "The Devil We Know" about how nearly impossible it was, despite overwhelming evidence, to establish the toxicity of manufacturing Teflon.

Any or all of these technologies may, in the long run (say, 200 years) be found inappropriate. Research into such questions will, obviously, be a very high priority, but there will be several decades to do the proper research and analysis. It will be the focus of an "industry" of investigators.

The manufacturing and uses of electricity will need careful investigation. Research into possible effects of cell-phone technology (towers and phones) has begun to show toxic effects of even earlier releases of electrical energies into our communities, pointing to a role in a number of modern degenerative diseases.[1] AC or DC, at what strengths and which frequencies, need to be looked at for possible effects on cell metabolism. Electrical industry, including its mode of transmission, may be an important exception to my previous claim that only in the past eighty or so years have we seen environmental destruction that has regional or global impacts, since even with the introduction of the telegraph in the 1860s serious health problems seem to have resulted. To maintain our ability to use our many machines fueled by electricity, how it is made, transported,[2] and used will quite possibly need to be redesigned in the coming decades.

All such investigations will begin to look into less mechanistic ways of intervening in nature, would, in fact, understand humanity's *partnership* with the natural world as a more appropriate model, anchoring our understanding in an awareness of the traditional four directions honored for millennia by indigenous people everywhere.[3]

---

[1] Arthur Firstenberg, *The Invisible Rainbow: A History of Electricity and Life* (Santa Fe, New Mexico: AGB Press, 2017).

[2] Thus, for example, some sort of Faraday cage-like insulator might be incorporated on the outside of wires.

[3] Though perhaps understandable, it would be a shame if *Marxism & Witchcraft* is seen as supporting a kind of technological determinism, wherein the machines determine our fates. Indeed, were that my belief, it would amount, horror of horrors, to *my* succumbing to the seductive spell of the mechanical philosophy! Though such causal claims are not my intention, it is easy to see why such an interpretation is possible, for do I not keep on returning to the machines — how the ways of production — create the toxins that seem invariably to flow into the ditches besides the factories, or up into the air around us? Indeed, I do, but not because the *machine* is the central agent. Rather, the machine and workers are the means of producing not just the goods, but the damaged landscape those goods create in the process of being made under social systems founded on the need for profit.

The machines are the locus of the damages inflicted onto the airs, waters, and places, but in a deeper sense they are expressions of deep social, economic, political, and ideological forces, and are merely tools by which those deeper forces express themselves on the natural world.

On some rivers, dams may have to be allowed into the near future.

Paper (without use of chlorine), cloth, and (with appropriate chemicals) paints will continue to be made. Casting, toolmaking, manufacture of metal pipelines, and machinery will need to be produced for some time. The building trades will always be needed into any future. Decades of ignoring critical infrastructure will initially provide an enormous list of things that need building or repairing. The kinds of gargantuan developments that are built not because they are useful, but because they will make huge profits for someone, will fade in the face of the senior centers, clinics, schools, wastewater pipelines, bridges, and mass transit that *must* and can be built.

Given that this conclusion follows a rather extended discussion in *Marxism & Witchcraft* of the many baneful cultural, political, epistemological, and, not at all least, environmental damages resulting from information technologies, it will surprise no one who has read so far that I believe its horrific toxicities create a strong case for its termination, but as I argued in Chapter 30, it is not my job to make such decisions. If they are made, such decisions will have to be the outcome of debates and deliberations of the hundreds of millions worldwide unable to find employment as a result of the job-extinction function of computers through downsizing, outsourcing and robotization, *and* of the billions of mothers and fathers worldwide who eventually figure out the close connection I believe I have demonstrated between a rising crisis in fertility and chip-production technologies.

Though in the form of "programmed learning" lessons, I believe they are used in excess for people with disabilities, I also argued in Chapter 30 that some limited uses of computers should continue: the example of the late Stephen Hawking demonstrates how hi-tech can be critical to a healthy functionality; so too for the use of VR for pain relief. Once more it is a question of scale, and of the principle that any toxic burdens from technologies seen as desirable must be widely shared.

And, of course, the getting of food, the source of all our vitality — how it will be gotten and brought to we who will eat it, the likely widespread practice of multitudes deciding to grow or raise some proportion of what they eat, all these will be especially critical questions as we move towards ecological balance.

It will be essential, of course, that those industries that are abolished for the good of all not thereby abolish the right of their workers to continue to be employed (by *whom*, under what kind of economic system, will be the subject of much debate).[1] Retraining and retooling must go hand-in-hand with curtailing.

It is almost certain that this future I have just depicted will unfold quite differently in its details from what I have outlined above. What I propose is meant primarily as *a* way of sketching how difficult questions might be ad-

---

[1] As emphasized by Marian Doub (personal conversation, October 26, 2014).

dressed. In the actual doing, the real priorities will reveal themselves as people work their way to concrete decisions.

I am convinced that the World War II environmental watersheds hold true, and provide us with a practical operational scaffolding on which can be organized a system of triage that will prove critical to our survival. Since for the most part the direst threats to our environments arise from practices and chemical and radioactive substances deployed only in the past eighty or so years (approximately the life expectancy in many industrialized countries), there is hope that an environmental recovery could be well within the reach of a concerted planetwide effort. (Getting there will be the real challenge.) Such a plan might enable us to frame in a proverbial ark for the short-term (50 to 200 years), capable of bearing as many of us as possible safely through the coming storms, taking us to drier, higher terrain, so to speak, to a quite transformed social and technological future; still toxic, to be sure, but sufficiently less so, which can be a temporary respite of sorts, as we set to the serious work.

It is in that respite that we can engage as a society in the kind of careful, less-frenzied analysis, debate, and trance-visions needed, thereby inventing the kind of long-term practices called forth by the urgency of our situation, by the dire need for long-range survival.

At the center of all that takes place in this imaginary world of ours where environmental balance is key, a world that may become real in the not-so-distant future — and yes, let us allow utopian visions to occupy our dreams, knowing it is the task of revolutionaries to make dreams become manifest — at its center will necessarily be people living and making the things they find useful and doing what it takes to feel part of the larger social enterprises set in motion by the gargantuan project of developing peoples' ways of rein-habiting this Earth so that its natural bounty is not destroyed. In so doing, we may be surprised to rediscover our humanity.

Skepticism about how utopian dreams can readily become nightmares — historically, it should be noted, frequently only after the armies of Property have already exacted blood vengeance from the dreamers, as in Münster in 1525 and the Paris Commune in 1871 — is tempered by my realization that our crisis is so dire that only through such a utopian vision miraculously becoming real does humanity, and all those creatures who survive or not, based on what we do, have a prayer of a chance of making it, and my faith (and it is a faith rooted, I would guess, in my larger sense of a cosmos teeming with life) that in the end, our will to survive will be triumphant. For it is my overriding belief that it is in the nature of most living creatures, and that includes humans, to fight for their survival.[1] Human history, the *real* history that isn't much taught in the schools, the history of the many Münsters

[1] I exclude those creatures (the octopus, salmon, black widow spider, etc.) where dying is intimately tethered to reproduction.

reaching back into paleolithic times[1] is replete with examples. I do not believe that instinct can ever really be smoothered, much as the State and as Capital will try, for like the grass that insists on growing up through the cracks in the pavement, we shall prevail.

It goes without saying, there are no guarantees. Agency is everything!

The future is ours only if we make it so. And only thus can we ensure that we do not allow the dead nature premised by the mechanical philosophy at the beginning of the modern era, indeed, to become a self-fulfilling prophecy.

---

[1] Albert, *op. cit.*

Bibliography

I — Interviews

Judy Berg, phone interview (September 18, 2014).
Jackie Cabaso, personal letter (March, 2017).
Marian Doub, personal communication (October 26, 2014).
Doug Henwood, phone interview (n.d.).
Roy King, personal letter (n.d.).
Joseph LaDou, phone interview (n.d.).
Jerry Mander, phone Interview (May 20, 2013).
Robert Proctor, phone interview (March 8, 2013).
Ted Smith, interview (August, 2012).
Shanna H. Swan, PhD, phone interview (August 14, 2013).

II — Manuscripts

Anon., Bodleian Ms Rawl. J4°, 2.
John Conduitt, King College Ms Keynes 130 n° II.
———, Ms Keynes 130 n° II (reprinted in Edmund Turner, *Collections for the History of the Town and sake of Grantham containing authentic memoirs of Sir Isaac Newton* [London, 1806]).
———, Ms Keynes 30 n° 7.
David Gregory, Royal Society MS Gregory.
Isaac Newton, Babson Ms 420.
———, "Qu[a]estiones quodam Philosophiae" Cambridge Add MS 3996; publ. (ed.) J.E. McGuire and Martin Tammy as *Certain Philosophical Questions: Newton's Trinity Notebook* (Cambridge, England, Cambridge University Press, 1983).
———, "[The Vegetation of Metals]" Burndy MS 16.
———, Cambridge University Add. MS 3970.
———, "[Notes] Out of La Lumière sortant des Ténèbres," in Dobbs, *Janus Face*.
———, "Out of Cudworth," William Andrews Clarke Memorial Library Ms Journal of the Royal Society.

III — Primary Sources

Carlos D. Abraham, "Chemical Handling Problems and Solutions for Semiconductor Plants," in *Electronic Packaging and Production* (July, 1976).

———, "In Sterile Workplaces, Every Move Counts," San Francisco *Chronicle* (July 17, 1985).

Georg Agricola, *De Re Metallica*, transl. Herbert Clark Hoover and Lou Henry Hoover (New York, Dover, 1950).

Francesco Algarotti, *Sir Isaac Newton's Philosophy Explained for the Use of the Ladies*, transl. Elizabeth Carter (London, England, 1739, from 1737 Italian edition).

Erin Allday, "Problems with sperm linked to death risk," San Francisco *Chronicle* (May 16, 2014).

Anon., "Voluntary Human Extinction: One Brick Shy of a Full Solution?," *These Exit Times* (Special *Earth First! Journal* Edition, 2000).

Elias Ashmole, *Theatrum Chemicum Britannicum: Containing Several Poetical Pieces of our Famous English Philosophers, who have written the Hermetique Mysteries in their own Ancient Language* (London, 1652; New York. Johnson reprint, April 1967, ed. Allen G. Debus).

———, "Annotations and Discourse upon some part of the preceding Worke," in *Theatrum Chemicum*.

Peggy V. Beck, Anna Lee Walters and Nia Rancisco, *The Sacred: Ways of Knowledge, Sources of Life* (Tsaile, Arizona, Navajo Community Press, 1992).

Thomas Birch, *A History of the Royal Society for Improving of Natural Knowledge* (London, 1756-57, repr. 1968) in 4 vol.

William Blake, *The Marriage of Heaven & Hell* (London, England and Paris, France, Oxford University Press & The Trianon Press, n.d.).

Ian Buruma, "China: Reeducation Through Horror", *The New York Review of Books* (January 9, 2014).

John Cairns, Julie Overbaugh and Stephen Miller, "The Origins of Mutants," *Nature* 335 (September 8, 1988).

Nigel Cameron, "Open Forum, Where will people work when robots take the jobs?," San Francisco *Chronicle* (December 2, 2014).

Samuel Clarke, *A Dissertation of the Being and Attributes of God: More Particularly in Answer to Mr. Hobbs, Spinoza and their Followers* (London, England, 1705).

Fernando Claudin, *The Communist Movement: From Comintern to Cominform*, transl. Brian Pearce and Francis McDonagh (Middlesex, England, Penguin Books, 1975).

Patricia Cohen, "Fending Off Digital Decay, Bit by Bit," *New York Times* (March 16, 2010).

Victoria Colliver, "Efforts to shift science on sugar," San Francisco *Chronicle* (September 16, 2016).

Lady Anne Conway, *The Principles of the Most Ancient Philosophy, Concerning God, Christ and the Creatures; viz. of spirit, and As well matter in general, whereby may be resolved all those problems or difficulties which neither by the school nor common modern philosophy nor by the Cartesian, Hobbesian or Spinosian could be discussed...* (London, 1692, reprint, The Hague Martinus Nijhoff Publishers, 1982).

J.T. Desagulier, *A Course of Mechanical and Experimental Philosophy* (n.p.,n.d.).

————, *The Newtonian System of the World, The Best Model of Government: An Allegorical Poem* (London, England, 1728).

J. K. Dineen, "Flawed Shipyard Cleanup Blasted," San Francisco *Chronicle* (August 16, 2018).

John Dury, *A Seasonable Discourse* (London, England, 1649).

Thomas Edwards, *Gangrena* (London, England, 1646).

Friedrich Engels, *The Origins of the Family, Private Property and the State, in Light of the Researches of Lewis H. Morgan* (New York, International Publishing, 1970.

Peter Femrite, "Study: Chemicals, pollutants found in newborns," San Francisco *Chronicle* (December 3, 2009).

Arthur Firstenberg, *The Invisible Rainbow: A History of Electricity and Life* (Santa Fe, New Mexico, AGB Press, 2017).

Johann Wolfgang von Goethe, *Goethe's Color Theory* (ed.) Rupprecht Matthei, (transl.) Herb Aech (New York, Van Nostrand Reinhold Co., 1971).

David Gregory, *The Elements of Physical & Geometrical Astronomy*, 2 vols. (London, England, 2nd ed. 1726).

Barry G. Hall, "Adaptive Evolution That Requires Multiple Spontaneous Mutations," *Genetics* (December, 1988).

Edmond Halley, "An Account of the Cause in the Change in the Variation in the Magnetical Needle" in *Philosophical Transactions of the Royal Society no.175* (1692).

————, "An Attempt to Find the Age of the World by the Saltiness of the Sea," *Philosophical Transaction, Abridged*, vol. V (London, England, various dates).

————, *Correspondence and Papers of...* (ed.) Eugene Fairfield MacPike (London, England, Taylor and Francis, Ltd., 1937).

————, "Of the Cause of the Deluge" in *Philosophical Transactions and Collections ... Abridged...* (ed.) John Lowthrop (London, England, various dates).

Thomas Hearne, *Remarks and Collections* vol.III (ed.) Ce. E. Doblem (Oxford, England, 1889).

G.W. von Hegel, *Lectures in the History of Philosophy* (transl.) E. S. Haldane and Frances H. Simson, M.A., 3 vols.(London, Routledge and Kegan Paul, 1965).

John Frederick Helvetius, *The Golden Calf. Which the World Worships and Adores. In Which is Discussed The Most Rare Miracle of Nature in the Transmutation of Metals: Viz: How at the Hague a Mass of Lead was in a Moment of Time Changed into Gold by the Infusion of a Small Particle of Our Stone* (1667, repr. Edmondson, Washington, 1987).

Jeffrey Herf, *Reactionary Modernism: Technology, Culture and Politics in Weimar and the Third Reich* (Cambridge, United Kingdom, Cambridge University Press, 1984).

B. Hessen, *The Social and Economic Roots of Newton's Principia* in *Science at the Cross Roads* (London, 1931).

Hippocrates, *Airs, Waters, and Places*.

Thomas Hobbes, *Leviathan Or the Matter, Form and Power of a Commonwealth Ecclesiastical and Civil* (London, England, 1651).

Robert Hooke, *Dect. de Potent Restito*.

———, *Diary of Robert Hooke*, M.A., M.D., F.R.S., 1672 - 1682 (ed.) Harry W. Robinson and Walter Adams (London, England, Taylor & Francis, 1935).

———, *The Posthumous Works of Robert Hooke... Containing His Cutlerian Lectures and Other Discourses Read at the Meetings of the Illustrious Royal Society...* (ed.) Richard Waller (London, England, 1705; repr. New York, Johnson Reprint Corp., 1969) (ed.) Richard S. Westfall.

David Hume, *Essays Moral, Political and Literary* (ed.) T.H. Green and T.H. Grose (London, 1882; reprint Dormstode, 1964) in 2 Vols.

Diarmuid Jeffreys, *Hell's Cartel: IG Farben and the Making of Hitler's War Machine* (London, Bloomsbury, 2008).

Heinrich Kramer and James Sprenger, *The Malleus Maleficarum* (1489).

G. W. von Leibniz, *The Monadology* (1717).

———, *Selections* (ed.) Philip P. Weiner (New York, Charles Scribner's Sons, 1951).

G. Gordon Liddy, *Will* (New York, St. Martin's Press, 1980).

Karl Marx and Friedrich Engels, *On Religion* (Moscow, Progress Publishers, 1975).

———, *The German Ideology*, Part I & III (New York, International Publishers, 1947).

Karl Marx, *Capital*.

———, "Introduction to Contribution to the Critique of Hegel's Philosophy of Law" in *On Religion*.

Thomas H. Maugh II, "UC study links ADHC, pesticides", San Francisco *Chronicle* (October 20, 2010).

China Miéville, *October: The Story of the Russian Revolution* (London, Verso, 2017)

Henry More, *Antidote against Atheism: Letters to Descartes & C.* in More, *A Collection of Several Philosophical Writings* (London, England, 1712).

———, *Conjectura Cabbalistica* in More, *A Collection of Several Philosophical Writings*.

———, *Enthusiasmus Triumphatus; or, a Brief Discourse of the Nature, Causes, Kinds, and Cure of Enthusiasm* (London, England, 1662; Los Angeles, California, W. Andrews Clark Memorial Library, 1966).

———, *Immortality of the Soul* in More, *A Collection of Several Philosophical Writings*.

H[enry] M[ore], *Psychathanesia, or the Second Part of the Song of the Soul Treating of the Immortality of the Soule* (Cambridge, England, 1647).

Isaac Newton, *A dissertation upon the Sacred Cubit of the Jews and the Cubits of Several Nations, in which, from the Dimensions of the Greatest Pyramid... the... Cubit... is Determined* in John Greaves, *Miscellaneous Works of...* (London, England, 1737), vol. 2.

———, *Correspondence of Sir Isaac Newton & Professor Cotes...* (London, England, 1850).

———, *Chronology of the Ancient Kingdoms Amended* (London, England, 1728).

————, *Mathematical Principles of Natural Philosophy and His System of the World* (ed.) Florian Cajori (Berkeley, California, University of California Press, 1687; 1934).

————, "Of nature's obvious laws & processes in vegetation," in Dobbs, *Janus Face*.

————, *Opticks, or A Treatise of the Reflections, Refractions, Inflections & Colours of Light* (New York, Dover Publications, 1952).

————, *The Correspondence of…* (ed.) H.W. Turnbull, FRS, vol. 1–4.

————, *Unpublished Scientific Papers of Isaac Newton* (ed.) A.R. and Marie Boas Hall (Cambridge, England, Cambridge University Press, 1962).

No Place To Hide, various issues.

Henry Oldenburg, *The Correspondence of Henry Oldenburg* (ed. and transl.) A. Rupert and Marie Boas Hall (Madison, Wisconsin, Univ. of Wisconsin Press, 1970).

Samuel Parker, *A Free and Impartial Censure of the Platonic Philosophy…* (Oxford, England, 1667).

Project for a New American Century, *Rebuilding America's Defenses: Strategies, Forces, and Resources for a New Century* (n.p., 2000).

Wilhelm Reich and Karl Teschitz, *Selected Sex-Pol Writings. 1934–37* (London, England, Socialist Reproduction, 1973).

Wilhelm Reich, *Sex-Pol Essays. 1929–1934* (ed.) Lee Baxandall, transl. Anna Bostock, Tom DuBose and Lee Baxandall (New York, Vintage Books, 1972)

Mike Reynolds, "Earth Under Fire," *Astronomy* (August, 2006).

Howard Rheingold, *Virtual Reality* (New York, Simon & Schuster, 1991).

————, "Hands Off Technology: Four Books on Virtual Reality," *Whole Earth Reviews* (Winter, 1992).

Aurelio Rojas, "High Rates of Disease in Bayview: Study Lends Weight to Pollution Fears," San Francisco *Chronicle* (June 9, 1997).

Jeff Rothenberg, "Ensuring the Longevity of Digital Documents," *Scientific American* (January, 1995).

Douglas Rushkoff, *Program or Be Programmed: Ten Commands for a Digital Age* (Berkeley, California, Soft Skull Press, 2011).

Kevin Schultz, "Pesticides tied to drop in child lung function," San Francisco *Chronicle* (after 2013).

Thomas Sprat, *The History of the Royal Society of London, For the Improving of Natural Knowledge* (London, England, 1667; St. Louis, Washington University Studies, 1985) ed. Jackson I. Cope and Harold Whitmore Jones.

Franklin W. Stahl, "Bacterial Genetics: A Unicorn in the Garden," *Nature* n° 335 (September 8, 1988).

Starhawk, *The Spiral Dance: A Rebirth of the Ancient Religion of the Goddess* (San Francisco, California, Harper & Row, 1979).

Mao Tse-Tung, "On Contradiction," *Selected Readings from the Works of…* (Peking, China, Foreign Language Press, 1967)

.[Thoma]S. [Vaugha]N., *Aula Lucis*, or *House of Light* (London, 1652). Unknown author, "Invisible Planet," *Discover* (nd).

Frank Waters, *The Man Who Killed the Deer* (New York, Pocket Books, 1971).

———, *Book of the Hopi* (New York, Viking Press, 1963).

William Whiston, *Memoirs of the Life and Writings of Mr. William Whiston: Containing Memoirs of Several of His Friends Also*, 2 vol. (London, England, 2nd ed., 1753).

John Wilkins, *Ecclesiastes: or, A Discourse of the Art of Preaching* (London, England, 1646).

Anthony à Wood, *The Life and Times of…* in *The Broadview Anthology of Seventeenth Century Verse and Prose* (ed.) Alan Rudrum; Joseph Black & Holly Faith Nelson (Peterborough, Ontario, Broadview Press, 2000).

IV — BOOKS AND ARTICLES

Alex Abella, *Soldiers of Reason; The RAND Corporation and the Rise of American Empire* (Orlando, Florida, Harcourt, Inc., 2008).

David Abram, *The Spell of the Sensuous; Perception and Language in a More Than Human World* (New York, Vintage Books, 1996).

Dariq Albright, Frans Berkhout, and William Walker, *Plutonium and Highly Enriched Uranium* (Oxford, England, Oxford University Press, 1997).

Bert Alpert, *Inversions: A study of Warped Consciousness* (Ann Arbor, Michigan, privately printed, 1973).

M. Kat Anderson, *Tending the Wild: Native American Knowledge and the Management of California's Natural Resources* (Berkeley, California, Univ. of California Press, 2005).

———, "Tending the Wilderness," *Restoration and Management Notes* 14(2).

Stanislav Andreski, "The Syphilitic Shock," in David Hicks (ed.) *Ritual and Beliefs; Readings in the Anthropology of Religion* (New York, McGraw Hill, 2002).

Wilbur Applebaum, "Friedrich Engels and the History of Science," M.A. thesis (State University of New York at Buffalo, 1964).

David Arnold (ed.) *Imperial Medicine and Indigenous Society* (Manchester, England, Manchester University Press, 1988).

Tom Athanasiou, *Divided Planet: The Ecology of Rich and Poor* (Boston, Massachusetts, Little Brown and Co., 1996).

G.E. Aylmer, "The Religion of Gerrard Winstanley," in McGregor and Reay, *Radical Religion in the English Revolution* (Oxford, England, Oxford University Press, 1986).

Michael Baigent, Richard Leigh and Henry Lincoln, *Holy Blood, Holy Grail* (New York, Dell Books, 1983).

Margaret Bailey, *Milton and Jakob Boheme, A study of German Mysticism in Seventeenth Century England* (New York, 1914).

Nicholson Baker, "Discards," in *The Size of Thoughts: Essays and Other Lumber* (New York, Random House, 1996)

Lee Balinger, "From Sea to Dying Sea", *CounterPunch*, vol. 24, No. 2 (2017).

Owen Barfield, *Saving the Appearances: A Study in Idolatry* (New York, Harcourt Brace & World, 1957).

Julio Caro Baroja, *The World of the Witches*, transl. O. N. V. Glendinning, (Chicago, University of Chicago Press, 1965).

Antony Beevor, "The Very Drugged Nazis," review of Norman Ohler, *Blitzed: Drugs in the Third Reich* (Boston, Massachusetts, Houghton Mifflin Harcourt, 2017), in *The New York Review of Books* (March 9, 2017).

Max Beloff, *Public Order and Popular Disturbances, 1661-1715* (Oxford, England, 1938).

Morris Berman, *The Reenchantment of the World* (Ithaca, New York, Cornell University Press, 1981).

———, *Coming to Our Senses: Body and Spirit in the Hidden History of the West* (New York, Bantam Books, 1990).

Jeremy Bernstein, *Plutonium: A History of the World's Most Dangerous Element* (Washington, DC, John Henry Press, 2007).

Wendell Berry, *The Unsettling of America: Culture & Agriculture* (San Francisco, California, Sierra Club Books, 1977).

Janet Biehl, "Ecology and the Modernization of fascism in the German Ultra Right" in Janet Biehl and Peter Staudenmaier, *Ecofascism: Lessons from the German Experience* (San Francisco, California, AK Press, 1995).

Sven Birkerts, *The Gutenberg Elegies, The Fate of Reading in an Electronic Age* (London, England, Faber & Faber, 1994).

Iain A. Boal, "A City for Idiots" in Chris Carlsson (ed.) *The Political Edge* (San Francisco, California, City Lights, 2004).

R. Bosher, *Making of the Restoration Settlement: The Influence of the Laudians 1649-1662* (Westminster, England, 1951).

Janet and Colin Bord, *Earth Rites: Fertility Practices in Pre-Industrial Britain* (London, England, Grenada, 1982).

Paulina Borsook, *Cyberselfish: A Critical Romp Through the Terribly Libertarian Culture of High Tech* (New York, Public Affairs, 2000).

Paul Bracken, *The Command and Control of Nuclear Forces* (New Haven, Connecticut, Yale University Press, 1983).

Stewart Brand, "Army Green," *Whole Earth Review* no.72 (Fall, 1992).

Harry Braverman, *Labor and Monopoly Capital: The Degradation of Work in the Twentieth Century* (New York, Monthly Review Press, 1974).

Kenneth Brechen and Michael Fertig (ed.) *Astronomy of the Ancients* (Cambridge, Massachusetts, Massachusetts Institute of Technology Press, 1981).

Gray Brechin, *Imperial San Francisco: Urban Power, Earthly Ruin* (Berkeley, California, Berkeley University of California Press, 2007).

Martin Brennan, *The Stars and the Stones. Ancient Art and Astronomy in Ireland* (London, England, Thames and Hudson, 1983).

Paul Broder, *The Great Power-Line Cover-Up: How the Utilities and the Government*

Are Trying to Hide the Cancer Hazard Posed by Electromagnetic Fields (Boston, Massachusetts, Little Brown and Company, 1993).

E. Richard Brown, *Rockefeller Medicine Men and Capitalism in America* (Berkeley, California, University of California Press, 1979).

Louise F. Brown, *The Political Activities of the Baptists and Fifth Monarchy Men in England During the Interregnum* (Oxford, England, 1912).

Peter Lancaster Brown, *Megaliths, Myths and Men; An introduction to Astra-Archeology* (New York, Harper & Row, 1976).

Peter Burke, *Popular Culture in Early Modern Europe* (New York, Harper & Row, 1978).

Shane Burley, *Fascism Today: What It Is and How to End It* (Chico, California, AK Press, 2017).

John Burnet, *Early Greek Philosophy* (New York, Meridian Books, 1892; 1960).

E. A. Burtt, *The Metaphysical Foundations of Modern Science* (Garden City, New York, Doubleday Anchor, 1952).

Herbert Butterfield, *The Whig Interpretation of History* (London, England, G. Bell, 1951).

George Caffentzis, "Rambo on the Barbary Shore," in Midnight Notes Collective, *Midnight Oil: Work, Energy, War, 1973–1992* (Brooklyn, New York, Autonomedia, 1992).

Jeremy Campbell, *The Improbable Machine: What the Upheavals in Artificial Intelligence Research Reveal About How the Mind Really Works* (New York, Simon & Schuster, 1989).

Bernard Capp, "The Fifth Monarchists and Popular Millenarianism," in *Radical Religion in the English Revolution* (ed.) V.F. McGregor & B. Reay (Oxford, England, Oxford University Press, 1986).

Nicholas Carr, *The Shallows: What the Internet Is Doing To Our Brains* (New York, W. W. Norton & Company, 2010).

Center for Ecoliteracy, *Computers in Education: a Critical Look* (Berkeley, California, 1995).

Alexander Cockburn, "A Short, Meat-Oriented History of the World. From Eden to Mattole," *New Left Review* 215 (January–February, 1996).

Theo Colborn, Dianne Dumanoski and Peter Myers, *Our Stolen Future* (New York, Dutton, 1996).

Jackson I. Cope, *Joseph Glanvill, Anglican Apologist* (St. Louis, Missouri, Washington University Studios, 1956).

Keith Critchlow, *Time Stands Still: New Light on Megalithic Science* (London, England, Gordon Fraser, 1979).

Critical Art Ensemble, *The Molecular Invasion* (Brooklyn, New York, Autonomedia, 2002).

Alfred W. Crosby, *Ecological Imperialism. The Biological Expansion of Europe, 900–1900* (Cambridge, England, Cambridge University Press, 1986).

Elizabeth Gould Davis, *The First Sex* (Baltimore, Maryland, Penguin Books, 1972).

Ralph Davis, *The Rise of the Atlantic Economies* (Ithaca, New York, Cornell University Press, 1973).

Wade Davis, *Lights at the Edge of the World* (Vancouver, Canada, Douglas & McIntyre, 2001).

———, *Shadows in the Sun: Travels to Landscapes of Spirit and Desire* (Washington, D.C., Island Press, 1998).

Allen Debus, *The English Paracelsians* (London, England, 1965).

———, *The Chemical Dreams of the Renaissance* (Cambridge, England, 1968).

Paul Devereux, *Places of Power: Secret Energies at Ancient Sites, A Guide to Observed or Measured Phenomena* (London, England, Bradford, 1999).

Paul Devereux, John Steele, and David Kubrin, *Earthmind: Communicating with the Living World of Gaia* (Rochester, Vermont, Destiny Books, 1992).

E. J. Dijksterhuis, *The Mechanization of the World Picture* (Oxford, England, Oxford University Press, 1961).

Betty Jo Teeter Dobbs, "Newton as Final Cause & First Mover," in *Rethinking the Scientific Revolution* (ed.) Margaret Oster (Cambridge, England, Cambridge University Press, 2000).

———, *The Foundations of Newton's Alchemy or 'The Hunting of the Greene Lyon'* (Cambridge, England, Cambridge University Press, 1983).

———, *The Janus Face of Genius: The Role of Alchemy in Newton's Thought* (Cambridge, England, Cambridge University Press, 1991).

Ricardo Dobrovolski, "Marx's Ecology and the Understanding of Land Cover Change," *Monthly Review* (May, 2012).

Hubert Dreyfus, *What Computers Can't Do: The Limits of Artificial Intelligence* (New York, Harper & Row, 1979).

———, *What Computers Still Can't Do: A Critique of Artificial Reason* (Cambridge, Massachusetts, Massachusetts Institute of Technology Press, 1992).

Steven M. Drucker, *Altered Genes, Twisted Truth* (Salt Lake City, Utah, Clear River Press, 2015).

Hans Duerr, *Dreamtime. Concerning the Boundaries between the Wilderness and Civilization* (Oxford, England, Basil Blackwell, 1985).

Roxanne Dunbar-Ortiz, *An Indigenous People's History of the United States* (Boston, Massachusetts, Beacon Press, 2014).

George Dyson, *Turing's Cathedral: The Origins of the Digital Universe* (New York, Viking Books, 2012).

Paul N. Edwards, *The Closed World: Computers and the Politics of Discourse in Cold War America* (Cambridge, Mass., Massachusetts Institute of Technology Press, 1996).

Barbara Ehrenreich, *Dancing in the Streets: A History of Collective Joy* (New York, Metropolitan Books, 2006).

————, "Terror Cells: Ain't No Cure for dystopian biology," in *The Baffler* no. 26 (2014).

Barbara Ehrenreich and Deirdre English, *Witches, Midwives and Nurses* (New York, Feminist Press, 2nd ed. 2010).

Paul Erlich, *The Population Bomb* (1968).

etc. Group, *Extreme Genetic Engineering: An Introduction to Synthetic Biology* (Canada, 2007).

Arthur Evans, *God of Ecstasy: Sex Roles and the Madness of Dionysius* (New York, St. Martin Press, 1988).

————, "The Mythic Proportions of Halloween," *Coming Up!* (October, 1984).

————, *Witchcraft and the Gay Counterculture: A Radical View of Western Civilization and Some of the People It Has Tried to Destroy* (Boston, Mass., Fag Rag Books, 1978).

Silvia Federici, *Caliban and the Witch: Women, the Body, and Primitive Accumulation* (Brooklyn, New York, Autonomedia, 2004).

Paul Feyerabend, *Philosophy of Nature* (ed.) Helmut Heit and Eric Oberheim (Cambridge, England, Polity Press, 2016).

————, *Killing Time: the Autobiography of Paul Feyerabend* (Chicago, 1999).

————, *Science in a Free Society* (London, Verso, 1978).

Karin Figula, "Newton as Alchemist," *History of Science* 15 (1977).

Daniel Ford, *Meltdown: The Secret Papers of the Atomic Energy Commission* (New York, Simon & Schuster, Inc., 1986).

————, *The Cult of the Atom: The Secret Papers of the Atomic Energy Commission* (New York, Simon & Schuster, Inc., 1984).

Michel Foucault, *Madness and Civilization* (New York, Vintage Books, 1965).

Sam Frank, "Come With Us If You Want to Live: Among the Apocalyptic Libertarians of Silicon Valley", *Harper's Magazine* (January, 2015).

David H. Freedman, "Can Science Save the Human?," *Discover* (November, 2011).

Peter J. French, *John Dee: The World of an Elizabethan Magus* (London, England, Routledge & Kegan Paul, 1984).

Benjamin M. Friedman, "'Brave New Capitalists' Paradise': The Jobs?," *The New York Review of Books* (November 7, 2013).

Otto Friedrich, *The End of the World: A History* (New York, Coward, McCann & Geoghegan, 1982).

John G. Fuller, *The Day We Bombed Utah: America's Most Lethal Secret* (New York, Signet Books, 1985).

Connie Garcia and Amelia Simpson, "Community Based Organizing for Labor Rights, Health, and the Environment: Television Manufacturing on the Mexican-U.S. Border," in *Challenging the Chip*.

Peter Gay, *The Enlightenment: an Interpretation, The Rise of Modern Paganism* (New York, Vintage Books, 1966).

Eugene P. Genovese, *Roll, Jordan, Roll: The World the Slaves Made* (New York, Vintage, 1976).

Carlo Ginzburg, *Ecstasies: Deciphering the Witches' Sabbath*, transl. Raymond Rosenthal (New York, Penguin Books, 1992).

———, *Witchcraft & Agrarian Cults in the 16th & 17th Centuries*, transl. John & Anne Tedeschi (New York, Penguin, 1983).

James Gleick, "How Google Dominates Us," *The New York Review of Books* (April 18, 2011).

Chellis Glendinning, *Off the Map: An Expedition Deep into Empire and the Global Economy* (Gabriela Island, British Columbia, New Society Publishers, 2002).

Global Electronics, "Issue No. 117" (December, 1992).

Donny Gluckstein, *Nazis, Capitalism and the Working Class* (Chicago, Illinois, Haymarket Books, 1999).

David Goodman, "Philip II's Patronage of Science and Engineering," *British Journal for the History of Science* 16 (1983): 62–65.

Nicholas Goodrich-Clarke, *The Occult Roots of Nazism: Secret Aryan Cults and Their Influence on Nazi Ideology. The Ariosophists of Austria and Germany, 1890–1935* (New York, New York University Press, 1992).

Susantha Goonatilake, *Aborted Discovery: Science & Creativity in the Third World* (London, England, Zed Books Ltd., 1984).

David Graeber, "Of Flying Cars and the Declining Rate of Profit," *The Baffler* no.19 (2012).

Chris Hables Gray, *Postmodern War: The New Politics of Conflict* (New York, The Guilford Press, 1997).

Susan Griffin, *A Chorus of Stones: The Private Life of War* (Doubleday, 1992).

Paul Gross and Norman Levitt, *The Higher Superstition: the Academic Left and Its Quarrels with Science* (Baltimore, Maryland, John Hopkins University Press, 1994).

Karl Grossman, *The Wrong Stuff: The Space Program's Nuclear Threat to Our Planet* (Monroe, Maine, Common Courage Press, 1997).

Sue Halpern, "Who Was Steve Jobs?," *The New York Review of Books* (January 12, 2012).

Graham Hancock, *Underworld: The Mysterious Origins of Civilization* (New York, Three Rivers Press, 2002).

Gerald Hawkins, *Stonehenge Decoded* (Garden City, New York, Doubleday, 1965).

Susanna Hecht & Alexander Cockburn, *The Fate of the Forest: Developers, Destroyers and Defenders of the Amazon* (New York, 1990).

Steve J. Heims, *John Von Neumann, and Norbert Wiener, From Mathematics to the Technologies of Death* (Cambridge, Massachusetts, Massachusetts Institute of Technology Press, 1980).

Nathan Heller, "Laptop U.: Has the Future of College Moved Online?," *The New Yorker* (May 30, 2013).

John Henry, "Robert Hooke, The Incongruous Mechanist," in *Robert Hooke: New Studies* (ed.) Michael Hunter and Simon Schaffer (Woolbridge, England, The Boyloll Press, 1984).

Doug Henwood, *After the New Economy: The Binge… And the Hangover That Won't Go Away* (New York, The New Press, 2003/05).

Stephen Hilgartner, Richard C. Bell and Rory O'Connor, *Nukespeak: The Selling of Nuclear Technology in America* (San Francisco, California, Sierra Club Books, 1982).

Christopher Hill, *The World Turned Upside Down: Radical Ideas During the English Revolution* (New York, Viking Press, 1972).

Jonathan Hill, "A Musical Aesthetic of Ritual Curing in the Northwest Amazon," in *Portals of Power: Shamanism in South America* (ed.) E. Jean Mattleson Langdon and Gerhard Baer (Albuquerque, New Mexico, Univ. of New Mexico Press, 1992).

Eric Hobsbawm, *The Age of Extremes: A History of the World, 1914–1991* (New York, Vintage Books, 1994).

———, *The Age of Revolution, 1789–1848* (New York, Vintage Books, 1996).

———, *Primitive Rebels: Studies in Archaic Forms of Social Movement* (New York, Norton, 1965).

Andrew Hodges, *Alan Turing: The Enigma* (New York, Simon & Schuster Inc., 1983).

Donald C. Hodges, *Intellectual Foundations of the Nicaraguan Revolution* (Austin, Texas, University of Texas Press, 1986).

Holt, *Science* (New York, Holt, Rinehart, and Winston, 1986).

Jim Holt, "How the Computers Exploded," *The New York Review of Books* (June 7, 2017).

Winthrop S. Hudson, "Mystical Religion in the Puritan Commonwealth," *Journal of Religion* XVIII (1948).

H. Stuart Hughes, *Consciousness and Society: the Restructuring of European Social Thought 1890–1930* (New York, Vintage, 1958).

Michael Hunter, "Alchemy, Magic, and Moralism in the Thought of Robert Boyle," *British Journal for the History of Science* 23 (1990).

Edward Hyams, *Soil & Civilization* (New York, Harper & Row, 1976).

Ivan Illich, *Medical Nemesis: The Expropriation of Health* (New York, Pantheon Books, 1976).

Walter Isaacson, *Steve Jobs* (New York, Simon & Schuster, 2011).

Invisible Committee, *To Our Friends* (South Pasadena, Semiotext(e), 2015).

J. R. Jacob, *Robert Boyle and the English Revolution: A Study in Social and Intellectual Change* (New York, Burt Franklin & Co., 1977).

———, "The New England Company, the Royal Society, and the Indians," *Notes and Letters* (n.d.).

———, *Henry Stubbe, Radical Protestantism and the Early Enlightenment* (Cambridge, England, Cambridge University Press, 1983).

Margaret Candee Jacob, "John Toland and the Newtonian Ideology," *Journal of the Warburg and Courtauld Institute* vol. XXXII (1969).

————, "The Church and the Formulation of the Newtonian World View," *Journal of European Studies* (1971).

Julian Jaynes, "The Problem of Animate Motion in the Seventeenth Century," *Journal of the History of Ideas* XXXI (April–June, 1970).

Thomas Harmon Jobe, "The Devil in Restoration Science: The Glanvill-Webster Debate," *Isis* 72 (1981).

Richard Foster Jones *et. al.*, *The Seventeenth Century: Studies in the History of English Thought and Literature from Bacon to Pope* (Stanford, California, Stanford University Press, 1969).

Peniel E. Joseph, *Stokely: A Life* (New York, Basic Civitas, 2014).

Didier Kahn, "The Rosicrucian Hoax in France (1623–24)," in *Secrets of Nature: Astrology and Alchemy in Early Modern Europe* (ed.) William R. Newman and Anthony Grafton (Cambridge, Mass., Massachusetts Institute of Technology Press, 2001).

David Kaiser, *How the Hippies Saved Physics: Science, Counterculture and the Quantum Revival* (New York, W. W. Norton, 2011).

Robert Kargon, *Atomism in England from Harriot to Newton* (Oxford, England, Clarendon Press, 1966).

————, "John Graunt, Francis Bacon and the Royal Society: The Reception of Statistics," *Journal of the History of Medicine and Allied Sciences* Vol. 18 (1963).

V. Karpenko, "Coins and Medals Made of Alchemical Metal," *Ambix* 35 (1988).

William M. Kaula, "The Earth as a planet," *Geophysical Monograph* 60 Vol.10 (1990).

Lierre Keith, "Culture of Resistance," in Annie McBay, Lierre Keith and Derrick Jensen, *Deep Green Resistance: Strategy to Save the Planet* (New York, Seven Stories Press, 2011).

Kevin Kelly, "Deep Evolution: The Emergence of Postdarwinism," *Whole Earth Review* no. 76 (Fall, 1992).

Lord Keynes, "Newton the Man," *Newton's Tercentenary Celebrations* (ed.) The Royal Society (Cambridge, English, 1947).

Stephen Kinzer, *Overthrow: America's Century of Regime Change from Hawaii to Iraq* (New York, Henry Holt and Company, 2006).

David L. Kirp, "Tech Mania Goes to College: Are Massive Open Online Courses the Utopia of Affordable Higher Education Or Just the Latest Fad?," *The Nation* (September 23, 2013).

Henry Kissinger, *American Foreign Policy: Three Essays* (New York, W.W. Newton & Co.1969).

Jack Ralph Kloppenburg Jr., *First the Seed: The Political Economy of Plant Biotechnology, 1492–2000* (Cambridge, England, 1988).

Elizabeth Kolbert, *The Sixth Extinction: An Unnatural History* (New York, Henry Holt & Co., 2014).

Karl Korsch, *Marxism and Philosophy* (New York, Monthly Review Press, 1970).

Thomas Kostigen, "Garbage Patch: How the Pacific Ocean Became the World's Largest Dump," *Discover* (July, 2008).

Alexandre Koyré, *From the Closed World to the Infinite Universe* (New York, Harper & Row, 1957).

——, *Newtonian Studies* (Cambridge, Mass., Harvard University Press, 1957)

Alexandre Koyré and I.B. Cohen, "Newton and the Leibniz-Clarke Correspondence," *Archives Internationale d'Histoire des Science* XV (1962).

E.C. Krupp, *Echoes of the Lost Skies: The Astronomy of Ancient Lost Civilizations* (New York, Harper & Row, 1983).

Yu-Ling Ku, "Human Lives Valued Less Than Dirt: Former RCA Workers Contaminated by Pollution Fighting Worldwide for Justice (Taiwan)," in *Challenging the Chip.*

David Kubrin, "Edmond Halley," in *Encyclopedia of the Scientific Revolution from Copernicus to Newton* (ed.) Wilbur Applebaum (New York, Garland Publishing, 2000).

——, "How Sir Isaac Newton Helped Restore Law 'n' Order to the West," in *Liberation Magazine* (March, 1972).

——, "Newton's Insides Out! Magic, Class Struggle and the Rise of Mechanism in the West," in Harry Woolf (ed.) *The Analytic Spirit: Essay in the History of Science in Honor of Henry Guerlac* (Ithaca, New York, Cornell University Press, 1981).

——, "Newton and the Cyclical Cosmos: Providence and the Mechanical Philosophy," *Journal of the History of Ideas*, Vol. XXVIII, no.3 (July–September 1967).

——, "Providence and the Mechanical Philosophy: The Creation and Dissolution of the World in Newtonian Thought. A Study of the Relation of Science and Religion in Seventeenth-Century England," doctoral diss., 1968, Cornell University.

——, "'Such an Impertinently Litigious Lady': Hooke's 'Great Pretending' vs. Newton's *Principia* and Newton's and Halley's Theory of Comets," in (ed.) Norman J.W. Thrower, *Standing on the Shoulders of Giants: A Longer View of Newton and Halley. Essays Commemorating the Tercentenary of Newton's Principia and the 1985–1986 Return of Comet Halley* (Berkeley, California, University of California Press, 1990).

——, "The dragon tracked to his lair?," in *W.I.S.E. Newsletter* (August, 1986). (Also in *The Ley Hunter* and in *Reclaiming Newsletter* [both 1986]).

——, "The Perils of Polling," *Propaganda Review* no. 4 (Spring, 1989).

——, "Toxic Ideologies," *Reclaiming Quarterly* (Summer, 1999).

——, "Scaling the Heights of Seattle," in *The Battle of Seattle: The New Challenge to Capitalist Globalization* (ed.) Eddie Yuen, Daniel Burton-Rose, and George Katsiaficas (New York, Soft Skull Press, 2001).

David Kubrin, Marcia Altman, John Kwasnik and Tina Logan, "The People's Healers: Healthcare and Class Struggle in the United States in the 19th Century" (ditto, 1974).

Mara Sonya Kubrin, "The Origins of Language: The Multilanguage Theory," paper for Seminar on Psycholinguistics, Columbia University (spring 2009).

Thomas Kuhn, *The Copernican Revolution* (Cambridge, Mass, 1965).

———, *The Structure of Scientific Revolutions* (Chicago, University of Chicago Press, 1970).

Katherine Kurtz, *Lammas Night* (New York, Ballantine Books, 1983).

Joseph LaDou, "Occupational Health in the Semiconductor Industry," in *Challenging the Chip.*

Christina Larner, *Witchcraft and Religion: The Politics of Popular Belief* (ed.) Alan Macfarlane (Oxford, England, Basil Blackwell, Ltd., 1985).

Peter Linebaugh, *The London Hanged: Crime and Civil Society in the Eighteenth Century* (Cambridge, England, Cambridge University Press, 1992).

———, *The Magna Carta Manifesto: Liberties and Commons for All* (Berkeley, California, University of California Press, 2008).

Peter Linebaugh and Marcus Rediker, *The Many-Headed Hydra: Sailors, Slaves, Commoners, and the Hidden History of the Revolutionary Atlantic* (Boston, Massachusetts, Beacon Press, 2000).

Charles E. Little, *The Dying of the Trees: The Pandemic in America's Forests* (New York, Viking, 1995).

J. Norman Lockyer, *The Dawn of Astronomy: A Study of the Temple Worship and Mythology of the Ancient Egyptians* (Cambridge, Massachusetts, Massachusetts Institute of Technology Press, 1894, 1964).

John Lukacs, *The Hitler of History* (New York, Harper Collins, 1997).

Ernst Mach, *The Science of Mechanics* (1897).

Nancy MacLean, *Democracy in Chains: The Deep History of the Radical Right's Stealth Plan for America* (New York, Penguin Books, 2017).

Jeff Madrick, "Computers: Waiting for the Revolution," *The New York Review of Books* (March 26, 1998).

André Malraux, *Man's Fate* (New York, Vintage Books, 1961).

Jerry Mander, *Four Arguments for the Elimination of Television* (New York, Morrow Quill Paperbacks, 1978).

Charles C. Mann, *1491: New Revelations of the Americas Before Columbus* (New York, Vintage Books, 2006).

Frank E. Manuel, *A Portrait of Isaac Newton* (Cambridge, Massachusetts, Harvard University Press, 1968).

Lynn Margulis and Dorian Sagan, *Microcosmos: Four Billion Years of Microbial Evolution* (New York, Touchstone, 1986).

John Markoff, *Machines of Loving Grace: The Quest for Common Ground Between Humans and Robots* (New York, Harper Collins, 2015).

Jeffrey Moussaieff Masson and Susan McCarthy, *When Elephants Weep: The Emotional Lives of Animals* (New York, Delacorte Press, 1995).

Peter Matthiessen, *In the Spirit of Crazy Horse* (New York, Penguin Books, 1992).

Nicole Maxwell, *The Jungle Search for Nature's Cures* (New York, Star, 1961).

James McCourt, "Worker Health at National Semiconductor, Greenock (Scotland): Freedom to Kill?," in *Challenging the Chip*.

J. E. McGuire, "Forces, Active Principles, and Newton's Invisible Realm," *Ambix* 15 (1968).

———, "The Origin of Newton's Doctrine of Essential Qualities," *Centaurus* 12 (1968).

Bill McKibben, *The End of Nature* (New York, Random House, 1989).

———, "Pause! We Can Go Back!," *The New York Review of Books* (January 9, 2017).

David McNally, *Global Slump: The Economics of Crisis and Resistance* (Oakland, California, PM Press, 2011).

William H. McNeill, *Plagues and People* (New York, Doubleday, 1976).

Betty Medsger, *The Burglary: The Discovery of J. Edgar Hoover's Secret FBI* (New York, Alfred A. Knopf, 2014).

Christine Mercer, *Leibniz's Metaphysics: Its Origins and Development* (Cambridge, England, Cambridge University Press, 2000).

Carolyn Merchant, *The Death of Nature: Women, Ecology and the Scientific Revolution* (San Francisco, California, Harper & Row, 1980).

John Theodore Merz, *A History of European Thought in the Nineteenth Century*, in 4 vol. (New York, Dover Publications, 1965).

John Michell, *At the Center of the World: Polar Symbolism Discovered in Celtic, Norse and Other Ritualized Landscapes* (London, England, Thames and Hudson, 1994).

———, *City of Revelation, Or the Proportions and Symbolic Numbers of the Cosmic Temple* (New York, Ballantine Books, 1972).

———, *The View Over Atlantis* (London, England, Sage Press, 196.

Sidney Mintz, *Sweetness and Power: The Place of Sugar in Modern History* (New York, Penguin Books, 1985).

Ida Mojadad and Laura Waxmann, "Toxic Relationship: The Fraud at Hunters Point," *SF Weekly* vol. 37, n° 95 (August 23, 2018)

F. T. Moran, "Alchemy, Prophecy, and the Rosicrucians: Raphael, Egonus and the Mystical Currents of the Early 17th Century," in (ed.) P.M. Rattansi and Antonio Clericuzio, *Alchemy and Chemistry in the 16th and 17th Centuries* (Dordrecht, Netherlands, Kluver Academic Publishers, 1994).

Mark Morrison, *Modern Alchemy: Occultism and the Emergence of Atomic Theory* (Oxford, England, Oxford University Press, 2007).

A. L. Morton, *A People's History of England* (London, England, Lawrence & Wishart, Ltd., 1968).

Lewis Mumford, *Technics and Civilization* (San Diego, California, Harcourt, Brace, Jovanovich, 1963).

Cullen Murphy, *God's Jury: the Inquisition and the making of the Modern World* (Boston, Massachusetts, Mariner Books, 2012).

Jeremy Narby, *The Cosmic Serpent: DNA and the Origins of Knowledge* (New York, Putnam, 1998).

Joseph Needham, *Science and Civilization in China* (Cambridge, England, Cambridge University Press, 1956), vol. 2.

Nicholas Negroponte, *Being Digital* (New York, Knopf, 1995).

J. U. Nef, *The Rise of the British Coal Industry* (London, England, 1932) in 2 vols.

William R. Newman, "Newton's Clavis as Starkey's Key," *Isis* 78 (1987).

Malcolm Nicolson, "Medicine and Racial Politics: Changing Images in the New Zealand Maori in the Nineteenth Century," in Arnold, *Imperial Medicine and Indigenous Societies* (1988) ch. 4.

David Noble, *Forces of Production: A Social History of Industrial Automation* (New York, Oxford University Press, 1986).

Douglas Noble, "Mental Material: The Militarization of Learning and Intelligence in US Education," in *Cyborg Worlds: The Military Information Society* (ed.) Les Levidow and Kevin Robins (London, England, Free Association Books, 1989).

Norman Ohler, *Blitzed: Drugs in the Third Reich* (Boston, Houghton Mifflin Harcourt, 2016).

Dan O'Neill, *The Firecracker Boys: H-Bombs, Inupiat Eskimos, and the Roots of the Environmental Movement* (Arizona, Basic Books, 2007).

Todd Oppenheimer, "The Computer Illusion," *Atlantic Monthly* (July, 1997).

Elaine Pagels, *The Gnostic Gospels* (New York, Vintage Books, 1981).

Trevor Paglen, *Blank Spots on the Map* (New York, Dutton, 2009).

Ann Pancake, *Strange As This Weather Has Been* (n.p., Shoemaker Hoard Publisher, 2008).

Talcott Parsons and Edward Shils (ed.), *Towards a General Theory of Action: Theoretical Foundation for the Social Sciences* (New York, Harper & Row, 1962).

R. Pascua, "Introduction" to Marx and Engels, *The German Ideology* (1947).

Raphael Patai, *The Hebrew Goddess* (New York, Avon Books, 1978).

Charles M. Payne, *I've Got the Light of Freedom: The Organizing Tradition and the Mississippi Freedom Struggle* (Berkeley, California, Univ. of California Press, 1995).

Corey Pein, "Blame the Computer," *The Baffler* no. 38 (March–April, 2018).

Charles Perrow, *Normal Accidents: Living With High-Risk Technologies* (New York, Basic Books, 1994).

Leonard Pitt, *A Small Moment of Great Illumination: Searching for Valentine Greatrakes, the Master Healer* (Emeryville, California, Shoemaker & Hoard, 2006).

———, "The History of Flight," *Somatic Magazine: Journal of the Mind/Body Arts & Science* vol. VIII, no. 1 (Autumn/Winter, 1988/1989).

J. H. Plumb, *The Growth of Political Stability in England* (London, England, 1967).

Neil Postman, *Technopoly: The Surrender of Culture to Technology* (New York, Alfred A. Knopf, 1992).

Lawrence M. Principe, *The Aspiring Adept: Robert Boyle and His Alchemical Quest* (Princeton, New Jersey, Princeton University Press, 2000).

Thomas de Quincey, "Historico-Critical Inquiry into the Origins of the Rosicrucians & the Freemasons," *London Magazine* (1824).

P. M. Rattansi, "The Literary Attack on Science in the 17th and 18th Centuries," doctoral diss. 1961, London School of Economics.

———, "Paracelsus and the Puritan Revolution," *Ambix* XI (1963).

Marcus Rediker, *Slave Ships: A Human History* (New York, Penguin Books, 2007).

G. Reichel-Dolmatoff, "Cosmology as Ecological Analysis: A view from the Rain Forest," in *Man, New Theories*, vol. XI, n°3 (September, 1976).

Don Robins, *Circles of Silence* (London, England, Souvenir Press, 1985).

P. G. Rogers, *The Fifth Monarchy Men* (London, England, Oxford Univ. Press, 1966).

Susan Ronald, *The Pirate Queen: Queen Elizabeth I, Her Pirate Adventurers, and the Dawn of Empire* (New York, Harper Perennial, 2007).

Hilary Rose and Steven Rose, *Genes, Cells and Brains: The Promethean Promises of the New Biology* (London, England, Verso, 2012).

Franklin Rosemont, *Marx and the Iroquois* (Brooklyn, New York, Red Balloon Collective, 1989).

George Rosen, "Social Attitudes to Irrationality and Madness in Seventeenth and Eighteenth Century Europe," in *Journal of the History of Medicine and Allied Sciences* vol. 18, n°3 (July, 1963).

———, *The History of Miners' Diseases: A Medical and Social Interpretation* (New York, Schuman's, 1943).

Hanna Rosin, "The Touch Screen Generation," *Atlantic Monthly* (April, 2013).

Theodore Roszak, *Bugs* (Garden City, New York, Doubleday, 1981).

———, *From Satori to Silicon Valley* (San Francisco, Don't Call It Frisco Press, 1986).

———, *The Cult of Information: The Folklore of Computers and the Art of Thinking* (New York, Pantheon, 1986).

Joel Rubin, "Monitor to Oversee School Payroll Repair," *Los Angeles Times* (September 17, 2007).

Richard Rudgley, *The Lost Civilizations of the Stone Age* (New York, Simon & Schuster, 2000).

Jacques Sadoul, *Alchemists and Gold*, (transl.) Olga Sieveking (New York, G.P. Putnam's Sons, 1972).

Richard Sasuly, *I. G. Farben* (New York, Boni & Goar, 1947).

Giorgio de Santillana, and Hertha von Dechend, *Hamlet's Mill: An Essay on Myth and the Frame of Time* (Boston, Massachusetts, Gambit Inc., 1969).

Eric Schlosser, *Command and Control: Nuclear Weapons, the Damascus Accident, and the Illusion of Safety* (New York, Penguin Books, 2014).

Mary Schulman, *Moses Hess: Prophet of Zionism* (New York, T. Yoseloff, 1963).

Hillel Schwartz, *The French Prophets: The History of a Millennarian Group in Eighteenth Century England* (Berkeley, California, University of California Press, 1980).

James C. Scott, *Against the Grain: A Deep History of the Earliest States* (New Haven, Connecticut, Yale University Press, 2018)

Gregorio Selzer, *Sandino* (New York, Monthly Review Press, 1981).

Michael Shallis, *The Electric Shock Book* (London, England, Souvenir Press, 1988).

Steven Shapin, "Social Uses of Science," in G.S. Rousseau and Roy Porter (ed.), *The Ferment of Knowledge* (Cambridge, England, Cambridge University Press, 1980).

Barbara Shapiro, *John Wilkins, 1614-1672: An Intellectual Biography* (Berkeley, California, University of California Press, 1969).

———, "Latitudinarianism and Science in Seventeenth Century England," in *Past and Present* n°40 (1968).

William Shea, *The Magic of Numbers and Motion: Scientific Career of René Descartes* (Canton, Massachusetts, Science History Publications, 1953).

Rupert Sheldrake, *The Presence of the Past* (1988).

———, *Science Set Free: Ten Paths to New Discovery* (New York, Deepak Chopra Books, 2012).

———, *The Rebirth of Nature: The Greening of Science and God* (London, England, Century, 1990).

Michael Shellenberger and Ted Nordhaus, "Environmentalism's Apocalyptic Daydream," San Francisco *Chronicle* (June 9, 2013).

Lenny Siegel and John Markoff, *The High Cost of High Tech: The Dark Side of the Chip* (New York, Harper & Row, 1985).

Dusty Sklar, *The Nazis and the Occult* (New York, Dorset Press, 1977).

Ted Smith, David A. Sonnenfeld, and David Naguib Pellow, *Challenging the Chip: Labor Rights and Environmental Justice in the Global Electronics Industry* (Philadelphia, Temple University Press, 2006).

Gary Snyder, *Earth House Hold: Technical Notes & Queries to Fellow Dharma Revolutionaries* (New York, New Directions, 1969).

Rebecca Solnit, *Savage Dreams: A Journey into the Landscape Wars of the American West* (New York, Vintage Books, 1994).

Starhawk, *Dreaming the Dark: Magic, Sex & Politics* (Boston, Beacon Press, 1982).

Clifford Stoll, *Silicon Valley Snake Oil* (New York, Anchor Books, 1995).

Lewis Strauss, *Men & Decisions* (New York, Popular Library, 1962).

Dirk Struik, "Introduction" to Karl Marx, *The Economic and Philosophical Manuscripts of 1844* (New York, International Publishers, 1964).

Han Suyin, *A Mortal Flower* (n.p., Putnam, 1966).

David Talbot, *The Devil's Chessboard: Allen Dulles, the CIA, and the Rise of America's Secret Government* (New York, Harper-Collins, 2015).

Dick Teresi, "Lynn Margulis," *Discover* (April, 2011).

Michael Taussig, *Shamanism, Colonialism, and the Wild Men: A Study in Terror and Healing* (Chicago, Illinois, University of Chicago Press, 1987).

———, *The Devil and Commodity Fetishism in South America* (Chapel Hill, North Carolina, University of North Carolina Press, 1980).

Gary Tauber, "A Clock More Perfect Than Time," *Discover* vol.17 n°12 (December, 1996).

Astra Taylor, *The People's Platform: Taking Back Power and Culture in the Digital Age* (New York, Picador Metropolitan, 2014).

F. Sherwood Taylor, *The Alchemists* (New York, Collier Books, 1962).

Arnold Thackray, "Matter in a Nut-Shell: Newton's *Opticks* and Eighteenth Century Chemistry," *Ambix* 15 (1968).

A. Thom, *Megalithic Sites in Britain* (Oxford, England, Clarendon Press, 1967).

———, *Megalithic Lunar Observations* (Oxford, England, Clarendon Press, 1978).

Keith Thomas, *Religion and the Decline of Magic: Studies in Popular Belief in Sixteenth and Seventeenth Centuries* (London, England, Weidenfeld & Nicolson, 1971).

E. P. Thompson, *Customs in Common* (New York, New Press, 1993).

———, "Time, Work-Discipline, and Industrial Capitalism," *Past & Present* n°38 (1967).

H. R. Trevor-Roper, *The European Witch-Craze of the Sixteenth and Seventeenth Centuries and Other Essays* (New York, Harper & Row, 1967).

Fred Turner, *From Counterculture to Cyberculture: Stewart Brand, The Whole Earth Network, and the Rise of Digital Utopianism* (Chicago, Illinois, University of Chicago Press, 2006).

Ellen Ullman, *Close to the Machine: Technophilia and Its Discontents* (San Francisco, City Lights Books, 1997).

Rick Vecchio and Paul Elias, "Root from Peru at Center of Dispute," San Francisco *Chronicle* (January 7, 2007).

Peter Viereck, *Metapolitics: The Roots of the Nazi Mind* (New York, Capricorn Books, 1961).

Virgil J. Vogel, *American Indian Medicine* (New York, Ballentine Books, 1973).

Scott Wallace, *The Unconquered. In Search of the Amazon's Last Uncontacted Tribes* (New York, Crown Publishers, 2011).

Richard Watson, *Cogito, Ergo, Sum: The Life of René Descartes* (Boston, David R. Godine, 2002).

Andrew Watterson, "Out of the Shadows and Into the Gloom? Worker and Community Health in and Around Central and Eastern Europe's Semiconductor Plants," in *Challenging the Chip*.

Jacob Weisberg, "We Are Hopelessly Hooked," *The New York Review of Books* (February 25, 2016).

David Weir, *The Bhopal Syndrome: Pesticides, Environment, and Health* (San Francisco, Sierra Books, 1987).

John Weiss, *Moses Hess: Utopian Socialist* (Detroit, Wayne State Univ. Press, 1960).

Joseph Weizenbaum, *Computer Power and Human Reason: From Judgement to Calculation* (New York, Freeman and Company, 1976).

Spencer Wells, *Pandora's Seed: Why the Hunter-Gatherer Holds the Key to Our Survival* (New York, Random House, 2010).

Margaret Wertheim, *The Pearly Gates of Cyberspace: A History of Space from Dante to the Internet* (New York, W. W. Norton & Co., 1999).

Richard S. Westfall, *Never at Rest: A Biography of Isaac Newton* (Cambridge, England, Cambridge University Press, 1983).

———, "Short-Writings and the State of Newton's Conscience," 1662(1), *Notes and Records of the Royal Society* 18 (1963).

———, "Newton's Reply to Hooke and the Theory of Colors," *Isis* 54 (1963).

———, "Newton Defends His First Publication: The Newton-Lucas Correspondence," *Isis* 56 (1966).

Lynn White Jr., "The Historical Roots of Our Ecological Crisis," *Ecology and Religion in History* (New York, Harper & Row, 1967).

Anne Whitelock, *The Queen's Bed: An Intimate History of Elizabeth's Court* (New York, Picador, 2013).

Jon Wiener, "Inside the Coursera Hype Machine," *The Nation* (September 23, 2013).

Naomi Wise, "Is Your PC Killing You? Tips, Advice and Products for Pain-free Computing," *Bay Area Computer Currents* (June 1–12, 1995).

Ellen Meiskins Wood, *The Origins of Capitalism* (New York, Monthly Review Press, 1999).

Benjamin Woolley, *The Queen's Conjuror: The Science and Magic of Dr. John Dee, Advisor to Queen Elizabeth I* (New York, Henry Holt and Company, 2001).

———, *Heal Thyself: Nicholas Culpeper and the Seventeenth Century Struggle to Bring Medicine to the People* (New York, Harper Collins, 2004).

Lee Worden, "Counterculture, Cyberculture, and the Third Culture: Reinventing Civilization, Then and Now," in *West of Eden: Communes and Utopia in Northern California* (ed.) Iain Boal, Janferie Stone, Michael Watts, and Cal Winslow (Oakland, California, PM Press, 2012).

Frances Yates, *The Rosicrucian Enlightenment* (Boulder, Colorado, Shambala, 1972).

Olivia Zalecky, "Helping Just Mayo Sales Cut the Mustard," San Francisco *Chronicle* (August 7, 2016).

John Zerzan, "Tonality and the Totality," in *Future Primitive and Other Essays* (Brooklyn, New York, Autonomedia & Anarchy: A Journal of Desire Armed, 1994).

V — NEWSPAPERS & MAGAZINES

John Abell, "Computer Crashes Costing Corporate America Plenty: Study Puts Tab at 4 Billion a Year for Downtime," San Francisco *Examiner* (August 30, 1992).

Shomial Ahmad and Peter Hogness, "A CUNYfirst breakdown," *Clarion* [Newspaper of the Professional Staff Congress] (October, 2014).

Chris Allbritton, "Future Glitches Make Y2K Seem Way 2 EZ," San Francisco *Chronicle* (October 9, 1998).

Erin Allday, "Male Infertility Linked to Host of Health Maladies," San Francisco *Chronicle* (December 11, 2014).

————, "Tracking Body's 100 Trillion Bacteria," San Francisco *Chronicle* (July 5, 2013).

————, "Virtual reality offers children a welcome respite from pain," San Francisco *Chronicle* (August 22, 2016).

Rick Anderson, "Inmates freed too early, for years," *Los Angeles Times* (April 16, 2016).

Anon., "6000 Complaints Flood New Hot Line on VDT," San Francisco *Chronicle* (February 12, 1984).

Anon., "As Benefits Go Paperless, Check-Day Rituals Vanish," *New York Times* (January 29, 2011).

Anon., "Argentina: Monsanto Denies Its Pesticides are Unsafe," San Francisco *Chronicle* (October 24, 2013).

Anon., "A Special Reason to Avoid Pesticides," San Francisco *Chronicle* (June 10, 1994).

Anon., "Campaign sets out to save Poland's complex alphabet," San Francisco *Chronicle* (February 22, 2013).

Anon., "Cancer Warning From 50's Tests," San Francisco *Chronicle* (August 2, 1997).

Anon., "Comet Lovejoy Found To Be All Hopped Up on Alcohol," San Francisco *Chronicle* (October 27, 2015).

Anon., "Deepwater Horizon's Final Hours: Missed Signals, Indecision, Failed Defenses, Acts of Valor," *New York Times* (December 26, 2010).

Anon., "Is Policy Out of Focus," San Francisco *Chronicle* (July 23, 2014).

Anon., "Japanese TV Leaves Hundreds of Viewers in Hospital, Shocking cartoon gives kids seizures," San Francisco *Chronicle* (December 17, 1999).

Anon., "Japanese TV Yanks Dangerous Cartoon Show Off the Air," San Francisco *Chronicle* (December 18, 1997).

Anon., "Magical Solar Etchings Left by Ancient Indians in Desert," San Francisco *Chronicle* (January 10, 1983).

Anon., "Magnetic Fields Linked to Illness," San Francisco *Chronicle* (September 20, 1982) .

Anon., "News of the Day From Across the Nation," San Francisco *Chronicle* (September 3, 2015).

Anon., "New Theory on the Origin of Life on Earth," San Francisco *Chronicle* (September 28, 1978).

Anon., "Quality Time Redefined," *New York Times* (May 1, 2011).

Anon., "Silicon Hell," San Francisco *Bay Guardian* (April 26, 2000).

Anon., "SmartMeters: Likely to Boost Shut-offs," San Francisco *Chronicle* (January 26, 2010).

Anon., "Suit Over a Chemical Linked to Death: Santa Clara Firm Accused," San Francisco *Chronicle* (January 2, 1984).

Anon., "The High Cost of a High Tech-Gadget Gorge May Drain Brain," San Francisco *Chronicle* (April 17, 2011).

Anon., "The Quest for Perfect Sound," San Francisco *Examiner*, This World (March 9, 1986).

Brian Awehali, "Slow Type," *East Bay Express* (May 7–13, 2014).

David Barboza, "Workers Poisoned at Chinese Factory Wait for Apple to Fulfill a Pledge," *New York Times* (February 23, 2011).

Anne Brice, "The Immortality Machine," *East Bay Express* (November 7–13, 2012).

William J. Broad, "Pentagon Reportedly Spent Millions on ESP," San Francisco *Chronicle* (January 11, 1984).

John M. Broder, "Bashing E.P.A. Is New Theme in G.O.P. Race," *New York Times* (August 18, 2011).

Pam Belluck, "To Tug Hearts, Music First Must Tickle the Neurons," *New York Times* (April 19, 2011).

California Teachers Association, *Action* (December, 1994).

Nigel Cameron, "Open forum, Where will people work when robots take the jobs?" San Francisco *Chronicle* (December 2, 2014).

Jon Carroll, "Modest do-gooders finding a place on the Net," San Francisco *Chronicle* (June 15, 2014).

Cathy Castillo, "Computers in California Schools," San Francisco *Examiner*, This World (April 29, 1984).

Steve Chawkins, "Parishioners See the Light at Mission During Solstice," San Francisco *Chronicle* (December 22, 2011).

David W. Chen, "Housing Agency's Computer Woes Put Aid Recipients in Limbo," *New York Times* (February 26, 2011).

Dawn Chmielewski, "Cat in the Hat or Mouse in the House," San Francisco *Examiner* (November 22, 1998).

John A. Clusman, "Friendly Fire," San Francisco *Chronicle*: Insight (August 7, 2005).

James Coates, "Machinery strikes fear," San Francisco *Examiner* (August 8, 1993).

Patricia Cohen, "Fending off digital decay, bit by bit," *New York Times* (March 16, 2010).

Chris Colin, "In the Mountains of Perú, an Ayahuasca Retreat Tailor-Made for the Start-Up Set," *California Sunday*, San Francisco *Chronicle* (2016).

Steve Connor, "Scientists Note Dramatic Decline in Sperm Count," San Francisco *Examiner* (March 8, 1992).

David Diamond, "RSI: How to Protect Yourself," *Clarion* (March, 2012).

David Dietz, "Boxer Scolds FAA Over Air Traffic Snarl," San Francisco *Chronicle* (April 1, 1992).

Bob Egelko, "Public Colleges Not Liable for Violence, Court Rules," San Francisco *Chronicle* (October 12, 2015).

Juliet Elperin, "EPA Decides Not to Limit Perchlorate," San Francisco *Chronicle* (September 22, 2008).

Benny Evangelista, "Teens, screens spend lots of time together," San Francisco *Chronicle* (November 3, 2015).

Laura Evenson, "At Home With Reader Rabbit," San Francisco *Chronicle* (April 25, 1994).

———, "Booming Market for New Kidware," San Francisco *Chronicle* (April 25, 1994).

Peter Femrite, "Big Animal Extinctions Leave Holes in Ecosystems," San Francisco *Chronicle* (October 27, 2015).

———, "6th Mass Extinction in Progress, Study Shows," San Francisco *Chronicle* (June 20, 2015).

Ben Fong-Torres, "The Heartbreak of High-Tech Anxiety," San Francisco *Chronicle* (February 15, 1984).

Leah Garchik, "How to kick back, unplug and forget it," San Francisco *Chronicle* (March 8, 2017).

Kirstin Downey Grimsley, "Workers Face a Daily Deluge of Messages, Study Shows," San Francisco *Chronicle* (May 21, 1998).

Peter Hogness, "A CUNYfirst upgrade is delayed," *Clarion* (January, 2015).

Nick Hoppe, "Putting Their Best Socks Forward," San Francisco *Chronicle* (July 12, 2016).

Michiko Kakutani, "Text Without Contexts," *New York Times* (March, 2010).

Rachel King, "What's next? Chips that think," San Francisco *Chronicle* (November 7, 2011).

Marissa Lang, "Attacks Put Huge Holes in Web," San Francisco *Chronicle* (October 22, 2016).

———, "Reducing screen time," San Francisco *Chronicle* (February 5, 2016)

Chris Langton, "Towards Artificial Life," *Whole Earth Review* no. 58 (Spring, 1988).

Evan Leatherwood, "For a Public Search Engine," *The Nation* (May 6, 2013).

Thomas Lee, "Beware the Real Big One: An Online Security Earthquake," San Francisco *Chronicle* (July 21, 2015).

Wendy Lee, "End-to-end email encryption still a struggle," San Francisco *Chronicle* (January 22, 2017).

———, "Kids Learn How to Code," San Francisco *Chronicle* (July 31, 2016).

Wendy Lee and Daniel De May, "Why the Web Went Down: DNS and DDoS Explained," San Francisco *Chronicle* (October 22, 2016).

Dan Levin, "Shaman's Spirits Control Air of Mongolian Capital," Ulan Bator Journal, *New York Times* (July 21, 2009).

Steven Levy, "A-Life Nightmare," *Whole Earth Review* no.76 (Fall, 1992).

———, "Artificial Life: The Quest for a New Creation," *Whole Earth Review* no.76 (Fall, 1992).

Gilbert A. Lewthwaite, "Pentagon Can't Keep Track of Its Money," San Francisco *Chronicle* (April 13, 1984).

Emily Listfield, "Generation Wired," Parade. San Francisco *Chronicle* (October 9, 2011).

Steve Lopez, "Wanted — Payroll Mr. Fix-It for L.A. Schools, Point West," *Los Angeles Times* (September 19, 2007).

Greg Lucas, "Computer Bumbling Costs State $1 Billion: Repeat Snafus in DMV, Other Agencies," San Francisco *Chronicle* (February 18, 1999).

A. Kent MacDougall, "The Gadgets That Run Our Lives," *Los Angeles Times* (n.d.).

John Maddox, "The Doomsday Syndrome," *Saturday Review of Books* (October 21, 1972).

Stephen Manes, "Time and Technology Threaten Digital Archives," *New York Times* (April 7, 1998).

Jon Mooallem, "Do-It-Yourself Genetic Engineering: In the Burgeoning Field of Synthetic Biology Even Amateurs Are Building Life Forms," *New York Times Magazine* (February 14, 2010).

Casey Newton, "Apple Tackles Labor Issues," San Francisco *Chronicle* (January 14, 2012).

Sean ODriscoll, AP, "Names with an apostrophe do not compute," San Francisco *Chronicle* (February 22, 2008).

Melisa Olmos, "Study Finds Computer-Related Student Health Problems," *The Lowell* (February 14, 2003).

AP, "Argentina, Monsanto denies its pesticides are unsafe," San Francisco *Chronicle* (October 24, 2013).

David Perlman, "Cal Academy Team Finds New Species," San Francisco *Chronicle* (December 26, 2016).

———, "Mysteries of Mass Extinction Cleared Up," San Francisco *Chronicle* (October 2, 2015).

Charles Petit, "Weak Microwaves May Alter Cells," San Francisco *Chronicle* (January 8, 1980).

Jeanne Phillips, "Dear Abby," San Francisco *Chronicle* (March 31, 2017).

Adam Piore, "Silent Warrior," *Discover* (April, 2011).

David Pogue, "The Past, From Tape to Drive," *New York Times* (April 15, 2010).

Andrew Pollack, "His Corporate Strategy: The Scientific Method," *New York Times* (September 5, 2010).

Neil J. Reley, "Education chief pushing for more tech in classroom," San Francisco *Chronicle* (September 13, 2012).

Elisabeth Rosenthal and Andrew W. Lehren, "Efforts to Curb Dangerous Coolant Falters, Sometimes at Home," *New York Times* (November 23, 2012)

Susan Rust, "Aquarium Can Dump Wastewater: State Regulators Exempt Monterey Bay Aquarium From a State Ban…," *East Bay Express* (November 2–8, 2000).

David Segal, "The Dirty Little Secrets of Search: Why One Retailer Kept Popping Up as No.1," *New York Times* (February 13, 2011).

Somini Sengupta, "Hacker Rattles Security Circles," *New York Times* (September 12, 2011).

Thom Shanker and Matt Richtel, "In New Military, Data Overload Can Be Deadly. Your Brain On Computers. Wired Warriors," *New York Times* (January 17, 2011).

Warren Siegel, "Computer error could land you in jail," San Francisco *Chronicle* (April 18, 1984).

Silicon Valley Toxics Coalition, *News* (various issues).

———, *Action* (various issues).

Bill Soiffer, "New Study Says Toxic Chemical Ruining the Bay," San Francisco *Chronicle* (December 8, 1983).

Sandy Stone, "Sex and death among the Cyborgs," *Wired* (May, 1996).

Rachel Swan, "Alameda County's new software blamed for wrongful arrests," San Francisco *Chronicle* (November 30, 2016).

Lindsey Tanner, "Addiction to Video Games Should Be a Disorder, AMA Says," San Francisco *Chronicle* (June 22, 2007).

Bernadette Tansey, "Leaving MIT for Stanford, assistant professor emphasizes collaboration in synthetic biology," San Francisco *Chronicle* (December 26, 2007).

James Temple, "Internet Vulnerable to Sophisticated Attacks, Dot Commentary," San Francisco *Chronicle* (January 22, 2012).

Jill Tucker, "High-grade gift to schools. Tech titan donates $2.7 million, tells SF officials to think big when they seek support," San Francisco *Chronicle* (October 7, 2013).

———, "Strike up the bandwidth. 3-year project brings cutting-edge technology to SF schools," San Francisco *Chronicle* (June 16, 2011).

University of California at San Francisco *Magazine*, "Is Well Enough?" (April, 1997).

U. P., "Cleveland Budget Left a Mess By One Small Computer Goof" (June 24, 1983).

Henry Weber, "FAA Glitch Wreaks Havoc on Flights," San Francisco *Chronicle* (November 20, 2009).

Mark Wheeler, "Fly Wars," *Discover*, vol.14:2 (February, 1993).

VI— FILMS, RADIO AND MUSIC

Caroline Casey, "The Visionary Activist", KPFA (March 2, 2017).

KPFA, "Evening News" (June 9, 2013).

Sasha Lilley, "Against the Grain," KPFA (February 4, 2013).

———, "Against the Grain," KPFA (October 21, 2014).

———, "Against the Grain," KPFA (October 31, 2014).

Pink Floyd, "Another Brick in the Wall (Part 2)" (song, 1979).

Silvia Rivera Cusicanqui, lecture, California Institute of Integral Studies (September 21, 2016).

Leon Rosselson, "The World Turned Upside Down" (song, 1975).

"Avatar," a film, directed by James Cameron (2009).

"Batman," a film, directed by Tim Burton (1989).

"Children of Men," a film, directed by Alfonso Cuarón (2006).

"Deep Waters," a film, directed by Todd Haynes (2019).

"The Devil We Know," a documentary, directed by Stephanie Soechtig and Jeremy Seifert (2018).

VII — INTERNET

Carl Frey and Michael Osborne, "The Future of Employment: How Susceptible are Jobs to Computerization?" (September, 2013) www.oxford-martin.uk.ca.uk

http://www.walter9.info/Cavendish/html/antwerp.html

San Francisco Public Library web-site, https://sfpl.org

Wikipedia, "Audio system measurements" https://en.wikipedia.org/wiki/Audio_system_measurements

Wikipedia, "Comparison of analog and digital recording" https:// en.wikipedia.org/wiki/Comparison_of_analog_and_digital_recording

Glossary

ANIMISM: The once-universal belief that the world (Earth, cosmos, etc.) as a whole is intrinsically alive, so too its various aspects, the rivers, mountains, springs, rocks, etc. Organized religions such as Judaism, Christianity, Islam, and Buddhism, among others, tend to suppress earlier animist beliefs, labelling them idolotrous. Some organized religions insist that the power of life can only come into matter from outside, from a God. "Anima," its root, referred to the breath or the soul.

ENTHUSIASM: Literally (from the Greek) means "full of gods," a term used by some conservative enemies to cast blame on the beliefs and actions of the far-left agitators in England's mid-17th century Civil War and revolution, men and women, often lay-preachers, whose spiritual visions formed a vital part of their political passions as they turned their world upside down, broadly challenging social privilege and the prerogatives of property. Critics emphasized the lower social class of the enthusiasts and that they were drawn to alchemy, astrology, caballa, and other magical pursuits.

HOLISM: Comprehension that takes as its premise that all things are interconnected, so seeking answers that take an extended view of all matters, their larger social contexts. Opposed to Cartesianism, which holds that analysis should proceed, part by part, separately, and to *reductionism*.

INERTIA: The scientific theory that matter once in motion (with no changes in speed or direction) will continue thus unless a force opposing or adding to the motion is brought to bear, and that matter at rest resists being put into motion unless, again, a force is applied. All changes in speed and/or direction require an outside force. Formulated as the first of Isaac Newton's Three Laws of Motion, but versions of inertia had been articulated by Kepler, Galileo, and Descartes. Since matter is unable to initiate its own motion, in effect, it is a mere passive lump of stuff, essentially dead. Earlier, "inert" had been used to describe "idle" men of the lower social classes, who later were labelled "vagrants."

LATITUDINARIANISM: A program of political/religous/scientific/literary moderation, eschewing "extremes" at either end, that characterized the thinking of leading writers and social figures as the ideological basis for the Restoration of the monarchy in England in 1660. Thus, religiously, latitudinarianism advocated a broad toleration of religous forms, but adamantly excluded both Catholics and the popular religions of the Civil War radicals. Latitudinarianism was very powerful in the formation of the Royal Society at the Restoration.

MACHINE-LIKE: Repetitive; predictable outcomes totally determined from starting points and subsequent inputs; controlled by an operator; without affect; (sometimes) moving jerkily and linearly.

MECHANICAL PHILOSOPHY: The reductionistic view that all phenomena, including everything our senses perceive, arise only as a result of the motion of the small particles that constitute all bodies. Some mechanical philosophers used the atomic theories of Democritus and Epicurus from antiquity to explain things like fluidity, cohesion, magnetic attraction, saltiness, etc., on the basis of the size and shape as well as the motion of the constituent particles. The mechanical philosophy swept through the extended community of natural philosphers in the mid-17th century. Their slogan of "matter and motion" expressed the suffiency of their twin agents.

POSITIVISM: There are quite a variety of positivisms, but they passionately base their beliefs on observable phenomena only, and tailor their doctrines to a perceived scientific understanding. Some notable positivists of different stripes and eras have been Auguste Compte, Ernst Mach, Rudolf Carnap and Bertrand Russell, but many of its tenets were influential during the scientific revolution.

REDUCTIONISM: The belief that all phenomena can be explained in terms of more fundamental principles, in the sciences usually the laws of physics, its fields and forces acting on the atoms and their particles explaining everything else, incuding chemical reactions, biological processes, and how you are (hopefully) able to understand this sentence.

THIRD INTERNATIONAL (COMINTERN): Created in 1919 out of the wreckage of the Second International (1891–1914), which had discredited itself when most of the socialist members in 1914 voted to fund their several national armies, despite longstanding antiwar rhetoric and predictions of the coming war of the imperialist powers that would betray the interests of the proletariat. Lenin and Rosa Luxemburg, condemning those votes as reflecting the choice of their national, over class, allegiances, were instrumental in establishing the alternative Third International in the aftermath of the Bolshevik Revolution.

Index